Internet Sources on
Each U.S. State

Internet Sources on Each U.S. State

Selected Sites for Classroom and Library

Compiled by
CAROL SMALLWOOD, BRIAN P. HUDSON,
ANN MARLOW RIEDLING, *and*
JENNIFER K. ROTOLE

McFarland & Company, Inc., Publishers
Jefferson, North Carolina, and London

ALSO BY CAROL SMALLWOOD AND FROM MCFARLAND

Free or Low Cost Health Information:
Sources for Printed Materials on 512 Topics (1998)

Recycling Tips for Teachers and Libraries (1995)

Helpful Hints for the School Library:
Ideas for Organization, Time Management
and Bulletin Boards, with a Resource Guide (1993)

Free Resource Builder for
Librarians and Teachers, 2d ed. (1992)

Reference Puzzles and Word Games for Grades 7–12 (1991)

Library Puzzles and Word Games for Grades 7–12 (1990)

Current Issues Resource Builder: Free and
Inexpensive Materials for Librarians and Teachers (1989)

Health Resource Builder: Free and
Inexpensive Materials for Librarians and Teachers (1988)

LIBRARY OF CONGRESS CATALOGUING-IN-PUBLICATION DATA

Internet sources on each U.S. state :
selected sites for classroom and library /
compiled by Carol Smallwood ... [et al.]
p.   cm.
Includes index.

ISBN 0-7864-2108-8 (softcover : 50# alkaline paper)

1. U.S. states—Computer network resources—Directories.
2. United States—Computer network resources—Directories.
3. Web sites—Directories. I. Smallwood, Carol, 1939–
E180.I58   2005   025.06'973—dc22   2005003511

British Library cataloguing data are available

Manufactured in the United States of America

McFarland & Company, Inc., Publishers
Box 611, Jefferson, North Carolina 28640
www.mcfarlandpub.com

To my cousin, Mary Lou Andrews.— CS
For Daniel, who made it all worthwhile.— BPH
To the lovely people of Oman.— AR
This one is for you, Mom.— JKR

Contents

Preface

This book is a guide to websites on the fifty U.S. states (and the District of Columbia). These sites have been selected for pre-kindergarten through college educational application and content, frequency of updating, and absence of commercialism. Anyone with an interest in a particular state — or the United States in general — will find valuable information here, but the guide is designed to be especially useful to students, teachers, library media specialists, parents, technology coordinators, counselors, administrators, curriculum directors, and other school staff. Several sites refer to their state's department of education standards, reflecting the No Child Left Behind Act. No site listed in this book requires log in or registration to access.

Each of the fifty states averages fifty entries, listed alphabetically by sponsor or topic. An appendix listing sites useful in all states has fifty entries, and a second appendix listing sites for Washington, D.C., has fifteen entries, making a total of 2,583 entries.

In assembling this book, the compilers have sought out sites that, taken together, offer a full picture of the life of each state. Topics of the sites are based heavily on the humanities and include history, geography, famous natives, authors, animals, artists, attractions, government, folk art, statistics, agriculture, forests, culture, state symbols, natural resources, native peoples, economy, art, music, and education. Each state has a site, often called the official state site, providing information about the governor and related state departments. Often the sponsor is listed as "State of — ," but not always. Maine's official site, for example, is sponsored by Information Research of Maine, and Minnesota's by North Star. To help the reader locate the official site for each state, the information on official sites is printed **entirely in boldface**.

Each entry includes a note about special features of the site, highlighting unique and especially helpful aspects.

To enhance the sites' usefulness for educators, each entry also suggests associations with curriculum areas that demonstrate inter-relationships in our increasingly interdependent society on a global scale.

ALABAMA

1 Academy of Achievement

www.achievement.org/autodoc/page/par0pro-1

Features individuals who have shaped our times by their accomplishments. Interviews with Academy inductees motivate and educate others by serving as inspiring role models in the: Arts, Public Service, Sports, Business and Science and Exploration.

Special Features: Curriculum Center, Photos
Curriculum: History

2 Alabama Agricultural Experiment Station

www.ag.auburn.edu/aaes/communications/pu
blicationslist.html

Leaflets, bulletins, reports, relating to Alabama farming, forestry and wildlife, rural life and economics, fisheries, and the environment grouped by type of publication, and by topic. Some PDFs.

Special Features: News Releases
Curriculum: Environmental Studies; Social Studies

3 Alabama Agriculture Statistics Service

www.aces.edu/department/nass/

Alabama agricultural survey, news releases, statistics, weather, annual bulletin, agriculture census, agriculture links.

Special Features: Graphical Overview includes Alabama's ranking in U.S. Agriculture, statistics of Alabama farms from 1930, Alabama crops since 1950, and related numbers.
Curriculum: Social Studies

4 The Alabama Center for Traditional Culture

www.arts.state.al.us/actc/actcmission.html

Operating within the framework of the Alabama State Council on the Arts, it was created in 1990 and is dedicated to the research, documentation and preservation of the state's folk cultures. Gospel jubilee singing, graveyard decoration days, American Indian basketry, Anglo-American folk pottery, west–Alabama blues, shape-note singing, coastal fishing lore, religious holidays, examples of Alabama folk life.

Special Features: Articles; Newsletters; Alabama Cultural Events Calendar; Performances for Schools
Curriculum: Art; Music

5 Alabama Commission on Higher Education

www.ache.state.al.us/Institutional%20Directory/
Inst.htm

Access to Public Institutions: Map of Institutions, Public Universities, Public Two-Year Colleges. Private Universities, Private Junior Colleges with data on enrollment, tuition, and fees.

Special Features: Student aid resources
Curriculum: Counseling; Education

6 Alabama Cooperative Extension System

www.aces.edu/

County offices offer county maps, county summaries, county crops, and related information along with address and e-mail contact. Several publications are available relating to Alabama agriculture, natural resources, food and health, forestry, community.

Special Features: Issues in the News; Monthly News Archive

Curriculum: Health; Home Economics; Social Studies

7 Alabama Department of Archives and History

www.archives.state.al.us/ts.html

Designed for teachers and students: Kids' Page, School Tours, Teacher Resources, Using Primary Sources, Youth Activity Sheets, Alabama Moments in American History, Selected Alabama History Books, Alabama History Online, Alabama History Timeline, Alabama Theses & Dissertations.

Special Features: This Month in Alabama History; Alabama Official Symbols and Emblems

Curriculum: History

8 Alabama Department of Education

www.alsde.edu/html/home.asp

Alabama ongoing Education News, Facts about Alabama Schools, Publications, Contact Information, Reports, Accountability Reporting, Statewide Parent Visitation Month, Alternative Approaches to Alabama Certification.

Special Features: Scholarships, Grants for Alabama teachers

Curriculum: Education

9 Alabama Forests Forever Foundation

www.alaforestsforever.org/

Alabama's forests improve the environment, provide material for nearly 5,000 different products, and offer recreational opportunities.

Special Features: Educational Interactive CD-ROM; Brochure on the Importance of Forests; Alabama Forestry Facts on a PDF file.

Curriculum: Environmental Studies; Science; Social Studies

10 Alabama Humanities Foundation

www.ahf.net/programs.htm

The Alabama Humanities Foundation makes available a wide variety of humanities programming throughout the state, from literacy promotion to a lending library of over 600 exhibitions and videos, to meet the humanities

enrichment needs in Alabama. Links offer a view of each of the programs.

Special Features: Educational media, teacher resources

Curriculum: Education; Library Media

11 Alabama Indian Affairs Commission

aiac.state.al.us/TRIBES_2.htm

Tribes recognized by the State of Alabama: name of the tribe, head, address, phone and also website, e-mail if available. Legislation, genealogy, programs, special events.

Special Features: Scholarships to download

Curriculum: Education; History

12 Alabama Info

www.alabamainfo.com/media/

Alabama e-zines (electronic publications), radio, television, newspapers, magazines, may be accessed. Arrangement of links is alphabetical.

Special Features: Driving Directions

Curriculum: Language Arts

13 Alabama Institute for Education in the Arts

www.artseducation.org/home.html

Helps provide a curriculum framework that educators may use to integrate arts into any school, any grade, and with any age student. Students study significant works of art using four disciplines.

Special Features: Summer sessions in music, theatre, visual arts and dance disciplined-based arts education, as well as an Administrator's Institute

Curriculum: Art

14 The Alabama Legislature

www.legislature.state.al.us/index.html

Current session, access to bills, committees, related information. Historical background including: Alabama's Six Constitutions, Past Legislative Leadership, Acts & Journals, Past Legislators, Researching Archival Records (Archives and History).

Special Features: Student and Teacher Page provides a large number of educational links for students, teachers, parents; information on our Legislative Page Program, as well as special pages on YMCA Youth Legislature, Boys State and Girls State

Curriculum: Government; History

15 Alabama Library Association

www.lib.auburn.edu/madd/docs/ala_authors/
contents.html

A compilation of Alabama authors and their works as compiled by the members of the Alabama Library Association's Bibliographic Committee over a number of years. Search by keyword, or a alphabetical list of authors. Covers: Occupation, Date and place of birth, Parents' names, Education, Marriage, Children, Employment or career, Honors, Miscellaneous information, and Works.

Special Features: States what sources were consulted in compiling

Curriculum: Language Arts; Library Media

16 The Alabama Men's Hall of Fame

www.samford.edu/groups/amhf/id38.htm

Formed to recognize the men native to or identified with Alabama who have made significant contributions. Inductees are organized by year of induction, and alphabetically at Samford University.

Special Features: Plaques of inductees may be selected and viewed

Curriculum: Social Studies

17 Alabama Museums Association

www.alabamamuseums.org/museum.htm

Alabama Museums include: Name, location, phone, e-mail, hours, admissions, tours, accessibility, demonstrations, special programs, purpose, description, last updated.

Special Features: One is spotlighted, featured

Curriculum: Art; History; Social Studies

18 Alabama Music Hall of Fame

www.alamhof.org/

Honors the state's music achievers from performers to songwriters, management to publishing. #1 Songs; Song writers in the Charts.

Special Features: Inductee websites; Achievers Birthdays; Links

Curriculum: Music

19 Alabama Network of Children's Advocacy Centers

www.ancac.org/

Promotes the multidisciplinary process in fostering an abuse-free society for Alabama's children and supports the development of the children's advocacy through public awareness, training and networking. The directory includes: center's name, address, director, phone, fax, e-mail alphabetically arranged by the name of the center.

Special Features: Map of Alabama

Curriculum: Education

20 Alabama Online Pet Resources

www.creatures.com/AL.html

Alabama Online Pet Resources of no-kill facilities. Links to animal rescues, humane societies, SPCA's in Alabama. Map of Alabama and cities mentioned having animal sites. Pet care tips, vet news, books, animal links, state by state guide of other no-kill facilities.

Special Features: Pet care tips, printed and audio books

Curriculum: Social Studies

21 Alabama Ornithological Society

www.bham.net/aos/

Founded in 1952 to foster a greater knowledge of birds and promote conservation of natural resources through: Alabama Birds e-mail discussion list; Alabama Bird Records Committee Checklist of Alabama Birds, including: web-based version of checklist; Breeding Bird Atlas Project; Rare Bird alerts for Alabama statewide.

Special Features: Contacts to society officers

Curriculum: Biology; Science

22 The Alabama Press Association

www.alabamapress.org/

Newspapers in Education, This Week in Alabama History, Alabama Press Archives, Updates and headlines about the newspaper world.

Special Features: Alabama Newspapers lets you make selections by newspaper, city, or clip the map for a list of newspapers within that county

Curriculum: History; Language Arts

23 Alabama Shakespeare Festival

www.asf.net/studyandexplore.cfm

Located in Montgomery, it is the sixth largest Shakespeare festival in the world, attracting over 300,00 annual visitors. Information about: Bringing a School Group; Classes, Lectures, & Tours; Camp; Resources for Teachers, Listening to NPR, and others.

Special Features: Windows Media Player (free download) presents festival history

Curriculum: Language Arts

24 The Alabama Sports Hall of Fame

www.alasports.org/

The Alabama Sports Hall of Fame (ASHOF), founded in 1967, is a place where heroes and their memories live forever. No other state can match the number of great sports legends that have ties to this state, either through birth or performance.

Special Features: Children's Outreach Program

Curriculum: Sports

25 Alabama Women's Hall of Fame

www.awhf.org/fame.html

The Alabama Women's Hall of Fame located in Marion, Alabama, was established to provide a permanent place of honor for Alabama's most outstanding women and a place for people to visit and learn about the contributions they have made to our state and nation. Stories are told through portraits, photographs, letters, and bronze plaques.

Special Features: Inductees may be located by induction year, or alphabetically; Information for Nomination

Curriculum: History; Women's Studies

26 AlabamaEd

www.alabamaed.com/

Vast educational resources for Alabama administration, counselors, librarians, parents, teachers K–College, school nurses, special education. Topics such as Language Arts as a second language, legal issues, physical education and sports, Alabama government, career testing, technology, lesson plans, updates on education.

Special Features: Grants and Funding; Jobs in Education; Homework Help

Curriculum: Counseling; Education; School Nurse; Sports; Technology

27 Animal Welfare (Sponsor: CLC Publishing)

www.saveourstrays.com/ala.htm

City location, name of organization, e-mail addresses of the humane societies in Alabama arranged alphabetically by name of city.

Special Features: Several such as the Mobile SPCA, Montgomery Humane Society, and West Alabama Animal Rescue are linked to the websites

Curriculum: Social Studies

28 Archaeology (Sponsor: University of South Alabama)

www.usouthal.edu/archaeology/ad-visit-site_index.htm

For over 20 years, archaeologists at the University of South Alabama have been excavating prehistoric and historic sites in the Mobile Bay area. Some of these sites are open to the public, others are restricted. You can "virtually visit" sites such as: Port Dauphin, Bottle Creek, Old Mobile, Dog River, and others.

Special Features: Educator's Page includes lesson plans and other teacher resources

Curriculum: History

29 Auburn University Marine Extension and Research Center: Alabama Sea Grant Extension

www.ag.auburn.edu/fisheries/aumerc/Publications/Publications.html

The Auburn University Marine Extension and Research Center (AUMERC), located in Mobile, Alabama, on the shores of Mobile Bay and a short distance from the Gulf of Mexico, to help ensure that Alabama's marine resources remain renewable. Publications such as The Zebra Mussel Invasion in Alabama, Coastal Wetlands of Alabama, Water: An Alabama Treasure.

Special Features: High School Aquaculture Programs; Workshops

Curriculum: Science

30 Booker T. Washington's *Up from Slavery: An Autobiography* (Sponsor: University of North Carolina at Chapel Hill)

docsouth.unc.edu/washington/menu.html

Full text of *Up from Slavery: An Autobiography* published 1901, can be downloaded; the ix, 330 pages (550K) includes illustrations. Washington founded Tuskegee Institute in 1881 in Alabama for people of his race.

Special Features: Short bibliography of books about him; Biographical Information

Curriculum: History

31 Consumer Affairs Division

www.ago.state.al.us/consumer.cfm

The Attorney General's Office of Consumer Affairs provides three primary services for the State of Alabama and its residents: serves as a mediator of consumers' complaints that relate to a retail transaction; investigates allegations of fraud or illegal practices by a business which may violate state or certain federal laws; and offers information and consumer education to the public about how to avoid becoming a victim of fraud.

Special Features: Consumer Alerts; Consumer Law & Info; Latest Alerts

Curriculum: Business

32 Department of Geography, University of Alabama

alabamamaps.ua.edu/

Historical and Contemporary Maps are indexed separately and may be viewed through JPEG, Plugin, and PDF. The Historical Archive begins with maps before 1826 and includes Civil War ones. Not all of the 4112 maps online are on Alabama but include regional areas and others. Contemporary Maps include: Agriculture, Climate, Education, Forestry and others relating to Alabama.

Special Features: Alabama Education information covers such topics as: Total Revenues Spent by Student; Average Teacher Salary; State Board of Education Districts

Curriculum: Education; Geography; History

33 Early Works Museum Complex

www.earlyworks.com/index.html

The complex, located in Huntsville, includes: Children's Museum; Historic Huntsville Depot; Alabama Constitution Village; Humphrey Rogers House. Virtual Tours, What's New, Fun Stuff are some of the features offered.

Special Features: Field trips are lined to national social studies standards, designed to engage students in a fun way

Curriculum: History

34 Geological Survey of Alabama

www.gsa.state.al.us/gsa/EQ2/eq.html

Myths about earthquakes, what structures in Alabama are the most likely to be damaged by earthquakes because of the land they occupy, how intensity and magnitude of earthquakes are measured.

Special Features: Map showing the locations of earthquakes in Alabama and their intensity and magnitude

Curriculum: Science

35 Heart of Dixie Railroad Museum, Inc.

www.heartofdixierrmuseum.org/

The Heart of Dixie Railroad Museum is the official railroad museum of the state of Alabama located south of Birmingham in Calera, Alabama, featuring operating standard gauge and narrow gauge trains, two restored depots, an indoor collection of railroad artifacts and memorabilia, and an outdoor collection of railroad cars, locomotives, and cabooses.

Special Features: What's New includes the latest events, special days, trips

Curriculum: History

36 Ivy Green

www.bham.net/keller/home.html

Birthplace of Helen Keller in Tuscumbia, Alabama. Background, accomplishments of this famous woman who overcame physical handicaps. The play, *The Miracle Worker,* is done annually on the grounds of Ivy Green in June and July.

Special Features: Photos of Helen's home built in 1820, a year after Alabama joined the union; poem by her

Curriculum: Language Arts

37 The Legend of Zelda

www.poprocks.com/zelda.htm

Zelda was born in Montgomery and married the author F. Scott Fitzgerald. Letters that F. Scott Fitzgerald wrote to his wife's doctor; "How Crazy Was Zelda?"; Bibliography of Zelda's novels, stories, articles; Chronology of both of the Fitzgeralds.

Special Features: Photos, comments by Ernest Hemingway about Zelda

Curriculum: Language Arts

38 Marshall Space Flight Center

www1.msfc.nasa.gov/

The Marshall Space Flight Center, a field installation of the National Aeronautics and Space Administration, was established in 1960 and named in honor of General George C. Marshall, the Army Chief of Staff during World War II, and Secretary of State. The History Office Library includes information on the early years of Dr. Wernher Von Braun to Rocket Power, from Redstone Rocket to Saturn V, and 20 years of Space Shuttle development.

Special Features: NASA's Educator Astronaut Program

Curriculum: Science

39 Montgomery Museum of Fine Arts

fineartsmuseum.com/home.cfm

The Museum's education programs are designed for pre-school through senior citizen to enrich the appreciation and understanding of art. Programs follow the philosophy that people learn by doing, by interacting with materials, objects and other people. Studio classes for children are offered after school and on weekends. Most classes are in multi-part series which focus on a single subject or technique. The Museum offers scholarships to these classes.

Special Features: Current Calendar of Events for programs now being offered

Curriculum: Art

40 National Inventors Hall of Fame

www.invent.org/hall_of_fame/30.html

Inductee George Washington Carver developed his crop rotation method at Tuskegee, which alternated nitrate producing legumes—such as peanuts and peas—with cotton, which depletes the soil. Carver then developed 325 different uses for the extra peanuts—from cooking oil to printers ink. Upon his death, Carver contributed his life savings to establish a research institute at Tuskegee.

Special Features: Biography has links to significant topics in his life

Curriculum: Science

41 19th Alabama Infantry Regiment, C.S.A, Inc.

www.19thalabama.org/

A non-profit living history and Civil War reenactment organization with headquarters in Huntsville, Alabama, organized in 1982, one of the largest and most active reenactment groups in Alabama. Provides: Civil War Facts, Orders of Battle, North/South alliance, Civil War Links, and related information.

Special Features: Photographs, Drill Manuals

Curriculum: History

42 North Alabama Railroad Museum

www.suncompsvc.com/narm/

The museum is located in Chase, Alabama, just east of Huntsville to preserve railroad history. The museum is open for visitors April through October. Visitors have a choice of a free self-guided tour or a special guided tour of the depot, museum grounds, facilities and historic display train.

Special Features: Train sounds and Songs on wav, audio, and midi files; Excursions for school children

Curriculum: History; Music

43 Old Alabama Rails

www.oldalabamarails.org/history.html

Articles such as: The West Point Route, Industrial Railroads of Montgomery, The Alabama Railpark. Stories and photographs submitted by former employees and their descendents include reflections on individual people as well as various tales of work on the railroad.

Special Features: Photo Album; Modelers Forum

Curriculum: History

44 Public Affairs Research Council of Alabama

parca.samford.edu/

A nonprofit, nonpartisan group that collects, synthesizes, and reports information on issues of public interest affecting state and local government in Alabama. Some topics covered are: State Constitution; K–12 Education; Higher Education; State Taxes, Finances, & Debt; County Government.

Special Features: Local Acts Database

Curriculum: Education; Government

45 St. Stephens Historical Commission

www.oldststephens.com/

Upon Mississippi gaining statehood, Alabama became its own territory and St. Stephens its capital. Alabama's first governor presided over the first meeting of the Territorial Legislature at the Douglass Hotel in St. Stephens. After taking the oath of office, the charter of Alabama's first bank, was created.

Special Features: Education Outreach for students and teachers; Links included in descriptive historical material

Curriculum: History

46 Slavery (Sponsor: Auburn University)

www.lib.auburn.edu/archive/aghy/slaves.htm

Between statehood and the end of the Civil War, the Alabama Supreme Court rendered numerous decisions on slavery, mostly pertained to slaves as property. the original cases appeared in the *Alabama Reports* and may be located there. Arranged by: Who Were Slaves, Rights and Powers of Ownership, Transfers of

Slaves, Hiring of Slaves, Fugitive Slaves, Manumission, and others.

Special Features: Links to specific case described

Curriculum: History

47 State of Alabama

www.alabama.gov

The official site of the state of Alabama includes: State Agency Directory, State Employee Directory, Help Center, Site Map, Media Center, Search Option, Recent News, Kids' Page.

Special Features: Education Section includes the state's K–12 schools; Libraries; Universities and Colleges, as well as Resources in Education.

Curriculum: Social Studies

48 Tuscaloosa Museum of Natural History

www.inusa.com/tour/al/tuscaloo/natural.htm

The Museum is located in historic Smith Hall near the Quadrangle on the University of Alabama campus. Exhibits of natural history, ethnology, geology and mineralogy. Fossils, rocks and minerals from the Coal Age, Ice Age and Dinosaur Age.

Special Features: Traveling exhibitions are featured regularly in the changing exhibits gallery; free admission

Curriculum: Science

49 University of Alabama, Museums; Moundville Archeological Park

www.ua.edu/academic/museums/moundville/home.html

Moundville, located 14 miles south of Tuscaloosa, Alabama, on Highway 69 South is known as the largest city 800 years ago in North America. Archaeological Sketch, Riverbank Overlook, Archaeological Museum, Programs and Events, and other attractions.

Special Features: Streaming seventeen minute video

Curriculum: History

50 Voices for Alabama's Children

www.alavoices.org/

To accomplish the mission of a decent childhood for every Alabama child, Voices for Alabama's Children researches the conditions of children in Alabama, communicates those conditions to those who can work for change, advocates for public policy and private programs that will improve lives.

Special Features: Includes a table showing how Alabama children rank nationally. *Programs:* Alabama Kids Count; Children's Legislative Agenda

Curriculum: Education; Social Studies

ALASKA

51 Adventure Learning Foundation

www.questconnect.org/AK_HOME.HTM

Far North Journal, Photographs, Geography and Climate, Alaska and Yukon links, History, Fauna and Flora, Environment vs. Oil, Archaeology, and other topics.

Special Features: Lesson plans such as Alaska and the Yukon; Alaska map

Curriculum: Environmental Studies; Geography; History; Science

52 Alaska Association of School Libraries

www.akla.org/akasl/bb/bbhome.html

Battle of the Books is an Alaskan reading motivational and comprehension program sponsored by the Alaska Association of School Libraries. Books are chosen, the students read them, and compete with one another. The previous year's state winners are listed.

Special Features: Divisions for K–2; 3–4, 5–6, 7–8, 9–12

Curriculum: Language Arts; Library Media

53 Alaska Center for the Environment

www.akcenter.org/action.html

Working for Alaska's natural environment since 1971, protection activities in state lands, wild forests, Prince William Sound, Mat-Su Valley, links to action, recycling resources.

Special Features: Scholarship information and registration for Trailwide Discovery, an outdoor experience for children ages 4–17

Curriculum: Environmental Studies; Social Studies

54 Alaska Department of Community and Economic Development

www.dced.state.ak.us/dca/commdb/CF_BLOCK.htm

Select a community alphabetically listed from Adak to Yakutat, select from one or more data types such as: General Overview, Schools, Population and Housing Characteristics, then click to retrieve.

Special Features: Overview includes a photo, locates the community on a map of Alaska and covers such topics as location by latitude and longitude; history; culture, economy; facilities; transportation; climate

Curriculum: Geography; Social Studies

55 Alaska Division of Public Health

www.ahelp.org/f_materials.html

Database of health education materials such as pamphlets, posters, publications, audiovisuals, and teaching materials on Alaska. Some can be downloaded.

Special Features: Health topics designed to be used by students

Curriculum: Health

56 Alaska Economic Information System

www.dced.state.ak.us/cbd/AEIS/AEIS_Home.htm

Economic overview of the geographic areas of Alaska. Just click the map where you want more information and a profile of the economics will present such information as: Economic Overview of Employment, Per Capital Income, Population, Net Migration, Below Poverty Level, and other statistics. Way of life, climate, wildfood subsistence harvests, tourism, infrastructure, minerals and related topics.

Special Features: Charts, graphs, photos; state statistics as a whole

Curriculum: Economics; Social Studies

57 Alaska! Image

www.state.ak.us/

News updates about Alaska, links to state's budget plan, governor's office, lieutenant governor's, Alaska Legislature, Alaska courts, Alaska communities; Alaska Facts & Visitor Information, and others.

Special Features: Kids' Web Stuff includes facts about Alaska, Wildlife Video Gallery; Search option for Alaska

Curriculum: Social Studies

58 Alaska Native Heritage Center

www.alaskanative.net/4.asp

Choices of school visits for Grades K–12 includes dance, stories, history, tours, in the Anchorage center. Day camps and adult classes and workshops are also offered. The center organized its material around five cultural groupings such as the Aleut and Alutiiq.

Special Features: Background about Alaska Native Culture includes a map showing the distribution of cultures

Curriculum: Dance; History; Language Arts

59 Alaska Native Language Center

www.uaf.edu/anlc/languages.html

The center was established by state legislature for research and documentation of the twenty Native languages of Alaska. Information about language classes and degree programs, more than a hundred research and teaching publications available, online resources include books, texts, newsletters, archives.

Special Features: Click on a map of Alaska divided by language for information

Curriculum: Language Arts; Social Studies

60 Alaska Natural History Association

www.alaskanha.org/about_us.html

Nonprofit organization dedicated to enhancing understanding and conservation of the natural, cultural and historical resources of Alaska's public lands.

Special Features: Children's books on Alaska

Curriculum: Social Studies

61 Alaska Public Lands Information Centers

www.nps.gov/aplic/fieldtrip/index.html

The centers were authorized by the Alaska National Interest Lands Conservation Act. Some of the resources include a 51 page, *Our Wild Neighbors: An Educational Resource Book about Alaska's Animals* to download that includes the areas it meets of the Alaska Content Standards adopted by the Alaska State Board of Education.

Special Features: Educational programs for students and teachers

Curriculum: Geography; Government; Technology

62 Alaska Rainforest Campaign

www.akrain.org/

Coalition to protect the remaining wild lands of the Chugach and Tongass National Forests. Information about the people and land, logging, action alerts, Alaska's Rainforest Conservation Act.

Special Features: Virtual tour, audio tour, map of the rainforest

Curriculum: Environmental Studies; Geography

63 Alaska State Library

www.library.state.ak.us/

What the Alaskan state library in Juneau offers such as: Alaska newspapers on microfilm 1866–1998; Books about Alaska, Library cards and catalog information, list of Alaska state holidays, Alaska photographs, Alaska Statistics Index, manual on book repair to download.

Special Features: Alaska's Gold: a Teacher Resource; Eight Stars of Gold: the Story of Alaska's Flag

Curriculum: History; Library Media

64 Alaska Studies Website (Sponsor: Cook Inlet Tribal Council)

www.akhistory.org/index.cfm

The Alaska Studies Website designed for Middle School and High School includes maps, glossary, bibliography, lessons, links. Information about the Aleut is grouped by: Student Summary, Readings, Worksheets, Makushin Village, Makushin Bay Map, Links, Lesson Help.

Special Features: A timeline provides dates of the lessons provided

Curriculum: History

65 Alaska Volcano Observatory

www.avo.alaska.edu/avo4/index.htm

The observatory if a joint effort of the United States Geological Survey, the geophysical Institute of the University of Alaska–Fairbanks, and the State of Alaska Division of Geological and Geophysical Surveys. Information on geology, remote sensing, seismology; publications for downloading such as: *Catalog of the Historically Active Volcanoes of Alaska.*

Special Features: Map of Alaska to click the area of volcanic activity to explore

Curriculum: Science

66 Alaska Wildlife Alliance

www.akwildlife.org/

Dedicated to the protection of Alaska's wildlife for its intrinsic value as well as for future generations. Wildlife facts, issues and campaigns, latest updates on the wildlife in Alaska.

Special Features: Flash presentation: The Killing of Wolves in Alaska

Curriculum: Social Studies

67 Alaska Women's Network

www.alaskawomensnetwork.org/

A nonprofit network to connect Alaskan women with each other, to the state, and the world. Information on such topics as: Domestic Violence, Health Issues, Women and Work, Calendar of Events, Women's Organizations, Subsistence, Government, Yellow Pages, Travelers to Alaska.

Special Features: Annotations of books by and about, or of interest to Alaskan women; Book Club

Curriculum: Social Studies; Women's Studies

68 Alaskan Natives (Sponsor: UAA-ISER)

www.alaskool.org/

The Institute of Social and Economic Research materials about Alaskan Natives, education, languages and cultures, land claims, government, traditional life and subsistence, biographies, literature, maps, and other resources.

Special Features: Teaching units, curriculum resources for various grade levels

Curriculum: Education; Social Studies

69 AlaskaNativeArts.net

alaskanativearts.net/index.htm

A resource directory of Alaskan Native Arts covering visual arts, crafts, writers, musicians, dancers, arts organization and resources, and related links.

Special Features: Locate artists by name, craft, tribe

Curriculum: Art; Dance; Language Arts

70 Bering Land Bridge National Preserve

www.nps.gov/bela/html/morebear.htm

Alaska's polar, brown, and black bears; bears and people interaction and what to do; what is the significance of Bering Land Bridge; information on continental glaciation.

Special Features: Bear chart of the three kinds of bears as to length, weight, coloring, number in Alaska

Curriculum: Biology; History

71 Challenger Learning Center of Alaska

www.akchallenger.org/kids/noflash.htm

Calendar for kids includes camps, classes, events of the center located in Kena, Alaska. Go to a Space Mission, Work on a Space Mission, Soaring Students of Science, are other features.

Special Features: Games, Quizzes, and Fun Stuff; What's the Buzz? Requires Flash

Curriculum: Science

72 Communities (Sponsor: McPhee Publications)

www.llovealaska.com/

Features a community of the day by profiling it and showing where it is located on an Alaskan map. An Alaskan photo gallery, Alaskan daily headlines from over 4,000 sources.

Special Features: Alaska Links Encyclopedia offers such topics as: Alaska Climate Records; Fun and Cool Stuff, and a search option

Curriculum: Geography

73 Consortium Library, University of Alaska Anchorage

www.lib.uaa.alaska.edu/archives/index.html

The Archives and Manuscript collection in the Consortium Library of the University of Alaska Anchorage is grouped by: Historical Manuscripts Collection List, and University Records List.

Special Features: Alaska Women's Oral History Project; Past and current exhibits

Curriculum: History; Library Media; Women's Studies

74 Dinosaurs (Sponsor: Division of Lands, Bureau of Land Management)

denali.ak.blm.gov:80/ak930/akdino.html

Dinosaur bones were first discovered in the mid–1980s in Alaska. Discusses DNA studies, Northern Alaska's 12 Known Dinosaurs, Where to See Dinosaur Remains in AK, and other topics.

Special Features: How to pronounce names of various dinosaurs; E-mail for more information on the dinosaurs of Alaska

Curriculum: Science

75 Everything Alaska

www.everythingalaska.com/index.html

Alaskan totem poles, statistics and facts, news, state and local government, archives, attractions, free stuff, fun stuff, bears, totem poles, volcanoes, parks, eagles, city guide, annual events, wildlife refuges, moments in history.

Special Features: Slide and word puzzles; coloring book; educational links

Curriculum: Geography; History; Social Studies

76 Fairbanks North Star Borough Public Library

sled.alaska.edu/akfaq/akfaqindex.html

Alaska Governor's Mansion, Alaska Native Claims Settlement Act, Maps of Alaska, State Symbols, Weather Influences in Alaska. Answers to such questions as: how to research mining claims of relatives, how much did the United States pay Russia for Alaska.

Special Features: Official Student Information Guide to Alaska

Curriculum: Geography; Government; History

77 Geography (Sponsor: Motion, Inc.)

www.AlaskaOne.com/travel/

Geography of Alaska from deserts to rain forests; city information for Juneau, Fairbanks and others; National Parks, State Parks, Wild and Scenic Rivers. Regional travel information for Kenai Peninsula, Southcentral, Inside Passage, Interior, Southwest, Arctic Region.

Special Features: Commonly used Alaskan lingo

Curriculum: Geography; Social Studies

78 Geophysical Institute

www.giseis.alaska.edu/Seis/seis.html

Earthquake safety and preparedness, notable earthquakes, searchable earthquake database. Educate and Outreach includes such resources

as: Science and Math Enrichment Program, Science Potpourri, Seismology Lab Tours, and others.
Special Features: Interactive Seismicity Map of Alaska
Curriculum: Science

79 Guide to Activities and Information (Sponsor: Alaska Internet Services)

www.alaskasearch.com/

Photo gallery, Alaska Regions, Alaska Communities, Weather Reports, Transportation, Alaska Attractions, Business Directory, Weather Reports, and other features.
Special Features: Alaskan Maps by region, Alaska Marine Highway System, Alaska Weather, Volcanoes in Alaska
Curriculum: Geography; Social Studies

80 Institute of Museums and Library Services

www.museumsalaska.org/

Museums Alaska is a statewide association of individuals and institutions to preserve Alaska's natural and human history, improve museums as educational institutions, and related goals. Art news, events calendar.
Special Features: Alaska museums are included with information on each one with links to websites if available
Curriculum: Art; History

81 Intersea Foundation

www.intersea.org/

Nonprofit corporation that conducts whale research voyages to learn natural history and enable lay people to help scientific study of cetaceans and their environment. Information about: History of Vessels; Scientific Achievements.
Special Features: Sound archives, photo exhibits, publications and presentations
Curriculum: Biology; Science

82 Kenai Peninsula Borough School District

www.kpbsd.k12.ak.us/akhistory/aktools.htm#famaks

Alaska Studies Teacher's Toolbox provides links to historical sites, science, geography, government agencies, and other topics as well as virtual visits to museums.

Special Features: Alaska studies lesson plans by teachers; Interactive Links; Photo albums
Curriculum: Education

83 Linkup Alaska

www.linkupalaska.com/

Links to Alaska Communities alphabetically arranged, Labor and Employment information, National Security Resources. Alaska Topical Directory begins with Aboriginal Alaska, and ends with USA (Federal Government Agencies).
Special Features: Kid's World; Education; Maps. Ice Alaska features photos of Word Ice Art Championships, articles on ice events
Curriculum: Art; Social Studies

84 Mental Health Association in Alaska

www.alaska.net/~mhaa/

Children's Mental Health Fact Sheet, Juvenile Justice, Alaska Mental Health Information Sources, Prevention, Community Outreach, Cabin Fever. Some information is on PDF files, on tapes.
Special Features: Legislative Alerts about Children's Issues; Children's Smart Start
Curriculum: Health; Psychology

85 Mineral Management Service, United States Department of the Interior

www.mms.gov/alaska/kids/index.htm

Topics relating to Alaska minerals include: Lab Experiments, People at Work, Photo Gallery, Cool Links, Short Subjects, Intern Program, Historical Films, Alaska Native Links, Campbell School Science Fair.
Special Features: Just for Kids Activity Pages to download such as an Alaska Crossword Puzzle, Match Alaska Animals With Their Name
Curriculum: Counseling; Geography; Science

86 Municipality of Anchorage

www.ci.anchorage.ak.us/History/

History of Anchorage beginning with 5000 B.C., the earliest known human habitation, the next when Russian traders established trading posts in the 18th century. The stages of history includes links for further information such as Anthropological Research, Alaska Railroad, Air Transportation.
Special Features: Photos trace Anchorage development with the text
Curriculum: History

87 National Weather Service

aprfc.arh.noaa.gov/

Map of Alaska to click on to zoom in or access graphs and text data. Hydrographs, snow graphs, precipitation maps, breakup and ice observation, model graphs are some of the resources on Alaska's weather.
Special Features: Current snow depth search; weather information by alphabetical search option
Curriculum: Geography

88 National Wildlife Federation

www.nwf.org/women/solace.html

Alaska Women's Environmental Network activities in Alaska and contact information. Conservation topics, Education E-Newsletter, features for teachers, articles on Alaska.
Special Features: Kid's environmental activities grouped by ages: 1–3; 3–7; 7–13; 13 and up
Curriculum: Environmental Studies; Social Studies; Women's Studies

89 Neal B. Brown's Radio Science Program

alaskascience.com/index.htm

Neal Brown hosts a weekly radio science program on KUAC-FM; past programs are available on Real Audio. Neal's Alaska Science Explained features: Build Your Own Rocket, Aurora Borealis, Remote Mapping, Scientific Links. Includes his e-mail.
Special Features: The feature, Aurora Borealis, includes a photo to enlarge, suggested reading, research milestones, induction demonstrators, K–12 lesson plan
Curriculum: Science

90 NetPets, Inc.

www.netpets.com/cats/catresc/alaska.htm

United States Postal Service address, phone, of Alaska shelters arranged by city. Pet tips, hours, directions, missions, link, for such places as: Humane Society of Kodiak, Alaska Pet News, Seward Animal Shelter.
Special Features: E-mail addresses, websites are provided when available
Curriculum: Social Studies

91 The North Slope Borough

www.north-slope.ak.us/

The borough, the size of Minnesota, is inhabited by 6,290 residents, mostly Inupiat. Borough Special Events, Wildlife Management, Search and Rescue, Health and Social Services, Fire Department, and related governmental departments.
Special Features: Map with eight communities like Barrow to click for more information. Another map shows the part the borough occupies in Alaska
Curriculum: Government; Social Studies

92 Northwest Arctic Borough

www.northwestarcticborough.org/

The Northwest Arctic Borough (county) covers about 36,000 square miles in northwest Alaska with a population of about 7,300. Monthly newsletter, FRE Scholarship, Borough Community Profiles, the Mayor's office and other governmental departments.
Special Features: Artist Index features local artists and their work
Curriculum: Art; Government

93 She-Wolf Works, Monty Sloan, others

www.wolfsongalaska.org/

Predator and Prey Relationship, Wolves and Humans, Wolves and Native Americans, Adopt a Wolf, Events Calendar, Intern Program, Wolves and Folklore, and related topics.
Special Features: Poems about wolves; Education Center
Curriculum: Language Arts; Science

94 Smithsonian Institution

www.mnh.si.edu/arctic/index.html

The Arctic Studies Center explores the history of northern peoples, culture, environment with topics such as: Yup'ik Masks, the Vikings, Arctic Wildlife, and publications.
Special Features: glossary of arctic vocabulary; tools for teachers
Curriculum: Environmental Studies; History

95 State of Alaska

www.state.ak.us/

Headline articles, Doing Business in Alaska, State Employee Directory, Alaska Governor and Lieutenant Governor, Legislation, Courts, Communities, Motor Vehicles, Alaska Marine Highway, Facts & Visitor Information, and related state information.

Special Features: **Kids' Web Stuff includes Wildlife Video Gallery, Student Guide, Safe**

Kids, Fish and Game Kids, Kids' Money, Healthy Kids. websites of Alaskan schools
Curriculum: Education; Geography; Social Studies

96 Trivia (Sponsor: Hilton Anchorage, and others)

www.alaska.com/akcom/trivia/trivcom/symbols/story/3005293p-3029500c.html

Alaskan question and answers on culture, geography, geology, history, government, jobs and business, fish, wildlife and plants, parks, people, sports, and other topics. Construction history, photo, of Alaska's state capitol.
Special Features: Search by article, activity, business; photo gallery
Curriculum: Geography; Social Studies

97 University of Alaska Anchorage

litsite.alaska.edu/uaa/

LitSite Alaska promotes literacy, cultural diversity, well being in Alaska. Information on Alaska traditions, reading and writing in Alaska, Alaska libraries, and related topics.
Special Features: Archive of lesson plans; peer work by Alaskan students
Curriculum: Education; Social Studies

98 Virtual Power Network

www.stateofalaska.com/media/news/news.htm

Links to fourteen Alaskan newspapers such as: *Alaska Journal of Commerce, Juneau Daily News, Anchorage Daily News, The Nome Nugget.*
Special Features: Radio, Magazines, Television links in Alaska
Curriculum: Language Arts

99 Visitors Information (Sponsor: Alaska Websites, Inc.)

www.alaskavisitorsinformation.com/

Information for visitors on the Northern Lights, whales, places of interest in Alaska to visitors, roads, and related topics.
Special Features: Photographs include zoom in, seasonal, wildlife
Curriculum: Geography

100 Women in Alaska History (Sponsor: Elizabeth Beckett and Sarah Teel)

library.thinkquest.org/11313/Gold_Rush/index.html

ThinkQuest's, Women in Alaska History, such as Nellie Cashman, Belinda Mulrooney, Klondike Kate, Mollie Walsh, through biographies, trivia, a time line, poetry, activities, recipes, crafts, and maps.
Special Features: Photos, maps; Women Today
Curriculum: History; Women's Studies

ARIZONA

101 ADOT, State of Arizona

www.arizonahighways.com/

Online articles from the magazine, *Arizona Highways*, famed for its photography, the latest magazine cover with table of contents. Includes Discover Arizona, Plants and Animals Nature Guide, among its topics.
Special Features: Virtual Tours of Arizona; Search site option
Curriculum: Art; Biology; Geography

102 American Forests

www.americanforests.org/news/display.php?id=102
Article about the Arizona Futbol Club, a non-

profit group supporting young soccer players in Arizona, helping to plant 800,000 trees in Arizona. Includes resources for kids about trees, access to the National Register of Big Trees, Sprawl Information, How to Plant Trees.
Special Features: Historic Tree Nursery Tour; Monthly e-mail newsletter and magazine
Curriculum: Biology; Science; Social Studies

103 Arizona Animal Welfare League

www.aawl.org/education.htm

Nonprofit group providing care, protection and compassion for animals entrusted to us and taking a leadership role in promoting humane values for the benefit of all animals and people. Includes a free behavior help line, list of events, press releases.

Special Features: Kids Education includes workshops, presentations for scouts, schools, and community groups at the shelter in Phoenix or offsite

Curriculum: Social Studies

104 Arizona Attractions (Sponsor: LifeWare Publishing)

www.azlife.net/Attractions.htm

Arizona Attractions grouped by: Scenic Areas, Historic Sites, Canyons and other groupings; Attractions by City or Town; Attractions by Name of Area such as Ajo Area; or by clicking on a map of Arizona.

Special Features: Many photographs; large map of Arizona can be printed out

Curriculum: Geography

105 Arizona Blue Book

www.sosaz.com/public_services/Arizona_Blue _Book/1999_2000/ch02.htm

History of Arizona from Prehistoric Times (12,000 years ago) beginning with the Cochise and Anasazi to the end of the Twentieth Century with photo links in the narrative.

Special Features: Arizona state symbols with background information and photos

Curriculum: History

106 Arizona Board of Regents

southwest.library.arizona.edu/azas/body.1_div. 21.html

Information about the most common wild animals of Arizona such as the bear, elk, deer, antelope, wild goat, cougar or California lion, wolf, fox, wild cat, prairie dog, hare, rabbit, skunk, squirrel, beaver, mink, muskrat.

Special Features: Many illustrations

Curriculum: Science

107 Arizona Child Abuse InfoCenter

www.ahsc.arizona.edu/ACAInfo/statistics/sta tistics.htm

Arizona Vital Statistics, Arizona Child Protective Services Reports, and others about child abuse. For example, a PDF by the Child Welfare League of America, provides information on the condition of vulnerable children in Arizona, using indicators of child protection, health, child care, education, and income support.

Special Features: Resources by County includes counties in Arizona; Reporting Laws

Curriculum: Social Studies

108 Arizona Commission of Indian Affairs

www.indianaffairs.state.az.us/townhall/index. html

The commission hosts the annual Arizona Indian Town Hall. Tribal State Agreements, Tribes of Arizona, Bills/Legislature, Business Development, Legal Issues, are some of the areas covered. PDF versions.

Special Features: Arizona Map of Tribal Lands

Curriculum: Social Studies

109 Arizona Department of Health Services

www.hs.state.az.us/plan/

Arizona statistics for: birth, deaths, marriages, divorces, pregnancies, abortions, fetal deaths by census, community, county, gender and others. Also covers trends, related sites.

Special Features: Teenage pregnancy; Reports are available on various topics

Curriculum: Social Studies

110 Arizona Department of Transportation

www.dot.state.az.us/ABOUT/atrc/Index.htm

The Arizona Department of Transportation (ADOT) conducts research to improve all aspects of transportation in Arizona. Specific goals include evaluation of new materials and methods, development of design and analysis techniques, and study of underlying causes of transportation problems.

Special Features: Latest news on Newsletters, and Implementation Reports

Curriculum: Driver Training; Social Studies

111 Arizona Education Association

www.arizonaea.org/frame.html

Articles under such topics as: Issues in Arizona Schools; Community Engagement; Coming Attractions; Quality Teaching and Learning; National Board Certification. Calendar of Events, Legislative Update.

Special Features: Teaching and Learning articles, links

Curriculum: Education

112 Arizona Education Foundation

www.azedfoundation.org/index.html

The Arizona Educational Foundation thinks that improving public education was too great a task for school districts to do alone; it fosters excellence by funding programs that enhance Arizona's school districts to strengthen the teaching profession, design high quality curricula and stimulate student achievement.
  Special Features: Teacher of the Year, Arizona Spelling Bee, School Recognition Programs
  Curriculum: Education

113 Arizona Geographic Alliance

alliance.la.asu.edu/azga/

Lesson Plans, Links, and other resources on geography. Maps of Arizona include an outline map of Arizona, map of Arizona counties, Arizona cities, Arizona rivers, population growth, state topography, and others; many can be downloaded.
  Special Features: Arizona State Geography Standards by the Arizona Department of Education K–12
  Curriculum: Education; Geography

114 Arizona Humane Society

www.azhumane.org/

Humane Education for different age groups, field trips, school visits, therapeutic program, pet partners animal-assisted therapy, project safehouse, and pet first aid are some of the activities offered.
  Special Features: Dogs in Art; Kids' Zone has such features as I Want to Be a Veterinarian!
  Curriculum: Counseling; Social Studies

115 Arizona Library Association

www.azla.org/

Promotes library services and librarianship in all types of Arizona libraries. News articles relating to legislative concerns, books for children, and reading are featured. Provides contact to submit an idea for a presentation, program, or workshop.
  Special Features: Site index to locate material on the website; links to Arizona academic, public, school, and special libraries, as well as others outside of the state
  Curriculum: Education; Language Arts; Library Media

116 Arizona Music Educators Association

www.arts.arizona.edu/amea/pub.html#AMN

Information about festivals, workshops, conferences, and their various types of publications such as directories, journal, magazines.
  Special Features: How to submit lesson plans for the *Arizona Music News*; articles for the *Arizona Music Educator*
  Curriculum: Music

117 Arizona State

www.dlapr.lib.az.us/

Dedicated to providing the Arizona legislature and Arizona citizens with needed information and the history of Arizona. Some of their programs include: the Arizona Newspaper Project, Cultural Inventory Project.
  Special Features: Arizona Library Directory, About Arizona, Arizona Reading Program, Children's Services Newsletter, Authors for Teens, Digital Maps
  Curriculum: Geography; History; Language Arts; Library Media

118 Arizona State Legislature

www.azleg.state.az.us/

Includes: The Legislative Process, Senate Information, House Information, links to legislative agencies and other government offices. The Recent News section includes, Who is My Legislator? Search option for bills by number.
  Special Features: Arizona Constitution; Floor Calendar; Committee Agendas
  Curriculum: Government

119 Arizona State Museum

www.statemuseum.arizona.edu/

The museum in Tucson, the oldest and largest anthropology museum in the Southwest. Events and Programs, Exhibitions, Collections, Research, and other aspects of the museum are featured. Spotlight articles.
  Special Features: K–12 School Programs, Teacher Workshops, Student Poetry. College Education; Continuing Education
  Curriculum: Social Studies

120 Arizona State University and the Arizona Board of Regents

www.artswork.asu.edu/arts/teachers/organizations/organizations4.htm

Name, address, phone, e-mail address, website, of organizations such as the Arizona Alliance for Arts Education involved with Arizona arts and cultural development. ArtsWork includes information for students, teachers, standards, lesson plans, assessment, and other resources.
Special Features: Search Option
Curriculum: Art

121 Arts and Entertainment (Sponsor: EMR Corporation)

aztec.asu.edu/AandE/aehome.html

Features Ballet Etudes, a youth ballet company in Phoenix's East Valley, the Tempe Community Chorus, West Valley Cadet Strings, and other arts youth groups.
Special Features: Auditioning, concert schedules, photos, news
Curriculum: Music

122 AZED

www.azed.us/weblog.html

News about Arizona education grouped for: Teachers, Students, Parents, in the areas of: Arizona, History, Language, Library, Math, Science, Writing.
Special Features: Recent articles about Arizona education in various publications such as *Arizona Republic, Capitol Media Services*; National educational news from such sources as *Time Magazine*
Curriculum: Education; Library Media

123 Central Arizona Museum Association

www.dlapr.lib.az.us/text/museum/index.html

Access museums to over 50 museums by type such as: Anthropology/Archaeology; by location such as: Phoenix Downtown; or by name such as Arizona Doll and Toy Museum.
Special Features: Photos; Mentoring Resources
Curriculum: Art; History; Science

124 Children's Action Alliance

www.azchildren.org/caa/welcome.asp

Nonprofit, nonpartisan group dedicated to research, education, and advocacy to promote the well-being of Arizona's children and families. Fact Sheets & Links allows access to fact sheets and provides links to other sites and organizations promoting the well-being of all children and families in Arizona.

Special Features: Most research publications are in PDF format
Curriculum: Education; Social Studies

125 College of Agriculture and Life Sciences, University of Arizona

ag.arizona.edu/AZWATER/

The Arizona Water Resources Research Center's mission is to provide statewide outreach and education focused on critical water issues affecting Arizona and to provide expertise on state and regional water management and policy. The WRRC provides information and services through outreach, conferences and symposia, and a publications program that includes two newsletters.
Special Features: Water Education for Teachers: interdisciplinary resources for ages 5–18.
Curriculum: Environmental Studies; Science

126 Desert Little Bear

www.rockartcreations.com/indian.html

Petroglyphs and their meaning, Arizona Indian Tribes, background and photos of the Arizona born and raised artist, Desert Little Bear Gonzales, Gallery of Art.
Special Features: Children's Pages include games, activities to instruct about Arizona's native culture
Curriculum: Art; History

127 Geology (Sponsors: Julia K. Johnson and Stephen J. Reynolds)

reynolds.asu.edu/azgeo3d/azgeo3d_home.htm

Arizona Geology 3D consists of QuickTime virtual reality movies of the geologic map of Arizona draped over digital topography, giving a 3D perspective the user can rotate.
Special Features: Directions for QuickTime, links to web resources related to Arizona Geology 3D
Curriculum: Geography; Science

128 Grand Canyon (Sponsor: Bob Ribokas)

www.kaibab.org/geology/gc_geol.htm

Geology of the Grand Canyon through illustrations, photos, and narration. Types of stone such as Kaibab Limestone, Hermit Shale are pointed out and questions such as how it was formed, where the rock came from and why it looks like it does, and related questions are answered.

Special Features: Links within the narrative provide added information
Curriculum: Geography; Science

129 History Reference Guides (Sponsor: Jeffrey Scott)

jeff.scott.tripod.com/reference.html

Arizona from Prehistoric times to the present, Arizona Politics, Arizona Crime and Criminals, Injustices in Arizona, Water in Arizona, Arizona Education, Arizona Multiculturalism, Native Americans, Arizona Cities, Arizona.

Special Features: Women in Arizona feature individual women, websites, lists those in the Arizona Women Hall of Fame, and books; search option for the site
Curriculum: Education; History; Women's Studies

130 Indian Country Today

www.indiancountry.com/

Articles, top stories, editorials, cartoons, trade, employment, columns in this Native American newspaper. It includes news other than Arizona, but the search option lets you locate the numerous Arizona articles such as: "Arizona Indians Fight to Preserve Petroglyphs in Phoenix Valley."

Special Features: Author Gallery of prominent columnists
Curriculum: Language Arts; Social Studies

131 Indians Web Quest

coe.west.asu.edu/students/amysjs/AZINDWeb_Quest.html

Study guide for the comparison of the Sinagua and Navajo Indians in Arizona by exploring resource sites of the two tribes, creating a design for a Navajo rung or a model for a home, database for the two tribes and related activities.

Special Features: Links, photos included in the narration.
Curriculum: Art; History

132 K–12 Outreach Program (Sponsor: University of Arizona)

www.biology.arizona.edu/

K–12 Outreach Program includes the BIO-TECH Program, Science Connection, Marine Discovery, and others. Kids Corner includes Art, Language, Math, Music, Science resources.

Special Features: Problem Sets and Tutorials
Curriculum: Art; Biology; Language Arts; Math; Music; Science

133 League of Arizona Cities and Towns

www.azleague.org/mission.htm

The league provides collective advocacy, education, training, technical assistance and information sharing for and among the cities and towns of Arizona. Includes legislative information, websites of Arizona city and towns with access to United States Census, and related information.

Special Features: Map shows legislative districts, contact information for state senators and representatives
Curriculum: Government

134 Museum Division

www.dlapr.lib.az.us/text/museum/index.html

How Arizona became a state, the Capitol Centennial Web Exhibit, the Arizona Hall of Fame Museum in the 1908 restored Carnegie Library, and the Arizona Capitol Museum in the restored 1900 Capitol Building are some of the features.

Special Features: Teacher Resource Guide
Curriculum: History

135 Museum of Art at Tucson (Sponsor: University of Arizona)

artmuseum.arizona.edu/

The Museum of Art at Tucson offers many educational experiences for students of all ages to connect to the visual arts including school tours, student gallery for all grades, K–6 Outreach, seminars in the museum for middle and high school, internships for high school and college.

Special Features: Exhibitions, Virtual Tours
Curriculum: Art

136 National Optical Astronomy Observatories

www.noao.edu/pubpage/pub.html

Kitt Peak is the home of research facilities for two divisions of the National Optical Astronomy Observatories (NOAO): Kitt Peak National Observatory and the National Solar Observatory, located 56 miles southwest of Tucson on the Tohono O'Odham Reservation. The summit of Kitt Peak is 6,875 feet.

Special Features: Visiting hours, what may be viewed on tours
Curriculum: Science

137 The Natural American

thenaturalamerican.com/tna.htm

Material on Arizona wildflowers, trees, grasses, reptiles, birds, mammals under the topic: Plants, Animals and Insects. History of Arizona with photos beginning with the Hohokam and the Anasazi, to the Navajo Code Talkers.

Special Features: Map of Arizona; Map of the Reservations and Four Corners
Curriculum: Biology; History

138 Office of Governor Napolitano
www.governor.state.az.us/global/az_kids.htm

The Governor offers a section for kids about Arizona that includes: Natural Wonders, State Facts, History, Wildlife, Arizona Pictures, and a Coloring Book to download. Includes access to the Governor's biography, speeches.

Special Features: Arizona World Game; Today in History
Curriculum: Social Studies

139 Research Advisory Services
www.azplansite.com/

Research Advisory Services (RAS) is a public policy and geo-demographic research consulting firm for state and local governments, private businesses, lobbyists, school districts and non-profit organizations. Contacts, websites, for Arizona State Government, Arizona Counties, Cities and Towns in Arizona are provided.

Special Features: Search option of major Arizona cities
Curriculum: Government

140 San Pedro Mesquite Company
www.spmesquite.com/articles/ancientfoods.html

Pima, Tohono, O'odham tribes of Arizona are being urged to go back to their ancient food to prevent being overweight and diabetic as well as to preserve their heritage.

Special Features: Illustrations and specific benefits of such wildfoods as: Amaranth, Prickly Pear Cactus, Tepary Bean
Curriculum: Health; History; Home Economics

141 Schools (Sponsor: DesertNet)
links.desert.net/links/Arizona/Education_And_Reference/K-12.html

Links to K–12 Arizona Internet school sites and Arizona school district home pages.

Special Features: Online K–12 Schools Across America
Curriculum: Education

142 State Capitol and Wesley Bolin Plaza Virtual Tours (Sponsor: A.L.I.S.)
www.azleg.state.az.us/museum/museum.htm

Virtual tour of the Wesley Bolin Plaza and the Arizona State Capitol Complex.

Special Features: Aerial views and ability to enlarge them
Curriculum: Government

143 Territorial Newspapers
www.azbiz.com/AZBIZ/myarticles.asp?S=358&PubID=11853&P=878880

Access to: The Daily Territorial, and Inside Tucson Business, newspapers serving the Tucson and Pima County areas. Includes current articles, columns, commentaries, features, as well as an archive.

Special Features: Article Search option
Curriculum: Language Arts

144 Tucson's Children's Museum
www.tucsonchildrensmuseum.org/

Upcoming Events, Featured Activity of the Week, Tykes Time, are some of the features along with information for teachers about tours and classes. Mazes, submarine rides, interactive attractions are available in this museum in Tucson.

Special Features: Photographs of exhibits such as Dinosaur Canyon with robotic animation
Curriculum: Science

145 United States Census Bureau
factfinder.census.gov/home/en/kids/funfacts/arizona.html

Statistics for children, 1990 and 2000, such as: population divided into male and female; statistics by age grouping; by urban and rural residence; educational attainment.

Special Features: Arizona state capital, date of statehood, and state symbols
Curriculum: Social Studies

146 United States Department of Commerce — Economic Development Administration
ag.arizona.edu/edrp/index.html

Dedicated to utilizing the resources of the University of Arizona to help economic development within the State of Arizona, with a special focus on economically distressed areas within the state.

Special Features: PDFs on Arizona retail sales, housing, employment, economic development, tourism, and related topics
Curriculum: Economics

147 University of Arizona Library

dizzy.library.arizona.edu/images/folkarts/welco me.html

Folk art of southern Arizona such as quilts made in Randolph and St. David, Arizona, Easter eggs, Chicano murals in Tucson, food, and other examples.
Special Features: Graphics such as color murals; Links to added material in narratives
Curriculum: Art; Home Economics; Library Media; Social Studies

148 Women's Organizations (Sponsor: Denise Osted)

www.euronet.nl/~fullmoon/womlist/countries/ usa/arizona.html

Name, address, phone, fax, of women's organizations in Arizona sorted by postal code such as: Arizona Coalition Against Domestic Violence, Phoenix Women's Commission, Women's Resource Center University of Arizona.

Special Features: websites are included as well as e-mail addresses if applicable
Curriculum: Women's Studies

149 Women's Studies Department, University of Arizona

www.u.arizona.edu/ic/mcbride/ws200/wsproj. htm

Information about Arizona women grouped in such categories as: Women in Arizona History, Women in Arizona Politics, Tucson Women Artists, Women in Southern Arizona in the Early Twentieth Century, and others.
Special Features: Photos, Illustrations
Curriculum: Women's Studies

150 Writing Groups (Sponsor: USPN Tech)

www.arizonaweb.biz/cgi-bin/search.cgi?key words=Arizona%20Writers%20Authors

Access to Arizona writing groups such as: Arizona Authors Association, Authors and Writers in Flagstaff, Arizona, and SCBWI Arizona (children's authors and illustrators).
Special Features: A directory A–Z makes for easy access
Curriculum: Language Arts

ARKANSAS

151 Anything Arkansas Directory

www.anythingarkansas.com/arkansas/county. html

Date created, parent country, progeny counties with dates, county boundary changes with dates, county records preservation and extent for Arkansas counties arranged alphabetically.
Special Features: Click a county on a map of Arkansas for more information on that county
Curriculum: Government; History

152 ARGenWeb Archives

www.rootsweb.com/~usgenweb/ar/ppcs-ar. html

A county-by-county display of penny postcards from Arkansas in black and white/color. Instructions on submitting. The postcards were

called penny postcards because they cost a penny to send.
Special Features: History of postcards divided by date/type from 1898 to the present
Curriculum: History

153 Arkansas Activities Association

www.ahsaa.org/

Fostering Arkansas education through activities. Links to: Arkansas High School Coaches Association, Arkansas Cheerleading Coaches Association; Arkansas Track Coaches Association; Arkansas Quiz Bowl, Chess Association for Arkansas Schools, and others.
Special Features: Hall of Fame; State Farm Arkansas High School Record Book
Curriculum: Physical Education

154 Arkansas Area Health Education Centers Program

www.rpweb.uams.edu/ArkansasHealthCareers/
ArkansasHealthCareers.htm

Health related problems and needs of Arkansas citizens. A map of Arkansas shows where health professionals are in short supply. Information about health careers in various professions such as: nursing, pharmacy, therapy, vision care, dentistry, veterinary medicine.
Special Features: A Guide to Life after High School in Arkansas
Curriculum: Counseling; Health

155 Arkansas Arts Center

www.arkarts.com/

Calendar of Events, Collection, Exhibitions, Museum School, State Services, Children's Theater, Young Arkansas Artists Exhibition Application, and other features of the Little Rock center.
Special Features: Educational offerings include: Lectures and Conversation, Teacher Resources, Community Outreach, Artmobile, *Curriculum* Study Guide, and others
Curriculum: Art; Drama

156 Arkansas Arts Council

www.arkansasarts.com/

The seventeen-member council appointed by the governor advances the arts in Arkansas through such programs as: Arts in Education, Arts on Tour, Grants, Art Scholarships, Governor's Arts Awards.
Special Features: Directory search by name of artist of discipline; local arts organizations
Curriculum: Art; Counseling; Education

157 Arkansas Child Abuse and Neglect Prevention Board

www.arctf.org/search/index.php

Information about Arkansas Children's Trust Fund, Local Councils, Links, Education Registry, and other resources. The Parenting Program Directory allows a search by county or program type in Arkansas.
Special Features: Adolescent Services, Child Care Education, Life Skills Education, Teen Parenting Education, are some of the topic resources in locations around the state
Curriculum: Counseling; Education; Health; Psychology

158 Arkansas Coalition Against Domestic Violence

www.domesticpeace.com/

Statistics from the FBI on violence on females in Arkansas, Domestic Violence Shelters in Arkansas, Contact numbers, Services and Projects, Events and Training, Cycle of Abuse.
Special Features: Power and Control Wheel includes summaries of the types of abuse, how children are used, how isolation relates to domestic abuse
Curriculum: Social Studies; Women's Studies

159 The Arkansas Comprehensive Testing, Assessment and Accountability Program (ACTAAP)

www.arkedu.state.ar.us/accountability/index.h
tml#ACTAAP

The program encompasses the state's Smart Start Initiative, which focuses on Grades K–4; the state's Smart Step Initiative, which focuses on Grades 5–8; and education for Grades 9–12: academic standards, professional development, student assessment, and accountability for schools and students.
Special Features: Academically distressed school districts are grouped according to phases
Curriculum: Counseling; Education

160 Arkansas Democrat Gazette

epaper.ardemgaz.com/Default/Client.asp?skin
=ArkDaily&Daily=ArDemocrat&GZ=T&AW=
1074702901420

Online edition of the newspaper, the Arkansas Democrat Gazette, that features the latest edition as well as access to past issues. Search option for Arkansas news, or by national/world news.
Special Features: Download the newspaper; Photo reprints
Curriculum: Language Arts

161 Arkansas Department of Economic Development

www.1-800-arkansas.com/energy/index.cfm?
page=education

Locate economic information on Arkansas by county, region, name, or search the alphabetically arranged index. Includes the Arkansas Energy Office, information about taxation, business and community development, and a message from the Governor.

Special Features: Teaching Materials; Kids Korner
Curriculum: Economics

162 Arkansas Department of Education

www.arkansasnews.com/

Curriculum Framework K–12 for: Mathematics, Language Arts, Science, Social Studies, Fine Arts, Music. Benchmarks, sample lesson resource lists, sample *Curriculum* models.
Special Features: Information Technology; Teacher Licensure
Curriculum: Education

163 Arkansas Department of Environmental Quality

www.adeq.state.ar.us/ep/arkwet.htm

Introduction, goals, benefits, responsibilities of participating schools, teaching resources. List of schools taking part in the Arkansas WET with contact information.
Special Features: Environmental projects, searchable databases, links
Curriculum: Environmental Studies; Science

164 Arkansas Department of Finance and Administration

www.arkansas.gov/dfa/motorvehicle/driverservices.html

Primary and secondary documents used as proof of identification in the issuance of driver's license/ID cards, and related information for Arkansas drivers.
Special Features: Graduated licensing for 14–18 year olds; changes in licensing regulations
Curriculum: Driver Education

165 Arkansas Department of Health

www.healthyarkansas.com/index.html

Regional offices; county health units in Arkansas: includes name of unit, photo of the building, address, city, phone, fax, administrator, hours, with option to click topics like Child Health, Food Services, Teenage Pregnancy.
Special Features: Services section includes information on several topics as: Product Safety, Fluoridation, Radon, Maternity
Curriculum: Health

166 Arkansas Department of Higher Education

www.arkansashighered.com/

Financial aid; websites of four and two year public universities and independent colleges; Students: First Choice Arkansas about students going to Arkansas colleges.
Special Features: Publications such as: Higher Education in Arkansas; Academic Degree Program Inventory of Arkansas Public Institutions for Higher Education
Curriculum: Counseling

167 Arkansas Department of Parks and Tourism

www.arkansasstateparks.com/things/events.asp

Guided walks, lake tours, historic sites, campfire programs, story telling living history, workshops, and others are offered at Arkansas state parks. Featured Events include information about specific current offerings.
Special Features: Option to search all the parks or by specific park, search by month, keyword, date; Kids Stuff
Curriculum: Social Studies

168 Arkansas Employment Security Department

www.careerwatch.org/

Occupations, Education, Getting a Job, Message from the Governor, Working Profiles, are some of the topics covered in the annual publication of the Arkansas Employment Security Department. Some resources are available on PDF.
Special Features: Financial Aid includes such resources as: Arkansas Academic Challenge Scholarships; Arkansas Student Loan Authority
Curriculum: Counseling

169 Arkansas Encyclopedia

www.geocities.com/arkencyclo/wiki/Governor_of_Arkansas/

Arkansas Territorial Governors, 1819–1836; Governors to the present. Information includes links to their political party, significant dates that were the same year as the years they held office as well as links to people, places, and events mentioned in their biographies.
Special Features: Information on important aspects of Arkansas as a state may also be accessed
Curriculum: Government; Social Studies

170 Arkansas Forestry Commission

www.forestry.state.ar.us/education/education.html

Contacts to the commission office for your county, free video tapes for teachers, forest management and protection, links to other education sites; fire statistics by month, cause, county.

Special Features: A 50-page booklet about establishing and developing an outdoor classroom

Curriculum: Science

171 Arkansas Historic Preservation Program

www.arkansaspreservation.org/

Youth education program includes such offerings as free classroom presentations, lesson plans, grants. Antebellum cotton plantation virtual tour, Arkansas Civil War Battlefield update, walking tours of National Register of Historic Places.

Special Features: E-mail newsletter
Curriculum: History

172 Arkansas History Commission

www.ark-ives.com/

Some of the commission's activities includes the preservation of the official archives of Arkansas, the collection of Arkansas historical materials, the encouragement of research. Features include: Frequently Asked Questions, History Facts, and others.

Special Features: Thousands of historical images of Arkansas
Curriculum: History

173 Arkansas Humanities Council, National Endowment for the Humanities

www.arkhums.org

Includes a link to a four-day lesson plan on Arkansas animals for Grades 1–4 about the different animals living in the wild. Provides a list of the wild animals, a website for other Arkansas lesson plans.

Special Features: Includes appropriate Arkansas *Curriculum* Frameworks
Curriculum: History; Language Arts; Science; Social Studies

174 Arkansas Judiciary

courts.state.ar.us/courts/kids_pages.html

Information for children about the third branch of government, the judiciary. Slide shows or text only versions to select.

Special Features: Citizen Resources; Professional Resources; Online Resources
Curriculum: Government; Social Studies

175 Arkansas News Bureau

www.arkansasnews.com/

The newspaper covers politics, government, business, general interest, sports, for Little Rock and across Arkansas. Includes Harville's cartoons, columnists, today's news, recent news and commentary.

Special Features: Archives
Curriculum: Language Arts

176 Arkansas PTA

www.arkansaspta.org/

Legislative issues such as: Arkansas PTA Accountability Statement; State Convention, Workshops for school staff, parents, community; Online newsletters.

Special Features: Electronic contact with the Arkansas PTA President, and the National PTA website
Curriculum: Education

177 Arkansas School Band and Orchestra Association

www.asboa.org/

Eligibility scholarships, all-state auditions, audition sheets, links to Arkansas Legislative Matters, Arkansas Phi Beta Mu Hall of Fame, and others. Arkansas music news.

Special Features: PDF of the Arkansas Symphony Orchestra and other PDFs
Curriculum: Music

178 Arkansas Secretary of State

www.arelections.org/index.php

Election results by type of office, election results by geographic location, information on Arkansas voter turnouts and candidates, frequently asked questions about elections, past election results, and related information.

Special Features: Election Ballot Issues PDF
Curriculum: Government

179 Arkansas State Highway & Transportation Department

www.arkansasinterstates.com/fpdb/TouristMap .asp

Photo Gallery of construction on Arkansas roads; Trivia game about Arkansas roads;

Alternate Arkansas routes and what attractions may be seen.

Special Features: Online request for free Arkansas state map

Curriculum: Geography; Social Studies

180 Arkansas State Library

www.asl.lib.ar.us/

A profile and access to Arkansas State Library services; Arkansas Libraries Online include academic, public, special libraries; Arkansas Public Library Information includes a map by county and a directory to download; Arkansas State Library Calendar of Events including state holiday; library related news.

Special Features: Homework help is included under Quick Reference

Curriculum: Language Arts; Library Media

181 Center for Youth and Families (Sponsor: CenterSite, LLC)

www.youthandfamilies.org

Centers for Youth and Families is a nonprofit corporation providing behavior health services for children, adolescents and their families in central Arkansas since 1987. It includes school services.

Special Features: Depression Checklist, Glossaries, Book Reviews

Curriculum: Counseling; Psychology

182 Central Arkansas Library System

www.cals.lib.ar.us/CALSkids/index.html

Events for kids at the library, homework help, kids' links, Internet safety tips for kids, Internet tips for parents, and other features.

Special Features: Book Lists for Kids includes such lists as: Arkansas Diamond Primary Book Awards Reading List; The Coretta Scott King Awards Book List

Curriculum: Language Arts; Library Media

183 Children's Defense Fund

www.cdfactioncouncil.org/arkansas%20children.htm

Statistics relating to the children in Arkansas such: child support enforcement, infant mortality, health insurance, low birth weight.

Special Features: Education rankings

Curriculum: Education; Health; Sociology

184 Civil War Round Table of Arkansas

www.civilwarbuff.org/

Searchable database about what happened during the Civil War in various Arkansas counties; Civil War stories about ancestors of current Arkansans; Interactive Message Board for sharing information about Arkansas in the Civil War.

Special Features: Arkansas Civil War Reading List, videos; Links to Arkansas Civil War Collections; New books and reviews on Arkansas in the Civil War

Curriculum: History

185 Civil War (Sponsor: Tom Martin)

www.rootsweb.com/~arcivwar/

Arkansas Civil War Information covers such topics as: Confederate Units, Feature Sites, Links, and others. One of the stories in the Stories section includes: *The Civil War Memories of Joseph M. Bailey,* written upon the requests of his grandchildren.

Special Features: Audio medley of patriotic songs from the South

Curriculum: History

186 Clinton Presidential Center

www.clintonpresidentialcenter.com/lib_index.html

Progress of the new center which will include the Presidential Library and Archives, renovation of the abandoned Rock Island Railroad Bridge, and the adaptive reuse of the historic Choctaw Station.

Special Features: Preview of exhibitions

Curriculum: Social Studies

187 Edward G. Gerdes Civil War Home Page

www.couchgenweb.com/civilwar/

Confederate Women of Arkansas 1861–1865; Arkansas Regimental Histories; The Arkansas Civil War Medal of Honor Winners; Arkansas in the Civil War Message Board; 1st Arkansas Cavalry Regiment, 2D Arkansas Mounted Rifles, First Arkansas Light Artillery, are just a few of the resources on this site.

Special Features: Search option by surname

Curriculum: History

188 Earthquakes (Sponsor: UALR)

quake.ualr.edu/

Arkansas geology, Arkansas earthquakes, the Madrid Fault Zone, research, from the Arkansas Center for Earthquake Education and Technology Transfer.

Special Features: School resources include activities, projects, virtual field trips and virtual earthquakes for: Pre-K, 1–6, 7–9, 10–12, and for Teachers/Administrators/Staff
Curriculum: Science

189 Historic Arkansas Museum

www.arkansashistory.com/

Historic grounds include pre–Civil War neighborhoods including the oldest home still standing in Little Rock. Exhibits of Arkansas-made art and artifacts. PDF on currently offered education programs; packet of educational material is also available.
Specific Features: Annual heritage events, living history reenactments, free teacher lesson plans on slavery in Arkansas
Curriculum: History

190 iHigh.com

arkansas.ihigh.com/

The High School Internet Network includes 287 Arkansas high school websites, boys sports, girls sports, and speech and debate. Some of the sports include: basketball, cross country, golf, gymnastics, ice hockey, soccer, swimming, and volleyball.
Special Features: School headlines, state sport records
Curriculum: Physical Education

191 Little Rock National Airport

lrn-airport.com/services/gallery.asp

The Arkansas Gallery is 1,740 square foot area near Gate 6 in the airport displaying the art of Little Rock and Arkansas with drawings, painting, sculpture, historic artifacts.
Special Features: List of current Arkansas exhibitors; what other art is also in the airport
Curriculum: Art

192 Maps (Sponsor: Sheila Farrell Brannon)

www.seark.net/~sabra/cnty.html

Outline maps of: Arkansas Territory 1819; Arkansas 1836; Arkansas 1850; Arkansas Present Day.
Special Features: Printable maps
Curriculum: History

193 Museum of Discovery

www.amod.org/

Collections, Events and Exhibits, Links and related features of the Museum of Discovery, and the Children's Museum of Arkansas in Little Rock. Teacher's Corner has information about services for children that are from 30 minutes to an hour long that are focused on the educational objectives of the Arkansas *Curriculum* Framework in several *Curriculum* areas for Pre-K through 12.
Special Features: Choice of In-Museum Programs, Interactive Rentals; Learning Resources, Outreach Programs
Curriculum: Biology; Health; History; Math; Science; Technology

194 Northeast Arkansas Humane Society

www.neahs.org/

Programs, Pet Photo Gallery, Lost and Found Pets, Calendar, Spaying and Neutering, Pet Safety, Links, Search option.
Special Features: Pet care information for those thinking of adopting as well as for those already owning a cat or dog
Curriculum: Social Studies

195 Old State House

www.oldstatehouse.com/

The multimedia museum of Arkansas history, people, and culture are a National Historic Landmark. A Just for Kids section is about what activities, programs, events, contests are available for children at the museum.
Special Features: Classroom aids, pre-arranged tours. Self-guided tours include floor plan and features to discover
Curriculum: History

196 School Directory (Sponsor: AS-IS)

www.as-is.org/

School directory of 310 school districts and 15 cooperatives in Arkansas, educational indicators, statistical trends, and related information on education in Arkansas.
Special Features: A detailed profile of Arkansas schools can be downloaded
Curriculum: Education

197 State of Arkansas

www.state.ar.us/

Government: State/Local Business; Community; Family; Travel; and others. Arkansas eNewsRoom provides recent articles that includes the date posted. Local information relating to your neighborhood is accessed by entering a zip code.

Special Features: Education in Arkansas includes Grades K–12 by county, city or zip code, or accessed alphabetically. Child Resources has links to online services and information relating to children.

Curriculum: Education; Government

198 University of Arkansas Cooperative Extension Service

www.kidsarus.org/

4-H Homepage, Arbor Day Poster Contest, Fire Ant Kids Corner, Safety, Cool Links, Open to All Youth, Volunteer, and other features for children.

Special Features: Leads you to: Evolution of Arkansas Agriculture Time Line/Panels from 1000 B.C. to the present

Curriculum: History; Social Studies

199 University of Arkansas for Medical Services

www.uams.edu/general_information/

Research, Technology, News, Outreach, Colleges and Student Services in Little Rock. Links to Arkansas Cancer Research Center, Get Healthy Arkansas, Arkansas Healthlink, Arkansas Cares, and others.

Special Features: Search for a doctor by name, department, condition/disease treated

Curriculum: Counseling; Health

200 U.S. Newspaper List

www.usnpl.com/arnews.html

Arkansas newspaper sites arranged alphabetically by city from Arkadelphia to West Memphis; Arkansas magazines by title; College newspapers by name of college such as the University of Arkansas at Fayetteville.

Special Features: Includes Arkansas television stations, radio stations, and useful links

Curriculum: Language Arts

201 Writers in the Schools

www.uark.edu/~wits/

Program by graduate students in the Program in Creative Writing at the University of Arkansas to encourage and guide Arkansas students to explore poetry and fiction. E-mail to contact if interested in a school visit.

Special Features: Five classroom activities; Links for teachers and poets

Curriculum: Language Arts

CALIFORNIA

202 Alcatraz Island/Golden Gate National Recreation Area

www.nps.gov/alcatraz/

Information on Alcatraz Island, one of Golden Gate National Recreation Area's most popular destinations. Useful information on the site includes online Tours of the famous prison island, plus articles on island Military, Penitentiary, Native Occupation, and Nature.

Special Features: FAQ-style document answering common questions about Al Capone, the Birdman, and escaping Alcatraz; photographic slide shows detail the island and accompany the topics

Curriculum: History

203 Association of California Water Agencies

www.acwanet.com/

Home page for a coalition for California's public water agencies, promoting leadership, advocacy, and information. Online resources include information on state water supplies, Issues & Outreach, News, Events, Products & Services.

Special Features: Comprehensive coverage of state water issues, including legislative matters; water facts and figures

Curriculum: Environmental Studies; Government; Science

204 Bristlecone Pine Tree (Sponsor: Leonard Miller)

www.sonic.net/bristlecone/

Discusses the science and history of the Ancient Bristlecone Pine, with emphasis on the White-Inyo mountain range of California. Includes scientific characteristics of the bristlecone, dendrochronolgy, gallery of .jpg images.
Special Features: Full-color photos; extensive links
Curriculum: Environmental Studies; History; Science

205 California Academy of Sciences

www.calacademy.org/

Homepage of Steinhart Aquarium, Natural History Museum, Morrison Planetarium. Contains a variety of K–12 friendly online exhibits and resources, including sections on the Earth, the Ocean, and Space; a Guide to California Seafood; Ants: the Hidden World Revealed; California Wildflowers; and more.
Special Features: Teacher Services area; Education resources
Curriculum: Biology; Education; Science

206 California Coalition for Youth

www.ccyfc.org/

This state-focused advocacy group promotes awareness and activism on issues affecting Californians ages 12 to 24. Maintains the California Youth Crisis Line, produces the online 'zine Youth Voices, provides a library of youth-related documents, offers memberships, links to related websites.
Special Features: Advocacy Calendar for local-area activism; full Spanish-language site
Curriculum: Social Studies

207 California Commission on the Status of Women

www.statusofwomen.ca.gov/default.asp

The government-funded Commission tracks women's issues in the state of California with an emphasis on legislative action and initiatives to further women's issues. Contains News, Issues, Legislation, Links, and a Calendar of events.
Special Features: Comprehensive links on women's issues; legislative and action alerts on current legislation
Curriculum: Government; Women's Studies

208 California Department of Education

www.clrn.org/home/

The California Learning Resource Network (CLRN) provides California educators with electronic supplemental resources that both meet local instructional needs and embody California curriculum frameworks and standards. Features standards-based reviews of commercial resources including textbooks, audio/video materials, and websites.
Special Features: A Lesson Plan Builder for creating curriculum-compliant courses; specific content areas for English-Language Arts, History-Social Science, Mathematics, and Science
Curriculum: Education; History; Language Arts; Math; Science; Social Studies

209 California Department of Water Resources

cdec.water.ca.gov/

The California Data Exchange Center is a central resource for state-specific hydrological data. Contents include Current River Conditions, Snowpack Status, Reservoir Data/Reports, Satellite Data, Water Supply, Weather Reports, others.
Special Features: Linked collection of comprehensive satellite images for weather, hydrology
Curriculum: Environmental Studies; Science

210 California Digital Library

www.californiadigitallibrary.org/

The California Digital Library is an online digital archive of California-specific materials made available to the public. Incorporates the University of California Digital Collections, the Online Archive of California (OAC), the Counting California statistical collection.
Special Features: Extensive range of tabulated statistics in the Counting California database; extensive historical and contemporary image collection at the OAC; extensive multi-topic document archive through the University of California Digital Collection
Curriculum: Economics; Education; Government; Social Studies

211 California Ethnic and Multicultural Archives

cemaweb.library.ucsb.edu/digitalArchives.html

A special collection that archives photographs, artwork, texts, and other digital collections by, for, and about ethnic and cultural minorities in California. Includes K–12 initiatives for classroom support. Backed by the University of California, Santa Barbara.

Special Features: Collections for African American, Asian American, Latin American, and Native American specialties; a constantly updated guide to Chicano Art

Curriculum: Art; History; Social Studies

212 California Historical Society

www.californiahistory.net/

California History Online contains articles on significant events and topics in California's history. Among the available topic areas are The First Californians, European Explorations, Mexican California, The Gold Rush, and The Great Depression. Each topic area features several informative articles.

Special Features: A clickable timeline that places topics in a visual chronology; full search features

Curriculum: History; Social Studies

213 California Labor Organization

www.calaborfed.org/

State AFL-CIO Organization, representing unions and labor organizations in the state. Contains valuable resources including areas About the Organization, Issues and Politics, Taking Action, Events, Workforce and Economic Development, News, Organizing, Resources.

Special Features: Organizational publications; fact sheets

Curriculum: Business; Social Studies

214 California Native Plant Society

www.cnps.org/

A statewide non-profit organization promoting interest and awareness in California's native flora. Website includes online Manual of California Vegetation, information on conservation and awareness, Action Alerts, membership information, more.

Special Features: Kid's Stuff page features basics of flowers, vegetation

Curriculum: Environmental Studies

215 California Science Teachers Association

www.cascience.org/

Professional organization of state science teachers. The website hosts information about CSTA; information about upcoming events and programs; their journal and other CSTA publications; membership information; and a variety of resources and links for science teachers both within and outside the state.

Special Features: Legislative resources pertaining to science education; K–12 curriculum resources

Curriculum: Education; Science

216 California State Association of Counties

www.csac.counties.org/

Comprehensive site on California counties. CSAC represents county government before the California Legislature, administrative agencies, and the federal government. Their website educates on the county structure, promotes county programs and services, and tracks legislative issues.

Special Features: Comprehensive list of every California county, including maps, links

Curriculum: Government

217 California State Legislature

www.legislature.ca.gov/

Official website of the state Legislature. Encompasses both state Senate and Assembly websites, plus Bill Information, Budget Information, Rules and Ethics, Calendar and Schedule, Oversight and Review, Legislators and Districts, Research and Publications.

Special Features: Comprehensive bill search; Find My District by zip code

Curriculum: Government

218 California State Library

www.library.ca.gov/

Information and services offered by the California State Library, Sacramento, and the Surtro Library, San Francisco. Information on and access to includes online catalogs, research databases, the California Research Bureau, genealogy resources, historical documents, and more. Some documents are in .PDF format.

Special Features: Fully searchable catalog of onsite stacks, Internet databases, and special collections

Curriculum: History; Library Media

219 California State Science Fair

www.usc.edu/CSSF/

The official home page for the state Science Fair, open to students in the 6th to 12th grade. Provides sections for Students, Judges, Volunteers, Sponsors, and the Media, as well as information on entering the Fair and a Reference Library.

Special Features: Complete listing of prior fairs, participants, projects, and winners

Curriculum: Science

220 California State University Department of Geography

geogdata.csun.edu/

Home to the California Geographical Survey, an online collection of California-specific and nationwide geographical resources, made publicly available. Includes an Electronic Map Library, Educational Materials, Cartographic Resources, and a Census Data Archive.

Special Features: Full-color digital images including topographical maps of major California regions, metropolitan maps of major cities, and statistic-oriented maps; course materials and syllabus examples

Curriculum: Geography; Science; Social Studies

221 California Voter Foundation

www.calvoter.org/index.html

A non-profit, non-partisan group providing voter resources and encouraging vote participation. Provides news, resources, voter guides, issues & publications of interest to Californian voters.

Special Features: Map Series provides comprehensive visuals for district, regional, and county divisions

Curriculum: Government; Social Studies

222 California Wildlife Center

www.californiawildlifecenter.org/homepage.htm

A publicly funded nonprofit organization wildlife rescue and release in Southern California. Content areas include What's New, How You Can Help, Emergencies, Education, and Living With Wildlife.

Special Features: Links and information about CWC school presentations; Argyle's Kids section for younger visitors

Curriculum: Geography; Science

223 California Wildlife Foundation

www.californiawildlifefoundation.org/

Website for the non-profit Foundation features information, links, and articles. Also contains links to contact the Foundation, ways to donate to the Foundation, and a subscription e-mail list.

Special Features: Articles on specific California species suitable for K–12 readers; articles are in .PDF format

Curriculum: Geography; Science

224 CaliforniaAuthors.com/California Writers.com

www.californiaauthors.com/

Contains resources for and about California writers. Site includes California author lists; lists of books by California authors and about California subjects; online essays by local (California) authors; submission opportunities within the state and of interest to local authors; and news of interest to local authors or those interested in local authors.

Special Features: A comprehensive list of California authors, including links to personal or professional web pages and lists of relevant works; resources for interested authors local to California

Curriculum: Language Arts

225 CaliforniaColleges.edu

www.californiacolleges.edu/

Information resource for California public and private schools, dedicated to getting students started in their college careers. Features school facts, application procedures, financial information, and career advice for current and prospective college students.

Special Features: Full range of online tools to assist in college selection

Curriculum: Education

226 The César E. Chávez Institute (Sponsor: San Francisco State University)

www.cesarechavezinstitute.org/home/

The César E. Chávez Institute (CCI) is an education and activism organization dedicated to the impact of social oppression on the health, education, and well being of disenfranchised communities. Based in San Francisco, the CCI is named for the famous Californian minority rights activist. Offers student training, as well as college-level internships and assistantships. Appropriate for older students.

Special Features: Extensive articles on youth, minority, and LGBT issues
Curriculum: Education; Social Studies

227 City of Los Angeles

www.ci.la.ca.us/

Government homepage for Los Angeles, the most populous California city. The first source for local government information, civic services, employment and business opportunities, city events calendar, resident and tourist resources.
Special Features: For Youth section, including links to LA-based kids programs, websites
Curriculum: Geography; Government

228 City of Sacramento

www.cityofsacramento.org/

Government homepage for California's capitol city. Contains resources for residents and visitors. Links to local departments and services, employment and business information, maps of the area.
Special Features: Sister Cities program unites Sacramento with cities in Europe, Asia, New Zealand
Curriculum: Geography; Government

229 Driving in California (Sponsor: Hamish Reid)

www.caldrive.com/

California Driving: A Survival Guide is an on-line book for native drivers, visiting tourists, and new residents. Summarizes and illustrates the laws, conditions, and quirks of surviving on California roads.
Special Features: "Test Your California Driving IQ" quiz
Curriculum: Driver Training; Social Studies

230 Golden Gate Bridge

www.goldengatebridge.org/

Official website for the famous bridge. Site includes fares and rates, driving and walking regulations, information about the bridge, news/events, photos.
Special Features: Student-friendly Research Library catalogs facts and statistics about construction, maintenance, traffic, history
Curriculum: Geography; History

231 Historical Landmarks (Sponsor: Donald Laird)

www.donaldlaird.com/landmarks/

Privately collected archive of state landmark facts and images. Features over 1000 pages of California State Historical Landmarks. Many provide images and text of plaques, and some even provide GPS coordinates. Sorted by county.
Special Features: Colorful map for easy navigation
Curriculum: History

232 History (Sponsor: Joel GAzis-SAx)

www.notfrisco.com/calmem/index.html

The California Reader is a collection of primary documents about California's past, assembled from a private collection. Poems, postcards, photographs, and eyewitness accounts detail subjects including Catalina Island, the Arrowhead formation, San Francisco Bay, the Chaparral, more.
Special Features: Great section on *ursus californicus*, the extinct California black bear
Curriculum: Geography; History; Social Studies

233 Humboldt County Office of Education

scorescience.humboldt.k12.ca.us/default.htm

Schools of California On-line Resources for Education (SCORE) provides this website dedicated to providing science resources to K–12 educators. Resources for earth, life, and physical sciences, plus group information.
Special Features: Kid's Corner featuring fun activities; Teacher's Place including lesson plans and collaborative projects
Curriculum: Education; Science

234 Legislative Council of California

www.leginfo.ca.gov/index.html

State-maintained official site for California legislative information. Contains current events, bill information, California law, legislature information, and legislative publications (requires Adobe Acrobat Reader).
Special Features: Completely searchable, full-text database of laws, statues, and codes
Curriculum: Government

235 Library of Congress

memory.loc.gov/ammem/afccchtml/

California Gold: Northern California Folk Music From the Thirties is an audio and graphical archive preserving cultural music from California's past. Contains the entire collection of the WPA California Folk Music Project, conducted circa 1940.

Special Features: Audio archive of folk music in .wav, .ra. and .mp3 format

Curriculum: History; Music; Social Studies

236 Natural History Museum of Los Angeles County Foundation

www.tarpits.org/

The Page Museum is dedicated to the La Brea Tar Pits. Website features include museum information, history and geology of the tar pits, and a children's section.

Special Features: "Shasta's Sticky Situation" online educational adventure

Curriculum: Biology; History; Science

237 Natural Resources Conservation Service

www.ca.nrcs.usda.gov/

State website for environmental studies and natural resource preservation. Includes information on soils, water, air, plants, animals, communities, farmers, policy, volunteering, and an education section for teachers and students. Supported by the USDA.

Special Features: "S.K. Worm Teaches About Soil" kid-friendly section

Curriculum: Environmental Studies; Science

238 Oakland Museum of California

www.museumca.org/

State museum dedicated to art, history, and natural science exhibits. Site contains a list of Exhibitions, Calendar, Online Resources, plus visitor and donation information.

Special Features: Virtual Exhibitions available online; California-specific curriculum resources for Latino history and the California gold rush

Curriculum: Art; History; Science

239 Orange Empire (Sponsor: Press-Enterprise)

www.orange-empire.com/

Website dedicated to the Orange Empire area of Southern California, also known as the Inland Empire (Riverside, San Bernadino, Ontario counties). History, OE Factoids, In the News, Photo Galleries, Data, City Pages.

Special Features: Regularly updated Orange Empire web log

Curriculum: Geography; History

240 Pacific Southwest Railway Museum Association

www.sdrm.org/

The Pacific Southwest Railway Museum chronicles the history of railroads in and around the state. Located in Campo, CA. Includes Museum information, History, Stories, Gallery, Sounds.

Special Features: Audio gallery with actual railroad sounds, calls

Curriculum: History

241 Phoebe A. Hearst Museum of Anthropology

hearstmuseum.berkeley.edu/exhibitions/ncc/splash.html

Native Californian Cultures exhibit, sponsored by the Phoebe A. Hearst Museum, provides images of artifacts on early California life. The images reflect the Hearst Museum collections, and include food objects, clothing, tools, ceremonial items, Ishi and Intercultural objects.

Special Features: High-quality images

Curriculum: History; Social Studies

242 Regents of the University of California

www.ca4h.org/

Homepage of the California 4-H Youth Development Program. User-friendly website contains resources for Newcomers, Members, Parents, Volunteers, and Educators; sections include News, Youth Leadership, Citizenship, Technology, more.

Special Features: Curriculum resources

Curriculum: Education

243 San Francisco Museum

www.sfmuseum.org/

The Virtual Museum of the City of San Francisco, an online arm of San Francisco's premier historical museum. Features major online exhibits of local interest, including the Gold Rush, the Golden Gate Bridge, and the Great 1906 Fire and Earthquake.

Special Features: Multi-function search by keyword, subject, or year

Curriculum: History

244 Sonoma County Wine Library

www.sonoma.lib.ca.us/wine/index.html

The Sonoma County Wine Library is a special collection dedicated to wine around the world, with a focus on California wines. Includes online articles, wine links, links to further areas of Sonoma County Library.
Special Features: WineFiles online database
Curriculum: Science; Social Studies

245 Southern California Earthquake Center

www.scec.org/

Organization devoted to tracking and informing on earthquakes in Southern California. Contains Research, Resources, and Education sections, as well as a link to the SCEC Data Center, an information-rich resource on seismic activity.
Special Features: K–12 and college earthquake resources, including links to USGS kid-friendly and teacher-friendly content pages, and curriculum guides; guide to commonly held Earthquake Myths
Curriculum: Science

246 State Humane Association of California

www.californiastatehumane.org/member.html

Statewide coalition of Humane Society, S.P.C.A., and other groups dedicated to the prevention of animal cruelty, formed in 1909 to pool resources and efforts. Contains a list of affiliated groups, including links to group websites (where applicable).
Special Features: List of career opportunities in the field; tracks and supports animal cruelty legislation
Curriculum: Social Studies

247 State of California, Forests

ceres.ca.gov/ceres/calweb/forests.html

The California Forests website, provided by the California Environmental Resources Evaluation System (CERES), is a summary site that lists every national forest in the state. Features a state forestland map, essays on coastal forests, and a compete list of forest areas.
Special Features: Links to forest and park specific websites
Curriculum: Environmental Studies; Geography

248 State of California, General Information

my.ca.gov/state/portal/myca_homepage.jsp

Welcome to California is a general information resource on the state. Content areas include Education and Training, Business, Health and Safety, Consumers and Families, Labor and Employment, History and Culture of California, Travel and Transportation, Environment and Natural Resources, Government.
Special Features: **California State and County QuickFacts; student reading and resources for Pre-School to 6th Grade, Middle School and High School, College and College-Bound**
Curriculum: **Business; Education; Geography; Government; Health; History; Social Studies**

249 Transportation and Land Use Collaborative of Southern California

www.tluc.net/

Organization dedicated to the growing problem of traffic, transportation, population, and land use in Southern California. Publishes information and editorials on transportation and land use, tracks legislation and policy issues, and serves as a coalition for more local California land use groups.
Special Features: Online articles and editorials; links to locale-specific and regional land use groups
Curriculum: Environmental Studies; Government; Social Studies

250 University of California Berkeley Seismological Laboratory

quake.geo.berkeley.edu/

The Northern California Earthquake Data Center is a comprehensive collection of data on seismic activity in Northern and Southern California. Contains information on recent and historical quakes, as well as an academic collection of data, maps, and links. Co-sponsored by the United States Geological Survey.
Special Features: Memento Mori real-time seismic activity meter; "Make Your Own Seismogram" allows location-specific activity tracking
Curriculum: Science

251 Yosemite Association

www.yosemite.org/

Not-for-profit educational organization that supports Yosemite National Park. Website contains visitor and membership information, seminar and event alerts, informative articles on Yosemite, and links of interest.

Special Features: Virtual Yosemite provides live webcam shots of Yosemite Valley and archives virtual Scenic Views

Curriculum: Environmental Studies; Geography; Science

COLORADO

252 Boulder Community Network

bcn.boulder.co.us/

The Boulder Area Sustainability Information network (BASIN) offers public access to area environmental information, with focus on waterways. Sections include Watershed, Water & Community, Personal Action, History, Learning, Current Events.

Special Features: Educator-oriented Learning section provides school activities, curriculum assistance, links

Curriculum: Education; Environmental Studies; History; Science

253 Bureau of Land Management

www.co.blm.gov/edu/kconnection.htm

The BLM's Kid's Connection website offers kid- and family-friendly pages on outdoor activities in Colorado. Stuff To Do, Things To See, Outdoor Activities, and Links to Other Environmental Education Sites, plus connections to the larger BLM website.

Special Features: Two online Wildflowers of Colorado coloring books (requires Adobe Acrobat Reader)

Curriculum: Geography; Science

254 City and County of Denver

www.denvergov.org/

Official homepage for both the city and county of Denver. Official information, History and Facts, Elected Officials, Safety, Neighborhoods, Employment, Doing Business, Online Services.

Special Features: Kid's page with interactive history timeline, virtual city tours

Curriculum: Government; History; Social Studies

255 City of Boulder

www.ci.boulder.co.us/

Official homepage and resource for Boulder, Colorado's state capitol. Informational sections on the site include Government, Things To Do, Weather & Conditions, News Releases, and Employment.

Special Features: Visitor's page includes full-color maps, photographs, links to other sites

Curriculum: Government; Social Studies

256 City of Colorado Springs

www.pikespeakcolorado.com/index.htm

Website dedicated to Pikes Peak, "America's Mountain," sponsored by the city of Colorado Springs. Offers visitor information, plus sections on history, wildlife, geography, recreation, a map of the region.

Special Features: Online streaming videos; Pikes Peak webcam

Curriculum: Geography; History

257 Colorado Alliance for Arts Education

www.artsedcolorado.org/

The CAAE promotes K–12 arts education in Colorado. Their website contains resources for teachers, parents, and art organizations, plus advocacy and "Get Involved" pages. Developed in cooperation with the Colorado Endowment for the Arts.

Special Features: Content standards and curriculum advice for Dance, Music, Theatre, Visual Arts

Curriculum: Art; Dance; Drama; Education; Music

258 Colorado Association of Libraries

cal-webs.org/

Informational website provides library resources for the state. Contains Association information and bylaws, national and state-specific library links, publications of the Association, legislative news, other library resources.

Special Features: Special section on Intellectual Freedom, including brochures on the USA Patriot Act and an Intellectual Freedom Handbook

Curriculum: Library Media

259 Colorado Children's Campaign

www.coloradokids.org/

Statewide non-profit organization dedicated to children's issues. Areas of concern include child development, health, education, and safety issues, as well as proactive and legislative action.

Special Features: KidsCount data archive provides profiles, graphs, maps, rankings, and raw data about state children

Curriculum: Government; Health; Social Studies

260 Colorado Counties, Inc.

www.ccionline.org/

Local website provides information about Colorado counties, legislative issues, and services provided by CCI. Contains information on Colorado counties, discussion of the county system, news items, membership information.

Special Features: Full-color, interactive map of Colorado counties

Curriculum: Government

261 Colorado Department of Education

www.coloradoliteracy.net/

The Colorado Family Literacy Consortium promotes CO literacy through program development, resource distribution, and literacy training. Resources for Parents, Communities, and Teachers/Service Providers.

Special Features: Recursos para Los Padres bilingual section

Curriculum: Education; Language Arts

262 Colorado Department of Personnel and Administration

www.colorado.gov/dpa/doit/archives/

The Colorado State Archives provides a wealth of information on the state. Content areas include state history, geography, and archive of state legal documents.

Special Features: Complete list of official symbols and emblems, along with brief history of their meaning and selection

Curriculum: Government; History; Social Studies

263 Colorado Department of Transportation

www.cotrip.org/

The CDoT Traveler's Information Guide provides a comprehensive resource for commuters and others traveling Colorado's highways. Available resources include Travel Information, Variable Message Signs, Traffic Cameras, Weather Conditions & Weather Stations, Commuter & Bicycle Traveler Information.

Special Features: Metro Denver Speed Map

Curriculum: Driver Training

264 Colorado Digitization Program

www.cdpheritage.org/

The Colorado Digitization Program aims to make Colorado historical and archive materials available online. Includes digital resources, historical newspaper collection, Colorado's Main Streets feature, Western Trails feature.

Special Features: Educator Resources offer state history curriculum suggestions, primary source reading materials, and lesson plans for grades 1–5, 6–8, and 9–12

Curriculum: Education; History

265 Colorado Division of Wildlife

wildlife.state.co.us/kids/index.html

The Discovery Pages of the Colorado Division of Wildlife is a kid-centered website featuring information and links on Colorado fauna. Puzzles, games, animal sights and sounds, informational essays, and a section for older students.

Special Features: Video and audio files of significant Colorado wildlife

Curriculum: Environmental Studies; Science

266 Colorado Endowment for the Humanities

asstudents.unco.edu/faculty/rjones/CWCC/index.htm

Colorado Writers For Colorado Classrooms is an online resource of Colorado authors and texts. Provides bibliographical and curriculum information divided by genre, reading level, author, and subject.

Special Features: Online critical summaries of major Colorado works
Curriculum: Education; Language Arts

267 Colorado Film Commission

coloradofilm.org/home.html

Commission organized by the Colorado Tourism Office to regulate and assist state filmmakers and film festivals. Website contains information for filmmakers, festival organizers, visitors, and film fans; current projects, film highlights, festival calendar, more.
Special Features: Complete Colorado filmography
Curriculum: Social Studies

268 Colorado Geological Survey

geosurvey.state.co.us/

State-sponsored organization for geological monitoring, information, and excavation. Includes the Colorado Avalanche Information Center, a reporting, monitoring, and historical archive for avalanche activity in the state.
Special Features: RockTalk online newsletter (requires Adobe Acrobat Reader)
Curriculum: Geography; Science

269 Colorado HealthSite

www.coloradohealthsite.org/

Website of a non-profit corporation that provides electronic access to medical information, support, and resources. Content areas include Chronic Illnesses, Holistic Therapies, Drug Information, Women's Issues, Food Safety, Youth Center, Minority HealthSite.
Special Features: School Projects page details educational outreach
Curriculum: Health

270 Colorado Historical Society

www.coloradohistory.org/

State organization that "collects, preserves, and interprets the history of Colorado for present and future generations." Provides information on Exhibitions, Programs, Activities, Museums, Libraries.
Special Features: Kid's section provides games, articles, information for educators
Curriculum: History

271 Colorado Humane Society and S.P.C.A.

www.coloradohumane.org/

State website dedicated to the rescue and care of animals in the state. Adoption information, services, volunteer information, off-site links.
Special Features: Community bulletin of events; links to local shelters, clinics, rescues
Curriculum: Social Studies

272 Colorado State Library

www.aclin.org/

The Colorado Virtual Library is a central resource for state libraries. Search libraries across the state, access online data and archives, find local libraries, request an interlibrary loan.
Special Features: Colorado for Kids section provides subject-divided, kid-friendly resources; Teachers section provides K–12 support in keeping with state curriculum standards
Curriculum: Education; Library Media

273 Colorado State University

waterknowledge.colostate.edu/

Colorado Water Knowledge collects information about state waterways, including flora and fauna. Basic state water facts, details and maps of state waterways, water quality facts, links to related sites. Co-sponsored by Colorado Water Resources Research Institute.
Special Features: CWRRI Kids page features kid-friendly links, water facts quiz
Curriculum: Biology; Environmental Studies; Science

274 Colorado State University Cooperative Extension

www.ext.colostate.edu/

CSU's Cooperative Extension site contains state-specific information and links about Cooperative Extension. Includes areas on Crops/Soil, Drought/Fires, Farm Management, Food & Nutrition, Insects, Livestock, 4-H, more.
Special Features: AnswerLink section with comprehensive Q&A on State Cooperative Extension issues
Curriculum: Science

275 Colorado State University Department of Atmospheric Science

ccc.atmos.colostate.edu/

Colorado Climate Center assists the state in monitoring climate in both short and long term studies. Links to regional climate centers and to the National Climate Data Center; provides additional data resources and links.

Special Features: Learn about the Climate of Colorado feature

Curriculum: Environmental Studies; Science

276 Colorado Technology in Teacher Education Consortium

soe.cahs.colostate.edu/cttec/

CTTEC addresses state and national technology requirements for new teacher licensures. In addition to organization and event info, website contains tutorials, resources for new teachers.

Special Features: Guide to WebQuest development

Curriculum: Education; Technology

277 Colorado Tourism Office

www.colorado.com/default.asp

Travel and tourism information for Co visitors. Includes vacation guide; Colorado Info; road, scenic, and regional maps.

Special Features: Kids Stuff pages with information, activities

Curriculum: Geography; Government

278 Colorado Wolf and Wildlife Center

www.wolfeducation.org/

CWWC focuses on protecting state wolf populations, promoting wolf education and awareness. Online publications & resources, Center information, scheduling Wolf Tours online.

Special Features: Online wolf gallery; streaming wolf video

Curriculum: Environmental Studies; Science

279 Colorado Women's Agenda

www.womensagenda.org/

State women's commission, dedicated to the economic, social, and political security of women. Tracks legislative issues, promotes grassroots action, offers group memberships.

Special Features: Legislative scorecard tracks representative's votes.

Curriculum: Government; Women's Studies

280 Colorado Women's Hall of Fame

www.cogreatwomen.org/

Traveling exhibits highlight the contributions of great women in Colorado. Website contains every contemporary and historical hall inductee, along with information on tours, exhibits around Colorado, etc.

Special Features: Readers can nominate new Colorado women to the hall

Curriculum: History; Social Studies; Women's Studies

281 DenverStories.com

www.denverstories.com/

This website collects the real stories of Denver residents, past and present. Set up in a weblog format, Denver residents log on and post essays, anecdotes, observations about the city.

Special Features: Local students have the ability to contribute

Curriculum: Social Studies

282 Department of Public Health and Environment

www.cdphe.state.co.us/stats.asp

Collected statistics and research data on various health and environmental topics, including birth, death, marriage, divorce statistics. Requires Adobe Acrobat Reader.

Special Features: Colorado Health Information Dataset with state, county and local level birth and death statistics

Curriculum: Health; Social Studies

283 Fort Collins Public Library

library.ci.fort-collins.co.us/

The Online Digital Archive provides online access to portions of the Fort Collins Public Library's Local History Archive. Most entries combine scholarly essays with images culled from the Local History Archive, and represent elements of the Archive that have fragile or limited-access.

Special Features: Local Anecdotes narrate Colorado history in the voices of those who lived it

Curriculum: History

284 Fourteeners Hiking Site (Sponsor: ColoradoWebsites.com)

www.coloradowebsites.com/fourteeners/

This website gathers information on the Colorado Fourteeners, 54 mountains over 14,000 ft. high. The site contains mountain descriptions, photographs of hiking expeditions, and advice for hiking the Fourteeners. Maintained by hiking enthusiasts.

Special Features: Complete index of Four-teeners by elevation
Curriculum: Sports

285 Genealogy for Students (Sponsor: Mary Ann Hetrick)

www.rootsweb.com/~cokids/

The COKidsGenWeb Project is an online resource for Colorado K–12 students to begin researching their family origins. Basic, Intermediate, and Advanced pages allow for kids of varying skill levels to begin researching their genealogy; provides state and national links for genealogical information.
Special Features: Teacher's Page gives advice for incorporating genealogical research into curriculum
Curriculum: History; Social Studies

286 Ghost Towns (Sponsor: Universal Systems)

www.coloradoghosttowns.com/

Colorado Ghost Towns & Mining Camps online. Informative website features fifteen prominent historical sites in Colorado, including detailed directions for those who with to visit the sites.
Special Features: Online tours of each site, including history, photos, maps
Curriculum: History

287 History (Sponsor: Savert Technologies)

www.coloradohistory.com/index.htm

General history site for the state, featuring state and county information. Includes a plethora of links for Chambers of Commerce, Museums, Historical Societies, county seats, more.
Special Features: Clickable county map includes map, brief history of each county
Curriculum: Government; History

288 Land Use History of North America

www.cpluhna.nau.edu/index.htm

LUHNA's Colorado Plateau page discusses the biology, ecology, geology, geography, population, and land-use history of the four-state area named for CO. Collects information from a broad range of sources, and collects them in an accessible form.
Special Features: Summaries of current scientific research on the plateau

Curriculum: Biology; Environmental Studies; Geography; History; Science

289 Lore, Legend, and Fact (Sponsor: Ellen's Place)

www.ellensplace.net/hcg_fac.html

Colorado Lore, Legend, and Fact is a well-designed site that collects historical anecdotes, along with images, statistics, and maps. Privately created, but of high-quality.
Special Features: Colorado Qwik Facts page
Curriculum: History; Social Studies

290 Morrison Natural History Museum

town.morrison.co.us/dinosaur/index.shtml

Dinosaurs of Colorado website collects information on dinosaur finds within the state. Data sorted by name, chronology, and taxonomic classification, and includes information on extinction.
Special Features: Finding details include dates, locations, contents of state finds
Curriculum: Science

291 National Park Service

www.nps.gov/romo/index.html

Home page for the Rocky Mountain National Park, Colorado. Subsections include Planning Your Visit, Natural & Cultural Resources, Downloads & Photos, Education, Park Planning and Management Issues.
Special Features: Full color, detailed map of the park; information on the Park as an educational area, including the Heart of the Rockies educational resource page
Curriculum: Education; Geography; Geology; Science

292 Old Colorado City Historical Society

history.oldcolo.com/default.htm

Website dedicated to local and state history. Includes many online articles, including oral histories and biographies, a signpost timeline, maps & architecture of Old Town, more.
Special Features: Catalog of useful research resources
Curriculum: Architecture; History

293 Paleontology (Sponsor: Steve Wagner)

www.paleocurrents.com/

PaleoCurrents is a public education resource dedicated to current paleontological projects in and around Colorado. Pages cover Efforts at the Denver Museum of Nature & Science, Other Topics in Paleontology, and Museum Virtual Tours. Developed with the cooperation of the DMNS.

Special Features: Virtual Tour of Dinosaur National Monument

Curriculum: Science

294 Pinecam.com

www.pinecam.com/

Community-run and community-supported site for the mountainous central region of CO. Gathers current conditions information, almanac statistics, panoramic webcams, forums and weblogs, local news, emergency information, highway conditions, more.

Special Features: Pinecam Panoramas; Radio Pinecam

Curriculum: Geography; Social Studies

295 Photographs of Life in The Colorado Rockies (Sponsor: Circles and Lines)

www.circlesandlines.net/index.cfm

Website collects historic and contemporary images of life in the Colorado Rockies. Mines, ghost towns, off road, seasons, wildlife, then & now sections. Also offers essay excerpts from Thoreau, Muir, Van Dyke.

Special Features: Full-color computer wallpaper of the region

Curriculum: Geography

296 Reference Site (Sponsor: John C. Wilson)

www.acoref.com/

Well-crafted reference site on Colorado, assembled by a state resident. Includes many photograph-heavy pages on history, tourism, ghost towns, national parks, weather, and more, plus links to state and local governments.

Special Features: Link list for all major Colorado sports teams and venues

Curriculum: Geography; Government; History

297 Rocky Mountain National Park (Sponsor: Jesse Speer)

www.explore-rocky.com/

Explore-Rocky.com is a guide to traveling and enjoying Rocky Mountain National Park. It is assembled and maintained by a professional nature photographer, and the website is replete with images of the range. Panorama shots, photo gallery, information on outdoor recreations, park history, more.

Special Features: The Weekly View, a new, high-quality image of RMNP updated weekly

Curriculum: Geography; History

298 SF-Colorado

www.sf-colorado.com/

Website collects information on writers of Speculative Fiction (science-fiction) in Colorado. Complete lists of authors, works, and websites (when available), online writings, plus convention, workshop, and membership information.

Special Features: On-site forum

Curriculum: Language arts

299 Southern Ute Indian Tribe

www.utelegacy.org/

Colorado Ute Legacy, an educational resource designed to work in conjunction with the Colorado Ute Legacy video presentation, which has been distributed to Colorado schools. The website contains a wealth of useful resources.

Special Features: Online curriculum support; color maps and photographs; discussion questions

Curriculum: Education; History; Social Studies

300 State of Colorado

www.colorado.gov/

Colorado government, laws, tourism, natural resources, transportation, taxes, colleges and universities, medical care programs, legislative information, consumer protection, and related topics.

Special Features: Kids and Students K–12 friendly resources; Public Schools K–12; Colorado's Missing Child Alert System

Curriculum: Education; Government; History; Science; Social Studies

301 Trails Illustrated (Sponsor: National Geographic Maps)

www.coloradoguide.com/

ColoradoGuide.com is dedicated to the outdoors and outdoor activities in Colorado. Sections on-site include recreational activities, rafting, parks & forests, ranches, wildlife, skiing & snowboarding, outdoor jobs.

Special Features: Wildlife Watch provides

good overview of Colorado animals, fishes, birds

Curriculum: Geography; Science

CONNECTICUT

302 Arts in Connecticut (Sponsor: Tito Victoriano)

www.hartnet.org/artsinct/

Arts in Connecticut resource contains a directory of important art and performance links, plus a calendar of arts and performance events. Also provides links of use to artists and art lovers.

Special Features: Full Spanish-language site
Curriculum: Art; Dance; Drama

303 Careers (Sponsor: Applied Information Management Institute)

www.connecticuthasjobs.com/

Career site for the state. Four main content areas, including For Job Seekers, For Employees, For Educators, and For Students. Designed for those exploring careers in the classroom, as well as for those seeking a job.

Special Features: Discover Your Career Strengths for students
Curriculum: Education; Social Studies

304 Children's Book Award (Sponsor: Bibliomation)

www.biblio.org/nutmegaward/

The Nutmeg Award is given out each year by CT's young readers. State students in grades 4–6 read nominated books and vote; their votes determine the winner. List of current nominees, past winners and nominees.

Special Features: Application for schools, classrooms to vote
Curriculum: Language Arts

305 City of Hartford

www.hartford.gov/

Official website for CT capitol. Major content areas for services, businesses, visitors, govern-

ment. "I want to …" quick links to most requested services, offices.

Special Features: Complete directory of civic websites
Curriculum: Government

306 City of New Haven

www.cityofnewhaven.com/

Official website of the city. Government and civic information, economic development, schools, visitors, links.

Special Features: A Guide to New Haven
Curriculum: Government

307 Connecticut Agricultural Experiment Station

www.caes.state.ct.us/

State-supported scientific research institution studies plants, pests, insects, soil, water, pesticides, more. Provides online resources, research efforts, and services.

Special Features: Online Plant Pest Handbook
Curriculum: Environmental Studies; Science

308 Connecticut Agriculture in the Classroom

www.ctaitc.org/index.html

Teacher's resources for using agriculture as a teaching focus in the classroom. Includes online curricular resources, plus information and links on Connecticut classroom opportunities.

Special Features: Online lesson plans, handouts (requires Adobe Acrobat Reader)
Curriculum: Environmental Studies; Science

309 Connecticut Association of Boards of Education

www.cabe.org/

CABE is a coalition of 151 state school boards.

Exists to serves local and regional boards and improving the quality of education throughout CT. Site offers info on membership, projects, events, services, staff.

Special Features: Advocacy services
Curriculum: Education

310 Connecticut Audubon Society

www.ctaudubon.org/default.htm

Website for the state chapter of the Society provides a wealth of online resources. Online nature articles, directories, photo gallery, backyard wildlife Q&A, advocacy, membership info, more.

Special Features: A Teacher's Guide and educational program info
Curriculum: Education; Environmental Studies; Science

311 Connecticut Children's Museum

www.childrensbuilding.org/

New Haven institution catering to young children, focusing on education in a variety of subjects. Museum guidelines, information on visiting, exhibits, field trips, special programs.

Special Features: Curriculum resources; schedule a field trip
Curriculum: Biology; Education; Language Arts; Math; Science; Social Studies; Technology

312 Connecticut Commission on the Arts

www.ctarts.org/

The CT Commission on Arts, Tourism, Culture, History & Film supports state arts and cultural resources. Website includes sections for News, Public, Schools, Artists, Organizations, Industry.

Special Features: Resources for Schools featuring ArtsConnectEd interactive resource
Curriculum: Art; Education; History; Social Studies

313 Connecticut Department of Environmental Protection

dep.state.ct.us/burnatr/wildlife/wdhome.htm

CDEP's Wildlife Division provides an informative website. Resources on CT wildlife include Fact Sheets, Endangered Species Information, Wildlife Slideshows, .PDF Library.

Special Features: Just For Kids section
Curriculum: Biology; Science

314 Connecticut Digital Library

www.iconn.org/index.html

iCONN allows CT residents to search libraries statewide and access digital content, all with their local or school library account. Registration at local library required.

Special Features: Information and resources for librarians and teachers
Curriculum: Library Media

315 Connecticut Fund for the Environment

www.cfenv.org/

CFE's environmental action site, a not-for-profit resource on CT endangered species, endangered lands, aquifer protection, clean emissions standards, environmental law, and related topics.

Special Features: Downloadable .PDFs (requires Adobe Acrobat Reader)
Curriculum: Biology; Environmental Studies; Government; Science

316 Connecticut Historical Commission

www.ctfreedomtrail.com/

Website dedicated to recognizing important CT sites associated with the Underground Railroad and African American history, collectively called the CT Freedom Trail. Essays, maps, location & information on historical sites.

Special Features: Online virtual tour
Curriculum: History; Social Studies

317 Connecticut History Online

www.cthistoryonline.org/

Site dedicated to preserving and presenting pictures, maps, documents, and essays on state history. Collaborative online effort between multiple state institutions, including the University of Connecticut and the Connecticut Historical Society.

Special Features: CHO in the Classroom provides curriculum guidance for teachers; Journey section provides complete presentations on Diversity, Livelihoods, Lifestyles, Environment, and Infrastructure
Curriculum: Education; History

318 Connecticut Humane Society

www.cthumane.org/

State home page dedicated to animal rescue, control, and care. Contains links to local shelters, clinics, programs, adoption, and opportunities.
  Special Features: Library section contains informative articles on animal care
  Curriculum: Social Studies

319 Connecticut Humanities Council

www.cthum.org/default.htm

Connecticut's Cultural Gateway provides online resources and information portal for state humanities, history, and cultural life. Created by the Connecticut Humanities Council.
  Special Features: Cultural Resources for Teachers; Activities for Readers of all ages
  Curriculum: Language Arts; Library Media; Social Studies

320 Connecticut State Library

www.cslib.org/faq.htm

The CSL Research Resources page is a well of information for students doing research in or on the state. Includes multiple on-site FAQs, as well as links to research databases and other resources.
  Special Features: Homework section provides compendium of state facts
  Curriculum: Government; History; Library Media

321 Connecticut Trust For Historic Preservation

www.towngreens.com/

The TownGreens project provides online information about state traditional civic features. GreenLink to 172 recognized town greens, online exhibits, informational DataCenter. Includes online articles.
  Special Features: Survey maps of each green
  Curriculum: History; Social Studies

322 Connecticut United for Research Excellence

www.biorap.org/

Biological Research for Animals and People (Bio-RAP) Is an online resource for medical and health information. Topics include Cancer, AIDS, Aging & Genetics, Sun & Skin, Product Safety. Each subject includes Student Issues, Teacher Guide.
  Special Features: Connecticut BioBUS touring classroom demonstration
  Curriculum: Health; Science

323 Connecticut Wildlife Division: Connecticut Department of Environmental Protection

dep.state.ct.us/burnatr/wildlife/wdhome.htm

Facts about Wildlife in Connecticut.
  Special Features: Links, PDF's
  Curriculum: Environmental Studies

324 Connecticut Women's Hall of Fame

www.cwhf.org/

Museum exhibits highlight the contributions of great women in Connecticut. Website contains essays on each hall inductee. Browse the Hall, Teaching & Learning, Community, Get Involved, Upcoming Events.
  Special Features: Comprehensive curriculum resources for teachers; For Students section
  Curriculum: Education; History; Social Studies; Women's Studies

325 CT Gravestones Network

www.ctgravestones.com/

Organization educates the public about graveyard and cemetery preservation in CT, gravestone carving as an art, and the importance of gravestones and cemeteries in CT and national history. Sources on rubbings, history, locations, conservation, reading list, more.
  Special Features: Teaching History promotes using gravestones as a classroom subject
  Curriculum: History; Social Studies

326 Waterfalls (Sponsor: David A. Ellis)

www.ctwaterfalls.com/

A guide to Connecticut's Waterfalls, created by a hiker and nature enthusiast. Includes an online tour of waterfalls, plus comprehensive list by name, county, height, waterflow. Includes clickable map.
  Special Features: Hear the sounds of each waterfall
  Curriculum: Geography; Science

327 The Eli Whitney Museum & Workshop

www.eliwhitney.org/main.htm

Hamden, CT museum celebrates the famous inventor. Online resources include multiple essays on Whitney, his inventions, his family, the cotton gin, archeological digs, plus museum information, available school programs, links.
  Special Features: Time Machine 1798
  Curriculum: Education; History; Technology

328 Folk Dancing and Folk Music (Sponsor: Walter Olson)

walterolson.com/local/musicdance.html

Online overview of folk dancing and folk music resources in Connecticut. Written by a folk dancing enthusiast.
Special Features: Extensive dance and music links
Curriculum: Dance; Music

329 Geology (Sponsor: Wesleyan University)

www.wesleyan.edu/ctgeology/

Connecticut Geology website for educators and students. Geology and the CT. Landscape, A Genius for Water, Dinosaur State Park, Groundwater Pollution, Stream Flow Duration, Glacial Geology, Geologic Hazards, Trap Rock Ridges, Virtual Field Trips, Ask a Geologist, Connecticut Geology Illustrated.
Special Features: Teaching Plans and Materials on site; full-color maps
Curriculum: Geography; Science

330 Golden Hill Indian Tribe

paugussett.itgo.com/

Information on the Paugussett Indian Nation and the Golden Hill Indian Tribe of CT. History of the tribe, current tribal issues, land-claim legislation, social issues, more.
Special Features: Question and Answers page
Curriculum: History; Social Studies

331 Highways (Sponsor: Kurumi)

www.kurumi.com/roads/ct/index.html

ConnecticutRoads is an information site for every numbered highway in CT. Includes living, extinct, and proposed roads, including "secret" roads. Lists & Indexes, In Depth pages, History, maps.
Special Features: Connecticut Roads Quiz
Curriculum: Driver Training; Geography; History

332 Historic Ship Nautilus and Submarine Force Museum

www.ussnautilus.org/

Official website for the USS *Nautilus*, docked as a museum in Groton, CT. The website offers virtual tours of submarine and museum, plus history, crew information, medal of honor recipients, information on visiting.
Special Features: 360-degree panoramic views of *Nautilus*
Curriculum: History

333 History (Sponsor: Mark Williams)

www.connhistory.org/

Connecticut History on the Web is a teacher-oriented site that provides materials and lesson plans for history and social studies teachers. Williams is an author and history teacher.
Special Features: Assessment and Evaluation sections provided for all covered topics
Curriculum: Education; History; Social Studies

334 Lighthouses (Sponsor: Jeremy D'Entremont/Coastlore Productions)

lighthouse.cc/ct.html

Comprehensive page of Connecticut Lighthouses. Each lighthouse includes a complete history, bibliography, photographs, maps.
Special Features: Includes historic, but no longer existing, lighthouses
Curriculum: History

335 The Mark Twain House

www.marktwainhouse.org/

Homepage for the state historic landmark, birthplace of Mark Twain. Online pages include a history of the house, virtual tour, Twain timeline, information on teaching Twain and visiting the house as part of a curriculum.
Special Features: Just for Kids section
Curriculum: History; Language Arts

336 Mystic Seaport

www.mysticseaport.org/library/initiative/intro.html

The G. W. Blunt White Library Digital Initiative collects a number of historical maritime collections online. Ship records, logbooks, bills of lading, ship registers, ships plans and more.
Special Features: Connecticut Ship Database, 1789–1939
Curriculum: History; Library Media

337 Neag School of Education at University of Connecticut

www.literacy.uconn.edu/

The Literacy Web gathers information and resources for promoting literacy in CT classrooms. Literacy Topics, Research, by topic or grade level.

Special Features: Literacy Web for Classroom Teachers

Curriculum: Education; Language Arts

338 New England Skeptical Society

www.theness.com/

Homepage for region-wide organization stationed in Hamden, CT, dedicated to the promotion of science/reason and the investigation of paranormal/pseudoscientific claims within New England. Online articles, organization and membership info, more.

Special Features: Online Encyclopedia of Skepticism and the Paranormal

Curriculum: Science

339 Quinnipiac University

www.quinnipiac.edu/x6776.xml

Quinnipiac's Digitized Connecticut History Books currently holds complete texts for thirteen titles. Books are valuable both as histories and as historical objects; many were written a century or more ago.

Special Features: Links to other digital collections

Curriculum: History; Library Media

340 Secretary of State's Office

www.sots.state.ct.us/RegisterManual/regman.htm

The Interactive State Register and Manual is the latest incarnation of a 200-year-old CT government publication. Covers state history, incumbent biographies, state government, counties, local government.

Special Features: Connecticut Towns In The Order Of Their Establishment, With The Origin Of Their Names

Curriculum: Government; History; Social Studies

341 SoundWaters

www.soundwaters.org/index.htm

Organization that educates the public about Long Island Sound and promotes Sound preservation. Resource guides online for parents, students, teachers, plus membership, programs, tours.

Special Features: Curriculum for teachers using SoundWaters programs

Curriculum: Education; Environmental Studies; Geography

342 Southeastern Connecticut Gang Activities Group

www.segag.org/

Information resource on gang activity in CT and nearby states. Contains information on CT gangs, hate & terrorist groups, regional & national gangs, resources for parents, teachers, & law enforcement.

Special Features: Parents & Teachers Guide to Gang Activity

Curriculum: Social Studies

343 State Climate Center (Sponsor: University of Connecticut)

www.canr.uconn.edu/nrme/cscc/

The Connecticut State Climate Center is a resource for weather and conditions around the state. Climate Overview, Climate Statistics, Links to related websites.

Special Features: Regional statistics from various points in the state

Curriculum: Science

344 State of Connecticut

www.ct.gov

Official state home page. Includes information on Working, Doing Business, Living, Learning, Visiting, and Governing Connecticut, as well as the CT.gov Reading Room provides convenient list of significant resources, grouped by area of interest.

Special Features: ConneCT Kids section features child-friendly discussion and information on the state.

Curriculum: Government; History; Social Studies

345 Talcott Mountain Science Center

g3.tmsc.org/face_of_ct/index.html

Online edition of *The Face of Connecticut* by Michael Bell. Book chronicles the people, geology, and land of CT. Includes photos, bibliography, index.

Special Features: Geologic Sketch map of CT.

Curriculum: Geography; Science; Social Studies

346 The Thornton Wilder Society

www.thorntonwildersociety.org/

Organization dedicated to the famous CT writer, three-time Pulitzer Prize winner and author of *Our Town*. Site contains biography, bibliography, newsletter, education resources.
   Special Features: Our Town study guide
   Curriculum: Education; History; Language Arts

347 Toxics Action Center

www.toxicsaction.org/ct/tic/index.html

Toxics in Connecticut is a database of hazardous and potentially hazardous sites in the state, including asphalt plants, landfills, incinerators, and power plants. Includes a Map of Sites, Top Ten Lists, Data Summary, Recommendations.
   Special Features: Town-by-town summary of sites, statistics
   Curriculum: Environmental Studies; Health; Science

348 University of Connecticut Libraries

digitalcollections.uconn.edu/

The Gateway to Digital Collections at the University of Connecticut Library, including the Melville Project, Colonial Connecticut Records, Invasive Plant Atlas of New England, Scanned Maps of Connecticut 1676–1900.
   Special Features: Links to digital collections worldwide
   Curriculum: Biology; Geography; History; Language Arts

349 University of Connecticut Marine Sciences

www.mysound.uconn.edu/

MYSound provides real-time monitoring of conditions, water quality, and wave data in Long Island Sound. Station reports, data archives, Sound webcams, water quality articles, resource links.
   Special Features: Clickable location map
   Curriculum: Environmental Studies

350 Yale University

www.yale.edu/

One of the most prestigious colleges in the nation. Complete resource for attending, visiting, learning about the university.
   Special Features: Facts about Yale; History of Yale
   Curriculum: Education; History

351 Yale-New Haven Teachers Institute

www.yale.edu/ynhti/

Homepage for the educational partnership between Yale University and the New Haven Public Schools. YNHTI's goals include enhancing teaching and learning in local CT schools. Includes Brochures & Reports, Online Publications, Published Reports, Curricular Resources, more.
   Special Features: Complete Curriculum Units (various subjects) by Fellows of the Yale–New Haven Teachers Institute from 1978
   Curriculum: Education

DELAWARE

352 AARoads.com

www.aaroads.com/delaware/

Delaware Highways is a comprehensive state road guide. Content on Interstates, SR1 Turnpike, U.S. Highways, State Routes, plus select city guides, exit guides, maps.
   Special Features: Delaware Highway Vidcaps
   Curriculum: Driver Education; Geography

353 African American History (Sponsor: University of Delaware)

www.udel.edu/BlackHistory/index.html

A History of African Americans of Delaware And Maryland's Eastern Shore, an online anthology of texts written by scholars and professors.
   Special Features: Series of Lesson Plans
   Curriculum: Education; History; Social Studies

354 Brandywine Zoo

www.brandywinezoo.org/

Wilmington, DE zoo presents exotic and indigenous animals. Website features short essays, images of zoo species; plus zoo info, programs & events, games, parent's resources, field trip and visitors guide, zoo games, links.

Special Features: Teacher Workshops & Loan Kits; Education Programs

Curriculum: Education; Science; Social Studies

355 Center for the Inland Bays

www.inlandbays.org/

Center promotes the protection and preservation of DE's Indian River Bay, Little Assawoman Bay, and Rehoboth Bay. Organization information, photo galleries, maps, online publications & reports, public policy initiative, news & events, contact info.

Special Features: Inland Bays Interactive Classroom program

Curriculum: Environmental Studies; Science

356 City of Dover

www.cityofdover.com/

Civic website for the DE state capital. Content for Residents, Visitors, Businesses, Government; plus civic services online, city departments, city Q&A, links.

Special Features: The Dover Guide

Curriculum: Government

357 City of New Castle

www.newcastlecity.net/

Civic website for DE's historic capital city features extensive historical information. New Castle's History, New Castle's Historic Buildings, New Castle Historical Society; plus civic info, departments, online services.

Special Features: Maps; Visitor's Bureau

Curriculum: Government; History

358 City of Wilmington

www.ci.wilmington.de.us/

Civic website for DE's largest city. About Wilmington, Mayor's Office, City Council, City Departments, Community Services, Business Services, Visitor's Guide Online.

Special Features: Access Wilmington; Sister Cities program

Curriculum: Government

359 Civil War (Sponsor: George W. Contant)

mywebpages.comcast.net/33dny/torbert.htm

Page discusses DE in the Civil War. DE History, DE regiments, DE officers, plus info on local recreation & preservation.

Special Features: Links to DE-related sites

Curriculum: History

360 Delaware Aerospace Education Foundation

www.dasef.org/

Organization educates DE students in math, science, technology and aerospace. Learn about events, presentations, professional development opportunities, and DASEF Exploration Center; read DASEF newsletter online.

Special Features: Educational programs; interesting NASA links

Curriculum: Education; Math; Science; Technology

361 Delaware Agricultural Museum and Village

www.agriculturalmuseum.org/

Organization dedicated to the preservation of DE's rural heritage. Take an online tour; info on museum & village visits, educational programs, events & programs, links.

Special Features: Use a visit to meet state educational standards

Curriculum: Education; History; Science; Social Studies

362 Delaware Art Museum

www.delart.org/

Dover, DE institution presents historic and modern works. Collections highlighted online; plus info on exhibitions, museum membership, education opportunities, the Helen Farr Sloan Library, programs & events, visitors info.

Special Features: Online exhibitions

Curriculum: Art

363 Delaware Audubon Society

www.delawareaudubon.org/

State organization for wildlife protection and habitat conservation. Activism news, opportunity, resources; conservation & education resources, articles; complete DE birding guide; contact info, links.

Special Features: Wetlands in DE; The Inland Bays of DE

Curriculum: Environmental Studies; Science; Social Studies

364 Delaware Center for Educational Technology

www.dcet.k12.de.us/

Works towards providing DE schools with modern educational technology. Provides teacher workshops, technical instruction, programs & events, state standards, resource links.
Special Features: Dial-up Internet access for all DE teachers
Curriculum: Education; Technology

365 Delaware Center for the Book

www.state.lib.de.us/Center_For_The_Book/DE_Reads/

Delaware Reads encourages K–12, adult literacy through programs, events. Website provides programs & events resources for libraries & classrooms, including reading lists, discussion questions, promotional materials, resource links.
Special Features: Sign up for a program
Curriculum: Education; Language Arts

366 Delaware Department of Education

www.k12.de.us/science/

The State of DE Science Page collects extensive resources, materials, info for state science teachers. The DE Science Van, Science Olympiad, teacher's resources, more.
Special Features: DE Science Comprehensive Assessment Program; DE Teachers of Science organization
Curriculum: Education; Science

367 Delaware Department of State

www.state.de.us/sos/dpa/

The DE Public Archives collects documents, photos of historical and cultural significance. Include the DE Digital Archives, featuring many online collections of historic photos, document exhibits, maps, and audio files.
Special Features: Historical Markers Program, with complete list
Curriculum: History; Social Studies

368 Delaware Department of Education

www.deldot.net/static/projects/archaeology/index.html

DelDOT Archaeological Exploration and Historic Preservation in DE; info on current and past projects; brief prehistory and history of DE; historic preservation.

Special Features: Delaware Bridge Book online; Hockessin Area Finds
Curriculum: History

369 Delaware Division of the Arts

www.artsdel.org/

DE's Division of the Arts serves as a statewide guide to arts, events, organizations. Areas for Artists, Arts Organizations, Arts Education, Community-Based Organizations; workshops & events info, applications; resource links.
Special Features: Artline Online; Educational Resources
Curriculum: Art; Dance; Drama; Language Arts; Music; Social Studies

370 Delaware Division of Libraries

www.answerline.lib.de.us/

DE Answer Online offers live, interactive research assistance to students, community. Connect with a librarian, technical assistance, partner libraries.
Special Features: E-mailed chat logs for future reference
Curriculum: Library Media

371 Delaware Division of Parks and Recreation

www.destateparks.com/

DE State Parks website features info, photos, maps, activity guides for each of DE's official recreation areas; plus, state Parks rules and regulations, FAQ, tourism info, links.
Special Features: Online reservation system
Curriculum: Environmental Studies; Social Studies

372 Delaware Division of Public Health

www.ysmoke.org/homepage.cfm

Kick Butts Generation is a state antismoking campaign focused on youth, teens. Mission & goals; programs & events; activism opportunities; facts, FAQs, links.
Special Features: NOT, TATU programs
Curriculum: Health; Social Studies

373 Delaware Division of Water Resources

www.dnrec.state.de.us/water2000/

State agency concerned with water quality, pollution, watershed, ecosystem. Online services, including permits; resident, business, contractor resources; Division publications; links.

Special Features: For the Educator
Curriculum: Environmental Studies; Science

374 Delaware Genealogical Society

www.delgensoc.org/

Organization collects, presents DE genealogical resources online. DE Families Project, Tax Transcription Project, Surnames List, events, news, general genealogy links.
Special Features: Resources for Delaware Counties, Hundreds and Towns and Places
Curriculum: History; Social Studies

375 Delaware Geographic Data Committee

www.datamil.udel.edu/

The DE DataMIL is an online mapping project, part of a national effort. Interactive Map Lab offers explorable digital map of DE with roads, political borders, cities, multiple levels of detail; plus project info, message boards, links.
Special Features: Create, print custom maps
Curriculum: Geography

376 Delaware Geological Survey

www.udel.edu/dgs/index.html

Collects, studies, and educates on geologic and hydrologic research and exploration in DE. Content on geology, hydrology, earth science, paleontology, geophysics; plus education resources, publications, links
Special Features: Earth Science Website of the Week
Curriculum: Environmental Studies; Geography; Science

377 Delaware Historical Society

www.hsd.org/

Organization chronicles and educates about DE history. Read about history; learn about events, programs, museums; take advantage of educational opportunities; HSD Kids page; contact info and links.
Special Features: DE History Explorer online encyclopedia
Curriculum: History

378 Delaware Humane Association

www.dehumane.org/

Organization supports animals through shelter, spay/neuter services, humane education programs, and adoption/placement resources.

Online resources, services; pet care & behavior articles; support, contact, links.
Special Features: Education & outreach opportunities
Curriculum: Social Studies

379 Delaware Institute for the Arts in Education

www.diae.org/

DIAE promotes quality art education in DE through programs, events, resources. Info on summer sessions, workshops for Dance, Music, Theatre, Visual Art, plus resource links, contact info.
Special Features: Delaware Wolf Trap Early Learning Program
Curriculum: Art; Dance; Drama; Education; Music

380 Delaware Library Association

www.wilmlib.org/bluehen.html

The Blue Hen Book Award is a state contest that encourages literacy. K–6 kids can participate by voting at their local library. See this year's nominees, past year's winners.
Special Features: Print voting ballot online
Curriculum: Language Arts

381 Delaware Nature Society

www.delawarenaturesociety.org/

Non-profit organization promotes education, advocacy, appreciation of DE's natural world. Educational programs, resources; events calendar; conservation resources and articles; contact & membership info.
Special Features: Ashland Nature Center; Abbott's Mill Nature Center
Curriculum: Environmental Studies; Science; Social Studies

382 Delaware River & Bay Lighthouse Association

www.delawarebaylights.org/

Group dedicated to preservation & restoration of historic DE and Bay lighthouses. Read about their restoration projects; programs & events; volunteer to help; news, contact info, links.
Special Features: The Light List
Curriculum: History; Social Studies

383 Delaware Science Coalition

www.sciencede.org/

Coalition of DE schools, government, and businesses dedicated to promoting and improving science education. Curriculum development & tools for each grade level, plus workshops & programs, resources, links.

Special Features: Register for modules, science kits, forums
Curriculum: Education; Science

384 Delaware SPCA

www.delspca.org/

Animal advocacy organization features online articles about animal care, ownership; plus services, spaying & neutering, rescue, vaccinations, contact info.

Special Features: Monthly statistics
Curriculum: Social Studies

385 Delaware State Education Association

www.dsea.org/

State teacher's organization provides extensive resources on its website. News & Events, Training & Professional Development, About DSEA, Salaries, Legislation, Pensions, Accountability, Membership.

Special Features: Teaching Tips; Great School program
Curriculum: Education

386 Delaware Tech

www.dtcc.edu/terry/htv/main.html

Homework TV broadcasts to Sussux and Kent counties during the DE school year. Provides kid-friendly educational programming. Online schedule, weekly themes, partner schools, links.

Special Features: Homework Help Links for summer sessions
Curriculum: Education

387 Delaware Women's Conference

www.delawarewomen.org/

Annual DE event celebrates accomplishments, lives, culture of women. Website provides info on upcoming event, including speakers, schedule, exhibitors, programs & events, plus registration, volunteer info.

Special Features: Conference History
Curriculum: Women's Studies

388 DelawareSports.com

www.delawaresports.com/

Delaware Sports provides news, information on DE sports, with a focus on high school athletics. News & Scores; Articles; Message Boards; athletic profiles; Athlete of the Year; Sports Videos; more.

Special Features: Competition schedules; Where Are They Now?
Curriculum: Physical Education

389 DiscoverSea Museum

www.discoversea.com/

DE maritime museum preserves nautical history, catalogs shipwrecks. Catalog of shipwrecks; coin beaches; colonial sites; photo gallery; museum info & visitor's guide; links.

Special Features: Featured Artifact
Curriculum: History

390 Fort Delaware Society

www.del.net/org/fort/

Organization supports the preservation and study of historic Fort Delaware. History and tour of the fort, troops stationed at the fort, Society info and history, publications, links.

Special Features: Research assistance
Curriculum: History

391 Kalmar Nyckel Foundation

www.kalmarnyckel.org/

Historical ship serves as DE museum, learning experience. Info on the Kalmar Nyckel, including ship specifications, history; scheduling a tour, voyage, or school trip; calendar of events, news, photo archive; contact and visiting info.

Special Features: Schedule a school trip
Curriculum: History

392 Kids Count in Delaware

www.dekidscount.org/

Collects data, presents findings on DE kid's health, economic, educational and social wellbeing. Kid's Count, Families Count, Kid's Voices Count, contact info, links.

Special Features: Online newsletter (requires Adobe Acrobat Reader)
Curriculum: Social Studies

393 Lewes Historical Society

www.historiclewes.org/complex/rfh.html

Collection of historical sites, museums in Lewes, DE. Online histories of a dozen sites, collection highlights, news & events, visitor's info, links; opportunities for educators, including a kid's page.

Special Features: Lewes History Online, with timeline, genealogical archives

Curriculum: History

394 The News Journal

www.delawareonline.com/

DE newspaper sponsors DelawareOnline, a comprehensive state web source. News, events, classifieds, web directory, more.

Special Features: Spark Weekly popular culture guide

Curriculum: Social Studies

395 Preservation Delaware

www.preservationde.org/

Organization dedicated to the preservation of DE architectural heritage and historic settings. Programs, Events, Resources, PDI & You, Success Stories, Endangered/Lost Sites, Advocacy, Search.

Special Features: Education & Outreach programs

Curriculum: History

396 State of Delaware

www.delaware.gov/

Official website for the state. Content areas for Government, Residents, Businesses, State Employees, Visitors, plus department sites, services online, Mayor's office, links.

Special Features: DE Kid's Page with Homework Help

Curriculum: Government

397 University of Delaware College of Agriculture & Natural Resources

www.ag.udel.edu/extension/

DE Cooperative Extension provides living resources to the community. Extension Publications, Agronomy, Pest Management, Family & Consumer Sciences, Food & Nutrition, Home Gardening, 4-H, educational resources, county contacts, links, more.

Special Features: The Safety Zone; Agricultural Resource List

Curriculum: Business; Economics; Educa-

tion; Environmental Studies; Health; Home Economics; Science; Social Studies

398 University of Delaware College of Geography

www.udel.edu/leathers/stclim.html

Office of the DE State Climatologist. Current conditions online; access real-time weather data; compiled climatological data; five-day forecasts; links.

Special Features: Delaware Environmental Observing System

Curriculum: Science

399 University of Delaware University Museums

www.museums.udel.edu/mineral/mineral_site/index.html

UD Mineralogical Museum displays a vast collection of mineralogical samples and promotes earth science education. View the collections online; learn about special exhibits; visitor's guide; links.

Special Features: Extensive Educational Resources

Curriculum: Science

400 Wildflowers (Sponsor: David G. Smith)

www.delawarewildflowers.org/

Hobby photographer and botanist collects images, info on DE flora. Wildflowers; Names, origin, and rarity; Pictures; References; Links.

Special Features: Further reading bibliography

Curriculum: Science

401 World Champion Punkin Chunkin Association

www.punkinchunkin.com/

Unique competition in Sussex County, DE; contestants build machine to fire pumpkins for record distances. Competition history, rules, scholarships, past winners, image gallery, news, FAQ, links.

Special Features: Youth League competition

Curriculum: Science; Social Studies; Technology

FLORIDA

402 American Civil Liberties Union of Florida

www.aclufl.org

ACLU is freedom's watchdog, working in the courts, legislature and communities to defend individual rights and personal freedoms guaranteed by the constitution and the Bill of Rights.

Special Features: Links such as Death Penalty, Free Speech, Immigrant Rights, Lesbian and Gay Rights, Racial Justice

Curriculum: Government; Social Studies; Sociology

403 Busch Gardens Florida Educational Programs

www.seaworld.org

Busch Gardens is committed to bringing the excitement, wonder and awe of the natural world to your home, school or business. It strives to provide an ever evolving kaleidoscope of animal and environmental information.

Special Features: Animal Information, Adventure Camps, Just for Teachers, Fun Zone, Conservation Matters

Curriculum: Environmental Studies; Social Studies

404 Department of Juvenile Justice

www.djj.state.fl.us/agency/index.html

Their purpose is to protect the public by reducing juvenile crimes and delinquency in Florida by providing strong prevention and early intervention.

Special Features: Juvenile Justice FAQs for teens

Curriculum: Government; Social Studies

405 Family Network on Disabilities of Florida

www.findfl.org

A statewide network of families and individuals who may be at-risk, have disabilities or special needs. It ensures free access to family-driven support, education, information, resources and advocacy.

Special Features: Various groups such as Parents Educating Parents (PEP) and Parent Education Network (PEN)

Curriculum: Special Education

406 Florida Aquarium

www.flaquarium.org

This is the story of water as it follows a "drop" of water from its underground source to the open seas. It explains over 10,000 aquatic plants and animals native to Florida.

Special Features: Wetlands, Bays and Beaches, Coral Reefs, Sea Hunt, Media Center (with high resolution photography)

Curriculum: Environmental Studies; Science; Social Studies

407 Florida Art Association

www.faea.org

The Florida Art Association has a rich history in developing substantive art programs. It focuses on art educators, realizing the passion for seeing students express themselves in special ways.

Special Features: Divisions, Teacher Institute, Resources, Conferences and Publications

Curriculum: Art; Education

408 Florida Arts and Culture Ring

d.webring.com/hub?ring=floridaarts

This website is a web ring for arts and cultural organizations, individual artists, and arts agencies in the state of Florida.

Special Features: Includes visual, performing and literary arts; arts education, history/heritage museums and media arts

Curriculum: Art; Education

409 Florida Association of Media Educators

www.floridamedia.org

Their purpose is to promote and publicize the school librarian's role in Florida, as well as to develop and implement statewide guidelines for teacher library specialists and media specialists.

Special Features: Media Festival, Conferences, New with FAME

Curriculum: Library Media

410 Florida Association for Music Therapy

www.floridamusictherapy.com

This Association was established in 1979 to insure professional services to the citizens of Florida by qualified music therapists.

Special Features: Related Sites, Calendar of Events, Colleges and Clinical Training
Curriculum: Education; Music

411 Florida Association of Museums

www.flamuseums.org/fam

Their searchable database of Florida's Museums is an online exploration of the cultural, historic and scientific resources of more than 340 museums in Florida.

Special Features: Resources link — annotated list of links to online resources about various types of museums
Curriculum: Art; History; Language Arts; Music; Social Studies

412 Florida Attorney General

www.myfloridalegal.com

The Attorney General is the constitutional, statewide elected official who serves as the attorney for the state of Florida. He/she is responsible for the enforcement of state consumer protection, antitrust laws and civil prosecution of criminal racketeering.

Special Features: Useful Government Links: Financial Services, Statutes, Constitution, Executive Office of Governor
Curriculum: Government; Social Studies

413 Florida Chamber of Commerce

www.flchamber.com/home/default.asp

The Florida Chamber of Commerce is Florida's largest federation of business, chambers of commerce and business associations. It includes over 120,000 member businesses.

Special Features: New Cornerstone: study to assess Florida's economic performance during the past decade
Curriculum: Business; Economics; Environmental Studies; Government; Social Studies

414 Florida Cultural Affairs Division

www.florida-arts.org/index.asp

The mission of this organization is to guide and facilitate cultural development and services for Florida's citizens and visitors through public and private partnerships.

Special Features: Florida Heritage Month, Feature Articles, Special Paintings and Displays, Tours
Curriculum: Art; Education

415 Florida Department of Citrus

www.floridajuice.com

This useful website includes information regarding health and nutrition for students, teachers and parents, as well as scientific research, citrus recipes, citrus related links and much more.

Special Features: Coloring book pages, recipes for kids, word scrabble.
Curriculum: Health; Home Economics; Science

416 Florida Department of Highway Safety and Motor Vehicles

www.hsmv.state.fl.us/html/dlnew.html

This website discusses Florida driver's license information, locations, identity protection, organ donations, voter registration, insurance laws and so forth.

Special Features: Classes, Requirements, Improvement Schools
Curriculum: Driver Training; Government

417 Florida Division of Consumer Services

www.800helpfla.com/~cs/aboutus.html

Its purpose is to protect, inform and empower Florida's consumers and businesses, while promoting a positive business environment in the state of Florida.

Special Features: File a Complaint, Consumer Resources, A to Z Guide to Government.
Curriculum: Business; Government; Social Studies

418 Florida Division of Emergency Management

www.floridadisaster.org

It includes such disaster areas as: County Emergency Management Contacts, Library, Training and Events Calendar, Online Mapping, Citizen Emergency Information, Hazard Assessment, Weather Links.

Special Features: Programs: Community Emergency Response Team, citizen Corps, Disaster Reservist program, Fire Assistance.
Curriculum: Environmental Studies; Geography; Government; Health; Social Studies

419 Florida Division of Forestry

www.fl-dof.com

This site includes studies of forest health, water resources and ecology, as well as conservation and forest management.
Special Features: Training — state forests and fire and forest protection
Curriculum: Geography; Science; Social Studies

420 Florida Education Association

www.feaweb.org

The Florida Education Association web site includes topics such as the Florida Legislature, Today's Headlines, Affiliates, Tips for Teaching and so forth.
Special Features: Legislative Update, Today's Headlines, Position Papers, Bills and Announcements
Curriculum: Education

421 Florida Historical Society

www.florida-historical-soc.org

The Alma Clyde Field Library of Florida History is owned and operated by the Florida Historical Library Foundation. It does not receive any operating funds from the State of Florida.
Special Features: Greatest living Floridian rules, Historical Society Quarterly.
Curriculum: History; Social Studies

422 Florida International Museum

www.floridamuseum.org

This international museum provides unique educational programs through diverse exhibitions in partnership with local and global communities.
Special Features: Exhibits, such as Russian Odyssey, Baseball in America; Classroom Resources and Teacher Guides
Curriculum: Education; Geography; Science; Social Studies

423 Florida Library Association

www.flalib.org

The Florida Library Association develops programs and undertakes activities to earn a leadership position for all areas of librarianship. It also works with professional organizations and professions relevant to librarianship.
Special Features: Publications: FLA News Digest, FLA Manual, Florida Libraries
Curriculum: Library Media

424 Florida Lighthouse Page

users.eros.com/lthouse/home.htm

The Lighthouse Page site provides a greater appreciation of Florida lighthouses, accurate recordings of their history and current conditions.
Special Features: Maps, Special Notes, Picture Previews and Kid's Questions
Curriculum: History; Science; Social Studies

425 Florida Marine Research Institute

www.floridamarine.org

The Florida Marine Research Institute studies/provides information regarding such areas as the red tide, manatees, fisheries and marine biology.
Special Features: Latest News— Educational Information, Teacher and Student Resource
Curriculum: Biology; Environmental Studies; Science

426 Florida Medical Network

www.floridamedicalnetwork.com

This network is produced by the Florida Medical Association. It brings Florida's medical community together online and includes such areas as: Today's Medical News, What's New This Month, Associations and Organizations, Products and Services.
Special Features: Knowledge Center: Topics by special areas; Conditions and Diseases, other medical topics
Curriculum: Health

427 Florida Museum of Natural History

www.flmnh.ufl.edu

The Florida Museum of Natural History is dedicated to understanding and preserving biological diversity and cultural history, such as "Florida Fossils" and "Evolution of Life and Land."
Special Features: Current Events, Classes and Tours, Virtual Exhibits
Curriculum: History; Social Studies

428 Florida Music Association

www.flmusiced.org

This is an association (public, non-public, home-school organizations) which regulates and monitors the activities of its component music associates.

Special Features: Florida Bandmaster's Association, Florida Orchestra Association, Florida Vocal Association
Curriculum: Education; Music

429 Florida Newspapers

www.floridalink.com/thenews/florida_news papers.htm

Florida Newspapers is a direct link to over 63 Florida newspapers, such as "Destin Log," "Florida Sports," "Miami New Times" and "Orlando Weekly."
Special Features: Maps, Beach Towns, Breaking News, Television Stations
Curriculum: Education; Language Arts; Social Studies

430 Florida Panther Net

www.panther.state.fl.us

Through this website, one can learn about Florida's state animal, the panther. It provides a rich source of knowledge about the panther, its habitat and plants and animals that share its home.
Special Features: highlights, such as New Panther Find Created to Help Save Florida Panther
Curriculum: Environmental Studies; Geography; Social Studies

431 Florida Parent Teacher Association

www.floridapta.org/about.htm

The Florida PTA is the largest statewide volunteer organization working exclusively on behalf of children and youth, including 368,000 members.
Special Features: Raise standards of home life and secure adequate protection for the care of children
Curriculum: Education

432 Florida Plants Online

www.floridaplants.com

Florida Plants Online is a directory of information sources on the Internet about Florida's plant life and environment, as well as a guide to Florida plant life.
Special Features: Bookstore, Flower shop, BOT-LINX=Biology, Botany, Horticulture, Teaching, General Plant Links
Curriculum: Environmental Studies; Science

433 Florida School for the Deaf and Blind

www.fsdb.k12.fl.us

The mission of this school is to utilize all available talent, energy and resources to provide free appropriate public education for eligible sensory-impaired students of Florida.
Special Features: The largest school for the Deaf and Blind in the U.S.; includes history, facilities, location and FAQs
Curriculum: Education

434 Florida Smart

www.floridasmart.com/education

Florida Smart includes a wealth of information regarding Florida Schools, such as: Ratings, Assessments, Educational Standards, Information and Organizations, Educational Resources.
Special Features: Teacher and parent resources link and Learn how to design a web page of your school or class
Curriculum: Education

435 Florida State Courts

www.flcourts.org

Florida State Courts discusses and includes the following: Supreme Court, Judicial Administration, State Court Funding, Education, Press Page, Judge's Page, Self-Help Center and more.
Special Features: Useful links to Federal and State Government, Legal Research Resources (databases, search engines, law libraries)
Curriculum: Government

436 Florida State Language Arts Standards Aligned with Big6 Skills

www.big6.com/showarticle.php?id=151

This is an inclusive website/article that aligns Michael Eisenberg and Robert Berkowitz's Big6 Skills with the Florida state language arts standards.
Special Features: Lessons, Links, News and Views, Research, Resources and Workshops
Curriculum: Education; Language Arts; Library Media

437 Florida State Parks

www.floridastateparks.org

Florida State Parks provides areas such as an inclusive online park guide, Find a Park, Park Information, Pet Rules, Calendar of Events and much more.
Special Features: Photo Gallery and Camping Frequently Asked Questions
Curriculum: Environmental Studies; Geography; Social Studies

438 Florida Trail Association

www.florida-trail.org

The Florida Trail Association is a voluntary organization responsible for building, maintaining and protecting hiking trails across the state of Florida.

Special Features: Maps, Guidebooks, Activities, Resources, "National Trials Days"

Curriculum: Environmental Studies; Geography

439 Florida Women in Government

www.bitmark.com/fwg

Florida Women in Government, Inc. (FWG) is a non-profit, self-sustaining group dedicated to the personal and professional development of women in government. FWG believes that all its members are entitled to be emotionally and financially independent and supports the attainment of educational, vocational, career and personal goals.

Special Features: Offers a degree, education, a chance to network, opportunities to develop leadership skills and help the community

Curriculum: Government; Women's Studies

440 Florida Wildflowers

www.flwildflowers.com

Florida Wildflowers features more than 200 original pictures, news and interesting movies, accompanied by old-time mountain music.

Special Features: Wildflower Index: Flowers and insects by categories

Curriculum: Environmental Studies

441 Historical Museum of South Florida

www.historical-museum.org

The Historical Museum of South Florida explores over 10,000 years of history and culture in greater Miami, southern Florida and the Caribbean.

Special Features: Shipwrecks, Rescue, Folk life, History, Kid Summer Camp, Tours

Curriculum: History; Social Studies

442 Holocaust Memorial Research and Education Center of Central Florida

www.holocaustedu.org

This website provides educational and cultural experiences to examine the past — in order to learn from it and to help people become aware of and alert to present changes to our freedoms, human rights and lives.

Special Features: Museum Exhibits, Programs, Library Education, Teacher Institute

Curriculum: History; Social Studies; Sociology

443 Hooked on Fishing — Not on Drugs

floridaconservation.org/educator/hooked.html

HOFNOD promotes and educates individuals about fishing, aquatic ecology and conservation and drug prevention. It includes areas such as: Aquatic Resources, Sport Fishing and Programs for Youth.

Special Features: Training Workshops that integrate the curriculum to educational goals

Curriculum: Education; Environmental Studies; Science

444 Hurricane Advisories

www.hurricaneadvisories.com

Hurricane Advisories tracks previous storms and provides information concerning climatology, current storms, water temperatures, storm shelters, tropical radars and much more.

Special Features: Hurricane Chat Room, Hurricane Web Cams

Curriculum: Geography; Science; Social Studies

445 Kids and Aquatic Education

www.florida.fisheries.com/kids/index.html

Kids and Aquatic Education realizes that the future of Florida resources is in the hands of youth. The vision and commitment of parents, teachers and friends help mold their ideals and values.

Special Features: Link to "Joe Budd Aquatic Information," Fun Stuff—Nine-Button Puzzle, Fish Painting Pad

Curriculum: Environmental Studies; Science

446 My Florida

www.myflorida.com

My Florida is the official portal of the state of Florida, and includes areas such as: Visitor, Floridian, Business, Government, Get Answers, Charts, Community Health, Maps, Data and so forth.

Special Features: Hot Topics such as Information of the Influenza Outbreak, Family

Preparedness Guide, Financial Literacy for Floridians
Curriculum: Economics; Education; Government; Health; Technology

447 National Parks Service: Everglades

www.nps.gov/ever/

Everglades National Park is the only subtropical preserve in North America; it contains both temperate and tropical communities. This website explains important issues regarding the Florida Everglades.
Special Features: "For Kids," Junior Ranger Program, Walks, Talks, Campfire Programs, Bike Hikes
Curriculum: Environmental Studies; Geography; History; Science; Social Studies

448 Online Sunshine

www.leg.state.fl.us

Online Sunshine is the official Internet site of the Florida Legislature. It links to other legislative and state government Internet sites, laws—statutes, the constitution and much more.
Special Features: KidsPage has state symbols, capitol tour, fun facts, games, puzzles
Curriculum: Government; History

449 Seaworld Orlando

www.4adventure.com/seaworld/fla

Seaworld Orlando provides free resources to all individuals and discusses Florida resources, such as: animal information, adventure camps, educational programs, education e-store and much more.
Special Features: "Base Station Wild Arctic"—

frozen wonderland of the arctic, including walruses, belugas, whales, bears
Curriculum: Biology; Environmental Studies; History; Social Studies

450 State of Florida

www.stateofflorida.com

This is "your source for Florida information," The site includes many links regarding the state of Florida, including: Adoption, Agriculture, Air Quality, Art Museums, Birds, Blind Services, Business Assistance, Child Abuse, Churches, Disabled, Education, Environmental News, and much more.
Special Features: Main links include Florida Business, Real Estate, Driver Licenses, Insurance Information, Law Enforcement, Public Records, Visitors and Travel and Florida Information
Curriculum: Art; Business; Driver Training; Economics; Education; Environmental Studies; Geography; Government; History; Science; Social Studies; Sociology

451 Wings Over Florida Junior Birder Program

myfwc.com/educator/JrBirder/default.htm

Wings over Florida Junior Birder Program was developed to help teachers introduce third and fourth grade students to bird watching in Florida.
Special Features: Teacher guides, activities, certificate and student resources—questions and answers
Curriculum: Environmental Studies; Geography; Social Studies

GEORGIA

452 Agricultural Economics Association of Georgia

www.agecon.uga.edu/~jab/aeag.htm

This Association provides opportunities for professional improvement of people interested in the field of agricultural economics. It also provides a forum for the discussion of economic problems and issues of mutual interest

to people working in agriculture, agribusiness and related fields.
Special Features: Activities include: Lecture Series, Agribusiness Forums, professional Meetings, Awards and Scholarships Programs, Visiting Lecturers, Student Papers Competition, Agribusiness Internships
Curriculum: Business; Economics; Environmental Studies; Science; Social Studies

453 City of Atlanta

www.ci.atlanta.ga.us

The site offers an excellent page for students (Kids), which discusses the history of Atlanta, life in Atlanta, people of Atlanta and much more. The website states that they challenge kids to dream, be kind, be proud, listen and achieve.

Special Features: Links include Mayor's Office, City Council, Government, Economic Development, City Services

Curriculum: Business; Economics; Government; History; Social Studies

454 Department of Drama and Theatre

www.drama.uga.edu

The Department of Drama and Theatre has provided theatrical productions and education since the early 1940s. It provides quality instruction and experience in the dramatic arts, as well as the study and production of screen plays on film and video and dramatic uses of the computer for animation.

Special Features: Links include Academics, Production, People, Spaces, Special Features, Contact Information

Curriculum: Drama

455 Geography (Sponsor: Carl Vinson Institute of Government)

www.cviog.vga.edu./Projects/gainfo/geograph. htm

The Humane Society of North Georgia includes numerous useful links, such as: Georgia Geoscience Sites, Georgia Wildlife, Severe Weather Hurricanes, Rivers of Georgia, Tropical Cyclone Facts and Figures and many more.

Special Features: Additional links include Georgia Tornadoes since 1850, World Time Zones. Geologic Information about Georgia, Map of Minerals of Georgia.

Curriculum: Environmental Studies; Geography; Science; Social Studies

456 Georgia Art Association

www.gaea.armstrong.edu

The GAEA is a professional organization or art educators in Georgia and is affiliated with the National Art Education Association. The purpose of the GAEA is to represent the art teachers to Georgia; to improve the conditions of teaching art; to promote the study of teaching art; to encourage research in art education.

Special Features: Includes links such as: District and Division Information, Conferences, Advocacy, Resources, Archives, Supporters and Vendors

Curriculum: Art

457 Georgia Association of Educators

www.gae.org

The GAE exists to support, protect, and strengthen those who nurture Georgia's children. Georgia's educational programs can be only as good as their educators. For the GAE, standing up for education means standing up for teachers. The Georgia Association of Educators is the most experienced and effective professional organization for teachers, administrators, and educational support professionals within Georgia's public schools.

Special Features: Links include Services, History, Focus, Advocacy, Gallery, Special Programs, Awards, Items of Interest

Curriculum: Education

458 Georgia Association of Homes and Services for Children

www.gahsc.org/nm/mem/2002/about.html

The GAHSC is an association dedicated to supporting those who care for children who are at risk of abuse and neglect. It carries out its mission through advocacy, lobbying, education, training, technical assistance and providing opportunities for networking.

Special Features: Services include Family Preservation and Support, Education Programs, Emergency Care, Family Foster Care, Children's Homes

Curriculum: Health; Psychology; Social Studies; Sociology

459 Georgia Canoeing Association

www.georgiacanoe.org

This Association is a Georgia canoe and kayak club. It is an affiliate of the American Canoe Association and the American Whitewater Affiliation. Its purpose is to promote recreational paddling, river courtesy, skill development and river safety.

Special Features: Links include Paddling Activities, Meetings and Special Events, Trips, Instruction Clinics, Publications, River Protection

Curriculum: Environmental Studies; Geography; Physical Education

460 Georgia Capitol Museum

www.sos.state.ga.us/museum/default.htm

The Georgia Capitol Museum is a public educational institution housed in the State Capitol building. The Museum seeks to preserve and interpret the history of the Georgia State Capitol building itself, as well as the events that have taken place within its walls.

Special Features: Provides links to New Georgia History Museum, Virtually Visit the State Capitol Museum, State Capitol Restoration, Flag Information, Teacher Resources
Curriculum: Government

461 Georgia Conservancy

www.georgiaconservancy.org

The Conservancy is a statewide environmental organization to assure that Georgians have healthy air, clean water, unspoiled wild places and community green space now and in the future.

Special Features: Offers Current Issues, Events, Fun for Teachers, Parents and Kids, Teacher Workshops, a newsletter, Archived Education Articles
Curriculum: Environmental Studies; Geography; Science; Social Studies

462 Georgia Council for the Arts (GCA)

www.web-dept.com/gca/about_history.asp

The mission of the Georgia Council for the Arts is to encourage excellence in the arts, to support the arts' many forms of expression and to make the arts available to all of the people of Georgia by providing funding, programming and services.

Special Features: Links include Art News, GCA News, Upcoming Events, Press Releases, Newsletters and Publications, Arts Education
Curriculum: Art

463 Georgia Department of Agriculture

www.agr.state.ga.us/html/mission.html

The Georgia Department of Agriculture is committed to providing superior agricultural products, service and leadership. Their mission is to provide excellence in services and regulatory functions, to protect and promote agriculture and consumer interests and to ensure an abundance of safe food for Georgia.

Special Features: Links include Farmers and Consumers Market Bulletin, International Trade, Organic Agriculture, Animal Protection Division

Curriculum Economics; Geography; Science; Social Studies

464 Georgia Department of Natural Resources

www.gadnr.org

The Georgia Department of Natural Resource's vision is to ensure that Georgia's natural, historic, cultural, environmental and economic resources will be: better tomorrow than they are today; abundant, diverse, clean, well-managed and protected; and available for everyone to use and enjoy.

Special Features: Georgia Department of Natural Resources links to Georgia Land Conservation Partnership and Georgia Water Resources Council; divisions include: Coastal Resources, Historic Preservation
Curriculum: Economics; Environmental Studies; Geography; Science; Social Studies

465 Georgia Department of Transportation

www.dot.state.ga.us

The Georgia Department of Transportation plans, constructs, maintains and improves the state's transportation systems—roads, mass transit. It also provides airport and air safety planning. The DOT is committed to a safe, efficient and sustainable transportation for all users.

Special Features: Links include Traffic, Plans, Business, What's New, Divisions, FAQs
Curriculum: Business; Driver Training; Economics; Government

466 Georgia Division of Public Health

www.ph.dhr.state.ga.us

The Georgia Division of Public Health's vision is a Georgia with healthy people, families, and communities, where all sectors unite by pooling their assets and strengths to promote health for all. GDPH is responsive to health needs, valued for expertise and innovation and dedicated to excellence.

Special Features: Links include Annual Health status Measures, Calendar of Events, Programs and Services
Curriculum: Health

467 Georgia Dome

www.gadome.com/html/about_dome.html

The Georgia Dome is the largest cable-supported domed stadium in the world. It is unique in many ways, such as: 8,300 tons of steel was used to construct the dome, it contains 1.6 million square feet, and much more.

Special Features: Links include Facts, Operation, Sponsors, Community Development, Tours.

Curriculum: Economics; Math; Science

468 Georgia Environment

www.dnr.state.ga.us/dnr/environ/gaenviron_fil es/gaenviro.htm

Information regarding the conditions of Georgia's environment, such as Air Quality, Drinking Water, Environmental Releases and Radiation, Fish Consumption Guidelines, Floodplains, Geologic Resources, Hazardous Sites, Land Resources.

Special Features: Links to Georgia's Clean Air Force, Clean Air Campaign, Greenhouse Gas Emissions Program, Toxics Release Inventory Report.

Curriculum: Environmental Studies; Geography; Health; Science

469 Georgia Forestry Commission

www.gfc.state.ga.us/Services/index.cfm

The Georgia Forestry Commission provides a wide range of educational services. Education efforts focus on providing accurate information about Georgia's forest resources and increasing public awareness and understanding about issues and factors affecting Georgia's forests.

Special Features: Project Learning Tree uses the forest as a window to help pre-kindergarten through twelfth grade students learn about the natural world around them, their place within this natural environment, and their responsibility for it.

Curriculum: Environmental Studies; Geography; History; Social Studies

470 Georgia Golf Hall of Fame's Botanical Gardens

www.gghf.org

The educational mission is to educate students and the public about plants and their environment, and about the value of conservation and inclusion of plants in urban and suburban settings.

Special Features: Includes links: Calendar of Events, Virtual Store, Membership, Sponsors and Links, Media Kit, Gallery.

Curriculum: Environmental Studies; Geography; Science; Social Studies

471 Georgia Health Policy Center

www.gwf.org

The Georgia Health Policy Center's mission is to improve the health status of al Georgians through research, policy development, and program design and evaluation.

Special Features: Core Functions: Consensus Building, Grants Management, Health Systems Change, Knowledge, Creation and Management, Knowledge Transfer

Curriculum: Economics; Health

472 Georgia Historical Society

www.georgiahistory.com

The Georgia Historical Society is a private, non-profit organization that serves as *the* historical society for the people of Georgia. The society has collected, preserved and shared some of the most important documents, rare books, maps, photographs and artifacts of Georgia.

Special Features: Links include Library, Archives, Affiliate Chapters, Public Programs, Publications, Historical Markers, Education Programs

Curriculum: Government; History; Social Studies

473 Georgia History

www.cviog.uga.edu/Projects/gainfo/gahist.htm

Georgia History includes useful educational information such as: Prehistoric Period, Spanish Presence in the Southeast, French Presence in the Southeast, Georgia as an English Colony, American Revolution to the Civil War, Georgia in the 20th Century and much more.

Special Features: Also includes General Information (documents, journals, speeches), Georgia Railroads, Historical Organizations, Societies, Libraries

Curriculum: History

474 Georgia Home Education Association

www.ghea.org

The Georgia Home Education Association is a website that provides a wealth of information for home-schooled students and parents. It offers support groups, regional leadership conferences, forms and much more.

Special Features: Links include Resources, Events, Helpful Links, Senior High and College, Testing, Special Needs, Article Library
Curriculum: Education

475 Georgia Humanities Council

www.georgiahumanities.org

The Georgia Humanities Council serves the state of Georgia through its projects and grant program. The council receives funds from the National Endowment for the Humanities, the state of Georgia, foundations, corporations and individuals.
Special Features: Links include About GHC; Calendar of Events; Newsletter; Projects; Resources; Humanities Links
Curriculum: Business; Economics; Government; Social Studies

476 Georgia Learning Connections

www.glc.k12.ga.us

The Georgia Learning Connections offers standards, lesson plans, Web resources, assessments and thousands of resources for Georgia educators.
Special Features: Links include Teacher Resource Center, Georgia Education Initiatives, Professional Development Center, Projects and Programs, Lesson Plan Builder, Sequenced Lesson Plans
Curriculum: Education

477 Georgia Library Association

www.library.gsu.edu

The GLA is dedicated to developing an understanding of the place that libraries should take in advancing the educational, cultural, and economic life of the state, as well as promoting the expansion and improvement of library services.
Special Features: Includes: About GLA, GA Jobs, Join GLA, GLA Events and Activities
Curriculum: Library Media

478 Georgia Music Educators Association

www.gmea.org

The GMEA is the fifth largest Music Educators Association in the country. It provides educational opportunities and in-service opportunities for its members, promotes music in Georgia.
Special Features: Includes such divisions as Choral Division, College, Elementary, Music News, Multi-Cultural, Music Camps, Music Links, Music Events, Orchestra Division, Piano Division, Recordings and more
Curriculum: Music

479 Georgia Music Hall of Fame

www.gamusichall.com

The Georgia Music Hall of Fame features musicians such as Little Richard, James Brown, Otis Redding, the Allman Brothers Band and many more. The museum is 43,000 square feet featuring permanent and changing exhibits that include music, video, memorabilia, instruments, and performance costumes.
Special Features: Links include Permanent Exhibits, Music Factory, Education, Library, Music Store, Rentals, Press Room, Inductee List
Curriculum: History; Music

480 Georgia Newspapers

www.usnpl.com/ganews.html

Georgia Newspapers includes numerous city newspapers (Such as the *Atlanta Journal-Constitution*, *Athens Banner-Herald* and *Augusta Chronicle*), radio stations, college newspapers, television stations, magazines (such as Atlanta's *Web*, *Savannah Insider* and *Valdosta Magazine*).
Special Features: Links include Utilities, Auctions, Weather, National News, Special Interest, Newspaper Links, Stock Quotes, Search Engines, Phone Book, Maps, Cool Sites
Curriculum: Language Arts

481 Georgia Office of Homeland Security

www.gahomelandsecurity.com

This office concerns all matters related to the defense of Georgia. It is now made up of seven state agencies and deals with disasters such as hurricanes, fires, floods, earthquakes, plane crashes, crime and other emergencies.
Special Features: Links include News, Terrorism, Funding, Preparedness, Training, Resources, Related Programs, Professional Practices, G-8 Summit
Curriculum: Economics; Environmental Studies; Geography; Social Studies

482 Georgia Ornithological Society

www.gos.org

The Georgia Ornithological Society's mission is to encourage the scientific study of birds by gathering and disseminating information on Georgia bird life. GOS actively promotes bird conservation by encouraging the preservation of habitats that are vital to the survival of resident and migratory birds. The GOS also gives scholarships, produces scientific publications, and provides fellowship among those interested in nature.

Special Features: Links include Graduate Student Research Grants, Publications, Birding Georgia, From the Field, Rare Bird Alerts, Georgia Bird Clubs.

Curriculum: Social Studies

483 Georgia Power

www.southernco.com/gapower/home.asp

Georgia Power is the largest of the electric utilities that make up Southern Company. It has been in existence for over a century. Georgia Power supports an array of environmental projects that make their air and water cleaner — and their land more beautiful.

Special Features: Includes: Energy Efficiency Guide, Energy at Home, Energy Facts, Economic Development, Lakes and Recreation

Curriculum: Business; Economics; Environmental Studies; Technology

484 Georgia Press Association

www.gapress.org

The Georgia press Association promotes the interests and well-being of the newspaper industry in Georgia. It includes Georgia Newspaper Service, Georgia College Press Association, Georgia Press Educational Foundation, and Georgia Press Association Member Listings.

Special Features: Links include Calendar, Conferences, Special Events, Contact Information, Contests, Educational Seminars, Georgia Sunshine Laws

Curriculum: Business; Language Arts

485 Georgia Professional Standards Commission

www.gapsc.com

The Georgia Professional Standards Commission covers topics such as: Approved Programs, Alternative Preparation, Certification Routes, Rules, Educator Training, Commission Information, Educator Links, and Data and Research.

Special Features: Provides information concerning: Troops to Teachers, Teacher Recruit-

ment Fails, New Computer Skill Competency Assessment, PRAXIS Workshops

Curriculum: Education

486 Georgia Public Library Service

www.public.lib.ga.us

The Georgia Public Library Service improves the quality of life for all Georgians by providing information and by encouraging reading, literacy, and education through the continuing support and improvement of Georgia's public libraries.

Special Features: Kids Page with information for children and youth, reading programs, facts

Curriculum: Language Arts; Library Media

487 Georgia Science Teachers Association

www.ceismc.gatech.edu/gsta/gsta.htm

The GSTA is a non-profit association of professional science teachers whose primary purpose is to encourage the development of science interests and abilities as a vital part of the total educational development of students.

Special Features: Encourages science teachers to actively participate in local teacher organizations, provide administrators with acceptance of aims and objectives of association

Curriculum: Science

488 Georgia Secretary of State: Archives and History Division

www.sos.state.ga.us/archives

The Georgia Archives works to make a difference on behalf of all Georgia citizens. The archives help state and local governments operate more efficiently. At the core of their mission, they identify and preserve Georgia's most valuable historical documents.

Special Features: Links include Search the Archives, Hot Links, What's New, Services and Publications, Exhibits, Georgia History

Curriculum: Library Media; Social Studies

489 Georgia State Parks and Historic Sites

www.gastateparks.org

Georgia's 63 state parks and historic sites teach about colonial life to Civil War battles; from Native American settlements to our nation's first gold rush. Through this site, one can also learn about new programs and events.

Special Features: Kids' Activities: Georgia's

48 state parks and 15 state historic sites provide a variety of resources for educators and parents.

Curriculum: Environmental Studies; Geography; History; Social Studies

490 Georgia Trails

goergiatrails.com

This website discusses walking, hiking, backpacking and driving trails of Georgia. Examples for trails include Vickery Creek, Dick's Creek Falls, Glen Falls, Amicalola Falls and more.

Special Features: Links include Trails with Waterfalls, Scenic Trails, Parks, Features, Bookstore, about North Georgia.

Curriculum: Environmental Studies; Geography; History; Science; Social Studies

491 Georgia Trust for Historic Preservation

www.georgiatrust.org

The mission of this trust is to promote an appreciation of Georgia's diverse historic resources and provide for their protection and use to preserve, enhance and revitalize Georgia's communities. Its vision is to encourage understanding and appreciation of the irreplaceable value of historic buildings and places.

Special Features: Links include What's New, What We Do, Publications, Visit Historic Sites, Get Involved, FAQs.

Curriculum: Geography; History

492 Georgia Wildlife Federation

www.gwf.org

The GWF began as a sportsman's organization and has grown to become Georgia's oldest and largest conservation organization. Members include bird watchers, educators, gardeners, hikers and so forth. GWF takes stands on issues based on ecological and wildlife principles.

Special Features: Links include Calendar of Events, Special Events, Programs, Projects, Educational Resources, Publications

Curriculum: Biology; Environmental Studies; Geography; Science; Social Studies

493 Georgia Women of Achievement

www.gawomen.org

First Lady Rosalynn Carter pointed to the need to for a method of honoring women as is done in other states by the National Women's Hall of Fame. She was the impetus for the Founding Committee; Georgia Women of Achievement began in 1990, honoring women of Georgia who made extraordinary contributions to society.

Special Features: Links include Goal, History, Honorees, Exhibit, Personal Women of Achievement, Bibliography.

Curriculum: Women's Studies

494 Georgia Writers Association

www.georgiawriters.org/visitors.html

Georgia Writers Association is an organization that works to encourage and strengthen the proficiencies of writers in both the creative and business aspects of writing life in Georgia. Its mission is to serve Georgia's diverse literary communities through communication, education, and cultural awareness.

Special Features: Offers a bi-monthly publication, including articles, works, speakers, opportunities. Also provides Author of the Year Awards and numerous satellite groups

Curriculum: Language Arts

495 Georgia Writers Hall of Fame

www.libs.uga.edu/gawriters

The University of Georgia Libraries established the Georgia Writers Hall of Fame to recognize Georgia writers, past and present, whose work reflects the character of the state — its land and people.

Special Features: About the Hall of Fame, Hall of Fame Honorees, Make a Nomination, Hall of Fame Library, and others.

Curriculum: Language Arts

496 Georgia's State Capitol

www.cvig.uga.edu/Projects/gainfo/capitol.htm

This site includes: The Story of Georgia's Capitol and Capital Cites, 1886 Sanborn Map of Georgia Capitol, 1931 Sanborn Map of Georgia Capitol, Monuments and Statues at Georgia's State Capitol, Why Study the Georgia Capitol and Capitol as a Symbol Lesson Plan.

Special Features The Story of Georgia's Capitols and Capital Cities includes: Savannah and Augusta as Rotating Capitals, Georgia's Third Capital — Louisville, Milledgeville as State Capital.

Curriculum: Government

497 Humane Society of North Georgia

www.petfinder.com/shelters/adoptabuddy.html

The Humane Society of North Georgia is an adoption service for pets that need homes. They do both onsite and offsite adoptions; also provide discount spay/neuter certificates to rescuers and pet owners.

Special Features: Links to Adoption Schedule, Save a Life, Great Adoption Websites, Our Pet List

Curriculum: Social Studies

498 Keep Georgia Beautiful

www.keepgeorgiabeautiful.org

Clean land, water and air are important to Georgians. Created by Governor George Busbee in 1978, Keep Georgia Beautiful became the first state affiliate of Keep America Beautiful. Their mission is to build and sustain community environmental activities and behaviors resulting in a more beautiful Georgia.

Special Features: Keep Georgia Beautiful includes useful educational programs, such as Waste in the Workplace, Workshops for Georgia's Educators and Trash Treasures for the Classroom

Curriculum: Environmental Studies

499 Native Americans in North Georgia

ngeorgis.com/history/findex.html

This web site includes Native Americans/information in North Georgia such as: Creek, Cherokee, Talking Leaves, Trail of Tears, Chieftains Trail, Chief Vann House, John Ross, Sequoyah, Benjamin Hawkins, Samuel Austin Worcester, and many more.

Special Features: Links to areas such as: Early Native Americans, History of the Cherokee, Land Cessions of Native Americans in Georgia, Etowah Indian Mounds, Recommended Reading

Curriculum: Geography; History; Social Studies

500 Parent to Parent of Georgia

www.parenttoparentofga.org

Parent to parent is a non-profit organization that provides support and information to parents of children with disabilities. Their services are based on the philosophy that one of the most meaningful sources of support are other parents who have experienced a child with a disability.

Special Features: Links include Chat, Support, Services, Resources, Message Board, Conference, Health, Newsletter, Special Needs Database (over 4,000 resources)

Curriculum: Health; Sociology

501 State of Georgia

www.georgia.gov/

This is the official site for the State of Georgia. It includes such areas as: Business and Labor, Education and Training, Family and Health, Government, Legal and Public Safety, Science and Technology, Tourism, Recreation and the Arts and Transportation.

Special Features: Includes the New Georgia Encyclopedia, Business Registration, State Legislature, Federal Government, and others

Curriculum: Government

502 Stone Mountain Memorial Association

www.stonemountainpart.org

This Association is a State authority that is self-supporting and is responsible for Georgia's Stone Mountain Park. Its mission is to preserve, protect and enhance the 3,200 acre natural resource for the people of Georgia and for visitors from around the world.

Special Features: Links include Confederate Hall, Attractions, Schedules, Special Events, Lodging.

Curriculum: Environmental Studies; Geography; History; Science; Social Studies

503 Visual Arts of Georgia

vsaartsga.org/index/about_us

VSA Arts of Georgia provides access to the arts for people with disabilities and those who are economically disadvantaged. VSA is a statewide resource working with artists and organizations to fulfill their vision of an inclusive community that encourages everyone to enjoy and participate in the arts.

Special Features: Links such as Arts for All Gallery, Arts Programming, Community Events, Technical Services, Photo Gallery, Newsletter, Resources

Curriculum: Art; Economics

HAWAII

504 Ala Mua Hawaii

www.alternative-hawaii.com/index.html

Traveler-oriented website explores alternatives to standard HI tourism, with focus on eco-tourism. HI Overview, Hawaiian Culture, Eco-Cultural Events, Heritage Tour Guides, Vacation Activities, more.

Special Features: Photo gallery
Curriculum: Environmental Studies; Social Studies

505 Bishop Museum

www.bishopmuseum.org/

Natural and historical museum dedicated to preserving all aspects of HI. Educational and scientific items can be found throughout, including geology guide, Educational Guides to Programs & Exhibits; plus museum info, arranging a tour, links.

Special Features: Hawaii Biological Survey; X-Treme Science for kids
Curriculum: Education; Environmental Studies; History; Science; Social Studies

506 City and County of Honolulu

www.co.honolulu.hi.us/

Civic website for HI's largest city and capitol. Government, Kama'aina, Business, Visitors, Kids, Seniors, On-Line Services, Economic Development, plus civic departments and services.

Special Features: Homework Help for Students
Curriculum: Government

507 Contemporary Museum Honolulu

www.tcmhi.org/sitemap.htm

Honolulu attraction collects, exhibits post–1940 artwork. Online exhibit highlights collections; plus exhibits info, museum info, arranging a visit, events & programs.

Special Features: Educational program opportunities
Curriculum: Art; Education

508 County of Hawaii

www.hawaii-county.com/

Civic government for the city of Hilo and the island of Hawaii. Mayor's office, County Council, Calendar, Employment, Public Works, Maps, Economic Development, Tourism.

Special Features: Civic departments, services
Curriculum: Government

509 County of Maui

www.co.maui.hi.us/

Municipal authority encompassing several HI islands. Info for businesses, residents, visitors, government, including departments, services online, current conditions, office of the mayor.

Special Features: Maui Youth Connections
Curriculum: Government

510 The Dolphin Institute

www.dolphin-institute.org/

Honolulu group studies dolphins & whales in HI's waters. Extensive summaries of research findings; Resource Guide with articles on behavior, biology, ecology; programs, institute info, more.

Special Features: Educational program opportunities
Curriculum: Science

511 Earthtrust

www.earthtrust.org/wlcurric/

Hawaii's Marine Wildlife: Whales, Dolphins, Turtles, and Seals offers curriculum, lecture, lessons for classroom study of HI's marine fauna. Includes references, appendices.

Special Features: Further reading bibliography
Curriculum: Environmental Studies; Science

512 Extreme Hawaii Fun

www.extreme-hawaii.com/pidgin/

Full On Pidgin is a humorous but informative site on the unique island language. Glossary and pronunciation guide, including audio; fun pidgin activities.

Special Features: Pidgin Rhymes
Curriculum: Language Arts; Social Studies

513 Harold L. Lyon Arboretum

www.lyonarboretum.com/

Tropical botanical garden at the University of Hawaii offers education, research, conservation about native and tropical flora. Extensive education resources, science resources, learning opportunities, Gardens info and visitor's info.
Special Features: Teacher's Brochure; Science Performance Standards
Curriculum: Environmental Studies; Science

514 Hawaii Center for Volcanology

www.soest.hawaii.edu/GG/hcv.html

Scientific group in HI who observes, studies, monitors HI's active volcanoes. Pages on the major volcanoes, volcano formation, HI geography, membership, links.
Special Features: Volcano Gallery; "Life in Hawaii" online book
Curriculum: Environmental Studies; Geography; Science

515 Hawaii Department of Education

marcopolo.k12.hi.us/

The Marcopolo program provides HI teachers with free standards-based Internet classroom content and professional development training. Hawaii Resources, MarcoGrams, Lesson Plans, MarcoPolo Statistics in Hawaii, Integrated Unit Plans, Training Resource Center.
Special Features: Lesson plans by grade, subject
Curriculum: Art; Biology; Drama; Economics; Education; Environmental Studies; Geography; Health; History; Language Arts; Math; Music; Science; Social Studies; Sociology; Technology

516 Hawaii Networked Learning Communities

www.hnlc.org/newhnlc/abouthnlc/index.php

HNLC unites state schools into a virtual community focused on math, science, technology curriculum. Access teaching/learning resources, become a member, forums, e-mail lists; access to some areas requires registration.
Special Features: Unit Plans; HNLC Documents
Curriculum: Education; Math; Science; Technology

517 Hawaii Radio and Television Guide

www.hawaiiradiotv.com/

Extensive info on, resources for, links to broadcast media in HI. Covers radio, television, print media; resources organized by island, format; includes comprehensive media links.
Special Features: Interactive forum
Curriculum: Social Studies; Technology

518 Hawaii State Commission on the Status of Women

www.state.hi.us/hscsw/

Group promotes women's issues, defends women's rights, encourages activism. Info on current & upcoming projects, data on HI issues, legislative issues, women's resource links, links to island commissions.
Special Features: The "Status of Women in Hawaii" Report
Curriculum: Women's Studies

519 Hawaii State Department of Health

www.state.hi.us/health/oeqc/garden/index.html

How To Plant A Native Hawaiian Garden: An On-Line Handbook provides extensive info on the creation and care of a native HI garden. Includes topical bibliography.
Special Features: OEQC Homepage
Curriculum: Environmental Studies

520 Hawaii State Internet Virtual Public Library

www.hawaiilibrary.com/

Virtual library offers extensive online materials to general public & patrons of HI libraries. eBooks, online journals, databases, reference works, image collections; some areas require HI library patron membership.
Special Features: eBooks in HTML, .PDF formats
Curriculum: Education; Language Arts; Library Media

521 Hawaii State Public Library System

www.librarieshawaii.org/

An online guide to the services and collections in HI's public libraries. Access databases; find a local library; learn about programs for kids, teens, adults; library policies, including lending policies; resource links; more.
Special Features: Holo I Mua Newsletter online; book recommendations
Curriculum: Library Media

522 Hawaii Water Environment Association

www.hwea.org/

Group studies HI water resources, educates on use and preservation. Some online resources; General information, HWEA Activities, Current Features, Additional Information.
Special Features: Lua Line newsletter online; CWA in HI
Curriculum: Environmental Studies; Science

523 Hawaii's Agricultural Gateway

www.hawaiiag.org/

Information resource for agriculture, aquaculture on the islands. Gardening & farming resources, including animal issues; info on HI ag business; resources for kids, teachers, & parents; links.
Special Features: History of Agriculture in HI; How Important Is Agriculture Today?
Curriculum: Business; Education; Environmental Studies; History; Science; Social Studies

524 Hawaiian Astronomical Society

www.hawastsoc.org/index.htm

Non-profit organization promotes amateur astronomy in HI. Website provides extensive resources including a deepsky atlas, astronomy news, views of the solar system, resource links.
Special Features: Charts by region, date, constellation
Curriculum: Science

525 Hawaiian Ecosystems at Risk Project

www.hear.org

The HEAR educates on the dangers to HI ecosystems and science-based management of harmful non-native species. Invasive species lists, info, images; online articles; extensive resource links.
Special Features: The Silent Invasion
Curriculum: Environmental Studies; Science

526 Hawaiian Historical Society

www.hawaiianhistory.org/

Group dedicated to preserving, researching historical materials of HI and the Pacific. Hawaiian History Moments, Society Library, publications, Reference Collection, resource links.
Special Features: Hawaiian Journal of History complete index
Curriculum: History; Social Studies

527 Hawaiian Humane Society

www.hawaiianhumane.org/

State chapter of the animal advocacy and protection organization. Programs & Services, Educational Programs, FAQ, Adoptions, Donations, Animal Care & Behavior, Animal Laws, Lost & Found, News & Events, contact info.
Special Features: Dog, cat, small animal care articles
Curriculum: Social Studies

528 Hawaiian Islands Humpback Whale National Marine Sanctuary

www.hihwnms.nos.noaa.gov/

Marine whale & habitat sanctuary encompasses the HI Islands. Learn about the humpback whale and its environment, the sanctuary's history, management plan, research, education, whale watching, more.
Special Features: Sanctuary maps (require Adobe Acrobat Reader)
Curriculum: Environmental Studies; Science

529 Hawaiian Language Online Collection (Sponsor: College of Hawaiian Language and the Native Hawaiian Library)

ulukau.org/english.php

Ulukau, a Hawaiian-language digital online collection offers Hawaiian-language readings to the general reader. Books, newspapers, journal articles, dictionary, essays. Interface in Hawaiian, English, or dual-language.
Special Features: Baibala Hemolele, the Hawaiian-language Bible
Curriculum: Language Arts; Social Studies

531 Hawaiian Roots

www.hawaiian-roots.com/

State genealogical page focused on those with native Hawaiian ancestry. Genealogy basics, Hawaiian naming practices, birth & adoption records, Hawaiian history, specific problems & issues of Hawaiian genealogy, resource links.
Special Features: Immigrant ship lists; newspaper obituaries
Curriculum: History; Social Studies

532 Historic Hawai'i Foundation

www.historichawaii.org/

State organization works to preserve Hawai'i's cultural heritage. HI Register of Historic

Places; plus Membership, Projects, Historic Residence Sign, Grants, Conferences & Events, Links.

Special Features: Heritage Education Video Curriculum

Curriculum: History; Social Studies

533 Honolulu Theatre for Youth

www.htyweb.org/

HI troupe performs theatre & drama education programs with a target K–12 schools audience. Performs for classrooms, families. Upcoming plays, education opportunities, about the HTY, links.

Special Features: Teacher's Guide

Curriculum: Drama; Education

534 Honolulu Zoo

www.honoluluzoo.org/

Website offers zoo info and visitor's info, plus extensive animal info. Content includes images, info, video, audio files, animal games, animal quizzes, zookeeper's journals, more.

Special Features: Animals Slideshow; educational programs

Curriculum: Education; Science

535 Institute for the Advancement of Hawaiian Affairs

www.opihi.com/sovereignty/

Perspectives of Hawaiian Sovereignty, essays, viewpoints on the past for HI to regain independence.

Special Features: Short story by student, Mauna' Ala Burgess

Curriculum: Government

536 Island Options

www.hawaiischoolreports.com/

Hawaii School Reports provides K–6 students with user-friendly HI information. Quick Facts, People, History, Language, Nature, plus HI puzzle, HI quiz, links.

Special Features: HI Activities for Kids

Curriculum: Education; History; Social Studies

537 Media-HI

www.aloha-hawaii.com/

Travel and visitor's guide to HI. Contains two useful sections: Natural Hawaii, including articles on royalty, language, culture; Hawaii Almanac, with maps, geography, geology, history, more.

Special Features: Native Hawaiian Glossary; The Monarchy in HI

Curriculum: Geography; History; Social Studies

538 National Park Service

www.nps.gov/havo/index.htm

Hawaii Volcanoes National Park website features extensive info. History of park, park facts, in-depth sections, kid's program opportunities, visiting info, events calendar.

Special Features: Plan an educational trip; available teacher's guide

Curriculum: Geography; Environmental Studies; Science

539 National Tropical Botanical Garden

www.ntbg.org/

Congressionally-chartered institution in Kalaheo, HI studies, preserves exotic and endangered plant species. Meet the Plants online; plus, conservation articles, news 7 events, learn about classes, institute info, arrange a tour.

Special Features: Taxonomy, gallery of exotic plant species

Curriculum: Environmental Studies; Science

540 Pacific Tsunami Museum

www.tsunami.org/

Hilo, HI museum educates on tidal disasters. Tsunamis FAQ, education & science programs info, photo archives, articles archive, museum info & events, links.

Special Features: Schedule a school trip

Curriculum: Environmental Studies; Science

541 Pearl Harbor (Sponsor: Don Schaaf)

www.my.execpc.com/~dschaaf/

Website collects info on the 1941 Pearl Harbor attack. History, map, timeline, primary documents, audio files, info on the modern memorial & visitor's guide, links.

Special Features: Live video feed from Pearl Harbor

Curriculum: History

542 Polynesian Voyaging Society

www.pvs-hawaii.org/

Non-profit research and educational group recreates traditional Polynesian voyaging methods. Learn about recreation & ancient voyaging techniques through articles, images; cultural &

educational programs & events; newsletters & articles; links.

Special Features: Polynesia Voyage History & Culture; Closing the Triangle; Educational Curriculum for Rapa Nui

Curriculum: History; Social Studies

543 R.E.A.D. for NENE

www.nene.k12.hi.us/

HI children's book award program. Encourages literacy by having K–6 students read, vote on NENE Award winner. Info on award, past winners, current nominees, participating schools.

Special Features: Sign up your classroom to vote

Curriculum: Education; Language Arts

544 State of Hawaii

www.hawaii.gov/portal/

Official state web portal. Features content for Business, Government, Community, Employment, Visiting, Education, plus state department web pages, online services, governor's pages.

Special Features: About Hawaii; kid's resource links

Curriculum: Government

545 State of Hawaii Department of Education

www.arch.k12.hi.us/

Accountability Resource Center Hawai'i provides educational assessment and accountability information for teachers, administrators, parents, community. School accountability resources, including NCLB assessments; system accountability, including HOPPE survey; assessment & accountability resource links.

Special Features: NCLB Workbook

Curriculum: Education

546 State of Hawaii Office of Planning

www.state.hi.us/dbedt/gis/index.html

Statewide GIS Program works to establish and coordinate geographic information systems (GIS) technology in HI. Offers topographical and thematic maps online, plus GIS data, HI I-Map, program info, resource links.

Special Features: 2000 Census maps

Curriculum: Geography; Social Studies

547 Turtle Talk: Fun Facts about Hawaii from Children's Author Tammy Yee

www.tammyyee.com/turtletalk.html

Turtle Talk: Fun Facts About Hawaii is an educational page put together by Hawaiian children's author Tammy Yee. Geography, Hawaiian History & Legend, Multiculturalism in Hawai'i, Hawaiian Wildlife, links to other children's pages.

Special Features: Many articles link to fun activities

Curriculum: Geography; History; Science; Social Studies

548 University of Hawaii at Hilo

www.olelo.hawaii.edu/

Kualono is a bilingual English/Hawaiian language education and information resource. Learn the Hawaiian language, access and order Hawaiian language materials, connect with other Hawaiian speakers, use online Hawaiian dictionary, more.

Special Features: View content in Hawaiian, English, or Dual-Language

Curriculum: Language Arts; Social Studies

549 University of Hawaii at Manoa Libraries

www.libweb.hawaii.edu/

UHM's Digital Archives feature images, texts, and other online content. Two Jean Charlot art collections; three Hawaiian Culture archives; two Pacifica collections; plus links to the UH Libraries system.

Special Features: The Annexation of Hawai'i: A Collection of Documents; Hawai'i War Records Depository

Curriculum: Art; History; Library Media; Social Studies

550 University of Hawaii at Manoa, Office of Cooperative Extension

www.ctahr.hawaii.edu/ctahr2001/Extension/index.html

UH cooperative extension resources & services. Content areas include Agriculture, Home & Garden, Community, Environment, Business, Food & Nutrition.

Special Features: County Facilities; 4-H Resources

Curriculum: Business; Environmental Studies; Health; Social Studies

551 University of Hawaii at Manoa, Women's Studies Program

www.soc.hawaii.edu/hwhp/

Hawaiian Women's Heritage Project presents exhibits on the experiences of HI women. Three major presentations, plus supporting materials, resource links.

Special Features: Hula: From a Native Perspective

Curriculum: Women's Studies

552 University of Hawaii School of Ocean and Earth Science and Technology

www.radlab.soest.hawaii.edu/atlas/

The Oceanographic Atlas of Hawaii is a general reference work on HI's marine climate, water properties, currents, tides, waves. Contains graphs, maps, articles.

Special Features: On-line references

Curriculum: Environmental Studies; Science

553 U.S. Geological Survey

www.hvo.wr.usgs.gov/

The Hawaiian Volcano Observatory monitors, studies, educates on HI's many active volcanoes. Kilauea, Mauna Loa, Earthquakes, Other Volcanoes, Volcanic Hazards; includes maps, images, articles.

Special Features: Eruption updates

Curriculum: Environmental Studies; Science

554 USS *Utah* Association

www.ussutah.org/

Site preserving the memory of the USS *Utah*, one of the ships sunk in the Pearl Harbor attack. Ship and Harbor history, attack accounts, personal profiles, images, events support the Association, resource links.

Special Features: Virtual Monument; extensive Pearl Harbor historic links

Curriculum: History

555 Waikiki Aquarium

www.waquarium.otted.hawaii.edu/

The nation's oldest aquarium attraction features extensive online content. Marine Life Profiles, Exhibit Facts, Virtual Tour, live webcams, aquarium history, visitor's info, more.

Special Features: Shark Cam; Classes & Programs

Curriculum: Environmental Studies; Science

IDAHO

556 All Idaho Internet

www.allidaho.com/idaho/index.html

All Idaho On the Net is a comprehensive web guide with extensive ID links. Idaho Area Recreation, Travel & Tourism, Opinion & Government, Media & Information, Schools & Education, Arts & Religion, Business, Health & Home.

Special Features: 360-degree panoramic views of ID cities

Curriculum: Education; Government; Health; Social Studies

557 Association of Idaho Cities

www.idahocities.org/

Civic coalition of ID municipal governments, working together to improve local government, provide civic services. Info on organization and affiliate cities, calendar of events, legislative news and issues, publications, election info, links.

Special Features: Incorporated cities list, with links; City Trees

Curriculum: Government

558 Basque Museum & Cultural Center

www.basquemuseum.com/

Boise, ID museum celebrates the largest Basque community in North America. Museum info, events, collections & exhibits, education, membership.

Special Features: Oral Histories online; education opportunities

Curriculum: Social Studies

559 Boise Art Museum

www.boiseartmuseum.org/

ID's largest art museum. Website contains exhibit and permanent collection info; some artworks online w/discussion, artist's biography; museum and tour info; events; links.

Special Features: Teacher Discussion Boards; Teacher Resources; arrange for a class visit
Curriculum: Art

560 Boise State Radio Network

www.radio.boisestate.edu/information/otherpr
ojects/potato/

The Idaho Potato, an informative website documenting the history of the ID potato industry. Ancient History of the Potato, Potatoes Come to Idaho, Farming Process, Nutritional Facts, Growing Process, Potato Processing, more.
Special Features: French Fries: Facts and History; Bagging Potatoes
Curriculum: History; Science; Social Studies

561 BYU David O. McKay Library

www.lib.byu.edu/online.html

Online Collections at BYU include a searchable database; specialized collections of BYU Campus Photographs; Religious Education Archives; BYU Museum of Art; images of the Indian Wars; BYU Thesis & Dissertation archive.
Special Features: Children's Book and Play Review; Trails of Hope: Overland Diaries and Letters, 1846–1869
Curriculum: Art; Education; History; Language Arts; Social Studies

562 City of Boise

www.cityofboise.org/

Official civic website for the state capitol. City Government, Services, Departments, Visiting Boise, plus links to civic service websites, services online.
Special Features: Boise Demographics; newspaper & television links
Curriculum: Government

563 City of Lewiston

www.cityoflewiston.org/

Civic website for ID's only seaport city. Government info, City Hall, Community Development, Employment, County Regional Airport, Parks and Recreation, Public Works, plus civic services.
Special Features: Valley Vision subsite
Curriculum: Government

564 Clearwater-Potlatch Timber Protective Association

www.cptpa.com/

Organization dedicated to preventing wildfires, educating about ID wildfire prevention. Pictures, FAQ, annual reports, equipment, resource links.
Special Features: History of fire prevention
Curriculum: Environmental Studies

565 Digital Atlas of Idaho

www.imnh.isu.edu/digitalatlas/

Comprehensive series of digital maps cataloging the geography, geology, biology, hydrology, climatology, archeology of ID. Includes road maps, topographical maps, regional maps, county maps.
Special Features: Teaching Resources, including lesson plans, diagrams, charts, mages for the classroom
Curriculum: Biology; Education; Geography; Science

566 Fort Lemhi Indian Community

www.lemhishoshone.com/

Tribal website for the ID Lemhi-Shoshone. Much historical content onsite, including articles on Sacajawea, who came from the tribe; plus timelines, tribal culture, restoration efforts, modern tribe, links.
Special Features: Sacajawea and the Lemni-Shoshone; gallery of historic images
Curriculum: History; Social Studies

567 Idaho Artists (Sponsor: Andyy Barr Productions)

www.idahoartists.com/

IdahoArtists.com gives modern IA creators a place to list their contact information and display their work. Divided into Visual Arts, Performing Arts, Creative Writing areas.
Special Features: Calendar of Arts Events; resource links
Curriculum: Art; Dance; Drama; Language Arts; Music

568 Idaho Association of Counties

www.idcounties.org/

Coalition of ID counties, working together to improve local, state government. Info on organization and affiliates, calendar of events, legislative news and issues, publications, election info, links.
Special Features: County map; list of counties, with website links
Curriculum: Government

569 Idaho Center for the Book

www.lili.org/icb/

Center established to encourage and promote reading, writing, and collecting books and preserving ID's bibliophilic heritage. Semi-annual newsletter, ICB publications, events, links.

Special Features: Booker's Dozen annual presentation

Curriculum: Language Arts

570 Idaho Commission of the Arts

www2.state.id.us/arts/index.html

Official state agency for the support and development of the arts in ID through promotion, education. Onsite info about events, programs, grants, arts education, publications of the Commission.

Special Features: Artists registry; folk art/folklife resources

Curriculum: Art; Dance; Drama; Language Arts; Music; Social Studies

571 Idaho Department of Commerce

www.visitid.org/index.html

Visit Idaho is a general reference & visitor's guide to the state. About Idaho, Festivals & Events, Attractions, Recreation, History, more.

Special Features: Maps, Images, & Video; Regional Flipbooks

Curriculum: Geography; Government; Social Studies

572 Idaho Digital Learning Academy

www.idla.k12.id.us/

Statewide, web-based educational program provides course access to traditional, home schooled, adult learners. View schedules, register for courses, attend classes; links for parents, students, faculty, teachers.

Special Features: ISAT review courses; employment opportunities for educators

Curriculum: Biology; Business; Economics; Education; Government; History; Language Arts; Math; Music; Science; Social Studies; Technology

573 Idaho Forest Products Commission

www.idahoforests.org/

Organization promotes managed use of state natural resources through education, advocacy. Extensive teacher's resources on website, including workshop and grant opportunities, curriculum resources, essays on forest health & management.

Special Features: Online lesson plans; Forests Are For Kids feature

Curriculum: Economics; Education; Environmental Studies; Science; Social Studies

574 Idaho Geological Survey

www.idahogeology.org/

Service and research agency that researches, collects, educates geologic and mineral data for ID. Online resources, including geologic maps, publications, compiled data, programs & services, organization info, links.

Special Features: Earth Science Education resources, opportunities; Idaho Fault Map & Earthquake Maps

Curriculum: Education; Environmental Studies; Geography; Science

575 Idaho Historic Preservation Council

www.preservationidaho.org/

Organization promotes, supports, preserves prominent & endangered historic elements in ID. Programs, including educational classroom presentations; news and events; endangered sites; preservation & history resources; links.

Special Features: List of Endangered Sites; Nominate an Endangered Site for consideration

Curriculum: History

576 Idaho Humane Society

www.idahohumanesociety.com/

ID animal welfare, rescue, activism organization. Promotes pet adoption, spaying & neutering; plus cruelty cases, legislation, care & training, organization info, resource links, more.

Special Features: General Care articles; links to local shelters

Curriculum: Social Studies

577 Idaho Humanities Council

www.idahohumanities.org/

Council dedicated to expanding public humanities programs in ID. Website resources include info on grants, teacher programs, resources, and opportunities in disciplines including literature, history, philosophy, ethics, more.

Special Features: Humanities curriculums free by mail

Curriculum: Education; History; Language Arts; Philosophy; Social Studies

578 Idaho Libraries' Special Collections (Sponsor: FARRIT)

www.lili.org/farrit/

ID info resource gathers bibliographies, info, links on resources held by ID libraries. Presents categorized links and reading lists, plus some in-site content.

Special Features: Notable Idahoans bibliography; Idaho Book Awards

Curriculum: Geography; History; Language Arts; Social Studies

579 Idaho Mining Association

www.idahomining.org/

Mining organization advocates for ID's significant industry. History of mining in ID, educational programs, mining technology, economics, environment, resources, links.

Special Features: Out of the Rock school program

Curriculum: Business; Economics; Environmental Studies; Science

580 Idaho Museum of Natural History

www.imnh.isu.edu/

Museum acquires, studies, displays natural & cultural artifacts/objects for education and preservation. Museum info, history, exhibits, programs, research, collections.

Special Features: Resources for educators; info on kid, family activities

Curriculum: Education; History; Science; Social Studies

581 Idaho Newspaper Association

www.idahopapers.com/

Interactive Online Resource for the Idaho Newspaper Industry collects resources, links. Newspaper listing, contact info, links for entire state, plus advertising, news clips, IdahoPress Online, ID Publisher's Exchange.

Special Features: Interactive map
Curriculum: Social Studies

582 Idaho Potato Commission

www.idahopotatoes.org/

State agency oversees, researches, promotes ID's most famous product. Online content for Consumers, Foodservice, Retail; Nutrition Facts, Recipes, Links, more.

Special Features: Spuddy Buddy kid's pages; agricultural production photos
Curriculum: Home Economics; Social Studies

583 Idaho Public Television

www.idahoptv.org/learn/

The ID PTV Learn Site is a teacher's resource for using Public Television in the classroom. TV Schedule, Classroom Calendar, News for teachers, Dialogue for Kids, Adult Education, Teacher Toolbox.

Special Features: Lesson plans; workshop opportunities
Curriculum: Education

584 Idaho Rangeland Resource Commission

www.idrange.org/

Promotes education, awareness, preservation of ID's private and public rangelands. Learn about rangelands, rangelands research, teacher's resources, student resources, ask a range manager, calendar of events.

Special Features: How to identify Range Plants; Rangelands Quiz; teacher workshops
Curriculum: Education; Environmental Studies

585 Idaho Rivers United

www.idahorivers.org/

Organization working to preserve ID's river systems, including the Snake and Clearwater rivers. River Protection, Hydro/Energy Support, River Activism, news, events & programs, resource links.

Special Features: Are You RiverSmart?
Curriculum: Environmental Studies; Social Studies

586 Idaho State Board of Education

www.idahoboardofed.org/saa/index.asp

ID's BOE Standards, Assessment, and Accountability website is a resource for teachers wanting to achieve curriculum standards. Includes Teacher's guides by subject area, ISAT guidelines, Accountability Workbook, more.

Special Features: State Achievement Standards; curriculum by subject, grade level
Curriculum: Education; Health; Language Arts; Math; Science; Social Studies

587 Idaho State Historical Society

www.idahohistory.net/

State organization promotes history education and historic preservation, supports local historical societies. Online content includes digital exhibitions, educator's resources, programs & events, organization history.

Special Features: Oregon Trail in ID virtual exhibition; ID-centered lesson plans

Curriculum: Education; History

588 Idaho State Library

www.lili.org/

Extensive resource for ID libraries, including online catalogs, online databases, State Documents Collection, reading & literacy programs, links to the ID library system.

Special Features: Training and other resources for librarians

Curriculum: Education; Library Media

589 Idaho State Parks and Recreation

www.idahoparks.org/

State website collects info, links on ID national parks, state parks, recreation areas. News & events, visitor's info, doing business, publications, data center, links, more.

Special Features: State Parks A to Z; Recreation Resources

Curriculum: Geography; Social Studies

590 Idaho Women's Commission

www2.state.id.us/women/

State-sponsored commission promotes and supports women's issues, including legislative and national issues. Website contains organization info, events, FAQ, resources & links.

Special Features: Significant Women in Idaho's History

Curriculum: History; Women's Studies

591 Idaho Writer's League

www.idahowritersleague.com/

The IWL promotes local writers, provides a resource for writers to gather, share writings, gain access to publication and promotion. Website offers up site info, members list & websites, contests and conference info, Leagazette online.

Special Features: Writer's resource links

Curriculum: Language Arts

592 IdahoSports.com

www.idahosports.com/

Website supports, promotes ID high school sports & recreation. Online content includes schedules, scores, stats, rosters, standings, more.

Special Features: Top athlete rankings; coaching resources

Curriculum: Physical Education

593 IdahoSummits.com

www.idahosummits.com/

Hiking enthusiast's webpage has extensive info on ID mountains. Images, peak lists, trip reports, essays, recreational hikes, message board.

Special Features: The ID 12ers; Class Ratings

Curriculum: Geography; Physical Education

594 INSIDE Idaho

www.inside.uidaho.edu

Demographics collection center for ID statistics. Concentrates on geographic and geospatial data. Geodata, Numeric Data, Atlases, Interactive GIS major info sections; plus technologies, FAQ, contacts, links.

Special Features: Interactive data mapper; tutorial

Curriculum: Geography; Social Studies

595 Learning Lab

www.learninglabinc.org/

Boise, ID institution promotes basic and adult education with a focus on literacy. Learn about literacy, search course catalog, sign up for classes, contact the Lab.

Special Features: Read student writings

Curriculum: Education; Language Arts

596 Lemhi County Historical Museum

www.sacajaweahome.com/

Celebrates the birthplace of Sacajawea, the native American guide on the Lewis & Clark Expedition. Archive articles on Lewis and Clark, Sacajawea, Lemhi County, plus visitor's info, links.

Special Features: The Legend of Sacajawea's Name

Curriculum: History; Social Studies

597 Lewis & Clark in Idaho

www.lewisandclarkidaho.org/

Official ID website commemorating the Lewis & Clark Expedition. Expedition Map, Native Peoples, Points of Interest, Plan a Trip, Maps & Images, Research, links.

Special Features: Interactive maps; student & teacher resources
Curriculum: History

598 Museum of Idaho

www.museumofidaho.org/

Historical & natural science museum features permanent exhibits, temporary displays. Website features exhibit info, tour & visitor info, exhibits, news & events, links.
Special Features: Educational Resources for incorporating museum visit into curriculum
Curriculum: Education; History; Science; Social Studies

599 National Park Service: City of Rocks National Preserve

www.nps.gov/ciro/

The City of Rocks National Preserve is a geologically significant area that also provides popular and challenging hiking/climbing routes. Visiting info, park facts, park history, features, natural resources, science of the park.
Special Features: Natural Features & Ecosystem; Cultural History
Curriculum: Environmental Studies; History; Science; Social Studies

600 National Park Service: Hagerman Fossil Beds

www.nps.gov/hafo/

The Hagerman Fossil Beds are some of the nation's most significant paleontology sites. NPS website gives park overview & facts, plus in depth look at fossils, nature & science of the park, visiting info, education opportunities.
Special Features: Prehistoric Critter Corner; Fossil bed Geology
Curriculum: Science

601 State of Idaho

www.accessidaho.org/

Access Idaho official state website. Content areas include About Idaho, Government, Health & Safety, Laws & Rules, Tourism & Transportation, Working, plus state department websites, services.

Special Features: Idaho History; Just for Kids
Curriculum: Government

602 University of Idaho College of Agriculture and Life Sciences

www.info.ag.uidaho.edu/

Resources for Idaho collects info, files, links on ID agriculture. Primary content includes publications information, services; plus, complete online collection of AgKnowledge and Home-Wise newsletters.
Special Features: Resource links
Curriculum: Environmental Studies; Science

603 University of Idaho Extension

www.uidaho.edu/ag/extension/

Cooperative Extension portal for the state. Extension & College Offices, ID 4-H, Events, Employment, Journals & Publications, resource links.
Special Features: Current Features; ID Impact Statement
Curriculum: Environmental Studies; Science; Social Studies

604 University of Idaho Extension Forestry

www.cnr.uidaho.edu/extforest/

Resource website offers info, resources, links for forested land management. Content areas include Alternative Forest Enterprises, Business of Forestry, Fire, Forest Health, Wildlife; articles, bibliographies, links.
Special Features: Natural Resource Education sections for teachers, students
Curriculum: Environmental Studies; Science

605 Wolf Recovery Foundation

www.forwolves.org/

Organization working to restore and protect the wolf populations of the northern Rocky Mountains and Yellowstone National Park. Information on wolves, preservation efforts, news, events, photos, wildlife journal, links.
Special Features: Student Learning Area with wolf resources
Curriculum: Science; Social Studies

ILLINOIS

606 The Abraham Lincoln Association

www.alincolnassoc.com/

State organization dedicated to the president and IL native. Online features include the Collected Works of Abraham Lincoln; The Lincoln Log: A Daily Chronology of the Life of Abraham Lincoln.

Special Features: Teacher's Resources, including curriculum guides (requires Adobe Acrobat Reader)

Curriculum: History

607 Alliance Library System

history.alliancelibrarysystem.com/

Suite of four history-centered educational sites: Early Illinois Women & Other Unsung Heroes; Illinois Alive; Vets on the Net Resource Page; Kids and Korea.

Special Features: Early Illinois Women timeline; Illinois Alive Tools or Educators

Curriculum: Education; History; Social Studies; Women's Studies

608 Center for Governmental Studies, NIU

www.illinoisatlas.com/index.htm

IllinoisAtlas.com presents the ongoing efforts of the Data & Mapping Services Division's digital mapping program. Map types include physical feature, historical, agricultural, climate/environment, census maps, more.

Special Features: Order prints of any map

Curriculum: Environmental Studies; Geography; Government; History; Social Studies

609 Chicago Historical Society

www.chicagohistory.org/

City historic preservation and education organization. Online Projects offers My Chicago and Teen Chicago, both community-contributed projects; plus exhibits & museum info, programs & events, research & collections, donations & support.

Special Features: Educators area; History Lab

Curriculum: History; Social Studies

610 Chicago Public Library

www.chipublib.org/digital/digital.html

CPL Digital Collections online presentations.

Includes Chicago's Front Door; Chicago Renaissance; Down the Drain; Remembering Harold Washington; Weapons of the Civil War; Then and Now; Windows to Our Past.

Special Features: Teaching With Digital Content

Curriculum: History; Library Media

611 City of Chicago

www.egov.cityofchicago.org/

Official website for IL's famous city. Content areas For Residents, For Business, Exploring Chicago, Your Government, plus links to city services, department websites.

Special Features: Chicago History & Facts; Education & Resource links

Curriculum: Government; History

612 City of Springfield

www.springfield.il.us/

Official website for IL's capitol. Officials/Council, City Depts., Police & Fire, Economic Development, Tourism, News, Links.

Special Features: Action Center

Curriculum: Government

613 The Ernest Hemingway Foundation of Oak Park

www.ehfop.org/

Organization and birth home museum of the famous author. Extensive section on Hemingway's Life and Work, Web Resources & Links; plus museum information, events, visitors information.

Special Features: Virtual Tour of Hemingway House

Curriculum: Language Arts

614 Fermi National Accelerator Lab

www.fnal.gov/

Fermilab, located in Batavia, IL, conducts research in high-particle physics and related fields. Learn about Fermilab, learn about science, events, inquires, links.

Special Features: Inquiring Minds science essays; education resources, including teacher Resources

Curriculum: Science

615 The Field Museum

www.fieldmuseum.org/

Chicago's Field Museum website offers information the museum and its floor exhibits, plus online content areas. Online exhibits include Sue on the Web; Man-Eaters at the Field Museum; Anthropology Collections of the Field Museum; Sounds From the Vault; more.

Special Features: Education Resources, including arranging tours, classroom resources
Curriculum: Science; Social Studies

616 Frank Lloyd Wright Preservation Trust

www.wrightplus.org/

Oak Park, IL foundation and museum for the famous architect. Features Home & Studio and Frederick C. Robie House. Biography of photos, museum info and house tours, events, links.

Special Features: Frank Lloyd Wright: Life & Work interactive Flash program
Curriculum: Architecture

617 Grand Prairie Friends of Illinois

www.prairienet.org/gpf/

Grassroots organization committed to preserving and restoring tallgrass prairie and woodlands in East-Central Illinois. Online information about prairies, prairie preservation, prairie gardens, membership info, events, resource links.

Special Features: About Prairies; Prairie Gardens
Curriculum: Environmental Studies; Science

618 Historic Lighthouses (Sponsor: Terry Pepper)

www.terrypepper.com/lights/state_illinois.htm

Essays on the four historic lighthouses of IL: Chicago Harbor, Grosse Point, Little Fort, Waukegan Harbor.

Special Features: Gallery images; reference resources
Curriculum: History

619 History (Sponsor: Infobahn Outfitters, Inc.)

www.outfitters.com/illinois/history/

Pages on IL history, with a focus on western IL. Famous Illinoisans, IL in the American Civil War, History of Western Counties, Growth of IL Railroads, Military Tract in Western IL.

Special Features: Extensive Civil War pages
Curriculum: History

620 Humane Society of Central Illinois

www.hscipets.org/

Regional Humane Society chapter with extensive website. Adoption and rescue info, cat & dog care tips, events, galleries of pets, spay/neuter info, links to other state societies, more.

Special Features: Humane education opportunities
Curriculum: Social Studies

621 Illini Confederation (Sponsor: Robert Fester)

www.members.tripod.com/~RFester/index.html

The Illini Confederation traces the history of IL's first inhabitants. Lengthy site produced as a referenced essay, with sub-pages and links throughout.

Special Features: Illiniwek Homework Help Project
Curriculum: History; Social Studies

622 Illinois Association of Minorities in Government

www.iamg1.com/

Organization that advocates on behalf of minority employees for jobs, promotions, job retention and protection against discriminatory acts. Organization and membership information online, conferences & scholarships, interactive forums.

Special Features: Myth & Fact about minority employment
Curriculum: Government; Social Studies

623 Illinois Bureau of Tourism

www.enjoyillinois.com/

General travel guide to the state. Provides overview of the IL and IL places of interest, leisure areas, calendar of events, IL roadmap.

Special Features: Bilingual site (Spanish)
Curriculum: Social Studies

624 Illinois Department of Commerce & Economic Opportunity

www.illinoisdata.com/

The northern IL business & economic data library. Contains compiled government statistics on agriculture, business, crime, demographics, education, housing, government, and labor, plus economic indicators, census info, more.

Special Features: Regional and state profiles
Curriculum: Business; Economics; Education; Government; Social Studies

625 Illinois Department of Education

www.enjoyillinois.com/

The Illinois Green Door serves as a portal for IL environmental education resources. Flowing water, groundwater, forest prairie, schoolyard, urban, wetland ecosystems; early & late elementary, middle, and high school content areas.

Special Features: Environmental Education Standards
Curriculum: Environmental Studies; Science

626 Illinois Historic Preservation
        Agency

www.alincoln-library.com/Apps/default.asp

The Abraham Lincoln Library is dedicated to the famous president from IL. Slated to open in 2005; website is active, contains info on Lincoln, chronology of his life, selected readings, info on museum & construction, links.

Special Features: Kid's Pages
Curriculum: History; Library Media

627 Illinois Historical Art Project

www.illinoisart.org/

IHAP collects original source material and biographical information on IL artists. Contains comprehensive A–Z List of Illinois Artists, with biographical info.

Special Features: Gallery of select images
Curriculum: Art; History

628 Illinois Humanities Council

www.prairie.org/

Online humanities organization provides extensive online content, including Detours online journal; plus Exhibits Kiosk, news & events, Council programs, more.

Special Features: Brown vs. Board of Education: 50 Years Later online exhibit
Curriculum: Art; History; Language Arts; Social Studies

629 Illinois Institute for Rural Affairs

www.iira.org/index.asp

IIRA works to improve rural areas by developing small business development and community development projects in rural areas. Program information, news, outreach programs, research & publications, Resources.

Special Features: Rural Information Resources; Illinois Municipal Price Index
Curriculum: Business; Social Studies

630 Illinois Municipal League

www.iml.org/

IML unites local IL governments for legislative and community action. News, events, legislation, activism related to municipal government.

Special Features: Community forums, directory
Curriculum: Government

631 Illinois Native Plant Society

www.ill-inps.org/

State society studies, collects, and promotes preservation of IL native flora. Society publications, membership info, events, resources & links.

Special Features: IL Invasive Plant Species list
Curriculum: Environmental Studies; Science

632 Illinois Natural History Survey

www.inhs.uiuc.edu/

Survey studies, records, protects, and educates on IL ecology and ecological history. Info on INHS Centers and Projects, plus Research, Outreach, and Resources.

Special Features: Explore INHS Collections, with essays, maps
Curriculum: Environmental Studies; Science

633 Illinois State Geological Survey

www.isgs.uiuc.edu/

State geological survey presents extensive online resources. Illinois Geology articles on earthquakes, bedrock geology, coal, more; Databases & Collections; Geoscience Education, including field trip info; Maps & Mapping Efforts; QuickLinks to useful sites; more.

Special Features: Illinois Fossils; the Trilobite — Early Inhabitant of Illinois
Curriculum: Science

634 Illinois State Historical Society

www.historyillinois.org/

Society dedicated to historical preservation. Pages contain information, events, resources. Includes Illinois History Resource Pages, with articles, links, and essay on Women's Suffrage in IL.

Special Features: JUST FOR KIDS: For Those Pesky School Reports

Curriculum: History; Social Studies

635 Illinois State Museum

www.museum.state.il.us/

State Museum presents online exhibits including At Home In the Heartland; Ice Ages; Harvesting the River; Mazon Creek Fossils; Prairies in the Prairie State; plus museum info, events, arrange a tour.

Special Features: Educational tours

Curriculum: History; Social Studies

636 Illinois State Water Survey

www.sws.uiuc.edu/

State water survey website. Online content includes Nitrogen, Illinois Water Cycle, Illinois Water Supply, plus data & maps, survey info, resource links, more.

Special Features: How Is Water Used in Illinois?

Curriculum: Science

637 Illinois Storytelling, Inc.

www.storytelling.org/

Organization committed to increasing public awareness of the art, practice and value of oral storytelling. Website directory of IL storytellers; membership information; events, including annual IL Storytelling Festival.

Special Features: Directory of IL Storytelling Guilds

Curriculum: Language Arts

638 Illinois Student Assistance Commission

www.collegeillinois.com/

College Illinois! statewide program is a 529 prepaid tuition plan for state residents. Also assists prospective students and families in funding for college, college selection. Research, enroll online.

Special Features: Bilingual Polish, Spanish sites

Curriculum: Education

639 Illinois Trail History and Genealogy

www.iltrails.org/

Not-for-profit group dedicated to putting historical and genealogical information online for free use. Military Data, State Data, Census Data, Events, Newspapers, Research Help, Mailing list.

Special Features: Query Boards

Curriculum: History; Social Studies

640 Institute of Government and Public Affairs at the University of Illinois

www.igpa.uillinois.edu/abstract/

The IL Statistical Abstract is a yearly picture of IL created through compilation of economic, demographic, and political data. Data areas include Housing, Health & Vital Statistics, Education, Labor, Employment, Personal Earnings, Agriculture, more.

Special Features: Purchase CD edition of yearly abstract

Curriculum: Economics; Education; Health; Social Studies

641 Jane Addams Hull House Association

www.hullhouse.org/

Modern descendant of the famous social-reform program, based in Chicago. Community outreach programs, community centers; info on aid, volunteering, supporting, contacting.

Special Features: Works by Jane Addams; Jane Addams links

Curriculum: Social Studies

642 Jazz Age Chicago (Sponsor: Scott A. Newman)

chicago.urban-history.org/mainmenu.htm

Jazz Age Chicago highlights urban living from 1893–1934, focused on the city's diversifying population. History from the perspective of city amusements, recreations. Includes links.

Special Features: City Scrapbook

Curriculum: History; Social Studies

643 John G. Shedd Aquarium

www.sheddaquarium.org/

Chicago's Shedd Aquarium provides online information about aquarium species, including habitat info and images. Also: exploring Shedd exhibits, museum and tour info, events, conservation projects, teach & learn, more.

Special Features: Teachers can set up aquarium visits, with curriculum resources; Kid's Quest guide

Curriculum: Education; Environmental Studies; Science

644 Landmark Preservation Council of Illinois

www.landmarks.org/

Organization promotes state preservation of architecturally and historically significant sites, structures, and districts. Supports preservation efforts, funds initiatives, educates through programs and events.

Special Features: Ten Most Endangered Places; Chicagoland Watch List
Curriculum: History; Social Studies

645 Lincoln Park Zoo

www.lpzoo.com/

Chicago-area zoological gardens. Website features Know the Animals with habitat, biological info on zoo exhibits, plus museum info, arranging tours, events calendar, conservation, education.

Special Features: ZEBRA Interactive Curriculum Resource for classes visiting the zoo
Curriculum: Environmental Studies; Science

646 Paul V. Galvin Library

www.gl.iit.edu/collections/dighis.htm

Digital History Collections of the Paul V. Galvin Library. Includes the IIT Campus Newspaper Project 1928–1980; Voices of the Holocaust archive; Wright Air Development Center; World's Columbian Exposition of 1893 exhibit.

Special Features: Related Resources and Links for subjects
Curriculum: History

647 Peggy Notebaert Nature Museum

www.naturemuseum.org/online/index. html

Nature Museum Online presents interactive science pages for K–12 students in IL and nationwide. The Butterfly Lab; My Water Supply; City Science Mural; Hands-On Habitat; Bird Alert!; Environmental Central.

Special Features: Teacher Resources accompany each exhibit
Curriculum: Environmental Studies; Science

648 Peoria Astronomical Society

www.astronomical.org/

Peoria, IL-based astronomical society maintains an informative website. Learning Topics on constellations, planets, the Solar System, stars; Beginner, Intermediate, and Advanced Astronomy content.

Special Features: 3D Panoramic constellation map; photo gallery
Curriculum: Science

649 Prairie Nations Page (Sponsor: Meredith Fay and Jim Fay)

www.prairienet.org/prairienations/index.htm

The Prairie Nations Page collects the history, culture, and folklife of the native nations who once lived in IL. Printable handbooks, essays on tribes & tribal languages, researching Native American ancestry, bibliography information.

Special Features: Prairie Poster Project
Curriculum: History; Social Studies

650 Prairies (Sponsor: Jan Strasma)

www.prairiepages.com/

Short but informative website introducing IL prairie lands. Good for kids; includes numerous links.

Special Features: Online Prairie Resources
Curriculum: Environmental Studies

651 Prairies Research Guide (Sponsor: University of Illinois at Urbana-Champaign [UIUC])

www.library.uiuc.edu/nhx/prairieresearchguide 1.htm

Prairies Research Guide: an annotated guide to prairie resources provides students and researchers with a broad collection of resources on IL's significant ecosystem.

Special Features: Resources divided by type
Curriculum: Environmental Studies; Science

652 Sears Tower (Sponsor: Randall Krause)

www.searstower.org/

Small but informative site on the history and architecture of the Sears Tower. Contains introduction, facts, links to related articles and websites.

Special Features: Tower Height Comparison Chart.
Curriculum: Architecture

653 State of Illinois

www.illinois.gov/

Official state website. Content areas include Living, Working, Visiting, Learning, Business, Public Safety, Technology, and Government; links to state departments, services.
Special Features: Illinois Gallery collection of historic and modern images
Curriculum: Government

654 University of Illinois at Chicago (UIC)

www.tigger.uic.edu/depts/ahaa/imagebase/index.html

UIC's Chicago Imagebase collects and presents digital information on the region's built environment, both historic and modern. Table of contents by subject, or search the database.
Special Features: Interactive map search
Curriculum: Art; History; Social Studies

655 University of Illinois at Chicago, College of Architecture and the Arts

www.uic.edu/jaddams/hull/hull_house.html

The Jane Addams Hull-House Museum, is a historic site and memorial to the famous social-reform program. Website features detailed timeline and photo essay about Jane Addams, museum & tour info, education & research resources.
Special Features: Urban Experience in Chicago: Hull-House and Its Neighborhoods, 1889–1963
Curriculum: History; Social Studies

656 University of Illinois Extension

www.urbanext.uiuc.edu/

Urban Programs Resource Network is UI's cooperative extension program. Major content areas include Horticultural Corner; Home & Money; Schools Online; Nutrition & Health; 4-H; Parenting & Seniors; Environmental Stewardship.
Special Features: Just for Kids area with included Teacher's Resources
Curriculum: Biology; Education; Environmental Studies; Health; Science; Social Studies

INDIANA

657 Arts Place

www.indianaarts.org/

Online connection for the IN arts community. Directory and profile of IN artisans, including visual arts, media arts, language arts, traditional arts; events calendar, features artists, resource links.
Special Features: Register for listing
Curriculum: Art; Dance; Drama; Music; Social Studies

658 Association of Indiana Counties

www.indianacounties.org/

Coalition of county governments working to represent the interests of local government at the state level. Organization info, list of member counties, legislative news, publications, news, more.
Special Features: Interactive County Map
Curriculum: Government

659 Children's Museum of Indianapolis

www.childrensmuseum.org/

Indianapolis institution provides fun, educational displays for kids. Extensive online content includes games, activities, readings for use alone, or in conjunction with a museum visit; plus, museum info, programs & events, arrange a visit.
Special Features: Teacher's resources, including classroom activates
Curriculum: Education; History; Science; Social Studies

660 City of Fort Wayne

www.cityoᴠortwayne.org/

Civic homepage for the significant northern IN city. Major content For Visitors, For Residents, For Businesses, plus links for civic government, services, online recourses.
Special Features: Maps; city demographics
Curriculum: Business; Government

661 City of Indianapolis and Marion County

www.indygov.org/

Official civic website for IN's capitol city and county. Content areas for Services, Local Government, Visiting, Business, Community; plus civic departments, mayor's office, news, events.
Special Features: Family Guide to Public Schools in Indianapolis
Curriculum: Education; Government

662 City of South Bend

www.ci.south-bend.in.us/

Civic website for the significant IN city, home of Notre Dame University. Mayor, City Directory, Government, Explore South Bend, Events & News, Employment, City Public Bids, plus online services, links.
Special Features: History of South Bend; Bilingual Spanish site
Curriculum: Business; Government

663 Civil War (Sponsor: Craig Dunn Enterprises)

www.civilwarindiana.com/

Website chronicles IN's role in the Civil War through original material, primary sources, resource links. Soldier Search, Photo Archive, Prominent Personalities, Regiments, Events, more.
Special Features: IN Civil War Quiz
Curriculum: History

664 College Football Hall of Fame

www.collegefootball.org/

South Bend, IN Hall commemorates college football. List of inductees, tour the hall, new nominees, events & programs, schedule a tour.
Special Features: Stay in Bounds education program info
Curriculum: Physical Education; Sports

665 Conner Prairie

www.connerprairie.org/

Historical museum & attraction in Fishers, IN. Website features Prairie History Online with articles, exhibits, and resources about historical life on the prairie.
Special Features: Foodways; Primary Sources
Curriculum: History; Social Studies

666 County History Preservation Society

www.countyhistory.com/

Society providing Internet accessible historical information for IN counties. Extensive articles, county-by county & statewide; search, timeline, news, resource links.
Special Features: Governors of IN; 2000 Pictures of IN's Past
Curriculum: History

667 Electronic Atlas (Sponsor: Trustees of Indiana University)

www.atlas.ulib.iupui.edu/

Electronic Atlas of Central IN contain extensive maps of the regional counties, including census, environmental, historical, aerial, educational; plus, some statewide maps.
Special Features: Educational Resources; Historical Maps of Indiana Cities and Counties
Curriculum: Geography

668 Falls of the Ohio State Park

www.fallsoftheohio.org/

Clarksville, IN natural park on the Ohio River. Features many fossil finds, park programs, visitor info, park geologic history, facilities & services, resource links.
Special Features: Education section, including articles on fossils
Curriculum: Geography; Science

669 Historic Landmarks Foundation of Indiana

www.historiclandmarks.org/

The largest private state preservation group in the U.S.; promotes the restoration and preservation IN historic landmarks. Database of landmarks, with info & maps; endangered properties; preservation opportunities; membership & support info, events, links.
Special Features: 99 Historic Homes of Indiana
Curriculum: History; Social Studies

670 Historic Southern Indiana

www.usi.edu/hsi/index.asp

Organization dedicated to preserving, enhancing, and promoting historic resources of southern IN. HSI Resource Center includes directories, educational resources, workshop/conference proceedings, symposium transcripts, tourism/economic development resources.

Special Features: Guide to Historic Sites; lesson plans
Curriculum: History

671 Humane Society of Indianapolis

www.indyhumane.com/

Chapter of the national animal welfare organization. Info on animal abandonment & adoption; pet care, advice, and training; volunteering; news, events, links.
Special Features: Dog, cat, small animal care guides
Curriculum: Social Studies

672 Indiana Arts Commission

www.state.in.us/arts/

State commission promotes the arts in IN. Content areas for Artists, Communities, Educators, Organizations; plus news, events, contact, grants, publications.
Special Features: Arts Education Resources
Curriculum: Art; Dance; Drama; Education; Music

673 Indiana Association of Cities and Towns

www.citiesandtowns.org/

Organization dedicated to improving municipal government education in IN schools & with local officials. Programs, events, conference info; list of IN cities & towns; business & education resources; publications; membership & contact info.
Special Features: Municipal Management Institute; youth development programs
Curriculum: Government

674 Indiana Black Expo

www.indianablackexpo.com/

State community service organization working for the social and economic advancement of IN African-Americans. Programs, outreach, news & events, IBE history, jobs, membership info, links.
Special Features: IBE Commit 2 Quit; IBE license plates
Curriculum: Social Studies

675 Indiana Commission for Women

www.in.gov/icw/

State organization promoting women's rights and issues. Website includes membership info, news, activities, articles, publications, links.

Special Features: Legislative Guide
Curriculum: Women's Studies

676 Indiana Department of Education

www.indianastandards.org/

Online resource for K–12 curricular standards in four major academic subjects, plus specialized subjects. Divided by subject, grade/specialty level. Some files require Adobe Acrobat Reader.
Special Features: Bilingual Spanish site
Curriculum: Education; Language Arts; Math; Science

677 Indiana DoE Office of Learning Resources

www.wvec.k12.in.us/hometown/

Project Hometown, IN is a K–12 initiative to enhance history education & online history resources through classroom programs, student efforts. Schools present their portions of the project online; plus, get info, resource links.
Special Features: Sign up your class/school
Curriculum: Education

678 Indiana Geological Survey

www.igs.indiana.edu/index.cfm

State survey collects, studies, and presents IN geological information. Features interactive maps & databases; IGS publications; IN Geology extensive section.
Special Features: Earth Science Issues; topographical maps for sale
Curriculum: Environmental Studies; Geography; Science

679 Indiana Higher Education Telecommunications System

www.ihets.org/

IHETS is a consortium of IN colleges & universities striving to provide educational technologies to classrooms, libraries, communities. Find out about available programs & services, news, events, contact administrators for access.
Special Features: Information for Educators
Curriculum: Education; Library Media; Technology

680 Indiana Historic Architecture

www.preserveindiana.com/

Indiana Historic Architecture promotes the appreciation, restoration, and preservation IN landmarks. Images & info on historic architecture, preservation activism, endangered buildings, resource links.

Special Features: 10 Simple Ways You Can Help Promote Historic Preservation
Curriculum: Architecture

681 Indiana Historical Bureau

www.statelib.lib.in.us/WWW/ihb/ihb.html

Organization supports programs, opportunities for learning IN history. Extended content, links on state history, native Americans, cemeteries, historical markers, past governors, state emblems, Underground Railroad; plus resource links, Bureau info, services, news, links.

Special Features: The Word "Hoosier"
Curriculum: History; Social Studies

682 Indiana Historical Society

www.indianahistory.org/

Organization committed to collecting, preserving, interpreting and disseminating IN history. Browse digital archives online; collections & exhibits info; conservation efforts; Society info, membership, events, links.

Special Features: Education Resources; Lessons & Materials
Curriculum: Education; History; Social Studies

683 Indiana Library Federation

www.ilfonline.org/Programs/YHBA/

The Young Hoosier Book Award promotes reading through a student nominating and voting competition. Current nominees, former winners, booklists, programs & events, participating schools, how to participate.

Special Features: Idea Sharing; nominate a title
Curriculum: Language Arts

684 Indiana Literacy Foundation

www.indianaliteracy.org/

State organization promotes literacy at K–12, adult learner levels through programs, events, resources. Become a volunteer, programs & events, literacy resource links.

Special Features: Literacy License Plates
Curriculum: Education; Language Arts

685 Indiana Pioneer Cemeteries
Restoration Project

www.inpcrp.org/

Project promotes restoration and generates public awareness about the neglected pioneer cemeteries of IN. Cemetery preservation resources, IN cemetery lists, cemetery legislation, news & events, resource links.

Special Features: Hall of Shame neglected cemeteries list
Curriculum: History; Social Studies

686 Indiana Schools SMART
Partnership

www.smartpartnership.org/aboutsmart.asp

IN schools and IN businesses partnership for strengthening state science & math curriculums. Schools can find out info online, contact SMART, register for SMART, log into SMART programs.

Special Features: Online newsletter
Curriculum: Education; Math; Science

687 Indiana State Library

www.statelib.lib.in.us/www/isl/whoweare/data center.html

The IN Data Center makes census and other state and federal, demographic and economic statistics available through a statewide network. Access data, maps, publications, resource links, categorized chronologically and/or by category.

Special Features: State 2000 Census data
Curriculum: Economics; Government; History; Social Studies

688 Indiana State Teacher's Association

www.ista-in.org/

Organization fosters IN teaching community to help improve IN classrooms & assist in professional development. Membership, Resources, News & Events, Government Relations, ISTA Directory, links.

Special Features: Teachers Rights Under the Law; Tips for Parents
Curriculum: Education

689 Indiana Township Association

www.indianatownshipassoc.org/

Affiliation of Trustees and Associates working to improve local government and to represent local government to the Legislature. About the ITA, Legislative Issues, Resources, News & Events.

Special Features: Interactive map of counties, townships
Curriculum: Government

690 Indiana Traveler (Sponsor: Bill Holden)

www.indianatraveler.com/index.html

Indiana Traveler collects a wealth of IN information & resources, including history, parks, recreation, education, knowledge, events, tourism. Extensive links.

Special Features: County Map; Famous People; Fun Facts

Curriculum: Education; History; Social Studies

691 Indiana University Libraries

www.dlib.indiana.edu/

The Digital Library Project at IN University presents a range of networked digital resources. Text, music, and image collections; plus reference tools, resource links, contact info.

Special Features: Steelmaker-Steeltown: U.S. Steel Gary Works Photograph Collection, 1906–1971

Curriculum: History; Library Media; Music; Social Studies

692 Indiana Web Academy

www.indianawebacademy.org/

Academy dedicated to integrating technology and the Internet into IN education through web courses, programs, resources. Students, educators, parents can register for programs, access classes & resources, contact the Academy.

Special Features: Online lesson plan resources for teachers

Curriculum: Education; Technology

693 Indianapolis Museum of Art

www.ima-art.org/

Website for the IN Museum has museum info, visitor's guide, virtual tour, exhibits & collections, events & programs, donations, links. Educational Programs section features classroom & adult learning opportunities, online activities.

Special Features: Art-Making For All Ages; teacher's Resources

Curriculum: Art; Education; Social Studies

694 Indianapolis Zoo

www.indyzoo.com/

Website for the major IN zoo. What's New, Visitor Info, Events, Zoo Info, Education, Donate, Jobs, Membership. Focused looks at the zoo's animal populations.

Special Features: Field Trips; Student Workshop; Teacher Resources

Curriculum: Education; Science

695 The Lincoln Museum

www.thelincolnmuseum.org/

Fort Wayne museum celebrates Lincoln's life, achievements. Essays, FAQs on Lincoln, the Emancipation Proclamation, the museum; plus museum info, programs & events, arranging a tour, links.

Special Features: Learn about educational programs

Curriculum: History

696 National Park Service

www.nps.gov/libo/

Lincoln Boyhood National Memorial preserves the farm where Abraham Lincoln grew up. Facts about the park, news, history, visitors info; in depth look at Lincoln's boyhood & history.

Special Features: Programs for kids

Curriculum: History

697 Northern Indiana Historical Society

www.centerforhistory.org/

Organization dedicated to preserving and promoting historic resources of northern IN. Exhibitions & Events; Oliver Mansion & Museum; visitor's info, including tours; school programs & tours available.

Special Features: Indiana History; Facts & Statistics About Indiana

Curriculum: History

698 President Benjamin Harrison House

www.presidentbenjaminharrison.org/

Home of the 23rd President, in Indianapolis, now a museum. Online biography of Harrison, including timeline; museum info, virtual tour, events, education opportunities.

Special Features: Benjamin Harrison in Person program; schedule a school tour

Curriculum: History

699 Purdue University

www.ces.purdue.edu/

Purdue Extension provides information, resources to the IN community. Major content for Agriculture & Natural Resources, Consumer & Family, Sciences Leadership & Community Development, 4-H, Environment, Food Safety, more.

Special Features: Ag Answers; New Ventures business resources

Curriculum: Education; Environmental Studies; Health; Science; Social Studies

700 Purdue University, Agronomy Department

www.state.in.us/dnr/soilcons/wet/index.htm

IN Project Wet is a teacher's resource for K–6 water education. Provides in-class materials, articles, programs & events, classroom equipment loans, educator's workshop.

Special Features: Curriculum resources in keeping with state science standards

Curriculum: Education; Environmental Studies; Science

701 State of Indiana

www.state.in.us/

Access Indiana, the official state website. Content for Business, Tourism, Labor, Education, Licensing, Family, Taxes, Agriculture, Travel, Law, Technology.

***Special Features:* In Your Neighborhood (myLocalIN.gov)**

***Curriculum:* Government**

702 Studebaker National Museum

www.studebakermuseum.org/

Fort Wayne museum chronicles the history of the famous cars. Museum History, Special Events, Archives, News and Notes, Collection Tour, Membership, Trivia Contest, Links.

Special Features: Images, brief essays

Curriculum: History; Technology

703 Virginia B. Ball Center for Creative Inquiry

www.bsu.edu/ourlandourlit/index.html

Our Land, Our Literature explores significant IN authors whose works connect to IN, and the environment that inspired them. Learn about authors and their works; IN environment & ecosystems; regions of IN and the works connected to them.

Special Features: Author bios, bibliographies

Curriculum: Environmental Studies; History; Language Arts

704 Virtual Library (Sponsor: INCOLSA)

www.inspire.net/

INSPIRE, Indiana's Virtual Library offers electronic magazines, encyclopedias, and other resources to IN residents. Access EBSCO, ERIC, MedLine, Middle Search Plus, more. Must be IN resident to apply for access.

Special Features: Hoosier Heritage

Curriculum: Library Media

705 The Woodland Steward

www.inwoodlands.org/

Quarterly publication promoting woodland education and proper use of woodland resources. Content on Woodland Management, Forest Industry, Insects, Tree Diseases, Tree Identification; plus publication info, resource links.

Special Features: Teacher's Page; Kid's Page

Curriculum: Education; Environmental Studies; Science

706 The Writer's Center of Indiana

www.indianawriters.org/

State organization dedicated to literary arts education & community. Classes & workshops, readings & events, MAIZE Literary Newsletter, organization info, membership opportunity, resource links.

Special Features: Publishing opportunities for IN writers; sign up for classes, workshops

Curriculum: Language Arts

707 Young Audiences of Indiana

www.yaindy.org/

YAIndy develops and promotes arts education in IN classrooms and communities. Catalog of IN artists, arts resources; YAIndy ArtCard; Y-ARTS program archive; events, programs, info, links.

Special Features: Teacher's Arts Resources

Curriculum: Art; Dance; Drama; Education; Music; Social Studies

IOWA

708 African American Historical Museum & Cultural Center of Iowa

www.blackiowa.org/

African American Historical Museum and Cultural Center of Iowa is located in Cedar Rapids. The museum exhibits African American artifacts from across the USA with focus on Iowans. With a mission to preserve black history, the museum site offers virtual tours, glimpses of the collections, and photos of the changing exhibits.

Special Features: Virtual tour, Black history moments, educational page, multiculturalism

Curriculum: Art; History

709 Amana Colonies Convention & Visitors Bureau

www.amanacolonies.com/welcome/index.html

The Amana Colonies were founded by a German religious group in 1855. An entire community of 1,200 people moved to Iowa to live in communalism to meet their religious ideals and goals. Today the communalism lives on through the Amana Society that owns the agricultural land (26,000 acres) and some of the businesses.

Special Features: Educational resources, frequently asked questions, historical overview, and calendar of events

Curriculum: Business; History; Home Economics; Sociology

710 Business and Professional Women of Iowa

www.bpwiowa.org/index.html

Business and Professional Women of Iowa (BPW/Iowa) is founded to elevate standards, promote interest and a spirit of cooperation to the workplace through advocacy, education, and information. It has twenty-nine local organizations in six regions throughout the state. It was founded on July 15th, 1919 for and by professional women.

Special Features: BPW/Iowa history, legislative platform, what's new and women related links

Curriculum: Women's Studies

711 Coal Mining (Sponsor: University of Northern Iowa)

www.fp.uni.edu/iowahist/Social_Economic/CoalMining_inIowa/coal_mining_in_iowa.htm

Coal Mining in Iowa from 1870 to 1940. A highly informative article on coal mining history including graphs, charts, and illustrations. Iowa map of mineral locations. Good information for junior high students. Part of the Explorations in Iowa History Project.

Special Features: Historical photos, bibliographic resources

Curriculum: Business; Economics; History

712 Des Moines Register

www.desmoinesregister.com/extras/iowans/index.html

A list of famous Iowans. Site lists the person's name includes a picture and short biography of their time in Iowa. Some names include: Herbert Hoover, Kate Shelley, John Wayne, Grant Wood, the Wright Brothers and Earl May.

Special Features: Alphabetical listings, searchable format, famous people are broken up into professions

Curriculum: Language Arts

713 Die Cast Collectables (Sponsor: RC2)

www.rcertl.com/

Located In Dyersville, Iowa. If you have ever owned or played with a die cast collectable or toy it is more than likely an Ertl toy. Collectables include farm and construction equipment, muscle cars, NASCAR, metal soldiers, and video game characters.

Special Features: Collector information, hard to find lists

Curriculum: Art

714 Gazette Communications

www.fyiowa.com/

An overall guide to the state of Iowa. Covers hunting, tourism, wedding planning, quick facts, trivia, and maps. In depth articles on the famous painter, Grant Wood, is included.

Three hundred sixty degree panoramic photos from around the state can also be seen.

Special Features: Events calendar, city and travel general information, Iowa chat room, statewide e-weather resources

Curriculum: Business; Geography; Social Studies

715 Glenn Miller Birthplace Society

www.glennmiller.org/

A tribute to the Big Band era icon, Glenn Miller. Includes history, his birthplace, music festival held in his honor and available scholarships.

Special Features: Link to Japanese branch of the society, historical photos

Curriculum: Dance; History; Music

716 Grotto of the Redemption

www.nw-cybermall.com/grotto.htm

A grotto is an artificial recess or cave. The largest grotto in the world is located in West Bend, Iowa. The grotto is frequently called "the Eighth Wonder of the World." It is the largest collection of minerals and petrifaction.

Special Features: Identification list of precious and semi-precious stones, photos, links

Curriculum: Art; Environmental Studies; Math; Sociology

717 Humanities Iowa

www.uiowa.edu/~humiowa/

Humanities Iowa, founded in 1971, is a non-profit organization bringing the humanities to the public through interactive programming, publications, and events. Programs include traveling exhibits, videos, speakers and reading discussion groups available to Iowans at a low fee.

Special Features: Current grant programs and forms, calendar of events, available speaker list

Curriculum: Art; Education; History; Library Media; Sociology

718 Iowa Artists

www.iowaartists.org/

A statewide listing of Iowa artists. Artists range from chainsaw sculptors, kaleidoscope makers, illustrators, jewelry makers to writers. Website lists museums, tourism sites and artisan forums.

Special Features: Searchable site, related links

Curriculum: Art

719 Iowa Association of Naturalists

www.ianpage.20m.com/index.html

Iowa Association of Naturalists strives to develop the art of interpreting natural and cultural environments through skill development and education. Founded in 1978, IAN sponsors newsletters, workshops, and internships.

Special Features: Extensive related links, nature stories

Curriculum: Environmental Studies; Language Arts

720 Iowa Association of School Boards

www.myiowaschools.org/

Site intends to help keep parents and citizens involved in Iowa public schools. Organized by the Iowa Association of School Boards, Iowa Education Association and the School Administrators of Iowa. Brings all Iowa educational issues to light and provides education advocacy tips.

Special Features: Lists state educational organizations, quick facts, newsroom, school links, current issues and find your legislator's address

Curriculum: Business; Economics; Education; Government

721 Iowa Beef Center

www.iowabeefcenter.org/

Anything and everything about cattle, beef production and the beef industry in Iowa. Originating in 1996, IBS helps support the growth and vitality of Iowa beef through programming, research based information dissemination, educational outreach, and works closely with state extension specialists.

Special Features: Full text library, hot topics, activities and research, calendar of events

Curriculum: Biology; Business; Environmental Studies

722 Iowa Corn Growers Association

www.iowacorn.org/

The ICGA or Iowa Corn Growers Association sponsors a highly useful and informative site. Research, development, promotion, and education of corn and corn products thorough programming and legislative action is covered. Kids page and educator's pages available.

Special Features: Full text corn production news, weather, ethanol industry, uses for corn, biotechnology in farming

Curriculum: Business; Economics; Environmental Studies

723 Iowa Council of Teachers of Mathematics

www.iowamath.org/

Iowa Council of Teachers of Mathematics (ICTM) promotes excellence on their resource page. Print blank graph paper, read math cartoons or use thought provoking questions for discussion.
Special Features: Math related links, membership information
Curriculum: Math

724 Iowa Dance Theatre

www.iowadancetheatre.com/

Established in 1983, Iowa Dance Theatre (IDT) strives to bring dance education, quality performances, and workshops to Iowans. Ballet, modern, jazz, and tap dancing can be seen throughout the year. Schedule available.
Special Features: Additional dance links, news
Curriculum: Dance; Physical Education

725 Iowa Department of Economic Development

www.traveliowa.com/

Iowa's most timely information about attractions and facilities. Includes an event calendar. Covers Iowa history, state symbols, statistics, special byways and scenic routes. All around coverage of the state of Iowa.
Special Features: Facts and fun, travel contacts, regional information, city search, quick fact sheets
Curriculum: Driver Training; Geography; History

726 Iowa Department of Natural Resources

www.iowadnr.com/

The department is organized into Conservation and Recreation, Environmental Services, and Management Services to maintain state parks and forests, protect the environment, manage energy, fish, wildlife, land and water resources.
Special Features: Information about planting trees and wildflowers, hunting and fishing laws, limits and regulations, water quality management and monitoring

Curriculum: Biology; Environmental Studies; Science

727 Iowa Federation of Humane Societies

www.ifhs.storycity.net/member.html

The statewide organization of humane societies. Free images for downloading, fun activities for kids, pet care, how to choose a pet. An animal behavior specialist is available for questions. Listing of accomplishments and successful laws passed in support of animal rights.
Special Features: Listing of shelters and rescues located throughout Iowa, extensive links to other animal related sites
Curriculum: Social Studies

728 Iowa GenWeb Project

iagenweb.org/

IAGenWeb is a group of Iowa volunteers working to provide websites for genealogical research. Select an Iowa county to find ancestors or use the interactive map. Read through archives and special projects such as gravestone photography. Civil War and listings of the Iowa militia are available.
Special Features: Special projects about Iowa history, learn more about ethnic group settlements
Curriculum: Geography; History

729 Iowa Geological Survey

www.igsb.uiowa.edu/browse/minerals/minerals.htm

"Minerals of Iowa" by Jean Cutler Prior is an illustrated article on Iowa's minerals and their identification. Perfect for the rock hound. This article details mineral formation and locations throughout Iowa.
Special Features: Rock and mineral identification
Curriculum: Geography; Science

730 Iowa Health System

www.ihs.org/

Iowa Health System (IHS) was created in 1993. Supporting communities statewide, the website includes twenty-four hour health information, an interactive health library containing over four thousand articles, physician finder, and body animations.
Special Features: Interactive health tools, reference index, searchable library
Curriculum: Biology; Health

731 Iowa High School Athletic Association

www.iahsaa.org/

Comprehensive coverage of Iowa high school athletics including statistics, schedules, records, constitution and bylaws. Basketball, baseball, cross country, football, golf included. Hall of Pride project information available.

Special Features: Printable forms, job openings

Curriculum: Physical Education

732 Iowa Legislature

www.legis.state.ia.us/

Homepage of the Iowa General Assembly. Follow a bill into a law, order governmental publications, look at budgets and fiscal reports. Peek into state employee salaries. Includes statistics on Iowa's government, economy, and population. Governmental and economic fun. Archives available.

Special Features: Guide to the general assembly, three branches of government, state symbols, tour the capitol, legislative page applications

Curriculum: Business; Economics; Government

733 Iowa Library Association

www.iowalibraryassociation.org/

The Iowa library Association (ILA) strives to promote and develop quality library service for Iowans. Founded in 1890 it is the second oldest library association in the country and currently holds fourteen hundred members. Full text bylaws and organization manual available.

Special Features: Legislation watch, membership information, posters, event calendar

Curriculum: Library Media

734 Iowa Natural Heritage Foundation

www.inhf.org/

The non-profit foundation conserves and protects Iowa's environment through donation and sales of land which become county or state owned and will always remain natural. These lands are then turned into nature centers, wildlife rescue areas, prairie reclamation projects and parks.

Special Features: Printable articles, outdoor guide, trails, contacts

Curriculum: Environmental Studies

735 Iowa Pork Producers

www.iowapork.com/

The Iowa Pork Producers or IPP works to bring leadership to the Iowa pork industry by promoting educational resources, strategic investment programs, and partnerships with retailers on a grassroots level. Meetings date back to the 1930's and association status was recognized in April of 1968.

Special Features: Seasonal recipes, economic reports, meeting notes, and scholarship programs

Curriculum: Business; Economics; Home Economics

736 Iowa Secretary of State

www.sos.state.ia.us/publications/redbook/history/7-1.html

The Iowa Official Register, "History of Iowa," written by Dorothy Schwieder. The full text concise article is perfect for educators. The article spans from 1673 to 1840 and includes explorers, Native Americans, and the population census from 1840 to 1990.

Special Features: Full text article, population census

Curriculum: Government; History; Social Studies

737 Iowa State Education Association

www.isea.org/

Iowa State Education Association (ISEA) lobbies for increased school resources, builds community support, promotes and supports quality education. ISEA makes sure the educational standard is at it's highest for the students of Iowa. Includes hot topics for educators and educational issues.

Special Features: Legislative action center, information for parents, membership, links to the National Education Association

Curriculum: Education; Government

738 Iowa State University Entomology Dept.

www.ent.iastate.edu/misc/insectsasfood.html

Iowa State University's tasty insect recipes. Includes a listing of the nutritional value of insects, how to cook them and where to buy bugs in bulk.

Special Features: Links to extensive insect photo gallery and pest control information

Curriculum: Home Economics; Science

739 Iowa State University Extension

www.extension.iastate.edu/

Iowa State University Extension (ISUE) improves Iowa lives by offering research based learning opportunities. Issues concerning family, community, business, or farming may be covered. Extensive informative full text articles available.

Special Features: Continuing education opportunities, agricultural and natural resource topics, searchable full text site

Curriculum: Education; Home Economics; Sociology

740 Iowa Technology and Education Connection

www.itec-ia.org/

Iowa Technology and Education Connection or ITEC promotes technology use through demonstrations to educators and the public. By showing how technology is appropriately used, ITECH hopes to impact teaching and learning. Yearly conferences and newsletters are available.

Special Features: Full text articles, swap and shop database for buying and trading school technology

Curriculum: Education; Technology

741 Iowa Tractors.com

www.iowatractors.com/

Tractors! Big, small, harvesting, hauling, tillage, spraying, fertilizing, livestock handling, haying, or irrigation, Iowa Tractors serves the machinery marketing business. Each entry includes photo, detailed item description and price.

Special Features: Extensive photos, tractors
Curriculum: Business; Economics; Math

742 Iowa Women in Public Policy

www.iowawipp.com/

Iowa Women in Public Policy (WIPP) was founded to "increase the number of women influencing public policy and…elected to public office." Founded in 2001, the organization has hosted leadership conferences, held women's receptions and fundraisers to support women's involvement in politics and public office.

Special Features: Statistics on Iowa women, full text articles, membership information
Curriculum: Government; Women's Studies

743 Living History Farms

www.lhf.org/

Living History Farms reenacts how Iowans turned the prairies into productive farmland. It is a six hundred acre open air working museum encompassing five historical time periods spanning three hundred years. Includes live demonstrations, seasonal activities, and Ioway Indian information.

Special Features: Detailed information on how to perform time period chores: churn butter, tan hides, hoeing with bone instruments, making bone needles and more

Curriculum: Drama; History; Home Economics; Social Studies

744 Madison County Chamber of Commerce

www.madisoncounty.com/index.html

The famous bridges of Madison County were built between 1870 and the mid 1880's. Originally nineteen bridges were in existence, only five remain. One bridge was destroyed by an arsonist on Sept. 3, 2002.

Special Features: History, tourist information, events, map
Curriculum: Architecture; History

745 National Archives and Records Administration

hoover.archives.gov/

Located in West Branch, Iowa, the Herbert Hoover Presidential Library and Museum includes an in depth look at Hoover, his boyhood, chronology of his accomplishments, and the "Hoover Ball." First Lady Lou Henry Hoover is also included.

Special Features: Virtual exhibits, historical photos, related sites
Curriculum: Government; History

746 National Czech & Slovak Museum & Library

www.ncsml.org/

Located in Cedar Rapids, the library holds over eighteen thousand items and five thousand cataloged artifacts from the nineteenth to twenty-first centuries. The museum includes special exhibits and events covering Czech and Slovak history. Educational packages are available for teachers.

Special Features: News releases, contact information
Curriculum: Art; History; Social Studies

747 National Nineteenth Amendment Society

www.catt.org/

Carrie Chapman Catt Childhood Home. Key coordinator of the woman suffrage movement and founder of the League of Women Voters, her history and home.

Special Features: Suffrage and women's history sites, FBI files, historical pictures

Curriculum: Government; History; Social Studies; Women's Studies

748 National Sprint Car Hall of Fame

www.sprintcarhof.com/

The National Sprint Car Hall of Fame & Museum Foundation opened its renovated doors in January 4, 1992. The four story facility promotes the future by preserving the past history of sprint and midget car racing. Full text news articles are available and contacts for detailed information are given.

Special Features: Complete listing of inductees since 1990, polling of sprint car favorites, latest news in racing

Curriculum: Sports

749 Office of State Archaeologist (Sponsor: University of Iowa)

www.uiowa.edu/~osa/

Office of the State Archaeologist. Responsible for Iowa prehistory and beyond, the office conducts research through out the state. Office manages data on all known sites, preserves burial grounds, and publishes books on Iowa archaeology. Wonderful Iowa history articles available for reading.

Special Features: Historical articles with illustrations, educational links, Native American interests

Curriculum: Geography; History; Social Studies

750 Official State of Iowa Website

www.iowa.gov/state/main/index.html

The official Iowa website includes governmental agencies, public safety, travel information, living and visiting Iowa, facts about the state, sites and attractions, along with homeland security. All encompassing information about the state.

Special Features: **Ask a librarian option, FAQ's and help desk available, weather and** road conditions, maps, kids page, and employment opportunities

Curriculum: Government

751 Public Library of Des Moines

www.pldminfo.org/Search/iowaauthors.htm

A comprehensive list of Iowa authors and children's book authors who were born in Iowa or who have lived here for twenty years or more. Alphabetical author listing including bibliography.

Special Features: Links to the Des Moines Public Library, kid's pages, coloring pages

Curriculum: Language Arts; Library Media

752 Silos and Smokestacks National Heritage Area

www.silosandsmokestacks.org

Located in Northeast Iowa covering thirty-seven counties and twenty thousand square miles Silos and Smokestacks is part of the National Park Service and is a designated National Heritage Area. Six themes of education include Fertile Land, Farmers and Families, Changing Farm, Higher Yields: Science and Technology of Agriculture, Farm to Factory: Agribusiness in Iowa, and Policies and Politics.

Special Features: Fun and learning, historical photos, see and do, events, printable brochures, maps

Curriculum: Business; Economics; History

753 State Historical Society of Iowa

www.iowahistory.org/index.html

With a mission of education and preservation, the State Historical Society of Iowa (SHISI) is organized to identify, record, collect, preserve, manage, and provide access to Iowa's historical resources. Continuing research and preservation keeps SHISI in the highest of professional standards.

Special Features: Tips for preserving photos and documents, list of recommended readings of Iowa history

Curriculum: Government; History; Library Media; Technology

754 State Library of Iowa

www.silo.lib.ia.us/index.html

The state library of Iowa was founded in 1838 as a territorial library. As Iowa became a state in 1846, it was to provide services to the state government. Over the years the mission now includes bringing excellence and innovation to the libraries and citizens of Iowa.

Special Features: Numerous catalogs, databases, and library websites, telling a story tool kit, lists of available programs and grants

Curriculum: Library Media; Technology

755 United States Department of the Interior

www.nps.gov/efmo/

Effigy mounds or ancient burial mounds constructed in the shape of mammals, birds, and reptiles were found along the Iowa banks of the Mississippi river. Effigy Mounds became a national park in October of 1949 and is located In Harpers Ferry, Iowa.

Special Features: Ariel photos of the mounds, fact sheets, short history of the park, Native American interest

Curriculum: Environmental Studies; History

756 Veteran's Association of the USS *IOWA* (BB-61)

www.ussiowa.org/index.htm

The largest and most complete website dealing with any one military unit or naval vessel is all about the USS *IOWA*. Fabulous history of the boat, pictures, statistics, full text articles about the boat are also included. A deck log was designed to read what veterans have to say about their battleship and shipmates.

Special Features: Historical photographs, complete history of the ship, virtual tour and gun information

Curriculum: Government; History; Sociology

757 Writer's Workshop (Sponsor: University of Iowa)

www.uiowa.edu/~iww/index.html

Iowa Writers' Workshop program was the first in the nation to offer a creative writing degree. It is a blueprint to other university creative writing programs. The program has produced many Pulitzer Prize winning authors. Faculty members have also been famous notable laureates.

Special Features: Current reading list, course descriptions, history of the program, application forms

Curriculum: Language Arts

KANSAS

758 Amelia Earhart Birthplace Museum

www.ameliaearhartmuseum.org/

Amelia Earhart was born in Atchison, Kansas, on July 24, 1897. Not only a famous aviator, Amelia Earhart was a fashion designer and writer. Today her birthplace is a museum and tribute to her life. Take a virtual tour and see her childhood home and fashion designs. Read her biography and find out more about the legend.

Special Features: Fashion design, virtual tour, historical photographs, fun facts, schedule of events

Curriculum: History; Women's Studies

759 Cherokee Strip Museum (Sponsor: CivicPlus)

arkcity.org/index.asp?ID=216

Cherokee Strip Museum is dedicated the his-

tory of the largest race ever, the Cherokee Strip Land Rush that occurred on September 16th, 1893. Over one hundred ten thousand people raced to claim a piece of seven million acres. Arkansas City, Kansas, was the largest of the registration points of the race. Forty-five thousand artifacts, pictures and documents are on exhibit.

Special Features: Photo gallery, history of the photographers of the "race"

Curriculum: Art; Geography; History; Social Studies

760 Emporia State University — School of Library and Information Management

slim.emporia.edu/globenet/globenet.htm

Located and researched in Emporia, Kansas, Globenet researches and publishes studies on the paradigmatic shift in information technology and global conversation. The flow of information around the world and the global systems that disseminate it along with economic forces are the focus of bi-annual worldwide conferences.

Special Features: Read previous conference session notes, view interview videos and contact organizers

Curriculum: Economics; Library Media; Sociology; Technology

761 First Hand Historical Accounts (Sponsor: Wesley Retirement Communities, Inc.)

www.iwitnesstohistory.org/

I, Witness to History. Founded in 1996, by a retirement community, the website strives to preserve first hand accounts of historical events, and earlier lifestyles. Subjects include: family, arts, travel, wars, holidays, and intergenerational interviews. The Special Collections Library at Wichita State University then preserves the historical accounts of various lives by adding them to its collection for all to use.

Special Features: Historical photos, oral history, folk art

Curriculum: Language Arts; History; Psychology; Social Studies; Sociology

762 Great Plains Nature Center

www.gpnc.org/

The Great Plains nature Center located in Wichita provides informational and educational experiences to the public about the Great Plains wildlife and plant resources. Their goal is to focus on environmental education and the importance of urban habitats. Extensive information on Kansas wildlife is available.

Special Features: Full text information on Kansas wildlife, photos, educational links

Curriculum: Biology; Environmental Studies; Geography; Science

763 Greyhound Hall of Fame

www.greyhoundhalloffame.com/

The Greyhound Hall of Fame is located in Abilene. Greyhounds breed back to almost four thousand years ago. The hall of fame hopes to document and display the history of greyhound racing and honor those who have played a notable part in its development.

Special Features: Inductee listing from 1963 to the present, scholarships

Curriculum: Business; Economics

764 Gunfighters, Outlaws, and Lawmen (Sponsor: University of Kansas)

www.ukans.edu/heritage/owk/128/guns.html

Kansas gunfighters, outlaws and lawmen. History buffs will love looking through names and biographies of the gunfighters, outlaws and lawmen who helped tame the West. Some famous names include Billy the Kid, Buffalo Bill, the Dalton Gang, Wyatt Earp, Wild Bill Hickok and Doc Holliday. Read the article on the general gunfighters' history. Site offers bibliography, cowboy links, fort information and photos.

Special Features: Kansas history, railroads, towns, trails and Native American Tribe information

Curriculum: History

765 Information Network of Kansas, Inc.

www.accesskansas.org/

The Official Website of Kansas. Look through online services, facts and history, government, employment, operating a business, education, travel information, and popular services. All encompassing information about the state. Look at featured photographs taken in Kansas or search the site.

Special Features: **Extensive links, online help, ask a librarian**

Curriculum: **Government**

766 Kansas Association of Counties

www.kansascounties.org/

Kansas Association of Counties or KAC strives to advance public interest by promoting effective, responsive county government in Kansas. Visit a Kansas county by clicking on the interactive map. Instructional services are available. Interesting and informative section dedicated to public health documents.

Special Features: Interactive map, full text articles, county news updates

Curriculum: Government

767 Kansas Association of Wheat Growers

www.wheatmania.com/

"Wheat Mania!" The website all about wheat;

planting, growing, harvesting, history, grain elevators, and trivia. Educational page for students and teachers, "awesome" activities, and "wacky" wheat photos too. Lots of information and things to do.

Special Features: Recipes, agricultural information, statistics, follow a farm family, records of wheat production
Curriculum: Economics; Home Economics; Math; Social Studies

768 Kansas Beef Council

www.kansasbeef.org/

Formed in 1973, the Kansas Beef Council's sole purpose is to promote beef. Kansas has the second highest number of cattle in the nation and has produced more than 5 billion pounds of red meat. Free educational material for preschools through high school. Nutritional information and recipes also offered.

Special Features: Recipes, food safety, nutrition, Kansas beef statistics
Curriculum: Business; Home Economics

769 Kansas Cosmosphere and Space Center

www.cosmo.org/home.html

Located in Hutchison, Kansas, Cosmosphere and Space Center. Features one of the largest collections of U.S. and Russian space artifacts in the world. The actual Apollo 13 command module and a flown Vostok spacecraft are part of museum along with a SR-71 spyplane, a T-38 astronaut training jet, and a full-scale Space Shuttle replica.

Special Features: Photographs, Cosmosphere newsletter, news and events, lease a space artifact
Curriculum: Science; Technology

770 Kansas Department of Agriculture

www.accesskansas.org/kda/

The Kansas Department of Agriculture ensures safety in milk, egg, and meat supply, protection of natural plants, water conservation, and responsible pesticide use. Drought information, mad cow disease, agricultural directory, environmental programs, FAQ's, Kansas products, and loan and grant information available.

Special Features: Informative article called, "Wheat: Kansas' Number One Crop," agricultural facts, kids learn about agriculture

Curriculum: Business; Economics; Environmental Studies; Geography

771 Kansas Department of Health and Environment

www.kdhe.state.ks.us/kdsi/index.html

Reduce, reuse, recycle. The Bureau of Waste Management in Kansas sponsors the slogan, "Kansas: Don't Spoil it!" It is found on billboards, posters and recycling centers across the state. Striving to keep Kansas clean, programming includes Kansas Kids Can! environmental stewardship for children K–8. Full text publication called "Trash Talk," available for youth education.

Special Features: Recycling, composting, environmental awareness
Curriculum: Environmental Studies; Health; Science

772 Kansas Department of Human Resources

www.hr.state.ks.us/kaaa/html/index.html

Also known as KAAAC, Kansas African-American Affairs Commission provides opportunities for the advancement of African Americans through training programs, public awareness, and dissemination of information. Strategic plan and related links included.

Special Features: Legislative contacts, news and upcomming events
Curriculum: Government; Social Studies

773 Kansas Department of Transportation

www.ksdot.org/

KDOT or Kansas Department of Transportation has a history dating back to 1917. Primary activities include road and bridge maintenance, transportation planning, data collecting, contract compliance and inspection of material, and administrative support. Special programs include highway safety, planting wildflowers roadside, and adopt-a-highway litter control.

Special Features: road conditions, publications and maps, safety tips
Curriculum: Driver Training

774 Kansas Department of Wildlife and Parks

www.kdwp.state.ks.us/

Managing and promoting wildlife and natural resources is the mission of the Kansas Department of Wildlife and Parks. The KDWP conserves and enhances the natural heritage of Kansas by providing the public with opportunities and appreciation of the land. With informational and educational programming, the KDWP hopes to become one of the nation's leaders in the stewardship of wildlife and park resources.

Special Features: Hunting, fishing, boating, parks, education, publications, and legislative updates

Curriculum: Biology; Environmental Studies; Geography; Science

775 Kansas Geological Survey

www.kgs.ukans.edu/kgs.html

Conducting geological studies across the state, the Kansas Geological Survey collects, correlates, preserves, and disseminates information leading to a better understanding of geology. It was established in 1889. Special emphasis and studies are made about natural resources of economic value, water quality and quantity, and geologic hazards and then published for the public. An excellent student friendly site is called GeoKansas also provided by KGS.

Special Features: Hydrology, geology, full text library and publications, educational resources, oil and gas, and maps

Curriculum: Environmental Studies; Geography; Science

776 Kansas Heritage Group

www.ku.edu/heritage/research/inter-gen/

The Kansas Heritage Group hosts a very large, extensive site all about Kansas genealogy. Search through cemeteries, obituaries, census records, ethnic groups, family names, military veterans, societies, news releases, and maps. Helpful for those interested in history. Historical photos.

Special Features: Extensive related links, add your own research, keyword searching

Curriculum: History; Social Studies; Sociology; Women's Studies

777 Kansas Humane Society

www.kshumane.org/

Founded in 1888, the Kansas Humane Society originally focused its efforts on horses when the automobile became popular. Now, over one hundred years later they provide shelter and promote welfare to homeless animals. See adoptable animals online, read pet care tips and find out more about the importance of spaying and neutering your pet.

Special Features: Animal pet tips include: cats, dogs, birds, seasonal information, overpopulation facts and figures.

Curriculum: Social Studies

778 Kansas Information Technology Office

da.state.ks.us/kito/

The Kansas Information Technology Office or KITO, supports all state branches of government for the development of policies, architecture and methodologies of information technology. Find out the information structure of the state and how it works. Flow charts are available. Planned projects can also be perused.

Special Features: Downloadable charts, mission statements, databases

Curriculum: Technology

779 Kansas Legislature

www.kslegislature.org/

Follow the Kansas Legislature live. Listen in as a committee goes to work. Website covers bills, statues, calendars within the house and senate. Searchable statutes, full text bills, track a bill, find a legislator. Covers current happenings, hot items, issues in education and the history of the legislature. Historical and current photos.

Special Features: Live coverage, searchable site, full text articles

Curriculum: Business; Economics; Government

780 Kansas Library Association

skyways.lib.ks.us/KLA/

Kansas Library Association or KLA is the state advocate for funding, laws, services, and issues of Kansas libraries. Bylaws, position statements, library directory included. Online news available with conference dates and job opportunities.

Special Features: Searchable site, full text articles, educational conference schedule

Curriculum: Library Media

781 Kansas Library Directory

skyways2.lib.ks.us/kld/

Find a library in Kansas. A directory of libraries, staff, and interlibrary loan. Search library location by city or county. Also search by library type including community colleges, corporate, schools, law libraries, and special collections.

Special Features: A searchable site, alphabetical listings

Curriculum: Library Media; Technology

782 Kansas Nature-Based Tourism Alliance

www.naturalkansas.org/welcome.htm

Natural Kansas! Visiting the Kansas prairie introduces a tremendous amount of natural diversity. Natural Kansas gives a state tour of the many landforms available. Prairie habitat, ancient forests, glaciated region, sand dunes, and more can be found. Nature based event calendar available.

Special Features: Regional interactive map, wildlife viewing tips, scenic byway information, bibliography available

Curriculum: Biology; Environmental Studies; Geography; Science

783 Kansas on the Net, LLC.

skyways.lib.ks.us/counties/

A concise statistical view of all Kansas counties. Includes alphabetic county name, year founded, population, and county seat. Clickable map of Kansas Counties. Good for quick glance assignments.

Special Features: One page at-a-glance information, links to genealogy, history, museums and towns

Curriculum: Geography; Social Studies

784 Kansas Originals

www.kansasoriginals.com/

Kansas artists, craftsmen, and food producers, especially those who are over 62, disabled, minority, low-income, or women who are in business for themselves showcase their exceptional arts, crafts and food products here. Browse Kansas art by category or by name. Kansas Originals Market opened on August 1, 1991.

Special Features: History of the store, full color photos, prices available

Curriculum: Art; Business; Home Economics; Math; Sociology

785 Kansas Public Radio

www.kansaskidshealth.org/

Kansas Kids' Health uses the power of radio to promote and challenge Kansans about health issues in the state. The program consists of in depth reporting about health issues rarely considered or discussed. View program titles, and listen to the program through downloading. Some subjects include: nursing homes, food borne illnesses, women and heart disease, and hepatitis C.

Special Features: Audio files, search programs by topic, hard to find health issues

Curriculum: Health; Physical Education

786 Kansas Sampler Foundation

www.kansassampler.org/

Kansas Sampler Foundation is a not for profit organization striving to preserve and sustain rural culture through the elements of architecture, art, commerce, cuisine, customs, geography, history and people. By educating Kansans about Kansas and networking and supporting rural communities goals will be met. Site promotes everything Kansas related.

Special Features: Extensive related links, questions for cuisine assessment, find out how to hold a garage sale art contest

Curriculum: Art; Business; History; Home Economics; Music; Sociology

787 Kansas Speedway

www.kansasspeedway.com/

"The track that will blow you away!" Located in Kansas City the Kansas Speedway was opened in 2001. The speedway seats more than 80,000 spectators and is a one and a half mile tri-oval track. Track records are available. The track also hosts stock and Indy car driving schools.

Special Features: Read full text racing news, schedule of events, maps and area information

Curriculum: Sports

788 Kansas Sports Hall of Fame

www.kshof.org/

Founded in 1961 and located in Wichita, the Kansas Sports Hall of Fame houses one hundred seven Kansas sports heroes. Lists high school all time record holders and current list of hall of fame inductees. Mission is to honor, preserve, educate, and inspire the public about Kansas' great moments, players and teams.

Special Features: Photos of hall of fame, searchable listings

Curriculum: Sports

789 Kansas State Conservation Commission

www.accesskansas.org/kscc/main.html

The Kansas State Conservation Commission traces its beginnings back to 1937. The need for soil conservation arose after the Midwest was a "dust bowl" during the Depression. The KSCC now strives to enhance natural resources through policies, guidelines and programs designed to assist local government and individuals in conserving renewable resources.

Special Features: History, program summaries, photos, education programs, contact information

Curriculum: Environmental Studies; Geography; Government; History; Social Studies

790 Kansas State Department of Education

www.ksbe.state.ks.us/Welcome.html

The Kansas Department of Education provides quality leadership, support, and service for continuous improvement of education in Kansas. Site includes information about assessments and standards, legislative actions, accreditation, pilot schools, scholarships, grants, special education, and school statistics.

Special Features: Just for parents' booklets, site map, what's new

Curriculum: Business; Education; Government; Math

791 Kansas State Library: Blue Skyways

www.skyways.org/

"Blue Skyways: A Service of the Kansas State Library," is the shared information service of the Kansas library community. Although the internet links are not official publications of the state government the information is useful and vital to Kansas research. Extensive links for general Kansas information, libraries, communities, education, and government.

Special Features: Search anything about Kansas, chat real time with librarians

Curriculum: Library Media; Technology

792 Kansas State Library: Lebanon, Kansas

skyways.lib.ks.us/towns/Lebanon/

Lebanon, Kansas, the geographical center of the United States was established in 1898 by a geodetic survey conducted by the government. An historical marker was dedicated in 1941 marking the site. It is now a crossroads for hunters searching for Kansas wildlife. Population: 364.

Special Features: Longitude and latitude figures, links to town information

Curriculum: Geography

793 Kansas State Treasurer

kansasstatetreasurer.com/cgi-win/kz_main.kst

Kansas State Treasurer Kids Zone: A place to have fun and learn about money. As Money WI$E the owl helps you with money facts, games, homework, budgeting and more. Contact the treasurer for a classroom visit.

Special Features: Treasurer biography, contact information, games

Curriculum: Economics; Government; Math

794 Wildflowers and Grasses (Sponsor: Kansas State University Library)

www.lib.ksu.edu/wildflower/

Professor Mike Haddock a librarian and web coordinator at Kansas State University identifies more than 375 species of wildflowers and grasses in Kansas. Site offers more than 1500 identification photos of flora sorted by color or grasses. Also identify plants by time of flowering. Site offers scientific and common names, bibliography, and glossary.

Special Features: Extensive photographs and drawings, useful links

Curriculum: Art; Biology; Environmental Studies; Science

795 Kansas State University Solar Car Racing Team

www.engg.ksu.edu/solarcar/

Ever wonder about solar power? Experience the life of a solar powered car as it races through New Mexico. The electrical and mechanical systems are available for viewing, descriptions of why technology was chosen, and color photos are included. Read the journal of the car from as far back as 2001.

Special Features: Full text journal, photographs, team information, contact information, adopt a solar cell on the race car

Curriculum: Driver Training; Environmental Studies; Science; Technology

796 Kansasphotos.com

www.kansasphotos.com/

Don Palmer, a Kansas photographer, covers the state using images and photo essays. Coverage includes such subjects as animals, birds, in-

sects, flowers and plants, Flint Hills, old buildings, nature trails, tombstones, and trains.
Commentary about the photos.

Special Features: Animals, wildlife
Curriculum: Art; Biology; Language Arts

797 Kids Voting U.S.A.

www.kidsvotingkansas.org/

Kids Voting Kansas believes by involving students in the voting process and education in
family involvement, civic education, and community volunteerism, children will be more
likely to become life long voters. After beginning in 1992, there has been an average voter
increase of five percent. Website includes history of the program, ideas for teachers, stuff for
students, and kids voting statistics.

Special Features: Ideas for teacher for each
grade level through high school
Curriculum: Government; Math; Social
Studies

798 National Agricultural Hall of Fame

www.aghalloffame.com/

Funded entirely by private and corporate
donations and onsite revenues the National
Agricultural Hall of Fame (otherwise known as
the Ag Center) is located in Bonner Springs. It
was created in 1960, by federal action to become the "national" agricultural museum and
memorial to farming leaders. One hundred
seventy-two acres is the setting for educational
workshops, historical reenactments, and youth
outreach.

Special Features: Virtual tours of the main
building, the museum, and Farm Town U.S.A.
Curriculum: Biology; Education; History;
Social Studies; Sociology

799 National Archives and Records Administration

www.eisenhower.utexas.edu/

The Dwight D. Eisenhower Library is located
near Abilene. As the thirty fourth president of
the United States the library preserves nearly
twenty three million pages of manuscripts.
Eisenhower's family, life and times are shown
through exhibits, programming, and educational outreach. The library also commemorates the Allied Expeditionary Forces of World
War II.

Special Features: Online documents, audio
recordings, photographs

Curriculum: Government; History; Social
Studies

800 National Park Service

www.nps.gov/brvb/

Brown Vs. Board of Education National Historic Site. Located in Topeka, Monroe Elementary School was one of four segregated schools.
Now the location is a national park, two acres
house the museum to the 1954 Supreme Court
decision ending segregation. Pictures of the
school are included with a short history.

Special Features: Photos, park hours, planning a visit and yearly operational costs
Curriculum: Education; Government; History; Social Studies

801 National Park Trust

www.parktrust.org/zbar.html

The Tallgrass Prairie National Preserve also
known as the Z Bar Spring Hill Ranch is located in the midst of the Kansas Flint Hills.
Created in partnership with the National Park
Service in 1996 almost 11,000 acres are being
preserved to the natural tallgrass prairie. Look
at photos and take a virtual tour of the vast ex-
panse of what once was called the great American desert.

Special Features: Full test news publications,
interview transcripts; Learn about one of the
largest limestone barns in the nation
Curriculum: Environmental Studies; Geography; History; Social Studies

802 Notable Women (Sponsor: Kansas State Historical Society)

www.kshs.org/people/women.htm

Notable Kansas Women. Famous women who
lived in or were from the state of Kansas. List
includes such names as Susan B. Anthony,
Amelia Earhart, and Carry Nation. A short biography of each woman and links are provided.

Special Features: Related links, pictures of artifacts, other minority lists available
Curriculum: History; Women's Studies

803 Oceans of Kansas

www.oceansofkansas.com/

Oceans of Kansas is an award winning site.
With hundreds of pictures of fossils and paleo-
life art this very large site contains more than
one hundred fifty sub-pages about ocean crea-

tures during the final stages of the dinosaur age. Such prehistoric marine animals include: mosasaurs, plesiosaurs, sharks, and bony fish. All creatures were found in the Smokey Hill Chalk of western Kansas.

Special Features: Educational scientific site, highly illustrated

Curriculum: Geography; History; Science

804 Prairie Fire Season (Sponsor: Rare Book, Manuscript, and Special Collections Library Duke University)

www.lib.duke.edu/exhibits/larryschwarm/

After twelve years of work, Larry Schwarm, from Emporia, Kansas, captures the Flint Hills in photographs during prairie fire season. View the tall grass prairie "on fire." Read excerpts from the book entitled *On Fire: Photographs.* Learn about the prairie ecosystem.

Special Features: Photographs

Curriculum: Art; Biology; Environmental Studies

805 Rush County Committee for Economic Development

www.rushcounty.org/barbedwiremuseum/

The Kansas Barbed Wire Museum is located in LaCrosse, Kansas. Barbed wire or "the devil's rope" is one of the Midwest's most significant inventions to American history. The museum exhibits over one thousand varieties and houses samples of the wire made between 1870 and 1890. An in-house research library is also available.

Special Features: Information about collect-

ing and swapping wire, history included, photos

Curriculum: Business; Economics; History; Technology

806 Territorial Kansas (Sponsor: Kansas State Historical Society)

www.territorialkansasonline.org/cgiwrap/iml-skto/index.php

Territorial Kansas 1854–1861. The maps, diaries, letters, and photos of Kansas during the bloody debates over slavery therefore the name, "Bloody Kansas." Serving as a rehearsal for the Civil War, read about the border warfare with Missouri. Large comprehensive historical site containing full text articles, photos, and lesson plans.

Special Features: Timelines, lesson plans, bibliographies, personalities of the time

Curriculum: Geography; Government; History; Social Studies

807 Wichita International Raceway

www.teamwir.com/

The Wichita International Raceway opened in 1963. The raceway site offers car math; calculators that figure rear wheel horsepower, estimated time per second and overall horsepower. Look through previous year photos, read over safety rules and regulations or ask a technician automotive questions.

Special Features: Site provides: weather, schedule, classes, safety regulations, points standings, and related links

Curriculum: Driver Training; Math; Technology

KENTUCKY

808 American Civil Liberties Union of Kentucky

www.aclu-ky.org/

The American Civil Liberties Union (ACLU) of Kentucky Strives to protect individual's rights and liberties protected by the Constitution of the United States and the Commonwealth of Kentucky. This website features news

stories, the history of the ACLU, and the program's legal program. It also features links to various Kentucky organizations striving for similar goals.

Special Features: Links include Our History, Legal Program, Action Alerts, Legislative Updates, Fairness Campaign, National ACLU, and Hot Issue

Curriculum: Government; History

809 Aviation Museum of Kentucky

www.aviationky.org

The Aviation Museum of Kentucky provides information regarding the history of Kentucky aviation and airplanes. This organization strives to educate people about aviation by providing people with access to learning materials and via first hand experiences.

Special Features: Links include New and Upcoming Events, Summer Camp, Mission, 20 Years of History, Aviation Hall of Fame, The F4 Phantom Page, Aviation Weather and others

Curriculum: History; Social Studies

810 Black Mountain (Sponsor: America's Roof)

www.americasroof.com/ky.shtml

This website provides information on Black Mountain, Kentucky, the site of the largest coal mining operation in the world. This site provides information on the mountain itself, as well as information on coal. Also included in this site are books, state songs, maps, and photos.

Special Features: Links include Coal Sculptures, Coal Museums, Coal Tipple, Lynch, Black Mountain Guide, Controversy, and Maps. The site also has links to the highest points in other states and throughout the world

Curriculum: Environmental Studies; Geography; History

811 Civil War Home

www.civilwarhome.com/jdavisbio.htm

This site features a descriptive biography of Jefferson Davis, President of the Southern Confederacy. Numerous other biographies of people involved in the Civil War are available. The site features in depth descriptions of Civil War events and battles, as well as a large compilation of other web pages on the Civil War.

Special Features: Links include The Armies, Overview of the Civil War, Letters About the War, Essays on the Civil War, the Confederate States of America, Civil War Medicine, Civil War Battles, Civil War Biographies, Abraham Lincoln Research Site, Civil War Educational Center

Curriculum: Government; History; Social Studies

812 Coal Education Web Site

www.coaleducation.org/

This website is designed to provide people information about the history of coal in Kentucky and its importance to Kentucky's heritage. The website has information on coal mine locations, the history of coal, Kentucky coal facts, and links to other Kentucky coal related websites. The website also features a special section for teachers to encourage students' education about coal.

Special Features: Links include Kentucky Coal Facts and History, Teacher Resources, Professional Resources, Kentucky Timeline, Mining Tourism

Curriculum: Economics; Environmental Studies; Geography; History; Science; Technology

813 Congress.org

www.congress.org/congressorg/state/main/?state=KY

This site is a comprehensive guide to Kentucky Legislature, including state officials, agencies, local officials, issues, and congressional delegation. This site has congressional members, state officials, and local officials available for all states in the U.S. Congress.org also has information on the presidential cabinet, bills in Congress, and a media guide.

Special Features: Links include Books, Media Guide, Agencies, Elected Officials, Issues and Action, Capitol Hill Basics, Current Elections

Curriculum: Government

814 Enchanted Learning: Kentucky

www.enchantedlearning.com/usa/states/kentucky/

This is a comprehensive website containing general facts about the state of Kentucky. The website features educational games and quizzes about Kentucky's flag and map, as well as various printable maps of Kentucky. The website features Kentucky's animal symbols, plant symbols, and earth symbols. This website also has links to various facets of education and learning, such as biology and geography.

Special Features: Links include Kentucky State Symbols, Kentucky Map/Quiz Printout, Biology, Geography, Physical Science, Art, History, Languages, Writing, Books, and links to other U.S. state facts, symbols, maps

Curriculum: Education; Geography; History; Science; Social Studies

815 Famous Kentuckians

www.bigdogdesign.com/famouskys.html

This website describes the famous faces of Kentucky in both the past and present. It includes people from a wide array of backgrounds, including Abraham Lincoln, Jefferson Davis, and Colonel Harland Sanders. Links are provided for in depth information for many of the famous Kentuckians.

Special Features: Links include Explorers, Pioneers, and Frontiersmen, Scientists, Inventors, Physicians, Artists, Authors, Journalists, Entertainers, Sports Personalities, Political, and Military Heroes

Curriculum: History; Social Studies

816 Geology of Kentucky

www.uky.edu/KGS/coal/webgeoky/kygeolgy.htm

Geology of Kentucky is a section of the University of Kentucky Web site. It provides a geological map of Kentucky, geological structures in Kentucky, Kentucky fossils, and geology for specific Kentucky counties. Information and links for geology in other states are also available.

Special Features: Links include Geology of Other States, U.S. Geological Survey, Tapestry of Time and Terrain, Geological Map, Beneath the Surface, Physiographic Map, Fossils of Kentucky, Rocks and Minerals of Kentucky.

Curriculum: Geography; Science

817 Kentucky Cabinet for Health Services

www.chs.state.ky.us

The Kentucky Cabinet for Health Services is an agency that coordinates programs to encourage the mental and physical health of people in Kentucky. It provides health information, statistics and publications. This site also includes numerous links to other health-related sites, both in Kentucky and throughout the United States.

Special Features: Links include KidSource Online, Kentucky Cares, National Mental Health Association, Kentucky Department of Public Health, Kentucky Education Rights Center and others

Curriculum: Health

818 Kentucky Center for the Arts

www.kentuckycenter.org/

The Kentucky Center for the Arts is home to numerous plays, musical performance, and art pieces. The Center for the Arts also has outreach programs and performance programs to encourage higher education and interaction with the arts. This website features an online art gallery, media center, and other tools for learning about the arts in Kentucky.

Special Features: Links include Louisville Orchestra, Stage One, Kentucky Opera, Louisville Ballet, Education, Our History, Media Corner, PNC Bank Broadway Louisville, Visitor's Corner

Curriculum: Art; Dance; Drama; History

819 Kentucky Child Now!

www.kychildnow.org

Established in 1998, Kentucky Child Now is a nonprofit organization working to assure that Kentucky meets the needs of children of all ages. The goal of this association is to support those efforts through education, public awareness, collaboration and special programs, and through the work of its members— individuals and organizations committed to the health and success of Kentucky's children.

Special Features: Their vision: The Commonwealth of Kentucky will be a state composed of caring communities where all children, youth and their families are valued and can prosper

Curriculum: Education

820 Kentucky Dance Foundation

www.folkdancer.org

The Kentucky Dance Foundation promotes the tradition of folk dancing and related arts. This organization hosts dance events and distributes dance materials, such as CDs and pamphlets, in order to keep the cultural heritage of folk dancing alive. This website features music samples from *The World of Folk Dance Series.*

Special Features: Links include Music Samples, Archive, Events, Catalogue

Curriculum: Art; Dance; Music

821 Kentucky Department of Fish and Wildlife Resources

www.kyafield.com/

This website is a comprehensive database containing information on wildlife and fishing in Kentucky. It provides detailed information on wildlife preservation, safety precautions, safe practices, conservation and allocation of resources, and animal habitations. The Kentucky Department of Fish and Wildlife Resources encourages people to boat, fish, and engage in legal outdoor activity, but enlightens and reminds people of the fragile nature of the environment.

Special Features: Links include Hunting, Fishing, Boating, Wildlife, Education, Maps, Special Awareness Programs, Kentucky Artisan Center; Kentucky Horse Park, Kentucky State Fair Board

Curriculum: Environmental Studies; Social Studies

822 Kentucky Department of Travel

www.kytourism.com/

The Kentucky Department of Travel provides an in-depth guide to exploring Kentucky. This site describes Kentucky's cultural heritage, history, entertainment, lodging, recreation, and general state facts. This site is both a tool for planning a visit to Kentucky and researching detailed aspects of the state.

Special Features: Links include Calendar of Events, Regional Travel, Local Tourism Offices, Kentucky.gov, Kentucky State Parks, Kentucky Artisan Center, Fish and Wildlife Resources

Curriculum: Geography

823 Kentucky Derby

www.kentuckyderby.com/2004/

This is the official website for the Kentucky Derby, the oldest and most anticipated horse race held every year on the first Saturday in May. This website features in depth information on past Derby winners, women in the Derby, minorities in the Derby, and numerous charts and statistics. In addition this website provides information on Churchill Downs, the location of the Derby, as well as links to Derby festivities, including Thunder Over Louisville.

Special Features: Links include Derby Museum, Festival, African-Americans, Women in the Derby, Derby Timeline, Derby News, the Garland, Attending Celebrities

Curriculum: Sports

824 Kentucky Down Under

www.kdu.com/

This website highlights Kentucky Down Under, an Australian themed animal park, and includes information on Australian animals and people, as well as animals native to Kentucky. This site also features Kentucky Caverns, focusing on Mammoth Cave. Educational information, student activities, and trip planners are all helpful and educational features within this website.

Special Features: Links include The Formation of Caves, Cave Ecology, Student Activities, Australian People and Animals, Bison and Sheep in Kentucky, Trip Planner, Mammoth Cave National Park

Curriculum: Education; Environmental Studies; Geography; History; Science; Social Studies

825 Kentucky Educational Television

www.ket.org/

Kentucky Educational Television is a statewide public broadcasting network providing educational television shows about local arts, heritage, history, and public affairs. The TV shows target a wide range of viewers, from workplace professionals to young children. The website features educational resources, television programs, and links to Kentucky Arts.

Special Features: Links include History, Nature, Arts, Public Affairs, Science, Kids and Families, Drama, Adult Basic Education, Lifelong Learning, Instructional Television

Curriculum: Art; Drama; Education; Geography; Government; History; Science; Technology

826 Kentucky Environmental and Public Protection Cabinet

www.environment.ky.gov/homepage_reposito ry/About+the+Agency.htm

The Kentucky Environmental and Public Protection Cabinet (EPPC) was created to help protect Kentucky's land, water, and environment. It id divided into four sectors: The Department for Environmental Protection; The Department for Natural Resources; The Department of Labor; and The Department of Public Protection. This website has a comprehensive list of agencies within the EPPC as well as educational tools.

Special Features: Links include Earth Day, Education and Outreach, Division for Air Quality, Division of Water, Environmental Quality Commission, Kentucky Heritage Land Fund, Public Service Commission, Division of Energy

Curriculum: Environmental Studies; Geography; Science

827 Kentucky Folk Art Center

www.kyfolkart.org/

The Kentucky Folk Art Center, located at Moorehead State University, was designed to preserve Kentucky folk art and encourage people to become educated about it. This website features information on folk art, as well as special exhibitions help at the museum. There is also a library at Moorehead State University, dedicated to Edgar Tolson, one of the greatest folk artists in Kentucky.

Special Interests: Links include Exhibitions and Events, Arts and Crafts, Appalachian Arts and Crafts Fair, News, Library, Museum Store, Moorehead State University

Curriculum: Art; History; Library Media

828 Kentucky Fried Chicken

www.kfc.com/about/colonel.htm

Colonel Harland Sanders was the founder of the famous fast food chain Kentucky Fried Chicken. This website provides information on the Colonel and the famed restaurant. This site also discusses the "secret recipe" used for making the chicken taste good.

Special Features: Links include Secret Recipe, Pressure Cooker, Press Releases, Animal Welfare Program, Party Preparation, Colonel's Recipes, Nutrition, UNCF Scholarship, a section for children

Curriculum: Home Economics

829 Kentucky Geographic Alliance

www.kga.org/

The Kentucky Geographic Alliance is an organization that strives to promote education about geography. This website provides an extensive number of resources and organizations to promote further knowledge of this topic. This site also has tools and activities for students and teachers.

Special Features: Links include Geographic Departments in Kentucky Universities, National Geography Organizations, National Earth and Science Organizations, General Geography, World Geography, Earth Science

Curriculum: Geography; Science

830 Kentucky High School Athletic Association

www.khsaa.org/

The Kentucky High School Athletic Association provides a thorough guide for high school athletics. It covers topics ranging from sports to health concerns. It also provides information on coach education and links to other athletic sites.

Special Features: Links include KHSAA sports, News Releases, Reports, Heat Recommendations, Cheer/ Spirit Links, Directory of Member Schools, Rules Clinics

Curriculum: Health; Physical Education

831 Kentucky Higher Education Assistance Authority

www.kheaa.com/

The Kentucky Higher Education Assistance Authority (KHEAA) is a public corporation and governmental agency which was designed to improve students' access to higher education. KHEAA offers several programs, such as Kentucky Educational Excellence Scholarship and Kentucky Tuition Grant, which assist students in financing higher education. This website also features several articles on preparing for higher education, as well as links to other scholarships and loans.

Special Features: Links include KHEAA Publications, Federal Programs, Financial Aid 101, Online Loan Counseling Program, KHEAA Work Study, Kentucky Educational Excellence Scholarship, College Access Program

Curriculum: Counseling; Education

832 Kentucky Historical Society

history.ky.gov/

The Kentucky Historical Society encourages people to become informed about and involved in the history of Kentucky. This society collects and preserves artifacts and documentation surrounding Kentucky's history. This website features information for teachers and students, research, publications, and information on the museums storing the artifacts.

Special Features: Links include Research Database, Museums and Exhibitions, Students and Teachers, Publications, Library, links to other historical venues

Curriculum: Government; History; Library Media; Social Studies

833 Kentucky Horse Park

www.imh.org/khp/

The Kentucky Horse Park is a beautiful attraction featuring nearly 50 breeds of horses. The park features two museums, twin theaters, special exhibitions, and a campground. The website includes a great deal of information on horses, including their history, famous horses, the Hall of Champions, and Educational Programs.

Special Features: Links include National Horse Center, Online History Exhibits, Virtual Art Gallery, International Museum of the Horse, and Southern Holiday Lights Festival. The website also displays an enormous number of links on equine health, history, horse farms, educational sites, magazines, publications, horse breeds, art, horse education, racing

Curriculum: Social Studies

834 Kentucky Humane Society

www.kyhumane.org/

The Kentucky Humane Society is an organization that promotes the humane treatment of animals. This organization provides basic needs for unwanted, abused, and neglected animals and helps to place the animals in loving safe homes. This site provides information on how people can become involved in their mission to protect animals' rights.

Special Features: Links include Summer Camp, Veterinary Care, Get Involved, Boarding, Adoptions, Animal Rescue, Kentucky Humane Society E-News, Grooming

Curriculum: Sociology

835 Kentucky Lakes

www.kylakes.com/

This website provides detailed information on the lakes in Kentucky. Each of the 11 lakes and rivers are thoroughly described and information on attractions surrounding the lakes is provided. This information includes camping, dining, attraction, antiques, fishing, hunting, and local services.

Special Features: Links include Cumberland Sea Ray, Conley Bottom, State Docks, Captain Cove's Resort and others

Curriculum: Environmental Studies; Geography

836 Kentucky Library Association

www.kylibasn.org/

The Kentucky Library Association strives to encourage the development and usage of Kentucky library and information services. This site provides information on the history of the association, online university education for librarians, as well as links to various library associations throughout Kentucky.

Special Features: Links include Kentucky School Media Association, American Library

Association, Kentucky Department for Libraries and Archives, Southeastern Library Association, University of Kentucky School of Library and Information Services

Curriculum: Library Media

837 Kentucky Marina Association

www.kymarinas.com/

The Kentucky Marina Association is an organization which represents marinas located throughout the state of Kentucky. This organization assists in meeting peoples' demands for recreational facilities and services. This website provides information on the group as well as links to various nature related websites.

Special Features: Links include Map of Kentucky, Fish and Wildlife, Marinas.com, The Marine Web, Heartland Boating Magazine, Marina Business Today, Meeting Information

Curriculum: Environmental Studies; Geography

838 Kentucky Museum of Arts and Design

www.kentuckyarts.org

The Kentucky Museum of Arts and Design strives to educate artisans and the public about the history and heritage of art in Kentucky. The museum holds numerous workshops and exhibitions each year, as well as an ongoing gallery of work. It also features educational events and information for students, adults and young children.

Special Features: Links include History, Pressroom, Special Events, Education, Scholarships, Retail Gallery, Kentucky Foundation for Women, Educational Events Calendar and others

Curriculum: Art; History

839 Kentucky Psychological Association

www.kpa.org/

The Kentucky Psychological Association strives to represent the interests of psychologists as wells as provide academic information to people studying psychology. This website provides a research directory, information on psychology, and tips for people wishing to pursue psychology as a career. The site also has links to other health and psychology related websites.

Special Features: Links include The American Psychological Association Practitioner Portal, American Academy of Clinical Psychology, Mental Health Infosource, Continuing Educa-

tion, Diversity, Book Corner, Kentucky Research Directory, Academic Psychology
Curriculum: Education; Psychology

840 Kentucky Railway Museum

www.kyrail.org

The Kentucky Railway Museum strives to educate people about Kentucky railways by providing information regarding their history and builders. It provides information about and pictures of various models of trains.
Special Features: Links include Rolling Stock, Motor Power, Model Train Center, Restoration Projects, Museum Store, Area Attractions
Curriculum: History; Social Studies

841 Kentucky Soybean Board and Kentucky Soybean Association

www.kysoy.org/

The Kentucky Soybean Board and Kentucky Soybean Association strive to create greater awareness about and demand for soybeans. This website includes an detailed description of soybean production, research, and uses. The site also has health information and legislative action regarding soybeans.
Special Features: Links include Kentucky Agriculture Statistics Service, Kentucky Department of Agriculture, UK College of Agriculture, Soybean Production Resources, Biotechnology, Weather Center, New Soybean Uses, Legislative Action Center
Curriculum: Social Studies

842 Kentucky Tourism Council

www.tourky.com/

This is a comprehensive website designed to provide visitors with an insight on Kentucky attractions, events and highlights. It features statewide events, such as the Kentucky State Fair, as well as local festivals and amusements. Information on Kentucky history, dining, entertainment, and the arts are also outlined.
Special Features: Links include The Kentucky Historical Society, the Kentucky Association of Museums, the Kentucky Festival Association, the Top Ten Kentucky Festivals, Travel Information by Region
Curriculum: Art; Dance; Drama; History; Social Studies

843 Kentucky Virtual Library

www.kyvl.org/

The Kentucky Virtual Library is a detailed and comprehensive method of locating information on the internet and in libraries. This website includes a digital library, advanced search methods, a reference desk, and numerous other helpful tools. In addition, this website provides tips on doing research and links to educational sites.
Special Features: Links include Kentucky Stats, Virtual Reference Desk, Digital Library, How to do research, Adult Education and Literacy, K–12 Schools, Kids
Curriculum: Education; Library Media

844 Lewis and Clark 200

www.lewisandclark200.com/state.phtml?state_id=d238fe610e32c6e962a7996147923b90

This website features information on Lewis and Clark who explored new lands to discover a water source across the U.S. The site includes numerous links to information about the explorers, including museums, libraries, and guides to the trail they took. Information on Lewis and Clark artisans, restaurants, hotels, and camping are also available.
Special Features: Links include Trail Information, Arts and Crafts, Education, Expedition Trail Fun, Trail Outdoor Fun, Food and Fun, Lewis and Clark Libraries, State Parks, Bicentennial Living History
Curriculum: Art; Geography; History; Social Studies

845 Lexington Herald-Leader

www.kentucky.com/mld/kentucky/

This website is the online version of the newspaper *Lexington Herald-Leader*. This website includes current news on local, national, and world levels. Topics range from information on the Kentucky Derby to international affairs. The newspaper covers all areas, including business, shopping, entertainment, politics, and special interest news.
Special Features: Links include Business, Shopping, Entertainment, Shopping, Politics, Weather, National News, Local News, and State News. Also, the website features an archive enabling people to access past reports and stories
Curriculum: Art; Business; Economics; Education; Government; Health; Home Economics; Social Studies

846 Louisville Science Center

www.louisvillescience.com/

The Louisville Science Center seeks to expand peoples' knowledge of science, mathematics, and technology through hands on exhibits, IMAX films, and educational programs. The website features information on IMAX films, exhibits, and special events. Science Center Facts and News are also featured on this site.

Special Features: Links include Science Center News, Science Center Facts, exhibits, IMAX theater, Daily Doings, The World Within Us, The World We Create

Curriculum: Math; Science; Technology

847 Louisville Slugger Museum

www.sluggermuseum.org/flash5.html

The Louisville Slugger Museum is a tribute to the most famous baseball bat in the world. This museum is also the production center for this world renowned product. This website features an in depth history of the Louisville Slugger as well as the famous faces of baseball. The site also features educational tools and baseball trivia.

Special Features: Links include The Story, Timeline, Batting Champs, Today's Pros, Trivia, Gift Shop, Visitor Information, and Archive. Also, the website features an online tour of the museum and factory

Curriculum: History; Sports

848 My Old Kentucky Home

www.myoldkentuckyhome.com/

This website is a source for information on Kentucky, focusing on central Kentucky and Bardstown. The site includes featured attractions in this area of Kentucky as well as a postcard tour of Bardstown. An extensive list of events and festivals throughout the region is available.

Special Features: Links include Postcard Tours of Bardstown and Federal Hill, Bardstown Aero Modelers, Kentucky Standard Online, Stephen Foster Collins: America's Favorite Folksong Writer, The Oldham Era

Curriculum: History; Music

849 My New Kentucky Home

kentucky.gov

My New Kentucky Home is an official Web site for the state of Kentucky. It included a multitude of areas, such as: Government, Education, Business, Health and Public Safety, Facts and History, Recreation and Travel and much more.

Special Features: **Additional links include, for example: Community: Kid's Pages, Resources, Arts and Culture, as well as Register to Vote, License My Business, Get Tax Forms**
Curriculum: **Business; Education; Government; Health**

850 My Old Kentucky Roots

www.myoldkentuckyroots.com/CIVILWAR.html

My Old Kentucky Roots provides information about Kentucky in the Civil War. The site includes Civil War biographies, rosters, regimental histories, and media. In addition, this site has other sections dedicated to other facets of Kentucky's history.

Special Features: Links include Daniel Boone, Kentucky Censuses, History, My Genealogy, Kentucky Pioneers, Kentucky Obituaries Project, East Kentucky Genealogy

Curriculum: History

851 Roadside America: Kentucky

www.roadsideamerica.com/map/ky.html

Roadside America's website provides a glimpse of attractions in various cities and towns around Kentucky. These attractions are eccentric ones, such as the largest stained glass window in Covington. Links to other attractions in U.S. cities are also available.

Special Features: Links include Electric Map, Latest Tips, Tourism News, Souvenir Hut, Travelbrain, HyperTours, The Pie

Curriculum: Geography; Social Studies

852 Site Atlas: Kentucky Information Page

www.sitesatlas.com/Maps/Info/usaky.htm

This website features a detailed map of Kentucky, including highways, parks, cities, and lakes. Destination guides for various cities and towns in Kentucky are also available. A wide variety of travel options and guides are featured.

Special Features: Links include Books and Guides, Maps, and Population. Destination Guides for U.S. states and various countries throughout the world are also available

Curriculum: Geography

853 Special Olympics Kentucky

www.soky.org/

Special Olympics is an international program of year round sports and activities for children and adults with a mental handicap. It provides people with the opportunity to show that even though they possess a mental impairment, they are capable of succeeding in athletics. This website features information on all aspects of the Kentucky location of Special Olympics, as well as links to Special Olympics in other states.

Special Features: Links include Calendar of Events, Families, Sports, Media Center, Resource Library, Unified Sports, World Games, Special Events, Healthy Athletes

Curriculum: Education; History; Library Media; Physical Education

854 Surnames of Kentucky

www.ket.org/

Surnames of Kentucky is a website dedicated to tracking people's ancestors. It features missing persons and hard to find ancestors. Kentucky's history is also featured in "Kentucky Folklore," a section highlighting Kentucky stories that have been passed down through generations.

Special Features: Links include Kentucky's Most Wanted Ancestors, Kentucky's Mysteries, Surnames, Kentucky Folklore, Genealogy Detective, Kentucky's Unsolved Mysteries

Curriculum: History; Sociology

855 Tobaccopedia

www.tobaccopedia.org/

This is a comprehensive website about tobacco. Topics covered in this site include environment, economics, smoke free areas and legislation, smoking cessation, health effects, addiction, and advertising. Each topic on tobacco provides numerous links to other websites describing a certain aspect of the product. The site provides tips for quitting and the health rewards achieved by quitting.

Special Features: Links include Brown University, Smokescreen Action Network, International Calendar of Tobacco Control, Quit Net, UICC Globalink, Global Partnerships for Tobacco Control, Center for Behavioral Epidemiology and Community Health

Curriculum: Economics; Government; Psychology

856 West Kentucky Corporation

www.thinkwestkentucky.com/index.html

The goal of West Kentucky Corporation is to create more opportunity for the people of West-

ern Kentucky by building and sustaining a competitive and powerful economy. The website features information on the counties of Western Kentucky, as well as information on business and industry, tourism and recreation, historic and Civil War, heritage, agriculture, and legislative issues.

Special Features: Links include 10,000 Trails, Coal Development, Horse Industry, Economic Development, Environmental Education, Kentucky Agriculture Department, Barn Trails of Kentucky, Food Products, Heritage Corridors, Ecotourism/Outdoor Recreation

Curriculum: Economics; Environmental Studies; Geography; History; Science; Technology

857 Western Kentucky Universities Library

www.wku.edu/Library/museum/

The Kentucky Library and Museum features various artifacts from Kentucky's history. Historical topics include politics, ancestry, politics, culture, war, geographical landmarks, music, and art. Collections and exhibits are available online, as are educational resources. Links to an online library databases and catalogues are also featured.

Special Features: Links include Library Catalogue, Library Databases, Kentucky Library and Museum, Calendar of Events, Events and Exhibitions, Topper InfoPortal, Research

Curriculum: Library Media

858 Women in Kentucky

www.womeninkentucky.com/

This website provides information on some of the most notable women in Kentucky's history. It provides information on the achievements of Kentucky women in the fields of religion, reform, sports, science, law, literature, business, health, music, journalism, military, political service, etc. Also includes a timeline of Kentucky women as well as a timeline of contributions from women throughout the United States.

Special Features: Links include Educational Tools, Selected Readings, Archival Collections, Children's Books, The Suffrage Movement, Civil Rights, National Women's Hall of Fame, KyTales, National Women's History Project

Curriculum: History; Women's Studies

LOUISIANA

859 America's Wetland

www.americaswetland.com/

Organization dedicated to preserving coastal LA. Wetlands Fact Sheet, News/Events, videos, brochures, education materials, getting involved.

Special Features: Wetland coloring books; Wetland quizzes

Curriculum: Environmental Studies

860 Atchafalaya Trace Commission

www.atchafalayatrace.org/index.htm

Website for tourism and study of the Atchafalaya heritage area, encompassing 13 LA parishes. History and information, maps, visitor information.

Special Features: .PDF map archive

Curriculum: Environmental Studies; Geography

861 Audubon Nature Institute

www.auduboninstitute.org/fhome.htm

Complex of learning centers in New Orleans, including the Audubon Zoo, Aquarium of the Americas, LA Nature Institute, IMAX Theatre. Each center website contains articles, resources, online tours, and kid's area, as well as complex info, tourism info.

Special Features: Audubon Research Center with online articles

Curriculum: Biology; Science; Social Studies

862 City of Baton Rouge

brgov.com/

Government website for the state capitol. Major sections include Online Services, Information, Government; live traffic and conditions updates.

Special Features: Extensive links for visitors

Curriculum: Government

863 City of New Orleans

cityofno.com/portal.aspx

City government website features four major content areas: Government, Business, Residents, Visitors. Portal to city agencies, services.

Special Features: Speech enabled browsing

Curriculum: Government

864 Creole History (Sponsor: Ambiance Studio Web Design)

www.gensdecouleur.com/

Les Gens de Couleur Libres presents historical resources and links about Creoles of Color in New Orleans. Photo gallery, genealogy data, plus links to Creole history, music, language, publications, more.

Special Features: Les Gans meeting room

Curriculum: History; Social Studies

865 Dogwood Press

dogwoodpress.myriad.net/dcm/redbone.html

Scholarly article on the Louisiana Redbones ethnic subculture, written and originally presented by Don C. Marler.

Special Features: Resource bibliography

Curriculum: History; Social Studies

866 Education Resource (Sponsor: Greg English)

www.louisiana101.com/

Extensive education resource geared towards K–6 teachers in LA. Actual lesson plans taught by LA teachers in LA schools, submitted for free distribution, along with web resources, lists of links, more. Covers several subjects.

Special Features: LA Fact of the Day; Shrimpy and the Bayou Mudbugs music section

Curriculum: Education; Environmental Studies; Geography; History; Music; Social Studies

867 Encyclopedia Louisiana

www.enlou.com/

Online webzine that catalogs economic and historical data to promote state cultural literacy. Site design is basic, but the "Two-Bit Tour" assists in familiarizing site content.

Special Features: LA Economic Information by Parish index; historical timeline index

Curriculum: Economics; History; Social Studies

868 Festival International de Louisiane

festivalinternational.com/site1.php

Annual festival entering its 19th year, celebrating the diversity of cultures, ethnicities, and lifestyles in LA. Information on the Festival and its history, information on attending the festival, lists of artists and vendors, opportunities to volunteer.

Special Features: French-language site
Curriculum: Social Studies

869 FrenchQuarter.com

www.frenchquarter.com/index.php

Visitor's guide to the French Quarter of New Orleans. Generally a commercial-oriented site, but with a good section on the history of the Quarter.

Special Features: Interactive Map of the Quarter
Curriculum: Geography; History

870 Lake Pontchartrain Basin Foundation

www.saveourlake.org/

Citizens-based not-for-profit organization dedicated to preserving and educating about Lake Pontchartrain. Site offers resources on water quality, habitat protection, public access, education, events, volunteering and activism, links.

Special Features: Learn about class programs; written materials for classrooms
Curriculum: Environmental Studies

871 Local History (Sponsor: Catherine Campanella)

www.stphilipneri.org/teacher/pontchartrain/

Excellent comprehensive, multi-faceted history page for New Orleans and Lake Pontchartrain. History, culture, arts, literature, decade-by-decade timeline, images, maps, more.

Special Features: Activates for students studying Lake Pontchartrain history
Curriculum: Art; Education; Environmental Studies; Geography; History; Language Arts; Music; Social Studies

872 Louis Armstrong House & Archives

www.satchmo.net/

Official site of the Louis Armstrong House, dedicated to preserving the history and legacy of the famous LA musician. Contains an Armstrong bio, some online archives, info for visiting the House & Archives.

Special Features: Louis Armstrong FAQ
Curriculum: History; Music

873 Louisiana Center for Educational Technology

lvs.doe.state.la.us/portal/index.php

The Louisiana Virtual School offers LA high school students access to standards-based courses delivered by LA teachers. Web portal offers information, curriculum, enrollment for state students, opportunities for LA teachers.

Special Features: Browse course basics/supply lists
Curriculum: Art; Biology; Education; Environmental Studies; History; Math; Science; Social Studies; Technology

874 Louisiana Challenge Grant

www.challenge.state.la.us

State initiative to integrate technology into education. Gathers lesson plans on a variety of subjects for elementary, middle, and high school; online projects, the Challenge Resource Hotlist, other resources and links for educators.

Special Features: Links to state regional pilot sites
Curriculum: Art; Business; Education; Geography; Health; Language Arts; Math; Science; Social Studies; Technology

875 Louisiana Department of Education

www.doe.state.la.us/slrc/index.htm

LA State Literacy Resource Center promotes reading through education, programs, and professional development. Site contains online publications, literacy bibliography.

Special Features: Teacher/Tutor Resources
Curriculum: Education; Language Arts

876 Louisiana Department of Wildlife and Fisheries

www.nutria.com/

LADWF website on the nutria, an imported semi-aquatic rodent that is damaging LA's wetlands ecosystem. History and biology of the nutria, how it damages the ecosystem, efforts to curb nutria populations.

Special Features: History of LA fur industry; useful links
Curriculum: Biology; Environmental Studies; History; Science

877 Louisiana Division of Archaeology

www.crt.state.la.us/crt/ocd/arch/homepage/index.htm

The Louisiana Division of Archaeology records, protects, and distributes information about the state's archaeological sites. Presents one dozen virtual books on state archaeology, list of National Registry sites, educational resources, more.
Special Features: Free anthropology books and activity booklets online
Curriculum: Science

878 Louisiana Division of the Arts

www.louisianafolklife.org/index.html

Folklife in Louisiana is an online database of resources on state cultures, ethnicities, and living traditions. A library of online articles and virtual books, audio and video files, lists and bibliographies, Louisiana Voices folklore in education project, introduction to folklore/folklife.
Special Features: Curriculum resources for teachers
Curriculum: Education; History; Music; Social Studies

879 Louisiana Environment (Sponsor: Bruce E. Fleury)

www.tulane.edu/%7Ebfleury/envirobio/enviroweb.html

This series of essays on the LA environment are used in college-level courses at Tulane University. Provided by Tulane's Environmental Biology Honor's Class.
Special Features: Essays on regional habitats and regional environmental problems
Curriculum: Environmental Studies; Science

880 Louisiana Genealogy (Sponsor: Edward J. Hayden)

www.lagenweb.org/

LAGenWeb collects LA genealogical data, information, and material online, and makes it freely available to Internet access. Search by parish or town, access USGenWeb resources.
Special Features: Clickable LA Parish Map
Curriculum: History; Social Studies

881 Louisiana Library Network

louisdl.louislibraries.org/

The LOUISiana Digital Library provides digital image and document collections. State topics include Frank B. Moore Photograph Collection, French Colonization of Louisiana and Louisiana Purchase Map Collection, Huey P. Long, Louisiana State Aerial Photograph Collection, others.
Special Features: Teaching American History Collection
Curriculum: Education; History

882 Louisiana Native Guards at Port Hudson (Sponsor: JGH)

www2.netdoor.com/~jgh/

Website about the Louisiana Native Guards at Port Hudson, the first black soldiers in the Union Army during the Civil War. Their story, their origins, their officers, and links to other sites of interest.
Special Features: Native Guard book list
Curriculum: History; Social Studies

883 Louisiana Office of Electronic Services/Louisiana GIS Council

wwwlamap.doa.state.la.us/

LouisianaMAP is a state-supported collection of geospatial data presented online. Contains digital, aerial, satellite, and survey maps, many with interactive content.
Special Features: Download geospatial data of Louisiana
Curriculum: Geography; Science

884 Louisiana Office of State Parks

www.lastateparks.com/

Office that oversees LA's parks, reservations, historic sites, and preservation areas. Complete list of park locations, maps, visitors guides, events, plus legislative and government issues related to parks.
Special Features: Free brochures by request (online form)
Curriculum: Environmental Studies; Government; History; Social Studies

885 Louisiana Office of Tourism

www.crt.state.la.us/crt/tourism/civilwar/civilwar.htm

Informative articles on Louisiana's Civil War history. Background and causes, major LA battles, regiments and generals, battle sites.
Special Features: Nicely illustrated map of Civil War battle sites
Curriculum: History

886 Louisiana Purchase (Sponsor: LSU Libraries)

www.lib.lsu.edu/special/purchase/

The Louisiana Purchase: A Heritage Explored presents a wealth of archival material online. Over 200 historical images, historical essay, search collections, related links.

Special Features: Teacher's Guides and Lesson Plans

Curriculum: Education; History

887 Louisiana SPCA

www.la-spca.org/

State chapter of the animal protection, shelter, and care organization. Website presents four major content areas: Dedication, Education, Prevention, and Adoption, each with multiple articles and resources.

Special Features: Animal Care Library

Curriculum: Social Studies

888 Louisiana State Museum

lsm.crt.state.la.us/

State Museum website contains a plethora of online resources. Several excellent online Exhibits on Mardi Gras, Louisiana Purchase, Mississippi River, more; plus audio and video files, bibliography resources, museum information.

Special Features: Educator's Corner with curriculum, materials; RealAudio New Orleans Jazz Club Vintage Radio Broadcasts

Curriculum: History; Music; Social Studies

889 Louisiana State University

www.lgs.lsu.edu/index1.htm#

The Louisiana Geologic Survey is the premier geological research institution in the state of Louisiana. Website offers department and program information, plus high-quality .pdf files suitable for classrooms. Requires Adobe Acrobat Reader.

Special Features: Earth Stuff educational materials available free upon request

Curriculum: Science

890 LSU AgCenter

www.lsuagcenter.com/

State source for agricultural information and cooperative extension. Articles on a wide range of related topics, plus statewide and parish centers, cooperative extension services, organizational information.

Special Features: Kids and teens section

Curriculum: Business; Economics; Environmental Studies; Health; Home Economics; Science

891 LSUE Office of Public Relations

www.lsue.edu/acadgate/

Central Acadiana Gateway focuses on the traditional cultures of southwestern LA. Geography, cities and parishes, cultural traditions of the area.

Special Features: Mardi Gras in Rural Acadiana; Contemporary LA Cajun, Creole, and Zydeco Musicians

Curriculum: Geography; Music; Social Studies

892 Mardi Gras (Sponsor: G. R. B. Enterprises)

www.mardigrasunmasked.com/

Colorful website offers both contemporary and historical info on Mardi Gras. Geared for both those attending Mardi Gras and those seeking information. Carnival and parade information, history, customs and traditions, music, images, more.

Special Features: Mardispeak dictionary; Carnival 4 Kidz

Curriculum: History; Music; Social Studies

893 Music (Sponsor: Greg Hardison)

www.satchmo.com/

The LA Music Archive & Artist Directory collects comprehensive information on the state music scene. Music news, events calendar, artists directory, history of LA music, LA musicians Hall of Fame, more.

Special Features: French Quarter Radio

Curriculum: Music; Social Studies

894 National Park Service

www.nps.gov/popo/

Poverty Point National Park preserves some of the largest prehistoric earth works in North America. NPS website features complete park information, schedule of activities, and online facts, in-depth information.

Special Features: Link to LA Park Service website

Curriculum: History; Social Studies

895 New Orleans (Sponsor: Jay Garcia and Stephen Garcia)

gatewayno.com/index.html

Gateway New Orleans is a commercial site but provides a good spread of information on New Orleans and its environs. Contains History, Cuisine, Culture, Music, the French Quarter, and area Business information.

Special Features: History section contains short, accessible, referenced articles on city and state

Curriculum: History; Music; Social Studies

896 New Orleans Public Library

nutrias.org/

The Library's NUTRIAS site holds a wealth of online content. Online exhibits, image galleries, online book club, "Images of the Month" feature, library and branch information, card catalog.

Special Features: Kid's page
Curriculum: History; Library Media; Social Studies

897 NOLA.com

www.nola.com/

Everything New Orleans can be found in this comprehensive community guide. Current events, weather, business, sports, radio, local guides, visitors info, more.

Special Features: Hosts the Times-Picayune online.
Curriculum: Social Studies

898 Notable Women in History (Sponsor: LSU Libraries)

www.lib.lsu.edu/soc/women/lawomen.html

Louisiana Leaders: Notable Women in History presents biographies of sixteen prominent LA women. Includes Kate Chopin, Pearl Rivers, Mahalia Jackson, more.

Special Features: Timeline of LA Women's History
Curriculum: History; Social Studies; Women's Studies

899 Office of Community Preservation at LSU

lhn.lsu.edu/

The Louisiana Heritage Gateway gathers resources about LA's cultural and natural heritage, with a focus on the Lower Delta Region. Main Heritage Database holds resources on Nature, Buildings and Gardens, Folkways, Economy, Heritage Corridors.

Special Features: Extensive links
Curriculum: Economics; History; Science; Social Studies

900 Ouachita River Foundation

www.ouachitariver.org/

A non-profit organization dedicated to the preservation of the Ouachita River in western LA. Several articles, photograph galleries.

Special Features: Useful links
Curriculum: Environmental Studies

901 Police Jury Association of Louisiana

www.lpgov.org/

Website explains the Parish government system of LA, its version of the common county system. Introduction to police jury & home rule charter, Parish directory, legislative news, links to resources.

Special Features: Clickable Parish map
Curriculum: Government

902 Railways (Sponsor: Michael M. Palmieri)

www.lrs.railspot.com/index.html

The Louisiana Rail Site is a compendium of historic and modern information on LA's railways. Image library, essays, railroads, accident statistics, history, more.

Special Features: All About *Smoky Mary* extended feature
Curriculum: History; Technology

903 Save Our Cemeteries

www.saveourcemeteries.org/index.htm

New Orleans organization fighting to promote, protect, and preserve historic gravesites in and around the city. Information on preservation, tours, events, newsletter, education opportunities.

Special Features: Directory of 31 city cemeteries
Curriculum: History; Social Studies

904 State of Louisiana

www.louisiana.gov/wps/portal/

Official state home page. Traveling, Business, Learning, and Government major content areas, plus links to departments, services online.

Special Features: Learning in Louisiana —

Just For Students collection of articles and links

Curriculum: Government, History, Social Studies

905 State Library of Louisiana

www.state.lib.la.us/la_dyn_templ.cfm?doc_id=113

The Center for the Book is a state literacy initiative. Encourages reading by developing reading and writing programs, supporting LA book community, and presenting or sponsoring public presentations. Program details and more online.

Special Features: LA Writers Directory; LA Book Festival

Curriculum: Education; Language Arts; Library Media

906 Tulane University Libraries

www.specialcollections.tulane.edu/Online_Exhibits.html

Online Exhibits from the Special Collections at Tulane. Content changes occasionally, but online exhibits generally have a state historical or cultural focus.

Special Features: Carnival Collection

Curriculum: History; Library Media; Social Studies

907 ULL Center for Cultural and Eco-Tourism

ccet.louisiana.edu/

LA visitor's guide with a focus on cultural and environmental attractions of the state. Collects efforts of University of Louisiana teachers, outside resources and weblinks, into three main content areas: cultural tourism, environmental tourism, folklore.

Special Features: Info on the Louisiana Folk Masters Series; Cajun and Creole Hour

Curriculum: Social Studies

908 USGS National Wetlands Research Center

www.lacoast.gov/

LaCoast collects and presents resources on LA's coastal wetlands. Funded by the Coastal Wetlands Planning, Protection and Restoration Act, pursues conservation projects, provides maps, articles, and online resources.

Special Features: Teacher's Guides; Kid's Corner

Curriculum: Education; Environmental Studies; Science

909 Voodoo in New Orleans (Sponsor: Lindsey Tubbs & Esther Liu)

studentweb.tulane.edu/~ltubbs/index.html

Voodoo in New Orleans is a brief but useful overview of the religious practice popularly associated with LA. History, Modern Practice, and a biography of Mary Laveau.

Special Features: Links to further Voodoo sites

Curriculum: History; Social Studies

MAINE

910 AllofMaine.com

www.allofmaine.com/

All of Maine is a directory search engine. All the websites in the directory are about or located in the state of Maine. The directory subject list includes: art and entertainment, automotive, business, community, computers, education, agriculture, financial, dining, health, gardening, kids, law, hobbies, real estate, recreation and sports, and tourism.

Special Features: Searchable, regional information

Curriculum: Business; Education; Government; Health

911 American Lighthouse Foundation

www.lighthousefoundation.org/museum.cfm

The Museum of Lighthouse History is located in Wells. The museum preserves lighthouse, lightship and lifesaving station artifacts and documents from all over America. Website provides a partial listing of items on display and includes a listing of preservation projects the foundation sponsors.

Special Features: Photos, lighthouse information

Curriculum: History; Sociology

912 Animal Welfare Society

www.animalwelfaresociety.com/

The Animal Welfare Society is a humane society located in West Kennebunk. Offering care for more than thirty-eight hundred animals annually they also offer adoption and education programs. Website offers photos of pets looking for a home and description of education programs available to the public.

Special Features: Animal photos, schedule of events, volunteering information

Curriculum: Social Studies

913 Blethen Maine Newspapers, Inc.

www.mainetoday.com/

MaineToday.com is an online newspaper offering daily news that includes news, sports, business and entertainment in Maine. Maps, travel tips, photographs, and eating establishments are listed. Information is updated throughout the day to ensure up to date and timely information.

Special Features: Teen writing section, photos, area information

Curriculum: Business; Language Arts; Sociology

914 Cat Fanciers' Association

www.cfainc.org/breeds/profiles/maine.html

The coon cat is longhaired breed originating out of the state of Maine. It is well known for its loving personality and great intelligence. The Maine Coon cat was bred for harsh winters and good mouse hunting. Along with its usefulness, the breed is popular for showing and has a history of winning "best cat."

Special Features: Photos, breed history

Curriculum: Science

915 Children's Museum of Maine

www.childrensmuseumofme.org/home2.html

The Children's Museum of Maine is located in Portland. Dedicated to child development and learning through discovery, imagination, ex-

ploration, and play the website is also child friendly and offers lots of fun facts that correlate with the exhibits. Links for children, grownups and educators are provided.

Special Features: Fun facts, schedule of events

Curriculum: Art; Science

916 Children's Book Author Jacqueline Briggs Martin)

www.jacquelinebriggsmartin.com/

Award winning children's book author Jacqueline Briggs Martin was born and raised on a farm in Maine. Her website offers biographical information, curriculum ideas, family photos, reader activities and a bibliography of her work. View images from her books.

Special Features: Handouts, school project ideas

Curriculum: Language Arts; Library Media

917 Desert of Maine

www.desertofmaine.com/

Located near Freeport, the "Desert of Maine" is a natural deposit of vast amounts of sand. In 1797, after clearing, over grazing and soil erosion, a three hundred acre farm grew into a desert. Today the land and farm is a tourist attraction and museum. The geologist attested natural phenomenon was deposited over eleven thousand years ago by a glacier.

Special Features: Photos, facts

Curriculum: Environmental Studies; Geography; Science

918 Fishing In Maine.com

www.fishing-in-maine.com/

Maine contains nearly six thousand lakes and ponds and thirty-two thousand miles of running water. Fishing in Maine offers all types of fishermen the information they need to catch record fish. Website offers interactive regional map for easy fishing spot location. Site includes photos, weather, moon phases, fishing reports and fishing regulations.

Special Features: Kid opportunity listing, state records, related links

Curriculum: Environmental Studies; Geography; Science

919 Henry David Thoreau's "The Maine Woods" (Sponsor: Richard Lenat)

www.eserver.org/thoreau/mewoods.html

"The Maine Woods" by Henry David Thoreau are three essays of the Main wilderness. This website offers the full text, comments on the literary work, maps of Thoreau's Main experience, plant and animal lists, and related links. More detailed information on Thoreau is available through the extended links.

Special Features: History, life, times, and biography of Thoreau's life

Curriculum: Language Arts

920 Information Resource of Maine

www.state.me.us/

The official website of the state of Maine. Website covers Maine government, living, visiting, working, business, and education. A featured link titled "Facts and History" is useful for projects and research. A kids' page is also included and offers contests and games, homework helpers, and cartoons.

***Special Features:* Online governmental services, news, tourism information**

Curriculum: Business; Government; Social Studies

921 Lighthouses of Maine (Sponsor: William A. Britten)

www.lighthousegetaway.com/lights/maine.html

Lighthouses of Maine, by William Britten is a virtual tour of lighthouses on the coast of Maine. With more than sixty lighthouses to offer, the website includes lighthouse name, location, photos, and brief history of each lighthouse. The brightest lighthouse is located at Cape Elizabeth.

Special Features: Photography

Curriculum: Geography; History; Technology

922 Maine Arts Commission

www.mainearts.com/

The Maine Arts Commission exists to promote public participation and interest in cultural heritage and arts of the state. Site offers artist directory, organizations, calendar of events, programs and news. Maine also holds an office of a poet laureate offered on this webpage.

Special Features: Poetry, featured art images

Curriculum: Art; Language Arts

923 Maine Audubon

www.maineaudubon.org/

Maine Audubon strives to connect people with nature. By conserving wildlife and habitat all people can enjoy nature in the future. Website contains extensive information on science and conservation, birding, issues and actions, nature centers and sanctuaries, trail maps and regional chapter information.

Special Features: Photos, legislative actions, newsletters

Curriculum: Biology; Environmental Studies; Science

924 Maine Boats and Harbors

www.maineboats.com/

Maine Boats and Harbors is a magazine dedicated to Maine's coastal lifestyle. Featuring magnificent scenery it also includes people, history, traditional boats, architecture and food. Published five times a year, a glimpse of the "magazine of the coast" is offered online.

Special Features: Free issue is offered, recipes

Curriculum: Geography; Home Economics; Language Arts

925 Maine Center for the Arts, University of Maine

www.ume.maine.edu/~mca/

The Maine Center for the Arts or MCA islocated in Orono. Live performances in music, dance and theatrical productions bring companies from all over the world to Maine. Website offers detailed information on the construction of the stage and the orchestral area. A schedule of performances is also provided.

Special Features: Detailed information of stage and systems

Curriculum: Dance; Drama; Music; Technology

926 Maine Diner

www.mainediner.com/index.cfm

The Maine Diner is famous for its fresh Maine cuisine and its wholesome Northeastern atmosphere. Lobster rolls and hot lobster pie are regional favorites and have been featured on the Today Show on television. Website offers the diner menu and pictures of the daily special. History of the diner is included.

Special Features: Video clips, menu, articles

Curriculum: Business; Home Economics

927 Maine Humanities Council

www.mainehumanities.org/

The Maine Humanities Council is home to the Harriet P. Henry Center for the Book. It is a statewide program using literature, history, philosophy and the arts to provide opportunities for people to come together in cultural enrichment events. The council is located in Portland and offers extensive literary programs for children and adults.

Special Features: Literacy programs, grant information, newsletters

Curriculum: Education; Language Arts; Library Media; Sociology

928 Maine Independent Media Center

maine.indymedia.org/

Maine Independent Media Center is a grassroots news and media coverage organization. Open to the public, news coverage is in the hands of the people who experience it. Subjectivity is up to the author and many points of view are offered. Website offers many categories of interest and photos.

Special Features: Photos; environmental issues

Curriculum: Environmental Studies; Government; Language Arts; Sociology

929 Maine International Film Festival

www.miff.org/

The Maine International Film Festival was founded in 1998. The festival lasts ten days and shows over one hundred American and international independent films. Directors, producers, writers, actors, and musicians attend and are scheduled for panel discussions, question and answer sessions and mingling.

Special Features: Ticket and pass information, schedule

Curriculum: Sociology

930 Maine Library Association

mainelibraries.org/

The Maine Library Association is a statewide advocate for all Maine libraries. It offers continuing education to librarians, a quarterly journal, networking and professional conferences. It is also the sponsor of the Maine Lupine Award for children's literature. Website offers library resources and job listings.

Special Features: Legislative news, publications, library reports

Curriculum: Library Media

931 Maine Lobster Promotion Council

www.mainelobsterpromo.com/

The name of the Maine Lobster Promotion Council is self descriptive to its mission. The website offers fact sheets, nutrition information, recipes, how to eat a lobster, and how to purchase and store lobster for eating. It also includes the journal of the day in the life of a lobster harvester.

Special Features: Newsletters, email mailing list

Curriculum: Business; Home Economics

932 Maine Maritime Museum

www.bathmaine.com/programs.asp

The Maine Maritime Museum holds gallery exhibits, an historic shipyard, education programs and narrated cruises. Located in historic Bath, the museum also includes an extensive research library, maritime artifacts, and the history of the Maine waterfront. Website offers historical Maine information, wooden schooner building and a virtual tour.

Special Features: Interactive map, related links, photos

Curriculum: History; Social Studies

933 Maine Memory Network, Maine Historical Society

www.mainememory.net/home.shtml

The Maine Memory Network is a searchable database full of photos, maps, paintings, museum objects, letters, diaries, and images for public use to enhance and promote knowledge of Maine history. Online exhibits and lesson plans are offered. Create your own gallery of knowledge or explore student made exhibits.

Special Features: Ready made educational albums arranged by topic

Curriculum: Art; History; Social Studies

934 The Maine Music Box (Sponsor: University of Maine)

mainemusicbox.library.umaine.edu/

The Maine Music Box is a project devoted to the collection and lending of printed music to professional musicians and educational use. It includes music literature, lyrics, scores, cover art and recordings. The collection is searchable and may be browsed by collection, subject, cover art and keyword.

Special Features: Artwork, sheet music, images

Curriculum: Dance; Music

935 Maine Narrow Gauge Railroad Co. and Museum

www.mngrr.org/

Located in Portland the Narrow Gauge Railroad Company and Museum is home to antique rail cars, steam and diesel locomotives. View the scrapbook of events, or browse the photo gallery. The equipment roster lists locomotives, motor cars, pump cars, passenger cars, freight cars and other materials.

Special Features: Discussion forum, photo gallery, related links

Curriculum: History; Social Studies

936 Maine Office of Tourism

www.visitmaine.com/home.php

The official website of the Maine Office of Tourism. From outdoor adventures to shopping or sandy beaches there is something for everyone in Maine. The website offers seasonal information, where to visit, lodging, things to do, trip planning or travel packages. Free travel books and brochures are available.

Special Features: Photos, maps, monthly events schedule

Curriculum: Business; Geography

937 Maine Parent Federation

www.mpf.org/

The Maine Parent Federation is an organization that provides information, advocacy, support, training and education to parents and professionals for the benefit of all children. Statewide assistance is available. Many programs are offered; these include an information network, parent resource center, home visiting program, a preschool, and more.

Special Features: Fact sheets, online training, newsletters

Curriculum: Health; Home Economics; Sociology; Women's Studies

938 Maine Potato Board

www.mainepotatoes.com/

Maine is one of the top potato producers in the United States. The website offers consumer and producer information. Read over the history of the potato in Maine or the yearly industry review. Recipes are offered and can be made for two to over fifty people.

Special Features: Contests, calendar, economic study

Curriculum: Business; Economics; Home Economics

939 Maine Public Broadcasting

www.mpbc.org/

Maine Public Broadcasting includes television and radio. By broadcasting news, information and educational programming the MPBC strives to open a window to the world and enlighten minds. Free to the public the MPBC includes children's programs, public affairs, culture, history, nature, documentaries and classroom materials.

Special Features: Radio and television program guides

Curriculum: Drama; Language Arts; Music; Sociology

940 Maine Resource Guide

www.maineguide.com/

The Maine Resource Guide is a website dedicated to the promotion of the Pine Tree State. Find outdoor recreation, events, accommodations, recreation, business, education and schools, travel and more. Searchable site helps find what you are looking for. Use the interactive regional map to find cities or travel interests.

Special Features: Photos, forums, forest reports

Curriculum: Business; Geography

941 Maine Rivers

www.mainerivers.org/

Maine Rivers was started in 1989. As the advocate for clean water in the state, Main Rivers is an information sharing action network. It offers information on clean water history, legislative actions, water profiles and water depth. News on watershed areas and their wildlife is also offered.

Special Features: Photos, maps, full text articles

Curriculum: Biology; Environmental Studies; Geography; Science

942 Maine Snowmobile Associations

www.mesnow.com/

There are over thirteen thousand miles of snowmobile trails in Maine. The MSA is the promoter and conduit of snowmobiling information in the state. Website offers maps, laws, events, weather conditions, issues, news, and links all about the snowmobiling sport.

Special Features: Hand signals, landowner information, membership information

Curriculum: Sports

943 The Maine Solar House (Sponsor: William and Debora Lord)

www.solarhouse.com/index2.html

The Maine Solar House is located in southern Maine and is privately owned. It is totally solar powered from water heating to lighting. As solar power is a free renewable resource the website offers information on planning, architecture and details of the house.

Special Features: Statistics, photos, technology news

Curriculum: Architecture; Environmental Studies; Science; Technology

944 Maine State Music Theatre

www.msmt.org/default.asp

The Maine State Music Theatre or MSMT brings professional musical theatre to the state. The mission is to bring live performances to the public to enrich them with culture. The MSMT is the only theatre troop dedicated to musical theatre alone. By preserving the classic American musical it can be passed onto the next generation.

Special Features: History, news, photographs

Curriculum: Business; Dance; Drama; Music

945 Maine Wolf Coalition

home.acadia.net/mainewolf/

The Maine Wolf Coalition was founded in 1994 to promote better understanding of the wolf and its importance. At one time the wolf disappeared from Maine even though there is suitable habitat for it to live. Website offers basic facts and information on the wolf and related sites about Canis lupus.

Special Features: Fact and fiction of the wolf, news, recovery updates

Curriculum: Biology; Environmental Studies; Science

946 Mainebirding.net

www.mainebirding.net/

Birding in Maine is an exciting hobby as it includes both seaside and mainland birds. Maine is the only state where Atlantic puffins breed. Website offers extensive information on puf-

fins, articles on birding, feeding wild birds, how to build a birdhouse and bird checklist.

Special Features: Photos; bird alerts, news and notes

Curriculum: Biology; Science

947 Mount Desert Oceanarium

www.theoceanarium.com/

Located in Bar Harbor, the Mount Desert Oceanarium offers education about lobsters, marsh ecology, whales, scallops, tides, weather and fishing. It is known as one of the best teaching oceanariums on the coast. It is also known for "hands on" exhibits.

Special Features: Map of the area, photos. Contact information

Curriculum: Biology; Environmental Studies; Science

948 National Park Service

www.nps.gov/acad/

Acadia National Park is located on the coast of Maine and includes more than forty-seven thousand acres of mountains and shoreline. It was the first national park east of the Mississippi. The park is home to diverse wildlife, scientific studies and recreational activity areas. Kid's page is included.

Special Features: Photos, history, educational programming

Curriculum: Biology; Environmental Studies, Geography

949 Natural Resources Council of Maine

www.maineenvironment.org/

Using the power of people, science, and law to protect the environment of Maine, the Natural Resources Council of Maine strives to preserve the land for future generations. Website offers extensive information on environmental issues and concerns. Full text articles and legislative news is provided. Search engine for the website offers opportunity to find specific issues.

Special Features: Publications, related links, contact information

Curriculum: Environmental Studies; Geography; Government

950 Old York Historical Society

www.oldyork.org/visiting_pages/elizabeth_perkins.htm

The Elizabeth Perkins House is one of the finest surviving examples of colonial revival architecture. The form was popular at the turn of the twentieth century. The original one room house was built in 1686 and then added onto until 1935 when the Perkins family transformed the building into a colonial home.

Special Features: Photos, information on the surrounding historical sights

Curriculum: Art; History; Social Studies

951 Penobscot Theatre Company

www.ptc.maineguide.com/

Founded in 1973 as a summer theater troupe the Penobscot Theatre Company now runs full season and attracts more than twenty two thousand people per year. The Bangor Opera House is home to the company's base of operations. The company also offers the largest drama outreach program in the state.

Special Features: Press releases, ticket information, performance schedule

Curriculum: Dance; Drama; Music

952 The Portland Museum of Art (Sponsor: Time Warner Cable of Maine)

www.portlandmuseum.org/

The Portland Museum of Art. This website offers a glimpse of the artistic heritage of *Maine*. Some pieces date back to the eighteenth century. The permanent collection includes European and American artists and over two thousand pieces of glass. Website also features current and future exhibits. Online images are available.

Special Features: Virtual tour, events, programming information

Curriculum: Art; History

953 Ski Maine Association

www.skimaine.com/

Ski Maine Association hosts an informational webpage on skiing in the state of Maine. Find snow conditions, weather, maps, facts, history, and more. Links to youth skiing, the ski hall of fame and news. Full text and searchable, the website offers extensive information on skiing in Maine.

Special Features: Ski quotations, images, photos

Curriculum: Physical Education; Sports

954 The Spanish-American War: "Remember the *Maine*" (Sponsor: Small Planet Communications)

www.smplanet.com/imperialism/remember.html

The Spanish-American War: "Remember the *Maine*." This is a full text article on the battleship the USS *Maine*. The *Maine* was summoned to Cuba to protect American interests there during the fight against imperialism. The *Maine* was then sabotaged and blown in half by the Spanish. American newspapers covered the news story extensively.

Special Features: Rare historical photos, interactive map, related articles

Curriculum: History; Social Studies

955 State of Maine Department of Economic and Community Development

www.mainemade.com/

This website is a collection of independent Maine retailers promoting the craftsmanship and products produced in the state. Look through jewelry, art, photography, books, toys, gourmet foods, furniture and music. Site offers photo and price of each product and is searchable.

Special Features: Images of all products, monthly giveaways

Curriculum: Business; Home Economics

956 University of Maine Cooperative Extension

www.umext.maine.edu/

The University of Maine Cooperative Extension is an educational research based outreach program with offices located throughout the state. Website offers extensive topics of interest such as: aging, farming, child development, safety, forestry, cooking and more. Brochures articles and publications are available.

Special Features: Schedule of classes, recipes, events

Curriculum: Education; Health; Home Economics; Women's Studies

957 University of Maine Folklife Center

www.umaine.edu/folklife/

The Maine Folklife Center in located in Orono. The center contains an extensive collection of folklore, oral history, interviews, academic papers, exhibits, topical surveys, traditional music, photographs and images. The collection is used in classrooms, and to promote the cultural heritage of the Northeast. Website offers descriptions of collections and photographs.

Special Features: Related links, correlating university courses
Curriculum: History; Language Arts; Music; Social Studies

958 Wadsworth-Longfellow House, Maine Historical Society

www.mainehistory.org/house_overview.shtml

Henry Wadsworth Longfellow was born and raised in Portland. As a famous American poet he sold his first poem at the age of thirteen. The house where he was born and raised is now a museum house and filled with the original Wadsworth artifacts and furnishings. The house was built in 1785. Website offers biographical information of the poet, family and poetry is included.

Special Features: Photographs, garden, teacher information
Curriculum: History; Language Arts

959 Waterboro Public Library

www.waterborolibrary.org/maineaut/

Waterboro Public Library offers extensive information about Maine authors, fiction set in Maine, mystery writers and more. The "Maine Writers Index" includes more than three hundred thirty writers. Index is listed in alphabetical order. Search engine is offered for the website.

Special Features: Each writer has a brief biography
Curriculum: Language Arts; Library Media

MARYLAND

960 African-American Heritage (Sponsor: ThinkQuest)

library.thinkquest.org/10854/?tqskip1=1

Exploring the African-American heritage in MD, including biographies of famous African-Americans and a timeline. Developed by students through the ThinkQuest program.

Special Features: Suggestions for Classroom Projects
Curriculum: Education; History; Social Studies

961 Babe Ruth Museum

baberuthmuseum.com/

Birthplace and Museum of Baltimore's famous baseball player. School Programs, Class Trips; Pre-School–3 Introduction to the Museum; Clues to the Past for Grades 4–8; History of Baltimore Baseball for Grades 4–12.

Special Features: Reading List includes: author, book, appropriate grade levels, and related information
Curriculum: Sports

962 Baltimore County Public Library

www.bcplonline.org/

Library's website contains extensive online resources for patrons and visitors. Online articles, encyclopedias on various subjects; local info & links; collection search. Some content requires a BCPL library card.

Special Features: "Got Homework?" informative kid's pages; Baltimore County Legacy Web
Curriculum: Business; Education; Geography; History; Language Arts; Library Media; Science; Social Studies

963 Baltimore Reads

www.baltimorereads.org/

Literacy initiative targeting high-risk and high-needs members of the Baltimore and MD community. Information on programs for children and adults, events, resources, donations.

Special Features: The Cal Ripken Learning Center
Curriculum: Education; Language Arts; Social Studies

964 Baltimore Symphony Orchestra

www.bsokids.com

BSO Kids attempts to make orchestral music fun for kids, and educate on the symphony and the music. Backstage tour, Meet the Artists, Online Games, Student Reviews, Fun Facts, Music Dictionary.

Special Features: Be a Music Critic; Teacher's Resources
Curriculum: Education; Music

965 The Battle of Antietam (Sponsor: Brian Downey)

aotw.org/

Antietam on the Web presents a historic, interactive look at the MD Civil War battlefield. Overview and chronology of the battle, site and combat maps, articles, exhibits, sources.
Special Features: Index of Official Reports [transcribed]
Curriculum: History

966 Chesapeake Bay Program

www.chesapeakebay.net/

Organization fighting to preserve and protect Chesapeake Bay through conservation and education efforts. Website maintains extensive pages on the Bay ecosystem, geology, history, population, the dangers to it, maps, more.
Special Features: Bay Plain and Piedmont online book traces geologic history
Curriculum: Environmental Studies; Geography; History; Science; Social Studies

967 City of Annapolis

www.ci.annapolis.md.us/

Official website for the MD capitol. In addition to Resident, Government, Business, and Visitors sections, contains links to city departments, city services, city maps.
Special Features: E-Gov
Curriculum: Government

968 City of Baltimore

www.ci.baltimore.md.us/

Official website of MD's largest city. Major content areas for Citizens, Visitors, Municipal, and Business, plus city services, online payments, maps.
Special Features: CitiStat program
Curriculum: Government

969 College Savings Plan of Maryland

www.collegesavingsmd.org/index.cfm

Website for the MD Prepaid College Trust and the MD College Investment Plan. Enrollment info, tuition and savings calculators, resources to assist in college selection/savings options.
Special Features: Enroll online

Curriculum: Economics; Education; Social Studies

970 A Compendium of Articles on Maryland (Sponsor: John T. Marck)

www.marylandtheseventhstate.com/

Maryland, the Seventh State, a compendium of articles on history, culture, and life in MD. Created and maintained by a private historian and author.
Special Features: The Founding of Maryland; Historical African-American Figures from Maryland
Curriculum: History; Social Studies

971 Crisfield & Smith Island Cultural Alliance

www.smithisland.org/

Online presence for Smith Island, MD's only inhabited island in Chesapeake Bay. Info on Island history, culture, community, ecology, visiting.
Special Features: Island Gallery
Curriculum: Geography; History; Social Studies

972 The Edgar Allan Poe Society of Baltimore

www.eapoe.org/

Comprehensive website covering the life and works of Edgar Allan Poe. Explores his connections with Baltimore, presents his complete works, pages on Poe-related sites in the city, information on the E. A. Poe society.
Special Features: Scholarly articles & lectures from the society
Curriculum: History; Language Arts

973 Enoch Pratt Free Library/State Library Resource Center

www.mdch.org/

MD Digital Cultural Heritage Online, with exhibits. H. L. Mencken Collection; Portraits of the Six Lords Baltimore; Great Baltimore Fire interactive exhibit.
Special Features: Digitization resources
Curriculum: History; Library Media; Social Studies

974 Fort McHenry (Sponsor: Gene Towner)

www.bcpl.net/~etowner/patriots.html

Informational site on historic Fort McHenry, "Home of the Star-Spangled Banner." Contains historical essays on the Fort, Francis Scott Key, the National Anthem, plus photo galleries, maps, visitor information, links.

Special Features: Virtual Tour; online Fort McHenry Quiz

Curriculum: History; Music

975 Historic St. Mary's City

www.stmaryscity.org/index.html

St. Mary's was the fourth permanent colony in America and MD's first capitol. The site is now dedicated to a historic museum. Website presents visiting information, site information, history, research.

Special Features: Schedule educational tours, events; online history & archaeology articles

Curriculum: History

976 History of Slavery (Sponsor: Maryland State Archives)

www.mdarchives.state.md.us/msa/homepage/html/homepage.html

Extensive online resource acts as central depository for government records of permanent value. Online archives include state vital records, records for genealogical research, atlas of historical maps, colonial records, All About Maryland, much more.

Special Features: Education & Outreach; Teachers Resources, including Documents for the Classroom

Curriculum: Education; Geography; Government; History; Social Studies

977 Maryland Association of Counties

www.mdcounties.org/

Affiliated network of MD counties provides government and legislative information, including a discussion of county structure and a complete list of MD counties.

Special Features: Links to each county's website

Curriculum: Government

978 Maryland Commission for Women

www.marylandwomen.org/

State organization promotes women's rights, educates on women's issues. Online presence includes membership info, news, events calendar, resources, links to local commissions, the Maryland Woman's Hall of Fame.

Special Features: Online brochures of women's issues, many bilingual (requires Adobe Acrobat Reader)

Curriculum: Women's Studies

979 Maryland Department of Business & Economic Development

www.choosemaryland.org/index.asp

Website directed towards encouraging economic investment in MD. Extensive economic, technological, and business-related information for small businesses, corporations, and investors.

Special Features: Orientation to MD; MD Data Center

Curriculum: Business; Economics; Social Studies

980 Maryland Department of Education

msp.msde.state.md.us/

The MD Report Card collects annual info on MD school performance. Reports on grade performance, attendance, teacher qualifications, student demographics, more.

Special Features: Sort by school or district

Curriculum: Education; Social Studies

981 Maryland Department of Housing and Community Development

www.marylandhistoricaltrust.net/

Maryland Historical Trust studies, evaluates, preserves, and educates on MD's significant historic items. Information on historical sites, preservation efforts, state museums, archeology, outreach and community programs, tourism, more.

Special Features: Explore MD's National Register Properties

Curriculum: History

982 Maryland Department of Natural Resources

www.dnr.state.md.us/wildlife/

MD's Wildlife and Heritage Service coordinates, protects, and regulates state fauna. Site content areas include Game Program, Natural Heritage Program, Education, Habitat for Wildlife. Extensive info on MD wildlife.

Special Features: Educational materials, programs; DNR's Animal Bites; endangered species list

Curriculum: Education; Environmental Studies; Science; Social Studies

983 Maryland Genealogical Society

mdgensoc.org/

State organization for collecting and preserving MD genealogy. Online databases offer Surname and First Name search; connect with other MD citizens and Society members; Society publications; event and membership info.
Special Features: Submit genealogical queries
Curriculum: History; Social Studies

984 Maryland Geological Survey

www.mgs.md.gov/

Extensive online guide to Maryland Geology, including essays and resources for general MD geology, maps, fossils, gold, caves, and geohazards. Data resources for downloading, available publications, geoscience events, education resources.
Special Features: A Gallery of Geologic Features in MD; MGS Educational Publications
Curriculum: Science

985 Maryland Historical Society

www.mdhs.org/

Collects and preserves state history, maintains a collection of artifacts, educates the public on MD history. Online exhibits, museum overview and directions, public and school program information, membership, MHS In the Classroom programs, Teacher Education opportunities.
Special Features: Maryland Memory project digital archive
Curriculum: Education; History

986 Maryland Humanities Council

www.mdhc.org/

A private non-profit organization that promotes public humanities education throughout MD. Info on programs, events calendar, MD History Day, *Maryland Humanities* journal.
Special Features: Bibliography of MD History and Culture, with essays
Curriculum: Education; History; Social Studies

987 Maryland Municipal League

www.mdmunicipal.org/mmlhome/index.cfm

Non-profit association of MD cities and towns strengthens municipal government through research, legislation, assistance, training and education. Website collects resources valuable to municipal governments, info and links to each participating municipality.
Special Features: Arrange educational presentations; Facts For Kids
Curriculum: Government; Social Studies

988 Maryland Office of the Secretary of State

www.mdkidspage.org/

MD Kid's page offers kid-friendly information on MD history, government, and geography. Includes links to other kid-friendly MD sites.
Special Features: Good information on State Symbols
Curriculum: Geography; Government; History; Social Studies

989 Maryland Public Libraries

www.sailor.lib.md.us/

The SAILOR system uses Internet technology to provide information and access to state information. Directories of MD information, free dial-up Internet access for MD residents, links to sites.
Special Features: SAILOR Kid's pages with homework help, online coloring books
Curriculum: Education; Government; Library Media; History; Social Studies

990 Maryland Public Television and Johns Hopkins University

www.thinkport.org/default.tp

ThinkPort is an interactive education site where MD educators, families, and community members contribute to online learning. Interactive lesson plans, online training, classroom websites, and community calendars, plus Career, Technology, Family & Community areas.
Special Features: Online Field Trips cover Historic MD, Edgar Allen Poe, Economics, more
Curriculum: Art; Biology; Business; Drama; Economics; Education; Environmental Studies; Geography; Health; History; Home Economics; Language Arts; Library Media; Math; Music; Science; Social Studies; Technology

991 Maryland Sea Grant

www.mdsg.umd.edu/CB/index.html

Extensive pages on the ecosystem and history of Chesapeake Bay. The Bay Science Gateway, Understanding the Ecosystem, Geologic History, Water & Sediments, Invasive Species, History & Culture, more.

Special Features: Online fact sheets; information on educational events, programs

Curriculum: Education; Environmental Studies; Geography; History; Science; Social Studies

992 Maryland SPCA

www.mdspca.org/

State chapter of the national animal welfare organization. Sections on pet adoption, spaying/ neutering, SPCA services, lost & found, membership, donations, plus a list of local shelters/rescues.

Special Features: Behavioral articles, and info on training classes

Curriculum: Social Studies

993 Maryland State Archives

mdslavery.net/

This special presentation, funded by the State Archives, chronicles the history of slavery in MD. Topics include Antebellum MD, the Underground Railroad, the Flight to Freedom, Stories of Flight, plus Internet resources, links.

Special Features: Interactive maps

Curriculum: History; Social Studies

994 Maryland State Arts Council

www.msac.org/

Supports the efforts of MD artists through grants, public presentations. Online Arts Resources, information on grant application, news and information about the Council and MD arts.

Special Features: MD Artists Rosters and Registry

Curriculum: Art; Dance; Drama

995 Maryland State Teacher's Association

www.mstanea.org/

Professional development organization for MD educators. Find out about issues and legislation; opportunities for professional development; educational resources and links; membership information; services.

Special Features: Q&As about the new Elementary and Secondary Education Act

Curriculum: Education

996 Maryland Writer's Association

www.marylandwriters.org/

Providing state authors with resources, promoting the art, craft, and business of writing. Membership and event info, writer's resources, member websites, annual conference.

Special Features: Pen in Hand online newsletter

Curriculum: Language Arts

997 Milton S. Eisenhower Library at JHU

levysheetmusic.mse.jhu.edu/index.html

The Lester S. Levy Collection of Sheet Music collects popular American music of 1780 to 1960. Collection is indexed and searchable.

Special Features: Full sheet music online for all public domain songs

Curriculum: History; Music

998 National Aquarium in Baltimore

www.aqua.org/

Aquarium information and tour information, plus exhibit info, news, events, make a donation. Learn more about aquarium species on website.

Special Features: Teacher and Student Opportunities

Curriculum: Education; Science

999 National Park Service

www.nps.gov/cato/index.htm

Catoctin Mountain National Park, home of Camp David. NPS website has park and visitor information, plus in-depth pages on history, geology, nature & science of the park.

Special Features: Education opportunities in the park

Curriculum: Social Studies

1000 Ocean City Life-Saving Station Museum

www.ocmuseum.org/

Historical museum showcases maritime disasters and life-saving efforts in the Chesapeake Bay area. History of the Station; history of life-saving services; Bay shipwrecks; arrange a visit.

Special Features: Local genealogical records; articles of interest

Curriculum: History

1001 Peerless Rockville

peerlessrockville.org/

Presents the historic places of Rockville, MD. Historic Places, Events & Tours, Preservation projects, more.
Special Features: The Civil War in Rockville
Curriculum: History

1002 Potomac River (Sponsor: Alice Ferguson Foundation)

fergusonfoundation.org/

Hard Bargain Farm Environmental Center educates on the history of the Potomac River and its natural environment. Kid-friendly tours and activates; includes extensive Kid's Zone website with essays, games, quizzes.
Special Features: Teacher's Resources, including online activities
Curriculum: Education; Environmental Studies; Science

1003 Rural Development Center at UM Eastern Shore

skipjack.net/

Skipjack.net collects info and links on RDC projects and enterprises, hosts project websites. Agribusiness, Business Development, History & Culture, Minority Interests, Seafood, Useful Links, Skipjack Fun.
Special Features: Accohannock Indian Tribe & Living Village; African-American Historic Sites on the Lower Shore
Curriculum: Business; Environmental Studies; History; Social Studies

1004 Star-Spangled Banner Flag House

www.flaghouse.org/index.html

Baltimore historical site dedicated to Mary Young Pickersgill and the American flag. Short history essay online, plus museum information, arranging tours, educational resources, links.
Special Features: Classroom curriculum for use with a museum tour
Curriculum: Education; History

1005 State of Maryland

www.maryland.gov/

Website for the state government features major content areas for Education, Government, Business, Travel & Recreation, Taxes, Family Health & Safety, Motor Vehicles & Transportation, Career Development, plus links to departments, services.

Special Features: State events calendar; informative kid's links
Curriculum: Business; Driver Training; Education; Government; Health

1006 University of Maryland College of Agriculture & Natural Resources

www.agnr.umd.edu/MCE/

UMCANR's Cooperative Extension division collects and connects resources on MD agriculture, ecology, industry, and culture. Extensive suite of links, articles, resources, and subcategories related to MCE.
Special Features: Maryland Center for Agro-Security; Education Resources
Curriculum: Education; Environmental Studies; Health; Science; Social Studies

1007 University of Maryland, College of Library and Information Services

oriole.umd.edu/~mddlmddl/791/frameset.html

The Maryland Immigration Digital Library collects data, records, images from 300 years of MD immigration. Online presentations include Legislation, Labor, Population, Communities, plus sources and links.
Special Features: Timeline of Eras of Immigration
Curriculum: History; Social Studies

1008 USS *Constellation* Museum

www.constellation.org/

The last all-sail warship built by the U.S. Navy, now a floating museum in Baltimore. Site features an extensive history section, as well as information about the museum, arranging tours, current news, photo gallery.
Special Features: Education opportunities for K–12; Adult Outreach education
Curriculum: History

1009 Western Maryland Public Libraries

www.whilbr.org/

WHILBR catalogs historical artifacts of western MD. Online collections include Accident, MD; Confederate Soldier's Burial.
Special Features: Cultural and historical links
Curriculum: History; Social Studies

MASSACHUSETTS

1010 Association for Gravestone Studies

www.gravestonestudies.org/

Greenfield, MA organization promotes the preservation and chronicling of historic cemetery sites. Publications, conferences & workshops, preservation materials, journal, resource links.

Special Features: Preservation Q&A
Curriculum: History; Social Studies

1011 Blue Hill Observatory and Climate Center

www.bluehill.org/

The oldest continuous weather observatory in America, located in Boston. Keeps a decade of climatologic data online, including temperature, rainfall, snowfall; plus long-term data graphs dating back 100 years.

Special Features: Weather gallery; Hands-on Weather Workshop for K–8 teachers
Curriculum: Environmental Studies; Science

1012 Boston Historical Society and Museum

www.bostonhistory.org/

Boston institution maintains extensive online history resources. Online image and manuscript archives; Boston History Research Guides; record of historical markers; education opportunities; museum info, exhibits, arrange a tour, links.

Special Features: Boston Massacre interactive learning site & detective game
Curriculum: Education; History

1013 Boston Irish Tourism Association

www.irishheritagetrail.com/

The Irish Heritage trail is a three-mile, self-guided walking tour that highlights Irish American culture in Boston. Online virtual tour contains images, text on each stop in the tour, divided into type categories.

Special Features: Interactive walking map
Curriculum: History; Social Studies

1014 Boston Regional Library System

www.massanswers.org/

Unique library service connects users with MS librarians to answer reference questions & help with research. Live, real-time chat interface, twenty-four hours a day.

Special Features: Chat logs for future reference
Curriculum: Library Media

1015 Boston Roads (Sponsor: Steve Anderson)

www.bostonroads.com/

Comprehensive look at Boston-area road system, designed for commuters and residents. Roads, including current conditions & history; bridges & river crossings; road maps & historic maps; events and links.

Special Features: Traffic & Agency Links
Curriculum: Driver Training

1016 Center for Coastal Studies

www.coastalstudies.org/

Provincetown group studies coastal marine life, ecosystem. Focus on whales, with whale info, rescue efforts; ongoing research, including Stellwagen Bay; Coastal Solutions Initiative; links.

Special Features: Education opportunities, including whale-watching
Curriculum: Environmental Studies; Science

1017 City of Boston

www.cityofboston.gov/

Civic website for MA's capital city. Content areas for Residents, Visitors, Business; plus the Mayor's office, city calendar, city council, e-services, links of interest.

Special Features: Boston Youth Zone
Curriculum: Government

1018 City of Cambridge

www.cambridgema.gov/

Civic website for the MA city, home of Harvard University. Major content areas for Living in, Working in, Visiting Cambridge, Calendar of Events, Mayor's Office, civic departments and services online.

Special Features: History of Cambridge
Curriculum: Government; History

1019 City of Springfield

www.cityofspringfieldmass.com/

Civic website for MA's significant city. Mayor's Office, Visitors, City Hall, Business & Commerce, Public Safety, Employment Services, Telephone Directory, plus city departments, services online.

Special Features: Visitor's Virtual City
Curriculum: Government

1020 Concord Lithics (Sponsor: Peter Waksman)

neara.org/lithic/

Concord Lithics is an artifact hunter's observations on MA prehistoric artifacts. Concord Geology, Conventional Archeology, Personal Archeology, Ethics of Collecting, image gallery, links.

Special Features: Sacred Sites of Concord
Curriculum: History; Social Studies

1021 COWASS North America, Inc.

www.cowasuck.org/

Website of the Cowasuck Band of Pennacook-Abenaki in MA. Extensive historical and cultural resources online, including tribal history, traditional lifestyles, Abenaki language, facts, stories & legends; plus modern tribal governance, services, issues.

Special Features: Abenaki Resources and Websites
Curriculum: Government; History; Social Studies

1022 Dennis Conservation Trust

www.savethecrowe.org/

Organization dedicated to preservation of Crowe's Pasture habitat & ecosystem on Cape Cod. About Crowe's Pasture, Rare & Endangered Species, Environmental Threats, Protection & Conservation Efforts, Current Events, Getting Involved, contact info, resource links.

Special Features: Catalog of wildlife with images, info
Curriculum: Environmental Studies; Science; Social Studies

1023 Freedom Trail Foundation

www.thefreedomtrail.org/

Organization preserves and promotes Boston's historic role in the American Revolution through tours, events, programs. Online Tour with timeline, walking map; info for Visitors, Students, Educators; field trips; event info & calendar, more.

Special Features: Sample lesson Plans; Primary Sources
Curriculum: History

1024 John Fitzgerald Kennedy Library Foundation

www.cs.umb.edu/jfklibrary/

Library and museum dedicated to the former President and MA native. Read JFK biography online, full text of speeches & press conferences, photo gallery, audio/visual archive, museum & library info, resource links, more.

Special Features: Student resources; Teacher's curriculum resources
Curriculum: Government; History

1025 Lighthouses (Sponsor: Russ Rowlett)

www.unc.edu/~rowlett/lighthouse/ma.htm

Website collects information, images, and extensive links concerning MA lighthouses. Cape Ann, Salem area, Boston Harbor, Plymouth County, Cape Cod, Nantucket, Martha's Vineyard sections.

Special Features: Info on lost lighthouses
Curriculum: History; Social Studies

1026 Massachusetts Agriculture in the Classroom

www.aginclassroom.org/

Promote awareness of agriculture and food industry to MA through classroom support. Extensive educational resources, grants info, newsletter, workshops and events, resource links.

Special Features: Available Comprehensive Agriculture Education Kit
Curriculum: Education; Environmental Studies

1027 Massachusetts Center for the Book

www.massbook.org/

Organization promotes reading, literacy, and libraries through education, programs. Learn about programs & events, including the MA Book Awards.

Special Features: Literary Map of MA
Curriculum: Education; Language Arts

1028 Massachusetts Commission on the Status of Women

www.mass.gov/women/

State commission promotes, advocates for, educates on women's issues. Calendar of Events, Hearings, Legislation, Resources, Publications, contact info.

Special Features: Links to local, regional, national commissions
Curriculum: Women's Studies

1029 Massachusetts Department of Fish and Game

www.mass.gov/dfwele/river/riv_toc.htm

MA Riverways Program promotes the restoration, protection and ecological integrity of MA waterways. List of rivers, restoration efforts, volunteering, newsletter, links.

Special Features: Complete rivers list, with local watershed programs
Curriculum: Environmental Studies

1030 Massachusetts Division of Fisheries and Wildlife

www.mass.gov/dfwele/dfw/

MassWildlife has extensive resources, links on MA fauna. Living With Wildlife; Lists & Guides to MA Wildlife; Wildlife Management; Fisheries; Hunting & Fishing; online licenses, services, links.

Special Features: Natural Heritage & Endangered Species Program
Curriculum: Environmental Studies; Science

1031 Massachusetts Foundation for the Humanities

www.mfh.org

Organization aims to promote education, understanding of MA cultural & intellectual heritage through programs, exhibits, activities. The Foundation, Grants, Resources, Special Projects, News & Events.

Special Features: State House Women's Leadership Project
Curriculum: Art; History; Language Arts; Social Studies

1032 Massachusetts Historical Society

www.masshist.org/welcome/

Society dedicated to MA history maintains several online resources, including: John Adams Family Papers; Battle of Bunker Hill exhibition; Jefferson Papers Archive; Maps of the French & Indian Wars; plus publications, resource links, more.

Special Features: Teacher's Guide; classroom course curriculums
Curriculum: History

1033 Massachusetts Municipal Association

www.mma.org/

Association of MA civic governments working to improve local, state living. Community Info, Innovations, Municipal Jobs, Municipal Events, MA Facts, Association info, contact, links.

Special Features: Comprehensive municipal listing with website links
Curriculum: Government

1034 Massachusetts Online Digital Library Initiative

www.bpl.org/modelconference/sitelist.htm

List of MA online digital archives, from the MODeL Initiative. Newton History Postcard Collection, Historic Collections and Documents from Old Sturbridge Village, Photographs from the Jones Library, Sound Archives from the Boston Public Library, more.

Special Features: Info on developing MODeL Initiative MA Archive
Curriculum: Library Media

1035 Massachusetts Reading Association

www.massreading.org/

Non-profit organization concerned with improving reading & language arts instruction in MA. Info on programs, grants, online resources for literacy.

Special Features: Teachers, Parents resources
Curriculum: Language Arts

1036 Massachusetts SPCA

www.mspca.org/

State chapter of the animal protection, care, and advocacy group. Resources for new and experienced pet owners, including adoption info, pet care, nutrition, spaying & neutering; plus animal cruelty resources, shelter info, advocacy, wildlife, links.

Special Features: Sections for Veterinarians/ Technicians
Curriculum: Social Studies

1037 Massachusetts Studies Project

www.msp.umb.edu/

Online project provides teachers with searchable databases, lessons, and texts to enhance MA-related historical and cultural curriculum. Lesson Plans & Activates, Primary Documents, themed Feature Projects, Maps, Texts, resource links.

Special Features: Students Page

Curriculum: Art; Education; History; Language Arts; Social Studies

1038 MassachusettsCivilWar.com

www.massachusettscivilwar.com/

The MA Civil War Research Center contains comprehensive info on MA soldiers, units, and regiments of the Civil War. Search database of soldiers; read brief histories of regiments, units.

Special Features: Request research

Curriculum: History

1039 MassStats.com

www.massstats.com/

Comprehensive statistical maps for many categories: Demographic, Economic, Education, Housing, Crime, Health, Political, Environmental, Transportation, General Purpose. Full color maps, map keys.

Special Features: Index; bibliography

Curriculum: Economics; Education; Environmental Studies; Government; Health; Social Studies

1040 MayflowerHistory.com

www.mayflowerhistory.com/

Historical & genealogical site chronicling the lives of the Mayflower Pilgrims. Mayflower Passengers List; Mayflower History; Full-text Primary Sources; Societies and Museums; links.

Special Features: Biographical info for each Mayflower pilgrim

Curriculum: History

1041 Museum of Fine Arts, Boston

www.mfa.org/

Museum in Boston features a significant collection of historical, contemporary art. Learn more about the MFA, take a virtual tour, browse the Online Collections Database, read about museum exhibits, become a museum member, arrange a tour, more.

Special Features: Guide to the Collections, with audio; teacher resources

Curriculum: Art; Education; History

1042 Museum of Science, Boston

www.mos.org/

Science-themed exhibits, IMAX Theatre, and learning opportunities in Boston. Website fea-tures virtual exhibits with interactive games, activities; plus museum info, arranging a class tour, links, more.

Special Features: Educator resources, workshops

Curriculum: Education; Environmental Studies; History; Science; Social Studies

1043 National Marine Sanctuaries

stellwagen.nos.noaa.gov/

Stellwagen Bank National Sanctuary studies, preserves the marine ecosystem beneath the mouth of Massachusetts Bay. About the Sanctuary, Management, Education & Outreach, Research & Monitoring, Wildlife Watching, Image Gallery.

Special Features: Online Courses; Tales From the Middle Bank essay series

Curriculum: Environmental Studies; Science

1044 National Park Service

www.nps.gov/bost/

Boston National Historic Park preserves locations, artifacts important to the fight for independence. Follow the Freedom Trail; virtual tour; maps & information; park info, arrange a visit, For Kids page.

Special Features: Educational Program opportunities

Curriculum: History

1045 Paul Revere Memorial Association

www.paulreverehouse.org/

House & museum records the legendary midnight ride of Paul Revere. Online resources include a full Revere bibliography, map of the ride, images, teacher's resources, visitors info, links.

Special Features: Just for Kids with activities, contests, links

Curriculum: History

1046 The Pilgrim Society

www.pilgrimhall.org/

Pilgrim Hall Museum educates through preserving, studying, exhibiting historical collections. Online historical essays on the Pilgrim Story, including the voyage, the Wampanoag natives, Pilgrim culture; museum info, tour of exhibits, arranging a tour, events.

Special Features: Online Curriculum Units; Learning Guides for Hall visits

Curriculum: Education; History

1047 Plimoth Plantation

www.plimoth.org/

Living history museum recreates the 17th-century lives of America's founders. Features three sites: Plimoth Village, Wanpanoag Homesite, Mayflower II recreation. Plymouth history FAQ, virtual tour, arrange a tour, volunteer.

Special Features: Educational Field Trip Guide
Curriculum: History

1048 PreservatiON MASS

www.historicmass.org/

State non-profit organization dedicated to preserving MA historic and cultural heritage. Community & Education Resources, including participation programs, newsletter; events, membership info, resource links.

Special Features: 10 Most Endangered Sites
Curriculum: History

1049 Quaboag Plantation (Sponsor: Becky Chickering)

www.college.holycross.edu/users/staff/rchicke r/quaboag/index.htm

Quaboag Plantation in central MA, now divided into five modern towns: West Brookfield, Brookfield, East Brookfield, North Brookfield, New Braintree and Warren. Plantation history, town histories, primary documents, historic maps, resources & links.

Special Features: Genealogical resources
Curriculum: History

1050 Salem Witch Trials (Sponsor: Douglas Linder)

www.law.umkc.edu/faculty/projects/ftrials/sal em/salem.htm

Extensive pages on the infamous Salem Witch Trials. Chronology/timeline, biographies of significant individuals, historical essays, primary documents, images, modern assessments, bibliography & links.

Special Features: Teacher's notes
Curriculum: History

1051 Springfield Library & Museums Association

www.quadrangle.org/

The Springfield "quadrangle" features four significant corners; Springfield art museums, Springfield Science museum, Connecticut Valley Historical Museum, Dr. Seuss National Memorial. Museums info, online content, arrange visits.

Special Features: All About Dr. Seuss; Springfield History & Timeline
Curriculum: Art; History; Language Arts; Science

1052 State of Massachusetts

www.mass.gov/

Official state website contains Resident, Visitor, Business, Public Employee major content areas; plus federal, state, local government; civic departments and online services.

Special Features: Track the Issues
Curriculum: Government

1053 Think College Early Massachusetts

www.thinkcollegeearly.org/

State-supported website promotes college planning. Advice on choosing a college; preparing for college; paying for college. Some files require Adobe Acrobat Reader.

Special Features: Teacher & counselor materials
Curriculum: Education

1054 Town of Nantucket

www.nantucket-ma.gov/

Website for the historic coastal island. Visitor Services, Getting To and Around Nantucket, Departments, Town Bylaws, Elections, Permits & Licenses, Employment, Links.

Special Features: Nantucket Historical Society
Curriculum: Government; History

1055 The Trustees of Reservations

www.thetrustees.org/index.cfm

Conservation and preservation efforts to save MA's shorelines. Find out about preserved properties, visiting guides, historic resources, natural resources, school programs info, publications, more.

Special Features: Dinosaur Footprints of Holyoke
Curriculum: Environmental Studies; History; Science

1056 University of Massachusetts

www.umassextension.org/

UMass Extension offers info, research, programs to the community. Agriculture & Landscape; Communities, Families & Youth; Natural Resources & Environmental Conservation; Nutrition Education; 4-H Programs; online services, resource links, more.

Special Features: Virtual Library (requires Adobe Acrobat Reader)

Curriculum: Environmental Studies; Health; Science; Social Studies

1057 University of Massachusetts — Amherst

www.umass.edu/tei/mwwp/

MA Water Watch Partnership connects, supports local organization monitoring water quality & condition. Learn about monitoring, start a monitoring effort, protocols, resources, MSA monitoring groups, links.

Special Features: Discussion Forum

Curriculum: Environmental Studies; Science

1058 U.S. Geological Survey

www.pubs.usgs.gov/gip/capecod/index.html

Extensive website explores the geologic history of Cape Cod. Glacial Cape Cod; Cape Cod and the Sea; Geologic Mapping; the Ultimate Cape Cod; Selected Reading.

Special Features: Color maps and images

Curriculum: Geography; Science

1059 Wampanoag Tribe of Gay Head (Aquinnah)

www.wampanoagtribe.net/

Homepage for the MA tribe associated with the Pilgrims. Tribal history & culture; current tribal structure, council, programs & services; departments online.

Special Features: Aquinnah Cultural Center

Curriculum: Government; History; Social Studies

MICHIGAN

1060 Canton Public Library

www.cantonpl.org/irs/michigan/michhist.html

Links to sites on Michigan history includes museums, photo galleries, news archives, libraries, societies, online collections. Some covered are: Alfred P. Sloan Museum, Ambassador Bridge, Detroit Almanac, Michigan in the Civil War.

Special Features: Kids Page; Teen Place

Curriculum: Art; History; Music; Science

1061 Central Michigan University Dept. of Teacher Education

miteachers.org/eddan/index.html

Michigan Teachers Online is sponsored by Central Michigan University's Department of Teacher education and Professional Development. It includes newsletters and articles to download, licensing of Michigan teachers.

Special Features: The State of Michigan Standards

Curriculum: Education

1062 Clarke Historical Library

www.lib.cmich.edu/clarke/treatyintro.htm

This web site explores the treaties that affect the people, Indian and Euro-American, who live in Michigan, and offers case studies to explain how treaties signed between 1795 and 1864 had relevance in the past and continue to have importance today.

Special Features: Link to a map of Indian reservations in Michigan today

Curriculum: History

1063 Department of Geological Services, University of Michigan

www.geo.lsa.umich.edu/

Lecture Series, Geosciences News, Field Trips, Geological Links at the University of Michigan.

Special Features: Poster-size 3.4 MB PDF color schematic illustration of the bedrock geology of Michigan with descriptive information available to download.

Curriculum: Geography

1064 The Detroit Institute of Arts

www.dia.org/

One of the largest art museums in the nation includes the General Motors Center for African

American Art. Holds events such as story telling musical presentations, artist lectures, Native American work. Offers onsite art classes, Art in the Schools, student tours, education for teachers as well as the general public. Changing exhibitions.

Special Features: Lesson Plans; Student Writings about Art

Curriculum: Art

1065 The Detroit News

info.detnews.com/history/index.cfm

Articles such as: Mackinac Island's Grand Hotel is History's Front Porch, Michigan Athletes Have Made Olympic History, The Building of the Ambassador Bridge, Michigan's Mysterious Indian Mounds, Detroit's Historic Indian Village. Michigan's Best Schools, Notable Events, Life in Michigan, Notable People.

Special Features: Search option; Index of Rearview Mirror Stories with photos

Curriculum: Language Arts; History; Social Studies

1066 Everything Michigan (Sponsor: KKZO Web Services)

www.everythingmichigan.net/

Michigan topics divided into categories of: Everything Official; Everything Outdoors; Everything Resourceful. Includes such sites as Michigan Economic Development Corporation, Michigan Morels, Michigan History Magazine, Michigan Maps, Michigan Library Links, Jobs in Michigan.

Special Features: New category, Entertainment in Michigan; Search Option

Curriculum: Library Media; Social Studies

1067 The Grand Traverse Regional Community Foundation

www.eTeach.net/home.cfm

The Foundation is formed of linked member organizations such as the Michigan Legacy Art Park, Great Lakes Children's Museum, Eco-Learning Center, Inland Seas Education Association.

Special Features: News stories such as: Everyday Ways to Protect Our Water

Curriculum: Geography; Science

1068 Great Lakes Commission

www.great-lakes.net/

Information for those who live, work or have an interest in the Great Lakes region. Topics include history, culture, geography, pollution, and careers for elementary through high school students. The modules, continually expanded and updated, include links to a glossary to help explain scientific terms and acronyms.

Special Features: Educational links to regional museums, historic sites, lighthouses, and the arts; Kid's Question of the Month

Curriculum: Counseling; Geography; Science

1069 Henry Ford Estate

www.henryfordestate.com/index.html

History of Fair Lane, a National Historic Landmark featured in several television specials located in Dearborn, Michigan, Virtual Tour, Programs, Events, Links to Related Sites.

Special Features: Lesson Plans, Oral Histories, Student Activities, Research Archives

Curriculum: History

1070 The Henry Ford Museum

www.thehenryford.org/explore/default.asp

Henry Ford Museum, Greenfield Village, Ford Rouge Factory Tour and other features. Online exhibits, information about field trips, classes, camps, scout programs. One of the nation's largest and most important collections highlighting our national heritage as well as Michigan's pioneering automotive industry.

Special Features: Teacher mailing list; MuseumQuests of web-based lesson plans

Curriculum: Art; History

1071 Historical Markers (Sponsor: James Brennan)

www.michmarkers.com/

About 1500 Michigan Historical Markers arranged by topics such as: Black History, Lighthouses, Historic Homes, Early Settlers, Events. The Michigan Registered Historic Sites can also be located by county, alphabetically, and by number, or searched by word or phrase. Includes photos, text from the marker, links to the text. The markers have been erected as part of a program begun by the Bureau of History of the Michigan Department of State.

Special Features: Map shows location.

Curriculum: History

1072 Historical Society of Michigan

www.hsmichigan.org/educator.php

A day by day look at historic events in Michigan for each month to download. Under January 1 appears seven significant events in Michigan arranged chronologically. The Historical Society of Michigan was formed in 1828.

Special Features: Annual state competition for Michigan History Day after regional competitions. Each year has a theme

Curriculum: History

1073 History of Michigan (Sponsor: Michigan State University)

www.h-net.org/~michigan/

Electronic discussion group providing a forum for historians to discuss issues related to study and teaching of Michigan history. H-MICHIGAN seeks dialogues in the discipline, publish syllabi, outlines, handouts, bibliographies, tables of contents of journals, term papers guides, listings of new sources, library catalogs and archives, reports on new software, datasets, cd-roms.

Special Features: Photographs, timelines

Curriculum: History; Library Media

1074 Isle Royale National Park (Sponsor: John William Uhler)

www.isle.royale.national-park.com/

A wilderness of 850 square miles only accessible by boat or float plane in Lake Superior. Island geological history, wilderness areas, wildflower guides, tree guides, insects and wild animals are featured and photographed.

Special Features: Junior Ranger Programs

Curriculum: Geography; Science

1075 The Library of Michigan

www.michigan.gov/hal/0,1607,7-160-17445_19270---,00.html

Sponsored by the Library of Michigan. Search the library's holdings by: Keyword, Author, Title, Author/Title, Call Number, or Subject. Includes library acronyms and terms commonly used. History of the Library of Michigan, newsletter, policies.

Special Features: Has the options, Search InMich, to search by libraries in Michigan through interactive and PDF versions, locate exhibits and events, rare Michigan books, and browse new library titles

Curriculum: Language Arts; Library Media

1076 Library of Michigan eLibrary

www.mel.org/

The Michigan eLibrary is an anywhere, anytime information gateway to selected Internet resources, full-text magazines, newspapers, electronic books online practice tests and more. Users may log on at home, work, or at your library or school. This service is funded in part by the State of Michigan and additional project support from the federal Library Services and Technology Act.

Special Features: Includes InfoTrack K12 Professional Collection and such helpful resources as eLibrary Elementary in full text

Curriculum: Counseling; Language Arts; Library Media

1077 Mackinac Bridge Authority

www.mackinacbridge.org/

The official site of the Mackinac Bridge includes: Current News and Bridge Conditions, Labor Day Bridge Walk, Frequently Asked Questions, Fare Schedule, History, Links. The Photo Gallery includes pictures of the bridge during each of the four seasons, construction of the bridge, the Michigan Ferry Service, the new Bridge View Park.

Special Features: Facts & Figures includes statistics about heights and depths, weight, concrete, cables, and related information

Curriculum: Geography; History

1078 Media Genesis

www.virtualmichigan.com/aboutvm.htm

Internet resources located in Michigan geographically by city; alphabetically by name; or by categories covering such categories as education, government, health, organizations.

Special Features: When searching by Category or Name, the City is also listed beside each resource for quick reference to geographic location

Curriculum: Education; Health; Social Studies

1079 Michigan Agricultural Experiment Station

www.maes.msu.edu/

Research on food safety, nutrition, water quality, environmental remediation, forestry, children and communities, tourism, animal health, and production agriculture is vital to the health and well-being of Michigan and its citizens. Publications such as Standards and Strategies in the Michigan Potato Industry, Analysis of Michigan Pesticide Complaints, are available in PDF or from the linked MSU Extension offices.

Special Features: Field Research Stations have field days and special events. News and articles updates
Curriculum: Environmental Studies; Health; Home Economics; Social Studies

1080 Michigan Artists

www.michigan-artists.com/

Online gallery for contemporary artists that includes resumes, examples of their work. Drawing, ceramics, mixed media, photography, sculptor, paintings, and others are featured.
Special Features: Some have links to their own websites
Curriculum: Art

1081 Michigan Association of School Boards

www.masb.org/page.cfm/6/

The mission of the Michigan Association of School Boards is to provide quality educational leadership services for all Michigan boards of education, and to advocate for student achievement and public education. Report includes: No Child Left Behind; Final Report of Michigan's Accountability Task Force.
Special Features: Legislative Alerts on current education with links on who to contact
Curriculum: Education

1082 Michigan Authors and Illustrators

mel.org/miai/miai.html

Sponsored by the Michigan Association of Media in Education, Library of Michigan, and Michigan Center for the Book. Biographical and bibliographical information on authors and illustrators who were born in, live or have lived in Michigan or have works about or settings in Michigan. This is based on three print editions of *Michigan Authors* (1960, 1980, 1993) and *Michigan Poets* (1964). Includes author photos, book covers.
Special Features: Tells whether the author or illustrator is available for school and library visits. Provides examples of the recommended citations for material from *Michigan Authors and Illustrators* using formats of the Modern Language Association, American Psychological Association
Curriculum: Art; Language Arts; Library Media

1083 Michigan Aviation Hall of Fame

www.michiganaviation.org/

Formed to honor Michigan's aviation and space pioneers by highlighting outstanding their achievements with an annual award. Biographies of enshrinees inducted since 1987 and how they are selected.
Special Features: Award winners may be searched by name or year
Curriculum: History

1084 Michigan Basin Core Research Laboratory

www.wmich.edu/geology/corelab/corelab.htm

Established in 1982 to promote research on Michigan subsurface geology, especially as it relates to petroleum exploration and development. The Core Lab is maintained as a data and geological sample repository and a basic and applied research facility.
Special Features: Links to Michigan Searchable Databases, Michigan Oil and Gas, Michigan Governmental Resources.
Curriculum: Geography

1085 Michigan Council for Maternal and Child Health

www.mcmch.com/

Provides information on maternal and child health advocacy in Michigan, alerts and bulletins on breaking issues, links and contact information for legislators, policymakers and others.
Special Features: The Archives include such articles as: Barriers to Learning; Uninsured and Newly Insured Children in Michigan
Curriculum: Health

1086 Michigan Department of Education

www.michiganepic.org/

Michigan EPIC is an educational technology project currently focused on the social sciences based on the need for Internet based resources to enrich K–12 students and teachers to obtain the new goals set by the state in Michigan *Curriculum* Framework.
Special Features: The Michigan Educator Forum is for teachers to discuss the MEAP and Michigan *Curriculum* Framework
Curriculum: History; Social Studies

1087 Michigan Economic Development Corporation

www.michigan.org/

Travel offers help from Michigan's official guide to travel and leisure; Careersite provides information about job opportunities in Michigan; Business is about locating, expanding, or starting a business in Michigan.

Special Features: Register to find a job; Michigan School Reports.

Curriculum: Business; Counseling; Social Studies

1088 Michigan Environmental Education

www.michiganenvironmentaled.org/linksmain. html

Reflects the changes in environmental issues, educational reform and national efforts to establish criteria for excellence in environmental education by the Michigan Department of Education. Links to: Environmental Organizations, State and Federal Agencies, Nature Centers, Field Trips and Traveling Naturalists, Workshops.

Special Features: Lesson Plans, Activities, Publications and Curricula Materials

Curriculum: Environmental Studies; Geography; Science

1089 The Michigan Federation of Humane Societies and Animal Advocates

http:my.voyager.net/~harriss/

The Federation is a 501 (c)3, non-profit animal advocacy organization devoted to helping individuals and organizations to help Michigan's non-human animals both domestic and wild. Includes links to: Michigan Humane Societies, Animal Rights Groups, Animal Rescue, Animal Sanctuaries, Wildlife Rehab Groups, and others.

Special Features: Current news around Michigan relating to animals. Links to state newspapers, radio stations, TV stations

Curriculum: Social Studies

1090 Michigan Government Television

www.mgtv.org/

To provide MGTV's audience with live and taped coverage of all branches of Michigan government. Educational materials target standards and benchmarks in the Michigan *Curriculum* Framework in government, history, and technology.

Special Features: How to locate local cable channels

Curriculum: Government

1091 Michigan Historical Center

www.michiganhistorymagazine.com/kids/index. html

Michigan history for kids online includes teaching materials. Activities center on teaching children about the history of Michigan.

Special Features: Covers Michigan historical events happening in the current week, Michigan state symbols to download, a collection of Michigan firsts

Curriculum: History

1092 Michigan Humane Society

www.mihumane.org/html//maintest/gbodyframe 1.htm

Helping Michigan animals in four Michigan locations including a Mobile Adoption Unit. Free Classroom Programs, Health Care & Tips, Kids Corner, Behavior Tips, Current legislation on Michigan animals, publications, volunteer stories, links of interest. The Michigan Humane Society was begun in 1877.

Special Features: School contact information for shelter tours and educational materials, classes offered, pet education center

Curriculum: Social Studies

1093 Michigan Humanities Council

www.michigan;shalloffame.org/

The Michigan Women's Historical Center, The Michigan Women's Hall of Fame, The Michigan Women's Studies Association, celebrate Michigan women. The women in the Hall of Fame may be found alphabetically by name or under categories such as Music, Politics, and if they are Contemporary of Historic, and others. The Michigan Women's Studies Association goal aims to change what is thought and taught about women's role in history, particularly Michigan women, in our public schools and at the college level.

Special Features: A Chronology of Michigan Women's History from 1702

Curriculum: History; Women's Studies

1094 The Michigan Native American Arts Initiative

www.minativearts.net/about.html

The Native American Arts Initiative (NAAI) is a project of the Michigan State University Museum and is funded by a grant from Michigan Council for the Arts and Cultural Affairs (MCACA). The project started in the fall of

2000 and has the purpose of strengthening Native American arts in Michigan. The goal is to find ways to creatively increase the sharing of information between and about artists and to strengthen opportunities for support and recognition of painting, dance, theater, writing, oratory, and music.

Special Features: Artist Gallery

Curriculum: Art

1095 Michigan Sea Grant

www.miseagrant.org/

A joint program of Michigan State University and the University of Michigan promoting greater knowledge of the Great Lakes through research and education through such projects as: Great Lakes Education Program, Great Lakes and Natural Resources Camp, Purple Loosestrife Project, Exotic Species Day Camp.

Special Features: Grants and Fellowships; Sea Grant Bookstore; Curriculum Lessons; Links

Curriculum: Geography; Science

1096 Michigan Wildlife Conservancy

www.miwildlife.org/

A nonprofit group working to restore and improve wildlife habitat provides information on: Wetlands, Streams, Urban Sprawl, Ponds, Cougars in Michigan, Bengel Wildlife Center, and related topics.

Special Features: Newsletter articles of their bi-monthly publication such as: How Consumers Choices Affect Wildlife; Kirtland's Warblers Choose Habitat Foundation Project

Curriculum: Geography; Science

1097 Michigan's Children

www.michiganschildren.org/

Michigan's Children was formed by business and philanthropic leaders, joined by labor and other community interests, recognizing the need for focused policy representation in Michigan regarding the needs of children. Features: What's Happening in the Capitol, The Children's Policy Information Center, Community Events Around Michigan, and related information.

Special Features: E-Bulletins provide weekly legislative updates on children's issues

Curriculum: Government; Social Studies

1098 Michigan Women's Foundation (MWF)

www.miwf.org/index.htm

Provides assistance and funds to nonprofit organizations serving women and girls; educates the public, policy makers and donors about the needs of women and girls; and encourages women and girls as philanthropists. One of their publications inform organizations and citizens of Michigan about the health status of women.

Special Features: Newsletters can be downloaded

Curriculum: Social Studies; Women's Studies

1099 Multimag

www.multimag.com/city/mi/

History, photos, location, information about organizations, events, for over six hundred Michigan cites and villages on the web alphabetically arranged.

Special Features: Includes county information that the city or village is located such as history, photos of county buildings, map indicating where it is located in Michigan

Curriculum: Social Studies

1100 Native American Research (Sponsor: Vicki Wilson)

hometown.aol.com/roundsky/introduction.html

Before the arrival of the first white man, Michigan was inhabited by 15,000 Indians, members of the Miami, Chippewa, Menominee, Ottawa, Potawatomi and Wyandot tribes. Federal Census, Indian Census, Church Records, Bureau of Indian Affairs, Cemeteries are some the sources included to find Native American previously living in Michigan. Links include such resources as Native Recipes, Notable Women, History of the Ottawa and Chippewa Indians of Michigan.

Special Features: Queries for Michigan (and Wisconsin) Native Americans may be posted on the board

Curriculum: History; Home Economics; Women's Studies

1101 Natural Resources Conservation Service

www.mi.nrcs.usda.gov/about/

Assistance to forest landowners for the sustainable management of private forests. Information on: Soils, Water, Air, Plants, Animals. Targeted to American Indians, Farmers, Homeowners, Michigan Teachers and Students, and others.

Special Features: Applications for students Grades 8–10 to learn about the opportunities, careers, enjoyment and importance of natural resource studies in a Protectors of the Earth Camp
Curriculum: Counseling; Science

1102 Public Section Consultants

www.michiganinbrief.org/edition06/text/appen dix/append-E.htm

Names of famous Michiganders by: Business and Philanthropy; Arts and Letters; Entertainment; Government and Public Affairs; Religion, Health, Education; Labor, and Social Causes, Science, Military, and Exploration; Sports, and Others. Some have links.
Special Features: Michigan government, Michigan's nonprofit sector, and issues like Aging, Domestic Violence
Curriculum: Language Arts; Government; Physical Education; Science; Social Studies

1103 The Rural Partners of Michigan (RPM)

www.ruralmichigan.org/resources.htm

A public/private partnership to develop new, collaborative approaches to build sustainable communities to enhance the future of Michigan citizens, finding new, innovative, non-traditional ways to address the problems.
Special Features: Links to several resources such as the Michigan Townships Association, Michigan Association of Counties, Michigan Municipal League, Michigan Center for Rural Health
Curriculum: Government; Social Studies

1104 Social Studies in the Classroom (Sponsor: University of Michigan)

www.artsofcitizenship.umich.edu/sos/edu/

The Students on Site (SOS) *Curriculum* is geared towards use in local third and fourth grade classrooms. It does not aim to replace district social studies curricula, but instead can be used as a supplemental resource for teaching about the histories of Michigan and Ann Arbor.
Special Features: The Archive is a growing collection of historical and contemporary materials such as maps, photographs, personal letters, and government records
Curriculum: Social Studies

1105 State Historic Preservation Office

michsite.state.mi.us/pictsrch.cfm

Photo and text for several historic sites arranged by groupings such as: Depots, Houses, Post Offices, Schools, Theater and Opera Houses, Ship and Shipwrecks, Military Sites, State Capitol. For example under Bridges, appeared twenty photos, mostly in color, of noteworthy Michigan bridges along with text with important aspects, dates.
Special Features: Includes School Tour
Curriculum: History

1106 State of Michigan

www.michigan.gov/

Access to the Governor, Lt. Governor, Michigan Newswire, Michigan Courts and the state of Michigan websites grouped by: Executive Branch; Agencies, Boards, Commissions; Legislative Branch, Judicial Branch, and others.
***Special Features:* Michigan Kids; Education. The Michigan Career Portal has categories for: Teachers; Students & Parents. Includes units and lessons for core *Curriculum* in Michigan schools.**
***Curriculum:* Counseling; Language Arts; Health; History; Math; Science; Social Studies**

1107 State of Michigan: Michigan Week

www.michigan.gov/hal/0,1607,7-160-17447_ 18630_22755---,00.html

Michigan Week is an annual tribute to the best of the Great Lakes State, began in 1954 as a way to promote state pride among citizens and to celebrate the rich heritage and unique features that make Michigan special. Youth Photo Contest, Awards Information, Events/Programs, Tools You Can Use may be accessed for Michigan Week.
Special Features: Who to contact for more Michigan Week information; Press Releases
Curriculum: Social Studies

1108 Technology Literacy Challenge Fund Grant Program

mtn.merit.edu/about/index.html

Michigan Teacher Network is designed for Michigan PK–12 parents, teachers, school administrators, school board trustees, librarians and media specialists, technology coordinators, students, professors, and others. Resources can be located through the Site Index or search option. Educators can search by keyword, title, author/sponsor, or resource type (such as lesson plans, primary resources, or professional periodicals).

Special Features: Allows searches for classroom resources in multiple ways, including grade level, intended use. Michigan *Curriculum* Content Standards, Michigan topics

Curriculum: Education; Library Media

1109 ThinkQuest for Tomorrow's Teachers (T3)

t3.preservice.org/T0211561/index.htm

Funded in part by a U.S. Department of Edu-

cation Preparing Tomorrow's Teachers to use Technology (PT3) Catalyst grant, T3 is a comprehensive effort, led by ThinkQuest, by universities, school districts, non-profit organizations and businesses to prepare teachers to have their students use technology to enhance learning.

Special Features: Michigan information is divided into: History; Waterways; Recreation; Facts. The grouping, Waterways in divided into: Great Lakes, Shipwrecks, and others

Curriculum: History; Social Studies; Technology

MINNESOTA

1110 Author and Conservationist Sigurd F. Olson (Sponsor: University of Wisconsin-Milwaukee)

www.uwm.edu/Dept/JMC/Olson/

This is a biographical webpage about Sigurd F. Olson, an author and one of the most influential conservationists of the twentieth century. He was an author of nine books and critical activist in preserving national parks, seashores, and wilderness areas. Although Olson was born in Illinois, he worked and lived in Minnesota and was a critical activist in preserving the Boundary Waters area.

Special Features: Photographs, biography, timeline, quotations

Curriculum: Environmental Studies; Geography; History; Language Arts; Science

1111 Boundary Waters Canoe Area Wilderness

www.bwca.cc/

The Boundary Waters is located in northeastern Minnesota. It includes approximately one million acres of wilderness and includes fifteen hundred miles of canoe routes. Site offers trip planning, information requests, maps and forums. Photo gallery, wildlife information and news releases are included.

Special Features: Searchable, weather information

Curriculum: Biology; Geography; Physical Education; Science

1112 Canoe Country.com

www.canoecountry.com/dorothy/

Dorothy Louis Molter is a legend of the Boundary Waters Canoe Area. She operated the Isle of Pines Resort for over twenty five years and was famous for her homemade root beer, flower gardens and colorful canoe paddle fences. Her death in 1986 turned her government owned resort into a museum and memorial. Over seven thousand people visit the area each year.

Special Features: Photos, biography, kid's page

Curriculum: History; Language Arts; Women's Studies

1113 Education Minnesota

www.educationminnesota.org

Education Minnesota was formed in 1998 after a merger of the Minnesota Education Association and the Minnesota Federation of Teachers. They strive to be the source of excellence in teaching in the state through democratic unionism. The legislative and political action department advocate for the educational system in the state.

Special Features: Licensure information, educational laws, suggestions and articles for parents

Curriculum: Education; Government

1114 Greater Minneapolis Convention and Visitors Association

www.minneapolis.org/index.asp

The official website of Minneapolis. Order travel books, experience different ethnic heritages or learn more about the history of Minneapolis. Since the mid 1800's the Twin Cities is home to unique neighborhoods and businesses. The banks of the Mississippi offer interests from golfing to book stores and everything in between.

Special Features: History, facts and trivia, people, tourism events

Curriculum: Business; Drama; Economics; Geography; History

1115 Hormel Foods

www.spam.com/

The SPAM Museum is in Austin, Minnesota. It opened in 2001 and is a tribute to the canned spiced ham made by Hormel. The website includes the history of SPAM, how SPAM was used in World War II, celebrities and SPAM, and a complete listing of SPAM products.

Special Features: Recipes, trivia, historical graphics, timeline of events

Curriculum: Business; History; Home Economics; Sociology

1116 Humane Society (Sponsor: Corecom)

www.ahshc.org/

The Animal Humane Society website serves the Twin Cities area. Established in 1891, the organization offers animal adoption services, therapeutic programs for the public and animal training programs. Site offers information on choosing a pet, reporting animal abuse, toll free pet hotlines and more.

Special Features: Animal photos, contact information, pet memorials

Curriculum: Biology; Psychology; Sociology

1117 International Wolf Center

www.wolf.org/

The International Wolf Center is located in Ely, Minnesota. They are dedicated to advancing the survival of wolf populations through educational programming and the conservation of the habitat of the wolf. Since 1993 the International Wolf Center has provided the public insight to the life and survival of the wolf.

Special Features: Photographs, fun facts, coloring pages, wolf history

Curriculum: Biology; Environmental Studies; Science

1118 Judy Garland Museum

www.judygarlandmuseum.com/

Judy Garland was born in Grand Rapids, Minnesota, in 1922. Although only living in there for four and a half years, the white house where she lived still stands and is home to the Judy Garland Museum. Website offers pictures and facts about the songbird and actress.

Special Features: Photos, virtual tour

Curriculum: Drama; Music; Women's Studies

1119 Lake Superior Railroad Museum

www.lsrm.org/index_2.htm

The Lake Superior Railroad Museum is located in Duluth. It is one of the largest railroad museums in the country with an historic collection of railroad artifacts and actual railroad cars, locomotives, cabooses, and equipment. Many educational programs are offered and summaries are available.

Special Features: Photos; train facts

Curriculum: History; Social Studies; Technology

1120 Laura Ingalls Wilder (Sponsor: Rebecca Lee Anne and Phil Greetham Irby)

webpages.marshall.edu/~irby1/laura.htmlx

Laura Ingalls Wilder was an American pioneer girl and author of the "Little House" books. Made famous by the television program, Laura Ingalls Wilder lived in various places throughout the Midwest and passed some of her childhood years in Minnesota. This is the official Laura Ingalls Wilder website designed to disseminate information on the life and times of the author and the places she lived.

Special Features: Biography, historical information, frequently asked questions

Curriculum: Geography; History; Language Arts; Library Media; Women's Studies

1121 Major League Baseball Advanced Media, L. P.

www.twinsbaseball.com/

The official website of the Minnesota Twins. Since 1960 the Twins have been playing baseball in Minnesota. Read over the history of the team the current roster of players, statistics and club records. Audio, video and news files are provided. Fan forum includes forum discussion, message board, newsletters, and free downloads.

Special Features: Free email accounts, free promotional contests
Curriculum: Business; Math; Physical Education

1122 Mayo Clinic

www.mayoclinic.org/rochester

The Mayo Clinic in Rochester is famous for expertise, thoroughness, team practice, professional opinions, tests and treatments all in one place. As a not for profit organization, the clinic strives to give the best care to each patient.
Special Features: Extensive health related links
Curriculum: Health; Physical Education

1123 Minneapolis Architectural History (Sponsor: James Lileks)

www.lileks.com/mpls/index.html

James Lileks is a journalist for the *Minneapolis Star Tribune* who maintains and eclectic website full of photos and tidbits of fun. This webpage is dedicated to Minneapolis architectural history. View historical skylines of the city, views of the lakes and the university. An index of the buildings is included.
Special Features: Historical Minneapolis photos
Curriculum: Art; Geography; History; Sociology

1124 Minneapolis Institute of Arts

www.artsmia.org/

Established in 1883 the Minneapolis Institute of Arts opened in 1915. It is dedicated to bringing arts and understanding of the world's diverse artistic background to the public. Exhibits include over one hundred thousand objects of which five thousand of them can be seen online. Search collection by artist, title or country.
Special Features: Online exhibits, interactive media, contact information
Curriculum: Art; History; Sociology

1125 Minnesota Board of Aging

www.mnaging.org

The Minnesota Board of Aging or MBA provides a gateway to services for seniors. The MBA listens to concerns, researches solutions and proposes governmental policies to address elderly needs. Established in 1956 the MBA today serves one out of every five Minnesotans.

Special Features: Statistics, programming information, data tables
Curriculum: Health; Math; Sociology

1126 Minnesota Canoe Association, Inc.

www.canoe-kayak.org/

Connecting paddle sport enthusiasts across Minnesota, the Minnesota Canoe Association is a great way to learn about canoeing. Read through river stories, trip reports and archives. Browse photographs or read *HUT! Magazine* the bi-monthly magazine of the association. Site offers timely information on safety, paddling and camping techniques plus conservation projects.
Special Features: Boat building plans, questions and answer section
Curriculum: Environmental Studies; Physical Education; Sports

1127 Minnesota Center for Book Arts

www.mnbookarts.org/

The mission of the center, located in Minneapolis, is to engage diverse artists and learners in finding creativity, expression, and inspiration through the book arts. It strives to preserve the traditional crafts of bookmaking. It offers an online tour of the center, online exhibits of artists, and news of upcoming visits of artists.
Special Features: Fieldtrips and workshops for students, and various classes.
Curriculum: Art; Language Arts; History

1128 Minnesota Department of Natural Resources

www.dnr.state.mn.us/index.html

The Minnesota Department of Natural Resources or MDNR is broken into four regions and includes eight divisions: ecology, forestry, trail and waterways, law enforcement, land and minerals, water, fish and wildlife, parks and recreation. Each division link contains information on the correlating subject.
Special Features: Informational brochures, hunting and fishing regulations
Curriculum: Biology; Environmental Studies; Science

1129 Minnesota Film and TV Board

www.mnfilm.org/

The Minnesota Film and TV Board was designed to develop and promote the film/video

industry in the state. Site offers guide to filming, locations, maps and weather, calendar of
events and information about the state. Fun
stuff link provides a listing of historical photos,
historical theaters, and event photos from
around the state.

Special Features: Contact information, hotline

Curriculum: Art; Business; Drama

1130 Minnesota Geological Survey, University of Minnesota

talc.geo.umn.edu/mgs/

The Minnesota Geological Survey or MGS conducts basic earth science research. Publications,
data and service activities provide the public
with geological education. The "virtual egg car-
ton" describes the major rock types commonly
found in Minnesota.

Special Features: Common Minnesota rocks,
full text articles

Curriculum: Environmental Studies; Geography; Science

1131 Minnesota Historical Society

www.mnhs.org/

The Minnesota Historical Society's mission is
to foster history awareness so the public may
learn from the past and draw strength from
what has gone before. Website offers extensive
publications, lists of museums and historic
places, preservation projects and school resources. Kids' history packet offers key facts
about the state.

Special Features: Curriculum

Curriculum: History; Social Studies

1132 Minnesota Historical Society, Minnesota Department of Transportation

www.mnhs.org/places/nationalregister/bridges/
bridges.html

Minnesota's Historic Bridges is an online exhibit featuring twenty seven historic bridges
with text and photographs. Locate the historic
places by location or type. History of the
bridges is included.

Special Features: Photos, addresses of bridges
provided

Curriculum: Driver Training; Geography;
History

1133 Minnesota Indian Community Guide (Sponsor: Rekha Inc.)

www.mnindia.us/

MNIndia.us is home to the Minnesota Eastern
India community guide. Find Eastern Indian
grocery stores, restaurants, temples and more.
Some subjects offered on the website include
India arts, associations, businesses, doctors,
grocery stores, immigration information, jewelry, politicians, restaurants and travel agents.

Special Features: Websites and links to India
related subjects, multiculturalism

Curriculum: Business; Social Studies

1134 Minnesota Links (Sponsor: Deckers)

www.deckernet.com/

Deckernet holds an extensive collection of
Minnesota related links. Arranged by category
almost anything Minnesotan is located here.
Take virtual tours; learn about Lake Superior,
towns, attractions, outdoors and events.

Special Features: Regional news, schedule of
events, school listings

Curriculum: Business; Geography; Sociology

1135 Minnesota Office of Tourism

www.exploreminnesota.com/index.cfm

The official tourism site of the state. Find out
about all the happenings and events, shopping,
state parks and more. The website offers destinations, activities, lodging, camping, photos
and golf courses. Order free brochures or sign
up for email newsletters. Toll free number is
provided for more information.

Special Features: Photographs, contests, and
multilingual option

Curriculum: Business; Geography

1136 Minnesota Orchestra

www.minnesotaorchestra.org/new_home/inde
x.cfm

Minneapolis is home to the Minnesota Orchestra. Established in 1903, the orchestra performs more than two hundred concerts per
year. Website offers interactive projects such as
virtual reality tours with the orchestra, recordings, audio clips, broad casts, and biographies
of musicians and artists.

Special Features: Orchestra history, photographic timeline,

Curriculum: Music

1137 Minnesota Ornithologists' Union, College of Biological Sciences University of Minnesota

http://biosci.cbs.umn.edu/~mou/

The Minnesota Ornithologists' Union is made up of professional and amateur bird watchers. The MOU tries to increase public interest in birding and promotes habitat preservation. Website offers extensive birding information such as bird counts, distribution maps, endangered species, birding hotspots, newsletters, and bird sighting forms.

Special Features: Birding checklists, guides and photos
Curriculum: Biology; Science

1138 Minnesota Public Radio

http://minnesota.publicradio.org/

Minnesota Public Radio or MPR has a goal to enrich minds and nourish spirits through radio and technological services. By enriching lives and perspectives by radio listening communities may be strengthened. Website offers music information, national and regional news, and special projects such as story collections.

Special Features: Programming schedule, station guide, opinion board
Curriculum: Drama; Language Arts; Music; Sociology

1139 Minnesota Sports and Entertainment

www.wild.com/

The official website of the National Hockey League team the Minnesota Wild. Find out about the team, coaches, statistics, press releases and injuries. Find the schedule or read over past game information. The fan center includes free downloads, contests, kids stuff and the Wild's anthem.

Special Features: Latest press releases, player appearances, community promotions
Curriculum: Business; Physical Education; Sports

1140 Minnesota State Arts Board

www.arts.state.mn.us/

Established in 1903 the Minnesota State Arts Board strives to give all Minnesotans an opportunity to participate in the arts. Artist directory includes performing artists, folk artists, galleries, grants and rehearsal spaces. Website offers grants, employment and volunteer opportunities, and workshop schedules.

Special Features: News, art links, contact information
Curriculum: Art; Dance; Drama; Language Arts; Music

1141 Minnesota Thunder

www.mnthunder.com/

The official website of the United Soccer League team, the Minnesota Thunder. Playing since 1994 the Minnesota Thunder website includes a team roster, statistics, schedule, history and news. Soccer camps, and volunteer information is available.

Special Features: Photographs, headlines, fan links
Curriculum: Business; Physical Education

1142 Minnesota United Snowmobilers Association

http://mnsnowmobiler.org/

Promoting, protecting and advancing the sport of snowmobiling, the MnUSA is an active organization in making snowmobiling fun in the state. Website offers trail and weather reports, safety information, a photo gallery, press releases and classified ads. The "Kids Korner" offers snowmobiling coloring pages.

Special Features: Articles, events, recent snowmobiling news
Curriculum: Physical Education; Sociology

1143 Minnesota Vikings

www.vikings.com/

The official team website of the Minnesota Vikings. The website includes any and all information about the NFL team. The team roster includes photos and a short biography of each player, injury reports, statistics, alumni of the past and employment opportunities. The game schedule is posted and news archives are available. History and audio clips are also provided.

Special Features: Fan links, frequently asked questions, cheerleader listing
Curriculum: Business; Sports

1144 Minnesota Zoo

www.mnzoo.com/

Located twenty minutes south of the Twin Cities, the Minnesota Zoo houses animals from A to Z. By using the alphabetical listing, all animals housed at the zoo have a short species description and photograph. Kids' corner includes games, environment information, dot to dots, and an art gallery.

Special Features: Schedule of events, conservation information, multi media videos and slide shows

Curriculum: Biology; Environmental Studies; Science

1145 Mississippi Headwaters Board

www.mississippiheadwaters.org/

Preserving the natural, cultural, scientific, and recreational area of the Mississippi's first four hundred miles in Minnesota. The Mississippi Headwaters Board was formed in 1980. Learn how to protect the river in your region or print maps and brochures. The oral history project preserves first person accounts of the headwaters through tape recorded interviews.

Special Features: Related links, schedule of events, contact information

Curriculum: Biology; Geography; History; Science

1146 Museum of Questionable Medical Devices

www.mtn.org/quack/welcome.htm

The Museum of Questionable Medical Devices is located in Saint Paul. The website offers photos and illustrations of quack medical devices, full text papers of useless medical value and a list of historical doctors who did more harm than good. A collection of extremely eccentric medical flops.

Special Features: Historical photos, articles, fraudulent medical cures

Curriculum: Health; Science

1147 NBA Media Ventures, LLC.

www.nba.com/timberwolves/

The official website of the Minnesota Timberwolves basketball team. Find out about the players as each has a brief biography and photo included. Follow the team schedule, read statistics, community events and fan photos. The Timberwolves dance team is also included.

Special Features: Game day information, music, schedule

Curriculum: Sports

1148 North Star, Minnesota State Government Online

www.state.mn.us/

The official website for the state of Minnesota. Website offers information on Minnesota government, business and jobs, education, social services, health and safety, natural resources, travel and leisure. Online services include vehicle registration, tax filing, child support, sex offender locator, and death certificates. Quick links are also included.

Special Features: Searchable, state facts and symbols, news and directories

Curriculum: Business; Geography; Government; Social Studies

1149 Prairie Home Companion, Minnesota Public Radio

http://prairiehome.publicradio.org/about/

A Prairie Home Companion is a radio show heard by over four million listeners every week named after a cemetery in Moorhead, Minnesota. The show hosts musical guests and plays commercials for imaginary products. Garrison Keillor is host of the program and author of many books.

Special Features: Trivia, audio clips, photos, scripts and musician information

Curriculum: Drama; Language Arts; Music; Sociology

1150 Science Museum of Minnesota

www.smm.org/

The Science Museum of Minnesota is located in Saint Paul. Permanent attractions include the human body, dinosaurs and fossils, Mississippi river, experiments hands-on gallery, science house, 3D Cinema, and the collections gallery which houses a mummy. Eight acres of indoor space and views of Mississippi are part of the museum.

Special Features: Education programs, research and collections, science activities

Curriculum: History; Science

1151 Special Education (Sponsor: George Byron Griffiths)

www.aspecialeducation.com/

"That Kid's My Light: Stories of Raising, Educating, and Loving Children with Disabilities" a photo-documentary book project by George Byron Griffiths. A webpage dedicated to three Minnesota children with disabilities and the families who take care and love them. Information about the parents, the kids and the photographer is available.

Special Features: Black and white photography, biographies
Curriculum: Special Education

1152 Special Olympics Minnesota

www.somn.org/

Special Olympics of Minnesota is a year round physical education program for peoples of mental retardation or related disabilities. By teaching values such as respect, community, choice, self-esteem, and accomplishment special athletes lives are enriched and developed.
Special Features: Information on how to become and athlete or volunteer, listing of sports offered, and list of area programs
Curriculum: Special Education

1153 Star Tribune

www.startribune.com/

The *Star Tribune* is the newspaper of the Twin Cities. Online newspaper publication offers regional and world news, classifies, business reports, opinion pages, and sports. Check the weather, recent movies, traffic and live camera shots of the cities. Variety section includes books, food, and health.
Special Features: Online comics, camping information, contests
Curriculum: Business; Language Arts; Sociology

1154 TIES

www.ties.k12.mn.us/

TIES was created in 1967 to provide Minnesota schools technology and information resources to administrators, educators and students. By offering products and services schools can use such programming as: creating school web pages, lesson plans, manage grade books, online class registration and individualized education plans (IEP).
Special Features: Publications, schedule of events, job opportunities
Curriculum: Education; Technology

1155 University of Minnesota Extension Service

www.extension.umn.edu/

Research based information on issues such as family, gardens, farming, environment, the community and home economics. Find recipes, insect control, food safety, animal science, weed control and more. Workshops, continuing education, and e-learning schedules are available. Toll free telephone number to answer questions is also listed.
Special Features: Listing of county office locations, full text brochures
Curriculum: Business; Education; Health; Home Economics; Sociology

1156 University of Minnesota Human Rights Center

www1.umn.edu/humanrts/

In 1988 the Human Rights Center was opened on the fortieth anniversary of the Universal Declaration of Human Rights. The main objective of the center is to train professionals and volunteers. There are five main programs to the center: research, educational tools, training, online resources and learning partnerships.
Special Features: Searchable site, numerous documents offered in five languages
Curriculum: Government; Psychology; Sociology

1157 Virtual North Woods

www.vnw.org/

Find out more about northern Minnesota. The Virtual North Woods website provides information on snowmobiling, maps, local artists and entertainers, recipes and more. Click on the outdoors link to find fishing, hunting, canoeing and hiking information. Snow reports are also available for America's most northerly continental state.
Special Features: Games, Spanish word of the day, maps
Curriculum: Business; Geography; Home Economics; Social Studies

1158 White Oak Society, Inc.

www.whiteoak.org/

The White Oak Society, Inc., hosts a learning center and fur trading post in Deer River. Located near the upper Mississippi in the north woods, the setting is perfect for fur trading, rendezvous and adventure. Learn about the three languages used, the uses of animals pelts, trade goods, fire arms and Native Americans.
Special Features: Newsletters, fur trade bibliography, online educational guide

Curriculum: Business; Economics; History; Social Studies

1159 Wilder Pageant Committee

www.walnutgrove.org/

Walnut Grove, Minnesota, is home to the Laura Ingalls Wilder Museum. The town also includes the Ingalls homestead, Plum Creek Park, and information on the Wilder festival and pageant. The website includes downloadable brochures illustrating the reenactments of the life and times of Laura Ingalls Wilder.
Special Features: Historical drama
Curriculum: Language Arts

MISSISSIPPI

1160 City of Gulfport

www.ci.gulfport.ms.us/

Civic website for the significant coastal town. Gulfport history, government, services, municipal courts, financial info, directory, links.
Special Features: City Pictorial
Curriculum: Government; History

1161 City of Jackson

www.city.jackson.ms.us/

Official website for the MS capitol. Content areas for Visitors, Services, Business, City Hall, City Jobs, News, Mayor's Office.
Special Features: History of Jackson
Curriculum: Business; Government; History

1162 City of Natchez

www.natchez.ms.us/

Civic website for the historic city. In addition to government, residential, business areas, visitor's guide, has extensive, informative essays on the history of the area, including the nearby Trail & Trace.
Special Features: Natchez Pre-History; Early History; Antebellum; Civil War; Postbellum
Curriculum: Government; History

1163 City of Vicksburg

www.vicksburg.org/

Civic website for MS's historically significant town. Vicksburg History, Government, Chamber of Commerce, Visitor's Center & Guides, Economics, more.
Special Features: Links, info on historic sites
Curriculum: History; Government

1164 C-R-E-A-T-E for Mississippi

www.create4ms.org/

MS teacher & student resource to help schools integrate technology into the classroom. Extensive classroom resources, including support, links for educators; professional development including video tutorials, training modules; school mentor model program.
Special Features: Online lesson plans; COSTA skills assessment
Curriculum: Education; Library Media; Technology

1165 Delta State University Library Services

http://library.deltastate.edu/aboutlib/departments/msdocsmain2.htm

Mississippi Documents section collects, organizes online resources for finding state documents, laws, statistics, info. Includes State Agencies, Research Guides, Mississippi Code, Mississippi Constitution, more. Some files require Adobe Acrobat Reader.
Special Features: State Statistics online
Curriculum: Economics; Government; Social Studies

1166 Governor's Mansion

www.mdah.state.ms.us/museum/mansion.html

MS Governor's Mansion is the second oldest continuously occupied governor's residence in the United States, also a museum. History of the mansion, by period, plus period furnishings with gallery; tour info, facility rental, FAQ.
Special Features: Floor plans
Curriculum: Architecture; History

1167 Fast Forward Mississippi

www.fastforwardms.com/

State imitative to school-to-careers initiative for K–12, college, and adult students. Major content areas for students, parents, teachers; financial aid assistance; career guides, career info, resources, links.

Special Features: Categorized by age, education level

Curriculum: Counseling; Education

1168 Faulkner on the Web (Sponsor: John B. Padgett)

www.mcsr.olemiss.edu/%7Eegjbp/faulkner/faulkner.html

Faulkner on the Web is a compendium of resources about the writer, born in MS. Lengthy biography, complete bibliography, character glossary, character genealogies, Faulkner fun, extensive links, much more.

Special Features: Teacher's resources; Faulkner screenplays and movie adaptations

Curriculum: Language Arts

1169 Information on the Mississippi Burning Case (Sponsor: Doug Linder)

www.law.umkc.edu/faculty/projects/ftrials/price&bowers/price&bowers.htm

Scholarly collection of essays, documents, links on the famous "Mississippi Burning" case, compiled and written by a University of Missouri professor. Chronology, maps, biographies, transcripts, images, more.

Special Features: Historic documents; In Quotes; resource links

Curriculum: History; Social Studies

1170 Jefferson Davis Beauvoir Home and Presidential Library

www.beauvoir.org/

Famous retirement house of the Confederate president. Online content includes history of Davis, Beauvoir, Beauvior Retirement/Widow's Home, Beauvoir Cemetery; Unknown Soldier of the Confederate States of America; virtual tour.

Special Features: Children's Page; documents for teachers, students

Curriculum: History

1171 Lower Mississippi River Conservation Center

www.lmrcc.org/

Nonprofit organization of state and federal agencies dedicated to preserving, renewing, managing the Lower Mississippi River. Ecosystem pages include socio-economic data, water data; plus group info, recreation, links.

Special Features: Short files on endangered/threatened species of the Lower Mississippi

Curriculum: Environmental Studies; Science

1172 Lynn Meadows Discovery Center

www.lmdc.org/

Gulfport, MS, center offers educational visits, programs, camps for children. Info on visiting, exhibits, attending, events, donations, links.

Special Features: Teachers can schedule visits, classroom demonstration, professional workshops

Curriculum: Art; Education; Environmental Studies; History; Science; Social Studies

1173 Marine Life Oceanarium

www.dolphinsrus.com/

Gulfport, MS, ocean life center offers oceanarium info, visitor's guide online; Tour the Oceanarium, with brief facts, statistics about each species type; view photo album and videos; Marine Life Coloring Book.

Special Features: Kid's tank pages; arrange a field trip

Curriculum: Environmental Studies; Science

1174 Mississippi Arts Commission

www.arts.state.ms.us/crossroads/

Crossroads of the Heart collects online content about MS folklife in the form of Music, Handmade Objects, Maritime Tradition, Quilting, and Narrative. Includes audio, images, essays.

Special Resources: Teacher's Resources, including curriculum guide for using Crossroads in the classroom

Curriculum: Music; Social Studies

1175 Mississippi Band of Choctaw Indians

www.choctaw.org/

MS Choctaw tribal page with extensive online resources. Major content areas for tribal history, including genealogy; cultural resources; tribal government, including education; economics, including tourism.

Special Features: Choctaw timeline; Through the Eyes of the MS Choctaw

Curriculum: History; Social Studies

1176 Mississippi Boll Weevil Management Corporation

www.bollweevil.ext.msstate.edu/

Organization provides info, resources to fight boll weevil infestation in MS. Boll weevil identification images, images of trapped pests, trapping resources, trapping efforts, organizational info, links.

Special Features: History of the Boll Weevil in the United States
Curriculum: Environmental Studies; Science

1177 Mississippi Commission on the Status of Women

www.geocities.com/mississippiwomen2002/index.html

State-supported effort to address issues, concerns of MS women, including health care, violence against women, discrimination, socioeconomic opportunities, sexual harassment, child care and support, more.

Special Features: Contact the Commission
Curriculum: Women's Studies

1178 Mississippi Department of Archives & History

www.mdah.state.ms.us/

Official department maintains state archives, libraries, museums, historic sites; oversees historic preservation programs, records management and archiving.

Special Features: Images, histories of state historic sites
Curriculum: History

1179 Mississippi Department of Education

http://marcopolo.mde.k12.ms.us/

MarcoPolo Discovers Mississippi provides Internet content for the MS classroom. Includes lesson plans, student interactive content, downloadable activity sheets, panel-reviewed websites, and additional resources.

Special Features: MS State Curricular Framework; Monthly Feature
Curriculum: Art; Dance; Drama; Education; Geography; Health; History; Language Arts; Physical Education; Science; Social Studies

1180 Mississippi Department of Information Technology Systems

www.its.state.ms.us/et/portal/MSSymbols/symbols.htm

Brief but informative page on State of MS Symbols. Covers all the officially declared symbols, with images, brief histories of the decisions.

Special Features: State song lyrics
Curriculum: Government; History; Social Studies

1181 Mississippi Forestry Commission

www.mfc.state.ms.us/

MS public service agency promoting forest protection, management, information through legislation, activism, education. Group & membership info, events, daily fire reports, links.

Special Features: Urban and Community Forestry
Curriculum: Environmental Studies

1182 Mississippi Governor's Office of Literacy

www.ihl.state.ms.us/gol/

State-supported literacy resource. Calendar of Events, Spotlight on Literacy, LEADERS Project, MS Literacy Resource Center, Other State Literacy Resource Centers, Literacy and Education Resources, Job Opportunities, Family Literacy, Adult Learners.

Special Features: LITERACY: A Mississippi Newsletter
Curriculum: Education; Language Arts

1183 Mississippi Historical Society

http://mshistory.k12.ms.us/

Mississippi History Now is an educator-oriented webzine that encourages interest in MS history. Includes searchable index of past issues.

Special Features: Lesson plans accompany each feature
Curriculum: Education; History

1184 Mississippi Land Trust

www.misslandtrust.org/

Organization dedicated to land conservation through easements, purchases, education, legislation. Info on conservation easements, federal easements, sustainable forestry, organization & membership info, applications, resource links.

Special Features: Habitats Needing Protecting informative articles
Curriculum: Environmental Studies; Science

1185 Mississippi Municipal League

www.mmlonline.com/

Economic and social partnership of MS municipal governments, for shared growth and development. Municipal directory, events, publications, legislative issues, resource links.
Special Features: Municipal employment opportunities; legislative alert
Curriculum: Economics; Government

1186 Mississippi Museum of Art

www.msmuseumart.org/

Jackson, MS, museum boasts extensive local, regional art collections, plus national exhibits. About MMA, Exhibits, Collections, Events, Visiting MMA, Education, Membership, Links.
Special Features: Arrange class tours; info on class workshops, summer camps
Curriculum: Art; Social Studies

1187 Mississippi Museum of Natural Science

www.mdwfp.com/museum/default.asp

Jackson, MS, museum promotes appreciation of MS ecosystems through research, education, exhibits. Online museum info, exhibits info, planning a visit, library info; plus searchable animal, plant databases.
Special Features: Plan a field trip, with teacher's classroom resources
Curriculum: Environmental Studies; Science

1188 Mississippi Musicians Hall of Fame

www.msmusic.org/

Museum celebrates successful Mississippi musicians and promotes interest and education about MS's music heritage. Complete list of inductees, teacher's resources, available recordings.
Special Features: Teaching Units for grades 4–9 (requires Adobe Acrobat Reader)
Curriculum: History; Music

1189 Mississippi Outfitters

www.outfitters.org/

Service group assisting outdoor sportspersons with info, guides, maps, more. Online resources include outfitter links, location maps, wildlife info, outdoor sports info.
Special Features: Facts About Mississippi's Fish And Wildlife Resources; Birds of Mississippi and the Mississippi Delta

Curriculum: Environmental Studies; Science; Sports

1190 Mississippi Public Broadcasting

www.etv.state.ms.us/educators/main.htm

MS Public Broadcasting educator's site provides information, opportunities to use broadcasts, resources, services for enhanced learning. Info on programs, teacher workshops, interactive video network, resources, School Resource Guide, links.
Special Features: Topic-oriented Teacher's Guides, including worksheets (requires Adobe Acrobat Reader)
Curriculum: Art; Economics; Education; Health; Language Arts; Math; Science; Social Studies

1191 Mississippi State Board for Community and Junior Colleges

www.colin.cc.ms.us/vcclib/

MELO, a virtual library created for MS community & junior colleges, but with many resources open to all visitors. Resources by subject area; online publications & databases; government & law links; more.
Special Features: Distance Education resources; site tutorial
Curriculum: Art; Business; Economics; Education; Health; Language Arts; Library Media; Social Studies; Technology

1192 Mississippi State University Extension Service

http://msucares.com/

MSUCares cooperative extension resources, including 4-H/Youth, Business Assistance, Crops, Food, Forestry, Leadership, Wildlife, more; plus branch offices, events, organization resources, links.
Special Features: Distance Education opportunities
Curriculum: Business; Economics; Education; Environmental Studies; Health; Science; Social Studies

1193 Mississippi Technology Alliance

www.msenergy.ms/

MS Alternative Energy Alliance promotes alternative energy development & education throughout MS. Organization info, current projects, alternative energy overviews, programs, events, links.

Special Features: Alternative Energy 101
Curriculum: Science

1194 MSGenWeb

www.rootsweb.com/~msgenweb/

MS genealogy resources online, as part of the USGenWeb project. City-Town List, County Records, MS Families on the Internet, MS History resources, archive file, resource lists & links.
Special Features: MS African-American, Native American Resource Pages
Curriculum: History; Social Studies

1195 NASA

www.ssc.nasa.gov/

John S. Stennis Space Center in southern MS offers educational programs and tours. Center info, history; pictures & video; public programs, educational resources, speaker's bureau; AstroCamp; more.
Special Features: Education Resource Center; "Ticktock Minutes" learning videos
Curriculum: Science

1196 National Agricultural Statistics Service

www.nass.usda.gov/ms/

MS agricultural statistics, compiled from state and national records. Daily MS Official Estimates, county estimates, reports, graphs, resources, links.
Special Features: Ag in the Classroom
Curriculum: Education; Environmental Studies; Social Studies

1197 National Park Service

www.nps.gov/vick/index.htm

Vicksburg National Military Park commemorates the famous MS battleground. Website provides Vicksburg history, info, visitor guide, maps, news, links.
Special Features: In-depth articles; plan an education program
Curriculum: History

1198 National Park Service Center for Cultural Resources

www.cr.nps.gov/aad/feature/feature.htm

Ancient Architects of the Mississippi explores the pre-colonial earthwork builders of the MS area. Culture, building practices, timeline, history, links.

Special Features: Links to the Past; Delta Voices
Curriculum: History; Social Studies

1199 Portal Mississippi

www.portalmississippi.com/

Portal MS provides extensive collections of resources, links to MS businesses, services, info, more. Includes State Info, Weather, Family & Children, Health & Fitness, more.
Special Features: Fully searchable
Curriculum: Social Studies

1200 State of Mississippi

www.mississippi.gov/

Official state website offers major content areas for Business, Government, Learning, Working, Visiting, Living in MS, plus links to state departments, services.
Special Features: A Treasure Chest of Educational Resources
Curriculum: Education; Government

1201 University of Mississippi, Biology Department

www.herbarium.olemiss.edu/

The Thomas M. Pullen Herbarium collects, studies, educates on MS flora. Online content includes projects in progress: Specimen Database, Rare Plants, MS Plants Checklist; plus department, collections, contact info.
Special Features: Herbaria resource links
Curriculum: Biology; Science

1202 University of Mississippi, Center for the Study of Southern Folklore

www.olemiss.edu/depts/south/index.html

The Center for the Study of Southern Folklore at UM studies, collects, preserves, and educates about regional culture. Features online Special Projects created by Center students and staff.
Special Features: Southern Foodways Alliance; Southern Culture Catalog
Curriculum: History; Social Studies

1203 University of Mississippi, English Department

www.olemiss.edu/mwp/

Internet guide to MS writers of all genres. Extensive MS writers listings, including biography, bibliography, resource links for each writer; literary history, writers resources, links.

Special Features: Region-by-region map of writers landmarks
Curriculum: Language Arts

1204 U.S. Army Corps of Engineers

www.wes.army.mil/

The Waterways Experiment Station at Vicksburg studies, plans, and executes engineering research and development studies. Station info, related organizations, library with online access for local users.
Special Features: Patriot's Grove, where historically significant trees are planted for Medal of Honor recipients
Curriculum: Science

1205 USM Center for Oral History and Cultural Heritage

www.usm.edu/crdp/

The Civil Rights Documentation Project at USM collects, catalogs primary resources on the Civil Rights Movement. Oral history transcripts, bibliography, civil rights timeline.
Special Features: Resource links
Curriculum: History; Social Studies

1206 USM Libraries

www.lib.usm.edu/~magnolia/magnolia.html

The MAGNOLIA system provides library database access for all MS libraries. Access EBSCO host, OCLC FirstSearch, Gale Products, Grolier, SIRS, Wilson Biographies. Requires a patron ID.
Special Features: Tiered access for K–12, college, public libraries
Curriculum: Education; Library Media

1207 USM McCain Library & Archive

www.lib.usm.edu/%7Espcol/crda/

Civil Rights in MS is a digital archive collecting primary, secondary historical documents. Includes oral histories, manuscripts, photographs, historical context essays.
Special Features: Civil Right in MS Timeline; A Brief History of the Civil Rights Movement in Hattiesburg
Curriculum: History; Social Studies

1208 Wildlife Mississippi

www.wildlifemiss.org/

MS fish & wildlife foundation educates on conservation, restoration of state ecosystem. Organization, publication, programs, events info; photography, screen images, resource links.
Special Features: Kids Korner with informative .PDF (requires Adobe Acrobat Reader)
Curriculum: Environmental Studies; Science

1209 Writers and Musicians (Sponsor: Starkville High School)

http://shs.starkville.k12.ms.us/mswm/MSWriters AndMusicians/

MS artisans lists, including MS writers, actors, musicians, artists. Most provide a brief biography; some include images, lists of works. Created and maintained by Starksville students.
Special Features: External links
Curriculum: Art; Drama; Language Arts; Music

MISSOURI

1210 American Kennel Club

www.akc.org/love/museum/

American Kennel Club Museum of the Dog is located in St. Louis, Missouri. It has the world's finest collection of dog art including over five hundred paintings, drawings, prints, sculptures and decorative arts. Web site also includes information on breeds, life with dogs, dog events, and clubs.
Special Features: Quotes about canines, humor, trivia about dogs, memorial to pets of the past, first aid, safety tips, nutrition
Curriculum: Art; Biology; Sociology

1211 Branson USA Online

www.branson.com/

Branson, Missouri, is the "Live Music Show Capital of the World." As a major vacation site Branson has much to offer such as shows, crafts, history, lakes, music, lodging and restaurants. There are also theme parks. In the heart of the Ozark Mountains, Branson was founded in 1903 in hopes of becoming a lumber or logging town. Today it is known for its entertainment industry.

Special Features: Extensive entertainment links, history of the area

Curriculum: Business; Dance; Drama; Economics; Music

1212 City of Kansas City

www.kcmo.org/kcmo.nsf/web/home?opendocu ment

Kansas City began as a trading post in 1821. It is now the thirty-sixth largest city in the nation and is known as the "Heart of America." It is known to have more fountains and boulevards than any other city in America. Jazz, steak and barbecue is also famous in Kansas City. Some of the famous headquarters located here include: Hallmark Cards, Russell Stover Candies, H&R Block and US Sprint.

Special Features: Employment, visitor information, businesses, neighborhoods, city council

Curriculum: Business; Economics; Geography; Social Studies

1213 City of St. Louis Community Information Network

http://stlouis.missouri.org/

St. Louis started as a French fur trading post in 1764. Populations then flourished in 1850's as German and Irish immigrants settled into the area. St Louis is now one of the largest and most popular cities of Missouri. Site offers calendar of events, press releases, community resources and sports information.

Special Features: Government, neighborhoods, housing, art, entertainment, maps

Curriculum: Business; Economics; Geography; Government

1214 Country Fish Farm, LLC

www.missourifishfarms.com/

Country Fish Farm, LLC, stocks Missouri lakes and ponds with sport and game fish. Learn about fish species and conditions in which they thrive. Download brochures and pamphlets on how many fish to stock or feeding and caring for pond fish. Read over the useful fish tips for pond vegetation and herbicide use.

Special Features: Fish species information, pond and lake control

Curriculum: Biology; Business; Science

1215 Department of Natural Resources

www.dnr.state.mo.us/

The Missouri Department of Natural Resources or DNR was created in 1974. It serves the state and it's citizens by preserving, protecting, restoring and enhancing natural, cultural and energy resources for now and future generations. Issues include air, energy, geology, land preservation, environmental problems, state parks and water information.

Special Features: Forms and permits, publications, state park information, current issues, keyword searches

Curriculum: Biology, Environmental Studies, Geography; Science

1216 Gateway Arch Riverfront

www.stlouisarch.com/

The great St. Louis Arch webpage. Plan your trip, buy your tickets on-line, and peruse the attractions surrounding the Gateway. There is much more to do than just go to the top. Watch the documentary on how the arch was built, shop, go on a riverboat cruise, or see the museum of the Westward Expansion.

Special Features: FAQ's include facts about the arch, lick on "Just for fun to take a quiz, play a game, and read fun facts

Curriculum: Architecture

1217 Governor's Office Kids Page

www.gov.state.mo.us/kids/

Easy reader kids' page. Perfect for at a glance lessons. Printer friendly option. Virtual tour of the capitol building. Fun facts about Missouri. Printable word search.

Special Features: Educator friendly, printable, reproducible fact pages, word search

Curriculum: Social Studies

1218 Harry S Truman Library & Museum

www.trumanlibrary.org/

Located in Independence, Missouri, the Harry S Truman Library and Museum houses the life, times and documents of his presidency. Look through online exhibits, the current exhibit schedule, play Truman trivia and check the program schedule for presentations on the thirty-third president.

Special Features: Online exhibits, kids' pages include student guide to Truman, fun facts, games, pictures, big events of his presidency and FAQ's

Curriculum: Government; History; Social Studies

1219 Holocaust Museum and Learning Center

www.hmlc.org

The St. Louis Holocaust and Learning Center was opened in 1995. Through exhibits, collections, and programs the center strives to educate the public about the Holocaust in hope of preventing such tragedy from happening again. A chronological look at the happenings with personal accounts of survivors, photographs, artifacts, and audio visual displays.

Special Features: Chronology, Holocaust terminology, common questions, bibliography, videography, and news

Curriculum: History; Language Arts; Psychology; Social Studies; Sociology

1220 Humane Society of Missouri

www.hsmo.org/

The Humane Society of Missouri is located in St. Louis and was founded in 1870. Today, they offer events and programs, obedience training, animal abuse information, veterinary care and pet adoption. Find information about choosing the right pet, adoption requirements and breed information. Teachers choose curriculum, classroom pets and alternatives to dissection.

Special Features: Historical photos, animal breed information, lesson plans

Curriculum: Biology; Psychology

1221 International Bowling Museum

www.bowlingmuseum.com/

As one of the largest participatory sports in the world with more than ninety-five million bowlers in over ninety countries the International Bowling Museum honors the ancient sport. Read about the history of bowling, view historical illustrations and see who is in the bowling hall of fame.

Special Features: Images from inside the museum, Hall of Fame listings, school programs and studies, history trivia,

Curriculum: Physical Education; Sports

1222 Kansas City Chiefs

www.kcchiefs.com/

Official National Football League website of the Kansas City Chiefs. Find out the latest team roster, stats, biographies, injury reports, coach information, cheerleader photos and biographies. Read through the hall of fame roster, buy tickets online and look over the schedule.

Special Features: Latest news about the team, virtual tour of Arrowhead Stadium

Curriculum: Sports

1223 Linda Hall Library of Science and Technology

www.lindahall.org/index.shtml

The Linda Hall library located in Kansas City is an independent public library housing around sixteen miles of shelving holding books of science, engineering, and technology. Site offers online exhibitions, searchable catalog, listing of databases offered at the library and educational programming.

Special Features: "Ask Linda Hall" a reference service, online exhibits

Curriculum: Library Media; Math; Science; Technology

1224 Missouri Arts Council

www.missouriartscouncil.org/

A division of the Department of Economic Development the Missouri Arts Council provides grants for stimulating growth and appreciation of the arts in Missouri. Find out where funding and grants come from, download your own applications and grant forms, check out the bulletin board for funding opportunities.

Special Features: Full text news releases

Curriculum: Art; Dance; Drama; Economics; Music; Sociology

1225 Missouri Botanical Garden

www.mobot.org/

Located in St. Louis, the Missouri Botanical Garden is an ornamental and scientific masterpiece. The gardens include many different types of landscapes to demonstrate the aesthetic and functional uses of plants. Through various displays they hope to enrich lives and emphasize the importance of plants in our lives. Also houses one of the world's finest botanical libraries founded in 1859.

Special Features: Virtual tour of gardens and collections, cultural days, butterfly house, horticulture information, searchable site

Curriculum: Art; Biology; Science

1226 Missouri Center for the Book

http://books.missouri.org/

Established in 1993 to bring books and reading into the lives of Missourians. A statewide organization that promotes the importance of books and reading, the state's literary heritage and the people that make up the literary arts such as authors, illustrators, publishers and librarians. Headquarters are in Jefferson City.

Special Features: Authors directory, literary contests, news and events, bookstores, publishers, book related links

Curriculum: History; Language Arts; Library Media

1227 Missouri Department of Agriculture

www.mda.state.mo.us/

French settlers first farmed the Missouri area around 1725. With a rich history behind it the Department of Agriculture was officially formed in 1933. Now the organization serves, promotes and protects the agricultural producers, processors and consumers of Missouri's food, fuel, and fiber products.

Special Features: Extensive links, full text articles, agricultural education, financial summary available

Curriculum: Biology; Business; Economics; Environmental Studies; Government; Science

1228 Missouri Department of Conservation

www.conservation.state.mo.us/

Dating back to 1937, the Missouri Department of Conservation has helped manage, control, restore and conserve the wild resources of the state. These resources include bird, fish, game, and forests. The MDC informs the public about the state's biodiversity through programming and creative partnerships.

Special Features: History of the department, permits, regulations, seasons and limits

Curriculum: Biology; Environmental Studies; Science

1229 Missouri Department of Economic Development

www.ded.mo.gov/

As the state's leading agency for economic, workforce and community development Missouri Department of Economic Development or MDED strives to make Missouri the best place to live, work, vacation and conduct business. Find statistics, start a business, learn more about communities, and regional areas.

Special Features: Business, communities, workers, vacation, statistics, zip code information search

Curriculum: Business; Economics; Math

1230 Missouri Department of Elementary and Secondary Education

www.dese.state.mo.us/

The Missouri Department of Elementary and Secondary Education or MDESE has a motto which states "making a positive difference through education and service." Website offers topics and resources for educators such as: school improvement, assessment, finance, certification, special education, school statistics, laws and legislation, publications and grants.

Special Features: School directory, "no child left behind" links, FAQ's

Curriculum: Education; Government

1231 Missouri Department of Health and Senior Services

www.dhss.state.mo.us/

Covering Missouri's health issues. Extensive information on numerous health issues such as: healthy living, disease, conditions, long term care, laws and regulations of health care. Site also offers fact sheets and profiles, information for seniors, community assistance programs.

Special Features: Searchable site, hot topics, full text resources

Curriculum: Health; Physical Education; Psychology

1232 Missouri Department of Transportation

www.modot.state.mo.us/

Missouri Department of Transportation or MoDOT provides the state with a safe efficient transportation system through public education, transportation partners, legislators, and local agencies. Although the DOT was not officially created until 1974, Missouri roads date back to 1735 to an unofficial road named "Three Notch Road."

Special Features: General information, funding, business, plans and projects, safety, travel services, community services, and publications

Curriculum: Driver Training

1233 Missouri Film Commission

www.stlfilm.com/

Established in 1983 the Missouri Film Commission was created to bring film, television, video and cable productions into the state. To promote the film industry within the state the commission has a network of contacts to help meet filming needs such as scouting areas, pre-production information and liaisons who work with local governmental officials.

Special Features: Production guide, press releases, weather information, incentives, permits

Curriculum: Social Studies

1234 Missouri Historical Society

www.mohistory.org/content/HomePage/
HomePage.aspx

The Missouri Historical Society hosts such programs and outreach as traveling exhibits, tours, theatrical and musical interpretations, family festivals, special events, workshops and lectures. The Missouri History Museum is located in St. Louis. Current exhibitions are listed and available for review.

Special Features: Historical photos, access to the historical library catalog

Curriculum: Art; History; Social Studies

1235 Missouri History

www.missouri-history.itgo.com/osage.html

The Osage Indians 1600–1830. A brief history of the Osage Indians in the early history of Missouri. Learn about what the Osage wore, ate and how they lived. Brief historical view of what happened to the Osage when United States was in settlement.

Special Features: Short factual article on Osage history

Curriculum: History; Social Studies

1236 Missouri Homeland Security

www.homelandsecurity.mo.gov/

After the disaster of September 11, 2001, Missouri was the first state in the nation to create an office for security that reports directly to the governor. The focus is to prevent and detect terrorist attacks specifically dealing in weapons of mass destruction. Year in review is available for reading.

Special Features: Related links, Homeland Security Newsletter

Curriculum: Government, Psychology; Social Studies

1237 Missouri Humanities Council

www.mohumanities.org/

The purpose of the Missouri Humanities Council is to build understanding within the fabric of the community through the use of history, literature, philosophy, arts, laws, religion, folklore and politics. By studying cultural forms and traditions MHC hopes to build powerful institutions such as libraries, museums, historical and civic organizations.

Special Features: History festival, grants, speakers, ethnic heritage recognition, reading programs for preschoolers

Curriculum: Art; Drama; History; Language Arts; Sociology

1238 Missouri Lewis and Clark Bicentennial Commission

www.lewisandclark.state.mo.us/home
page.asp

Lewis and Clark began the greatest military expedition in U.S. history from St. Charles, Missouri. The trip began in 1804. They kept very detailed journals and now the public can retrace their footsteps through Missouri. Use the interactive map to visit the same stops as the explorers. Look through features attractions, events, the virtual resource center, education pages, and related links.

Special Features: Extensive downloadable curriculum, kid's page

Curriculum: Environmental Studies; Geography; History; Social Studies

1239 Missouri Library Association

http://molib.org/

The Missouri Library Association strives to promote library service, the librarian profession, and the cooperation of all types of libraries and organizations dealing in library service. It was founded in 1900. Read through the MLA awards, bylaws, and news.

Special Features: Join the email discussion list, read conference materials, check the job line, related links

Curriculum: Library Media

1240 Missouri State Fair

www.mostatefair.com/

The ultimate showcase of what Missouri has to

offer. Pigs, cows, sheep, and art all judged and rated as the best in the state. It is also a great business opportunity as nearly 350,000 people attend the fair each year. Contact information available.

Special Features: Full text news releases
Curriculum: Social Studies

1241 Missouri State Government Homepage

www.state.mo.us/

The official website for the state of Missouri. Learn about living, traveling, working, business, learning, news, government and statistics in Missouri. Messages from the governor are included. Read current events, look through online services and extensive resources. Searchable format.

Special Features: Links to all governmental offices and state organizations
Curriculum: Economics; Government; Social Studies

1242 Missouri State Parks and Historic Sites, Bennett Spring State Park

www.mostateparks.com/bennett/insects.htm

Bennett Spring State Park website offers a list of insects and invertebrates most commonly found in Missouri. List offers common and scientific classification name. List includes: moths and butterflies, aquatic insects, common insects and invertebrates.

Special Features: Page also offers park information, maps, and hours of operation
Curriculum: Biology; Environmental Studies; Science

1243 Missouri Women's Council (Sponsor: Missouri Department of Economic Development)

www.womenscouncil.org/

Established in 1985, the Missouri Women's Council was created to identify and address economic and employment status of women in Missouri. The mission of the council is to provide women the information to obtain economic social and political parity. Site lists women's programs.

Special Features: Press releases, informational fact sheets, photographic scrapbook, events calendar, women's history

Curriculum: Economics; Government; Health; Women's Studies

1244 MissouriArtsAndCrafts.com

www.missouriartsandcrafts.com/

A multiuse craft resource for everyone. Look at calendars of shows and fairs, submit a crafting event of your own for free, or leave a message for other crafters. Read through the craft resources for links to magazines, organizations, and resources. The crafter's business showcase is a list of crafting categories such as candles, leather goods, nature, paintings, pottery and more.

Special Features: Free advertising and messaging for crafters, contacts available
Curriculum: Art; Business; Home Economics

1245 Negro Leagues Baseball Museum

www.nlbm.com/

Opened in 1997, the Negro League Baseball Museum is dedicated to preserving the history of African American baseball. Multimedia displays, historical photos, and artifacts from the late 1800's to the 1960's. Read through the rich history, available programming, and traveling exhibits.

Special Features: Athletics, contact information, history of the league
Curriculum: History; Sports

1246 Office of the Secretary of State, Missouri State Library

www.sos.mo.gov/library/

The Missouri State Library performs three major functions: service to the executive and legislative branches of government, service to blind and handicapped Missourians and to promote and develop library services for the state. Meet the state librarian. Many other library related links.

Special Features: News and announcements, scholarships and grants, directory of Missouri libraries, demographics, related links
Curriculum: Government; Library Media

1247 Roy Rogers

www.royrogers.com/museum-index.html

The Roy Rogers Dale Evans Museum is located in Branson, Missouri. The museum is a collection of their personal items from scrapbooks, tools, pictures and Trigger the horse rearing up on his hind legs. Find out more about the famous couple by browsing the official website.

Special Features: Historical photos, museum information

Curriculum: Music; Sociology

1248 Saint Louis Cardinals

http://stlouis.cardinals.mlb.com/NASApp/mlb/index.jsp?c_id=stl

Official site of the Major League Baseball team the Saint Louis Cardinals. Look up timeline of the team dating back to 1876, awards and honors, all-time rosters, club records. Watch videos and listen to audio recordings. Schedules, stats, promotions, and a fan forum. Kids' pages include tips from the professionals.

Special Features: Statistics and standings, radio broadcasts, ballpark pictures, searchable site

Curriculum: Sports

1249 St. Louis Walk of Fame

www.stlouiswalkoffame.org/

Founded in 1988, the St. Louis Walk of Fame strives to promote and showcase the cultural heritage of St. Louis. Brass stars and bronze plaques honor people who have made cultural contributions. Each star contains the name and brief biography. Site offers alphabetical listing, year of birth, and achievement.

Special Features: Brief biography and photo of inductee available, individualized links to each personality

Curriculum: History; Sociology

1250 Southwest Missouri State University

www.smsu.edu/folksong/maxhunter/

The Max Hunter Folk Song Collection. An archive of around 1600 Ozark Mountain folk songs from 1956 to 1976. Max Hunter was a traveling salesman who took his reel to reel recorder with him and recorded the heritage of the Ozarks by taping songs and stories. Each song is accompanied by sound byte and lyrics.

Special Features: Lyrics, some sheet music, audio files, searchable by title, singer and catalog number

Curriculum: Dance; Drama; History; Language Arts; Music; Sociology

1251 Sullivan Public Schools

http://eagles.k12.mo.us/sumner/missouri/culture.html

Mrs. Sumner is a fourth grade teacher in Sullivan, Missouri. She and her students have compiled a great deal of Missouri information. "The First Missourians" looks at the Native Americans in Missouri. Extensive Indian links and resources for the classroom.

Special Features: Look into four Missouri cultures: Paleo-Indians, Woodland Indians, Mississippi people, and the Osage

Curriculum: History; Social Studies

1252 Truman State University's Division of Language and Literature

www2.truman.edu/~adavis/mfs.html

The Missouri Folklore Society was organized in 1906. The society collects, studies and preserves folklore of all ethnic backgrounds including the following mediums: customs, institutions, beliefs, signs, legends, language, literature, musical arts, and arts and crafts throughout state.

Special Features: Traditional music, links to projects, exhibitions, and publications, contact information

Curriculum: Art; History; Language Arts; Music; Social Studies; Sociology

1253 University of Missouri-Kansas City

www.umkc.edu/orgs/kcjazz/mainpage.htm

Club Kaycee is a tribute to the golden age of Kansas City jazz. Enjoy the sights and sounds of the people of jazz. Famous names include: Count Basie, Eddie Durham, Charlie Parker and more. Each personality includes biography, photo and sound bytes. Full text articles and bibliographies included.

Special Features: Historical photos, historic hot spots, nightclubs, ballrooms and pavilions

Curriculum: Dance; Music; Sociology

1254 University of Missouri–St. Louis

www.umsl.edu/services/library/blackstudies/

African Missouri. The little known history of slaves, freedmen and women, settlers, teachers, soldiers, farmers etc. Homepage offers links to information, articles, narratives, and photos. Full text slave narratives, family history research, and partial list of lynchings are available.

Special Features: Extensive information links, full text articles, historical photos

Curriculum: History; Social Studies; Sociology

1255 USS *Missouri* Memorial Association

www.ussmissouri.com/

Launched on January 29, 1944, the USS *Missouri* or the "Mighty Mo" served in World War II and Korea before it was donated and opened as a memorial in Pearl Harbor, Hawaii. The United States accepted the unconditional surrender of the Japanese on the deck of the *Missouri.* Read about the battleship's daily routine in 1943.

Special Features: Detailed narrative timeline of the battleship, listing of dignitaries present at the surrender, Korean War diary, sea skills, photo gallery, videos, schematics, figure fuel consumption

Curriculum: History; Math; Technology

1256 VisitMO.com

www.visitmo.com/mainpage.cfm?SectionID=1&LeftNavID=0

The official Missouri tourism website. An easy to read site promoting tourism for the state. Links include: fast facts, road conditions, weather, history and culture, communities, conservation and parks, government and economy, plan your trip and publications. Quick search is available.

Special Features: Fast easy site, famous Missourians, Louis and Clark information, promotions for rural Missouri

Curriculum: Business; Economics; Geography; Social Studies; Sociology

1257 Vitalrec.com and Amazon.com

http://vitalrec.com/mo.html

Find out where and order vital records virtually. Search for birth and death certificates, marriage licenses and divorce decrees by first and last names. County by county vial record office information. Extensive searchable databases and helpful links to Missouri archives. Helpful for genealogical research.

Special Features: Searchable databases, contact information

Curriculum: History; Sociology

1258 Washington University in St. Louis

http://library.wustl.edu/vlib/dredscott/

The Dred Scott case is landmark slave hearing which lasted eleven years back in 1846. The decision declared Scott remain a slave and added to tension between states before the Civil War. The original file is located in St. Louis; this site offers eighty-five documents from the collection in JPEG and digital formats in chronological order to navigate easily through the documents.

Special Features: Digitized photos of the original documents, chronological order of documents from the famous case

Curriculum: History; Social Studies

1259 Wildlife Rescue Center

www.mowildlife.org/home.htm

The Wildlife Resource Center was founded in 1979 and is located in Ballwin, Missouri. It is dedicated to rescue, rehabilitation, and release of Missouri wildlife. The WRC has twenty-two acres to care for the more than three thousand animals per year that are brought to the center. The center offers programs for schools and the public on topics such as endangered species, earth day, bats and wild dogs.

Special Features: Animal information, wild orphans, wildlife conflicts, contact information

Curriculum: Biology; Environmental Studies; Science

MONTANA

1260 Art from Montana LLC

www.artfrommontana.com/

Art From Montana is an online collection of western art. Many art mediums are represented

such as pen and ink drawings, marble art , wood working, leather workings, and belt buckles. The website is searchable for finding specific artwork. Some artwork includes photographs, picture frames, etchings, religious based, Lewis and Clark trail maps and laser art.
Special Features: Art images and photos
Curriculum: Art

1261 Art Montana, Rattlesnake Valley Press

www.artmontana.com/

Art Montana is a website used for the purpose of promoting Montana arts. The site includes listings of artists, art centers, foundries and bronze castings, museums, galleries, art supplies, competitions and resources and links. The online directory also supplies a featured artist and includes photos of their artwork.
Special Features: Searchable site, art images and photos
Curriculum: Art; Business

1262 Big Sky Fishing.com

www.bigskyfishing.com/

Montana is known for good fly fishing. Big Sky Fishing.com is a webpage dedicated to fly fishing information and fishing gear. Choose between river, lake or mountain fishing. Site also includes travel and tourism information, links to the national parks, gear for fishing, hiking and camping or techniques and tips.
Special Features: Photo gallery and real time web cams of habitats in the state
Curriculum: Biology; Business; Environmental Studies; Geography

1263 Bitterroot National Forest (Sponsor: GORP)

http://gorp.away.com/gorp/resource/US_National_Forest/MT_BITTE.htm

The Bitterroot National Forest straddles the Idaho-Montana border. It includes one thousand six hundred miles of trails and is native ground to the Bitterroot Salish and Nez Perce Indians. The forest is over one and a half million acres in area and is considered to be one of America's most rugged wilderness areas.
Special Features: Photographs, travel information, related links
Curriculum: Biology; Environmental Studies; Geography; Social Studies

1264 Census and Economic Information Center

www.ceic.commerce.state.mt.us/

Statistics and data about the state of Montana. Economic and demographic information can be used for research, planning, decision making, economic development and for growth stimulation. Interesting quick facts include: bear facts, county, state and K–12 resources.
Special Features: Census information, American Indian data
Curriculum: Economics; Math; Sociology

1265 City of Helena, Montana

www.ci.helena.mt.us/

The city of Helena is the capitol of Montana. The official website offers city government, community affairs, parks and recreation, public health and safety, employment opportunities and animal control. City council minutes are available. Helena, Montana, is known as the "Queen of the Rockies." Related links offers more opportunities to explore the city.
Special Features: Information technology section is provided
Curriculum: Geography; Government; Social Studies

1266 Discovering Montana

www.discoveringmontana.com/

Discovering Montana is the official state website. This serves as the state's portal to governmental agencies, services and information. Learn facts about the state, plan a trip, find out more about Montana businesses, or explore educational opportunities. Information for school reports is included under the tourism and recreation link.
Special Features: Photographs, easy state facts
Curriculum: Business; Economics; Geography; Social Studies

1267 Fact and Fiction Books for All Ages

http://factandfiction.booksense.com/NASApp/store/IndexJsp

Fact and Fiction is an independent bookseller specializing in Montana regional books. By clicking on the "Local Authors and Signed Editions" link this provides a list of Montana author's websites. It is located in Missoula. Information and history about the store and Missoula are available.

Special Features: Browse booklists and bibliographies
Curriculum: Business; Language Arts; Library Media

1268 Gallatin National Forest Avalanche Center

www.mtavalanche.com/

The Gallatin National Forest Avalanche Center or GNFAC is located in Bozeman. It helps provide avalanche education, mountain weather information. Snow and avalanche articles are available. Read advisories or check out related avalanche sites though their related links.
Special Features: Photos, real-time weather reports
Curriculum: Environmental Studies; Science

1269 Holter Museum of Art

www.holtermuseum.org/

The Holter Museum of Art is located in Helena. The museum is committed to outreach and educational programming about the visual arts. National and international programs are brought into the region for viewing. Website includes exhibit schedule and educational activities.
Special Features: Related links, calendar of events
Curriculum: Art

1270 Indian Law Resource Center

www.indianlaw.org/

The Indian Law Resource Center is located in Helena. The center provides legal protection of native peoples, human rights, culture, and lands so the tribes and lands may be used in future generations. The website provides information on current topics and covers many law issues. Some of these issues include: land rights, mining information, environmental protection and self governance.
Special Features: Related links, legal papers, and employment
Curriculum: Government; Social Studies

1271 Lake County Directory

www.lakecodirect.com/

Lake County Montana is home to Glacier National Park. Lake County Directory is home to extensive information about the area, history and its Native Americans. View photographs, read over historical documents, learn more about the habitat and wildlife. Maps of the area and lake maps are also available for downloading.
Special Features: Photographs, historical documents, National Bison Range
Curriculum: Biology, Environmental Studies; Geography; History; Social Studies

1272 Montana Bureau of Mines and Geology, Montana Tech

www.mbmg.mtech.edu/

The primary source of earth science information for the state comes from the Montana Bureau of Mines and Geology formed in 1919. The MBMG develops mineral and water resources and provides technical and information services such as land reclamation after mining. Visit at the Mineral Museum site including many of the world's mineral specimens.
Special Features: Earthquake studies, environmental assessment, geologic map
Curriculum: Environmental Studies; Geography; Science

1273 Montana Center for the Book

www.montanabook.org/

The principal mission for the Montana Center for the Book is to celebrate and promote Montana literature, libraries and literacy. The site provides information on statewide literary programs and opportunities. Including the Montana Festival of the Book, Letters About Literature and One Book Montana.
Special Features: Related links, archives, contact information
Curriculum: Language Arts; Library Media

1274 Montana Festival of the Book, Montana Committee for the Humanities

www.bookfest-mt.org

The Montana Festival of the Book is an annual event occurring in September. The Festival occurs over two to three days with sessions of readings, literary panels, exhibits, performances, receptions and a literary contest. Held in Missoula, the festival attracts more than four thousand visitors. Many significant "Voices of the West" and western literature authors are featured.
Special Features: Schedule of events, archives, contact information

Curriculum: Language Arts; Library Media; Sociology

1275 Montana Fish, Wildlife and Parks

www.fwp.state.mt.us/parks/default.aspx

Montana Fish, Wildlife and Parks or FWP has much to offer. Website includes limits and regulations concerning hunting, fishing and camping. "Wild Things" link provides details on wildlife such as species of special concern, threatened and endangered species and living with wildlife. Educational opportunities include traveling trunks and programming.

Special Features: Photographs, wildlife statistics and details

Curriculum: Biology; Environmental Studies; Geography; Science

1276 Montana Forest Owners Association

www.forestsmontana.com/mtforestfacts/mtforestfacts.html

Montana has over twenty-two million acres of forestland. This is a webpage dedicated to Montana forest facts. Find statistics on land ownership, sawtimber volumes, wood harvest statistics, economy and forest types. Link to wildlife facts and history facts are also available.

Special Features: Statistics, contact information

Curriculum: Business; Economics; Environmental Studies

1277 The Montana Forum (Sponsor: Lee Enterprises)

www.montanaforum.com/

The Montana Forum is published by Montana based newspapers and deals with politics, public policy, the environment and other expansive issues of interest to the public. Discussion of the current events and issues is also welcome. Full text articles are available and the top ten interest list is also viewable.

Special Features: Top ten most read stories, frequently asked questions

Curriculum: Government; Social Studies

1278 Montana High School Association

www.mhsa.org/

The MHSA or Montana High School Association helps provide leadership and support in interscholastic activities and their coordination. Participation and sportsmanship helps promote citizenship. The website includes rules and regulations, forms, and handbooks for all high school athletics and includes speech and drama.

Special Features: News, school directory, athletic handbooks, coaches education

Curriculum: Drama; Physical Education

1279 Montana Historical Society

www.montanahistoricalsociety.com/

The Montana Historical Society was created in 1865 to preserve the past for future generations. Preservation includes Montana's Museum, historical publications, and Montana's Memory and Research Center. The Society also helps preserve historic buildings and sites.

Special Features: Online curriculum resources, student guide to the history of the state

Curriculum: History; Social Studies

1280 Montana Labor and Industry

http://dli.mt.gov/

The department that promotes the well-being of Montana's workers, employers, and citizens. It serves as an employment agency, distributes employment statistics, provides training and technical help.

Special Features: Job Service Workforce Center Directory; Subject Search

Curriculum: Counseling

1281 Montana Lewis and Clark Bicentennial Commission

www.montanalewisandclark.org/

Two hundred years after the expedition of Lewis and Clark through the United States, Montana is supporting the exploration by promoting the education of the history of the land, the native peoples, and what the famous explorers did in the state. The website is information based and supplies maps, brochures, publications, visuals and a reading list. It also includes American Indian resources and traveling exhibit information.

Special Features: Museum listing and contact information

Curriculum: Geography; History; Social Studies

1282 Montana Library Association

www.mtlib.org/

The Montana Library Association or MLA supports and promotes libraries and information science through workshops, seminars, conventions and online forums. Other programs include grants and scholarships, specialty promotions and previous conference notes and videos.

Special Features: Brochures, related links, contact information
Curriculum: Library Media

1283 Montana Library Network, Montana State Library

http://montanalibraries.org/

Montana Library Network is an online information network for patron resources, librarian resources and a Montana statewide shared catalog. Resources include references, school listings, digital maps, online magazines and newspapers. Site also offers library news, Montana authors, trivia and bibliography of Montana books.

Special Features: Statewide library catalogs, full text articles
Curriculum: Library Media; Technology

1284 Montana Living, New West Communications LLC

www.montanaliving.com/

Montana Living Magazine covers life in Montana through photographs and articles. Stories include subjects such as fine arts, business, recreation, homes and lifestyles. It is published semi monthly. The website does provide articles, photos, recipes and a peek into beautiful homes. Subscription information is available.

Special Features: Full text articles, recipes, tourism tips
Curriculum: Art; Business; Home Economics; Sociology

1285 Montana Magazine

www.montanamagazine.com/

With all that Montana has to offer it is no wonder there is a whole magazine just on the grandeur of the state. The magazine offers photography, geography, history, outdoor recreation, communities and people. It also includes current state issues, conservation, economic issues and unique businesses. A free trial subscription is offered.

Special Features: Current issue highlights, calendar of events, subscription forms

Curriculum: Environmental Studies; Geography; Social Studies

1286 Montana Pets on the Net

www.montanapets.org/

Montana Pets on the Net is an all encompassing website for the humane societies in Montana. The website strives to increase adoption of non-show quality animals. The site also offers listing of pet classes and seminars. Pet memorials and their pictures are available for perusal. A waiting list form is provided if a certain animal is desired.

Special Features: Photos, pet stories
Curriculum: Language Arts; Sociology

1287 Montana State Library

http://msl.state.mt.us/

Serving every Montana citizen, the Montana State Library provides maximum information services to the state. Services include: a talking book library, the natural resource information system, Montana library network, and services and development. Website offers news, related links, reference and governmental information.

Special Features: Searchable, contact information, online publications
Curriculum: Education; Library Media

1288 Montana State University Extension Service

http://extn.msu.montana.edu/

The Montana State University (MSU) Extension Service strives to improve the public's lives by disseminating research based information about families, communities, and agricultural interests. The Extension's website provides online information on the following subjects: agriculture, 4-H, environment, fire safety, home and family, insects and plants, nutrition, and tribal colleges.

Special Features: Full text information resources, schedule of events
Curriculum: Environmental Studies; Health; Home Economics; Women's Studies

1289 Montana State University, Museum of the Rockies

http://libmuse.msu.montana.edu/epubs/nadb/

Indian Peoples of the Northern Great Plains Online Images; this website is a searchable online photographic database. The organization format is by tribe. The collection consists mainly of photographs but does include some explanatory text and drawings or sketches. Search formats include subject, date, location, tribes, artists and biographical.

Special Features: Historical photos, Native American tribal information

Curriculum: Art; History; Social Studies

1290 Montana Territories, Internet Connect Services

www.montana.com/territories/text.html

This webpage is an online, full text, extensive collection of information about the state of Montana. Subjects include facts and basic information, commerce, education, government, recreation, news and discoveries. Links are provided for radio, television, newspapers, magazines, sports and more.

Special Features: Full text articles, searchable

Curriculum: Business; Economics; Government; Social Studies

1291 Montana Traveler

www.montana.ms/

"Montana Traveler: A Friendly Travel Guide." Montana has a lot to offer the traveler. Mountains, plains, wildlife are all available for viewing and exploring. Find museums, events and outdoor activities throughout the regions in the state. Site also includes city guides and a brief history of the state.

Special Features: City histories, travel tips, photographs

Curriculum: Business; Geography; Social Studies

1292 Montana Wilderness Bitterroot Valley National Forest information

www.bitterroot.net/usdafs/cover.html

The Bitterroot National Forest is located in west central Montana. It is part of the Northern Rocky Mountains. It is made up of over one and half million acres. The website includes safety information about the wildlife, camping, hiking, and trail etiquette. History of the Nez Perce Indians is also offered.

Special Features: Montana owl identification, mountain biking, and virtual tours

Curriculum: Biology; Environmental Studies; Geography; Health; Physical Education; Science

1293 Montanakids.com

www.montanakids.com

Montanakids.com is a webpage designed for kids. Easy to browse and full of information such as agriculture, business, activities and games, plants, animals, facts, history, special stories, things to do and see, plus Lewis and Clark information. Fun graphics make the page enticing.

Special Features: Montana quiz, special contests for kids

Curriculum: Geography; History; Social Studies

1294 Montana Web! (Sponsor: CenturyTel Web Solutions LLC)

http://search.montanaweb.com/

MontanaWeb! is an index to Montana businesses and associations. Subjects include: arts and entertainment, business and economy, computers and the net, education, environment and nature, government and politics, health and medical, news and references, real estate, science, shopping, sports and recreation, society and people, travel and tourism, and weather information.

Special Features: Searchable site

Curriculum: Social Studies

1295 MTLinks.com and Montana Capitol Restoration Foundation

www.montanacapitol.com/

This is the official website of the Montana State Capitol building. Virtual tours are offered of the artwork and of the Hall of Governors. A history of the capitol is available from the years of 1864 to 2002. Historic photos are provided. Site is searchable.

Special Features: Brief biography of each Montana governor is available

Curriculum: Geography; Government; History; Social Studies

1296 MyMontana.Com (Sponsor: FlexPortal)

www.mymontana.com/

For the latest news and event happenings anywhere in the state, check on mymontana.com. Site includes statewide news, related Montana links, Montana news sources, weather, entertainment, home and family, health and chat forums about the state.

Special Features: Searchable, events calendar, word of the day
Curriculum: Business; Economics; Sociology

1297 Myrna Loy Center for the Performing and Media Arts

www.myrnaloycenter.com/

The Myrna Loy Center is located in Helena. The center strives to promote the arts including media, performing, literary and visual for the education and enrichment of the public. Some of the performances include theater, dance, jazz, folk performance art, and cinema.
Special Features: Biography of Myrna Loy, schedule of performances, and history of the arts center
Curriculum: Art; Dance; Drama; Music; Women's Studies

1298 National Park Service

www.nps.gov/glac/home.htm

Glacier National Park is part of Waterton-Glacier International Peace Park. Established in 1932, Canada and the United States voted to share the land in an International Peace Park. Website offers camping guides, maps, schedule of events, park research, photo gallery and bookstore.
Special Features: Frequently asked questions, park history
Curriculum: Biology; Environmental Studies; Geography; Physical Education; Science

1299 Outdoor Radio Show (Sponsor: Cooper Tire, Tirerama, more)

www.montanaoutdoor.com/

Website homepage of Montana Outdoor Radio Show; specializing in hunting and fishing news. Site provides any and all information on hunting and fishing in the state. Information includes fishing conditions, wild game recipes, photo gallery, outdoor trivia and related links. Outdoor seminars and clinics listed.
Special Features: Hunting and fishing photos, calendar of events
Curriculum: Biology; Environmental Studies; Science

1300 Travel Article (Sponsor: Sundancer's West)

www.sundancerswest.com/easternmontanarivercountry.html

"Eastern Montana's River Country," by Gerry Watkins. This is an online travel article about the treasures and secret spots not often traveled by tourists. The article includes information about restaurants, historical forts, towns and sites, museums, Indian reservations and state parks. Bibliography is included.
Special Features: Photographs, full text article
Curriculum: Geography; Sociology

1301 Travel Montana

http://visitmt.com/

Travel Montana is the perfect site to begin planning a visit or view pictures of "Big Sky Country." Website offers stories, historical heritage, pictures and recipes. Games, Montana facts and trivia. The state is broken up into six travel regions to explore by using the interactive map.
Special Features: Searchable site, Lewis and Clark information
Curriculum: Economics; Geography; Home Economics; Social Studies

1302 Travel Montana, Montana Indian Nations

http://indiannations.visitmt.com/

Montana has seven Indian reservations in the state. With rich Native American heritage, culture, history, and sacred landscapes the reservations are popular tourist attractions. Find attractions, events and places to stay. Indian tribes include Blackfoot, Crow, Flathead, Assiniboine, Sioux, Gros Ventre and Chippewa.
Special Features: Detailed information on each tribe and reservation
Curriculum: Art; History; Social Studies; Sociology

1303 Vacation Montana

www.vacationmontana.com/

Vacation Montana is a website dedicated to making tourism easier. Find lodging, maps, photos, recreation and travel information. Site also offers information on golfing, fishing, boating, skiing, and snowmobiling. Visit the virtual bookstore to find out more about Montana books. Glacier National Park is also included.
Special Features: Poetry, news, and weather
Curriculum: Business; Geography; Sociology

1304 West Yellowstone News

www.westyellowstonenews.com/

Known as the "Best Little Newspaper in the West" the *West Yellowstone News* is published out of West Yellowstone, Montana. Just a few blocks away from the west entrance to the national park, the paper is published once a week and includes local news, national news, and community events. Articles about the local wildlife are often included.

Special Features: Full text articles, wildlife news

Curriculum: Business; Language Arts; Sociology

1305 Western Heritage Center

www.ywhc.org/aithp/index.php?topgroupid=&
groupid=1

The Western Heritage Center is located in Billings. It is a history museum illustrating and preserving life in the Yellowstone River region. There is seventy-two thousand miles of watershed. The American Indian Tribal Histories Project includes long term exhibits of the American Indian culture sharing their history though partnership with the tribes.

Special Features: Photographic essay book, virtual exhibits

Curriculum: Art; History; Social Studies; Sociology

1306 Wibaux Museum

www.directu.com/Museum/

Known as the "First and Finest Montana Museum" the Wibaux Museum is located in Wibaux, Montana. It includes the Pierre Wibaux house and office, the Montana centennial train car, the old Wibaux barber shop and livery stable. Includes historical timeline of events in Wibaux.

Special Features: Photos, online tour, news and message board

Curriculum: History; Social Studies; Sociology

1307 World Museum of Mining

www.miningmuseum.org/main.htm

Located on thirty three acres in Butte, the World Mining Museum is on the site of the Orphan Girl Mine. This mine operated between 1875 and 1956. The museum includes hundreds of original mining artifacts and a reproduction of a mining town. In 2002, an underground exhibit opened illustrating the steps of the mining process.

Special Features: Extensive photographs, online tours, mining history and facts

Curriculum: Business; Environmental Studies; Geography; History; Science; Technology

1308 Yellowstone Art Museum

www.artmuseum.org/

The Yellowstone Art Museum is located in Billings. As the premier museum of contemporary art in the Rocky Mountain area, it holds over three thousand objects in the collection. Many works of famous cowboy illustrators and Western artists are held in this permanent collection. A short biography of the artist Will James is available.

Special Features: Images from the permanent collection, history of the museum

Curriculum: Art; History; Sociology

1309 Yellowstone Historic Center

www.yellowstonehistoriccenter.org/

Located in West Yellowstone, the Yellowstone Historical Center is located in the old railroad buildings of the Union Pacific Railroad. The federal government of the early 1900s developed tourism to the national parks. These classic buildings are in the grand western architecture style. The museum is a showcase to the history of Yellowstone, travel to the area, and its visitors.

Special Features: Historical photographs, railroad history

Curriculum: History; Sociology; Technology

NEBRASKA

1310 ARTnetNebraska

http://artnet.nde.state.ne.us/

"ARTnet Nebraska is an online resource for general classroom teachers and art specialists, which focuses on the exploration, integration and application of the visual arts in education settings." Site offers links to Nebraska art museums, art resources and the Nebraska educational framework for visual and performing arts.

Special Features: Art lessons and unit plans, Nebraska arts and educational sites, extensive art links

Curriculum: Art; Dance; Drama

1311 Carhenge.com

www.carhenge.com/

A replication of Stonehenge, Carhenge is a memorial to the father of the artist, Jim Reinders. Thirty-eight cars are placed approximately in the same shape and size as the original Stonehenge. Family members built the memorial in 1987. It is located just north of Alliance, Nebraska. All automobiles are American made.

Special Features: Photographs, related links
Curriculum: Art; Sociology

1312 City of Valentine (Sponsor: GD Media Group)

www.heartcity.com/

Valentine, Nebraska, was named in 1883 after the Congressman, E.K. Valentine, not the holiday. This does not stop many lovebirds from sending valentines there to have them postmarked from the famous town nestled in the sandhills of Nebraska. Read the history of the city, see historical photos and explore tourist spots.

Special Features: Valentine's Day information, how to get the Valentine postmark, photo gallery

Curriculum: Geography; History; Sociology

1313 Cooper Foundation, Architectural Foundation of Nebraska

www.capitol.org/

This website contains the history of Nebraska's three Capitols. This page is dedicated to their history, construction and explanation of the ornate décor on the outside of the current building. The frequently asked question page offers many answers to touring the facility. The history of the current building references art and architecture history.

Special Features: Online virtual tour, plan a tour, photographs

Curriculum: Architecture; Government; History; Social Studies

1314 Cornhusker State Games

www.cornhuskerstategames.com/index.sp

Nebraska promotes physical fitness, personal health and well being though the event called the Cornhusker State Games. Founded in 1985, the games are a statewide amateur sports festival providing quality competition in a range of events such as: track and field, gymnastics, swimming, chess and horseshoes. The games are held annually in the third week of July.

Special Features: online registration, special events, contact information

Curriculum: Physical Education; Sports

1315 Frank H. Woods Telephone Pioneer Association

www.woodstelephonepioneers.org/museum/about.htm

Opened in 1996, the Frank H. Woods Telephone Pioneer Museum strives to educate the public about the history of the telephone industry. Frank H. Woods founded the Lincoln Telephone Company in 1903 and was the "first large automatically operated" phone company west of the Mississippi.

Special Features: Biography of Frank H. Woods, historical photos, virtual tour of museum

Curriculum: History; Sociology; Technology

1316 Friends of Crane Meadows Nature Center

www.cranemeadows.org/

Crane Meadows Nature Center is located on the Platte River near Grand Island on two hundred fifty acres of river habitat. The perfect setting for viewing wetland wildlife such as wood ducks, turtles, frogs, and of course, cranes. The mission of the nature center is to provide environmental education and natural recreation for the public.

Special Features: Trail information, schedule of events, contact information

Curriculum: Biology; Environmental Studies; Science

1317 Great Platte River Road Archway Monument

www.archway.org/

Opened in 2000, the Great Platte River Road Archway Monument is a tribute to the westward movement. The Archway spans Interstate 80 and provides educational opportunities about pioneers, the telegraph and railroad systems. Check the educational link for tours, testimonials and curriculum.

Special Features: Full text curriculum, lesson plans, fiber optic information

Curriculum: History; Social Studies; Technology

1318 History (Sponsor: Educational Service Unit Number Three)

www.esu3.k12.ne.us/nebraska/nshm.html

A collection of Nebraska State Historical Sites. This webpage is compiled for students studying Nebraska history. Sites include: Arbor Lodge, Fort Atkinson, Fort Kearney, Mormon Pioneer Cemetery, Nebraska State Capitol, Rock Creek Station and historical markers.

Special Features: Historical sites and their stories, photos

Curriculum: History; Social Studies

1319 Lester G. Larsen Tractor Test and Power Museum

http://tractormuseum.unl.edu/history.htm

After a bum deal on a tractor, a law was passed in 1919 to ensure tractor performance in Nebraska. Soon after a tractor test laboratory was created to test tractors and their performance claims. This laboratory was then turned into an historic landmark and museum in 1980.

Special Features: Historical photos, artifacts

Curriculum: History; Science; Technology

1320 Lincoln City Libraries

www.lcl.lib.ne.us/depts/hr/childrensauthors. htm

A compiled list of children and young adult authors from Nebraska. The list includes author's name and date they lived or are still living, the Nebraska location in which they resided, the genre they wrote and titles of their books. Searchable site.

Special Features: Alphabetical listing of Nebraska authors

Curriculum: Language Arts; Library Media

1321 Michael Forsberg's Photographs

www.michaelforsberg.com/news.shtml

Michael Forsberg is an award winning photographer who lives in Lincoln. His photographs have appeared in such magazines as *National Geographic*, *Audubon*, and *National Wildlife*. Forsberg is recognized for his photos of Sandhill Cranes of which half a million land in the Platte River during the spring.

Special Features: Photo Gallery, news, biography

Curriculum: Art; Biology; Environmental Studies; Science

1322 Museum of the Fur Trade

www.furtrade.org/

Most western trails were blazed by trappers and traders. The museum of the Fur Trade preserves this history in Chadron. The museum is located on the original site of the American Fur Company trading post dating back to 1837. Exhibits include trade goods, munitions, cutlery, axes, firearms and more.

Special Features: Botanical exhibit of Indian agriculture, detailed information on historical firearms, textiles, beads and silver

Curriculum: Business; Economics; History; Social Studies

1323 National Arbor Day Foundation

www.arborday.org/

The first Arbor Day occurred in April of 1872. It was estimated over one million trees were planted on that day in history. Today, the tradition of Arbor Day is kept strong by the National Arbor Day Foundation. Foundation headquarters is located in Nebraska City.

Special Features: Tree guide, tree bibliography

Curriculum: Environmental Studies; Science

1324 National Museum of Roller Skating

www.rollerskatingmuseum.com/

The National Roller Skating Museum is located in Lincoln. The museum opened in 1982 and is filled with historical artifacts, photos, memorabilia, and information all on the sport of roller skating. It hold the largest collection of historical roller skates; some dating back to 1819. The museum also includes a library holding over fifteen hundred volumes of books and periodicals.

Special Features: Extensive roller skating links, newsletters, contact information
Curriculum: Sports

1325 Nebraska Arts Council

www.nebraskaartscouncil.org/

Formed in 1974 by the legislature, NAC or Nebraska Arts Council strives to promote the arts for cultural purposes and business. The website is broken up into five categories: resources, news, about the NAC, grants and programs. News information includes stories and events for children.

Special Features: Includes artist directory
Curriculum: Art; Dance; Drama; Music

1326 Nebraska Center for Writers (Sponsor: Creighton University)

http://mockingbird.creighton.edu/NCW/

Nebraska Center for Writers is the Nebraska resource for writers of fiction, non-fiction, poetry and creative non-fiction. Find Nebraska writers, booksellers, libraries, magazines and publishers. References and resources are available. Look up agents, jobs and programs.

Special Features: Buy books on site, searchable site, contact information
Curriculum: Language Arts; Library Media

1327 Nebraska Central Telephone Company

www.nctc.net/counties/index2.html

Look at Nebraska through photos of the state countryside. Images through out the state give a better understanding of the beauty to be found in Nebraska. The photos are separated by areas such as eastern, western and central locations. Some other photo subjects include buffalo, rural mailboxes, winter and agricultural fields.

Special Features: Listing of all state symbols, trivial and aerial photos
Curriculum: Geography; Social Studies

1328 Nebraska Department of Economic Development

www.neded.com/

The Department of Economic Development or DED is dedicated to business growth. The DED offers information and resources to assist business in their success. Program services include business development, travel and tourism, rural community development, and administration and operations.

Special Features: Includes industry and business listings
Curriculum: Business; Economics

1329 Nebraska Department of Education

http://reportcard.nde.state.ne.us/

Coinciding with the No Child Left Behind System Nebraska has a report card for education accountability. This webpage addresses three levels of education: state, school district and school buildings. Family literacy development activities are included.

Special Features: School district recognition link
Curriculum: Education; Government

1330 Nebraska Department of Natural Resources

http://dnr.state.ne.us/

The Nebraska Department of Natural Resources or NDNR oversees the use and management of the states resources such as soil and water. This also includes irrigation, hydropower, rivers, lakes, ponds and reservoirs. Site offers information on such issues as surface water, ground water, planning and assistance and floodplain safety.

Special Features: Newsletters, hot topics, weather
Curriculum: Biology; Environmental Studies

1331 Nebraska Division of Travel and Tourism

www.visitnebraska.org/

The Department of Travel and Tourism promotes its state by providing an up to date website of all the events and happenings. Plan a visit, view pictures from scenic byways or request brochures. Links to online Nebraska newspapers. Site also offers information just for kids.

Special Features: Photo gallery, extensive links
Curriculum: Geography; Social Studies

1332 Nebraska Film Office

http://filmnebraska.org/welcome.htm

The Nebraska Film Office is available for film-makers to research the surroundings and beauty of Nebraska in hopes of luring productions to the state. Site provides a listing of films produced in the state, a photo gallery of film sites, information of Nebraska facts and attractions.

Special Features: Nebraska facts, famous Nebraskans, weather, crop information and permits, taxes, and laws
Curriculum: Business; Drama; Social Studies

1333 Nebraska Forest Service, University of Nebraska

www.nfs.unl.edu/

Nebraska is the home state of Arbor Day. But, back in the mid–1800s Nebraska was a natural prairie and almost devoid of trees. Today, the Nebraska Forestry Service provides information on planting, protection, care and utilization of forests and trees. Fire control is also a Forestry Service issues and addressed on this website.

Special Features: Forest pest management, listing of state programs
Curriculum: Biology; Environmental Studies; Science

1334 Nebraska Game and Parks Commission

www.ngpc.state.ne.us/

The Nebraska Game and Parks Commission are the stewards of Nebraska's fish, wildlife, parks, and recreation resources. The NGPC is made up of many divisions. Information and details on Nebraska wildlife, fishing, hunting, state parks and boating are included. A public photo gallery is available to display wildlife photos.

Special Features: Wildlife features, hunting information and guides, environmental programming
Curriculum: Biology; Environmental Studies; Science

1335 Nebraska Hall of Fame

http://info.neded.org/stathand/parttwo/hallfame.html

The Nebraska Hall of Fame is located in the state capitol building in Lincoln. The Hall of Fame was established in 1961 to recognize prominent Nebraskans. To be honored, a person must be inducted ten years or longer after their death. Only one person every two years is nominated. Some famous names included in the roster are: Willa Cather, Edward J. Flannagan, William "Buffalo Bill" Cody and J. Sterling Morton.

Special Features: Lists Medal of Honor winners and notable Nebraskans, many of the famous people include short biography or link to website of their life
Curriculum: Government; History; Language Arts; Sociology

1336 Nebraska High School Sports Hall of Fame

www.nebhalloffame.org/

The Nebraska High School Hall of Fame is located in Lincoln. It honors high school athletes and preserves the history of high school sports for future generations. Lists of inductees since 1994. Inductee criteria is listed onsite. Awards for family, great moments and inspiration are also listed.

Special Features: Each inductee has a brief sports biography and photo
Curriculum: Physical Education; Sports

1337 Nebraska Humane Society

www.nehumanesociety.org/

The Nebraska Humane Society was founded in 1875. Originally it was founded to care for animals and children. Then in the mid 1940s state run agencies took over child care. Today, the Nebraska Humane Society is located in Omaha. They offer adoption services, educational programming and community outreach.

Special Features: Photos, animal laws, newsletters
Curriculum: Social Studies; Sociology

1338 Nebraska Library Commission

www.nlc.state.ne.us/

Nebraska Library Commission sponsors extensive online resources to the Nebraska public. Search electronic full text resources, browse the electronic library or use the library directory. A good information source for teachers, librarians and educators.

Special Features: Library announcements, searchable site

Curriculum: Education; Language Arts; Library Media

1339 The Nebraska Newspaper Project (Sponsor: UNL Libraries)

www.unl.edu/nebnews/newshis.html

The Nebraska Newspaper Project is seeking every issue of every newspaper ever printed in Nebraska from territorial times to the present. The program is made possible through an alliance of five different organizations. The first Nebraska newspaper was published from Fort Atkinson and no surviving copies are available today.

Special Features: History of Nebraska newspapers, images of historic newspaper headings
Curriculum: History; Language Arts; Library Media; Social Studies

1340 Nebraska Online

www.state.ne.us/

The official website for the state of Nebraska. Find facts, capitol tour, community information, famous Nebraskans, state symbols and frequently asked questions. Site includes agricultural and natural resources, health and safety, government, visitor and community information. Searchable site with ask a librarian option. Links to related Nebraska sites.

Special Features: Newly featured Nebraska sites, tourism links, meet the governor
Curriculum: Government; Social Studies

1341 Nebraska State Historical Society

www.nebraskahistory.org/

Founded in 1878, the Nebraska State Historical Society strives to preserve and promote Nebraska history. The website can be translated into eight different languages, offers an alphabetical listing of topics, and is searchable. Extensive historical sites and facilities are also listed. Social studies lesson plans included.

Special Features: Table of contents, news and online museum store
Curriculum: History; Social Studies

1342 Nebraska State Paper

http://nebraska.statepaper.com/

The Nebraska State Paper is an online newspaper specifically and only about the state. It includes daily Nebraska headlines and governmental updates. Nebraska sporting events and

results are also included. The State Paper also takes submissions for publication. Contact the paper for submission information.

Special Features: Archives available, searchable site
Curriculum: Government; Language Arts; Social Studies

1343 Nebraska State Parks (Sponsor: iboats.com)

http://nebraska.state-park.org/

An annotated list of Nebraska state parks. Each park is summarized with activities, facilities, playgrounds, camping sites, boat use and trails. Links to boat rentals, dealers, sales and lessons. Links to each park connects to its official site.

Special Features: Listing of state parks, boating information
Curriculum: Environmental Studies; Geography; Sports

1344 Nebraska State Square and Round Dance Association

www.sqdancer.com/nebraska/

The Nebraska State Square and Round Dance Association provides the state with a schedule of dancing activities. Read over the schedule of events, find a square dance caller or locate lesson centers. Learn the ten commandments of square dancing, manners, and statistics.

Special Features: Related dancing links, list of health benefits of dancing
Curriculum: Dance; Health; Physical Education; Sociology

1345 Nebraska Statewide Arboretum, University of Nebraska

http://arboretum.unl.edu/

The Nebraska Statewide Arboretum is a living museum of trees and plants. It is not located in one area but "statewide" in a network of sites. It is used for research, enjoyment, and education. Read through the list of affiliate gardens to find locations within the state. An extensive list of wildflowers and grasses found in Nebraska is included.

Special Features: Plant information, bibliography
Curriculum: Biology; Environmental Studies; Geography; Science

1346 Nebraskastudies.org

www.nebraskastudies.org/

Find out facts and viewpoints about Nebraska history. Nine timelines range from pre–1500 to 2000. Read about people, letters, view photographs and documents. Teacher resources and lesson plans are provided. Extensive information on the Kansas-Nebraska Act and Native Americans is available.

Special Features: Full lesson plans, multicultural information

Curriculum: Education; Geography; History; Social Studies

1347 Nebraska Wildlife Federation

www.omaha.org/newf/

This is the website for the Nebraska state affiliate to the National Wildlife Federation. The NEWF protects endangered species, promotes conservation and follows public policies concerning wildlife habitats. The NEWF supports classroom education by sending out packets to classrooms across the state.

Special Features: Contact information and membership forms

Curriculum: Biology; Environmental Studies; Science

1348 Nebraska Women's Caucus for Art

http://chem-mgriep2.unl.edu/nwca/nwca.html

Supporting women committed to the visual arts, the Nebraska Women's Caucus for Art was founded in 1992. Meetings, regional exhibitions, events and activities support members and increase the visibility of their work. View images of artists work and short explanations of their mediums.

Special Features: Listing of Nebraska women artists

Curriculum: Art; Women's Studies

1349 Old-time Nebraska

www.olden-times.com/OldtimeNebraska/

Learn Nebraska history through personal testimonies, rhymes and nostalgic memories of how the way things were. Famous Nebraskans include genealogy of Buffalo Bill, speech from William Jennings Bryan, and news on notorious rustlers. Subjects include: stories, settlement information, photos, Nebraska history, reference articles and poetry.

Special Features: Full text articles, contact information

Curriculum: History; Language Arts; Social Studies

1350 Omaha Henry Doorly Zoo (Sponsor: Lozier IMAX Theater)

www.henrydoorlyzoo.com/

Dating back to 1894 the Henry Doorly Zoo in Omaha is famous for its conservation, research, recreation and education for the public. The website to the zoo is highly educational as it offers photos, website cameras and a virtual tour. IMAX information is also available.

Special Features: Summaries of zoo exhibits, visitor and contact information

Curriculum: Biology; Environmental Studies; Science

1351 Rowe Sanctuary, Audubon

www.rowesanctuary.org/

Owned by the National Audubon Society the Lillian Annette Rowe Bird Sanctuary is located in Gibbon. It includes one thousand two hundred forty-eight acres of river, wet meadows and agricultural fields. It is dedicated to the conservation of cranes and migratory birds. The sanctuary and center offer year round nature based education for the public.

Special Features: Sandhill crane information and viewing schedule, wildlife information

Curriculum: Biology; Environmental Education; Science

1352 Stuhr Museum of the Prairie Pioneer

www.stuhrmuseum.org/

Located in Grand Island, Nebraska, the Stuhr Museum of the Prairie Pioneer is a living museum that tells the story of early town building. Spanning the time period of 1840 to 1920, artifacts and information about the life and times of settlers have been collected and are now reenacted. The Stuhr Museum is a nationally known educational and cultural landmark.

Special Features: Virtual tour, photos, history of museum

Curriculum: History; Social Studies

1353 Traditional Fine Art Online, Inc.

www.tfaoi.com/aa/1aa/1aa395.htm

Museum of Nebraska Art is located in Kearney and was opened in 1993. The museum is housed in the renovated historic Kearney post office. Online essays accompany exhibitions. Contact information is available.

Special Features: Articles and essays from *Resource Library Magazine*
Curriculum: Art

1354 University of Nebraska State Museum, Division of Entomology

www-museum.unl.edu/research/entomology/

In 1969 over two million pinned, fluid preserved, papered or slide mounted insects and arachnids were moved into the University of Nebraska State Museum's Research Collection. Learn more about scarab beetles, hawk moths, and the endangered American burying beetle. Historical photos and illustrations are included.

Special Features: Entomological information, contacts
Curriculum: Biology; Science

1355 U.S. Fish and Wildlife Service

www.r6.fws.gov/ne.html

The U.S. Fish and Wildlife Service is separated into regions. Nebraska is located in the Mountain-Prairie Region. This webpage lists offices in Nebraska, wildlife refuges (there are six in the state) and wetland management areas of the state. The Federal government does grant the state yearly monies and amounts are listed onsite.

Special Features: Endangered species listing, environmental programming
Curriculum: Biology; Economics; Environmental Studies; Science

1356 Wessels Living History Farm

www.livinghistoryfarm.org/

Wessels Living History Farm is located in York, Nebraska. One hundred forty-five acres of farmland is now home to an historical farm that can be experienced by visitors as to how farming was done in the nineteen twenties and thirties. No modern amenities were available such as plumbing and electricity. Food storage did not include refrigerators to keep from spoiling nor did they all have tractors. Hear stories and see photos of how life was lived in rural Nebraska.

Special Features: Explore historic agricultural techniques in such issues as machines, crops, pests and weeds, water and making money

Curriculum: History; Home Economics; Technology

1357 Westward to Nebraska

www.westnebraska.com/index.htm

Explore western Nebraska; its wildlife, Native American history, military history, railroad history and its westward expansion trails. This website offers extensive links to area attractions. Look at the photo gallery to virtually tour the sights of western Nebraska. Travel planning and local business sites available.

Special Features: Native American historical sites
Curriculum: Business; Economics; Environmental Studies; Geography; History; Social Studies

1358 Wildlife Forever-Nebraska

www.wildlifeforever.org/nebraska.html

Wildlife Forever is dedicated to conserving and preserving wildlife habitat, facilitating conservation education and management of fish and animals. The Nebraska chapter has been active in elk restoration and fowl propagation in the state. Searchable site leads to latest news about the state.

Special Features: Wildlife education lesson plans, wildlife species information, photos included
Curriculum: Biology; Environmental Studies; Science

1359 Willa Cather Pioneer Memorial and Education Foundation

www.willacather.org/

Located in Red Cloud, Nebraska, the Willa Cather Pioneer Memorial and Education Foundation has been preserving the places of Cather's novels since 1955. The site includes many educational links about Cather and her writings. Extensive bibliographies can be found. Online e-texts and group guides are also offered.

Special Features: A short biography of Cather's life, schedule of related events, news
Curriculum: History; Language Arts; Women's Studies

NEVADA

1360 Agriculture (Sponsor: Nevada Agriculture Education)

www.nvaged.org/agedwhatweare.htm

The mission of agriculture education is to prepare and support individuals for careers, build awareness, and develop leadership for the food, fiber, and natural resource sysems. Agriculture education combines Classroom Instruction, Supervised Agricultural Experience, and the FFA organization through integral instruction. The agriculture education model is supported by both federal and state law.

Special Features: Covers agriculture science and advanced sciences, and gives students a practical approach to the theories of science and how they are used in agriculture
Curriculum: Education; Social Studies

1361 Boulder City Hoover Dam Museum

www.bcmha.org/

The Boulder City Hoover Dam Museum is ideally located just fifteen minutes from the dam and thirty minutes to Las Vegas. The museum tells the story of the men and women who braved the Nevada desert to build the dam and Boulder City. The collection offers photos, oral histories, and artifacts.

Special Features: History of the dam, genealogical information
Curriculum: Geography; History; Social Studies

1362 Central Nevada Emigrant Trails Association, Inc.

http://ourworld.compuserve.com/homepages/trailofthe49ers/

The Trail of the Forty-Niners or Emigrant Trail crossed Nevada for a difficult five hundred miles. The CNETA strives to promote the history of this trail. In twenty years over two hundred thousand people took the trail through Nevada to California. This website provides extensive information about this historical movement.

Special Features: Images, maps, lesson plans, bibliography
Curriculum: Geography; History; Social Studies

1363 City of Reno

www.cityofreno.com/

Reno was first created in 1859 when Charles Fuller created a toll bridge over the Truckee River. Making money off gold prospectors, the spot soon included a grist mill, stable, inn and more. The official city was founded in 1868; it is now home to over one hundred eighty thousand people. Website offers information on Reno business, government, and community.

Special Features: Photos, maps, news
Curriculum: Business; Geography; Government; Social Studies

1364 Department of Conservation and Natural Resources

http://dcnr.nv.gov/

The Department of Conservation and Natural Resources or DCNR is responsible for the state's natural resources. The organization is in charge of environmental protection, forestry, state lands and parks, water, environment, wild horses, and conservation. Reports and publications are available on any of these subjects.

Special Features: Site map, searchable, full text documentation
Curriculum: Environmental Studies; Science

1365 Department of Cultural Affairs, Nevada State Library and Archives

http://dmla.clan.lib.nv.us/docs/nsla/services/nevada-news.htm

This website offers a listing of Nevada newspapers, television, radio, and general news. List includes links to each station or publisher. Find regional information and news. Also offered are library information and "Ask a Librarian" option.

Special Features: Headline national news, searchable, extensive news links
Curriculum: Language Arts; Library Media; Sociology

1366 Department of Energy, Nevada Office

www.nv.doe.gov/news&pubs/photos&films/photolib.htm

The Department of Energy Nevada is host to a photo library of images taken onsite in Nevada. Some of the photo subjects include: general interest, nuclear test preparation, craters, drilling, underwater, waste management, atmospheric views, wildlife and artifacts.

Special Features: Thumbnail photos and description, contact information

Curriculum: Environmental Studies; Government; Science

1367 Desert Research Institute, University and Community College System of Nevada

www.dri.edu

The DRI was created in 1959 when a small group of scientists combined academics and research to promote management and understanding of the arid land in Nevada. Today every continent in the world is studied by the institute and global scale studies are conducted to solve scientific questions.

Special Features: Publications, K–12 programming, events

Curriculum: Environmental Studies; Geography; Science

1368 Division of Museums and History, Nevada Historical Society

http://dmla.clan.lib.nv.us/docs/museums/reno/his-soc.htm

The Nevada Historical Society was founded in 1904. Along with the state's oldest museum the society also maintains a library. The website offers a listing of the permanent exhibits, virtual exhibits, publications, and Nevada history. A listing of Nevada museums is provided and a listing of Nevada high school yearbooks.

Special Features: Photos, publications, schedule of events

Curriculum: History; Social Studies

1369 Eureka County Yucca Mountain Information Office

www.yuccamountain.org/

Yucca Mountain is the site of the national nuclear waste repository. Beginning in 2010 the first nuclear waste is scheduled to be delivered to Nevada. This website is designed to keep the public notified of the status and progress of the nuclear waste repository. Website offers timeline, frequently asked questions, photos, maps, documents and more.

Special Features: International nuclear waste program details, newsletters

Curriculum: Environmental Studies; Government; Science; Technology

1370 FieldnotesWest.com

http://fieldnoteswest.com/hal.html

Hal Cannon is a western folk life author, radio and television producer, and musician. Having spent time in Elko, Cannon is a famous for his National Public Radio show and founding director of the Western Folklife Center in Elko.

Special Features: Short biography, photos

Curriculum: Language Arts; Library Media; Music

1371 Friends of Nevada Wilderness

www.nevadawilderness.org/

The education and advocacy group Friends of Nevada Wilderness strives to keep the state's wilderness areas wild. The website is divided into regions of the state and provides information such as plant life, Mojave Desert ecology, wildlife and elevation information.

Special Features: Photos, maps, extensive regional information

Curriculum: Biology; Environmental Studies; Geography; Science

1372 A History of Native Nevadans through Photography (Sponsor: State of Nevada Department of Cultural Affairs)

http://dmla.clan.lib.nv.us/docs/museums/reno/expeople/people.htm

"A History of Native Nevadans through Photography." This is an online exhibit of fifty-four photographs of Native Americans in Nevada. The photographs are indexed and an explanation of the photographic processes is included. A map of Native Nevadans is also offered.

Special Features: Historical photos

Curriculum: Art; History; Library Media; Social Studies

1373 Geological Society of Nevada

www.gsnv.org/

The Geological Society of Nevada strives to promote geological sciences in the state. Presentations, field trips, symposiums, publications, grants and scholarships help disseminate the information and knowledge of the society. The website offers newsletters and publications.

Special Features: Schedule of events, school field trip information

Curriculum: Environmental Studies; Geography; Science

1374 Ghost Towns (Sponsor: Shawn Hall)

http://nvghosttowns.topcities.com/

This website is home to "Shawn Hall's Nevada Ghost Towns." Site is organized into county and then alphabetical by town name and includes a brief history with photos. There are over seventeen-hundred photos. Ghost town visitation etiquette is also offered. Booklist included.

Special Features: Interactive county site, ghost town chat room

Curriculum: Geography; History; Social Studies

1375 Guinness World Records Museum

www.guinnessmuseum.com/

The Guinness Book of World Records began in 1951. Sir Hugh Beaver decided to create a book containing factual information of the world's greatest statistics and accomplishments. The book has been published every year since 1955. The Museum of World Records is located in Las Vegas. The website contains historical information and photos of the museum.

Special Features: Photos, exhibit information

Curriculum: Sociology

1376 Inter-Tribal Council of Nevada

http://itcn.org1377)/

The Inter-Tribal Council of Nevada or ITCN is the political body for all twenty six tribes. ITCN promotes health, education, social, economic and employment programs. The Paiute language is included with audio files and phrases. Services such as aging, abuse and women and children programming is offered.

Special Features: Individual tribe information, program listing

Curriculum: Government; Social Studies

1378 Las Vegas Convention and Visitors Authority

www.vegasfreedom.com

Las Vegas is known as the "Neon Capital of the World." This is the tourism website for the oasis in the desert. Website offers a free visitor's guide, Vegas stories, shopping, shows, gaming facts, photos, facts and more. Interactive clickable website is easy to navigate and explore for Las Vegas information.

Special Features: Historical facts, photos, tourism book

Curriculum: Business; History; Sociology

1379 Liberace Museum

www.liberace.org/

The Liberace Museum is located in Las Vegas. The famous piano player was known for his candelabra and flamboyant dazzle. Being of Polish decent his real name was Wladziu Valentino Liberace and was born in Wisconsin. The museum includes his collection of rare antique pianos, cars, flashy costume wardrobe, stage jewelry and memorabilia.

Special Features: Photos, virtual tour, scholarship information

Curriculum: Music; Sociology

1380 Library of Congress

http://memory.loc.gov/ammem/ncrhtml/

"Buckaroos in Paradise: Ranching Culture in Northern Nevada, 1945–1982." The Library of Congress created a virtual documentary on ranch life in Northern Nevada. The collection includes over twenty four thousand photos, video clips, and audio files. Information on haying, irrigation, branding is included.

Special Features: Bibliography, glossary, classroom related publications

Curriculum: History; Social Studies

1381 National Park Service

www.cr.nps.gov/nr/travel/nevada/intro.htm

Three Historic Nevada Cities: Carson City, Reno, and Virginia City. These three cities were established after the Comstock Load in 1859. They are located along the Sierra Nevada Mountains. The National Park Service offers itineraries of the cities to see fifty seven historic places. Website offers historical information on each of the fifty seven sites and the people who made them great.

Special Features: Extensive historical information and links

Curriculum: Geography; History; Social Studies

1382 Native Nevada Classroom

www.unr.edu/nnap/

Designed for kindergarten through sixth grade teachers, this website offers lesson plans on the Indian culture, environment, and history. The Great Basin tribes of Washoe, Paiute and Shoshone are covered. The lesson plans are available for all classrooms and are copyrighted by the University of Nevada.

Special Features: Detailed lesson plans, related links

Curriculum: History; Social Studies

1383 Nevada Appeal

www.nevadaappeal.com/apps/pbcs.dll/front page

The Nevada Appeal is Carson City's online newspaper. The capitol city newspaper covers news, sports, opinions, classifieds and special sections. Place an ad, read archives, forecasts or find other area newspapers. Full text articles give regional, state and national news.

Special Features: Photos, searchable archives, tourism information

Curriculum: Business; Government; Language Arts; Social Studies

1384 Nevada Bureau of Mines and Geology

www.nbmg.unr.edu/

The Nevada Bureau of Mines and Geology or NBMG is a clearinghouse of information on mineral resources, engineering geology, environmental geology, hydrogeology, and geologic mapping. This includes earthquake hazards, disposal of nuclear and hazardous wastes, mapping, precious metals, and related publications in the state.

Special Features: Online documents, searchable bibliography, digital maps

Curriculum: Environmental Studies; Geography; Science

1385 Nevada Business Journal

www.nevadabusiness.com/

The Nevada Business Journal is for the business minded seeking information on companies in business in Nevada. The website conducts two formats for ranking Nevada's best businesses; public favorites and traditional rankings such as revenue and employees. Some choices include best bank, golf course, public relations and more.

Special Features: Subscription information, advertising, business lists

Curriculum: Business; Economics

1386 Nevada Commission on Tourism

www.travelnevada.com/

The Nevada Commission on Tourism is responsible for marketing Nevada as a travel destination. Site offers planning, accommodations, activities, facts, and a free magazine. Explore historic mining towns, parks and recreation, motor sports and museums. The name Nevada means "snow capped" in Spanish.

Special Features: Nevada facts, maps, attractions

Curriculum: Business; Geography; Social Studies

1387 Nevada Department of Wildlife

http://ndow.org

The Nevada Department of Wildlife or NDOW is responsible for managing fish and wildlife resources in the state. There are over seven hundred ninety varieties of native animals in Nevada and more that have been introduced into the state. As the driest state in the United States, Nevada receives less than seven inches of rain per year. The NDOW website provides information on hunting, fishing and boating.

Special Features: Animals of Nevada, regulations

Curriculum: Biology; Environmental Studies; Science

1388 Nevada Division of State Parks

http://parks.nv.gov/

The website of the Department of Conservation and Natural Resources. Nevada is known for its western history. Many of the state parks offer the wild scenic feel of the old west. A complete listing of the park regions, parks, and projects is offered. Recreational trails and photos are also available.

Special Features: Park activity lists, park fees, contact information

Curriculum: Environmental Studies; Geography

1389 Nevada Film Office

www.nevadafilm.com/home/index.php

Nevada Film Office is dedicated to help promote the film industry in Nevada. The website offers information for producers, actors and filmmakers. Location spots, equipment, stages and studios, permits and law information is provided. Fun facts about films made in Nevada is included.

Special Features: Photos of filming areas, maps, film festivals
Curriculum: Business; Drama; Sociology

1390 Nevada Institute for Children

www.unlv.edu

The Nevada Institute for Children provides research, reports, and community collaboration. Services provided include childcare, welfare, abuse, education, health, and prevention. Website includes kids' page, recommended reading, legislative information and research publications.
Special Features: Safety, fun and games, parent pages, Nevada facts
Curriculum: Education; Health; Sociology

1391 Nevada Library Association

www.nevadalibraries.org/

The Nevada Library Association or NLA was started in 1946. The NLA acts as a network for librarians in the state. It promotes libraries, library services and literacy programs. Yearly conferences, publication and legislative actions help disseminate the importance of libraries in the state.
Special Features: Past conference notes, newsletters, legislative agenda
Curriculum: Library Media

1392 Nevada Magazine

www.nevadamagazine.com/

Nevada Magazine is a bi-monthly publication dedicated to the Silver State. The online version of the magazine is a sampler of what the publication includes. Website offers a peek into the current issue, special features, guides and subscription information. Nevada gift shop includes Nevada artists.
Special Features: Photos, regional information; entertainment calendar
Curriculum: Business; Geography; Sociology

1393 Nevada Mining Association

www.nevadamining.org/

Nevada is the leader in mining the industrial mineral gypsum. The Nevada Mining Association believes everything harvested, manufactured, or transported require some sort of mining. This website offers insight to the importance of mining in daily life. It also offers the economical overview of the state's mining industry.

Special Features: mineral of the month, games and fun
Curriculum: Economics; Environmental Studies; Science

1394 Nevada Movie Page

www.intercomm.com/koala/home.htm

The Nevada Movie Page is an extensively researched information cache of all the movies filmed in Nevada. Find frequently asked questions, photos, stories about the movies, trivia, alphabetical listing, year by year listing, locations where movies were filmed, new releases and related links. History about Nevada films is also provided.
Special Features: Bibliography information, interactive county map
Curriculum: Sociology

1395 Nevada Museum of Art

www.nevadaart.org/

The Nevada Museum of Art is located in Reno. Founded in 1931, the museum is a cultural resource to the state. The NMA sponsors an outreach education program to expand the public's knowledge and appreciation for art. The website offers a glimpse into the permanent collection.
Special Features: History of NMA, newsletter, museum schools
Curriculum: Art

1396 Nevada Northern Railway

www.nevadanorthernrailway.net/

Nevada Northern Railway is a historical operation railroad museum located in Ely. Over thirty two miles of track are home to museum, steam engine, machine shops, roundhouse, yards and depot. Find out the mining history of the region, view photos, or read through roster of railroad equipment.
Special Features: Area information, related links, photos
Curriculum: History; Technology

1397 Nevada Seismological Laboratory (Sponsor: University of Nevada, Reno)

www.seismo.unr.edu/

The Nevada Seismological Laboratory is located in Reno. The website offers extensive information on earthquakes in Nevada, California and the world. Past earthquakes, present activity and future hazards are listed. Kindergarten through high school educational information is offered and safety tips as well.

Special Features: Question and answer, living with earthquakes

Curriculum: Geography; Science

1398 Nevada Shakespeare Company

www.nevada-shakespeare.org/

The Nevada Shakespeare Company is a professional theatre troupe located in Reno dedicated to bringing culture to the community through linguistic expression. Website offers schedule of programming, archives of productions and press releases.

Special Features: Quotations, theatrical reviews

Curriculum: Drama; Language Arts

1399 Nevada Travel Network (Sponsor: NevadaWeb)

www.nevadatravel.net/

The Nevada Travel Network is an online guide to Nevada. Nevada is the seventh largest state in the United States; it is the most mountainous and fastest growing. This website features an interactive map, city selection or highway. It also offers historical information, Nevada facts and a bibliography.

Special Features: Monthly reports, drawings and giveaways

Curriculum: Business; Driver Training; Geography

1400 Nevada.com (Sponsor: WebMagic, Inc.)

www.nevada.com/

"Nevada.com: Guide to the Silver State's Best Sites." This is a comprehensive guide to the state including fun, tourism, business, real estate, Reno, Las Vegas, and Tahoe. This site is a directory of sites for the state and offers extensive links. Subjects include education, facts and maps for classroom utilization.

Special Features: Extensive Nevada links

Curriculum: Business; Economics; Education; Sociology

1401 Madame Tussauds International

www.madametussaudslv.com/

Marie Grosholz was born in 1761. She became the famous wax artist known as Madame Tussaud. Since 1770, the Tussaud art of wax models has intrigued the public. The Las Vegas museum specializes in interactive wax figures where anyone can sit next to their favorite star.

Special Features: History of the Tussaud's wax empire

Curriculum: Art; History

1402 Poetry (Sponsor: Suzanne Alexander)

www.saddlesong.com/

Suzanne Alexander is a professional writer of poetry, western prose and nonfiction books. Her cowboy poetry was featured at the Cowboy Poetry Festival in Elko. "Saddle Song," is Suzanne Alexander's website filled with her poetry and photographs about the West and its culture.

Special Features: Haiku, free verse poetry, related links

Curriculum: Language Arts; Women's Studies

1403 Public Campgrounds (Sponsor: Herron Web Publishing)

www.herronweb.com/campgroundguide.html

Robert Herron is author of the website dedicated to camping in Nevada's Great Basin and the Sierra Nevada area of California. Created for campers, hikers, explorers, and outdoor recreation, only public campgrounds are included. Website includes maps, photos, side trips, the top ten least crowded campgrounds and more.

Special Features: Campground secrets, favorite places, camping tips

Curriculum: Geography

1404 Reno-Tahoe: America's Adventure Place

www.renolaketahoe.com/

This is a tourism website for the Reno-Tahoe area. Find vacation packages, lodging, transportation, business and recreation. Read news of the area, virtual web-cams and schedule of events. Website is searchable and lists extensive travel opportunities.

Special Features: Seasonal ideas, arts and culture links

Curriculum: Business; Economics; Sociology

1405 State of Nevada

www.nv.gov/

The official website for the state of Nevada. The "Silver State" is known for Las Vegas, the Hoover Dam, the Great Basin and the Mojave Desert. Much of the population is involved in the tourist industry supporting casinos in the Las Vegas and Reno areas. The website offers information on government, business, education, senior citizens, and news.

Special Features: Photo gallery, weather, schedule of events
Curriculum: Business; Geography; Social Studies

1406 State of Nevada Nuclear Waste Project Office

www.state.nv.us/nucwaste/

The website for the Agency for Nuclear Projects in Nevada is full of information regarding testing, waste, and disposal of nuclear refuse. The link titled "Of Interest" is a cache of articles dealing with the issues of nuclear engineering and its side effects.

Special Features: Maps, articles, new projects, health effects
Curriculum: Environmental Studies; Health; Science

1407 TechAlliance

www.newnevada.com

The mission to foster technology and entrepreneurial development in Nevada is accomplished through partnerships and networking facilitated by New Nevada. Volunteers broken up into the five groups of: recruiting, support, communications, education and the web team. Find out about the technology and advantages of business and living in Nevada.

Special Features: Technology resources, jobs and news
Curriculum: Business; Technology

1408 United States Bureau of Reclamation, Hoover Dam

www.usbr.gov/lc/hooverdam/

The United States Bureau of Reclamation manages, develops and protects water resources environmentally and economically. The Hoover Dam was built between 1930 and 1936 on the Nevada Arizona border. Building the dam created Lake Mead, one of the world's largest manmade lakes. The dam stands as one of the symbols of human industry.

Special Features: Hoover Dam essays, historical articles, frequently asked questions
Curriculum: Geography; History; Social Studies; Technology

1409 United States Navy

www.nevada.navy.mil/

The USS *Nevada SSBN 7333* is the fourth ship named after the state. The current USS *Nevada* is a nuclear powered fleet ballistic missile submarine. The history of all the *Nevada* ships is offered on this website along with current news. Crew information is available.

Special Features: Statistics, photo gallery, guestbook
Curriculum: Government; History; Social Studies

1410 Western Folklife Center

www.westernfolklife.org/site/

The Western Folklife Center is located in Elko. It strives to preserve and promote the folk arts of the West. The center supports research, documentation, public performances, media, exhibits and educational programming to enhance the contemporary culture and people of the West.

Special Features: News, events, mailing list
Curriculum: Art; Language Arts; Music; Sociology

NEW HAMPSHIRE

1411 Abenaki Indians (Sponsor: IMDiversity)

www.tolatsga.org/aben.html

The Abenaki Indians were first located across northern New England. A concentration of the tribe was located along the Merrimack River in southern New Hampshire. This webpage offers extensive information of the Abenaki people, their population, names, language and culture.

Special Features: Extensive Abenaki history
Curriculum: Geography; Government; History; Social Studies

1412 Artists-nh.com

www.artists-nh.com/

The website is organized by an alphabetical listing of New Hampshire artists or by a subject and style listing. Each fine artist includes samples of their work, a short biography, a description of the artist's method of work, and contact information.

Special Features: Collection of varied art mediums and styles
Curriculum: Art

1413 AskART.com

www.askart.com/interest/cornish_a.asp

AskART is home to an article entitled, "Cornish Colony of Artists— New Hampshire." Between 1895 and 1925 almost one hundred fine artists, writers and politicians lived in the Cornish area. The colony although spread out included Cornish and Windsor. The article provides a listing of artists, photographs of artwork and links to biographies of the artists.

Special Features: Bibliography; related links
Curriculum: Art; Geography; History; Sociology

1414 Audubon Society of New Hampshire

www.nhaudubon.org/

The Audubon of New Hampshire strives to protect and enhance the natural environment for wildlife and people. Learn more about birding, birding ethics, bird surveys and populations. A listing of centers, sanctuaries, and chapters is provided. Read about ospreys and peregrines in New Hampshire.

Special Features: Ask a naturalist, conservation fact sheets, contact information
Curriculum: Biology; Environmental Studies; Science

1415 Authors and Books for Children

www.elliemik.com/boylston.html

This website contains the article, "Helen Dore Boylston: Nurse From New Hampshire." Helen Dore Boylston was an actual nurse who took her experiences and turned them into stories for children. She was born in Portsmouth, served in the First World War, and wrote the Sue Barton nursing series. The website offers a brief biography of her life and touches upon the writing of her books.

Special Features: Related links, quotations
Curriculum: Library Media; Women's Studies

1416 Canterbury Shaker Village

www.shakers.org

Canterbury Shaker Village is a National Historic Landmark museum. It includes twenty-five original buildings on almost seven hundred acres of land including gardens, trails, forests, ponds and meadows. Located in Canterbury it covers over two hundred years of Shaker history. The website features virtual tours, photos and historical summary.

Special Features: Menus, shopping, photos of the area
Curriculum: History; Social Studies

1417 Children's Authors (Sponsor: Nora LeDuc)

www.concord.k12.nh.us/schools/kimball/leduc/nhauthors.html

New Hampshire's Children's Authors is an alphabetical index to authors who lived or is living in the state. Each author includes name, living location, and a brief list of their work. Each famous author's name links to Barnes and Noble which provides a bibliography and price listing.

Special Features: Alphabetical listing, biographical information
Curriculum: Language Arts; Library Media

1418 Civil War (Sponsor: Todd Grzywacz)

www.geocities.com/nh_heritage/

This webpage is dedicated to the role New Hampshire played in the Civil War. "New Hampshire Heritage 1861–1865" is written and maintained by Todd Grzywacz. Information on New Hampshire's units, the roles of towns, and the importance of women in the war are included.
Special Features: Civil War photos, related links
Curriculum: Government; History; Social Studies; Women's Studies

1419 Franklin Pierce (Sponsor: University of Virginia)

www.americanpresident.org/history/franklinpierce/

Franklin Pierce was the fourteenth president of the United States. Before becoming president he was a two term governor of New Hampshire. He was a strong advocate of the Kansas-Nebraska Act and served in the Mexican American War. He was born in Hillsboro and after serving as president he retired to Concord.
Special Features: Biographical information
Curriculum: Government; History; Social Studies

1420 General Information (Sponsor: NSTATE, LLC)

www.netstate.com/states/intro/nh_intro.htm

New Hampshire was named after Hampshire, England. Captain John Mason named it after the land where he grew up. The website includes such information as state symbols, maps, weather and people. Take the trivia test, read about the state's nicknames or see the state quarter.
Special Features: Photos, trivia, games, history
Curriculum: Geography; History; Social Studies

1421 Heritage New Hampshire

www.heritagenh.com

Located in Glen, Heritage New Hampshire is a walk through theatrical museum depicting New England's historical heritage from wilderness to the twenty-first century. Heritage opened in July 1976 in celebration of the nation's bicentennial. A study guide is offered online for educators and a virtual tour is provided.
Special Features: Photos, online game
Curriculum: Drama; History; Social Studies

1422 Historic Highlanders

http://historichighlanders.com/

The Historic Highlanders is an educational cultural group dedicated to preserving the culture of the Scottish specifically between the years of 1314 to 1746. The group selects periods of Scottish history and then produces, garb, skills, weaponry, utensils, language, music, and other art forms to share with others. The group is then available for festivals and other living history events.
Special Features: Detailed information on garb, blacksmithing, weaponry, or folk medicine
Curriculum: Dance; Drama; History; Music; Social Studies

1423 Library of Congress

www.americaslibrary.gov/cgi-bin/page.cgi/es/nh

The Library of Congress provides the history of New Hampshire and the highlights of its interesting moments. The webpage provides interesting articles on the culture and peoples of the state as well. New Hampshire is a relatively tax free state which corresponds with the motto of "Live free or die."
Special Features: New Hampshire images and related stories
Curriculum: Government; History; Social Studies

1424 Mount Washington Observatory

www.mountwashington.org/

The Mount Washington Observatory is located in the White Mountains and is New England's highest peak. The first summit house was built in 1852 and is now known as the "City Among the Clouds." The observatory is home to the highest wind speed ever recorded and is available for virtual tour. Website offers extensive weather information.
Special Features: Mountain history, educational programming, weather discovery arcade for kids

Curriculum: Environmental Studies; Science; Technology

1425 New Hampshire Astronomical Society

www.nhastro.com/

The New Hampshire Astronomical Society or NHAS is a not for profit organization that strives to educate, demonstrate and observe astronomical events, discussions and slide shows for the public. The website provides images and information on astronomical events such as comets. Finder charts and references are provided.

Special Features: Observation tips, events calendar, related links
Curriculum: Math; Science

1426 New Hampshire: Beyond a Picture Postcard (Sponsor: ExxonMobil Masterpiece Theatre's American Collection)

www.ncteamericancollection.org/litmap/new_hampshire.htm

"New Hampshire: Beyond a Picture Postcard." is an article written by Elizabeth H. Juster, a teacher from Londonberry High School. The article includes a listing of writers from New Hampshire and authors who have spent time in the state. Some of the famous names include: J.D. Salinger, E.E. Cummings, Lois Lowry and John Irving. Short biographies are provided.

Special Features: Author links, biographical essays
Curriculum: Language Arts; Library Media

1427 New Hampshire Division of Parks and Recreation State Parks

www.nhstateparks.org/ParksPages/franconianotch/oldman.html

This is home website of the Old Man of the Mountain Historic Site. Franconia Notch State Park was home to the Old Man of the Mountain or the Great Stone Face. Unfortunately the profile collapsed in 2003. The man was made up of granite ledges and is the state symbol of New Hampshire. The website offers information on the rock formation history and includes a scrapbook in its honor.

Special Features: Timeline, photos, first person accounts
Curriculum: Geography; History; Social Studies

1428 New Hampshire Division of Travel and Tourism

www.visitnh.gov/

This is the official site of the New Hampshire Division of Travel and Tourism. Directory includes: maps, lodging, events, recreations, state information, trip planner, free travel guide, seasonal package buys and contact information. Find seashores and mountains, bike trails and golfing. Tourism links included.

Special Features: Extensive tourism information
Curriculum: Business; Economics; Geography; Sociology

1429 New Hampshire Fish and Game Department

www.wildlife.state.nh.us/

The New Hampshire Fish and Game Department runs the state's fish, wildlife and marine resources. The website offers information on hunting and fishing reports, licenses, frequently asked questions and safety education classes. Wildlife information gives animal profiles, endangered animals and kids' activities.

Special Features: Journal articles, related links, photos
Curriculum: Biology; Environmental Studies; Science

1430 New Hampshire Gathering of the Scottish Clans

www.nhscot.org/default.htm

The New Hampshire Highland Games is home to the annual World Scottish Heavy Events Championships. The annual games are located in Contoocook. The games promote the culture and continuance of the Scottish people and the Gaelic culture. Information on such sporting events as stone put, weights, hammer throwing, sheaf toss, caber toss, and stone walking is included.

Special Features: Field records, musical performances, photos
Curriculum: History; Music; Physical Education; Sociology

1431 New Hampshire Historical Society

www.nhhistory.org/

Founded in 1823 the New Hampshire Historical Society or NHHS runs a museum, library and promotes the history of New Hampshire.

Some programs and events include furniture artistry, political history, musical concerts, and traveling exhibitions. Sample lesson plans about NH history are included.

Special Features: School programming, what's news, related links

Curriculum: History; Social Studies

1432 New Hampshire Humane Society

www.nhhumane.org/

Located in Laconia, the New Hampshire Humane Society offers online information about domestic pets. Guides for dog and cat owners are available for download. The resources link includes related links about pets and other NH humane societies. A memorial page is dedicated to beloved animals that have passed away.

Special Features: Animal photographs, newsletters, classes

Curriculum: Biology; Sociology

1433 New Hampshire International Speedway

www.nhis.com/

The New Hampshire International Speedway is an oval shape with a one and six tenth mile course. It is located in Loudon. An interactive map is provided for directions to the speedway. The grandstands hold more than one hundred thousand people. The website provides ticket information, racing schedule, track facts and news.

Special Features: Race results and records, technical information

Curriculum: Sports

1434 New Hampshire Interscholastic Athletic Association

www.nhiaa.org/

The NHIAA was formed in 1947 to establish athletic programs in the public schools. It has also ensured equality in competition and regulations have changed with the times. The development of youth is the NHIAA's main objective. The website includes champions, history, schools, schedules, scores and tournament information.

Special Features: School standings, rules and regulations

Curriculum: Physical Education

1435 New Hampshire Lakes Association

www.nhlakes.org/

The New Hampshire Lakes Association or NHLA was established in 1992 for the purpose of protecting shoreland and watershed areas, water quality improvement, boating safety, lake education and preservation. The website offers educational research articles, legislative accomplishments, educational events and related links.

Special Features: Research papers, kids' pages

Curriculum: Biology; Environmental Studies; Geography; Science

1436 New Hampshire Library Association

www.state.nh.us/nhla/

The Hampshire Library Association is a networking springboard for librarians in the state. This website offers constitution and bylaws, newsletters, intellectual freedom manual and other useful library publications. Conference information, scholarships, session notes and photographs are offered.

Special Features: Library links

Curriculum: Library Media

1437 New Hampshire Links (Sponsor: Union Leader Corporation)

www.newhampshire.com

New Hampshire.com is an index to the state. It has extensive links to such topics as: basic facts, accommodations, arts and theatre, business, cities, dining, education, events, regions, fall foliage, golf, holidays, maps, music, outdoor recreation, shopping, sports, travel and winter recreation.

Special Features: Agricultural statistics, haunted places, unusual laws

Curriculum: Business; Geography; Social Studies; Sociology

1438 New Hampshire Magazine

www.nh.com/apps/pbcs.dll/section?Category= NHM

New Hampshire Magazine is dedicated to promoting the beauty and culture of the Granite state. The online version of the monthly magazine includes cover art, cuisine, health and the seacoast scene. The website also offers the best of New Hampshire and is searchable.

Special Features: Related links, subject index

Curriculum: Home Economics; Language Arts; Sociology

1439 New Hampshire Music Festival

www.nhmf.org/

Established in 1952, the New Hampshire Music Festival originated on an island near Wolfeboro by two piano teachers. The event grew and grew and now presents more than one hundred ten events per year. Currently, headquarters are located in Center Harbor. The NHMF is committed to educational outreach and is highly active in the regional schools.

Special Features: Educational opportunities, contact information
Curriculum: Education; Music

1440 New Hampshire Phantoms

www.nhphantoms.com/index.htm

The Phantoms are New Hampshire's professional soccer club. Created in 1996 there are both men's and women's leagues and camps are offered. The website offers player biographies, laws of the game, soccer facts and a coach's corner.

Special Features: Camps, soccer photos, clinic information
Curriculum: Sports

1441 New Hampshire Political Library

www.politicallibrary.org/

The New Hampshire Political Library is located in Concord. It holds a comprehensive collection of papers and paraphernalia of the New Hampshire presidential primaries. The collection was started in 1952 and contains books, periodicals, speeches, audio and video clips, papers, strategy memos, debates, diaries, photos, bumper stickers, posters and more.

Special Features: Digital archives, photo gallery, news events
Curriculum: Government; History; Library Media; Social Studies

1442 New Hampshire Society for the Prevention of Cruelty to Animals

www.nhspca.org/

The NHSPCA is located in Stratham. The organization receives more than four thousand animals and each is provided with a safe environment. Dog training classes are provided to the public along with community programming that encourages compassion, kindness and respect for animals. The website offers an adoption center, learning center and information on cruelty prevention.

Special Features: Kids' projects and education pages
Curriculum: Biology; Sociology

1443 New Hampshire Society of Photographic Artists

www.nhspa.org/

Photographic Artistry is means for expression and cultural insight. The NHSPA provides education and artistic development to its members and the public. The society offers exhibitions, publications, education and outreach programming. The website provides an online art gallery.

Special Features: Online photo gallery, related links
Curriculum: Art

1444 New Hampshire State Library

www.state.nh.us/nhsl/

Established in 1717 the state library is located in Concord. The online resources provided include: library catalogs, genealogy resources, patents depository, talking book program, ask a librarian, family resources, and World War II posters. The library publishes statistics, standards, directory of libraries, almanac, author list, technology plan and other library resources.

Special Features: Librarian resources, related links
Curriculum: Library Media

1445 New Hampshire Symphony Orchestra

www.nhso.org/main.htm

The New Hampshire Symphony Orchestra or NHSO is located in Manchester. The website offers ticket information, season schedule, press releases and related links. Season reviews include short biographies of musicians.

Special Features: Performance reviews, related links
Curriculum: Music

1446 New Hampshire Theatre Project

www.nhtheatreproject.org/

The New Hampshire Theatre Project specializes in bringing theater to the community through schools, organizations and the workplace. Artist in residence positions are created for full time artists to share their expertise.

Classes and camps are offered for youth programming.

Special Features: Artist biographies
Curriculum: Drama

1447 NH Outdoors

www.nhoutdoors.com/

NH Outdoors offers an internet index to the outdoor activities, tourism and resources New Hampshire has to offer. Recreation in New Hampshire includes: fishing, hunting, golf, camping, skiing, boating, hiking, biking, and lodging. Seasonal activities such as fair going, gardening, and children's camps are included.

Special Features: Seasonal events, wildlife and animals
Curriculum: Business; Sports

1448 NHTunes.com

www.nhtunes.com/

NHTunes is dedicated to the New Hampshire music scene. Promotion of New Hampshire artists and bands is free. An alphabetical listing of artists is provided and each band provides, name, contact and music type. Audio files are downloadable. Studios are also listed and CD reviews are included.

Special Features: Audio files, contact information
Curriculum: Music; Sociology

1449 Parent to Parent of New Hampshire

www.parenttoparentnh.org/

Parent to Parent of New Hampshire is a support organization for parents of children with special needs. Located in Lebanon, the network provides emotional support, matches parents who have similar situations, it offers information and community resources, and training for volunteers. The website includes books, quotes, poetry, stories and essays.

Special Features: Just for kids section, message board, contacts, related links
Curriculum: Education; Health; Psychology; Sociology

1450 Public Service of New Hampshire, Northeast Utilities

www.psnh.com/

Safety and Health are the topics of focus at Public Service of New Hampshire. Find information on classroom presentations, facts for school projects, conservation tips, teacher consultants and more. Energy project reviews are also provided. The Sheep Project includes information on weed control and natural resources controlling natural problems.

Special Features: Full text articles, environmentalism
Curriculum: Business; Environmental Studies; Health; Science

1451 SeacoastNH.com

www.seacoastnh.com

SeacoastNH.com is a highly educational website containing extensive history about the seacoast of New Hampshire. Subjects include: seacoast history, famous people, Black history, seacoast women, timeline of the coast and historical events. The webpage is also a cache of cultural information and artistic happenings in the state.

Special Features: Events, full text historical articles
Curriculum: History; Social Studies; Women's Studies

1452 Society for the Protection of New Hampshire Forests

www.spnhf.org/

The Society for the Protection of New Hampshire Forests was founded in 1901. The society now protects over one hundred twenty-five thousand acres and promotes conservation through education and example. The website features maps, news, legislative actions, a list of educational field trips and conservation center exhibits.

Special Features: Forest news, e-newsletter
Curriculum: Biology; Environmental Studies; Science

1453 State of New Hampshire

www.state.nh.us/

This is the official website of the state of New Hampshire. Directories include residents, visitors, state employees, businesses, government, and just for kids. Online maps are included. Kids' links offers information on senate pages, aviation education, government history, how the government works, and a New Hampshire almanac.

Special Features: News and events, ask a librarian, searchable site
Curriculum: Business; Government; Social Studies

1454 State Report (Sponsor: ClassBrain. com)

www.classbrain.com/artstate/publish/article_525.shtml

This webpage is dedicated to the famous people from New Hampshire. The listing includes a link for authors, famous people, and biographies of some of the founding fathers. Some names include: J.D. Salinger, Robert Frost, S. Christa McAuliffe and more.

Special Features: Alphabetical listing, biographies

Curriculum: History; Language Arts; Social Studies

1455 University of New Hampshire Cooperative Extension

http://ceinfo.unh.edu/index.htm

The University of New Hampshire Extension offers researched based information to the public in hopes of strengthening families and communities. Some topics included on this website include agriculture, family issues, nutrition, forestry, gardening, money management, water, wildlife and youth.

Special Features: Publications, brochures; educational programming, events

Curriculum: Business; Education; Health; Home Economics; Sociology

1456 University of New Hampshire, Library Government Documents Department

http://docs.unh.edu/nhtopos/NewHampshire.htm

This website is a collection of New Hampshire maps dating back as far as the nineteenth century. The collection originates from the United States Geological Survey. The maps are interactively broken up into longitude and latitude fifteen minute sections.

Special Features: Interactive detailed historic maps

Curriculum: Geography; History; Social Studies

1457 Websites for Kids (Sponsor: Kathi Mitchell)

www.kathimitchell.com/NH.html

"New Hampshire: Websites for Kids (and Grownups, too)" was created and maintained by Kathi Mitchell a teacher for over thirty years. The webpage is an index to New Hampshire and includes such subjects as regions, famous people, authors, history, facts, trivia, census data and maps.

Special Features: Extensive New Hampshire links for kids

Curriculum: Education; Geography; Social Studies

1458 White Mountain Art and Artists

www.whitemountainart.com/index.html

This educational website is dedicated to the art and artists who painted the White Mountains during the nineteenth century. There were more than four hundred painters who were known to have painted the mountains; these are included with a biography and their images when available.

Special Features: Art history, images, photo comparisons, bibliography

Curriculum: Art; History

1459 White Mountain National Forest (Sponsor: Dartmouth College)

www.cs.dartmouth.edu/whites1460)/

The White Mountain Info Server. This website is dedicated to the recreation of the White Mountain National Forest. Read about hiking, backpacking, skiing, and snowshoeing. Included in the website are essays, suggested hikes, trail conditions, trip reports, pictures and wildlife.

Special Features: White Mountain photographs, video files

Curriculum: Environmental Studies; Physical Education; Science

1461 Wikipedia

http://en.wikipedia.org/wiki/Live_free_or_die

The New Hampshire motto, "Live free or die" is famous. This online article explains the history of the motto, what it has meant in history and common themes throughout history. The phrase was coined by a man named John Stark. A short biography of Stark is also included.

Special Features: Searchable, related historical links

Curriculum: Government; History; Social Studies

NEW JERSEY

1462 BlackLab Productions

www.njahof.org/

The New Jersey Aviation Hall of Fame and Museum is located in Teterboro on the airport grounds. This website features extensive photos of historical airpower and information on the preservation of these machines.
Special Features: Photographs
Curriculum: History; Technology

1463 Brady Associates

www.visitac.com/history/

"Historic Atlantic City: A Guide to Points of Interest in Atlantic City and Vicinity." This webpage is divided into counties surrounding the Atlantic City area and focuses on the historical interest points. Some historical landmarks include lighthouses, beaches and museums. View the Atlantic City photo documentary, or read over the history of African American communities in southern New Jersey.
Special Features: Photos, multicultural links
Curriculum: Geography; History; Social Studies

1464 Canal Society of New Jersey

www.canalsocietynj.org/

The Canal Society of New Jersey was formed in 1969 to study the history of towpath canals, preserve and restore remains and artifacts, and educate the public about towpath canals. The webpage offers facts, photo documentary, photo gallery, audio files, video files and related links.
Special Features: Historical information and photos
Curriculum: Economics; Geography; History; Social Studies

1465 Culinary History Timeline (Sponsor: Morris County Library)

www.gti.net/mocolib1/kid/food1.html

This webpage is entitled, "Culinary History Timeline." The Morris County Library provides an extensive index to web pages containing links to articles on culinary history, manners and menus. Some links include: American history, military rations and social aspects. The webpage is then listed by year from prehistory to 2003.
Special Features: Menu collections, future food trends
Curriculum: History; Home Economics

1466 Delaware Valley Poets

www.delawarevalleypoets.com/

The Delaware Valley Poets began in 1952. Today, the group has published four books and is open to the public. A listing of public poetry readings and links is provided. The website also includes a listing of poets published and their personal websites.
Special Features: List of New Jersey poets
Curriculum: Language Arts; Women's Studies

1467 Edisonnj.org

www.edisonnj.org/menlopark/

The birthplace of recorded sound is located in Edison, New Jersey, in Menlo Park. Menlo Park is home to the laboratory of Thomas Edison. This website offers extensive information on the history of recorded sound, the invention of the phonograph and other Menlo Park inventions. Listen to audio files or take a virtual tour.
Special Features: Recordings, photographs, full text articles
Curriculum: History; Science; Technology

1468 History of New Jersey (Sponsor: New Jersey City University)

http://faculty.njcu.edu/ckarnoutsos/index.htm

This website is an online reference for the history of New Jersey. Website offers a chronology of events in the state, a listing of New Jersey governors, Revolutionary War facts, facts about the state and historical documents and maps. Instructor's page also includes contact information.
Special Features: Related links
Curriculum: Geography; History; Social Studies

1469 Home Port Alliance

www.battleshipnewjersey.org/index.cfm

This is the homepage for the battleship *New Jersey*. The ship is permanently docked in Camden. Built in 1940 to 1942, the *New Jersey* then went straight into World War II and on into the Korean War and Vietnam. The website preserves the naval history of the ship by providing fact sheets, history of the boat and a photo gallery.

Special Features: Ship data, virtual tour, frequently asked questions

Curriculum: Government; History; Social Studies; Technology

1470 Images of American Political History (Sponsor: William J. Ball)

http://teachpol.tcnj.edu/amer_pol_hist/

"Images of American Political History." This is a collection of over five hundred photos of political history in America. The photos included in this collection are in public domain and collected from sources such as government collections or expired copyrighted materials. Each image is briefly described.

Special Features: Organized by era and topic

Curriculum: Art; Government; History; Social Studies; Sociology

1471 Liberty Hall Museum

www.libertyhallnj.org/

Liberty Hall was built in 1772 in Union. The hall was home to New Jersey's first governor William Livingston. This website offers historical information of the estate, map of the property, garden information, digital postcards and educational programming summaries. The house is unique in that it has stayed with in a family and spans centuries.

Special Features: Photos, historical information

Curriculum: History; Social Studies

1472 Library of Congress

www.americaslibrary.gov/cgi-bin/page.cgi/es/nj/

Find out what the Library of Congress has to say about the Garden State. This webpage provides an overview of the state, a short history and state symbols. Also included are links to articles about the state its people and culture. Photos are included.

Special Features: Stories about New Jersey

Curriculum: Social Studies; Sociology

1473 Memorable Quotations (Sponsor: Carol Dingle and Diana J. Dell)

www.memorablequotations.com/NewJersey.htm

"Memorable Quotations: Famous People from New Jersey." This website is a collection of quotations by such people as: Grover Cleveland, James Fennimore Cooper, Allen Ginsberg and Dorothy Parker. Famous quotations are good for opening speeches, papers and reports about the state.

Special Features: Quotations

Curriculum: Language Arts; Library Media

1474 Minerals (Sponsor: Herb Yeats)

http://simplethinking.com/franklinminerals/

This website contains in-depth, scientific information on the minerals found in the Franklin-Sterling Hill area of New Jersey. It includes photos of fluorescent minerals, mineral events and basic information on minerals. Also included are full text references on minerals of this area.

Special Features: Fluorescent photos, biographical information, video files, scientific texts

Curriculum: Geography; Science

1475 Museum of Early Trades and Crafts

www.rosenet.org/metc/

The Museum of Early Trades and Crafts or METC is located in Madison. The museum contains exhibits of pre-industrial New Jersey such as tools, products and household objects. Website features permanent exhibits, museum map, kids club, programming, and special exhibits. The mementos link includes extra interesting collection of things part of the virtual museum.

Special Features: Related museum links, schedule of events

Curriculum: History; Home Economics; Social Studies

1476 National Endowment for the Arts

www.pbs.org/georgesegal/index/

"George Segal: American Still Life." Based in New Jersey, sculptor George Segal is internationally known for his life sized plaster casts frozen in a single moment. This website is based on the documentary made about his life and work. Information on the documentary,

Segal's own statements, time line of events, and memorials are provided.

Special Features: Video tour, teacher resources, photographs

Curriculum: Art; Sociology

1477 Navy Lakehurst Historical Society

www.nlhs.com/

The Navy Lakehurst Historical Society's homepage offers information on the historical event of the Hindenburg explosion of 1937. Find a list of the crew members aboard the zeppelin airship. Also included: airship history, hanger inventories and historical photos.

Special Features: Photos, articles, manuscripts

Curriculum: Government; History; Science; Technology

1478 NBA Media Ventures, LLC.

www.nba.com/nets/

This is the official website of the New Jersey Nets. Find statistics, player information, schedules, community information, audio and video files. View photos, download free computer wallpaper and see highlights of the year. Ongoing community programming and events are included.

Special Features: Online literacy promotions

Curriculum: Sports; Technology

1479 New Jersey Academy for Aquatic Sciences

www.njaquarium.org/index2.php3

The New Jersey Aquarium is located in Camden. The website includes information on aquatic animals and online exhibits such as sea dragons, seals, nutrias and Caribbean beach birds. Lesson plans and units are offered online. The virtual museum includes information on how fish sleep, online coloring book, rainy day activities and games.

Special Features: Lesson plans, games, virtual tour

Curriculum: Biology; Environmental Studies; Science

1480 New Jersey Center for Visual Arts

www.njcva.org/contents.html

Located in Summit, the New Jersey Center for the Visual Arts promotes understanding of the contemporary arts. NJCVA provides workshops, classes, kid classes and events. The web-

site provides glimpses of current exhibitions and images of works. Summary of the current exhibit is also offered.

Special Features: Virtual exhibits

Curriculum: Art; Sociology

1481 New Jersey Commerce and Economic Growth Commission

www.nj.gov/travel/index.html

This is the official website for New Jersey tourism. Order free travel guides and brochures. The kids section includes facts and fun, a kid's hangout and book club. Find statewide events, attractions, traffic reports, accommodations and maps. Business news and industry information is also included.

Special Features: State tourism, regional information

Curriculum: Business; Economics; Geography

1482 New Jersey Department of Education

www.state.nj.us/education/

The New Jersey Department of Education provides leadership and direction to the schools and children of the state. The website offers contact information, school data, reports, frequently asked questions and an interactive regional map. The site also offers sections for parents, educators, students and financial partners.

Special Features: Standards, assessments, grants

Curriculum: Education; Government

1483 New Jersey Department of Health and Senior Services

www.state.nj.us/health/eoh/rtkweb/rtkhsfs.htm

"Right to Know Hazardous Substance Fact Sheets." This website is a collection of fifty fact sheets of hazardous substances. Substance scan be found in alphabetical order and is also available in Spanish. Each sheet includes common name, identification, exposure limits and ways of reducing exposure.

Special Features: Reproducible fact sheets

Curriculum: Health; Home Economics; Science

1484 New Jersey Department of Parks and Forestry

www.state.nj.us/dep/parksandforests/

The New Jersey Department of Parks and Forestry offers a website that contains information on historical sites and villages, forest fire information, land management, educational resources and park events. Virtual tours are available for many forest, parks, and historical sites. New headlines are also provided.

Special Features: Curriculum, individual park details

Curriculum: Biology; Environmental Studies; Geography; Science

1485 New Jersey Department of Transportation

www.state.nj.us/njcommuter/html/bikemaps.htm

The New Jersey Department of Transportation offers more than motor vehicle and road information. This link provides information on tour guides for bicyclists in waterproof foldable format. Each tour is available online along with newsletters, biking clubs, trails, and pedestrian safety.

Special Features: Biking, walking, rollerblading, routes

Curriculum: Driver Training; Health; Physical Education

1486 New Jersey During the Revolution (Sponsor: Glenn Valis)

www.doublegv.com/ggv/index.html

"New Jersey During the Revolution." is an educational website containing information about the battles and activities of the Revolutionary War in the state. The website includes overview of activities and related links to specific battles. Some images are included.

Special Features: Extensive Revolutionary War information

Curriculum: Geography; History; Sociology

1487 New Jersey Historical Commission, Rutgers University Libraries

www.scc.rutgers.edu/njh/

"Electronic New Jersey: A Digital Archive of New Jersey History." This is an educational website containing extensive information on the history of the state. The span of history includes homesteading to the social protest of the sixties and seventies. Subjects covered also include technology, science, mass culture and consumerism.

Special Features: Historical images, discussion links, related links

Curriculum: History; Social Studies; Sociology; Technology

1488 New Jersey Historical Society

www.jerseyhistory.org/

The New Jersey Historical Society provides the public with archives, a library and a museum dedicated to collecting the preserving the political, social, cultural and economic history of the state. Proving exhibitions, programming, and publications contributes to the identity of the peoples in the state. The website offers online collections, teacher resources and volunteer opportunities.

Special Features: Searchable site, maps, photos

Curriculum: History; Sociology

1489 New Jersey Institute of Technology

www.library.njit.edu/archives/lit-hall/

The New Jersey Literary Hall of Fame is located in Kupfrian Hall on the campus of the New Jersey Institute of Technology. The hall is "dedicated to remembering and perpetuating the work of authors" of the state. Some famous New Jersey authors include Stephen Crane, Walt Whitman, Mary Higgins Clark, Mary Mapes Dodge and more.

Special Features: List of inductees, history of the hall

Curriculum: Language Arts; Library Media

1490 New Jersey Library Association

www.njla.org/

The New Jersey Library Association or NJLA was established in 1890 to support intellectual freedom and promote literacy. The NJLA also provides a network to librarians and continuing education programming. The website offers information on statewide literacy programs and resources for libraries.

Special Features: Professional links, youth related topics

Curriculum: Library Media

1491 New Jersey Life Magazine (Sponsor: Olsten Publishing)

www.newjerseylife.com/

New Jersey Life: Best of the Garden State is a magazine dedicated to featuring life, culture and entertainment in the state. Website includes features of the current issue, things to do, places to go, dining and more. Find links to restaurants, seasonal activities, sports, theatre, and festivals.

Special Features: Photos, events, tourism
Curriculum: Art; Business; Drama; Geography; Sociology

1492 New Jersey Light House Society

http://njlhs.burlco.org/

The New Jersey Light House Society or NJLHS was founded in 1989 to preserve the history of lighthouses and to restore the lighthouses themselves. The society holds quarterly meetings, publishes a newsletter and has begun an archive. The website offers lighthouse information, photographs and historical documents.

Special Features: Time line of events, extensive historical documents
Curriculum: Geography; History; Sociology

1493 New Jersey Reading Association

www.njreading.org/

The New Jersey Reading Association promotes literacy through collaboration and professional development. The NJRA believes reading is the foundation of knowledge and should be facilitated and promoted. The website provides information on conferences, grants, legislation and local councils.

Special Features: Full text position papers, grant applications
Curriculum: Education; Language Arts; Library Media

1494 New Jersey State Library

www.njstatelib.org/

The New Jersey State library located in Trenton was established in 1796. It provides library and information services to the public. The website includes library laws, electronic resources, research guides and ask a librarian feature. The electronic resources include databases, electronic journals and e-books.

Special Features: Government periodicals, medical journals, state information
Curriculum: Government; Library Media

1495 New Jersey Times Radio Series (Sponsor: Rutgers)

http://njtimes.rutgers.edu/

New Jersey Times is a radio show dedicated to the culture and contemporary issues of the state. The show explores the past and present offing insight to the state's offerings. The website offers station listings, audio samples, program schedule and commentaries.

Special Features: Book reviews, historical commentaries
Curriculum: History; Library Media; Social Studies; Sociology

1496 Nike Missiles (Sponsor: Donald E. Bender)

http://alpha.fdu.edu/~bender/nike.html

"Nike Missiles and Missile Sites," by Donald E. Bender is a website of historical and technical information on Nike missile systems. The Nike missile was one of the first successful anti-aircraft missile systems. This site focuses on the missile sites in New Jersey, New York and Pennsylvania.

Special Features: Missile overview, articles, site locations
Curriculum: History; Math; Science; Technology

1497 NJ Restaurants and Dining Guide

www.njdiningguide.net/

This is an online guide to dining, restaurants, reception facilities and catering in New Jersey. Site includes guides to cuisine, county location, contests, and discounts. Find information on menus, reviews of restaurants and multicultural cuisine. Good for menu ideas.

Special Features: Photos, advertising
Curriculum: Business; Home Economics

1498 NJ.com

www.nj.com/lindbergh/

On the night of March 1, 1932, twenty-month-old Charles Lindberg, Jr., was taken from his crib. A ransom of fifty thousand dollars was left behind. Known as the "crime of the century" the remains of the Lindberg baby was finally found two months later a few miles from the home. This webpage chronicles the crime and gives in depth information on the historical happening. The trial was held in Flemington, New Jersey.

Special Features: Photographs, timeline of events, biographies
Curriculum: History; Psychology; Sociology

1499 Rutgers School of Communication, Information and Library Studies

http://njcenterforthebook.org/

The New Jersey Center for the Book was established in 1977 to stimulate interest in books, libraries and reading. The center celebrates literacy and the heritage it has in New Jersey. The website offers author interviews, youth literature information, news, books as art, and the history of books.

Special Features: Related links, literacy organizations

Curriculum: Language Arts; Library Media

1500 Seeing Eye, Inc.

www.seeingeye.org/aboutus.asp

Founded in 1929 the Seeing Eye specially breeds and trains seeing eye dogs in Morristown. Seeing Eye dogs enhance independence, dignity and confidence for blind people. The frequently asked question section of the website provides a great deal of information about the process of acquiring and training the dogs. Facts about blindness and history of seeing eye dogs is also available.

Special Features: First person testimonies, virtual tours, audio files

Curriculum: Health; Psychology

1501 Small Towns, Black Lives (Sponsor: Wendel A. White)

www.blacktowns.org/

"Small Towns, Black Lives" is a website and published book including photographs of black communities in rural settings in southern New Jersey. The website includes a virtual photo gallery of the towns of the state. Each virtual photo includes explanatory texts.

Special Features: Photographs, historical landmarks

Curriculum: Art; Geography; History; Language Arts; Social Studies

1502 Society of African Missions

www.smafathers.org/society/tenafly.htm

Tenafly is home to the Society of African Missions African Art Museum. The museum serves the public and schools providing talks, tours, presentations, and lectures. The website offers images of African art and a listing of publications.

Special Features: Each image has origination place name

Curriculum: Art; Geography

1503 State of New Jersey

www.state.nj.us/

This is the official state of New Jersey website. Website contains an alphabetical listing of services, departments and agencies, legislature, judiciary, and frequently asked questions. Maps, homeland security, military information, and business services are also listed. Get to know the governor and spouse or join the state book club.

Special Features: Interactive guide to NJ, citizen issues

Curriculum: Business; Geography; Government; Social Studies

1504 State of New Jersey Department of Environmental Protection, Division of Fish and Wildlife

www.state.nj.us/dep/fgw/

The New Jersey Department of Fish and Wildlife or NJDFW is dedicated to the protection and management of fish and wildlife in the state. The website offers education information on endangered species, hunter safety, fish species, fishing spots, teacher resources, black bear news and wildlife articles.

Special Features: Species studies, schedule of events, regulations

Curriculum: Biology; Environmental Studies; Science

1505 Thomas Edison's Muckers (Sponsor: About Inc.)

http://inventors.about.com/library/inventors/bl edisonmuckers.htm

This web link is titled, "Thomas Edison's Muckers." Edison would call his young inventors "muckers" and they came from all over the country to Menlo Park, New Jersey, to work with the famous inventor. Read short biographies of the men who helped Edison rise to history.

Special Features: Biographies, photographs, related links

Curriculum: History; Science; Technology

1506 Thomas Edison Papers (Sponsor: Rutgers)

http://edison.rutgers.edu/

The Thomas A. Edison Papers is an online documentary of Edison's papers, patents, family, bibliographies, and companies. The project began in the mid–1970s in celebration of the centennial of the incandescent lamp. Edison had over five million pages in his collection. Over three hundred fifty thousand documents are available here.

Special Features: Photographs, audio files, video files

Curriculum: History; Library Media; Science; Technology

1507 Thomas S. Warren Museum of Florescence

www.sterlinghill.org/warren/

The Thomas S. Warren Museum of Florescence, founded in 1999, is located in Ogdensburg. Home to more than five-hundred-fifty brightly glowing minerals the museum showcases the beauty of fluorescence. The website offers a short biography of Thomas S. Warren, specimen photos, facts and information on fluorescence, and related links.

Special Features: Educator information, searchable site

Curriculum: Science

1508 United States Census Bureau

http://factfinder.census.gov/home/en/kids/fun facts/new_jersey.html

"New Jersey Fun Facts." The Census Bureau put together the population numbers into an easy to read fact page. The kid friendly census data is good for math and logical problems and configuring. Subject ideas include: total population, age, housing, household residence, households, and native languages.

Special Features: 1990 and 2000 data comparison listing

Curriculum: Economics; Government; Sociology

1509 Wild New Jersey

www.wildnj.com/

Wild New Jersey strives to "foster understanding and respect for the wildlife and places in the Garden State." The website is filled with informative articles about bugs, birds, Native Americans, wildlife, photography and fish. The full text articles are insightful to the wildlife in the state. It is organized into four divisions: columns, reports, connections and reactions.

Special Features: Extensive annotated links

Curriculum: Biology; Environmental Studies; Science

1510 William Patterson University English Department and Alumni Association

http://euphrates.wpunj.edu/faculty/parrasj/con ference/WritersConferencemain.htm

The English Department of William Patterson University holds an annual spring writer's conference. Join workshops, readings, creative writing sessions and panel discussions. Authors and poets are available for conversations. The webpage offers conference details and a listing of featured writers.

Special Features: Conference reviews, contact information, related links

Curriculum: Education; Language Arts

1511 William Patterson University New Jersey Project

www.wpunj.edu/icip/njp/

The New Jersey Project is a statewide curriculum program striving for nonsexist multicultural education ideals. The program was developed in 1986 for the development of inclusive scholarship, curriculum and pedagogy for educators. The project publishes journals and resource collections, sponsors classes and networks, and conducts a scholarship competition.

Special Features: Related links

Curriculum: Education; Women's Studies

1512 Workshop on Plagiarism (Sponsor: Janice Cooper)

http://mail.nvnet.org/~cooper_j/plagiarism/

Janice Cooper of Northern Valley Regional High School in Old Tappan, has put together a workshop on plagiarism. This website offers an overview, a list of the materials needed, lesson plans relating to plagiarism and media examples. Website also includes extensive links to copyright related sources.

Special Features: Extensive plagiarism and copyright links

Curriculum: Education; Language Arts; Library Media

1513 Yogi Berra Museum and Learning Center

www.yogiberramuseum.org/

The Yogi Berra Museum and Learning Center is located in Little Falls. The center promotes values such as social justice, respect, sportsmanship through educational programs and exhibits. The website offers a biography of Yogi Berra and a list of educational programming open to the public.

Special Features: Bibliography, summary of baseball literature, classroom resources

Curriculum: Education; History; Physical Education; Sociology; Sports

NEW MEXICO

1514 Alamogordo Chamber of Commerce

www.alamogordo.com/activites/trinty.html

The Trinity Site is where the first atomic bomb was tested on July 19, 1945. Over fifty-one-thousand acres was declared a National Historic Landmark. Radiation is still active around the site although the levels are extremely low. The site is only open two Saturdays a year.

Special Features: Landmark details

Curriculum: History; Science; Technology

1515 American International Rattlesnake Museum

www.rattlesnakes.com/

The American International Rattlesnake Museum is located in Albuquerque. This museum holds the largest collection of different species of rattlers in the world. The website offers detailed information about snakes, photos, artwork, artifacts and memorabilia.

Special Features: Snake information

Curriculum: Biology; Science

1516 Animal Humane Association of New Mexico

www.ahanm.org/

The Animal Humane Association of New Mexico or AHANM was created in 1965. They strive to slow pet overpopulation, supply shelter for lost or unwanted animals, education for the public and promote animal friendships. Website offers pet adoption information, program details, a list of needs and related links.

Special Features: News, programs, services, links

Curriculum: Biology; Sociology

1517 Aztec Ruins (Sponsor: National Park Service)

www.nps.gov/azru/

Aztec Ruins National Monument is located in Aztec. The ruins are preserved structures and artifacts of the Pueblo people dating back to 1100 to 1200. The park was created in 1923 and the grounds include over three hundred acres of land. Website offers facts, kids' corner, history and culture, nature and science.

Special Features: Photos, news

Curriculum: Geography; History; Social Studies

1518 Birding (Sponsor: Robert B. Hole)

www.interaktv.com/NM/NMBirding.html

New Mexico Birding and birding related links. The state bird of New Mexico is the Greater Roadrunner. This website supplies birding resources for the state. Find species checklist, places to go birding, trip reports and other ornithological information.

Special Features: Wildlife checklists, nature centers, Audubon societies

Curriculum: Biology; Environmental Studies; Science

1519 Carlsbad Caverns (Sponsor: National Park Service)

www.nps.gov/cave/galleries.htm

Carlsbad Caverns National Park is located in southern New Mexico. The caves are some of the oldest and most famous in the world for their expansive underground chambers of many colors and shapes. The website offers trip planning, park information and interesting stuff for kids. A virtual tour, fast facts, manuals for teachers and history of the park is included.

Special Features: Bats, photo galleries, related links

Curriculum: Environmental Studies; Geography; History; Science

1520 Centinela Traditional Arts

www.chimayoweavers.com/

Centinela Traditional Arts is gallery of tapestries specializing in hand-woven wool, natural dyes, handspun yarns, and traditional styles. Several weaving works are represented in the website catalog. Products include: blankets, rugs, vests, coats and more. Information on how to use and display weaving in the home and history of regional style is available.

Special Features: Weaving process information, style details
Curriculum: Art; Business; History; Home Economics

1521 Children's Author Carolyn Meyer

www.readcarolyn.com/

Carolyn Meyer lives in Albuquerque. As an author of more than fifty books for young adults and children, her current works focus on strong female characters mostly of the princess or bound to be queen types. Her website offers information on her latest books, grammar problems and a short biography.

Special Features: Author's journal, writing tips for kids and teacher information
Curriculum: Language Arts; Library Media

1522 Children's Author Judy Blume

www.judyblume.com/menu-main.html

Judy Blume is a famous young adult fiction writer who has won more than ninety awards for her work. Although she was born in New Jersey she is a former New Mexico resident. Her site includes a biography, writing tips, related sites, and a kid's page. A favorite question pages answers many questions about the author and her writing.

Special Features: Writing tips, related links
Curriculum: Language Arts; Library Media; Women's Studies

1523 Chile Pepper Institute

www.chilepepperinstitute.org/

The Chile Pepper Institute is dedicated to the education, research, and archival of chile pepper information. The institute is located on the campus of New Mexico State University and collaborates with the chile pepper breeding and genetics program. The site offers extensive chile facts, statistics, bibliographies, nutrition and related links.

Special Features: Photos, terminology, growing tips
Curriculum: Biology; Health; Science

1524 Department of Cultural Affairs, New Mexico Museum of Natural History and Science

www.museums.state.nm.us/nmmnh/nmmnh.html

The New Mexico Museum of Natural History and Science is located in Albuquerque. The museum houses such permanent exhibits as dinosaurs, fossils and volcanoes of New Mexico. The website offers teacher materials and museum details of current exhibits.

Special Features: Dinosaur information
Curriculum: History; Science

1525 Desert USA

www.desertusa.com/mag00/mar/stories/pueblito.html

"Northwestern New Mexico's Pueblitos: A Navajo Legacy," by Jay W. Sharp. This webpage is an article about the Navajo ruins called "pueblitos" or "small villages." The pueblitos were designed in highly defensible areas and are still available for exploration. Photographs of remains are features and rock carving can be viewed.

Special Features: Photos, historical information, related links
Curriculum: Geography; History; Social Studies

1526 Discoverers Web, Andre Engels

www.win.tue.nl/cs/fm/engels/discovery/coronado.html

The famous explorer Francisco Vasquez de Coronado passed through New Mexico in 1540 looking for the legendary cities of gold. This website is a short introduction to the man and his exploration route. Although he never found the gold Coronado experienced impressive geologic formations throughout the Southwest and returned to Mexico to be governor until he died.

Special Features: Related internet resources
Curriculum: Geography; History; Social Studies

1527 El Rancho De Las Golondrinas

www.golondrinas.org1528)/

El Rancho de las Golondrinas or "Ranch of the Swallow" is a living history ranch located on two hundred acres near Santa Fe. Since 1972 the living museum has been bringing the culture of Spanish Colonial New Mexico to life through programming, festivals and theme weekends. The website offers photos, area maps, history and events.

Special Features: Photos, contact information history

Curriculum: Drama; Geography; History; Music; Sociology

1529 From Revolution to Reconstruction, Department of Humanities

http://odur.let.rug.nl/~usa/B/geronimo/geronixx

Geronimo is a famous Apache Indian leader; some of his life was spent in New Mexico. This webpage documents the life of the leader and provides an autobiography organized into parts. View photographs of the great leader and read his story.

Special Features: Photos, biography
Curriculum: History; Social Studies

1530 Georgia O'Keefe Museum

www.okeeffemuseum.org/indexflash.php

The Georgia O'Keefe museum is located in Santa Fe. Although O'Keefe was not born in New Mexico she loved the area and lived and died in the state. The website offers her biography, information about her works and exhibition details. An online gallery of O'Keefe's artwork is offered.

Special Features: Press releases, online exhibits
Curriculum: Art; Women's Studies

1531 Ice Caves Trading Company

www.icecaves.com/

Located on the Continental Divide, the "Land of Fire and Ice" is actually Ice Cave and Bandera Volcano. The Bandera Volcano is a large cinder cone of an erupted volcano and the ice cave is an empty lava tube where the temperature never raises above freezing. The website offers photographs and an education corner for online activities and information.

Special Features: Maps, trail information, related links
Curriculum: Environmental Studies; Geography; Science

1532 International UFO Museum and Research Center

http://iufomrc.org/

The International UFO Museum is located in Roswell. A UFO is rumored to have crashed in Roswell in 1947 and is famously known as the "Roswell Incident." This website offers a summary of this famous occurrence along with a virtual tour, related links and a sightings report form.

Special Features: Kids Club, newsletter, searchable library
Curriculum: History; Psychology; Science; Sociology; Technology

1533 KiMo Theater (Sponsor: City of Albuquerque)

www.cabq.gov/kimo/

The KiMo Theater is a famous Pueblo Deco style picture palace that opened in 1927. The word KiMo is a fusion of two words that means "mountain lion" and has been interpreted as "king of its kind." It was saved from destruction in 1977. Today the KiMo is an art gallery and working theatre. The webpage offers history, schedule of events and restoration documentation.

Special Features: Photos, anniversary news
Curriculum: Art; Drama; History

1534 Library of Congress

http://memory.loc.gov/ammem/rghtml/rghome. html

"Hispano Music and Culture of the Northern Rio Grand: The Juan B. Rael Collection." This is an online presentation of religious and secular music. Collected in 1940, residents of rural New Mexico and Southern Colorado offered hymns, folk drama, wedding songs, and dance tunes for recording. Manuscripts and publications are also provided for insight.

Special Features: Essays, maps, glossary, bibliography
Curriculum: Art; Dance; History

1535 Monterey County Historical Society

http://users.dedot.com/mchs/index.html

The Monterey Country Historical Society was founded in 1935. This society has put together a website full of hundreds of pages dedicated to local history. The site included the Treaty of Guadalupe Hidalgo the document that created California, Nevada, Utah, New Mexico and Arizona and ended the Mexican War.

Special Features: Natural history, people, places, artists, facts and stories

Curriculum: Geography; History; Social Studies

1536 Museum of International Folk Art

www.moifa.org/home.php

The Museum of International Folk Art is located in Santa Fe. It was established in 1953 and is home to more than one hundred thirty thousand international folk art artifacts. It is currently home to one of the largest collections of folk art in the world. The website includes photos of folk art images and current exhibitions.

Special Features: Bilingual, reproducible curriculum

Curriculum: Art; Geography; Social Studies

1537 Museum of New Mexico

www.nmculture.org/

"New Mexico's Cultural Treasures" is an information based catalog of cultural interests from New Mexico. The website offers an index to museums, parks and monuments. The website is organized into alphabetical, interest categories, timelines and regions and is also searchable. A statewide calendar of events is also provided.

Special Features: Cultural events

Curriculum: Art; Geography; History; Library Media; Social Studies

1538 National Atomic Museum

www.atomicmuseum.com/tour/index.cfm

The National Atomic Museum is located in Albuquerque. The homepage offers extensive information of the atomic age from early research to today's peaceful uses. The historical perspective page includes the beginnings, the Cold War and special projects information.

Special Features: Photos, biographies

Curriculum: Government; History; Science; Technology

1539 National Hispanic Cultural Center

www.nhccnm.org/

The National Hispanic Cultural Center is located in Albuquerque. The center or NHCC strives to preserve, interpret and showcase Hispanic culture and art. This webpage offers information on performing arts, visual arts, media arts, culinary arts, and literary arts. Images are also offered.

Special Features: Calendar of events, contact information

Curriculum: Art; Dance; Drama; Language Arts; Music; Social Studies

1540 New Mexico

www.state.nm.us/index.html

This is the official website of the state of New Mexico. The website offers an index of information about the state such as living, working, government, education, tourism, online services and state employee links. Find fast facts, statistics, environment, geography, community information and educator links.

Special Features: School directories, government agency listings

Curriculum: Business; Economics; Geography; Government; Social Studies

1541 New Mexico Arts, Division of the Department of Cultural Affairs

www.nmarts.org/

The New Mexico Arts offers financial support for arts services and programs across the state. This website offers contact information, art links, arts education, news, grants, apprenticeships, and public displays. New Mexico Arts also publishes newsletters.

Special Features: Art advocacy, related links

Curriculum: Art

1542 New Mexico Economic Development, Office of Science and Technology

www.edd.state.nm.us/TECHNO/

The Office of Science and Technology offers a website providing information on entrepreneur resources, a technology directory, telecommunications, and a technology fact book. Its mission is to be the state's advocate for high technology businesses.

Special Features: Aerospace, biotechnical, energy, information technology, optics

Curriculum: Business; Economics; Science; Technology

1543 New Mexico Farm and Ranch Heritage Museum

http://spectre.nmsu.edu:16080/frhm/

The New Mexico Farm and Ranch Heritage Museum offers historical insight to three thousand years of farming and ranching within the state. Located on forty-seven acres in Las Cruces, the interactive living demonstrations of ranch life offer educational opportunities.

The website provides games, online exhibits, educational curriculum and peeks behind the scenes are offered.

Special Features: History of the ranch, programming schedule

Curriculum: History; Social Studies; Sociology

1544 New Mexico Game and Fish

www.wildlife.state.nm.us/

The website of New Mexico Game and Fish includes extensive information on hunting, fishing, conservation, education, and applications for permits. It also includes coloring books, species information and interactive media about wildlife. Find out more about New Mexico's endangered species and wildlife viewing guides.

Special Features: Endangered species, wildlife photographs

Curriculum: Biology; Environmental Studies; Science

1545 New Mexico Kids!

www.newmexico-kids.com/

New Mexico Kids! is a family magazine published bi-monthly filled with activities, directories of youth programs and other resources. It includes cover art by a New Mexico child and provides articles of tips and ideas for children living in the state. The website provides the cover story, a let's draw section and an overview of the current issue.

Special Features: Art, kid ideas, calendar of events

Curriculum: Art

1546 New Mexico Magazine

www.nmmagazine.com/

New Mexico Magazine is in partnership with the State Department of Tourism to publish monthly the culture and heritage of the state. The magazine was started in 1923. The online version offers articles of the current issue and subjects such as history, Native Americans, attractions, geology, and memorials.

Special Features: Cuisine, bibliographies, travel information

Curriculum: History; Home Economics; Sociology

1547 New Mexico Museum of Space History

www.spacefame.org/

The New Mexico Museum of Space History is located in Alamogordo. The complex includes a space museum, planetarium, IMAX theater, Hubbard Space Science Education Facility and the International Space Hall of Fame. The website offers information on each division of the museum and extensive articles on space technology and events.

Special Features: Photos, articles

Curriculum: History; Science; Technology

1548 New Mexico Photographs (Sponsor: Sarbo)

www.sarbo-photo.com/

Sarbo is a photographic reproduction company specializing in New Mexico. The website offers photographs of New Mexico landscapes, historic buildings, Indian pueblos, Indian ceremonial dress, cliff dwellings, national monuments, natural formations and more. These photographs are then available for purchase in stationary format such as note cards.

Special Features: New Mexico photographs

Curriculum: Art; Geography

1549 New Mexico State Department of Education

http://reta.nmsu.edu/reading/

The New Mexico Reading Initiative is a program designed to provide information resources to implement and evaluate comprehensive reading programs. The website offers articles, strategies and conferences on literacy. A bibliography of literacy books is provided.

Special Features: Literacy related links

Curriculum: Education; Language Arts; Library Media

1550 New Mexico State Library, New Mexico Department of Cultural Affairs

www.stlib.state.nm.us/

The New Mexico state Library offers literacy resources such as youth services, interlibrary loan, library for the blind and physically handicapped, and rural services. It also includes a tribal libraries program and books by mail offer for rural New Mexicans. A newsletter is also available for the latest library trends, issues and concerns in library media services.

Special Features: Literacy programs, grants, services

Curriculum: Library Media

1551 New Mexico State Parks Division

www.emnrd.state.nm.us/nmparks/

The New Mexico State Parks website offers extensive information on recreational activities within the state. Plan a visit, learn about boating, find kids' activities or look up a specific park. Breaking news and teacher resources are offered. Online exhibits and related links are listed. Free junior ranger activity book is provided for downloading.

Special Features: Photographs, park details, trails

Curriculum: Environmental Studies; Geography; Science

1552 New Mexico Tourism Department

http://newmexico.org/index2.php

New Mexico is known as the "Land of Enchantment." The geography offers mountains, deserts, lakes and forests. The culture includes ancient peoples, Native Americans, Latino, and more. This website promotes tourism and provides facts and interest points in the state. Find online brochures, order a visitor's guide or plan a trip.

Special Features: Maps, culture, arts and entertainment

Curriculum: Business; Economics; Geography; Social Studies

1553 Office of Child Development

www.newmexicokids.org/

New Mexico Kids is a resource site for support of child care providers, professionals, parents and health educators. It is a network of information, technical assistance and resources. A current list of recalled child care item and toys is posted. Find local child care centers, insurance information, head start programs, county resources and state care regulations.

Special Features: Question and answer toll free numbers, nutrition

Curriculum: Health; Home Economics

1554 Office of the Secretary of State

www.sos.state.nm.us/BLUEBOOK/BLUEHOME. htm

This website holds a great deal of information about the state and its resources. Find the history of New Mexico's state capitol buildings. American Indian culture and history is also available. Symbols, history, government, cultural resources, leisure resources, facts, and media are all listed.

Special Features: Newspapers, statistics, state agencies

Curriculum: Government; History; Social Studies

1555 PBS Weekend Explorer, Nikon

www.pbs.org/weekendexplorer/newmexico/in dex.html

Ruidoso, New Mexico, is an interesting destination with information about Billy the Kid, the Lincoln County Wars, Smokey the Bear and the symbolism of the New Mexico flag. Carlsbad is also an interesting stop as it offers information on bats, cavern facts, and the Living Desert Zoo.

Special Features: Photographs, fast facts

Curriculum: Geography; History; Science; Social Studies

1556 Random House, Inc.

www.randomhouse.com/features/garypaulsen/

Gary Paulsen is one of America's most famous young adult authors. He lives in New Mexico and has written more than one-hundred-seventy-five books. This webpage offers biographical information, questions and answers, survival tips, teacher's information, guides and excerpts.

Special Features: Cover images, reader's guides

Curriculum: Language Arts; Library Media

1557 Regional Educational Technology Assistance

http://reta.nmsu.edu/

RETA strives to integrate technology into the classroom and assists administrators and teachers. This website offers a searchable lesson plan database. Lesson teacher guides are also offered and are provided by grade level. Technology workshops are also offered.

Special Features: Lesson plans and teacher guides

Curriculum: Education; Technology

1558 Santa Fe Opera

www.santafeopera.org/

The Santa Fe Opera was established in 1957. The theater itself is known for its artistic design and contemporary lines. The history of the opera is offered in a timeline format and includes photographs. Biographies are provided of directors and performers. A summary of community education programs is provided.

Special Features: Press releases, publications, schedule of events
Curriculum: Drama; Music

1559 United States Department of Energy

www.lanl.gov/worldview/

The Los Alamos National Laboratory offers the history of the lab, the people who created it and the history that would change the world. Extensive information on the atomic bomb is offered and the history since the bomb is included. Historical photos and biographies can also be found.

Special Features: Article archives, photos
Curriculum: Government; History; Math; Science; Technology

1560 University of New Mexico, Institute of Meteoritics

http://epswww.unm.edu/iom/

The Institute of Meteoritics was founded in 1944. It is dedicated to the study of meteorites using geochemical and microbeam theories. The IOM houses more than six hundred meteorites. A museum is also housed on campus. The website offers photos of the meteorites and meteorite facts.

Special Features: Searchable catalog, images
Curriculum: Science; Technology

1561 VIVA New Mexico, Public Service Company of New Mexico

www.vivanewmexico.com/nm/food.recipes.cocinas.glossary.html

This website is a glossary of New Mexican foods. By understanding New Mexican foods appreciation for the culture grows. The glossary includes basic ingredients, southwestern dishes, deserts, fruits and vegetables, beverages and a list of the most commonly used spices.

Special Features: Alphabetical listing
Curriculum: Home Economics

1562 White Sands (Sponsor: National Park Service)

www.nps.gov/whsa/

The white sands of New Mexico span over two hundred seventy-five miles and are the world's largest dunes of gypsum. The dunes lie at the northern end of the Chihuahua Desert in the Tularosa Basin. Website offers fact sheets, suggested reading, photos and a nature and science section.

Special Features: Plants, animals, ecosystems
Curriculum: Biology; Environmental Studies; Geography; Science

1563 Wheelwright Museum of the American Indian

http://wheelwright.org/

The Wheelwright Museum of the American Indian is located in Santa Fe. The museum hosts historical Native American art intermixed with Southwestern art. Contemporary art is also included featuring sculptures and weaving. The website includes current and past exhibitions and calendar of events.

Special Features: Art images
Curriculum: Art; Social Studies

1564 Woodharvest Writers' Workshops

www.sfworkshops.com/

The Woodharvest Writers' Workshops are one day classes in Santa Fe featuring local and regional published writers. Writing fiction and non-fiction workshops offer a creative outlet with experienced authors. Website offers information of current programs and workshops.

Special Features: Writing programs
Curriculum: Language Arts

NEW YORK

1565 The Adirondack Museum

www.adirondackhistory.org/

Network for NY teachers and students to aid in the study of state and local history. Collects primary sources, historical records, and archival material; presents narrative units.

Special Features: Fully searchable archive database
Curriculum: History

1566 Alliance for the Arts

www.nyckidsarts.org/

Resource for kids and parents seeking arts and cultural experiences in NYC. Arts Guide, Cultural Events Calendar, Family Guide, Links to Cultural Resources.
Special Features: Arts Education Curriculum Guide
Curriculum: Art; Dance; Drama; Education; Music; Social Studies

1567 Catskill Guide (Sponsor: Timothy J. Mallery)

www.catskillguide.com/guide.htm

The Catskill Guide is an online resource for the popular mountain range. FAQ, Forum, Gallery, History, Links sections, plus a bookstore.
Special Features: "The Catskill Archive" with history essays, online books
Curriculum: Geography; History

1568 Citizens Committee for Children of New York

www.kfny.org/youthactionnyc/index.html

YouthInActionNYC is designed to help kids take an interest in the political process and become advocates in their communities. Online resources maintained by NY high school students.
Special Features: How Government Works feature
Curriculum: Government; Social Studies

1569 City Lore

www.citylore.org/

Urban cultural organization focused on the lore, life, and tradition of New York City, but with national subfocus. Online exhibits, projects, resources, and links, plus information about organization, membership, events.
Special Features: NYC celebrations calendar
Curriculum: Social Studies

1570 City of Albany

www.albanyny.org/

Official website for the state capitol. Major content areas for residents, businesses, visitors, government. Fast-find links to city services, offices.
Special Features: Links to local news sites
Curriculum: Government

1571 City of Buffalo

www.ci.buffalo.ny.us/

Civic homepage for the largest Western NY city. Content areas include Leadership, City Services, City Information, News/Calendar.
Special Features: Interactive GIS maps
Curriculum: Government

1572 City of New York

www.nyc.gov/portal/index.jsp?front_door=true

NYC.gov, the official homepage for New York's most famous, most populous city. Major sections for residents, visitors, business, government; content areas include city agency websites, maps, city guides, online civic services, more.
Special Features: NYC For Kids guide to kid-friendly city attractions
Curriculum: Business; Government

1573 Cornell Cooperative Extension

www.cce.cornell.edu/index.php

NY program to enhance environmental and economic well-being of the state through research and education. Community Development, Environment, Family & Youth, Agriculture, Nutrition & Health, Gardening topic areas.
Special Features: Catalog of online fact sheets
Curriculum: Environmental Studies; Health; Social Studies

1574 Department of Earth and Atmospheric Sciences, Cornell University

http://nysc.eas.cornell.edu/

The NY State Climate Office is part of a national climate-monitoring program. Collects and presents data on NY climate, conditions, weather, nationally & regionally.
Special Features: Climate Summaries for Selected Cities
Curriculum: Environmental Studies; Science

1575 Ellis Island Immigration Museum (Sponsor: ARAMARK Sport and Entertainment, Inc.)

www.ellisisland.com/

Official Ellis Island Immigration Museum website. Museum information, events, genealogy resources; plus extensive island history section.

Special Features: 360° QuickTime Virtual Reality Images of Ellis Island
Curriculum: History

1576 Empire State Building Company LLC.

www.esbnyc.com/index2.cfm

Official website for the iconic NYC landmark, the Empire State Building. Take a virtual tour, read about history, construction, business in the ESB, more.
Special Features: ESB for Kids with facts, games, coloring pages
Curriculum: Architecture; Business; History

1577 Empire State Development

www.empire.state.ny.us/

I[Love]NY Online provides information on Travel and Tourism, Doing Business in NY, Starting or Expanding a Small Business, NY High Tech, Filmmaking in NY.
Special Features: World Trade Center Disaster Assistance Programs
Curriculum: Business; Social Studies; Technology

1578 Erie Canal (Sponsor: University of Rochester)

www.history.rochester.edu/canal/

History of the Erie Canal is a scholarly website chronicling the famous waterway. Site is currently incomplete, but already contains a chronology, population statistics, bibliographical documents, topographical maps, more.
Special Features: Biographies of Canal designers, builders
Curriculum: Geography; History

1579 Geophysics at Rensselaer

http://gretchen.geo.rpi.edu/roecker/nys/nys_edu.pamphlet.html

Comprehensive article on New York geology, by professors at Rensselaer University. Covers bedrock composition, geology; information is comprehensive and detailed, but would be difficult for younger students.
Special Features: Many large, color maps
Curriculum: Geology; Science

1580 History of Long Island (Sponsor: Newsday.com)

www.newsday.com/extras/lihistory/

A complete history of Long Island, told by Newsday journalists. A series of essays divided into nine chapters, plus photos, source documents, audio, video and more.
Special Features: Special Topics expands on subjects of interest
Curriculum: History

1581 The Humane Society of New York

www.humanesocietyny.org

Organization dedicated to the care and rescue of animals in NY. Adoption information, services, donations, Rescue Files, off-site links.
Special Features: Focus on animal legislative issues
Curriculum: Social Studies

1582 Letchworth State Park (Sponsors: Tom Cook & Tom Breslin)

www.letchworthparkhistory.com/

Website informs on the history of Letchworth State Park in the Genesee Valley. An Introduction to the Park's History, plus essays, photographs, artifacts, historical documents, maps, and links.
Special Features: Sign their visitor's register
Curriculum: Geography; History

1583 The Metropolitan Museum of Art

www.metmuseum.org/home.asp

Online home of the famous NYC museum. Features over 3000 viewable art images, essays, activities, educational materials, and activities, plus Museum information and history.
Special Features: Education Resources; Timeline of Art History
Curriculum: Art

1584 National Geographic Society

www.nationalgeographic.com/features/97/ny underground/docs/nymain.html

A guide to the New York Underground, featuring information on every strata beneath New York City, from street level, through pipes, wires, subways, sewage, and deep water lines. Plenty of graphics provide comprehensive visuals. Audio tours of the three major levels.
Special Features: Myths of the Underground game
Curriculum: Geology; Science

1585 National Park Service

www.nps.gov/stli/

The Statue of Liberty, national symbol of America and official national monument. Website contains information on visiting the Statue, education programs, facts, kids section, history & culture, employment opportunities.
Special Features: Statue of Liberty (1954) Historic Handbook Online
Curriculum: History

1586 National Public Radio

www.sonicmemorial.org/

The Sonic Memorial Project is a unique memorial to the 9/11 tragedy. Primarily collects and preserves audio traces of the World Trade Center, its neighborhood, and the events of 9/11. Features personal stories, recordings, news broadcasts, a WTC timeline, more.
Special Features: For Educators section discusses using 9/11 and the Sonic Memorial in the classroom
Curriculum: Education; History; Social Studies

1587 Natural History Museum of the Adirondacks

www.adkscience.org/

Adirondack Science Online is a compendium of facts and essays on the northern NY mountain range. Sections of the natural history, flora, fauna, and weather of the area, including a relief map.
Special Features: Online Discussion Area
Curriculum: Biology; Geography; Science

1588 New York Bight Beaches (Sponsors: Phil Stoffer and Paula Messina)

www.geo.hunter.cuny.edu/bight/index.html

Academic site chronicles the natural history, geology, and geography of NY bight beaches. Bight or "bent" beaches stretch along the southern NY coastline, into NJ. Contains multiple articles, plus educational materials, links.
Special Features: Curriculum advice for teachers
Curriculum: Education; Environmental Studies; Science

1589 New York City Roads (Sponsor: Steve Anderson)

www.nycroads.com/

New York Area Roads, Crossings and Exits compiles resources into a navigational aid for drivers in the greater NYC area. The Roads, the Crossings, History & Maps, Links, more.
Special Features: Historical maps
Curriculum: Driver Training; Geography; History

1590 New York History Net

www.nyhistory.net/

New York History Net archives articles, essays, for historians and students of NY history and culture. Includes a section on the history and destruction of World Trade Center Towers.
Special Features: "Drums Along the Mohawk: The American Revolution on the New York Frontier" presentation
Curriculum: History; Social Studies

1591 New York Paleontology (Sponsor: Karl A. Wilson)

http://bingweb.binghamton.edu/~kwilson/home.htm

New York Paleontology presents information on NY fossil finds and the geologic strata in which they were found. Pages divided by geologic period, then by specific location. Spotlights finds of interest.
Special Features: Many pictures of NY fossil finds
Curriculum: Geology; Science

1592 New York Public Library

www.nypl.org/digital/

The NYPL's Digital Archive presents tens of thousands of digital images, sound recordings, and writings from library collections. Content areas include NY state, history, literature, maps, performing arts, science, technology.
Special Features: In Motion: The African American Migration Experience
Curriculum: Library Media

1593 New York State

www.state.ny.us/

Official state website. Provides general state and government information, plus a compendium of links to state-run departments, divisions, organizations, and programs, plus visitor information.
Special Features: Online Citizen's Guide
Curriculum: Government

1594 New York State Archives Partnership Trust

www.nysarchives.org/gindex.shtml

The Archives Partnership Trust presents the holdings of the New York State Archives in a digital form. Ongoing project currently features records, images, essays on historical NY topics collected into subject databases including Family, Agriculture, Rediscovering New York, more.

Special Features: Educational Resources
Curriculum: Education; History; Social Studies

1595 New York State Association of Counties

www.nysac.org/

NYSAC is a nonprofit, statewide municipal association representing the interests of NY counties. Contains information on NY counties, tracks legislative issues, discusses the county system, provides county statistics & research.

Special Features: Interactive County Map with links to county websites
Curriculum: Government

1596 New York State Covered Bridge Society

www.nycoveredbridges.org/

State organization catalogs historic covered bridges, supports preservation efforts, and works to register bridges as Historic Landmarks. Includes maps, photos, a history of bridges.

Special Features: Glossary of Bridge Terms
Curriculum: History

1597 New York State Economic Development Council

http://nysedc.org/

Promotes the economic development of the state and its communities through advocacy, education. Online resources, organization information, membership opportunities.

Special Features: EDC Advance newsletter online
Curriculum: Business; Social Studies

1598 New York State Education Department

www.emsc.nysed.gov/ciai/

Curriculum, Instruction, & Instructional Technology resources for state and national teachers. Covers a wide variety of subjects; each subject provides Information, Assessment, Publications, Resources subsections. Requires Adobe Acrobat Reader.

Special Features: State curriculum standards
Curriculum: Art; Biology; Education

1599 The New York Times

www.nytimes.com/specials/nyc100/contents.html

NYC 100 chronicles the history of NY's most populous city, decade by decade. Also features Special Feature essays. Written by the staff of the *New York Times.*

Special Features: The Big Picture: The New Born City, Seen From Above
Curriculum: History; Social Studies

1600 New York's World Trade Tower: A Living Archive (Sponsors: M. R. Petit/Eric Darton

http://ericdarton.net/

New York's World Trade Towers: A Living Archive is both a tribute to and an exploration of the buildings felled in the 9/11 terrorist attacks. A "cultural living history" the author has collected official documents, apocryphal anecdotes, drawings, photographs, and essays.

Special Features: Afterwords/Afterimages collection of poems, stories, popular culture references
Curriculum: History; Social Studies

1601 Niagara Falls (Sponsors: Rick Berketa and James Brown)

www.niagarafrontier.com/

Niagara Falls Thunder Alley is dedicated to the famous waterfall. Comprehensive coverage of history, geology, tourism, weather, attractions, famous individuals, more. Supported by local interests.

Special Features: Excellent article/index on daredevils who have gone over the Falls
Curriculum: Geography; Geology; History

1602 The Norman Rockwell Museum

http://nrm.org/

Museum dedicated to the iconic American artist and state native. Online biography, gallery highlights, Eye Opener examination of several paintings, museum information, more.

Special Features: Teacher Resources
Curriculum: Art; History; Social Studies

1603 NYSOL Inc.

www.nysol.com/

New York Sports Online covers a wide range of sport activities in NY, from amateur to professional levels. In addition to traditional sports like football, baseball, covers arm wrestling, badminton, bocce, fencing, lacrosse, swimming, more. Provides articles, resources, links.
Special Features: Weekly e-mail list
Curriculum: Physical Education

1604 OldNYC.com

www.oldnyc.com/

Old New York City explores NYC's transportation infrastructure, from abandoned railroad lines to existing roads and planned but never constructed expressways.
Special Features: Virtual tours feature photograph-heavy exploration of sites.
Curriculum: Driver Training; History; Technology

1605 People's History Coalition

www.buffalonian.com

The Buffalonian.com collects history about the city of Buffalo and western New York. Site includes a News Archive, Buffalo History, Video, Forum, more.
Special Features: People Pages allow Buffalo residents to share their own history
Curriculum: History

1606 Rochester Regional Library Council

http://winningthevote.org/

Western New York Suffragists: Winning the Vote chronicles the history of the women's suffrage movement in and around Rochester, NY, one of the birthplaces of the movement. Suffrage history, biographies, timelines, images, links.
Special Features: Images, essays on all the major regional suffragists
Curriculum: History; Social Studies; Women's Studies

1607 Rochester's History (Sponsor: Genesee Gateway)

www.vintageviews.org/vv-tl/

Rochester's History ~ An Illustrated Timeline provides a broad range of resources about the history of the region. Prehistoric geology, native tribes, early settlers, statehood, the Civil War, and modern history are covered, plus numerous sidebar topics.
Special Features: Line Art of Early Rochester
Curriculum: Geography; Geology; History

1608 Senecaindians.com

www.senecaindians.com/default.htm

The Seneca Tribe, one of the Iroquois League of 6 nations, is settled primarily in Western NY. This page collects folklore, history, and culture of the Seneca tribe, as well as modern tribal situations and web resources on the larger Iroquois Nation.
Special Features: Discussion board
Curriculum: History; Social Studies

1609 The Statue of Liberty-Ellis Island Foundation

www.ellisisland.org/

The American Family Immigration History Center preserves immigrant records, passenger lists, information on Ellis Island immigrants. Features section on The Immigrant Experience, including an immigration timeline.
Special Features: Searchable database of Ellis Island immigrants
Curriculum: History; Social Studies

1610 SUNY College of Environmental Science and Forestry

www.esf.edu/pubprog/

Environmental Information Series provides scholarly written articles on NY flora and fauna. Topics include the Adirondack black bear, coyotes, soil pH, more.
Special Features: References
Curriculum: Environmental Studies; Science

1611 The Susan B. Anthony House

www.susanbanthonyhouse.org/

Museum preserves the Rochester home of the famous woman's suffrage activist. Short biography online, timeline, Susan B. Anthony dollar, plus museum information, directions, history, more.

Special Features: Online virtual tour
Curriculum: History; Women's Studies

1612 Traditional Arts in Upstate New York

www.northcountryfolklore.org/

North County Folklore Online collects traditional culture of the Adirondack Mountains and St. Lawrence River Valley. Still a work in progress, it aims to be a collection of educational modules about folk culture and traditional arts in northern New York State.
Special Features: Teacher Resources
Curriculum: Art

1613 Underground Railroad (Sponsor: MKL.Net)

www.freedomtrail.org/

Forging the Freedom Trail is dedicated to the African-American history in NY, especially concerning the Underground Railroad. Provides historical information and links to related resources.

Special Features: Timeline of Black History
Curriculum: History; Social Studies

1614 Upstate New York (Sponsor: R. A. Wood Associates)

www.rawood.com/upstateny/

Upstate New York is a broad collection of informational links about NY. Describes itself as "grassroots," with links collected and maintained by NY residents. Includes links for business (including Chambers of Commerce), education, weather, agencies, visitors.
Special Features: List of, and links for, all major NY universities
Curriculum: Business; Education

1615 Wolf Conservation Center

www.nywolf.org/

Protects and educates about NY's wolf population. Website contains center information, plus articles, photographs, resources, links.
Special Features: Learn About Wolves fact section
Curriculum: Environmental Studies; Science

NORTH CAROLINA

1616 Audubon North Carolina

www.ncaudubon.org/

Established in 1902, Audubon North Carolina is committed to the conservation of birds and their habitats. The website includes a list of sanctuaries, chapters, conservation news, and a newsletter. Birding information includes colonial water birds.
Special Features: Conservation
Curriculum: Biology; Environmental Studies; Science

1617 Autism Society of North Carolina

www.autismsociety-nc.org/

Autism effects one out of every two hundred-fifty people. The Autism Society of North Carolina serves the needs of people with autism and their families. This website offers definitions, starting points, news, bibliographies,

summer camps and events. The home office is located in Raleigh.
Special Features: Fast facts, bibliography
Curriculum: Counseling; Health; Sociology

1618 Carolina Raptor Center

www.carolinaraptorcenter.org/

Conserving birds of prey, their environment and environmental education is the mission of the Carolina Raptor Center. Located north of Charlotte, the center takes care of more than seven hundred injured birds a year. The website includes a question and answer section, a listing of raptor species, fun and games, school programming, news and events.
Special Features: Each species includes facts and statistics
Curriculum: Biology; Environmental Studies; Science

1619 Division of Marine Fisheries, North Carolina Department of Environment and Natural Resources

www.ncfisheries.net/

The Department of Marine Fisheries is responsible for stewardship of the marine and estuarine resources. As early as 1822 the division has been taking care of the North Carolina coastal waters. Educational information on this webpage includes web guides of crustaceans, fish and shellfish. A photo gallery is also offered.

Special Features: Red drum, blue crab industry facts
Curriculum: Biology; Environmental Studies; Science

1620 Greensboro Sit-ins (Sponsor: NRinteractive)

www.sitins.com/index.shtml

This is the story of the Greensboro sit-ins which occurred on February 1, 1960. The website chronicles the events and includes a timeline with historical photos, stories, links to the Greensboro library collection, and an electronic bulletin board for person reflections of the historical sit-ins.

Special Features: Headlines, timeline, related links
Curriculum: History; Social Studies; Sociology

1621 iHigh.com

http://northcarolina.ihigh.com/

This is North Carolina's high school internet network. This website includes high school athletic standings, polls and ratings, playoff updates and championship results. Find tournaments, sports awards, school headlines, audio and video clips, record books and more. Boys and girls athletics are separated by gender and sport.

Special Features: High school sports headlines
Curriculum: Health; Physical Education

1622 Information on the Civil War (Sponsor: Jeffrey C. Weaver)

http://members.aol.com/jweaver303/nc/nccwhp.htm

This webpage is a virtual repository of information about North Carolina and the Civil War. Subjects include general resources, Confederates, Union Units, medical terms, and descendant organizations. Find statistics, election results, ordinances and biographies.

Special Features: County information, genealogy
Curriculum: History; Social Studies

1623 Institute of Museum and Library Services

www.handsoncrafts.org/001.htm

"Hands on Crafts." is a website for bringing crafts, children and families together. The website offers lessons in pottery, weaving, quilting, and basketry. Online studios let you play with clay and create a pottery creation or introduce yourself to weaving and create clothes or baskets.

Special Features: Virtual studios
Curriculum: Art

1624 Kids' Page (Sponsor: North Carolina Department of the Secretary of State)

www.secretary.state.nc.us/kidspg/

Designed especially for students this kids' page offers a wealth of information on the state. Find the North Carolina almanac, state symbols, legends and ghost stories, fun and games, homework help, how ideas become a law, fun facts and a photo gallery. Great kid related links are included.

Special Features: Online stories, curriculum ideas
Curriculum: Government; Social Studies

1625 National Forests in North Carolina

www.cs.unca.edu/nfsnc/

There are four national forests in North Carolina; Nantahala, Pisgah, Croatan, and Uwharrie. This webpage offers outdoor recreation, news releases, forest facts and figures, forest planning and resources and management. Find such information as waterfalls, fishing and air quality readings. Links for requesting forest information and office phone numbers and addresses are given.

Special Features: Trail maps, campsites, forest acreage figures
Curriculum: Geography

1626 National Park Service

www.nps.gov/calo/kids.htm

Cape Lookout, located on the Outer Banks, may seem isolated but this webpage for kids' offers a guide to learn about what is offered in and around the ocean. Find information about birds, plants, shells and sea turtles. Each subject includes photos, identification guides and basic facts.

Special Features: Birding information, North Carolina wildlife

Curriculum: Biology; Environmental Studies; Science

1627 North Carolina Administrative Office of the Courts

www.aoc.state.nc.us/www/public/aoc/kids/index.html

This website designed specifically for children provides information about the North Carolina courts system. Subjects include: kid's window to the court system, guide for educators, and a poem about the state's first African-American supreme court justice, Henry Frye.

Special Features: Educational materials for teachers

Curriculum: Government; Social Studies

1628 North Carolina Aquarium Society

www.ncaquariums.com/

This webpage is a guide to North Carolina's aquariums. There are five aquariums located throughout the state; each is listed here with details about each location and what they have to offer. The aquariums were established in 1976. Educational information on this website includes a kids' page with video clips, games, a coloring book and web cameras.

Special Features: News, research program details

Curriculum: Biology; Environmental Studies; Science

1629 North Carolina Cooperative Extension

www.ces.ncsu.edu/

North Carolina State Extension is an educational organization of research based knowledge helping people for economic prosperity, environmental stewardship and quality of life. Statewide offices and the internet site offer information on agriculture, food, community, environment, forestry, health, gardening, youth and 4-H.

Special Features: Site offered in Spanish, full text publications

Curriculum: Environmental Studies; Health; Home Economics

1630 North Carolina Dance Theatre

www.ncdance.org/

North Carolina Dance Theatre is located in Charlotte. Offering classical and contemporary dance the dance theatre website includes season information, photos, news and reviews, and short biographies of the choreographers and dancers. Educational information includes "Dance 101" a link describing the seven movements of dance.

Special Features: Meet the ballet, dance school information

Curriculum: Dance

1631 North Carolina Department of Agriculture and Consumer Services

www.agr.state.nc.us/cyber/kidswrld/

Kids World is a webpage filled with games quizzes and information about agriculture and its history, plant nutrition, food safety and general nutrition. Find coloring pages, soil facts, puzzles and matching games. The agricultural overview offers statistics and facts about farming and production in the state.

Special Features: Interactive industry map

Curriculum: Business; Home Economics; Social Studies

1632 North Carolina Department of Cultural Resources

www.qaronline.org/

"*Queen Anne's Revenge*: Investigating, Interpreting and Preserving the Remains of Blackbeard's Flagship." *Queen Anne's Revenge* is the name of Blackbeard's flagship that was known to have been lost in 1718 in the Beaufort inlet. This website is the official site to the archeological assessment of the shipwreck. Site offers artifacts, conservation, education, and history.

Special Features: Biography of Blackbeard, history of shipwrecks

Curriculum: Geography; History; Science

1633 North Carolina Department of Environment and Natural Resources

www.enr.state.nc.us/

The NCDENR is that state's stewardship agency for natural resources such as air and water quality. It also works to protect wildlife and wilderness areas. Educational information offered on the website include: data, statistics, maps, reports, environmental education, rules, regulations and permits and licensure for hunting, fishing, mining and more.

Special Features: Kids page, environmental news, pollution prevention

Curriculum: Biology; Environmental Studies; Health; Science

1634 North Carolina Department of Public Instruction

www.ncpublicschools.org/students.html

Provided by the Department of Public Instruction this page is for students of the state. Find cool places to go, homework helpers, state facts and government, volunteer opportunities and information for graduation and beyond. News for teachers and parents is included.

Special Features: Curriculum guides, documentaries, subject guides

Curriculum: Education; Geography; Social Studies

1635 North Carolina Department of Public Instruction, Instructional Services

www.learnnc.org/dpi/instserv.nsf/Category7

This webpage offers instructional services for mathematics. Kindergarten through twelfth grade resources are provided such as weekly essentials, classroom strategies, questions and miscellaneous supplies. Grade level competencies are also included.

Special Features: Curriculum, lesson plans, related links

Curriculum: Education; Math

1636 North Carolina Egg Association

www.ncegg.org/

The North Carolina Egg Association was established in 1960 to promote eggs. North Carolina is twelfth in the United States for egg production. Recipes offered onsite include appetizers, dinners, desserts, side dishes, holiday recipes, pickled eggs, picnic ideas and vegetarian. Egg handling and safety is also provided.

Special Features: Related links, contact information

Curriculum: Business; Home Economics

1637 North Carolina Folklore Society

www.ecu.edu/ncfolk/

The North Carolina Folklore Society was founded in 1913. It promotes the appreciation and study of the cultural heritage of folklife in the state. The website offers definitions and explanations of folklore. It is also a directory to statewide agencies and publications. A bibliography is included.

Special Features: Related links

Curriculum: History; Language Arts; Sociology

1638 North Carolina Library Association

www.nclaonline.org/

The NCLA was established to promote libraries, information services, librarianship, intellectual freedom and literacy in the state. The website provides library news, handbook and library directory. NCLA is also responsible for grants and scholarships.

Special Features: Related links, Status of Women in Librarianship

Curriculum: Library Media; Women's Studies

1639 North Carolina Museum of History

http://ncmuseumofhistory.org/

The North Carolina Museum of History is located in Raleigh. Find different timelines of North Carolina such as women's history, American Indian, or pre–sixteenth century to current day. Find kids section, family fun, teacher information and current exhibits. A schedule of events includes kids' camps and adult education interests.

Special Features: Frequently asked questions, hot topics

Curriculum: Art; History; Social Studies

1640 North Carolina Office of Archives and History

www.ah.dcr.state.nc.us/

This website offers public history services such as publications, state historical records and government records. Find such special features as a timeline of North Carolina events, historical maps, Civil War roster, documentaries, publications, bibliographies, colonial records and more.

Special Features: Site offered in Spanish, related links

Curriculum: History; Social Studies

1641 North Carolina Office of State Archaeology, North Carolina Archaeological Society

www.arch.dcr.state.nc.us/

The North Carolina Archaeology website offers online reports and articles, publications on archaeology and history, underwater archaeology, a listing of archaeologists and websites and cultural resource management. Many educational papers and reports can be read online. The historical highlights of North Carolina are especially interesting.

Special Features: Historical reports, American Indian information

Curriculum: Geography; History; Social Studies

1642 North Carolina Pottery Center

www.ncpotterycenter.com/

The North Carolina Pottery Center is located in Seagrove. The center includes permanent and changing exhibits of pottery from around the state. In addition to exhibits the center interprets the history and technology of pottery, promotes public appreciation and awareness of the heritage pottery has in the state.

Special Features: Pot of the month, student showcase

Curriculum: Art

1643 North Carolina Sweet Potato Commission

www.ncsweetpotatoes.com/

The North Carolina Sweet Potato Commission was established in 1961 to promote sweet potato consumption with programming, research, development projects and information dissemination. Educational information includes: recipes, nutrition facts, statistics, growing instructions, featured chefs, and a kids page.

Special Features: New sweet potato breakthroughs

Curriculum: Business; Home Economics

1644 North Carolina Symphony

www.ncsymphony.org/

The North Carolina Symphony is located in Raleigh. Since the 1930s the symphony has been entertaining the public. The symphony website offers history, educational opportunities for schools, biographies of the conductors and musicians and a musical quiz.

Special Features: Symphony news and schedule

Curriculum: Music

1645 North Carolina Zoo

www.nczoo.org/

The North Carolina Zoo is located in Asheboro. Exhibits and plants are in the "natural habitat" presentation as they would be found in the wild. Find such ecosystems as African plains, the prairie, or the Sonora desert. Educational information includes a species list, biodiversity glossary and a kids' page.

Special Features: Site offered in Spanish, virtual tour, contact information

Curriculum: Biology; Science

1646 North Carolina Zoological Society

www.fieldtripearth.org/

Field Trip Earth although created by the North Carolina Zoological Society is a global resource for students, teachers and those interested in wildlife conservation. The site offers interviews, discussion groups and field reports on wildlife and their habitats. Read diaries, letters, and articles. View photos, and video clips. Students can virtually become part of field studies and research teams.

Special Features: Tools for teachers, essays from experts

Curriculum: Biology; Environmental Studies; Geography; Science

1647 North Carolina's Outer Banks

www.outer-banks.com/

A long chain of sand covered islands extends along the Atlantic coast of North Carolina. These islands are known as the Outer Banks. This website is all about life on these barrier islands. Educational information includes lighthouses, fishing reports, campgrounds, beaches and historical island stories.

Special Features: Wildlife refuges, historical articles

Curriculum: Geography; Social Studies, maps

1648 North Carolina's Writer's Network

www.ncwriters.org/

The NCWN was founded to connect, educate, and encourage writing and writers of all kinds. Established in 1985 the network today offers conferences and competitions. A literary hall of fame is listed on-site. A short biography and photo is provided for each writer.

Special Features: Literary hall of fame
Curriculum: Language Arts; Library Media

1649 Public Library of Charlotte and Mecklenberg

www.bookhive.org/

The Bookhive is an online guide to children's literature and books. Read book recommendations, read stories written by other children, listen to a story or discover fun activities. The website is designed for children age birth through age twelve. Free downloads and activities are provided.

Special Features: Coloring pages, book reviews
Curriculum: Language Arts; Library Media

1650 Regents of the University of Michigan, School of Information

www.ipl.org/div/kidspace/stateknow/nc1.html

The "Internet Public Library" offers facts and figures about North Carolina. Find population, motto, state nick name, state symbols and sports teams. The site includes major industries, historical sites, points of interest and bordering states. Links to encyclopedias and almanacs are included. State related helpful links are also offered.

Special Features: Facts, famous people
Curriculum: Geography; Library Media; Social Studies

1651 Special Olympics North Carolina

www.sonc.net/

Special Olympics North Carolina is a year round sports training and competition for peoples with mental retardation. Special Olympics offer opportunities to develop physical fitness, courage, and experience the joys of friendship with in the community. The website offers fact sheets and history of the program and a listing of sporting events.

Special Features: Annual reports, news, contact information
Curriculum: Health; Physical Education; Sociology

1652 State Library of North Carolina, Department of Cultural Resources

www.startsquad.org/

Lee the Librarian of the "Start Squad" guides kids to the best stuff for children offered on the internet. This program is used to promote the role of librarians and the library in a child's life. The website is organized for preschoolers, elementary, and middle school students. A guide on using the internet with children is provided.

Special Features: Grade level selection, customizable
Curriculum: Education; Library Media

1653 State Library of North Carolina, Information Services Branch

http://statelibrary.dcr.state.nc.us/nc/cover.htm

The North Carolina Encyclopedia is a reference page giving an overview of the state's people, government, history and other resources. Subject categories provided include: counties and communities, education, geography, health, society, history, people, government and symbols.

Special Features: Quick state references and facts
Curriculum: Government; History; Social Studies

1654 State of North Carolina

www.ncgov.com/

This is the official website of the state of North Carolina; the best and original direct source for information about the "Tar Heel State." Find information about the government, citizens, business, tourism, or browse the kids' page. Quick facts and frequently asked questions are provided. North Carolina products are also available for browsing.

Special Features: Transportation maps, natural attractions, job bank
Curriculum: Business; Economics; Government; Social Studies

1655 State of North Carolina Department of Transportation

www.ncdot.org/kids/

The NCDOT kid's page offers educational age appropriate lessons in transportation. "Beauty Fly" talks about beautification programs and talks about recycling and the proper place for trash. "Dot" the littlest civil engineer offers transportation games. Find out about riding trains in North Carolina or download the ferry system activity book.

Special Features: Career ideas, games, activities

Curriculum: Environmental Studies; Technology

1656 TEACH Toolkit (Sponsor: North Carolina State University)

www.lib.ncsu.edu/scc/legislative/teachkit/

The TEACH Toolkit website stands for "technology, education, copyright harmonization act." This is an online resource for teachers to help understanding copyright laws and distance education. TEACH glossary, guidelines, checklist and tutorial is provided.

Special Features: Frequently asked questions, related resources
Curriculum: Education; Government; Technology

1657 University of North Carolina Chapel Hill, Interaction Design Laboratory

http://open-video.org/

The Open Video project began in 1998 it is a repository of digitized videos. The website offers a searchable database by genre, duration, color, sound or origin. View the featured video or the most popular video for down loading. Project news is offered for the latest happenings in the project.

Special Features: Classic television commercials, lectures, documentaries
Curriculum: Library Media; Technology

1658 University of North Carolina Chapel Hill, National Library of Medicine

www.nchealthinfo.org/

North Carolina Health Info offers a listing of health services, providers and programming. Information on conditions, diseases and wellness is available. Drug information, and a medical encyclopedia and health issues are also listed. The website is available in Spanish.

Special Features: Ask a librarian, related medicine and health links
Curriculum: Health; Physical Education; Science

1659 University of North Carolina Chapel Hill, School of Education

www.learnnc.org/

"Learn NC is the North Carolina teacher's network." This is the slogan for Learn NC. Find lesson plans, hot topics, articles, a professional library and online courses for teachers. For students a media center, web quests and a virtual classroom is offered. The website if searchable and includes quick references such as fact books and encyclopedias.

Special Features: Online reference materials, lesson plans
Curriculum: Education; Library Media

1660 University of North Carolina Press, North Carolina Arts Council

www.ibiblio.org/ipa/

The Internet Poetry Archive is sponsored by the University of North Carolina Press. The website offers poetry, a photo of the poet, and a short biography. Audio files are available for listening to the poetry aloud.

Special Features: Audio files; photos
Curriculum: Language Arts; Library Media

1661 USS North Carolina Battleship Commission

www.battleshipnc.com/

The first USS *North Carolina* existed in the 1820s. This webpage is dedicated mostly to the battleship but includes all seven naval vessels. Educational information provided on the webpage includes learning Morse code, the boat's mission statement, or war memorial information.

Special Features: Photos, war history
Curriculum: History; Social Studies

1662 Western North Carolina Nature Center

www.wildwnc.org/

WildWNC is a website filled with nature information. The searchable site offers facts on animals, native trees, naturalist notes, endangered species and upcoming events. Fact sheets are available for students and educators on animals and trees and may be reproduced for the classroom but may not be reprinted otherwise.

Special Features: Related links, nature news, nature center exhibits
Curriculum: Biology; Environmental Studies; Science

1663 Wild Flowers and Plants of North Carolina (Sponsor: NCNatural)

http://ncnatural.com/wildflwr/flowrpg.html

"Wild Flowers and Plants of North Carolina."
This website offers flower and plant information. Browse by common name, Latin name,
color, bloom time and poisonous plants. A list
of endanger plants is included and articles on
special plants and trees are offered.
   Special Features: Wildflower photography
   Curriculum: Biology; Science

1664 Wildflowers of the Southern Appalachian Mountains

www.wncwildflowers.info/

This website is an index to an extensive collection of photographs and descriptions of wildflowers located in North and South Carolina
in the Appalachian Mountains. The flowers are
organized by color, season, and alphabetical by
name. Some species of flowers include related
links.

Special Features: Wildflower photos
Curriculum: Biology; Environmental Studies; Science

1665 The Wright Brothers in Photographs (Sponsor: OhioLINK Digital Media Center)

www.libraries.wright.edu/special/wright_brot
hers/dmc.html

"The Wright Brothers in Photographs." The
airplane has revolutionized American transportation. In 1903 at Kill Devil Hill near Kitty
Hawk, North Carolina, the Wright brothers
tested the first self powered plane. This page is
the brothers' photograph documentation or
collection of powered flight and their lives.
   Special Features: Thesaurus for graphic materials
   Curriculum: History; Science; Technology

NORTH DAKOTA

1666 Birding (Sponsor: Great Blue Media Works)

www.virtualbirder.com/vbirder/realbirds/rbas/
ND.html

This website is dedicated to birding in North
Dakota. The website offers a statewide rare bird
alert; an in depth report of where the bird was
found, who found it and how many. Contact
information is provided for questioning. Other
nature organizations are provided and online
resources are linked to the page.
   Special Features: Rare birds, contact information
   Curriculum: Biology; Environmental Studies; Science

1667 Bowman County Historical Society

www.ptrm.org/

This is the Pioneer Trails Regional Museum
homepage. The museum strives to preserve the
history of the Bowman, North Dakota, area.
Find such areas of study as anthropology, archaeology, astronomy, botany, genealogy, local
history, and paleontology. Each subject includes a bibliography and related links.

Special Features: Virtual tours, photo exhibits
Curriculum: History; Social Studies

1668 Center for Western Studies (Sponsor: Augustana College)

www.augie.edu/CWS/

The Center for Western Studies preserves interprets and promotes the culture of the Northern Plains. The center also includes a repository of over thirty-five thousand books on the
American West. Art and artifacts have also
been collected. The website offers general center information, recent publications, events
and details of the art and artifact holdings.
   Special Features: Online painting images,
artist information
   Curriculum: Art; History; Social Studies

1669 Central Dakota Humane Society

www.cdhs.net/

The CDHS or Central Dakota Humane Society
is located in Mandan and also serves Bismarck.
The webpage offers successful adoption stories
from previous resident animals. Find photos
of dogs and cats. The online library holds a

great deal of information on domestic animal behavior, "how to" instructional articles, and training tips.

Special Features: Pet/domestic animal information

Curriculum: Sociology

1670 Children's Author Jane Kurtz (Sponsor: Leitich Cynthia Smith)

www.cynthialeitichsmith.com/auth-illJaneKurtz.htm

"Interview with Children's Book Author Jane Kurtz," by Cynthia Leitich Smith. Jane Kurtz lives with her family in Grand Forks. She is an author of children's and resource books for teachers and librarians. This page offers insight to the author, her inspirations, writing, and advice for future writers.

Special Features: Conversation with the author

Curriculum: Language Arts; Library Media

1671 Dakota Dinosaur Museum

www.dakotadino.com/

The Dakota Dinosaur Museum is located in Dickenson. The museum includes full scale skeletal casts, dinosaur replicas of an Allosaurus, Albertosaurus, Thescelosaurus, Stegosaurus and more. The Museum opened in 1994. The webpage offers summary of program activities online.

Special Features: Dinosaur photos, virtual tour of exhibits

Curriculum: Science

1672 Dakota Graphics

http://artworkdakota.com/

Artwork Dakota is a website dedicated to promoting the artist Sylvia Lee of Burlington. Find western motifs, wildlife, horses, paintings, and photography. The website offers images of artwork and links to North Dakota history and other area artists.

Special Features: Painting ideas

Curriculum: Art; Business

1673 Dakota Science Center, Grand Forks Public Schools

www.natureshift.org/

Nature Shift: Linking Learning to Life; the mission for this website is to engage learners using higher order thinking connecting humans, history and the world. Find thinking games, science experiments, learn the night skies, Ranger Rosie explores ecosystems, Native peoples, survival adventures, memories and stories for history timelines.

Special Features: Kids, teacher and community use guides

Curriculum: Biology; Environmental Studies; Geography; History; Science; Social Studies

1674 Dakota West Adventures

www.dakotawestadventures.com/

Dakota West Adventures promote the beauty, recreation and opportunities offered in the Badlands. Special features include the Theodore Roosevelt National Park, Maah Daah Hey Trail, and the Little Missouri National Grasslands. Educational information includes wildlife, scenic wonders, and recreational opportunities.

Special Features: Trail information, hunting, birding

Curriculum: Business; Geography; Physical Education; Social Studies

1675 Dakota Zoo

www.dakotazoo.org/

The Dakota Zoo is located in Bismarck. Educational offers of the zoo website include animal pictures of amphibians and reptiles, birds, fish, insects, mammals, primates and animal babies. The zoo offers programming such as adopt an animal, summer kid camps, story time with the animals and more.

Special Features: Photo features include animal facts

Curriculum: Biology; Science

1676 Fargo, North Dakota (Sponsor: John Caron)

www.fargo-history.com/

"Fargo, North Dakota: Its History and Images," written and collected by John Caron. Fargo was founded in the 1870s. Most images found on this site came from postcards; each comes with descriptions and historical comments. Over one thousand images are offered. The website is organized by location, subject and links.

Special Features: History of Fargo before 1900, resident biographies

Curriculum: Geography; History; Social Studies

1677 Fargo Flood (Sponsor: North Dakota State University)

www.ndsu.edu/fargoflood/

This is the "Fargo Flood" homepage. The Red River Valley has flooded many times. This webpage contains information on the histories of the floods, the geology of the Red River Valley, flood gauges and hydrographs of the water levels, and flood emergency resources for the public.

Special Features: Historical flood photos, bibliographies, maps

Curriculum: Environmental Studies; Geography; Science

1678 Fargo Public Schools

www.fargo.k12.nd.us/project/ndwebsite/ND HOME.htm

Washington Elementary School in Fargo designed an educational website about North Dakota. "Welcome to North Dakota! Liberty and Union, Now and Forever, One and Inseparable." Find state information about: agriculture, industry, famous people, history, animals, tourism, letters from immigrants, Native Americans, government and geography.

Special Features: Fourth grade level design

Curriculum: Geography; Government; History; Social Studies

1679 Fishing in the Sioux State (Sponsor: Ocean of Invoman Services)

www.invoman.com/

North Dakota Fishing. This website provides a great deal of information on fishing in the Sioux State. Fishing reports are provided for the major rivers and lakes or find a fishing location by county. Fishing etiquette, tournaments and licensing details are also offered. Hunting in North Dakota is a related link.

Special Features: Ice fishing, maps, humor, photographs

Curriculum: Environmental Studies; Geography; Sociology

1680 Greater North Dakota Association

www.ndhorizons.com

North Dakota Horizons is a magazine emphasizing the people, places and events of the state. The quarterly magazine features such items as history, wildflowers, golf, wildlife, agronomy, quilting, and parks. A feature article is available online. Contact information is available for subscription and mail.

Special Features: Photos and articles about North Dakota

Curriculum: Business; Language Arts; Sociology

1681 Lewis and Clark Fort Mandan Foundation

www.fortmandan.com/

The Lewis and Clark Interpretive Center is located in Washburn. In the winter of 1804 to 1805 Lewis and Clark lived at Fort Mandan with the Indians and met Sacagawea. The fort is now reconstructed and sits next to the Interpretive Center filled with artifacts, displays, and exhibits. Extensive information on Lewis and Clark is provided.

Special Features: Daily journal entries, related links

Curriculum: Geography; History; Social Studies

1682 Lewis and Clark in North Dakota (Sponsor: Senator Byron L. Dorgan)

http://dorgan.senate.gov/lewis_and_clark/con tents.html

Senator Dorgan offers a webpage entitled, "Lewis and Clark in North Dakota." This page offers a detailed, dated itinerary of Lewis and Clark's experience in the state. Find maps, journal entries, and historical documents.

Special Features: Illustrations, diary entries

Curriculum: Geography; History; Social Studies

1683 Library of Congress

http://memory.loc.gov/ammem/award97/ndfa html/ngphome.html

The Library of congress has combined the photographic collections of Fred Hultstrand and F.A. Pazandak to create the online documentary, "The Northern Great Plains, 1880–1920." The online collection includes more than nine hundred photographs or rural and small town life at the end of the nineteenth century. Also includes information on North Dakota immigration.

Special Features: Extensive historical photos

Curriculum: History

1684 Louis L'Amour Enterprises, Inc.

www.louislamour.com/

The famous modern Western novelist Louis L'Amour was born and raised in Jamestown. This website offers a biography, articles, photos, discussion forum and frequently asked questions. He wrote over one hundred books and more than thirty became movies.

Special Features: Bibliography of L'Amour's books in print

Curriculum: Language Arts; Library Media

1685 Minot Public Schools

www.minot.k12.nd.us/mps/cc/ourstate.html

Minot Public Schools hosts a highly educational webpage entitled, "Our State — North Dakota." This website offers information on North Dakota facts and fun, postcard, the top ten reasons to visit the state, history, weather and statistics.

Special Features: Culture, western legacies, energy development

Curriculum: Education; Geography; History; Social Studies

1686 Mni Sose Intertribal Water Rights Coalition, Inc.

www.mnisose.org/profiles/strock.htm

Standing Rock Sioux Tribe Community Environmental Profile. This article about Standing Rock provides information on tribal government, history, land, culture, climate, transportation, tribal economy, education, recreation, public utilities, community services, housing, future and an environmental summary.

Special Features: Reservation overview

Curriculum: Government

1687 National Buffalo Museum

www.jamestownnd.com/promotiontourism/buffalomuseum.htm

The National Buffalo Museum is located in Jamestown. Dedicated to the history of the American bison or buffalo the museum holds artwork, artifacts, and Native American items. Featured items include a ten-thousand-year-old buffalo skull, wildlife mounts, oil paintings and amore.

Special Features: Related links, albino buffalo information

Curriculum: Biology; History; Sociology

1688 National Park Service

www.nps.gov/thro/

This is the website for the Theodore Roosevelt National Park. Roosevelt spent time and money in the cattle business of the state. By spending time in the badlands he experience destruction of wildlife, overgrazing of cattle and therefore conservation was on of Roosevelt's major concerns. The park is over seventy thousand acres and sees almost a half a million visitors per year.

Special Features: Park programs, kids' page, photos

Curriculum: Environmental Studies; Geography; History

1689 Native American Rhymes

www.nativeamericanrhymes.com/women/erdrich.htm

Louis Erdrich is a well known Native American author. She grew up in Wahpeton. Her Chippewa heritage gave her insight and incentive for writing. This webpage is a brief biographical overview of her life and touches upon her writing.

Special Features: Biographical information

Curriculum: Language Arts; Library Media; Women's Studies

1690 Nature Conservancy

http://nature.org/wherewework/northamerica/states/northdakota/preserves/art9058.html

The Davis Ranch, acquired in 1997, is one of the largest prairie landscapes in the area. Made up over seven thousand acres, mixed grass prairie, wetlands, and shrub land can all be found. The region is a natural environment for waterfowl. Educational information on the website includes animals, plants, and location.

Special Features: Prairie information

Curriculum: Biology; Environmental Studies; Geography; Science

1691 Norsk Hostfest

www.hostfest.com/

Norsk Hostfest is "North America's largest Scandinavian American festival." Each year the festival is held in October in Minot. The goal of the festival is to preserve the heritage and culture and weave it into current and future generations. The festival was started in 1978 and today features folk dances, music, heritage exhibits, and authentic Scandinavian cuisine.

Special Features: Hostfest history, hall of fame, school programming

Curriculum: Dance; Music; Sociology

1692 North Dakota Buffalo Association

www.ndbuffalo.org/

The North Dakota Buffalo Association or NDBA offers a great deal of information on the buffalo market and its benefits. Educational information includes production news such as reproduction, characteristics, health, and pasture needs. Buffalo products information includes hunting, meat, tours, hides and processors.
Special Features: Buffalo details of market and needs
Curriculum: Biology; Business

1693 North Dakota Department of Tourism

www.ndtourism.com/

The North Dakota Department of Tourism offers all the best of the state. Find scenic wonders, outdoor adventures, parks, arts and culture, Lewis and Clark, outdoor recreation and more. The online schedule of events offers the most up to date schedule of events in the state. The online photo gallery lets you glimpse what North Dakota has to offer.
Special Features: Photos, trip planner, state wide events
Curriculum: Business; Economics; Geography; Sociology

1694 North Dakota Department of Public Instruction

www.dpi.state.nd.us/

The North Dakota Department of Public instruction offers information on state standards, school district profiles, food and nutrition, Title One, and more. This valuable resource for teachers includes: bringing technology into the classroom, school maps, financing facts, scholarships and grants.
Special Features: State educational guidelines
Curriculum: Education; Government

1695 North Dakota Game and Fish Department

www.state.nd.us/gnf/

Find information about hunting, fishing, boating and the regulations and licenses in the state. Learn about aquatic nuisance species, chronic wasting disease and wildlife. Education classes include hunter safety, boating safety, or women in the outdoors.
Special Features: Birding information, maps, photography

Curriculum: Biology; Environmental Studies; Sociology

1696 North Dakota High School Activities Association

www.ndhsaa.com/

The NDHSAA's mission is to administer interscholastic activities, promote good sportsmanship and citizenship, encourage pride and supplement fine arts as well as athletic activities. The official webpage offers athletic rules and regulations, state results, schedules, and clinic schedules.
Special Features: Athletic and fine arts rules and regulations
Curriculum: Health; Physical Education

1697 North Dakota Indian Affairs Commission

www.health.state.nd.us/ndiac/tribes.htm

The North Dakota Indian Affairs Commission is a liaison between state government and the Indian tribes located in North Dakota. This webpage offers statistics, publications and links to the individual tribes of the state. A searchable tribal resources directory is provided.
Special Features: Tribal website links
Curriculum: Government; Social Studies

1698 North Dakota Information Technology Department

http://discovernd.com/

Discover North Dakota is the state's official webpage filled with facts, history and tourism information. Find facts and symbols, local government, photographs, elected officials, history, and travel. Business, education, employment, health and safety and law are also covered. There is something for everyone.
Special Features: Kids' page, coloring pages
Curriculum: Government

1699 North Dakota Library Association

http://ndsl.lib.state.nd.us/ndla/

The North Dakota Library Association or NDLA offers networking and literacy resources for the state's librarians. The annual conference is held in September. The state's children's book award is called the "Flicker Tale." Contact and membership information is provided.
Special Features: Legislative information, grants
Curriculum: Library Media

1700 North Dakota KIDS COUNT! (Sponsor: North Dakota State Data Center)

www.ndkidscount.org/

North Dakota Kids Count is a project that tracks the status of children across the state. Ten indicators are taken including: educational, social, economic, and physical well being. Website offers fast facts, data, education news, child advocacy, and presentations.

Special Features: Statistics, childcare information

Curriculum: Economics: Education; Geography; Health

1701 North Dakota Maps (Sponsor: University of Texas at Austin)

www.lib.utexas.edu/maps/north_dakota.html

The Perry-Castaneda Library Map Collection includes North Dakota maps. Some map subjects include state maps, cities, historical, national parks and historic sites. Some maps are topographical.

Special Features: Outline and topographical maps

Curriculum: Geography; Social Studies

1702 North Dakota Mill

www.ndmill.com/

The North Dakota Mill is the only state owned milling outfit in the United States. It opened in 1922 after freight costs rose too high for North Dakota farmers and elevators to profit. Today there are five milling unites and elevator and a packaging warehouse. The mill is in Grand Forks.

Special Features: History, retail information, frequently asked questions

Curriculum: Business; Economics; History

1703 North Dakota Museum of Art

www.ndmoa.com/

The North Dakota Museum of Art is located in Grand Forks. Educational information provided at the website includes: current exhibits, past exhibitions, images of the permanent collection, and related artistic links. Admission to the museum is free and is located on the campus of the University of North Dakota.

Special Features: Art images, programming information, events

Curriculum: Art

1704 North Dakota Parks and Recreation Department

www.ndparks.com/

The guide to outdoor adventure in North Dakota is provided by the North Dakota Parks and Recreation Department. Activities such as biking, hiking, canoeing, cross country skiing, snowmobiling, birding and plant identification is included.

Special Features: Environmental centers, nature preserves, parks

Curriculum: Biology; Environmental Studies; Geography; Science

1705 North Dakota Reading Association

http://ndreadon.utma.com/intro.htm

The North Dakota Reading Association or NDRA was founded in 1968 to promote literacy in all areas of education. The NDRA offers professional development, networking, and literacy awareness. The website provides conference information, state authors, newsletter and related links.

Special Features: Legislative updates, reading resources

Curriculum: Education; Language Arts; Library Media

1706 North Dakota State Extension Service

www.ext.nodak.edu/

The North Dakota State University Extension Service is a statewide research base information service. Established in 1914, the service offers a partnership for communities to facilitate programming in areas of critical need such as agriculture, family and youth. Find articles, brochures and field studies on subject such as nutrition, food safety, health, fitness, agronomy, crop production and more.

Special Features: Publications, research, events, directories

Curriculum: Biology; Education; Health; Home Economics; Science

1707 North Dakota State Library

http://ndsl.lib.state.nd.us/

The North Dakota State Library is located in Bismarck. Established in 1907, today it offers leadership and library services for the public. The website offers user friendly links for librarians, state government, the public and volunteers. A manual for the online catalog is included.

Special Features: Online publications, grant information, library directory
Curriculum: Library Media

1708 North Dakota State University, Department of Geosciences

www.ndsu.edu/nd_geology/

"Geology in North Dakota: Resources for students, teachers, geologists, and the public." This website holds information on geologic features and landforms in the state. Read about glacial features, mass wasting, stream features and look at the state from space. Each feature includes location, explanations, and photos.
Special Features: Educational geological links, bibliographies
Curriculum: Environmental Studies; Geography; Science

1709 North Dakota State University, Institute for Regional Studies Home Page

www.lib.ndsu.nodak.edu/welk/

Lawrence Welk was born and raised in Strasburg. The Lawrence Welk Collection was given to NDSU in 1993. The collection includes over ten thousand musical arrangements, scrapbooks, manuscripts, photographs, artifacts, record albums, and oral histories.
Special Features: Summary of Welk's work
Curriculum: Music; Sociology

1710 Plains Art Museum

www.plainsart.org/

The Plains Art Museum is located in Fargo. The art museum opened in 1997 after renovating the old International Harvester warehouse located in downtown Fargo. The webpage offers exhibition information of current shows and permanent collections. The education link offers teacher resources and kid quest.
Special Features: Art images; gallery talks
Curriculum: Art

1711 Sitting Bull (Sponsor: Public Broadcasting System)

www.pbs.org/weta/thewest/people/s_z/sitting bull.htm

Tatanka-Iyotanka or Sitting Bull lived on the North Dakota reservation Standing Rock. This website is a biography of Sitting Bull, his life and accomplishments as the great Lakota leader. A great deal of historical information is provided about related topics.
Special Features: Photo, related links
Curriculum: History; Social Studies

1712 State Historical Society of North Dakota

www.state.nd.us/hist/

The State Historical Society of North Dakota is organized into four divisions; historical preservation, museums and education, archives and library, and support services. The educational information offered on this webpage includes educational resources for teachers, history of North Dakota, North Dakota Governors, Lewis and Clark, Sacagawea, and more.
Special Features: Historic sites, bibliographies, publications
Curriculum: Geography; History; Social Studies

1713 United States Geological Survey

www.npwrc.usgs.gov/

This is the official website of the Northern Prairie Wildlife Research Center. Opened in 1965, the center focuses on waterfowl production, wetland ecology and wetland ecology. Educational information offered on this website includes fact sheets on plant ecology, mammals, migratory birds, river studies, wetland ecosystems, and more.
Special Features: Birds, mammal, reptiles, fish, plants, insects, endangered species
Curriculum: Biology; Environmental Studies: Science

1714 University of North Dakota, Chester Fritz Library

www.und.nodak.edu/dept/library/Collections/spk.html

This is the website of the Elwyn B. Robinson Department of Special Collections. Robinson was a professor at the university famous for writing a six volume history of North Dakota. The educational information provided includes Robinson's biography, a listing of the special collection holdings, extensive papers, documents, photos and maps about or relating to the history of the state.
Special Features: Digital collection of land, and death certificates
Curriculum: Geography; History; Social Studies

1715 Volcano World (Sponsor: University of North Dakota)

http://volcano.und.nodak.edu/vw.html

"Volcano World: The Web's Premier Source of Volcano Information." This is an extensively informative site on volcanoes. Find current eruptions, listings of volcanoes around the world, Mount Saint Helens, volcano adventures, interviews, history, and more. A kids' page is provided. Teaching and learning section offers lesson plans, facts and how to build your own volcano.
  Special Features: Teacher resources, location of world volcanoes
  Curriculum: Geography; History; Science

OHIO

1716 Cincinnati Art Museum

www.cincinnatiartmuseum.com/

Major metropolitan art museum featuring extensive online resources. Virtual tours of museum exhibit halls; explore images from museum collections; research resources and cultural links; museum info, visitor guide, arrange a tour, links.
  Special Features: Teacher's Guides; classroom activities; arrange a class tour
  Curriculum: Art; Education; History

1717 City of Cincinnati

www.cincinnati-oh.gov/

Civic homepage for the OH city. Content areas include Do Business, Live & Work, and Play, plus city departments, civic services online.
  Special Features: Online maps
  Curriculum: Government

1718 City of Cleveland

www.city.cleveland.oh.us/

Civic homepage of the major OH city. Citizen Services, Vendor Services, Government, Mayor's Office, Around Town, Information, Career Center, Kid's Corner.
  Special Features: Telephone Directory; kid's attractions, links
  Curriculum: Government

1719 City of Columbus

www.ci.columbus.oh.us/

Civic government website for OH's capitol. Major content areas include For Citizens, For Business, About Columbus, Where Can I?, City Departments, Civic Services, Links.
  Special Features: Kid's Columbus area with parents, teachers resources
  Curriculum: Government

1720 Civil War (Sponsor: Larry Stevens)

www.ohiocivilwar.com/

OH in the Civil War is a chronicle and bibliography of the units, people, and places involved in the Civil War. Complete regiments list, with histories and bibliographies; plus prisons, war stories, musicians, message boards, resource lists, links.
  Special Features: OH Civil War Research Sites; searchable database
  Curriculum: History

1721 Cleveland Museum of Natural History

http://resource-center.cmnh.org/

Cleveland Museum of Natural History presents the Science Resource Center, providing OH teachers with resources, information, materials for science & social studies courses. Professional development, educational resources, teacher field trips, student programs; many in connection with CMNH visits.
  Special Features: Teacher workshops; educational student field trips
  Curriculum: Science; Social Studies

1722 COSI

www.cosi.org/

Web portal for two COSI science & activity centers in OH, Toledo & Columbus. Online Center info, visitor's guide, tour scheduling; educational resources, including schedules of science programs, camps, events; links.

Special Features: Online classroom activities, optimized for use with a COSI visit
Curriculum: Education; Science

1723 CSU Library

web.ulib.csuohio.edu/SpecColl/cdl/

The Cleveland Digital Archive collects texts, maps, images concerning the history of northeastern OH. Search by subject, date, format, or location, plus bibliography, resource links.
Special Features: Educational Resources for Cleveland History Topics
Curriculum: Education; History; Social Studies

1724 Glenn Research Center

www.grc.nasa.gov/WWW/K-12/

NASA center in Cleveland presents Learning Technologies Project, providing K–12 science & aerospace resources for teachers. Aeronautics; Math/Science Resources; NASA Digital Learning Network; Gallery; Teacher's Corner.
Special Features: Download lessons & activities; teacher's workshops
Curriculum: Education; Math; Science; Technology

1725 Great Lakes Science Center

www.greatscience.com/

Educational center geared towards K–12 learning. Provides several online educational resources, including activities, games, resource links; plus museum info, educational tours, events.
Special Features: Printer Projects; Internet projects; Just Add Water science projects
Curriculum: Science

1726 History Teachers (Sponsor: Ohio Historical Society)

www.ohiohistoryteachers.org/

OHS presents Ohio History Teachers, an extensive educational resource. Teacher Resources, Educational Outreach, Field Trips, Distance Learning, Lesson Plans, Social Studies Content.
Special Features: My Town, Ohio, special third-grade curriculum project
Curriculum: Education; History; Social Studies

1727 Humane Society of Greater Dayton

www.humanesocietydayton.org/

Central OH organization dedicated to animal welfare. Find info on adoption, spaying & neutering, animal cruelty, local shelters, events programs. Part of the Humane Society network.
Special Features: Educational articles; resource links
Curriculum: Social Studies

1728 Jack Nicklaus Museum

www.nicklausmuseum.org/

Museum dedicated to the famous OH golfer, and the sport of golf. Biographical, achievements of Nicklaus online, including career stats, victories; plus museum info, map, links.
Special Features: Virtual Museum Tour
Curriculum: Sports

1729 Lakewood Historical Society

www.lkwdpl.org/buckeye/index.html

The Buckeye Chronicles compiles facts about Ohio's history in an online format. Topic-based directory explores historic events, significant places & people, cultural events, more.
Special Features: Our "Buckeye" Nickname
Curriculum: History; Social Studies

1730 Living History Productions

www.livinghistoryproductions.com/default.aspx

OH historical reenactment society focused on education through performance. Reenacts native culture, colonial, Victorian, early twentieth-century for schools, festivals, and other state events.
Special Features: Schedule a performance for school or classroom; educational resources to accompany performance
Curriculum: Drama; History

1731 Motts Military Museum

www.mottsmilitarymuseum.org/

Columbus, OH museum dedicated to preserving the memory United States Military personnel. Online exhibit information & images, virtual tour, museum & tour information, resource links.
Special Features: Life of General Tibbets; the Schwarzenegger Tank
Curriculum: History

1732 National Park Service

www.nps.gov/hocu/index.htm

Hopewell Culture National Park is dedicated

to historical mound building tribes in OH and the eastern U.S. History of the culture, history of the park, virtual museum, teacher's resources, kid's corner, museum info, links.
Special Features: Curriculum Guide
Curriculum: Education; History; Social Studies

1733 National Underground Railroad Freedom Center

www.freedomcenter.org/

Historical center located in Cincinnati celebrates the struggle for freedom in America. Major content areas include Learn, with online exhibits; Act, with events and activism opportunities; Give, for donations; Visit, with Center info.
Special Features: Educator's resources, including lesson plans
Curriculum: Education; History; Social Studies

1734 The Ohio and Erie Canal: A Photo Essay (Sponsor: Photojournalistas Publishing)

www.photojournalistas.com/Jan_2003/Ohio&Erie_Canal/O&E_canal_index.html

The Ohio & Erie Canal: A Photo Essay, chronicles the over 100 miles of the famous canal system in OH, through a series of pictures and brief essays. Includes technical details on the photographing effort.
Special Features: Canal Source Bibliography
Curriculum: Art; History

1735 Ohio Art League

www.oal.org/

Non-profit organization dedicated to representing and promoting OH artists. Events, membership, publications info, links.
Special Features: OH artists registry with contact info, links to websites
Curriculum: Art

1736 Ohio Biography

www.ohiobio.org/

Not-for-profit site chronicling all the achievements of prominent and famous OH residents. Biographies by name, by county, by occupation.
Special Features: Images; website links
Curriculum: History; Social Studies

1737 Ohio Caverns

www.cavern.com/ohiocaverns/

OH's largest natural cave system, open for tours and educational field trips. Learn about the caves, tours, rates, weather, plus photos, maps.
Special Features: Eight cave-related activities for students & classrooms
Curriculum: Environmental Studies; Geography; Science

1738 Ohio Department of Education

www.ohioreads.org/index.asp

State child literacy initiative promotes reading through programs, materials, educational resources. Find out about OhioReads, get involved, become a tutor, access resources.
Special Features: OhioReads Handbook; Summer Reading Challenge; Happy Birthday, Ohio
Curriculum: Education; Language Arts

1739 Ohio Department of Natural Resources

www.dnr.state.oh.us/geosurvey/

OH Geological Survey collects, researches, and educates on OH's geologic conditions, history. Features publications, digital maps, geologic data; Geology of OH with essays, downloadable maps.
Special Features: Educational Resources
Curriculum: Environmental Studies; Geography; Science

1740 Ohio Department of Transportation

www.dot.state.oh.us/dist1/planning/ohio_maps.htm

ODOT presents a series of state and regional maps for online viewing, printing. Includes historical and modern transportation, county, city, biking maps.
Special Features: Order print copies
Curriculum: Geography

1741 Ohio Ecological Food and Farm Association

www.oeffa.org/

OEFFA promotes and supports local, organic growers & agriculture, and the ecosystem they thrive in. Action Alerts, Consumer Info, Grower Info, Extension Toolbox, Events, Resources.

Special Features: 12 Reasons to Eat Local and Organic; Guide to Ecological Farms and Gardens
Curriculum: Environmental Studies; Science; Social Studies

1742 Ohio Geographic Alliance

www.geography.ohio-state.edu/oga/

State organization develops resources for OH teachers, classroom use; works to establish geography education as a priority; conducts the Ohio Geography Bee. Extensive online state, national Resource Links.
Special Features: Ask-the-Geographer
Curriculum: Geography; Science

1743 Ohio Historical Society

www.ohiohistory.org/

State organization dedicated to historic preservation and education. Multiple extensive and valuable online/digital presentations/collections, plus events, membership, resources, links, more.
Special Features: OhioKids pages; Ohio History Central online encyclopedia; Ohio Memory Scrapbook; OhioPix historical images
Curriculum: Education; History; Social Studies

1744 Ohio Learning Network

www.oln.org/olnhome.php

A consortium of OH colleges and universities enhancing education through technology. Ohio Learns! online course catalog; E4ME electronic learning tutorial; student services; teaching & learning; funding, grants, scholarships.
Special Features: Teacher's resources, development
Curriculum: Education; Technology

1745 Ohio Literacy Resource Center

http://literacy.kent.edu/

OLRC supports adult literacy efforts in OH through programs and materials. Online resources include fact sheets, resource lists, programs info, membership info, links. Includes teacher/tutor resources.
Special Features: ABLE Resources; Eureka AGORA; Women and Literacy Webliography
Curriculum: Education; Language Arts; Women's Studies

1746 Ohio Municipal League

www.omunileague.org/

Organization of OH municipal governments, working together to address statewide issues and concerns of municipal governments. Legislation, news, publications, affiliates.
Special Features: Resource Links
Curriculum: Government

1747 Ohio Public Library Information Network

www.oplin.org/ohkids/index.htm

OHKids offers three levels of kid-friendly websites: Webtots, Webkids, and Webtweens. School Stuff, Clubs, Fun Things to Do, Be Safe areas, more.
Special Features: Homework Help page, divided by subject
Curriculum: Art; Language Arts; Math; Music; Science; Social Studies

1748 Ohio SchoolNet

www.ohioschoolnet.k12.oh.us/

Online suite of resources helps coordinate, oversee responsible use of technology in OH schools. Technical training, teacher professional development, technology procurement, servicing, maintenance, repair, disposal.
Special Features: Educator listserv
Curriculum: Education; Technology

1749 Ohio Wildlife Center

www.ohiowildlifecenter.org/

Wildlife rehabilitation center promotes awareness and appreciation of native wildlife. Info on Rehabilitation, Education, Research, Volunteering, Membership, News & Events.
Special Features: Rabies Report; educational programs
Curriculum: Environmental Studies; Science; Social Studies

1750 Ohio Women's Hall of Fame (Sponsor: Ohio Department of Jobs and Family Services)

www.jfs.ohio.gov/women/Halloffame/

The OH Woman's Hall of Fame recognizes over 300 OH women have benefited state, nation and world. Database of inductees, searchable by name, category, date; HOF History; video history; current nominees; newsletters, news, links.

Special Features: Essay Contest; Resource links
Curriculum: History; Language Arts; Social Studies

1751 OhioDance

www.ohiodance.org/

Statewide resource for dance and movement arts. Events & performances, jobs & rehearsals, membership, dance resources, workshops & classes offered.
Special Features: Dance Education
Curriculum: Dance

1752 Ohioline (Sponsor: OSU)

·http://ohioline.osu.edu/

OhioLine is OSU's extension resource, offering information, news, and education. Online content areas include Yard & Garden, Food, Youth, Family, Farm, Environment, Business, Community, Home.
Special Features: Extension Fact Sheets; OSU Extension Bulletin online
Curriculum: Economics; Education; Environmental Studies; Geography; Health; Science; Social Studies

1753 Ornithology (Sponsor: Victor Fazio)

www.aves.net/

AVES.net Natural history Website is devoted to ornithology, with focus on OH birds. OH Birder Resources, OH Birds & Natural History Magazine, OH Winter Bird Atlas, more.
Special Features: The Birds (Aves)of Ohio list
Curriculum: Environmental Studies; Science

1754 Pro Football Hall of Fame

www.profootballhof.com/

Canton, OH, attraction dedicated to pro football. Hall info, including visitor guide; complete list of Hall inductees; Hall history; NFL history; multimedia files.
Special Features: Educational programs
Curriculum: Sports

1755 Rock & Roll Hall of Fame

www.rockhall.com/

Famous hall of fame in Cleveland honors rock & roll music and its roots. Website content includes complete list of inductees, exhibits information, museum & visitors info, programs for students with teacher's resources.
Special Features: The History and Heritage of Rock & Roll interactive timeline
Curriculum: History; Music; Social Studies

1756 State of Ohio

http://ohio.gov/index.stm

Official government website. Major content areas for government, residents, business, visitors, state employees, plus services, press room, links.
Special Features: Links to all state department websites
Curriculum: Government

1757 State Library of Ohio

www.infohio.org/

INFOhio is a state-funded resource center for OH's K–12 students and teachers. Core Collection, Media Resources, plus specific areas for K–6, 4–8, 9–12, Technology, Teachers.
Special Features: Curriculum Resource Catalog
Curriculum: Library Media

1758 The Toledo Zoo

www.toledozoo.org/

Website for the premier OH zoo. Meet the Animals online, including biological, habitat information; virtual zoo tour; visitor information, maps, events, more.
Special Features: KIDS Corner; teacher resources
Curriculum: Science

1759 UrbanOhio.com

www.urbanohio.com/

Website celebrates OH's urban areas. Collects maps, photographs of urban areas, brief essays, links. Sorted by region.
Special Features: Interactive forums
Curriculum: Social Studies

1760 Weather (Sponsor: Kurt Kovaleski)

www.weatherohio.com/

Weather Ohio compiles resources, links to provide detailed state, local forecasts, plus radar maps, 5-day forecast, OH weather facts.
Special Features: Interactive map provides county-by-county forecasts
Curriculum: Science

1761 Westerville Library

www.westervillelibrary.org/AntiSaloon/

Online presentation on the OH Anti-Saloon League, one of the major forces behind Prohibition. Extended essays on league history, leaders; digital archive of League printed materials; info on Anti-Saloon League Museum.

Special Features: Classroom Activities
Curriculum: History; Social Studies

1762 The Wilds

www.thewilds.org/

Cumberland, OH, animal park and preserve featuring animals from Asia, Africa, North America. Online animals list with images, facts; library of scholarly articles; MultiMedia; Events; membership & support.

Special Features: Learn about educational opportunities
Curriculum: Science

1763 Wm. McKinley Presidential Library & Museum

www.mckinleymuseum.org/

Official library & monument to the former president & OH native, with museum & learning centers. Learn about McKinley & monuments; science exhibits, including Hoover-Price Planetarium; historical collections & library info; programs & events.

Special Features: Teacher's Guide; Schedule a Visit
Curriculum: History; Science

1764 Wright Brothers Aeroplane Company

www.first-to-fly.com/

A virtual museum with extensive essays, images, resources on the Wright Brothers of Dayton, OH. History of flight; history of the Wright Brothers; images, essays of Wright-designed planes; the science of flight; research resources, links, more.

Special Features: Help With Homework; Wright Timeline
Curriculum: History; Technology

1765 Wright-Patterson Air Force Base

www.wpafb.af.mil/museum/

The USAF Museum chronicles the history and traditions of the United States Air Force through displays and exhibitions. Website contains extensive aircraft galleries, plus features on people, history, engines, weapons; museum info, visitor guide, contact, links.

Special Features: Aircraft of the Week; Educational Programs and Services
Curriculum: Education; Government; History; Technology

OKLAHOMA

1766 Asher Public School

http://rolemodel.asher.k12.ok.us

Asher Public Schools has designed a website featuring Oklahoma role models. The page is divided into subjects including: politicians, country singers, entrepreneurs, athletes, astronauts, authors, heroes and actors. Each role model includes a short biography and photo.

Special Features: Famous Oklahomans, role models
Curriculum: Sociology

1767 Bricktown

www.bricktownokc.com/

Bricktown is located in Oklahoma City. It was once the city's first wholesale district. Today it houses tourist attractions of dining, shopping, baseball and more. The website has documented the creation of Bricktown from its beginnings in the 1880s to the renovated leisure area it is today.

Special Features: Photos, newspaper articles
Curriculum: Business; History; Sociology

1768 Cable News Network LP, LLLP

www.cnn.com/SPECIALS/2001/okc/

"The Execution of Timothy McVeigh." The Oklahoma City bomber Timothy McVeigh was

executed on June 11, 2001. This website contains information about the terrorist. Extensive news reports and articles are provided.
Special Features: Timeline of events, photo gallery
Curriculum: Government; History; Psychology; Social Studies

1769 Cherokee National Historical Society

www.powersource.com/heritage/center.html

The Cherokee Heritage Center is located in Tahlequah. The center is made up of the Cherokee National Museum, Tsa-La Gi Ancient Village, Adams Corner Rural Village and current events and programming. The Tsa-La-Gi Ancient Village is a living Museum that recreates the Cherokee lifestyle in the Sixteenth Century.
Special Features: Online newsletter, contact information, bibliography
Curriculum: History; Social Studies

1770 Children's Author Wilson Rawls (Sponsor: Jim Trelease)

www.trelease-on-reading.com/rawls.html

Wilson Rawls was born in Scraper, Oklahoma. Growing up there had no school for Rawls to attend. Wilson's mother then taught the family. When the family moved to an area with schools, the Great Depression led Wilson to drop out of school at eighth grade. His book "Where the Red Fern Grows" took over twenty years to write.
Special Features: Image of Rawls, biography
Curriculum: Language Arts; Library Media

1771 The Dust Bowl, Men, Dirt and Depression (Sponsor: Paul Bonnifield)

www.ptsi.net/user/museum/dustbowl.html

"The Dust Bowl, Men, Dirt and Depression" by Paul Bonnifield is excerpted here to explain the significance and occurrences of dust storms in Oklahoma. Read about agricultural practices that left the land barren. See photos of incoming dust storms. This is a good glimpse of what happened in the Dust Bowl.
Special Features: Historical accounts of dust storms, photographs
Curriculum: Environmental Studies; History; Social Studies

1772 Enchanted Learning

www.enchantedlearning.com/usa/flags/oklahoma/oklahomaflag.shtml

Enchanted learning offers a printable image of the Oklahoma flag. The page also includes Oklahoma facts, map, and symbols. A short quiz is included for education enhancement.
Special Features: Reproducible worksheet
Curriculum: Art; Social Studies

1773 Gene Autry Oklahoma Museum

www.cow-boy.com/museum.htm

The Gene Autry Oklahoma Museum is a dedication to the "Singing Cowboys." Although Orvon Gene Autry was born in Texas, he was raised in Ravia. Today, a town is named after "America's Favorite Cowboy." The museum holds memorabilia of the musical western movies of the 1930s and 1940s.
Special Features: Biography of Autry's life and times
Curriculum: Dance; Drama; History; Music

1774 Geological Survey (Sponsor: University of Oklahoma)

www.ogs.ou.edu/index.htm

The Oklahoma Geological Survey investigates land, water, mineral, and energy resources for the state. The website offers information on fossil fuels, geologic mapping, earthquakes, publications, and photo essays. Many reports and maps are available.
Special Features: Bibliographies
Curriculum: Environmental Studies; Geography; Science

1775 Geronimo (Sponsor: Houghton Mifflin)

http://college.hmco.com/history/readerscomp/naind/html/na_013300_geronimo.htm

The famous Apache leader, Geronimo or Goyathlay was shipped to Fort Sill in 1892. There he learned ranching and farming. He became a celebrity after appearing with President Roosevelt and the St. Louis World's Fair. He died in 1909 of pneumonia and is buried at Fort Sill. This website provides a biography of his life and battles.
Special Features: Bibliography
Curriculum: History; Social Studies

1776 Ghost Riders

www.ghostriders.org/

Ghost Riders is a living history stunt company dedicated to reenacting frontier people and events. Each scene or representation of daily life in the Old West is based on research of the Reconstruction Era of history. The organization is based out of Tulsa. The website offers a list of clients, Old West locations in the state and reenacting links.

Special Features: Western stunt information, firearm safety

Curriculum: Drama; History; Social Studies

1777 Gilcrease Museum

www.gilcrease.org/index2.html

Located in Tulsa, the Gilcrease Museum was founded by the oil businessman Thomas Gilcrease. Pride in his Creek Indian ancestry the art of the American West became the focus of Gilcrease's collection. He deeded his art collection to the city of Tulsa in 1955. The collection includes over ten thousand works of art.

Special Features: Gilcrease biography, virtual exhibits

Curriculum: Art

1778 Information on Oklahoma City Bombing (Sponsor: About, Inc.)

http://history1900s.about.com/cs/crimedisaster/p/okcitybombing.htm

On April 19,1995, at nine o'clock in the morning, the Oklahoma City Federal building was attacked by terrorists and blown up with a truck bomb. One hundred sixty-eight people were killed. This historical disastrous event is summarized into a short article by Jennifer Rosenberg.

Special Features: Related articles

Curriculum: History; Social Studies; Sociology

1779 International Gymnastics Hall of Fame

www.ighof.com/

The International Gymnastics Hall of Fame is located in Oklahoma City. The website includes selection criteria; there are two categories for induction: gymnast and lifetime achievement. Tour the facilities with portraits, memorabilia, exhibits, artwork and a library.

Special Features: Watercolor portraits, gymnast biographies

Curriculum: Health; Physical Education

1780 International Photography Hall of Fame and Museum

www.iphf.org/

The International Photography Hall of Fame and Museum opened in 1977 in Oklahoma City. The mission of the museum is to promote the innovators, technologies, arts and chronology of photography. The list of inductees includes biographies and a photo of the artists.

Special Features: Photographer biographers

Curriculum: Art; History; Sociology

1781 Jim Thorpe Association

www.jimthorpeassoc.org/jimthorpeassoc.org asp/home.asp

Jim Thorpe was born in 1888 near Prague, Oklahoma. His Indian name was Bright Path. He indeed lived a bright path in life as he was known as the world's greatest athlete in his time. Jim played football, won gold medals in the decathlon and pentathlon and went on to play professional baseball. This website offers information on his legacy and how it lives on.

Special Features: Youth programs, biography

Curriculum: Health; History; Physical Education

1782 Kids' Page (Sponsor: State of Oklahoma)

www.youroklahoma.com/?c=112&sc=135

The official kids' page of Oklahoma offers information, activities, fun stuff, research, and school report resources for kids. Find coloring pages, booklists, fact sheets, encyclopedias, statistics, histories and more. Virtual fun includes postcards and games.

Special Features: Student resources

Curriculum: Geography; Government; History; Science; Social Studies

1783 Museum of Musical Instruments

www.themomi.org/museum/Guthrie/index_10 24.html

"Bound for Glory: The Life and Times of Woody Guthrie." This webpage is a virtual exhibition about the folk hero Woody Guthrie. Woody Guthrie was born in Okemah in 1912. The span of his life, works, articles, and music is included. He is best known for writing the song, "This Land is Your Land." He wrote over three thousand songs.

Special Features: Photographs, quotes, lyrics, sheet music

Curriculum: History; Music; Sociology

1784 National Cowboy and Western Heritage Museum

www.cowboyhalloffame.org/

The National Cowboy and Western Heritage Museum is located in Oklahoma City. The museum features such exhibits as art, firearms, paintings, and photographs. The hall of fame includes Westerners, Western performers, rodeo riders and more. Website also includes a kids' page providing songs, games and exhibits.

Special Features: Research center, popular culture

Curriculum: History; Social Studies

1785 National Memorial Institute for the Prevention of Terrorism

www.mipt.org/

NMIPT is the world's largest collection of unclassified information on terrorism available to the public. Terrorism subjects include: aviation, agricultural, Al Qauda, bibliographies, boarder security, combating terrorism and more. Research, outreach, feedback and conference information, publications are provided

Special Features: Searchable, counter terrorism efforts

Curriculum: Government; Sociology

1786 Oil Heritage of Oklahoma (Sponsor: Share Your State)

www.shareyourstate.com/OK/oil.htm

"The Oil Heritage of Oklahoma." This webpage is a short history of the oil industry in Oklahoma. Originally it is said Indians bathed in oil springs believing it would cure ailments. This article includes the "boom and bust" history of oil in the Sooner state.

Special Features: Oil industry links, suggested reading

Curriculum: Business; Economics; History; Social Studies

1787 OKGenWeb

http://marti.rootsweb.com/law/law.htm

This website includes an alphabetical listing of lawmen and outlaws in the Oklahoma and Indian Territory. The listing includes: given and surnames, position or crime, county or territory, and source of information. The website also includes reports, genealogy, hangings, and news.

Special Features: Photos; African American lawmen

Curriculum: Government; History

1788 Oklahoma Authors (Sponsor: Oklahoma State Department of Education)

title3.sde.state.ok.us/literatureanda/

"Oklahoma Authors." This webpage holds a grade level directory for all the authors who were born, lived or wrote stories about Oklahoma. Grade level divisions include kindergarten through third, fourth through sixth, seventh through ninth, and tenth through twelfth grades.

Special Features: Author photos, lesson plan links

Curriculum: Language Arts; Library Media

1789 Oklahoma Baptist University

www.okbu.edu/academics/natsci/planet/index.htm

The OBU Planetarium is located on campus in Shawnee. This webpage explains what a planetarium is, current shows, and offers technical specifications of the projector. Find links to constellations, cosmology, and celestial phenomenon.

Special Features: Constellation identification

Curriculum: Science

1790 Oklahoma Children's Theater

www.okchildrenstheatre.com/index2.htm

The Oklahoma Children's Theatre is located in Oklahoma City. The mission is to provide children opportunity to develop creative potential through theatrical participation and interactive educational experiences. The program began in 1986.

Special Features: Theatrical classes for children and teens

Curriculum: Art; Drama; Education

1791 Oklahoma City Convention and Visitors Bureau

www.okccvb.org/history/ok_history.htm

"Oklahoma History: From Clovis to Statehood" is an article offered by the Oklahoma City Visitors Bureau. The one page article includes a timeline of events that made the state what it is. Other historical articles offered include: Oklahoma City history, statistics, state government, and historical societies.

Special Features: Oklahoma City links
Curriculum: Geography; History; Social Studies

1792 Oklahoma City National Memorial

www.oklahomacitynationalmemorial.org/

9:02 am, April 19, 1995. The Alfred P. Murrah Federal building was attacked by Timothy McVeigh using a rental truck filled with explosives. The blast killed one hundred sixty-eight people. The building was demolished and become the home of the Oklahoma City National Memorial and Museum. The memorial is open all year round.

Special Features: Articles, history, news, educational materials
Curriculum: Government; History; Psychology; Social Studies

1793 Oklahoma City Zoo

www.okczoo.com/

The Oklahoma City Zoo was established in 1904. It is considered to be a living museum and botanical garden. Educational information offered on the website includes species information on wildcats, apes, fish, butterflies, and island life.

Special Features: Photos, schedule of events
Curriculum: Biology; Environmental Studies; Science

1794 Oklahoma Commission on the Status of Women

www.opm.state.ok.us/OCSW/html/hall_of_fame.html

First established in 1965, the commission was created to examine current legal status, potential bias, and quality of life issues for women in the state. Today, the commission includes such topical committees as incarcerated women, domestic violence, geriatric care, health, and poverty. The Oklahoma Women's Hall of Fame is located at the State Capitol.

Special Features: Legislative action, critical women's issues
Curriculum: Sociology; Women's Studies

1795 Oklahoma Department of Libraries

www.odl.state.ok.us/ocb/authors.htm

Oklahoma Center for the Book offers Oklahoma authors, journalism publishers, and booksellers on the web. This is an alphabetical listing of authors that includes "fan pages, profiles, finding aids, and author" websites. The website includes a literary map of Oklahoma.

Special Features: Related links
Curriculum: Geography; Language Arts; Library Media

1796 Oklahoma Historical Society

www.ok-history.mus.ok.us/

The Oklahoma Historical Society strives to "preserve and perpetuate history" of the state. Special project endeavors include encyclopedia project, folk life center, WWII, Korean War, immigrants and more. Archives and historical library links are offered.

Special Features: Interactive map includes museums and interest sites
Curriculum: Geography; History; Library Media

1797 Oklahoma Library Association

www.oklibs.org/

The Oklahoma Library Association is dedicated to promoting and strengthening the quality of libraries, services, and librarianship. The association offers networking, educational opportunities, professional development and conferences. The website offers meeting minutes, hot issues, by-laws, scholarships and employment opportunities.

Special Features: Related literacy links
Curriculum: Library Media

1798 Oklahoma Living

ok-living.com/

Oklahoma Living is the magazine published by Oklahoma electric cooperatives. This webpage offers recipes, restaurant reviews, farmer news, gardening, classified ads and more. Find local weather or search the site for anything Oklahoma.

Special Features: Archives, cover art photos
Curriculum: Home Economics; Sociology

1799 Oklahoma Reading Association

www.oktagagent.com/ora/

The Oklahoma Reading Association strives to increase literacy and promote the love of reading to the people of Oklahoma. The association holds conferences, programs, councils, awards, scholarships and classes for reading and literacy.

Special Features: Reading lists for kindergarten through second grade
Curriculum: Language Arts; Library Media

1800 Oklahoma Route 66 Association

www.oklahomaroute66.com/

The Oklahoma Route 66 Association is dedicated to the preservation and promotion of the classic road Route 66. Follow the virtual trip guide summary across the state featuring historic buildings, roadside attractions, people, history, bridges, museums and more. Educational information includes a town by town tour, fact sheet, and suggested reading list.
Special Features: Virtual museum tours, photo galleries, businesses
Curriculum: Driver Training; Geography; History

1801 Oklahoma State Department of Education

www.sde.state.ok.us/home/defaultie.html

The OSDE offers a World Wide Web resource page including Oklahoma Public School System websites. Schools are divided into elementary through high schools, charter schools, private schools, higher education and a few schools outside of the state. Additional resources include home schooling, administration, curriculum, and technology.
Special Features: Educational and curriculum links
Curriculum: Education

1802 Oklahoma Tourism and Recreation

www.travelok.com/

This is the official Oklahoma Tourism website. Find information needed to plan a getaway to Sooner State. Find attractions, activities, lodging, restaurants, festivals, and recreation ideas. Order free brochures. Website includes photography, facts about the state and related links.
Special Features: State parks, regional interests
Curriculum: Business; Economics; Geography

1803 Oklahoma's Native American Ballerinas (Sponsor: LookSmart, Ltd., Dance Magazine)

www.findarticles.com/p/articles/mi_m1083/is_n2_v72/ai_20187601

Dance Magazine featured the article, "Oklahoma salutes its five Native American ballerinas—Moscelyne Larkin, Marjorie Tallchief, Maria Tallchief, Rosella Hightower and Yvonne Chouteau" written by Camille Hardy in 1998. This article celebrates the dance heritage of Oklahoma. Indian culture is intermixed with classic ballet information.
Special Features: Related terms, multiculturalism
Curriculum: Dance

1804 Sam Noble Oklahoma Museum of Natural History

www.snomnh.ou.edu/homepage/index.shtml

The Oklahoma Museum of Natural History is on the campus of the University of Oklahoma. Established in 1899, the museum has acquired over five million objects. It is said a person can see over three million years of Oklahoma's natural history in one place.
Special Features: Resources for teachers, programming for all ages
Curriculum: History; Science

1805 Samuel Roberts Noble Foundation, Inc.

www.noble.org/imagegallery/

The Noble Foundation Plant Image Gallery is an online educational resource for identifying vascular plants of the Texas and Oklahoma region. The exhibit includes over six hundred species of plants. The plants are organized into forbs, grasses, and trees, shrubs and woody vines. It is a searchable site.
Special Features: Scientific publications and research, agricultural news
Curriculum: Biology; Environmental Studies; Science

1806 State Capitol Building (Sponsor: Frankfurt Short Bruza)

www.oklahomadome.com/home2.htm

Oklahoma State Capitol Dome website. Find all there is to know about the state capitol building. Website includes trivia, press releases, ceremonies, photos, anatomy of the dome, 3D animation, construction methods, timeline, dome builder team and more.
Special Features: Extensive engineering information
Curriculum: Architecture; Math; Science; Technology

1807 Student Guide to Oklahoma (Sponsor: Oklahoma Tourism and Recreation)

www.otrd.state.ok.us/StudentGuide/

"A Look at Oklahoma: A Student's Guide." This student friendly webpage holds information about Oklahoma history, western heritage, emblems, facts, and more. Each subject includes more links coordinating with each subject. Oklahoma has more than sixty-seven tribes of Native Americans and is one of the youngest states in the nation.

Special Features: Photos, images, related links

Curriculum: Geography; History; Social Studies

1808 Tornado Disaster Relief (Sponsor: American Red Cross, CNN interactive, IBM)

www.disasterrelief.org/Disasters/990601Torna doScience/

The website "Disaster Relief: Worldwide Disaster Aid and Information via the Internet" provides extensive information about the May 3, 1999, barrage of tornadoes that hit Oklahoma City. Seventy-six tornadoes touched down in the area with in a twenty-four hour period of time.

Special Features: Tornado safety information
Curriculum: Geography; Health; History; Science

1809 Things Uniquely Oklahoma (Sponsor: David Beatty)

www.geocities.com/Athens/3250/ok/okstuff.ht ml

"Things Uniquely Oklahoma" is an organized index to all things Oklahoma. Subjects include: state treasures, festivals and events, heritage, food, flora, holidays, sports, online publications, maps, web cams, emblems, icons, symbols, fauna, arts, minerals, commemorative days, and related Oklahoma websites.

Special Features: Oklahoma culture
Curriculum: Sociology

1810 Tornado Project

www.tornadoproject.com/alltorns/oktorn.htm

The Tornado Project is a collection of dates and locations of all the tornadoes occurring in Oklahoma between the years of 1950 to 1995. The page includes and alphabetical listing of each county and is organized by date, time, number of people killed and scale of intensity.

Special Features: Extensive tornado information links

Curriculum: History; Science

1811 Tulsa City-County Library

http://kids.tulsalibrary.org/books/okauthors.htm

The Tulsa City-County Library offers a website featuring Oklahoma authors and illustrators. Each author/illustrator includes a short biography and a bibliography database. Over thirty five authors are featured.

Special Features: Books and reading resources
Curriculum: Language Arts; Library Media

1812 Tulsa Race Riot (Sponsor: Nation)

www.thenation.com/doc.mhtml?i=20010820& c=1&s=1921tulsa

Tulsa, Oklahoma, 1921. Many well known dates live in history. The Tulsa Race Riot killed more people than the Oklahoma City Bombing yet no one knows the details. This website contains an eighty year old article covering the horrors of what happened.

Special Features: Race riots, historical news coverage

Curriculum: History; Social Studies; Sociology

1813 WildCare Foundation

www.wildcareoklahoma.org/index.html

Just outside of Noble, volunteers work with injured wildlife at WildCare. WildCare is a wildlife rehabilitation center that cares for more than three thousand animals per year. The website offers animal success stories, education awareness, virtual web cam and species information.

Special Features: Photos, wildlife information

Curriculum: Biology; Science

1814 Wilma Mankiller: Principal Chief of the Cherokee Nation (Sponsor: Powersource)

www.powersource.com/gallery/people/wilma. html

Wilma Mankiller was the first female to lead a major Native American Tribe. She was born in Tahlequah in 1945. Her position of Principal Chief of the Cherokee Nation was hard won as she survived death threats and slashed tires. She is famous for revitalizing her community and promoting interconnectedness of all things.

Special Features: Biography
Curriculum: Sociology; Women's Studies

1815 Your Oklahoma (Sponsor: State of Oklahoma)

www.state.ok.us/

The official state website of Oklahoma is called, "Your Oklahoma." Your Oklahoma offers online services to agencies, businesses, tourism, and resident needs. Find such topics as working, living, recreation, education, health, government, history, and facts. A list of the top ten most popular sites is offered.

Special Features: Governor's web site link
Curriculum: Business; Geography; Government; Social Studies

OREGON

1816 All Oregon Directory

www.all-oregon.com

There are currently over 5,000 links to Oregon-based websites on the All Oregon Directory. From the Oregon coast to the high deserts east of Bend, the state is full of surprises. This directory was created to bring business, real estate, maps, travel, recreation, and employment information about Oregon.

Special Features: Links include Oregon Cities, Oregon Vineyards, Oregon Trail, Education and Instruction, Health and Medicine, Home and Garden, Business to Business and many others
Curriculum: Business; Economics; History; Social Studies

1817 American Civil Liberties Union of Oregon

www.aclu-or.org

The American Civil Liberties Union of Oregon provides services in the following ways: Classroom Aids, Speakers Bureau, Educational Materials, Curriculum Resources, Educators Email Network, Historic Supreme Court Cases, Legal Information Institute Supreme Court Collection and much more.

Special Features: Links include Jobs/Internships, Chapters, Litigation, Politics, Publications, Resources, Students, Teachers, Issues, Quotes, Action, Speakers and others
Curriculum: Business; Economics; Social Studies

1818 Cave Junction, Oregon

www.cavejunction.com

Cave Junction is a small town that is the gateway to the Oregon Caves National Monument and the commercial, service and cultural center for a rural community of small farms, woodlots, crafts people, and families just living apart from the crowds.

Special Features: Links include Area Information, Brief History, Business and Services, Local Links, Local Pictures, Maps, Calendar, Points of Interest, Outdoor Activities and others
Curriculum: Business; Economics; Geography; History; Social Studies

1819 Electronic Universe

http://zebu.uoregon.edu

The Electronic Universe is an educational outreach server at the University of Oregon. Via this Web site, one can find materials and courseware on sciences of all fields, from Physics to Geology.

Special Features: Links include Space Science, Earth Science, Physics Courses, Our Environment, Javalab, Pine Mountain Observatory, McKenzie Page and others
Curriculum: Biology; Geography; Math; Science

1820 End of the Oregon Trail

www.endoftheoregontrail.org

End of the Oregon Trail preserves culture and educates the public about the history, heritage and spirit of the people at the end of the Oregon Trail. Students, Teachers, Homeschoolers and the Public may download any of the information provided for educational use.

Special Features: Links include End of the Oregon Trail Interpretive Center, Oregon Trail History Library, Touring the Oregon Trail and others

Curriculum: Geography; History; Social Studies

1821 Independence Heritage Museum

www.open.org/~herimusm

The mission of the Independence Heritage Museum is to preserve and display the history and culture of the river town of Independence and Polk County Oregon through collections of artifacts, documents and photographs and to make this available to the public by means of tours, programming and access to files and work with other historical groups and community organizations.

Special Features: Links include Exhibits, Willamette River, Independence History, Local Business, Artifacts and Photos, Schools and Churches, People of Independence

Curriculum: History

1822 On This Day in Oregon

www.onthisdayinoregon.com

On This Day in Oregon Web site offers unique history day-by-day. One can view the day's historical event, search a website or look at information via a calendar — January through December. It explores history, names, cities, rivers, pioneers and so forth.

Special Features: One can navigate this Web site by selecting a month link that appears on all pages. That will take you to the first day of that month, then you can select any day — and discover the history of Oregon

Curriculum: History

1823 Oregon Anglers

www.oregon-anglers.org

The purpose of the Oregon Anglers is to further the interests of present and future generations of recreational anglers in Oregon; goals include: promotion of the interests of Oregon's sports fishing community by taking a proactive role in government affairs and many more.

Special Features: A widespread perception is that salmon from hatcheries adversely affect the genetic diversity and fitness of wild fish. Most of the attack on hatchery salmon is based on comparisons between divergent stocks of fish, which is not a true comparison between wild and hatchery fish from the same stock.

Curriculum: Biology; Economics; Science; Social Studies

1824 Oregon Art Glass

www.oregonartglass.com

Oregon Art Glass offers creations in stained glass that are inspirational and a source of joy to behold. It includes an understanding of light and hue, as well as texture and depth.

Special Features: Their mission is to provide quality stained glass windows and artwork for churches, home builders and individuals. Links include Gallery, Catalog and others

Curriculum: Art

1825 Oregon Arts Commission

www.oregonartscommission.org

The Oregon Arts Commission was established in 1967 to foster the arts in Oregon and ensure their excellence. Funding for the commission and its programs is provided by the state of Oregon and the National Endowment for the Arts.

Special Features: Links include Serving Commissioners, Oregon Gallery Guide, Oregon Local Arts Agencies, Oregon Regional Arts Council, and others

Curriculum: Art

1826 Oregon Bioscience Online

www.oregon-bioscience.com

The Oregon Bioscience Online was formed in 1990 to promote the economic development of biotechnology in the state. It provides a continuing forum in which government agencies, business and academia can work together to address the long-term development issues facing biotechnology.

Special Features: Links include BioHistory, Business Development, Communications, Economic Development, Technology Transfer, BioEd Reading and others

Curriculum: Business; Government; Science

1827 Oregon Business Council

www.orbusinesscouncil.org

The Oregon Business Council is an association of more than 40 top business executives focused on public issues that affect Oregon's life and future. Its mission is to contribute to Oregon's long-term social and economic well being.

Special Features: Links include About, Alliances, Members, Policy Focus, Policy Documents, Oregon Business Plan, Employers for Educational Excellence, Oregon Performance Internship and others

Curriculum: Business; Economics; Social Studies

1828 Oregon Children's Theatre

www.octc.org

The Oregon Children's Theatre's mission is to present professional live theatre for youth at a price affordable to schools and families. By educating young people to the wonders of live theatre, this organization enriches lives today, while helping children develop a lifetime appreciation of the arts.

Special Features: Links include Our Plays, Box Office, Education, Our History, Who We Are, Gallery, Calendar, Support Us, Contact Us and others

Curriculum: Drama

1829 Oregon Climate Service

www.ocs.orst.edu

The Oregon Climate Service is the state repository for weather and climate information. They are affiliated with the College of Oceanic and Atmospheric Sciences at Oregon State University. Their mission is to collect, manage and maintain Oregon weather and climate data and much more.

Special Features: Links include Forecasts, Observations, Climate Data, Climate Maps, Satellite, Weather Maps, Periodicals, Reports, What's New, Links and others

Curriculum: Geography; Science; Social Studies

1830 Oregon Coast Aquarium

www.aquarium.org

The Oregon coast Aquarium is a private, nonprofit aquatic and marine science educational facility offering a fun and interesting way to learn about Oregon's unique coastal ecosystem. It is dedicated to teaching marine wildlife and ocean preservation through responsible management and exhibition of marine life.

Special Features: Links include Event Calendar, Membership, Volunteer, Jobs, Education, News and others

Curriculum: Biology; Environmental Studies; Science; Social Studies

1831 Oregon Department of Fish and Wildlife

www.dfw.state.or.us

The mission of the Oregon Department of Fish and Wildlife is to protect and enhance Oregon's fish and wildlife and their habitats; their vision is to provide thriving, healthy habitats for the fish and wildlife of Oregon.

Special Features: Links include News and Highlights, Hunting and Fishing Resources, Wildlife, Natural Resources, Native Fish and Hatcheries program, Marine Program and others

Curriculum: Biology; Environmental Studies; Geography; Science; Social Studies

1832 Oregon Department of Geology and Mineral Industries

www.oregongeology.com/portoff/portoffice.htm

The Oregon Department of Geology and Mineral Industries was created in 1937 as an independent state agency. It has evolved to become Oregon's major source of information to help Oregonians understand and prepare for the vast array of natural hazards that accompany the state's geology.

Special Features: The site explains, for example: Geological Hazards, Strategic Geological Mapping, History and General Information, The Mined Land Regulation and Reclamation Program and many others

Curriculum: Environmental Studies; Geography; History; Science; Social Studies

1833 Oregon Education Association

www.oregoned.org/oea/index.htm

The Oregon Education Association has five goals for assuring quality public education: Promote Safe Schools, Prepare Students for Future Jobs, Provide Adequate and Stable School Funding, and Preserve Education Employee's Benefits.

Special Features: Links include About, Contact, For Members (teachers, education support professional, community college, retired, student), For Parents, Bulletin, Newsflash, Publications and others

Curriculum: Education

1834 Oregon Educational Technology Consortium

www.oetc.org

The Oregon Educational Technology Consortium is a nonprofit organization dedicated to maximizing the value of educational technology by working with software and hardware vendors to procure the most effective and appropriate technological resources at the lowest price possible.

Special Features: Links include About, Price Lists, Newsletter, Software Reviews, Resource Centers, Professional Development, Educational Links, Technology Guidelines and others
Curriculum: Education; Technology

1835 Oregon Electric Railway Museum

www.trainweb.org/oerhs.oerm.htm

The Oregon Electric Railway Museum moved from its original location in 1996. The new museum was built from scratch and includes over a mile of track with overhead wire and yarn leads, a car barn with four tracks, a powerhouse and a small depot. It is run by volunteers; in their collection are a variety of trolleys and traction equipment.
Special Features: Links include About, Trolley Museum, Willamette Shore, News and Events, Schedule and Fares, Equipment Roster, Trolley History, Museum Links and others
Curriculum: History; Social Studies

1836 Oregon Flora Project

www.oregonflora.org

The Oregon Flora Project provides a wide variety of information regarding all of Oregon's fascinating plants; the state is blessed with an enormous diversity of plants ranging from insectivorous cobra lilies of southern serpentines to the stunning mountain heathers of the Wallowas.
Special Features: Links include Newsletter, Participants, Vascular Plant Checklist, Plant Atlas, Flora of Oregon, Contact Information, Herbarium and others
Curriculum: Biology; Environmental Studies; Science; Social Studies

1837 Oregon Forest Resources Institute

www.forestresourceinstitute.com

The Oregon Forest Resources Institute was created by Oregon Legislature in 1991 to improve public understanding of their state's forest resources. The institute provides information on forestry in Oregon and encourages sound forest management.
Special Features: Links include Events, Tours, Education, Rediscovery Forest, Forest Facts, Case Study Game, Flora and Fauna, Wildfires and others
Curriculum: Economics; Environmental Studies; History; Science; Social Studies

1838 Oregon Garden

www.oregongarden.org

The Oregon Garden offers thousands of plants that are displayed in over 20 specific gardens. It includes water features, garden art, wetlands, the Rediscovery Forest, a playful garden for kits, the 400-year-old Signature Oak and Gordon House and much more.
Special Features: Every year, their education department sees nearly ten thousand children participate in their educational programs; they work with the Environmental Education Program and the Forestry Education Program
Curriculum: Biology; Environmental Studies; Science

1839 Oregon Health and Science University

www.ohsu.edu

The Oregon Health and Science University is focused on one central goal — improving the well-being of Oregonians. It educates health and high-technology professionals, scientists and environmental engineers; it undertakes the functions of patient care, community service and biomedical research.
Special Features: Links include Community Relations, Government Relations, Leadership Team, History, Your County and many others
Curriculum: Education; Health; Science

1840 Oregon Historical Society

www.ohs.org

The Oregon Historical Society artifacts collection comprises over 85,000 artifacts, including ancient objects from the earliest settlements, and objects that illustrate exploration in the Oregon Country, the growth of business and industry, the development of artwork and crafts, and maritime history.
Special Features: The Education and Public Programs Department of this Society is actively engaged in educational outreach through the state of Oregon
Curriculum: History

1841 Oregon Humane Society

www.oregonhumane.org

With the help of over 7,000 donors, the Oregon Humane Society completed its most ambitious project in its 132 year history. The new animal resource center and educational facilities began a successful history as a progressive animal welfare organization.

Special Features: Links include Adoptions, You Can Help, What's New, Services, Resources, About Us, Contact Us, Frequently Asked Questions and others
Curriculum: Social Studies

1842 Oregon Library Association

www.olaweb.org

The purpose of the Oregon Library Association site is to keep Oregon's library community informed about events and issues important to association members, libraries, library trustees and friends of libraries across the state.

Special Features: Links include Publications, Calendar, Jobline, Conference, Membership, Continuing Education, Organization, Legislative Agenda and others
Curriculum: Library Media

1843 Oregon Military Museum

www.swiftview.com/~ormilmuseum

The purpose of the Oregon Military Museum is to stimulate scientific literary and educational matters as they relate to State and National Military Departments; to train citizen soldiers and their communities and to accept contributions for preservation of events concerning the Oregon National Army and Air Guard.

Special Features: Links include Location and Visiting Hours, Pictures, Projects, Purpose, Other Museums
Curriculum: Government; History

1844 Oregon Museum of Science and Industry

www.omsi.edu

The Oregon Museum of Science and Industry includes such areas as: Field Trips, Workshops, Outreach Programs, Outdoor School, Camp-Ins, JASON Project, Public Science Day, Science Resources and much more.

Special Features: Links include What's Happening, Camps and Classes, Science Online, Sales and Services, General Information, For Teachers and others
Curriculum: Science

1845 Oregon National Historic Trail

www.nps.gov/oreg

"As the harbinger of America's westward expansion, the Oregon Trail was the pathway to the Pacific for fur traders, gold seekers, mis-

sionaries and others. Beginning in 1841 and continuing for more than 20 years, an estimated 300,000 emigrants followed this route from Independence, Missouri to Oregon City, Oregon on a trip that took five months to complete."

Special Features: This trail is 2,170 miles long and passes through Missouri, Kansas, Nebraska, Wyoming, Idaho and Oregon
Curriculum: Geography; History; Science; Social Studies

1846 Oregon Newspaper Hall of Fame

www.orenews.com/About/halloffame

The Oregon Newspaper Hall of Fame recognizes Oregon newspaper people who have made outstanding contributions to Oregon newspaper journalism or, through Oregon journalism, to newspaper journalism generally or to their communities, region or state.

Special Features: Examples of inductees include: Gov. Elmo Smith, George Putnam, Wendell Webb, Robert C. Ingalls, Paul W. Harvey, William Tugman, William A. Hillard, Walter McKinney and many others
Curriculum: Language Arts

1847 Oregon Newspapers

http://newslink.org/ornews.heml

The Oregon Newspaper Web site includes not only newspapers, but magazines, radio, and television. It is an important business and individual source of media information.

Special Features: Oregon Newspapers include, for example: Albany Democrat-Herald, Ontario Argus Observer, Portland Business Journal, Gresham Outlook, Lincoln City News Guard, Portland Northwest Neighbor, Eugene Weekly, and many others
Curriculum: Language Arts

1848 Oregon Online Highways

www.ohwy.com

"The two-thirds of Oregon that lies on the eastern side of the Cascades receive far less moisture than the coast. Much of the land is occupied by agriculture and cattle ranches, and feels like it has more in common with the Old West than western Oregon."

Special Features: Links include Agri-tourism, Cities, Events, History, Natural Features, Outdoors, State Parks and others
Curriculum: Environmental Studies; Geography; Science; Social Studies

1849 Oregon Pilots Association

www.oregonpilot.org

The objectives and mission of the Oregon Pilots Association is to promote flying safety, promote flying to the non-flying public, monitor regulatory and legislative activities and provide a social forum for pilots and their families.

Special Features: Includes Current Aviation Events, such as (for example): EAA 105 Pancake Breakfast, EAA Gathering at Arlington, Family Fly-In, Stearman Fly-In, Seafair and many others

Curriculum: Social Studies

1850 Oregon Pioneers

www.oregonpioneers.com/ortrail.htm

The Oregon Pioneers Web site focuses on the pioneers of the Oregon Territory up to and including 1855. It is broken down into three sections: The Settling of Oregon, Emigrant Lists, and Researching the Pioneers.

Special Features: Under "Researching the Pioneers," one can link to: Oregon History Timeline, Medical Terms, Trail Links, Maps, Deaths on the Trail, Pioneer Cemeteries and many others

Curriculum: Geography; History; Social Studies

1851 Oregon Public Broadcasting

www.ophb.org

The mission of Oregon Public Broadcasting, an independent, nonprofit corporation, is to provide lifelong learning that informs, educates and enriches people through the development and delivery of exemplary programming and services.

Special Features: Links include Community, Internships, Newsletters, Funding, Directory, Newsroom, Frequently Asked Questions and others

Curriculum: Music

1852 Oregon School Activities Association

www.osaa.org

The Oregon School Activities Association is a nonprofit organization comprised of its member schools, both public and private. It is dedicated to ensuring equitable competition for Oregon high school students. The foundation for that goal lies in the belief that no school,

team or individual should be treated as any more or less than another.

Special Features: Links include Band/Orchestra, Baseball, Basketball, Choir, Cross country, Dance/Drill, Football, Golf, Soccer, Softball, Solo Music, Speech, Swimming, Tennis, Track and Field, Volleyball, Wrestling

Curriculum: Education; Health; Physical Education

1853 Oregon Shakespeare Festival

www.osfashland.org

The mission of the Oregon Shakespeare Festival is to create fresh and bold interpretations of classic and contemporary plays in repertory, shaped by the diversity of American culture, using Shakespeare as their standard and inspiration.

Special Features: They envision their Festival as a creative environment where artists and audiences from around the world know they can explore opportunities for transformational experiences via the power of theatre.

Curriculum: Drama; Language Arts

1854 Oregon Sports Hall of Fame and Museum

www.ohwy.com/or.oresport.htm

The Oregon Sports Hall of Fame and Museum provides exhibits that range from the Oregon Sports Timeline to Terry Baker's Heisman Trophy to catching a major league fastball. The museum is emotional, entertaining, educational and highly interactive. It features 9000 square feet of Oregon sports history.

Special Features: This museum includes hands-on displays, exciting videos, unique photo opportunities, uniforms, trophies, plaques and much more for the sports enthusiast

Curriculum: Health; History; Social Studies

1855 Oregon State Library

www.osl.state.or.us

The mission of the Oregon State Library is to provide quality information services to Oregon state government; provide reading materials to blind and print-disables Oregonians; and provide leadership, grants, and other assistance to improve local library service for all Oregonians.

Special Features: Links include Performance Measures, Administrative Rules, Leadership, History, Directions and Map, Organizational Chart, Government to Government and others

Curriculum: Library Media

1856 Oregon State Marine Board

www.boatoregon.com

The Oregon State Marine Board offers a wealth of information regarding boating. Their first goal is to promote safe boating; their second protecting the environment.

Special Features: Links include Online Boating Guide, Boating and Water Safety, Boating Education, Library — Publications, Laws and Regulations, News, Meetings, Events, Performance Measures and others

Curriculum: Geography; Physical Education; Social Studies

1857 Oregon Symphony

www.orsymphony.org

The Oregon Symphony serves the state of Oregon through the Community Music Partnership, a music residency program specifically designed to serve rural or remote communities. It provides varied music of the highest artistic standards to diverse audiences, with close attention paid to educating children as the musicians and audiences of tomorrow.

Special Features: Links include Season Performances, Tickets and Purchases, News and Events, Support the Symphony, Education and Community, The Orchestra and others

Curriculum: Music

1858 Oregon Trail

www.isu.edu/~trinmich/Oregontrail.html

The Oregon Trail Web site is offered by Mike Trinklein and Steve Boettcher, creators of the Oregon Trail, an award-winning documentary film that aired nationally on PBS. The Web site is to assist teachers and home schoolers — and anyone who wants to learn about the Oregon Trail.

Special Features: The Oregon Trail was the only practical corridor to the entire western United States. What we now know as Washington, Oregon, California, Nevada, Idaho and Utah would probably not be a part of the U.S. today were it not for the Oregon Trail

Curriculum: Geography; History; Social Studies

1859 Oregon Trout

www.ortrout.org

The Oregon Trout was founded in 1983 by a small group of committed conservations. It has long worked to protect and restore native fish and the habitats upon which they depend. Through its advocacy, education and on-the-ground restoration efforts, Oregon Trout has grown into one of the largest, most effective conservation organizations in the Pacific Northwest.

Special Features: Public education is one of the most important services provided by Oregon Trout; examples are Salmon Watch, Stream Adventures, Fish Factoids and others

Curriculum: Biology; Environmental Studies; Science; Social Studies

1860 Oregon Women for Agriculture

www.owaonline.org

The purpose of Oregon Women for Agriculture is to educate the public about the importance of agriculture to the economy and to the environment; to improve the image of agriculture; to support and encourage research that will benefit agriculture and much more.

Special Features: Links include Mission, Membership, Events, Education, Books, Links, Chapters, Contact Us and others

Curriculum: Science; Social Studies; Women's Studies

1861 Oregon Women Work

www.oregonwomenwork.homestead.com

Oregon Women Work is a nonprofit organization that supports the work of Oregon's fourteen Transition programs that assist women entering, re-entering, and/or training for the workforce. Services to single parents and displaced homemakers began in 1985.

Special Features: Examples of purposes include: promote the issues and concerns of single parents and displaced homemakers; work toward the economic self-sufficiency of single parents and displaced homemakers and others

Curriculum: Business; Economics; Psychology; Women's Studies

1862 Oregon.gov

www.oregon.gov

Oregon.gov is the official Web site for the state of Oregon. This useful site includes areas such as: A to Z Agency List, Administration, Business and Consumer Services, Economic Development, Education, Human Services and Health, Local Governments, Natural Resources, Public Safety, Transportation and much more.

Special Features: Additional Links include

Governor's Office, Jobs in Oregon, Online Services, Oregon Quarter Designs, Transportation News, Laws and Rules and others

Curriculum: Business; Education; Environmental Studies; Government; Health; Social Studies

1863 Portland Art Museum

www.pam.org

The mission of the Portland Art Museum is to serve the public by providing access to art of enduring quality, by educating a diverse audience about art and by collecting and preserving a wide range of art for the enrichment of present and future generations.

Special Features: Links include About Us, Visits, Exhibitions, Collections, Calendar and Events, Education, Membership and others

Curriculum: Art

1864 Southern Oregon Visitors Association

www.sova.org/attractions/information.htm

The Southern Oregon Visitors Association works to promote diversified economic development and stimulate the local economy while maintaining Southern Oregon's livability.

Special Features: Links include Attractions, Adventure, Information, Business and Relocation, Driving Tours, Parks and Campgrounds, Services and Shopping and others

Curriculum: Business; Economics; Social Studies

1865 Special Olympics Oregon

www.soor.org

Special Olympics Oregon was founded in 1972 and is a year-round program offering 14 different Olympic-style sports to athletes with mental retardation. Over 5,000 athletes participate in the Special Olympics Oregon.

Special Features: Events include, for example: Law Enforcement Torch Run, Blazers Street Jam, The Bite of Oregon, Governor's Gold Awards, Snow Sports Regional Competition and many others

Curriculum: Psychology; Physical Education; Sociology

1866 State of Oregon

www.stateoforegon.com

The State of Oregon Web site was created to enable all businesses in Oregon to market through an online Web presence at a reasonable cost. It is their hope that the Web site will not simply be a bullet on a checklist of starting a business, but rather that it becomes an extension of the business.

Special Features: Links include Local Information, Business Directory, Local Events, News and Headlines, Link List, Advertise with Us, Web Services, Frequently asked Questions and others

Curriculum: Business; Economics

1867 Welcome to Oregon

www.el.com/To/Oregon

"Oregon is a dramatic land of many changes. From the rugged seacoast, the high mountain passes of the Oregon Cascades, the lush greenery and magnificent waterfalls of the Columbia Gorge, to the lava and Ponderosa pines of the high desert, Oregon's natural beauty has been preserved for all to experience and enjoy."

Special Features: Links include Communities, Activities, Education, The Land, Culture, Facts, Internet, Map, Appreciation Links

Curriculum: Geography; Social Studies

PENNSYLVANIA

1868 Amateur Astronomers Association of Pittsburgh

http://3ap.org/

Astronomy website for hobbyists. Features astronomical guides, special interest groups, info on A3P observatories, feature articles, calendar of events, membership & contact info.

Special Features: Light Pollution Guide

Curriculum: Science

1869 Carnegie Museum of Natural History

www.carnegiemnh.org/

Pittsburgh museum featuring scientific ex-

hibits. Museum info, Plan Your Visit, Exhibits, Education, Research & Collections, Member Center, museum news, contact info.
Special Features: Dinosaur PaleoLab online
Curriculum: History; Science

1870 Citizens for the Arts in Pennsylvania

www.paarts.org/

Organization committed to advancing the arts in PA through advocacy, programs, services. Advocacy, Arts in Education, Cultural Tourism, Funding Resources, *The Citizen Online*, Members Links, Membership.
Special Features: Links to Art Education Sites
Curriculum: Art; Dance; Drama; Education; Music

1871 City of Harrisburg

www.harrisburgpa.gov/

Civic website for the PA capital. Careers, Special Events, Visitor Information, Economic Profile, Press Releases, Downtown Parking; plus city departments, services online.
Special Features: Harrisburg History project (requires Adobe Acrobat Reader)
Curriculum: Government; History

1872 City of Philadelphia

www.phila.gov/

Civic website for PA's largest city. Content areas for Visitors, Residents, Businesses; plus Mayor's office, City Council, City Departments, online directory, features, news, events, links.
Special Features: Online civic services
Curriculum: Government

1873 City of Pittsburgh

www.city.pittsburgh.pa.us/

Civic website for the significant PA city. Website sections for City Services, Community & Visitors, Businesses, Mayor, Council, Departments, Jobs, links.
Special Features: City of Pittsburgh Maps; photo gallery
Curriculum: Government

1874 Coal Region Enterprises

www.coalregion.com/home.htm

Website about life, lore of Anthracite Coal Region of PA. CoalSpeak dialect dictionary; Patch Towns; famous Coal Crackers; Message Boards; more.
Special Features: Historic and modern images
Curriculum: Geography; History; Social Studies

1875 County Commission Association of Pennsylvania

www.pacounties.org/

CCAP provides support for PA counties to better regulate and legislate. County news, legislation, info; support resources; contact and links.
Special Features: Doing Business with PA Counties
Curriculum: Business; Government

1876 Covered Bridges (Sponsor: Roger A. McCain)

william-king.www.drexel.edu/top/bridge/CB1.html

A Guide to Old Covered Bridges of Southeastern Pennsylvania features, essays, photos of existing and historic covered bridges. Guides to bridges sorted by locality, route.
Special Features: Photo essays
Curriculum: Art; History

1877 Daniel Boone Homestead (Sponsor: BerksWeb)

www.berksweb.com/boone.html

The Daniel Boone Homestead preserves the birthplace of the pioneer hero. History of the homestead, map, Daniel Boone biography, images, the Boones in PA, links.
Special Features: Ben Franklin's Mortgage on the Daniel Boone Farm
Curriculum: History

1878 Flagship Niagara League

www.brigniagara.org/

The U.S.S. *Brig Niagara*, based in Erie, PA, and the Erie Maritime Museum. *Niagara*'s history, specs, sailing schedule & calendar of events; Museum info, tours, events; Flagship *Niagara* league info.
Special Features: *Niagara* Education opportunities; image gallery
Curriculum: History

1879 The Franklin Institute

www.fi.edu/

Online presence of the Philadelphia science museum has extensive online content. Learn, Explore, Visit; online exhibits & activities; Benjamin Franklin, the Wright Brothers, virtual tours, live webcams; education resources; museum info, visitor's guide, field trip guide, links, more.

Special Features: Community Science Action Guides for teachers; Online Math Collection; Educational Hotlists

Curriculum: Biology; Education; Environmental Studies; Health; History; Science; Social Studies; Technology

1880 German Society of Pennsylvania

www.germansociety.org/

Group dedicated to significant PA ethnic heritage. History, Calendar of Events, Library Project, German and English Courses, Directions, Membership, Scholarship Information and Application, Links.

Special Features: Society bylaws
Curriculum: History; Social Studies

1881 Gettysburg National Military Park (Sponsor: National Park Service)

www.nps.gov/gett/index.htm

Gettysburg National Military Park preserves the site of the famous Civil War battle. Extensive info, including battle history, virtual battlefield tour, the Life of a Soldier, nature & science; plus Kid's activities, plan a visit, contact info.

Special Features: Gettysburg Teacher's Guide & Resources
Curriculum: Education; History

1882 Gettysburg.com

www.gettysburg.com/

Extensive historical site with essays, maps, resource links. The Story of the Battle of Gettysburg, Battlefield Maps, Battle News, History Stories Archives, Living History Center, General Lee's Farewell Address, reenactment events & info; plus modern regional info, maps, visitor's guide.

Special Features: Attend a Living History reenactment
Curriculum: History

1883 Harvey's Lake (Sponsor: F. Charles Petrilo)

www.harveyslake.org/

Extensive history of Harvey's Lake in Luzerne County PA, serves as cultural history of the area. Take the History Tour; Photo Gallery; classic postcards; Ice Cutters; the Railroad; the Trolley; Schools; Myths & Legends.

Special Features: Articles in either HTML or .pdf format for printing (requires Adobe Acrobat Reader)
Curriculum: History; Social Studies

1884 Historical Society of Pennsylvania

www.hsp.org/

Historical studies organization collects, preserves, educates on PA history, artifacts, sites. Exhibits, including online; educational resources; Online Catalogs, Research Guides, Library Services; events, news, links.

Special Features: Pennsylvania Ethnic History; Philadelphia History; History; Education Links
Curriculum: Education; History

1885 History (Sponsor: WITF, Inc.)

www.explorepahistory.com/

ExplorePAHistory.com, an extensive website with essays, exhibits, images, activities. Explore PA History, Visit PA Regions, Teach PA History; plus Features, Upcoming Events, PA Travel.

Special Features: Online lesson plans; Interact With History
Curriculum: History

1886 Independence National Historical Park (Sponsor: National Park Service)

www.nps.gov/inde/

Independence National Historical Park in Philadelphia preserves the "birthplace of America." Famous features include the Liberty Bell, Independence hall, Ben Franklin National Monument; in depth history, images, Park info, more.

Special Features: Teacher's Guide for Park visits; Following Franklin's Footsteps
Curriculum: Education; Government; History

1887 James Buchanan Foundation

www.wheatland.org/

Wheatland, estate and museum for James Buchanan, fifteenth President of the United States. Read Buchanan, Harriet lane Johnston bios; Mansion history, floor plan; Special Events, Hours and Location, Education Programs, Group Tours, Membership, Volunteer.

Special Features: Schedule an educational tour

Curriculum: History

1888 Landis Valley Museum

www.landisvalleymuseum.org/

Living history museum collects, conserves, exhibits, and interprets PA German culture, history, and heritage. Museum, collections, visitor's info; 360-degree virtual tour; educational resources; children's programs; activity pages; contact and links.

Special Features: Field trip planning guide, including curriculum materials

Curriculum: History; Social Studies

1889 Lehigh University Library

digital.lib.lehigh.edu/

Lehigh University's Digital Library features four collections. Digital Bridges; Lehigh Valley Geology; Illuminated Manuscripts; The Problem of the Planets.

Special Features: Color geological maps; printable PDFs (requires Adobe Acrobat Reader)

Curriculum: Environmental Studies; Geography; Language Arts; Science

1890 Local Government Academy

www.localgovernmentacademy.org/

Education institution works to improve municipal government by training PA citizens for local service. Find out about info, programs, services; Academy info, contact, links.

Special Features: Register for courses

Curriculum: Education; Government

1891 Maps of Pennsylvania (Source: Harold Cramer)

www.mapsofpa.com/

Historic Maps of PA features online collections of 16th, 17th, 18th, 19th, 20th century maps; map lists, references, links.

Special Features: Site goal is to provide a map for every year since founded

Curriculum: Geography; History

1892 National Constitution Center

www.constitutioncenter.org/

Organization dedicated to increasing understanding of, and appreciation for, the Constitution, its history, and its contemporary relevance. Explore the Constitution online, including full text, scholarly analyses; access educational resources; Center info, events & programs, news, links.

Special Features: Curriculum Resources; Current Events For the Classroom; Save the Bill of Rights game

Curriculum: Education; Government; History

1893 Pennsylvania Department of Conservation and Natural Resources

www.dcnr.state.pa.us/topogeo/index.aspx

PA Geological Survey collects, studies, educates about PA geology. Online Field Guide, Geologic Hazards, Groundwater; For Teachers; Kid's Corner; library with photos, maps; publications; GeoLinks.

Special Features: Digital Geospatial Data; curriculum resources

Curriculum: Education; Geography; Science

1894 Pennsylvania Dutch (Sponsor: Horseshoe.cc)

www.horseshoe.cc/

Pioneers and Patriarchs provides extensive writings on the history, culture of the Pennsylvania Dutch (Germans). Culture, Family, History, Graveyards, Places, People, Old Trades, Religion, Food, plus links.

Special Features: PA Dutch country maps; Quaint Idioms and Expressions of the Pennsylvania Germans

Curriculum: History; Social Studies

1895 Pennsylvania Environmental Council

www.watershedatlas.org/index.html

PA Watershed Atlas presents an educational look at PA water systems. What is a Watershed?; Explore the Allegheny and Monongahela Watersheds; Resource Center; maps; glossary; resource links.

Special Features: Full color diagrams; A Watershed Primer for Pennsylvania

Curriculum: Education; Environmental Studies; Science

1896 Pennsylvania Game Commission

http://sites.state.pa.us/PA_Exec/PGC/endangered/

PA Endangered and Threatened Species. Complete list, with species profile, habitat notes, nesting patterns. Includes links to related resources.

Special Features: Page on the extinct PA passenger pigeon

Curriculum: Environmental Studies; Science; Social Studies

1897 Pennsylvania Highways (Sponsor: Jeffrey J. Kitsko)

www.pahighways.com/

PA Highways is a complete guide to state roads. Interstate Highways, U.S. Highways, State Highways, Toll Highways, Regional & Local Highways, Exit Guides, Highways History, links.

Special Features: Highways Gallery; "Worst Roads" tracking

Curriculum: Social Studies

1898 Pennsylvania Historical and Museum Commission

www.fortpittmuseum.com/

The Fort Pitt Museum & Bushy Run Battlefield state historic sites, dedicated to the French & Indian War in PA. History of both sites; exhibits & events; tours & field trips; links.

Special Features: French & Indian War lesson plans

Curriculum: History

1899 Pennsylvania Humanities Council

www.pahumanities.org/

Organization promotes cultural education and appreciation through programs, presentations, publications. Community Resources, Events, Initiatives, membership and contact info.

Special Features: Book Discussion programs

Curriculum: Art; Education; Language Arts; Social Studies

1900 Pennsylvania League of Cities & Municipalities

www.plcm.org/

Nonprofit, nonpartisan group dedicated to preserving local autonomy and improving municipal government. Legislation, Programs & Services, Training, Headlines, Membership, Annual Conference, resources, links.

Special Features: Home Rule Network

Curriculum: Government

1901 Pennsylvania Parent Information Resource Center

www.papirc.org/

Website initiates opportunities for parents, promotes education and outreach. Parent Choices, Education Systems, Parent Programs & Services, events, resources, about PA PIRC, links.

Special Features: Starting Points

Curriculum: Education; Social Studies

1902 Pennsylvania Partnership for Children

www.papartnerships.org/

Group advocates for PA children's health, education, and well-being. Resources & Publications; Children and the Elections; online news, events, legislation; volunteer and activism; contact info and links.

Special Features: Annual State of the Child report

Curriculum: Social Studies

1903 Pennsylvania Spatial Data Access

www.pasda.psu.edu/

Geospatial information clearinghouse, part of the National Spatial Data Infrastructure (NSDI). Download data; search data sets; GIS Community; explore PA; About PASDA.

Special Features: Teacher Resource Center

Curriculum: Education; Geography

1904 Pennsylvania SPCA

www.pspca.org/

PA chapter of the animal advocacy organization in Philadelphia. Shelter, Clinic, Employment & Volunteering, Education, Lost & Found, Branches, news from the SPCA.

Special Features: Health & pet care tips

Curriculum: Social Studies

1905 Pennsylvania State Archives

www.phmc.state.pa.us/bah/dam/overview.htm

State document resource contains much online archival content. ARIAS Online Archives, Conservation of the William Penn Charter, PA History Day; plus visiting the State Archives, genealogical assistance, publications, more.

Special Features: Doc Heritage online collection with text, images of significant documents

Curriculum: History; Social Studies

1906 Pennsylvania State Climatologist

http://pasc.met.psu.edu/PA_Climatologist/index.php

State Climatologist provides complete climatological data available for PA. Online data presented in several ways for maximum flexibility. Current data, historical, compiled, city-level, state-level, more.
Special Features: PA Water Watch; Agricultural Climate Center
Curriculum: Environmental Studies; Science

1907 Pennsylvania State College of Agricultural Sciences

www.extension.psu.edu/

Penn State Cooperative Extension provides education, services to the community. 4-H & Youth, Agriculture, Families 7 Children, Horticulture/Gardening, Community Development, Natural Resources, Nutritions & Health, more.
Special Features: Outreach offerings; resource links
Curriculum: Economics; Education; Environmental Studies; Health; Science; Social Studies

1908 Pennsylvania Wildlife Federation

www.pawildlife.org/

Wildlife advocacy & conservation organization. Important Mammal Areas Project (IMAP); Backyard Wildlife Habitat program; National Wildlife Week; Membership Info.
Special Features: Learn how to participate in IMAP, Backyard Habitat
Curriculum: Environmental Studies; Science; Social Studies

1909 Philadelphia Zoo

www.philadelphiazoo.org/

Major animal attractions in PA. Website features zoo info, visitor's guide; attractions & exhibits; animal profiles, with video gallery; programs; group tours.
Special Features: School trips with educational lesson plans
Curriculum: Education; Environmental Studies; Science; Social Studies

1910 Preservation Pennsylvania

www.preservationpa.org/

Organization dedicated to the protection of historically and architecturally significant PA properties. Advocacy & legislation, preservation efforts, events & conferences, publications online, membership, links.

Special Features: Pennsylvania at Risk; Preservation Newsletter
Curriculum: History

1911 Society for Pennsylvania Archeology

www.pennsylvaniaarchaeology.com/

Group promotes the study of prehistoric and historic PA archaeological resources. Discover & preserve PA artifacts; Archeology Month; SPA Chapters, Awards, Meetings, membership, publications, links.
Special Features: Recording & Protecting Sites
Curriculum: History

1912 State Museum of Pennsylvania

www.statemuseumpa.org/

State institution presents historical, cultural, natural science exhibits. Online exhibit highlights; collections info; learning opportunities; kid's page; museum info, visiting guide.
Special Features: Teacher Resources
Curriculum: Art; Education; History; Social Studies

1913 State of Pennsylvania

www.state.pa.us/

PA PowerPort is the official state website. About PA, Business in PA, Learning in PA, Government in PA, Living in PA, Technology in PA, Working in PA, plus links to state agencies, services online.
Special Features: Virtual Newsstand; Kids, Parents & Teachers pages
Curriculum: Education; Government

1914 University of Pittsburgh Library System

http://digital.library.pitt.edu/

The University of Pittsburgh's Digital Library provides online projects, licensed databases. Some areas require library patron status.
Special Features: Historic Pittsburgh; the Parallax Project
Curriculum: Education; History; Library Media; Science

1915 Virtual Museum of Coal Mining (Sponsor: The 20th Century Society of Western Pennsylvania)

http://patheoldminer.rootsweb.com/index.html

The Virtual Museum of Coal Mining in Western PA. Coal mine index by county, maps, local history sites, images, resource links.
Special Features: Digital library
Curriculum: History

1916 Wyck
www.wyck.org/

Central PA national Historic Landmark, Wyck House served nine generations of the same Quaker family. Read the history of the house, family, architecture, gardens; Germantown timeline; museum info, visiting info, contact.
Special Features: Educational programs; teacher's resources
Curriculum: History

RHODE ISLAND

1917 Animal Rescue League of Southern Rhode Island

www.petfinder.org/shelters/RI02.html

Directions on how to reach the shelter located in Wakefield, e-mail, phone. Adoption process for homeless cats, dogs, and ferrets, includes how old adopters must be to adopt. How to volunteer to help the nonprofit organization.
Special Features: Pet of the Month; Pet List; Search Options; Information
Curriculum: Social Studies

1918 Audubon Society of Rhode Island

www.asri.org

At the Audubon Society of Rhode Island, an independent state environmental organization, one can walk, snowshoe or cross-country ski on a beautiful refuge, borrow a book or vides, arrange a classroom programs, learn about bird feeding and how animals survive in the winter, and participate in a wide menu of programs.
Special Features: Links include Environmental Education Center, About, Education, Conservation/Advocacy, Refuges, Nature Shops, Hathaway Library, Refuge Programs
Curriculum: Biology; Environmental Studies; Geography; Physical Education; Science; Social Studies

1919 Butterfly Society of Rhode Island

www.geocities.com/RainForest/84.htm

The mission of the Butterfly Society of Rhode Island is to promote public awareness and appreciation of moths and butterflies, to locate, inventory, create and encourage preservation of butterfly habitats, and to help people understand the effects of habitat loss, pesticide use and degradation of butterfly populations.
Special Features: Links include Visit RWP Zoo, Butterfly Count, Amateur Photography Contest, Lepidopterists' Society, North American Butterfly Association and others
Curriculum: Biology; Environmental Studies; Geography; Science; Social Studies

1920 Famous Rhode Islanders

www.visitrhodeisland.com/history/famous.html

Famous Rhode Islanders includes facts and history, family fun, arts and places to be, recreation and outdoors, accommodations and transportation and others. This website tells the history of Rhode Island, along with the people who made it what it is today.
Special Features: Rhode Island history states that, "Roger Williams founded the first permanent white settlement in the state at Providence in 1636 on land purchased from the Narragansett Indians ... and so on"
Curriculum: History

1921 Grow Smart Rhode Island

www.growsmartri.com

Grow Smart Rhode Island is a statewide public interest group representing a broad coalition of partners fighting sprawl and leading the charge for better-managed growth through innovative policies and programs.
Special Features: Grow smart intends to: revitalize city, town and village centers; preserve cultural and natural resources; and expand economic opportunity for all Rhode Islanders
Curriculum: Business; Economics

1922 International Institute of Rhode Island

www.iiri.org

Services of the International Institute of Rhode Island include: Interpreting and Translating, Feinstein Center for Citizenship and Immigration Services, Refugee Resettlement, Education and Training, International Charter School and so forth.

Special Features: Their vision includes, for example: a future in which refugees to Rhode Island are offered essential services to make their transition into the American mainstream and self-sufficiency as rapid and smooth as possible

Curriculum: Business; Economics; Education; Language Arts; Social Studies

1923 Literary Resources: Rhode Island

www.brown.edu/Departments/Swearer_Center/
Literacy_Resources

Literary Resources Rhode Island was established to expand existing professional capacity within Rhone Island's adult education community, increase educators' and learners' capacity to use and interact with online technology, and assist in improving delivery of services to adult learners.

Special Features: Links include Advocacy, Bulletin Archives, Current Bulletin, ESOL and EL/Civics, Inquiry Projects/Participatory Research, Learners, Learning Disabilities, Literacy Centers and Community Resources and many others

Curriculum: Education; Technology

1924 Preserve Rhode Island

www.preserveri.org

The mission of Preserve Rhode Island is protecting the state's historic structures and unique places for present and future generations. Rhode Island is rapidly losing the historic buildings, neighborhoods and landscapes that embody their state's rich heritage. If one recycles existing buildings and reuses a community's existing infrastructure of water, sewage and services, one can protect the natural environment and open spaces, among other things.

Special Features: Links include, for example: Real Life Preservation Stories, Public Service Announcement Campaign, Help for Historic Homeowners, Preservation Learning Laboratory, What is Dendrochronology?

Curriculum: Economics; Environmental Studies; Geography; History

1925 Providence Athenaeum, Rhode Island

www.providenceathenaeum.org

The Providence Athenaeum, Rhode Island, is an independent membership library that provides a collection of books and other materials to anyone who loves reading, appreciates literature and enjoys cultural discovery. It develops, conserves and maintains its collections and historic buildings in the spirit of its founders.

Special Features: Links include Home, General Information, Services and Collections, Member Community, Programs and Events, Membership Libraries, Our History, The Building, The Organization, Publications and others

Curriculum: History; Library Media

1926 Recycling for Rhode Island Education

www.rric.org

Recycling for Rhode Island Education is a nonprofit educational and environmental organization that has as its mission to encourage preservation of the environment by diverting clean non-toxic reusable excess inventory from the business community to educators and community organizations.

Special Features: Links include What's New, Events Calendar, Office Information and Warehouse, Workshops, Project Ideas, Newsletters, Business Sponsors, Cooperative Partners, and others

Curriculum: Business; Environmental Studies

1927 Retro-Computing Society of Rhode Island

www.osfn.org

The Retro-Computing society of Rhode Island exists to further the preservation of historic computers and to increase the awareness of the history of computers and their development. One of its primary goals is to restore historical systems to operational conditions.

Special Features: Links include Events, Open Houses, What's New, Computer Festival, Collections, Kronos BBS Computer, Contact Information

Curriculum: Technology

1928 Rhode Island Art Education Association

www.ri.net/RIAEA.html

The mission of the Rhode Island Art Education Association is to promote art education through professional development, service, advancement of knowledge and leadership. It promotes quality instruction in visual arts education conducted by certified teachers of art and numerous others.

Special Features: Links include Directory, News, Executive Board, President's Page, Professional Development, Museum and Gallery news, Scholastics Art, Student Gallery, Internet Resources

Curriculum: Art; Education

1929 Rhode Island Assistive Technology Access Partnership

www.atap.state.ri.us

The Rhode Island Assistive Technology Access Partnership provides workshops and training so individuals and organization learn about assistive technology, what it is, how it can be obtained and what are their rights; advocates on behalf of individuals to help them obtain appropriate assistive technology from publicly-funded programs, and many others.

Special Features: This site explains Assistive Technology, for example: Assistive Technology is any tool, equipment or service designed to help develop, maintain or improve one's ability to function in all aspects of life

Curriculum: Education; Technology

1930 Rhode Island Ballet Theatre

www.riballet.org

Rhode Island's Ballet Theatre is a classical ballet company training talented young dancers for regional professional companies and college dance scholarships. Its goal is to help young dancers reach their full potential through a pre-professional training program, learning experiences with professional ballet companies and opportunities to enhance dancer's stage presences.

Special Features: Links include About, Current Season, Company Auditions, Performances, Meet the Dancers, Private Performances, Nancy McAuliffe, artistic director, Board of Directors, Repertoire and others

Curriculum: Dance

1931 Rhode Island Cancer Council

www.ricancercouncil.org

The Rhode Island Cancer Council is a state supported community program whose mission is to help lower cancer's toll on the state. It achieves its mission by providing programs in public education, professional education and public information.

Special Features: Ways the Council helps: easy to read information on specific cancers, assistance with locating financial and/or pharmaceutical assistance, locating smoking cessation programs, nutritional supplements and others

Curriculum: Health

1932 Rhode Island Civic Chorale and Orchestra

http://members.cox.net/riccoweb/Home.html

The Rhode Island Civic Chorale and Orchestra is a musical organization made up of singers from Rhode Island and surrounding areas. Its mission is to provide artistic enrichment to the public and the singers through presentation of major choral works.

Special Features: Links include Auditions, Concert Schedule, Tickets, Subscribe, Donations, Contact Us, Music Samples, Mailing List, Conductor, Home

Curriculum: Music

1933 Rhode Island Coalition Against Domestic Violence

www.ricadv.org

The purpose of the Rhode Island Coalition Against Domestic Violence is to eliminate domestic violence in Rhode Island. Their mission is to support and enhance the works of member agencies and to provide leadership regarding the issue of domestic violence.

Special Features: The coalition, for example: fosters communication, resource sharing, networking and collaboration, raises awareness and responds to community needs, educates the public about domestic violence and others

Curriculum: Psychology; Sociology

1934 Rhode Island Computer Museum

www.osfn.org/ricm/prj.html

The Rhode Island Computer Museum is a nonprofit organization incorporated under the laws for "procuring and preserving whatever relates to computer science and its history;" disseminating knowledge and encouraging research in computer sciences by means of visits, lectures, discussions, publications and correspondence.

Special Features: Links include Wang Hardware Catalogue, Word Processor Catalogue, Other Present and Future Projects, Time Line, Schedules, Teachers' Informational Packet, Instructional Programs, Slide Show

Curriculum: Technology

1935 Rhode Island Department of Business Regulation

www.dbr.state.ri.us

The Rhode Island Department of Business Regulation is an organization of dedicated professionals responsible for regulating and licensing a broad array of the state's businesses in order to protect the public. This site includes: Central Management, Board of Accountancy, Insurance Regulation and Forms, Banking Regulations and much more.

Special Features: Their mission is to assist, educate and protect people through the implementation and enforcement of state laws mandating regulation and licensing of these industries while recognizing the need to foster a sound business environment

Curriculum: Business

1936 Rhode Island Department of Elementary and Secondary Education

www.ridoc.net

The Comprehensive Education Strategy of this Department is an action plan for preparing all Rhode Island's children to be lifelong learners, productive workers and responsible citizens.

Special Features: Links include Directory, Schools and Districts, Standards: Introduction and Student Assessment, Special Education, School Improvement and Accountability, Field Service, Charter Schools and others

Curriculum: Education

1937 Rhode Island Department of Transportation

www.dot.state.ri.us

Via the Rhode Island Department of Transportation website, one can discover its mission and organization, as well as all the opportunities for bicycle riding in the State. One can also check a personal global positioning device with the information posted on their Survey Section.

Special Features: Links include Traffic, News, Frequently Asked Questions, Construction, Highway Maintenance, GIS Map, Walkable Community Workshops Program and others

Curriculum: Business; Driver Training; Economics; Geography; Physical Education; Social Studies

1938 Rhode Island Developmental Disabilities Council

www.riddc.org

The Rhode Island Developmental Disabilities Council promotes the ideas that enhance the lives of people with developmental disabilities. They stay abreast of and share information about new programs and services, as well as important issues, trends and ideas that are of concern to people with developmental disabilities, families, service agencies, business and so forth.

Special Features: Links include News, Recreation, Web Guide, State Plan, About Us, Contact the Council, Upcoming Events, Service Learning and others

Curriculum: Education; Psychology; Sociology

1939 Rhode Island Economic Development Corporation

www.riedc.com/riedc/blue_sky

The Rhode Island Economic Development Corporation promotes the state and all that it offers, including an ideal business environment with innovative economic development programs and state-of-the-art transportation infrastructure.

Special Features: Under the "Simply, a Great Place" link, it explains that Rhode Island is both business and pleasure — theatre and Tall Ships, Jazz Festivals, livable cities, authentic villages and so on

Curriculum: Business, Economics, Geography, History, Social Studies

1940 Rhode Island Education Exchange

http://riedx.uri.edu

The Rhode Island Education Exchange collects, organizes and presents resources that support school communities in Rhode Island. Using their interactive capabilities, it continually refines and adds to its collection of opportunities, regulations, databases and documents.

Special Features: Links include Discussion Forum, Events Calendar, Resource Directory,

Tools for Educators, Teachers' Cabinet and others

Curriculum: Education

1941 Rhode Island Family Guide

www.rifamilyguide.com

The Rhode Island Family Guide is a complete resource for fun, adventure and well-being in Rhode Island. The "Help for New Moms" section includes, for example Lifespan Health Connection, Mothers and More, Moms Club, New Moms Clubs, Parents of Only Children, Toddlers Group and many more.

Special Features: Links include New Parents, Child Care, Child Development, Family Services, Health Care, Education, Outdoor Fun, Activities, Entertainment, Shopping, Family Events, Special Features and others

Curriculum: Economics; Psychology; Sociology

1942 Rhode Island Foundation

www.rifoundation.org

The Rhode Island Foundation is the state's center for philanthropy. Eighty-eight years ago, it received its first gift of $10,000; it now approaches $400 million and growing.

Special Features: Links include Welcome, Board, Staff, Foundation's 88-year History, Mission, What is a Community Foundation, Press Releases and Articles, Free Publications and others

Curriculum: Business; Economics

1943 Rhode Island Genealogical Society

http://users.ids.net/~ricon/rigs/html

The Rhode Island Genealogical Society began in 1975 and now includes over 900 members from across the country. The Society publishes a quarterly, Rhode Island Roots, which features many records, such as cemetery, tax lists, General Assembly petitions, civil and military records and genealogical articles.

Special Features: Examples of publications include: "The Diary of Captain Samuel Tillinghast of Warwick, Rhode Island, 1757–1766," "Elm Grove Cemetery of North Kingtown, Rhode Island," Daniel Stedman's Journal," and many others

Curriculum: History

1944 Rhode Island Geography Education Alliance

www.ri.net/RIGeo/regea/home.html

The Rhode Island Geography Education Alliance was established in 1991 to increase and improve the teaching of geography in Rhode Island Schools. This Alliance is supported by money raised in Rhode Island, and matched by the National Geographic Society.

Special Features: Goals include: to strengthen geography education in Rhode Island, to provide a variety of educational opportunities for all teachers, to teach relevant geographic concepts, to distribute innovative classroom materials

Curriculum: Geography

1945 Rhode Island Government

www.ri.gov

Rhode Island Government is the official Web site for the state of Rhode Island. It includes a multitude of links, such as: Government, Living in Rhode Island, Working in Rhode Island, Health and Public Safety, Business and Industry, Visiting Rhode Island, Education and Training, Facts and History and much more.

Special Features: Additional information/ links via this site include: Weather, News and Press Releases, Photographs from around Rhode Island, Business eServices, Citizen eServices and others

Curriculum: Business; Economics; Environmental Studies; Government; Health; Social Studies

1946 Rhode Island Heritage Hall of Fame

www.rilin.state.ri.us/studteaguide/HallofFame/notables.html

The Rhode Island Heritage Hall of Fame was founded in 1965. Its activities are endorsed by the state's Historical Preservation and Heritage Commission. It was established for the purpose of spotlighting the contributions of those whose efforts have added significantly to the heritage of Rhode Island.

Special Features: Examples of "Hall of Famers" include: Dr. Stanley M. Aronson (medical educator and researcher), Thomas G. Corcoran (advisor for Franklin D. Roosevelt), Darius and Lyman B. Goff (prominent industrial men), Sylvia K. Hassenfeld (civic, cultural and philanthropic leader)

Curriculum: Business; Economics; Education; Government; History

1947 Rhode Island Historical Society

www.rihs.org

The Rhode Island Historical Society is a privately endowed organization dedicated to collecting, preserving and sharing Rhode Island's history. The nation's fourth oldest state historical society, it houses a distinguished museum and library collections that comprise over 30,000 objects and 500,000 written, recorded and photographed items.

Special Features: Links include About, Calendar, Library, Education, Goff Institute, Publications, Summer Walks, Time Keepers Program, Summer Concert Series and others

Curriculum: History

1948 Rhode Island Homeschooling Laws

http://homeschooling.gomilpitas.com/laws/blR
l.htm

Rhode Island Homeschooling Laws is not intended to be legal advice, bur rather information for parents and students dealing with homeschooling. Books cited include, for example, "The Complete Home Learning Source Book: The Essential Resource Guide for Homeschoolers, Parents and Educators."

Special Features: Links include Associations, Legal Information, Support Groups, Support Group Lists, Articles, Beginning to Homeschool, Community, Networking, Concerns, Exploration 4 Kids, Laws and Legislation and others

Curriculum: Education; Government

1949 Rhode Island Interscholastic League

www.riil.org

The mission of the Rhode Island Interscholastic League is to provide educational opportunities for students through interscholastic athletics and to provide governance and leadership for its member schools in the implementation of athletic programs.

Special Features: Links include About the League, Member Schools, Tournament Information, Rules and Regulations, Meeting Dates, Online Directions, Monthly Bulletin, Online Documents, Sponsors, Local Media and others

Curriculum: Physical Education

1950 Rhode Island Kids Count

www.rikidscount.org

Rhode Island Kids Count is a statewide children's policy organization dedicated to improving the health, education and economic well-being of the state's children. It collects and disseminates data regarding child advocacy and facilitates the development of responsive policies and programs.

Special Features: Links include Policy and Advocacy, Child Watch, Making Connections, Leave No Child Left Behind, School Readiness, Child Indicator Projects, Health, News and Events, Legislative Information and others

Curriculum: Education

1951 Rhode Island Music Educators Association

http://rimea.org

The mission of the Rhode Island Music Educators Association is to advance music education by encouraging the study and making music by all. This Association represents state music educators and plays a significant role in representing all phases of music education in school, colleges and universities in Rhode Island.

Special Features: Links include About, Members, Resources, Applications, Gallery, Contact Us, Events, as well as Rhode Islands Beginning Teacher Standards

Curriculum: Education; Music

1952 Rhode Island Nature Conservancy

http://nature.org/wherewework/northamerica/s
tates/rhodeisland

The Rhode Island Nature Conservancy preserves the white pine forests, rivers, wetlands and habitats that make Rhode Island unique. It has protected over 24,000 acres of critical land and waters throughout the state of Rhode Island.

Special Features: Links include Places We Protect, Field Trips and Events, Press Releases, Estate Planning, Gift Ideas, Activities, Magazine, Field Guide, E-Newsletter and others

Curriculum: Economics; Environmental Education; Science; Social Studies

1953 Rhode Island Parks and Recreation

www.riparks.com

The objective of the Division of Parts and Recreation is to provide all Rhode Island residents and visitors the opportunity to enjoy a diverse mix of well-maintained, scenic, safe, accessible areas and facilities within their park system, and to offer a variety of outdoor recreational opportunities and programming.

Special Features: Their "Disability" link

includes: Handicap-Assisted Surf Chairs, Self-Propelled All Terrain Handicap Surf Chairs, Recreational Hand Cycle, Handicap-Accessible Boat Ramp and others
Curriculum Environmental Studies; Geography; Health; Physical Education

1954 Rhode Island Philharmonic

www.ri-philharmonic.org

The mission of the Rhode Island Philharmonic is to encourage lifelong involvement with music and with their program of Music-based Arts Education, a nationally recognized Outreach program and Community Involvement through privately funded performances, workshops and classes in schools and neighborhood centers throughout the state.
Special Features: Links include About Us, Season and Tickets, Education and Outreach, Support Us, News, E-mail Club, Contact Us, Artists and others
Curriculum: Music

1955 Rhode Island Resource Recovery Corporation

www.rirrc.org

The Rhode Island Resource Recovery Corporation is the state environmental agency dedicated to providing the public with environmentally sound programs and facilities to manage solid waste.
Special Features: Links include Annual Reports, Board of Commissioners, Directions, Holidays, Solid Waste Comprehensive Plan, News, Tour Request, Mixed Recyclables Sorting Illustration, Paper Sorting Illustration
Curriculum: Environmental Studies

1956 Rhode Island Rose Society

www.rirs.org/rwrg.htm

The Rhode Island Rose Society aids in choosing the varieties of roses planted and maintaining the garden in cooperation with Roger Williams Park. This park was restored and replanted in 1999; the original Victorian Woodwork was designed by noted garden designer, Chuck Carberry.
Special Features: Links include Interactive garden map Rose Show, Contacts, Photos, News, Learn! and others
Curriculum: Biology; Science

1957 Rhode Island School for the Deaf

www.rideaf.net/front/front.htm

The Rhode Island School for the Deaf offers links such as: Academics, Services, Summer Institutes, Special Projects, Learning Links, For Parents, Awareness, History and much more.
Special Features: The "Learning Links Page" provides games, fun and homework help for students. For teachers, there are teaching resources, lesson plans, book lists and reviews
Curriculum: Education

1958 Rhode Island School of Design: Museum

www.risd.edu/museum.cfm

The Rhode Island School of Design Museum traces the history of art from antiquity to the present through a collection of more than 85,000 works of art in all media from cultures around the world.
Special Features: Links include Degree Programs, Lifelong Learning, Calendar, Education, Architecture, Community Programs, The Collections and others
Curriculum: Art

1959 Rhode Island Sea Grant College Program

http://seagrant.gso.uri.edu

The Rhode Island Sea Grant College Program conducts research and outreach on important marine issues. Outreach topics include coastal management and fisheries, aquaculture and seafood safety. It conducts scientific, research, education and extension projects designed to help people better understand and use ocean and coastal resources.
Special Features: Links include Strategic Plan, Publishing Sea Grant-Sponsored Work, Knauss Fellowships Links, Coastal Management, Fisheries and Aquaculture, Bookstore and others
Curriculum: Science

1960 Rhode Island State Council on the Arts

www.arts.ri.gov

The Rhode Island Council on the Arts serves as a catalyst for the advancement, appreciation and promotion of excellence in the arts by encouraging leadership, participation and education in the arts for all Rhode Islanders.
Special Features: Information includes: Grant Programs at the Council, Technical Assistance, Information Services, Slide Registry, Partnerships, Education, Folk Arts and others
Curriculum: Art

1961 Rhode Island Technology Council

www.ritec.org

The Rhode Island Technology Council is a non-profit organization that champions technology growth and innovation in Rhode Island. They build their programs around three core functions: membership, workforce development and entrepreneurship.

Special Features: Links include Membership, Workforce Development, Entrepreneurship, Photo Gallery, Events, News, About Us, plus others, such as Membership Spotlight

Curriculum: Technology

1962 Rhode Island Wild Plant Society

www.riwps.org

The Rhode Island Wild Plant Society is a non-profit conservation organization dedicated to the preservation and protection of Rhode Island's native plants and their habitats.

Special Features: The educational component of this Society includes offering plant inventories and informal plant lists or surveys for private or public properties, as well as materials and lesson plans for youth education programs

Curriculum: Biology; Environmental Studies; Geography; Science

1963 Rhode Island Workforce Literacy Collaborative

www.riwlc.org

The Rhode Island Workforce Literacy Collaborative is a group of non-profit agencies and other companies funded by the Human Resource Investment Council to provide workforce or worksite literacy services to adults in Rhode Island.

Special Features: Advocate for consumer empowerment

Curriculum: Business; Economics; Education

1964 Rhode Island Yellow Pages for Kids with Disabilities

www.yellowpagesforkids.com/help/ri.htm

The Yellow Pages for Kids with Disabilities was created so people could obtain reliable information and support. It includes many resources, such as government programs, grassroots organizations, and parent support groups.

Special Features: This is a free service; they are adding evaluators, educational consultants, academic tutors, advocates, attorneys and others

Curriculum: Education

1965 United Cerebral Palsy Association of Rhode Island

www.ucp.org/ucp_localsub.cfm/141/9615/9615-9632

For more than 55 years, the United Cerebral Palsy Association has been committed to change and progress for persons with disabilities. It recognizes the value of people's contributions and potential; encouraging their expanding possibilities and exploring their choices. The Association focuses on individual needs, want and dreams.

Special Features: Links include Children and Family Services, Supportive Living, Arts and Adult Education, Questions and Answers, Resources and Links, Who We Are, Jobs and others

Curriculum: Health; Sociology

1966 Volunteer Center of Rhode Island

www.vcri.org

The mission of the Volunteer Center of Rhode Island is to connect people and opportunities for effective volunteer community service. They are they only statewide volunteer center that provides services to all ages and from all communities.

Special Features: Examples of the center's missions include: Promoting volunteerism statewide, through weekly or monthly columns in major state newspapers, connecting volunteers to community needs, training volunteers and their managers to be more effective and others

Curriculum: Economics; Social Studies; Sociology

1967 Women in Rhode Island History

www.projo.com/specials/women

According to the Women in Rhode Island History website, "Women have long made their mark in this state — even before it was one. This website showcases their achievements in a collection of series and stories from the Providence Journal.

Special Features: Links include Local News, Opinion, About Providence, Bulletin Board, Calendar, About the Newspaper, Newspaper in Education and numerous others

Curriculum: Women's Studies

SOUTH CAROLINA

1968 City of Columbia

www.columbiasc.net

As the capital of South Carolina, Columbia is a city rich with history. There are numerous things to see and do throughout the city. This includes visiting places of importance in history, enjoying the arts, playing or watching sports, attending festivals or participating in outdoor activities.

Special Features: Links include All about Columbia, Visit Columbia, Neighborhoods, Parks and Recreation, Area Links, News, City Events, City Views and others

Curriculum: Business; Economics; Government; History; Social Studies

1969 Civil War Music — Second South Carolina String Band

www.civilwarband.com

The purpose of the Second South Carolina Civil War String Band is to recreate (as authentically as possible) the music of the Civil War. In the "Southern Soldier" album, the listener hears the music of the 19th century played on 19th century period instruments in the appropriate style.

Special Features: Their music evokes the days when soldiers entertained their comrades around the campfire with the tunes of mistral composers like Dan Emmett and Stephen Foster

Curriculum: Music

1970 DISCUS — South Carolina's Virtual Library

www.scdiscus.org

South Carolina's Virtual Library gives all South Carolinians free online access to the best subscription library resources. One can locate magazine and newspaper articles, reference materials, maps, pictures, student and teacher resources and best Web links.

Special Features: Links include New, About DISCUS, How to Access K–12 Users and Other Users, Librarian's Toolbox, Calendar, Promotion, Training, Technical Toolbox

Curriculum: Library Media

1971 Family Connection of South Carolina

www.familyconnectionsc.org

Family Connection of South Carolina is a support network for families who have children with special needs. Founded in 1990, they exist to help thousands of children in South Carolina reach their potential by providing parent-to-parent connections, linking families to community resources, and sponsoring numerous educational and support programs.

Special Features: Links include Programs, Newsletter, Locations and Staff, Upcoming Events, Resources, Press Releases, Legislative Updates, PUNCH: New Support Group, Special Children Special Care and others

Curriculum: Education; Health; Psychology; Sociology

1972 Fine Arts Emporium: Original Art from South Carolina

www.fineartsemporium.com

Try "A Moment in Time the Artist's Tour of York County, South Carolina." Also, visit the Dottie's Kudzu Cafe and find out what kudzu is, get your fortune told, read current news headlines, horoscopes— all in the back room, of course.

Special Features: Links include Of Interest to Painters, For the Occasional Tourist, Featured Artists, What's New, Art Links, Artist's Book Store and Resource Center, South Carolina Watercolor Society and others

Curriculum: Art

1973 Huguenot Society of South Carolina

www.huguenotsociety.org

The Huguenot Society of South Carolina, established in 1885, is dedicated to the preservation of the history and genealogy of the members of the Protestant Reformation that took place in France during the 16th Century. The origin and history of the French Huguenots is a fascinating and compelling account of Protestant religious persecution.

Special Features: Examples of the Society's

objectives include: perpetuating the memory and promoting the principles and virtues of the Huguenots, commemorating the principal events in the history of the Huguenots, discovering and preserving all existing documents, and many others

Curriculum: History

1974 Humanities Council of South Carolina

www.schumanities.org

The Humanities Council of South Carolina funds, promotes, counsels and coordinates all manners of thoughtful (and thought-provoking) endeavors ... exhibits, documentaries, discussion forums, research, planning, workshops, dramatizations, lectures and so forth that pertain to the humanities.

Special Features: Links include Staff, Board, Mission, Vision, Statement of Purpose, Values, Events, Projects, How to Give, How to Receive, Affiliations, Accolades, Newsletter

Curriculum: History; Language Arts; Psychology; Social Studies; Sociology

1975 League of Women Voters of South Carolina

www.lwvsc.org

The League of Women Voters of South Carolina's mission is to encourage the informed and active participation of citizens in government, work to increase understanding of major public policy issues and influence public policy through education and advocacy.

Special Features: This organization believes in: respect for individuals, the value of diversity, the empowerment of the grassroots, the power of collective decision making for the common good

Curriculum: Government; Women's Studies

1976 Municipal Association of South Carolina

www.masc.sc

The Municipal Association of South Carolina represents and serves the state's 269 incorporated municipalities. The Association is dedicated to the principle of its founding members to offer the services and programs that will give municipal officials the knowledge, experience and tools for the best possible public decisions in the complex world of municipal government

Special Features: The "About Research/Resources" links includes information such as: Court Cases, White papers, Model Ordinances/Resolutions, Model Policies/Procedures, Federal and State Regulations, Publications, Video Library and many others

Curriculum: Government

1977 MySCGov.com

www.myscgov.com

This is the official Web site for the state of South Carolina. It includes information/links such as: Government, Education, Business, Health, Public Safety, Environment, Tourism, Online Services, Weather and much more.

Special Features: "Quick Links" include: Statewide Calendar, State Jobs, State Agencies and Boards, SC Phone Directory, Downloadable Forms and many others

Curriculum: Business; Economics; Environmental Studies; Government; Health; Social Studies

1978 South Carolina Academy of Science

www.erskine.edu/scas/home.htm

The mission of the South Carolina Academy of Science is to promote the creation and dissemination of scientific knowledge within the state of South Carolina by stimulating scientific research and publication, to improve the quality of science education and more.

Special Features: Links include History, Activities, Annual Meeting, Newsletter, Governance, Advantages, Awards, Science Fairs, Discovery Fairs, Opportunities for Young Scientists and others

Curriculum: Science

1979 South Carolina African-American History Online

www.scafricanamerican.com

The individuals honored each year have excelled in their respective fields and are role models of all of our children. They have succeeded in the areas of medicine, law, broadcasting, business, civil rights, community service, counseling, education, the arts, entertainment, government and military service.

Special Features: Links include Calendar, Current Honoree, All Honorees, Search, History Timeline, Resources, Photo Gallery

Curriculum: Business; Economics; Education; Government; History; Language Arts; Science

1980 South Carolina Aquarium

www.scaquarium.org

The South Carolina Aquarium is a self-sup-porting educational institution dedicated to ex-cellent displays and interpretations of the aquatic environments of South Carolina.

Special Features: The Education link in-cludes, for example, the following: Free School Programs, Teacher Programs and Resources, Homeschool Programs, Online Curriculum, Education and Animal Events, and others

Curriculum: Biology; Environmental Stud-ies; Science

1981 South Carolina Association of Counties

www.sccounties.org

The South Carolina Association of Counties is the only organization dedicated to statewide representation and improvement of county government in South Carolina. It is a non-profit organization that represents county gov-ernments (not county employees).

Special Features: This Association's purpose is to: promote more efficient county govern-ments, study and recommend improvements in government, investigate and provide means for the exchange of ideas and experiences be-tween county officials, and others

Curriculum: Economics; Government

1982 South Carolina Association of Nonprofit Organizations

www.scanpo.org

The mission of the South Carolina Association of Nonprofit Organizations is to sustain and strengthen nonprofit organizations for a better South Carolina. Its vision is to be a nationally recognized model and the provider of choice for charitable nonprofits in South Carolina.

Special Features: Links include History, Sup-porters, Programs and Services, Board and Staff, Press Center, Annual Report, Education and Training, Technical Assistance, Advocacy and Policy, Annual Conference, Resource Cen-ter

Curriculum: Business; Economics; Govern-ment; Social Studies

1983 South Carolina Autism Society

www.scautism.org

The mission of the South Carolina Autism So-ciety is to enable all children and adults in South Carolina who have autism spectrum dis-orders to reach their maximum potential. This occurs via facilitation of partnerships, infor-mation and referral services, regional support groups, annual conference and workshops and many other activities.

Special Features: Links include Annual Con-ference, Awards Nomination, Support Groups, Staff and Board, Site Map, Projects, Informa-tion on Autism, Links, Calendar of Events, Newsletters and others

Curriculum: Health

1984 South Carolina Botanical Garden

www.clemson.edu/scbg

The South Carolina Botanical Garden is a di-verse 295-acre garden of natural and mani-cured landscapes within the South Carolina Piedmont ecosystem. It includes a nationally recognized nature-based sculpture collection, youth, education and outreach programs as well as a Geology Museum.

Special Features: Links include Calendar of Events, Virtual Garden, Garden Programs, Sculpture Programs, Fran Hanson Discovery Center, Betsy Campbell Carriage House, Bob Campbell Geology Museum and others

Curriculum: Biology; Environmental Stud-ies; Geography; History; Science; Social Stud-ies.

1985 South Carolina Council for the Social Studies

www.sccss.org

The South Carolina Council for the Social Studies is a professional organization for per-sons interested in any aspect of social studies instruction. It is affiliated with the National Council for the Social Studies and offers its members the opportunity to share in the de-velopment of ideas and programs with educa-tors from the state and nation.

Special Features: Teacher Resources and Standards include, for example: Cowpens Na-tional Battlefield, Fort Sumter Educational Tours Information, Gideon vs. Wainwright, Lesson Plan Databases, Teaching Democracy and many others

Curriculum: Social Studies

1986 South Carolina Department of Alcohol and Other Drug Abuse Services

www.daodas.state.sc.us/web

The South Carolina Department of Alcohol and Other Drug Abuse Service is the cabinet-level agency charges with ensuring the provision of quality services to prevent or reduce the negative consequences of substance use and addictions.

Special Features: Links include Agency Overview, Services, Local Resources, News, Training Calendar, Funding Opportunities, Kid's Power: Tools for the Journey and others

Curriculum: Health; Psychology; Science; Sociology

1987 South Carolina Department of Commerce

www.callsouthcarolina.com

The Department of Commerce is South Carolina's lead agency for the growth and development of business and industry. This Department, in partnership with communities, claims to be the nation's most effective organization for locating new, quality investments and expanding existing investments to create wealth and a high quality of life for South Carolinians.

Special Features: Links include Press Releases, Resources, European Office, Aeronautics, Allies, Team South Carolina, South Carolina Film Office, International Trade and others

Curriculum: Business; Economics; Government

1988 South Carolina Department of Health and Environmental Control

www.scdhec.gov/board.htm

The mission of South Carolina's Department of Health and Environmental Control is to promote and protect the health of the public and the environment; their vision is healthy people living in healthy communities.

Special Features: Examples of "what they do" include: respond to environmental emergencies 24 hours a day, inspect restaurants, counsel patients on family planning, provide home health care services, and many others

Curriculum: Health

1989 South Carolina Education Association

www.thescea.org

The South Carolina Education Association is the professional association for educators in

South Carolina. Educators from pre–K to 12th grade comprise this association. Classroom teachers, guidance counselors, librarians, principals, middle managers, superintendents, as well as bus drivers, teaching assistants, lunch room operators, maintenance engineers, clerks and others are members.

Special Features: Links include About Us, Legislative News, Calendar, Meetings, Officers, UniDistricts, Staff, Teachers, Students, Parents, Programs, Publications and others

Curriculum: Education

1990 South Carolina Farm Bureau Federation

www.scfb.org

The South Carolina Farm Bureau Federation represents all South Carolina farmers and farm land owners. They serve the entire agricultural community through education and a unified voice in government for the benefit of everyone, since agriculture is an integral part of the state.

Special Features: The Education section contains: Ag in the Classroom, Youth Leadership Conference, College Scholarships; the Organization section offers: Women's Programs and Conference, Queen's Contest, Talent Contest and others

Curriculum: Business; Economics; Environmental Studies; Geography; Science; Social Studies.

1991 South Carolina Forestry Association

www.scforestry.org

The South Carolina Forestry Association's vision is one of sustainable forests, managed to meet the nation's needs without sacrificing the birthright of future generations—clean air and water, abundant wildlife, and renewable resources for recreation and the wood products upon which future society will depend.

Special Features: This Association is a partnership of landowners, loggers, foresters, educators, researchers, conservationists and sportsmen; joined by lumber mills, pulp and paper mills, wood processors and equipment dealers

Curriculum: Environmental Studies; Geography; Social Studies

1992 South Carolina Genealogical Society

www.scgen.org

The South Carolina Genealogical society is a non-profit organization. The aims of the Society are to raise the standards of genealogical research and to promote the preservation of records of the Colony and State of South Carolina.

Special Features: Links include Membership, "The Carolina Herald" online, Chapters of the State Society, Constitution, By-Laws, Current Projects, Meeting and Events Calendar, Archives, Research and Help, Histories of South Carolina counties

Curriculum: History

1993 South Carolina Hall of Fame

www.myrtlebeachinfo.com/chamber/aboutarea/sc_halloffame.htm

The South Carolina Hall of Fame, dedicated in 1973, was created to recognize and honor those contemporary and past citizens who have made outstanding contributions to South Carolina's heritage and progress. It is a non-profit corporation conducted under a state charter.

Special Features: Examples of Inductees include: Dizzy Gillespie, General William C. Westmoreland, J. Strom Thurmond, Major General Andrew Jackson, Bobby Richardson, James Lide Coker, Robert E. McNair and others

Curriculum: Business; Economics; Education; Environmental Studies; Government; History; Women's Studies

1994 South Carolina Historical Society

www.schistory.org

The mission of the South Carolina Historical Society is to collect information respecting every portion of the State, to preserve it, and when deemed advisable to publish it. The Society's holdings, located in the historic Robert Mills in Charleston, SC, are vast and grow constantly with the addition of materials from 200 years ago and from two weeks ago. It is especially rich on South Carolina's colonial and antebellum eras and the American Civil War.

Special Features: Regarding the link, "Explore Our Collection," it is noted that the first major accession was in 1856—the papers of Henry Laurens, who was merchant, planter and president of the Continental Congress.

Curriculum: History

1995 South Carolina History

www.state.sc.us/histro.html

The South Carolina History Website explores areas such as the following: State History, State Symbols, Quick State Facts. State Symbols and Emblems, South Carolina Firsts, Archives and History, South Carolina Library, South Carolina State Museum and many others.

Special Features: Includes virtual tours to the War of Independence, War of 1812, Mexican War, Civil War, UCV Collection, Conflict Comes Home, Medicine and Surgery, Spanish American War, World Wars I and II

Curriculum: History

1996 South Carolina Hospital Association

www.scha.org

The South Carolina Hospital Association is a private, non-profit organization consisting of over 100 hospitals and health systems and approximately 900 personal members associated with their institutional members.

Special Features: Links include Advocacy, Expertise, Education, Projects, Vendors, News, and topics such as Diversity, Trauma System, Geriatrics and others

Curriculum: Health

1997 South Carolina Library Association

www.scla.org

The South Carolina Library Association includes the following areas: College and University, Youth Services, Special Library, African American Concerns, Health Sciences, Archives and History, Continuing Education and numerous additional areas.

Special Features: Links include Calendar, News, Membership, Your Association, Governance, Jobs, Legislation, South Carolina Libraries, Awards, Resources, Updates

Curriculum: Library Media

1998 South Carolina National Heritage Corridor

www.sc-heritagecorridor.org

The South Carolina National Heritage Corridor was established by the U.S. Congress in 1996 as one of a select number of National Heritage Areas—regions in which entire communities live and work, and where residents, businesses, and local governments have come together to conserve special landscapes and their own heritage. It comprises 240 miles and fourteen counties in South Carolina.

Special Features: Links include About the Corridor, In the Press, Photo Album, Agricultural Entertainment Events, Discovery Route, Nature Route, Mountain Lakes, Freshwater Cost, and others

Curriculum: Business, Economics, Environmental Studies, Geography, Government, History, Social Studies.

1999 South Carolina Native Plant Society

www.scnps.org

South Carolina has a rich botanical heritage. Their distinct geographical provinces and abundance of water provide habitat for a diversity of flora. The South Carolina Native Plant Society was founded in 1996 by a diverse group of people interested in promoting the awareness and education of native plant species and their importance in South Carolina's landscape and history.

Special Features: This Society provides programs and activities designed to educate and inform members and the general public about the importance of native plants, promotes the commercial availability of native plant materials and more.

Curriculum: Biology; Environmental Studies; Geography; Science; Social Studies

2000 South Carolina Newspapers

www.usnpl.com/scnews.html

The South Carolina Newspapers Website includes Mailing Address Downloads, Newspapers, Radio Stations, College Newspapers, Television Stations, College Newspapers and Magazines.

Special Features: Examples of South Carolina newspapers include: *Charlestown Post and Courier, Columbia Free Times, Georgetown Times, The Greenville News, Hilton Head Carolina Morning News, Spartanburg Herald-Journal* and many others

Curriculum: Business; Economics; Language Arts

2001 South Carolina Nurses' Association

www.scnurses.org

The purpose of the South Carolina Nurses' Association is to promote the professional status of nurses and to improve health care in South Carolina. It works with standards of nursing and the public well being.

Special Features: Links include Philoso-

phy, Officials, By-Laws, Districts, Calendar, Practice Councils, Continuing Education, Links, others

Curriculum: School Nurse

2002 South Carolina Philharmonic

www.scphilharmonic.com

The South Carolina Philharmonic feels strongly about the education of today's youth. It is reflected in their mission statement — to provide opportunities for South Carolina's youth to develop their understanding of and skills in the performance of music. This organization offers a variety of programs to educate children of all ages.

Special Features: Links include Meet the Philharmonic, Concerts and Tickets, Get Involved, Educational Outreach, SCP Youth Orchestras, Symphony 101, Press Box, Site Map

Curriculum: Music

2003 South Carolina Ports

www.port-of-charleston.com

The mission of the South Carolina Ports is to contribute to the economic development of South Carolina by fostering and stimulating waterborne commerce and shipment of freight. In pursuit of this mission, the Authority seeks to develop and operate efficient marine terminals and attract high-quality steamship services.

Special Features: The General Information link includes: Contacting the Port, Our Leadership, Foreign Trade Zones, Port Statistics, Weather, Glossary of Shipping Terms, Frequently Asked Questions and others

Curriculum: Business; Economics; Geography; Social Studies

2004 South Carolina Reptiles and Amphibians Home Page

www.snakesandfrogs.com

The South Carolina Reptiles and Amphibians answers questions such as the following: I found a snake in my house! What kind is it? By far, the snake species that is most often found in houses and buildings is the Black Rat Snake (*Elaphe obsoleta obsoleta*). Black Rat Snakes are large nonvenomous snakes which eat rats, mice, squirrels and birds.

Special Features: Links include Herp Images and Information, What's New, Observation Notes, Herp Tales, Nature Commentaries, Herp Links, Herps Worldwide, South Carolina

Birds, South Carolina Mammals, South Carolina Beetles

Curriculum: Biology; Environmental Studies; Science; Social Studies

2005 South Carolina Research Associates

www.scra.org

The vision of the South Carolina Research Association is to stimulate economic growth through science and technology; its mission is to provide leadership in creating innovative solutions through advanced technology that enhances customers' performance.

Special Features: This Association's strategy includes: engaging in internationally competitive research and development by teaming with technology leaders, attracting advanced technology companies to strategically locate research parks and others

Curriculum: Business; Economics; Science; Technology

2006 South Carolina Resource Conservation

www.myscgov.com/SCSGPortal/static/home_t
em4.html

The South Carolina Resource Conservation is about new and improved methods for state agencies, colleges and universities, school and school districts to conserve natural resources, protect the environment and save money.

Special Features: Links include Statewide Calendar, State Jobs, State Agencies and Boards, Search South Carolina Phone Directory, Printable Classifies, Downloadable Forms, Books and Publications and others

Curriculum: Economics; Environmental Studies

2007 South Carolina School Boards Association

www.scsba.org

The South Carolina School Boards Association is a non-profit organization that serves as a source of information, as well as a statewide voice for boards governing the 85 public school districts.

Special Features: Links include Advocacy, Training, Reports, Marketing, Services, Board Information, Education News, Legal News, For the Media and others

Curriculum: Education

2008 South Carolina School of Library and Information Science

www.libsci.sc.edu

The mission of the University of South Carolina School of Library and Information Science is to provide and promote education and leadership in library and information science, services, and studies through the highest levels of teaching, research and service.

Special Features: Goals include, for example: to support the development and improvement of library and information services to the people of South Carolina, to maintain a strong program of basic professional education, to provide continuing education and development, and others

Curriculum: Library Media

2009 South Carolina Shakespeare Company

www.scshakespeare.org

The South Carolina Shakespeare Company's educational programs are an important component of the company's missions. They believe that drama teaches people of all ages; it is versatile enough to visit schools around the state to help students discover aspects of Shakespeare's works or to concentrate on one show in particular.

Special Features: For students age from age 7 to 18, taught by professional theatre artists from the company

Curriculum: Drama

2010 South Carolina Square and Round Dance Federation

web.ftc-i.net/~earley1/main1.html

The purpose of the South Carolina Square and Round Dance Federation is to promote Western style Square and Round Dancing throughout the state of South Carolina; to seek to improve and better Square and Round Dancing as a source of pleasure, physical and mental heath.

Special Features: Links include Directory of Clubs, Coming Events, Meeting Schedule, Hall of Fame, Club Highlights, Convention Information, "Sleep Over," Square Dancing Today and others

Curriculum: Dance

2011 South Carolina State Library

www.state.sc.us

The mission of the South Carolina State Library is to improve library services throughout the state and to ensure all citizens access to libraries and information resources adequate to meet their needs.

Special Features: Links include Online Library Catalog, Talking Books Services Catalog, Electronic Resources, South Carolina Reference Room, South Carolina Public Libraries Directory

Curriculum: Library Media

2012 South Carolina State Trails

www.sctrails.net/trails

South Carolina offers hundreds of scenic trails. It includes trail descriptions, maps, research of trail publications, and input from trail users. One visiting this site can click for trails by type or usage, descriptions, directions to and simple maps.

Special Features: Links include Trails Map; Trails Inventory (database); About the Trails Program; State Trails Plan; Agencies and Organizations; Trails Bibliography; National Trails Day

Curriculum: Environmental Studies; Geography; Science; Social Studies

2013 South Carolina: Teaching, Learning, Connecting

www.sctlc.com

This website includes curriculum, instruction and assessment resources for each of the eight subject areas for which there exist South Carolina Academic Standards. It uses a local database of resources that returns lesson plans from a select group of websites chosen by Educational professionals in South Carolina.

Special Features: The eight subject areas include: Foreign Language, Health and Safety, Language Arts, Math, Physical Education, Science, Social Studies and Visual and Performing Arts

Curriculum: Education

2014 South Carolina Technology Alliance

www.sctech.org

The South Carolina Technology Alliance was established to complete the following goals: prepare a technology-capable workforce, create a business environment that is friendly to technology-intensive companies and others.

Special Features: This Alliance's vision is to prosper in the 21st century as a recognized leader in attracting, creating, growing and retaining world-class technology-intensive companies while preserving South Carolina's quality of life

Curriculum: Business; Economics; Technology

2015 South Carolina Waterfowl Association

www.scwa.org

The South Carolina Waterfowl Association awards scholarships that allow kids to attend a camp that offers something for every outdoor enthusiast. Campers from ages 8–12 learn the basics of waterfowl and wildlife conservation, boating and many other hands-on wildlife programs. Campers aged 12–16 focus on wildfowl heritage skills.

Special Features: Links include Habitat, Camp Woodie, Wood Ducks, Mallards, Banding, Events, News, Conservation and Educational Programs, Mid-Continent vs. Eastern Mallard Model, Outfitter Reviews and others

Curriculum: Biology; Environmental Studies; Geography; History; Science; Social Studies

2016 South Carolina Wildlife Federation

http://secure.authoritychannel.net/scwf_org

The South Carolina Wildlife Federation represents people who care about preserving outdoor heritage. Sportsmen and outdoor enthusiasts, business and professional leaders, industry and South Carolinians from all walks of life support the Federation.

Special Features: This includes numerous links, such as: Kids Page, Programs, Legislative Updates, Archives, Resources, and workshops (for example: Vernal Pond and Wetlands Workshop, Butterfly Identification Skills Training, Turtles in South Carolina Sill in Grave Danger)

Curriculum: Biology; Environmental Studies; Geography; History; Science; Social Studies

2017 South Carolina World Trade Center

www.scwtc.org

The mission of the South Carolina World Trade Center is to promote and support all aspects of international commerce through education, networking, trade development services and institutional business opportunities throughout South Carolina.

Special Features: Links include About Us, Services, Programs, Membership, News, International Relations, Annual Events, Community Connections and others
Curriculum: Business; Economics

SOUTH DAKOTA

2018 A.B.A.T.E. of South Dakota

www.abatesd.com

A Brotherhood for Awareness, Training and Education of South Dakota is committed to serving the motorcycling public with objectives such as the following: improve road conditions, making roads safer for motorcyclists; help prevent accidents through rider awareness and education and many more.

Special Features: Links include Contact Your Legislature, Motorcycle Safety Education, Newsletter, South Dakota Motorcycle Registration and Licensing Information, South Dakota Motorcycle Laws and others
Curriculum: Driver Training

2019 Arts Alive South Dakota

www.sdarts.org

Arts Alive South Dakota provides information for arts organizations and administrators, arts educators and students, legislators and policy makers, artists and performers, anyone interested in the arts and culture of and by South Dakotans.

Special Features: Links include Protecting the Arts, Programs and Events, Arts and News, Arts Resources, Publications, Festivals and Directory, Touring Arts Roster, Folk Arts Program and others
Curriculum Art; Dance; Drama; Music

2020 Associated School Boards of South Dakota

www.asbsd.org

The Associated School Boards of South Dakota promotes excellence in school board governance by providing support, service, knowledge and training to local school boards. It speaks for school boards on the state level.

Special Features: Their Online Learning Center and Technology Leadership Network offer affordable, accessible and flexible professional development opportunities
Curriculum: Education

2021 Badlands National Park

www.nps.gov/badl

Located in southwestern South Dakota, Badlands National Park consists of 244,000 acres of sharply eroded buttes, pinnacles and spires blended with the largest protected mixed-grass prairie in the United States. It covers over 64,000 acres and is the site of the black-footed ferret — the most endangered land mammal in North America.

Special Features: Links include Accessibility, Activities, Education Programs, Facts For Kids, History and Culture, In Depth, Management Documents, News and others
Curriculum: Biology; Environmental Studies; Geography; History; Science; Social Studies

2022 Black Hills of South Dakota and Wyoming

www.theblackhills.com

The Black Hills of South Dakota and Wyoming reside on an oasis of pine-clad mountains on the Great Plains. The Black Hills offer five national parks, scenic drives, waterfalls, abundant wildlife, recreation trails and trout fishing — where the bison and wild horses still roam free.

Special Features: Links include Black Hills

Area Directory, Black Hills Area Map, Belle Fourche Historiography, Information Request Form, Communities, Attractions, Locals News and others

Curriculum: Environmental Studies; Geography; History; Science; Social Studies

2023 Corn Palace

www.cornpalace.org

Mitchell, South Dakota offers the world's only Corn Palace. It was established in 1892; it now serves as a multi-use center for the community and region. The facility hosts stage shows, as well as sports events in its arena. It is a structure that stands as a tribute to the agricultural heritage of South Dakota.

Special Features: Links include World's Only Corn Palace, Visitors Guide, Calendar and Special Events, About Mitchell, Hunting, Convention Services, Economic Development, Mitchell Chamber Directory, Links

Curriculum: Economics; Environmental Studies; History; Science; Social Studies

2024 Discover South Dakota

http://discoveresd.net

Discover South Dakota is an innovative telecollaborative journey of learning and discovery. For example: Opportunity and challenge for students and teachers to experience learning in innovative ways; Curriculum frameworks and resources to guide engaging classroom experiences, and much more.

Special Features: Links include The Journey: Launching, Beginning, Continuing, Sharing; also Model Classroom (teachers) and Model Classroom (students)

Curriculum: Education

2025 Focusing on the South Dakota Discovery Center

www.sd-discovery.com

The South Dakota Discovery Center and Aquarium is designed to offer opportunities to discover the excitement of science and technology. An example of the Center's goals is: To become a valued community resource by expanding, improving, and maintaining exhibits, programs and facilities.

Special Features: Links include Home, Exhibits, Join Us, Programs, Events, Activity, Friends, Program Reference, Mission, Email Newsletter and others

Curriculum: Science; Technology

2026 Great Lakes of South Dakota Association

www.sdgreatlakes.org

The Great Lakes of South Dakota Association provides a wealth of information regarding fishing, hunting and travel in the Great Lakes Region. It discusses campgrounds, recreation areas, golf courses, trails for hiking, biking and riding, as well as hunting and fishing in South Dakota.

Special Features: Links include Communities, Events, Great Outdoors, Lakes, Services, Lewis and Clark, Campgrounds, Department of Game, fish and Parks, Fishing, Hiking, Biking, Riding Trails and others

Curriculum: Environmental Studies; Geography; Physical Education; Science; Social Studies

2027 Minnesota-South Dakota Dairy Foods Research Center

www.fsci.umn.edu/dairycenter/mndak.html

The objective of the Minnesota-South Dakota Dairy Foods Research Center is to increase the viability and to ensure the future competitiveness of the United States dairy industry, as well as to develop expertise in dairy foods research.

Special Features: Links include About the Center, Mission Statement, Dairy Center Faculty Members, Completed Projects, Operational Advisory Committee, Links to Other Dairy Foods Research Centers and others

Curriculum: Economics; Health; Science

2028 National Association of Mental Illness South Dakota

http://sd.nami.org

The National Association of Mental Illness South Dakota offers practical support, useful education, sympathy and understanding to people who are living and coping with neurobiologically based brain diseases. It also works to increase public awareness and to advocate for increased research.

Special Features: Links include Purpose, Who Needs Us,? Here's Help, Workshops, Family Education, Conferences, Affiliate Bulletin Boards and others

Curriculum: Health; Sociology

2029 National Music Museum

www.usd.edu/smm

Founded in 1973 on the campus of the University of South Dakota, the National Music Museum is one of the great institutions of its kind in the works. Its renowned collections, which include more than 10,000 American, European and non–Western instruments from virtually all cultures and historic periods, as the most inclusive anywhere.

Special Features: Links include Frequently Asked Questions, Calendar of Events, Virtual Tours, Special Exhibitions, Recent Acquisitions, Collections, Research, Newsletter, Technical Drawings and many others

Curriculum: Music

2030 Pioneer Daughter's Collection

http://discovered.tie.net/continuing/resources/daughter/default.htm

The Pioneer Daughter's Collection are stories that were selected from 500 biographies of South Dakota pioneer women that were compiled by the General Federation of Women's Clubs of South Dakota and distributed to South Dakota schools in 1989.

Special Features: Begun by Marie Drew who stated, "It has to do with people and what they did, what they thought and how they felt, their joys, their sorrows and their emotions"

Curriculum: History; Women's Studies

2031 Small Business Association South Dakota District Office

www.sbs.gov/sd

The United States Small Business Administration is the only independent agency of the federal government with the sole mission of assisting small businesses to start, grow and prosper. The South Dakota District Office is responsible for the delivery of the Small Business Association's many programs and services for the state of South Dakota.

Special Features: Links include News, Training Calendar, Counseling and Training Resources, Startup Kit, Financing, Opportunities, Laws and Regulations, Assets for Sale, Disaster Assistance, Local Resources and others

Curriculum: Business; Economics; Government

2032 South Dakota Army National Guard

http://sdguard.ngb.army.mil/guard.asp

The South Dakota Army National Guard traces its history back to the earliest English colonies in North America. The militias protect their fellow citizens from attacks and invaders.

Special Features: Links include The Guard, Programs, News and Events, Careers, Join the Guard, Links, Home Security, Privacy and Policy Information and others

Curriculum: Government

2033 South Dakota Art Museum

www3.sdstate.edu/Administration/SouthDakotaArtMuseum

The South Dakota Art Museum serves, educates and provides access to a diverse constituency through public programming, collecting, preserving and exhibiting of art that reflects the creative nature of humanity, while increasing understanding and appreciation of their common heritage and culture.

Special Features: The Museum is designed to provide permanent housing and display of the Harvey Dunn paintings, the Marghab Collection, and other works of art, provide a program of changing exhibitions of contemporary and traditional works of art

Curriculum: Art

2034 South Dakota Arts Council

www.state.sd.us/deca/sdarts.htm

The mission of the South Dakota Arts Council is to serve South Dakotans and their communities through the arts. Its purpose: recognizing the importance of creativity in the lives of all South Dakotans, the Council makes quality arts accessible throughout the state by providing grants, services and information to artists, arts organizations, schools and the public.

Special Features: Links include Current News and Events, Grants to Artists, Grants to Organizations and Schools, Arts Directory, Directory of Arts Festivals, Artists-in-School Roster, Touring Arts Roster and others

Curriculum: Art

2035 South Dakota Bankers Association

www.sdba.com

The South Dakota Bankers Association is the professional and trade association for South Dakota's financial services industry; it serves as an advocate that promotes and enhances the profitability, leadership and image of South Dakota's banks.

Special Features: The range of services include: Board of Directors, Staff, Committee

Members, Associate Members, Calendar of Events, Consumer Information, Education, Media Center and others
Curriculum: Business; Economics

2036 South Dakota Community Foundation

www.sdcommunityfoundation.org

The mission of the South Dakota Community Foundation is to promote philanthropy, receive and administer charitable gifts and invest in a wide range of programs promoting the social and economic well being of the people of South Dakota.

Special Features: Links include Services, Why Invest, Example Fund, Rate of Return, Grants Awarded, Gift Law, Permanently Endowed Funds and others
Curriculum: Economics

2037 South Dakota Department of Environment and Natural Resources

www.state.sd.us/denr/denr_organization.htm

The mission of the South Dakota Department of Environment and Natural Resources is to provide assessment, financial assistance and regulation in a customer-service manner that protects the public health, conserves natural resources, preserves the environment and promotes economic development.

Special Features: Links include Scheduled Events, Frequently Asked Questions, Laws/Rules, Documents, Data/Technical Information, Air Quality, Drinking Water, Ground Water Quality, Minerals and Mining and others
Curriculum: Environmental Studies

2038 South Dakota Destination Imagination

www.rapidnet.com/~cozyom/DInfo.php

Destination Imagination is based on the concept of divergent thinking—understanding that there is more than one way to solve a problem. It challenges one to be creative, to apply the skills in which you know you are good, be they technical, theatrical, analytical, comic, linguistic, as well as to develop skills.

Special Features: How it works: There are two components—Team Challenges and Instant Challenges. Team Challenges allows the team to choose the challenge and devote creative energies into solving it; and Instant Challenge give the team a challenge that needs to be solved right now
Curriculum: Education; Psychology; Sociology

2039 South Dakota Education Association

www.sdea.org

The South Dakota Education Association's Learning Organization: shares a vision of the future of education, promotes dialogue with an involvement of all components of the association, values the strengths and diversity of individuals regardless of their role, and much more.

Special Features: Links include About the Association, Student Chapter, For Educators, For Parents, National Education Association, National Board Certification and others
Curriculum: Education

2040 South Dakota EDWeb

www.sdedweb.com

The South Dakota EDWeb connects educators, students and parents to the worldwide web. For example, the educator section is designed to provide links to services and resources for both instructors and administrators—and so forth.

Special Features: Each website has been reviewed by South Dakota educators or parents to ensure links to appropriate material that is generally free of extensive advertising; all sites have been evaluated for a user-friendly format; content that is reliable, useful and rich; and is published by a reputable source.
Curriculum: Education

2041 South Dakota Folk Dance

www.folkdancing.org/south_dakota.htm

The South Dakota Folk Dance website features ballroom dance, Balkan folk dance, Cajun dance, Clog dance, Contra dance, English country dance, International fork dance, Irish dance, Israeli dance, Morris dance, Ritual dance, Scottish country dance, Tap dance, Traditional square dance, Vintage dance, Western square dance and Zydeco dance.

Special Features: Links include South Dakota Classes and Sessions, Navigation Shortcuts, Websites, Have We Overlooked You,? Folk Dance Association Website Add-ons and others
Curriculum: Dance

2042 South Dakota Game, Fish and Parks

www.sdgfp.info

The purpose of the Department of Game, Fish and Parks is to perpetuate, conserve, manage, protect and enhance South Dakota's wildlife resources, parks, and outdoor recreational opportunities for the use, benefit and enjoyment of the people of this state and its visitors.

Special Features: Links include Wildlife — Prairie and Recreation, Licensing and Reservations; Outdoor Recreation Publications; Parks and Wildlife Foundation and others

Curriculum: Biology; Environmental Studies; Geography; History; Science; Social Studies

2043 South Dakota Governor's Office of Economic Development

www.sdgreatprofits.com

The South Dakota Governor's Office of Economic Development site contains information regarding taxes, employment, available property, county statistics, financing options, business startup information and current information about what is happening in economic development in South Dakota.

Special Features: Links include Doing Business in South Dakota, Labor Force, Financing Incentives, South Dakota Profile, Cities and Counties, Available Properties, E-Publications, In the News, Student's Corner

Curriculum: Economics

2044 South Dakota Hall of Fame

www.sdhalloffame.com

The South Dakota Hall of Fame honors those who built their great state and those individuals who continue to contribute to future developments of the state. It is the only resource in the state dedicated exclusively to the preservation and extension of South Dakota's heritage.

Special Features: Links include Inductees, The Beginning, Our Support, Facilities, Nomination Form, History, Membership, Special Events, Board and Staff

Curriculum: History

2045 South Dakota Health Care Association

www.sdhca.org

The South Dakota Health Care Association is the leading trade association representing long term care organizations, including skilled nursing care, assisted living and congregate living throughout South Dakota. It was founded in 1951 as a means of bringing together concerned providers to improve the quality of extended care.

Special Features: Links include Calendar of Events, Products/Video Library, Legislative Issues, Councils/Committees/Task Forces, Members/Association, Resources/Links, Consumer Information and others

Curriculum: Health; Social Studies

2046 South Dakota Highway Patrol

http://hp.state.sd.us

The South Dakota Highway Patrol uses the Internet as a means of communication to inform, educate and aid their communication with the public. Their mission is to serve the citizens of South Dakota with pride and distinction. They safeguard lives and property and respect the Constitutional rights of all men and women.

Special Features: Links include South Dakota Road and Weather Conditions, Road Construction Information, Office of Driver Licensing, Office of Highway Safety, Accident Records, South Dakota Laws.

Curriculum: Driver Training; Government

2047 South Dakota Historical Society

www.sdhistory.org/soc.htm

The South Dakota Historical Society first established its official relationship with state government in 1901 through the former Department of History. Originally housed in the state capitol, the Society moved in 1932 to the Soldiers' and Sailors' Memorial Building. In 1989, South Dakota celebrated its centennial and to showcase the state's history, the Cultural Heritage Center was build as the new headquarters for this Society.

Special Features: Links include Archaeology, Archives, Historic Preservation, Museum, Publishing, Site Index, Frequently Asked Questions, Organization, Heritage Fund, History Awards and many others

Curriculum: History

2048 South Dakota Home School Association of Sioux Falls

www.southdakotahomeschool.com

The South Dakota Homeschool Association of

Sioux Falls is an inclusive, non-profit home-school group that serves the city of Sioux Falls and its surrounding communities. This Association is a social and educational group, respectfully promoting members' diversity, monitoring state and local legislation, as well as informing and empowering their members on their educational journey.

Special Features: Links include membership Information, Getting Started with Home-schooling, Events and Calendar, Event Pictures, Links, and others

Curriculum: Education

2049 South Dakota Humanities Council

http://web.sdstate.edu/humanities

The South Dakota Humanities Council explores and promotes state, regional and national programs focusing on ideas, history and culture. Since 1972, the Council has awarded nearly $5,500,000 to organizations using the disciplines of the humanities.

Special Features: Humanities includes: philosophy, ethics, comparative religion, jurisprudence, history, literature, archaeology, languages, linguistics, the arts

Curriculum: Art; Dance; Drama; History; Language Arts; Music; Psychology; Sociology

2050 South Dakota Indian Tribes

www.kstrom.net/isk/maps/dakotas/sd.html

The South Dakota Indian Tribes website provides a wealth of information regarding Indian tribes in this State, such as the following links: Map of Great Sioux Nation, Exhibit from National Archives, Fort Laramie Treaty of 1868, Bear Butte, Lakota Sacred Constellations, Oglala Lakota Timeline and many others.

Special Features: Page buttons include: Aberdeen Area Office, Cheyenne River Agency, Crow Creek Agency, Lower Brule Agency, Pine Ridge Agency, Rosebud Agency, Sisseton Agency, Yankton Agency

Curriculum: Geography; History; Science; Social Studies

2051 South Dakota Internet Crimes Against Children Enforcement Unit

www.sdcybersafe.com

It is the mission of the South Dakota Internet Crimes Against Children Enforcement unit to provide public education and prevention of Internet crimes, facilitate Internet criminal investigations, and to provide computer forensics expertise.

Special Features: A message for this Units explains, "None of us would leave a child unsupervised in the middle of a large city, and yet, the Internet is just like that city.... Did you know that one in four kids today have received unwanted exposures to sexual materials online?"

Curriculum: Technology

2052 South Dakota Library Network

www.sdln.net

The mission of the South Dakota Library Network is to enable all libraries within South Dakota to provide the State's residents with the information they need, when they need it, and where they need it.

Special Features: Links include Search Online Catalog, Search Other Resources, member Libraries, Patron Information, Library Information, Technical Support, Future Automation

Curriculum: Library Media

2053 South Dakota Literacy Resource Center

http://literacy.kent.edu/~sdakota

The South Dakota Literacy Resource Center is a member of Midwest LINCS, funded in part through grant support from the National Institute for Literacy. It is one of four regional technology hubs. Through this network, it strives to provide access to national, regional and state resource materials for adult literacy practitioners and students.

Special Features: Links include About LINCS, South Dakota LINCS, Literacy Resources, News and Events, NIFL, Collections, Discussions, My LINCS, Hot Sites and others

Curriculum Education; Language Arts

2054 South Dakota Natural Resources Conservation Service

www.sd.nrcs.usda.gov

The South Dakota Natural Resources Conservation Service assists owners of South Dakota's private land with conserving soil, water and other natural resources. They deliver technical assistance based on sound science suited to a consumer's specific needs.

Special Features: The service of this mission is to provide leadership in a partnership effort to help people conserve, maintain and improve natural resources and environment; its vision is harmony between people and the land

Curriculum: Environmental Studies; Science; Social Studies

2055 South Dakota Newspapers

www.usnpl.com/sdnews.html

The South Dakota Newspaper List includes: Mailing Address Downloads, Newspapers, College Newspapers, Radio Stations, Television Stations, Magazines, Search Engines, Phone Book, Maps and Cool Sites. Examples of Magazines include: *Faith A Prairie Oasis, Fish and Game Finder* and more.

Special Features: Examples of Newspapers include: *Brookings Register, Madison Daily Leader, Miller Press, Pierre Capital Journal, Rapid City Journal, Sioux Falls Argus Leader, Vermillion Plain Talk* and others

Curriculum: Business; Economics

2056 South Dakota Parent Connection

www.sdparent.org

The South Dakota Parent Connection is a parent training and information center. It believes a child's needs are best met by parents who are informed and active in the development of services for the children. This organization provides training, information, assistance and resources to families and professionals who work with children with disabilities.

Special Features: Links include Calendar of Events, Parent to parent Program, Volunteer Parent Trainer, Sibshops, FILE, Current Workshops, Speed Machine Expo, Family Voices and others

Curriculum: Education

2057 South Dakota Safe Schools

www.sdsafeschools.com

South Dakota's Safe Schools site is a collection of links to other sites that specialize in various aspects of making a safer school. The single most important factor contributing to safe, high quality schools is concerned parents who are informed and involved in their children's school.

Special Features: Links include Aggression/ Anger, Behavior Patterns, Bullying, Communities, Conflict, Crime, Crisis Planning, Discipline, Dress Code, Drugs and Alcohol, Firearms/Weapons, Gangs and many others

Curriculum: Education; Psychology; Sociology

2058 South Dakota School for the Blind and Visually Impaired

www.sdsbvi.edu

The role and mission of the South Dakota School for the Blind and Visually Impaired is to provide statewide services to meet the educational needs of sensory impaired children from birth through twenty-one in South Dakota by serving in a dual leadership and resource role in the statewide efforts to serve these students.

Special Features: Links include Mission Statement, Instructors, Administration and Departmental Contacts, Outreach Services and Staff, History, Pioneer Newsletter, Summer Program, Links Related to Blindness, and others

Curriculum: Education

2059 South Dakota School for the Deaf

www.sdbor.edu/institutions/sdsd.htm

The South Dakota School for the Deaf is the only State resource serving children who are deaf, hard of hearing or have Cochlear implants. Useful links include: Legislative Affairs, Academic Information, K–12 Educators, Prospective Students, Current Students, Institutions, Publications and much more.

Special Features: Under "K–12 Educations," one can locate links such as: Curricular Resources, EveryTeacher, K–12 Schools of the Web, Advanced placement and others

Curriculum: Education

2060 South Dakota Service Direct

www.sd.gov/Main_Login.asp

Within the South Dakota Service Direct website, one can locate all of South Dakota's state forms. Locating the correct form is made easy via a life events timeline for locating services used by a specific age group, and so forth.

Special Features: Service Direct of South Dakota is a one-stop shop for state forms and services. Their goal is to provide successful interaction with the South Dakota state government

Curriculum: Government

2061 South Dakota State Agricultural Heritage Museum

www.agmuseum.com

The South Dakota State Agricultural Museum displays the role of agriculture in South Dakota's past, present and future. The museum offers a variety of programs including book signings, exhibit openings and lecture series. Its extensive connections provide opportunities for researchers to learn more about South Dakota history, agricultural technology and rural life.

Special Features: Links include Who We Are, Hours and Location, Exhibits, Tours and Programs, Membership, Museums and Gardens, Links, Kids, Barn Again, and others

Curriculum: Social Studies

2062 South Dakota State Library

www.sdstatelibrary.com

The mission of the South Dakota State Library is to lead the State in access to resources, advance literacy, and promote lifelong learning in the information age.

Special Features: Examples of Frequently Asked Questions include: Who may use your library services? What is the State Library's Internet policy? Do you have a list of all the materials in your library? and others

Curriculum: Library Media

2063 South Dakota State Medical Association

www.sdsma.org

The mission of the South Dakota State Medical Association is to promote the art and science of medicine, protect and improve the health of the public, and provide leadership and advocacy in the field of quality health care.

Special Features: Links include Bylaws, History, Governance, Specialty Societies, Affiliate Organizations, Medical Education, Legislative Advocacy, Public Health Campaigns, Publications and others

Curriculum: Health

2064 South Dakota Symphony

www.sdsymphony.org

The mission of the South Dakota Symphony is to provide musical excellence, education and cultural leadership throughout the region of South Dakota. This organization provides concerts and educational programs for all ages.

Special Features: Links include Concert Season, Chamber Season, Education and Touring, Special Events, About the Conductor, Washington Pavilion, Orchestra Personnel, Symphony Soloists and others

Curriculum: Music

2065 South Dakota Tobacco-Free Kids Network

www.sdtobaccofree.org

The South Dakota Tobacco-Free Kids Network is a statewide alliance of health, medical, education, parent, youth, law enforcement and other civic organizations advocating for laws, policies and funding of effective programs that will result in significant reductions in tobacco use and addiction, especially among children and high-risk groups.

Special Features: Links include Home, Calendar, Youth in Action, About Us, Advocates, News, Resource Center, Media Center, Tobacco Settlement Money and others

Curriculum: Health

2066 Water Resources of South Dakota

http://sd.water.usgs.gov

The U.S. Geological Survey is the Nation's largest earth-science agency and has the principal responsibility within the Federal Government for providing hydrologic information and for appraising the Nation's water resources. The water resources of South Dakota consist of streams, springs, lakes and aquifer systems.

Special Features: Links include Our Cooperators, Budget Status, Historicand Real-Time Water Data, Drought, Selected Projects and Research, Interests, Publications, GIS Resources, Outreach and others

Curriculum: Economics; Environmental Studies; Government; Science; Social Studies

2067 Welcome to South Dakota

www.state.sd.us

This is the official Web site for the state of South Dakota. It includes a wealth of information and links to other sites, such as: Government, Business, Family Health, Education, Employment, Travel/Parks, State News Web, Public Broadcasting, Public Training and much more.

Special Features: "Government Headlines" include, for example: Flood Cleanup Guidelines, Korean War Memorial Web site, West Nile Virus Information

Curriculum: Business; Economics; Environmental Studies; Government; Health; Social Studies

TENNESSEE

2068 Arc of Tennessee

www.thearctn.org

The Arc of Tennessee is a non-profit organization affiliated with the Arc of the United States. It is a membership organization composed of people with mental retardation and other disabilities, their parents, friends and the professionals who assist them in reaching their goals.

Special Features: Calendar of Events, Local Chapters, Related Disability Links, The Arc of the United States, Awards, Real Lives, The Arc Connection

Curriculum: Education; Health; Sociology

2069 Center for Appalachian Studies and Services: Governor's Schools

http://cass.etsu.edu/cass/govsch.htm

The Governor's School is a school for Tennessee heritage. Students who are talented in drama, storytelling, folk music, archeology, historic preservation or figuring out how drama works should attend this four-week school at East Tennessee State University.

Special Features: Cool stuff students will study: Historic Preservation, Governmental Growth and Development, Archeology, Folklore and Music, Storytelling, Multi-cultural Heritage, Dramatic Interpretation of History

Curriculum: Drama, Environmental Studies; Geography; Government; History; Science; Social Studies

2070 Department of Environment and Conservation

www.state.tn.us/environment

The Department of Environment and Conservation for the State of Tennessee ensures that Tennessee has the cleanest and safest environment, the greatest recreation opportunities, and the most valued natural and cultural resources of any state.

Special Features: Links include Air Pollution Control, Archaeology, Community Assistance, Geology, Ground Water Protection, Natural Heritage, State Parks, Water Pollution Control

Curriculum: Economics; Environmental Studies; Geography; Science; Social Studies

2071 Department of Safety

www.tennessee.gov/safety/tleta.html

The Tennessee Department of Safety's mission is to: provide instruction in Tennessee Law Enforcement; teaching methods best suited for the subject taught and the students' particular learning needs; stimulate inquiry and provide fresh perspectives about Tennessee's law enforcement.

Special Features: Driver License Information and Insurance, Defensive Driving Schools, Title and Registration

Curriculum: Driver Training; Government

2072 Elephant Sanctuary

www.elephants.com

The Elephant Sanctuary is located in Hohenwald, Tennessee. Founded in 1995, it is the nation's single natural habitat refuge developed specifically for endangered African and Asian elephants.

Special Features: Education about the crisis facing these creatures

Curriculum: Environmental Studies; Geography; History; Science; Social Studies

2073 Face of Immigration in Tennessee

http://web.utk.edu/~tnlatina

During the last decade, the State of Tennessee has begun to experience unprecedented growth in the numbers of Latinos and Latinas who live and work in Tennessee for all or part of a year. This site speaks of the experiences of Latino immigrants with Tennessee's legal system; the purpose is to identify special needs of this group.

Special Features: Legal Rights and Responsibilities Links include Banks and Money, Consumer Law, Discrimination, Education, Employment, Public Benefits

Curriculum: Economics; History; Social Studies; Sociology

2074 Family Voices of Tennessee

www.tndisability.org/familyvoices/default.html

The purpose of Family Voices of Tennessee is to assist families as they navigate public and private health systems and insurance plans; to education families about how to access services and resources for their children; to work with families, health care providers, public and private agencies and support promotion of family-centered care.

Special Features: Tennessee Disability Coalition, Tennessee Family Pathfinder, Children's Emergency Care Alliance, Tennessee Health Care Campaign

Curriculum: Health

2075 History of Country Music

www.roughstock.com/history/begin.html

Although musicians had been recording fiddle tunes in the southern Appalachians for several years, it wasn't until August 1, 1927, in Bristol, Tennessee, that country music actually began. On that day, Ralph Peer signed Jimmie Rodgers and the Carter family to recording contracts for Victor Records.

Special Features: The Beginnings, Acuff and the Grand Ole Opry, Cowboy Music, Western Swing, Bill Monroe and Bluegrass, Honky Tonk Music and others

Curriculum: History; Music

2076 Humanities Tennessee

http://tn-humanities.org

Humanities Tennessee examines the narratives, traditions, beliefs and ideas that define them as individuals and as participants in community life. Their Tennessee Young Writers' Workshop gives students with an interest in writing the opportunity to explore that interest and to devote time to their work in a unique environment with knowledgeable faculty and supportive peers.

Special Features: Links include Festival of Books, Motheread Fatheread Tennessee, Community History, Digital Humanities Tennessee; workshops, community development, teacher resources

Curriculum: Language Arts

2077 State of Tennessee

www.tennesseeanytime.org

State of Tennessee directories include: A to Z Departments and Agencies, State Employee Phone Directory, A to Z Site Contents, and FirstGov Federal Government. Links offered are Online Services, State News, About Tennessee, Government, Travel, Residents, Education, Business and so forth.

Special Features: **State News includes nu-merous up-to-date pieces of information about the State of Tennessee, such as: Presidential Scholar Semifinalists, EPA Reports on Tennessee Air Quality, Road Project Plans**

Curriculum: **Business; Economics; Geography; Government; History**

2078 Tennessee Animal Rescue

www.petfinder.org/shelters/TN229.html

The Tennessee Animal Rescue Organization is dedicated to helping homeless animals find permanent and loving homes.

Special Features: Featured pet, Adopting a Friend, What are Puppy Mills, Come Visit Us

Curriculum: Science; Social Studies

2079 Tennessee Aquarium

www.tnaqua.org

The Tennessee Aquarium inspires wonder and appreciation for the natural world. Useful links include: Events and Travel, Meet Our Animals, Kids and Teachers, Online Gift Shop, Newsroom and much more.

Special Features: The Kids and Teachers links discusses: Field Trips, Outreach, Summer Camps, Teacher Training, Preschool Opportunities, Homeschool, Environmental Learning Lab, Education Technology

Curriculum: Environmental Studies; Geography; History; Science; Social Studies

2080 Tennessee Archaeology Network

www.mtsu.edu/~kesmith/TNARCH/index.html

The Tennessee Archaeology Network, established in 1996, promotes and publicizes the contributions and significance of archaeological research in the State of Tennessee. This Network is the central information source for Tennessee archeology.

Special Features: Links include Events, A New Journal, FAQs about Tennessee Archaeology, Learn More, In the News, Careers in Archaeology, Current Research, Organizations, Law and Ethics

Curriculum: Geography; History; Science; Social Studies; Sociology

2081 Tennessee Art League

www.tennesseeartleague.org

The mission of the Tennessee Art League is to function as a cultural arts center for both artists and the general public, essentially as an educational facility and gallery. It also promotes creativity and art appreciation by workshops, exhibitions, classes, lectures.

Special Features: Includes links such as: In the News, Artist Links, Classes and Workshops. Exhibits include dates and information regarding upcoming galleries by educational institutions

Curriculum: Art

2082 Tennessee Association of Audiologists and Speech/ Language Pathologists

www.taaslp.org/home.htm

This association meets the needs of persons with hearing, communication and swallowing disorders. It also enhances the professional development of audiologists and speech and language pathologists.

Special Features: Links include Forum, Foundation, Leadership, Publications, Legislative Council, State Advocacy, Calendar, Additional Links

Curriculum: Education

2083 Tennessee Association of School Librarians

www.korrnet.org/tasl

The purpose of the Tennessee Association of School Librarians is to encourage the professional growth and development of school library media specialists, school administrators, classroom teachers and others interested in school library programs— and to strengthen school library media services in Tennessee.

Special Features: Links include Tennessee State Board of Education Requirements for School Library Media Centers, Volunteer State Book Awards, Links for Librarians, Tenn-Share

Curriculum: Library Media

2084 Tennessee Civil War Home Page

http://members.aol.com/jweaver303/tn/tncwhp.htm

The Tennessee Civil War Home Page creates a virtual central repository for information about Tennessee in the American Civil War. This site includes Biographies of Tennessee Military and Civilian Personalities, Statistics about the Civil War in Tennessee, Tennessee Civil War Research Sources, and much more.

Special Features: Includes Confederate Resources, Federal Resources, Links to Other Useful Civil War Sites, Descendant Organizations, Resources

Curriculum: History

2085 Tennessee Classical Association (TCA)

www.vroma.org

The Tennessee Classical Association is a nonprofit organization that promotes the study of Latin, Greek, and the Classics. It also facilitates communication among classicists across the State of Tennessee. The TCA includes links to seminars and additional similar organizations.

Special Features: Lists University Classics Programs and Secondary School Classics Programs, such as Clarksville High School, Germantown High School, Hume-Fogg High School, Vanderbilt University, Rhodes College

Curriculum: Language Arts

2086 Tennessee Clean Water Network Information

www.tcwn.org

While Tennessee's waters are among its most precious natural resources, many have been degraded too long. They continue to be polluted by toxic and other pollutants. This organization protects and recovers the watersheds in the State of Tennessee.

Special Features: Public Participation Opportunities, TCWN Library, Newsletter Archives, Related Links, A Little History, Our Goals, Our Projects

Curriculum: Environmental Studies; Science; Social Studies

2087 Tennessee Coalition to Abolish State Killing

www.tcask.org

TCASK's purpose is to end executions in the state of Tennessee by promoting alternatives to capital punishment. This organization is a secular one, heavily influenced by supporters who come to their opposition from faith-based perspectives. They include more than 1,700 active supporters.

Special Features: Links include Tennessee Case Information, News, Events, Fact Sheets, Press Releases, Resources

Curriculum: Government; Psychology; Social Studies; Sociology

2088 Tennessee Commission on Children and Youth

www.state.tn.us/tccy

The Tennessee Commission on Children and Youth is an independent agency created by the

Tennessee State Legislature to: advocate for legislation, policies and programs to promote and protect the health, well-being and development of children and youth.

Special Features: Links include Advocacy, Annual Report, Commission, Regional Councils, Events, Juvenile Justice, KIDS COUNT, News Releases, Publications

Curriculum: Economics; Education; Government; Health; Social Studies

2089 Tennessee Department of Education

www.state.tn.us/education/

The goal of the Tennessee Department of Education is to serve school districts in their efforts to ensure equal educational opportunities for all children in Tennessee and to equip them with the skills necessary to succeed in higher education, the workplace and society.

Special Features: Links include Curriculum, Grants/RFPs, Operations, News and Issues, No Child Left Behind, Smart from the Start, Special Education, Vocational Technical Education

Curriculum: Education

2090 Tennessee Education Association

www.teateachers.org

The state's leading association of educators, TEA is the voice of both Tennessee's teachers and their public schools. In recognizing the central role that teachers and other school staff play in making schools work for children, TEA is the leading positive force for schools in Tennessee.

Special Features: Links include: E-mail Your Legislator, National Education Association, News Center, Public Schools: The Facts, Parent Center, Teaching Center

Curriculum: Education

2091 Tennessee Eastman Hiking and Canoeing Club

www.tehcc.org

The Tennessee Eastman Hiking and Canoeing Club is a non-profit outdoors club that offers a year-round program of hiking, paddling and other outdoor activities. Their mission is to provide a program of hiking, paddling and similar outdoor recreational activities.

Special Features: Links include Appalachian Trail Information, Hiking Information, Paddling Information, Activities, Newsletters, Photo Gallery

Curriculum: Geography; Physical Education

2092 Tennessee Education Association

www.teateachers.org

The Tennessee Education Association is Tennessee's teachers. As the state's leading association of educators, this association is the voice of both Tennessee teachers and public schools. In recognizing the central role that teachers play in making schools for Tennessee's children, the Tennessee Education Association is the leading positive force for schools in the State.

Special Features: Links include Radio and Television Ads, E-mail Your Legislator, Legislative Report, National Education Association, Member Benefits

Curriculum: Education

2093 Tennessee Environmental Council

www.tectn.org

The Tennessee Environmental Council's mission is to educate and advocate for the protection of Tennessee's environment and public health. Accomplishments include: Preservation of the Wetlands and State Parks Land Acquisitions Fund.

Special Features: Links include Accomplishments, Issues, Get Involved, Tennessee Stewardship Project, Upcoming Events, Newsletter, Press Releases

Curriculum: Environmental Studies

2094 Tennessee Fainting Goats

www.webworksltd.com/webpub/goats/fainting goat.html

The origin of the Fainting goat has been traced back to the 1880s in Marshall County, Tennessee. A man by the name of Tinsley came to town bringing along a few goats and a "sacred" cow. The story continues ... and Fainting goats are now in existence in Tennessee and are not endangered.

Special Features: Facts: A Fainting goat does not faint; it averages between 17–25 pounds; they can be horned or hornless; they come in a variety of colors

Curriculum: Biology; History; Science; Social Studies

2095 Tennessee Farm Bureau Federation

www.tnfarmbureau.org

The Tennessee Farm Bureau Association's purpose is to improve the economic and social well-being of farm and rural people in Tennessee. Each unit of this organization operates autonomously from the other units, which assures that efforts are driven by the desires at the county level.

Special Features: Federation includes "Agriculture in the Classroom," which provides curriculum and enrichment materials for students in K–12 in Tennessee. All resources are interdisciplinary in nature

Curriculum: Business; Economics; Environmental Studies; Science; Social Studies

2096 Tennessee Horse Council

www.thehorsecouncil.com

The Tennessee Horse Council is a statewide coalition of horse people and other related concerns joining together to unify the equine industry in Tennessee. It is a volunteer, nonprofit organization representing all breeds and equine disciplines

Special Features: Links include Accomplishments, Committees, Meetings, Tennessee HorseSource, TennEquine Report, Horse Fair, Calendar of Events and more

Curriculum: Business; Science; Social Studies

2097 Tennessee Land History

http://users.rcn.com/deeds/tenn.htm

Overview of Tennessee Land History, beginning with Tennessee as a part of North Carolina, becoming a state in 1796.

Special Features: Provides copies of Surveyor District Records and Further Reading, "Struggle for the Frontier," "The Land Laws of Tennessee," "The Public Lands of Tennessee"

Curriculum: Geography; Government; History; Social Studies

2098 Tennessee Llama Community

www.tennllama.com

The TLC is an active group of people in and around Tennessee who love llamas and alpacas. It sponsors several major events each year, in addition to seminars, talks, demonstrations and discussions about all aspects of llamas and alpacas.

Special Features: TLC members range from professional Llama and alpaca breeders to those who have them as pets. Llamas and alpacas can attend performance classes

Curriculum: Science; Social Studies

2099 Tennessee Music Education Association

http://tnmea.org

The Tennessee Music Association includes vocal, orchestra and band. Related associations include: West Tennessee Band, Orchestra, Music; East Tennessee Band, Orchestra, Music; Middle Tennessee Band, Orchestra, Music; Tennessee Elementary Music Education Association and Collegiate MENC Chapter.

Special Features: Announcements, Officers, Associations, All State, Handbook, Special Awards, History

Curriculum: Music

2100 Tennessee National Wildlife Refuge

http://tennesseerefuge.fws.gov

The Tennessee National Wildlife Refuge encompasses over 50,000 acres on or around Kentucky Lake in northwest Tennessee. The refuge has three units: Big Sandy, Duck River and Busseltown. It serves as a resting and feeding area for wintering waterfowl and migratory birds.

Special Features: Links include Refuge Facts, Maps, Internships, Student Employment, Environmental Education, Refuge Brochures

Curriculum: Environmental Studies; Geography; History; Science; Social Studies

2101 Tennessee Nature Conservancy

http://nature.org/wherewework/northamerica/states/tennessee

The Tennessee Chapter of The Nature Conservancy has protected approximately 200,000 acres of critical natural lands in Tennessee and protects places such as, West Tennessee (Hatchie River), Middle Tennessee (Duck River, Taylor Hollow), Northeast Tennessee (Clinch River, Shady Valley) and Southeast Tennessee (Hubbard's Cave)

Special Features: Links include Press Releases, Virtual Preserve, Tour, Ways of Giving (estate planning, gift ideas, activities, events, merchandise, magazine, science publications, field guide, e-newsletter)

Curriculum: Environmental Studies; Geography; Science; Social Studies

2102 Tennessee Ornithological Society

www.tnbirds.org

The Tennessee Ornithological Society provides information on birds and birdwatching in Tennessee. It was founded in 1915 to promote the enjoyment, scientific study and conservation of birds. This society publishes a quarterly journal, a newsletter and holds local and state-wide meetings.

Special Features: Links include Publications and Other Literature, Events, Birding in Tennessee, Tennessee Bird Records Committee, Grants and Awards, What's New

Curriculum: Environmental Studies; Science

2103 Tennessee Overhill Experience

www.tennesseeoverhill.com

The Tennessee Overhill in Southeast Tennessee is also known as the "museum without walls." These museums and historic sites tell tales of minors, railroad town, Indians, forts, traders, camps, loggers and much more.

Special Features: Links include Calendar of Events, Outdoor/Adventure, Area Attractions, Educational Resources, Scenic Drives, Thematic Trails, Rivers and Lakes, Cherokee Heritage

Curriculum: Geography; History; Social Studies

2104 Tennessee Performing Arts Center

www.tpac.org

A part of the Tennessee Performing Arts Center takes TPAC into the community by providing opportunities for adult learners (18 and older) to enhance their understanding and appreciation for the performing arts and to enrich their experiences at TPAC performances.

Special Features: Links include Shows and events, Education and Outreach; Special Events

Curriculum: Drama

2105 Tennessee Psychological Association

www.tpaonline.org

The Tennessee Psychological Association advances psychology as a science, profession and means of promoting human welfare.

Special Features: Links include Tennessee Psychology Newsletter, Legislative and Professional Affairs and Developments, Public Education

Curriculum: Psychology

2106 Tennessee River Gorge

www.trgt.org

The Tennessee River Gorge is 27,000 acres of land carved through the Cumberland Mountains by 26 miles of the Tennessee River. It is one of the most unique natural treasures in the southeast, the fourth largest river canyon east of the Mississippi.

Special Features: Protected Areas, Newsletters, Events Calendar, Circle of Conservators, Pot Point House

Curriculum: Geography; History; Science; Social Studies

2107 Tennessee School for the Blind

www.tsb.k12tn.net

The Tennessee School for the Blind is a state school that serves K–12 students who are blind or visually impaired across the state of Tennessee.

Special Features: Links include Vision Information, Resource Center

Curriculum: Education

2108 Tennessee School for the Deaf

http://tsdeaf.org

The Tennessee School for the Deaf offers an individualized and comprehensive educational program for students with hearing difficulties. The school provides a total learning environment that utilizes state-of-the-art curricula, materials and methods to prepare students for adult life.

Special Features: Links include History, Purpose, Programs and Services, Student Living, Comprehensive Educational Resource Center, Outreach Services, Health Care, Technology

Curriculum: Education; Health

2109 Tennessee Sports Hall of Fame

http://tshf.net/

The Tennessee Sports Hall of Fame was founded by a group known as the Middle Tennessee Sportswriters and Broadcasters Association.

Special Features: Links include Important Dates, Field Trips and Group Tours. Nomination Process, Honorees, Inductees, Museum

Curriculum: Sports

2110 Tennessee State Museum

www.tnmuseum.org

The Tennessee State Museum is one of the largest state museums in the nation. Its interpretive exhibits begin 15,000 years ago and continue through the early 1990s, displaying Tennessee's history during the Prehistoric, Frontier, Age of Jackson, Antebellum, Civil War and Reconstruction periods.

Special Features: Links include History, In

the News, Exhibitions, Event Calendar, Children's Corner, Teacher Talk, Museum Store
Curriculum: History

2111 Tennessee Theatre

www.tennesseetheatre.com

The Tennessee Theatre is one of the few great movie palaces from the Roaring Twenties still in operation! Today, the theatre is used for much more than stage shows. It now represents the Historic Tennessee Theatre Foundation, the Symphony Orchestra, the Knoxville Opera Company, the Appalachian Ballet and much more.
Special Features: This theatre is a true multi-purpose performing arts venue, serving arts organizations, national touring productions
Curriculum: Drama

2112 Tennessee Trails Association

www.tennesseetrails.org

The Tennessee Trails Association is a non-profit organization whose mission is to promote the development of a state-wide system of hiking trails. It is also a member of the Southeast Foot Trails coalition, which promotes an interconnected trail system in the southeast.
Special Features: Chapters, Leadership, Grants, History, Photos, Newsletter Archives, Cumberland Trail Conference
Curriculum: Environmental Studies; Geography; History; Physical Education; Social Studies

2113 Tennessee Valley Authority

www.tva.gov

The Tennessee Valley Authority works in concert with other public agencies to protect the Tennessee Valley's water supply for the present and in the future.
Special Features: TVA has a website just for kids—to learn how TVA makes electricity, prevents floods, protects wildlife and much more (a section for teachers, too)
Curriculum: Economics; Environmental Studies; Geography; History; Science; Social Studies

2114 Tennessee Valley Railroad Museum

www.tvrail.com

The Tennessee Valley Railroad Museum offers a multitude of experiences. Grand Junction Station displays locomotives and cars from the late 1800s to present. Educational tours are offered regarding railroad history and progress. Displays and a theatre are available.
Special Features: Links include Day Out With Thomas, News and Updates, About Our Rides, Tour the Railroad, External Links
Curriculum: History; Social Studies

2115 Tennessee Walking Horse

www.twhnc.com

The Tennessee Walking horse National Celebration is credited to the late Henry Davis of Wartrance, Tennessee. Davis became an enthusiast about Tennessee Walking Horses in 1939 and is renowned for his contributions and celebrations.
Special Features: Links include Tennessee Walking Horse National Celebration, Fun Show, Music Show, News and Views
Curriculum: History; Social Studies

2116 University of Tennessee Space Institute Home Page (UTSI)

www.utsi.edu

The UTSI is a graduate educational and research institution in Middle Tennessee. Since 1964, it has become internationally recognized for study and research in engineering, physics, mathematics, and computer science. It maintains state-of-the-art expertise in both technical and managerial areas.
Special Features: This Institute has made important research contributions in the areas of airplane missile aerodynamics, jet engines, computational fluid dynamics, space propulsion, laser processing
Curriculum: Science; Social Studies; Technology

2117 Women in Tennessee History

www.mtsu.edu/~library/wtn/wtn-home.html

Women in Tennessee History include significant Tennessee women throughout the ages, with links to such areas as: African-Americans, American Indians, Arts and Literature, Civil War, Education, Politics, Religion, Social Reforms, Sports, Women's Rights, Work.
Special Features: Includes "Why This Is Needed and What Information Sources are Included," containing over 800 references to books, journal articles, theses, manuscript collections, publications, online links
Curriculum: Women's Studies

TEXAS

2118 Art Museum of Southeast Texas

www.amset.org

The Art Museum of Southeast Texas includes the following: Exhibitions and Collections, Gallery Tours, Café Arts, Photography and Sketching, Programs for Schools and Teachers, Public Education Programs, International Freedom Fest and the Children's Computer Lab and Kidsnet.

Special Features: The Programs for Schools and Teachers include: Teacher Resource Library/Klein Library, Tours, Art-To-Go, Protégé High School Art Competition and Exhibition, Odom Junior Docents

Curriculum: Art

2119 Association of Texas Professional Educators

www.atpe.org

The Association of Texas Professional Educators is a member-owned, member-governed professional association. ATPE is the leading educators' association in the state with 100,000 members. What's more, the Association of Texas Professional Educators is the largest independent association for public school educators in the nation.

Special Features: Links include Legal Issues, Education Issues, Legislative Advocacy, TAKS Resources, Para-educators, Student Teachers, Publications, Calendar and others including online resources

Curriculum: Education

2120 Bob Bullock Texas State History Museum

www.thestoryoftexas.com

The Bob Bullock Texas State History Museum tells the "Story of Texas" with three floors of interactive exhibits, the special effects show, The Star of Destiny and an IMAX theatre featuring "Texas—The Big Picture."

Special Features: Links include About the Museum, Museum Background, Education, State Preservation Board, Frequently Asked Questions, About Bob Bullock, Exhibits, Theaters, Press Room and others

Curriculum: History

2121 Denison Texas

www.denisontx.com

Denison Texas is located on the Texas and Oklahoma boarder near Lake Texoma and Dallas. It is unique because it has remained an active and thriving business district and a source of pride to the entire state of Texas for over three decades.

Special Features: Former President Dwight D. Eisenhower was born in Denison, Texas near Lake Texoma. The city of Denison is a National Register District with 20th century architecture

Curriculum: History

2122 Educators

http://utopia.utexas.edu/educators/index.html

Educators provides all Texas educators with easy access to an array of K–12 lesson plans and student activities from the University of Texas at Austin. All materials are searchable by grade and subject, and most of the lesson plans are TEKS-aligned.

Special Features: Links include Language Arts, Math, Science, Social Studies, Foreign Language, Theme Learning, Teacher's Toolkit, Counselors, Professional Development, Field Trips, Tenet

Curriculum: Education

2123 Famous People That Once Lived in Reagan, Falls County, Texas

www.forttumbleweed.com/famous.html

The town of Reagan that existed up until the early 1950s, for the most part, no longer exists. Most of the older inhabitants (who formed the bulk of the town) now rest in peace in their local cemetery. However; looking back at this town, it produced some individuals that made their marks on history.

Special Features: Links include Reagan Homecoming News, Map of the Reagan Community, History of Reagan, Former Residents of Reagan, Early-Day Businesses of Reagan and others

Curriculum: History; Social Studies

2124 Gateway to Texas Travel

www.tourtexas.com

One can make the most of traveling through Texas by visiting this inclusive website. Gateway to Texas Travel includes: Destinations and Attractions, Fairs, Festivals and Events, Maps, Free Travel Information, Texas Nature Trails and Outdoor Activities.

Special Features: Via Gateway to Texas Travel, one can access destinations and attractions by city or region; events by date, region and category, free brochures, links to other travel sites

Curriculum: Business; Economics; Geography; History; Physical Education; Social Studies

2125 Guide to Texas Outside

www.texasoutside.com

The Guide to Texas Outside offers information regarding hiking, biking, camping, boating, fishing, sailing, hunting, parts, scuba diving and just about anything one can do outside in the state of Texas.

Special Features: Areas include: Central Texas, San Antonio, Wichita Falls, East Texas, West Texas, Southern Texas, Northeast Texas, Highland Lakes, Amarillo area and others

Curriculum: Geography; Physical Education; Social Studies

2126 Kimbell Art Museum

www.kimbellart.org

The Kimbell Art Museum is widely regarded as one of the most outstanding modern public art gallery facilities in the world. Its holdings range in period from antiquity to the 20th century. This museum provides an ongoing program of interpretative exhibitions and publications.

Special Features: Links include Information, collection, Exhibitions, Education and Events, News, Award-Winning Building, Vision of the Founders, Mission Statement and others

Curriculum: History

2127 Lone Star Junction: A Texas and Texas History Resource

www.lsjunction.com

The Texas Lone Star Junction is a Texas history resource provided for the benefit of both Texans and "foreigners." It is an non-profit organization whose service, an online resource about Texas and its early history.

Special Features: Links includes such areas as: Archives, Forums, Classics Online, Texans,

Book Reviews and Texas Connections, Songs of Texas, A Texas Scrapbook, Images of Texas, Sites That Cite Our State

Curriculum: History; Social Studies

2128 North Texas Institute for Educators on the Visual Arts

www.art.unt.edu/ntieva/index.htm

This Institute's mission is to conduct research and staff development in the implementation of discipline-based art education. It is a comprehensive approach to learning art that centers instruction on works of art and derives content from four foundational disciplines that contribute to the creation, understanding and appreciation of art.

Special Features: Links include Programs, Newsletters, ArtLinks Study Prints, Curriculum Resources, Transforming Education through the Arts Challenge, Marcus Fellows Programs, School of Visual Arts and others

Curriculum: Art

2129 North Texas Technology Council

www.nttc.ws/goals.html

Examples of goals of the North Texas Technology Council include: Build a strong public image for the technology community in North Texas by promoting industry stars, products, technologies and member companies; Promote North Texas as a place for technology companies to start, locate, grow, prosper, invest, work, live and plan.

Special Features: Links include Goals, Mission, Events, Committees, Get Involved, Careers, Links, About Us, Frequently Asked Questions and others

Curriculum: Business; Technology

2130 School of Rural Public Health

www.srph.tamushsc.edu/index_SmRes.html

The mission of the School of Rural Public Health is to improve the health of communities, with an emphasis on rural and underserved populations through education, research, service, outreach and creative partnerships.

Special Features: Links include Academics, Student Services, Centers and Programs, Distance Education, About the School of Rural Public Health, Links and others

Curriculum: Health

2131 Songs of Texas

www.lsjunction.com/midi/songs.htm

The Songs of Texas website offers song files that conform to the Musical Instrument Digital Interface (MIDI) standard. These songs are categorized into: Uniquely Texas, Texas School Songs, Regional Favorites, Down Mexico Way, Campfire Classics, Honky-tonk Heaven and much more.

Special Features: Lyrics are also available for most of these Texas songs; one must have a sound card installed and one's browser must be linked to the MIDI player software to play the songs online.

Curriculum: Music

2132 State and Local Government on the Net: Texas

www.statelocalgov.net/state-tx.htm

Directory of official state, county and city government websites. It includes such areas within the Texas State and Local Government as: State Home Page, Statewide Offices, Boards and Commissions, Regional, County, City, Town, Village and more.

Special Features: Examples of Boards and Commissions of Texas include: Commission for the Blind Home, Ethics Commission, Geographic Information Council, Public Finance Authority, Veterans Commission

Curriculum: Government

2133 TAHPERD Physical Education

www.tahperd.org/LINKS/links_physical_ed.html

Because of its unique and essential contribution to the total education program, the Texas Association for Health, Physical Education, Recreation and Dance strongly recommends quality daily physical education instruction for all K–12 students.

Special Features: Links include Event Calendar, Resources, Publications, Programs, Issues and Legislation, Membership, Meetings and Conventions and others

Curriculum: Physical Education

2134 Tenet Web: The Texas Education Network

www.tenet.edu

The Tenet Web provides useful, current resources for the Texas Education Community. It includes sections of Administrators, Teachers, Professional Resources for All Educators, Parents and Students.

Special Features: Links include Educational Headlines, About Tenet, Professional Partners, Schools on the Web and others

Curriculum: Education

2135 Texas Art Education Association

www.coe.uh.edu/taea

The mission of the Texas Art Association is to promote quality visual arts education in Texas by promoting visual arts education as an integral part of the curriculum through professional development of knowledge and representation of the art educators of Texas, service and leadership opportunities and so forth.

Special Features: Links include About TAEA, Membership, Calendar, Divisions, Areas, Special Programs, Advocacy, Publications, Resources

Curriculum: Art

2136 Texas Association for Educational Technology

www.taet.org

The general purpose of the Texas Association for Educational Technology is the improvement of education through a joint effort with other educational organizations dedicated to teaching and learning. Its role is directed toward the improvement of instruction through effective utilization of educational technology.

Special Features: Links include Awards and Scholarships, Information Resources, Calendar of Events, Leadership, Constitution, Bylaws and Mission, Member Services, Vendors

Curriculum: Education; Technology

2137 Texas Association of Counties

www.county.org/counties/index.asp

More than ever before, the complex demands of modern society are focused on the traditional framework of local government — Texas' 254 counties. The Texas Association of Counties delivers a growing list of services and is working smarter and harder to respond to the ever-changing needs of Texas.

Special Features: Links include About Texas Counties, Texas County Websites, Texas County Courthouses, County Government, County Official Information, Related Sites

Curriculum: Business; Economics; Government; History; Social Studies

2138 Texas Association of Music Schools

www.tmea.org/085

The purpose of the Texas Association of Music Schools is to advance the cause of music in education and to improve the quality and program of the music educational system in Texas via the promotion of cooperation between universities and the exercise of educational leadership.

Special Features: Links include Our Mission, Member Institutions, Membership Information, History, Constitution, Bylaws, Ethics, Leadership, Presidential Address, Commissioned Survey

Curriculum: Music

2139 Texas Beyond History

www.texasbeyondhistory.net

Texas Beyond History is a public education project of the Texas Archeological Research Laboratory at the University of Texas at Austin. Its purpose is to interpret and share the results of archeological and historical research on the cultural heritage of Texas with the citizens of Texas and the world.

Special Features: Links include The Texas Archeological Research Laboratory, Staff, Editorial Assistants, Future Plans (including thematic exhibits covering every major culture and time period and from every area of Texas)

Curriculum: Geography; History; Social Studies

2140 Texas Business and Education Coalition

www.tbec.org

The Texas Business and Education Coalition was formed in 1989 to bring business and education leaders together in a long-term effort to improve the performance of the Texas public school system.

Special Features: Links include Policy Statements, Strategic Plan, Corporation and Educational Partners, Public Education Issue Briefs, Business to Teaching and others

Curriculum: Business; Education

2141 Texas Computer Education Association

www.tces.org

The mission of the Texas Computer Education Association is the improvement of teaching and learning through the use of computer technology. It is the largest state organization devoted to the use of technology in education.

Special Features: Links include Convention, Training, Contests and Awards, Special Interest Groups, Calendar, Publications, What's New

Curriculum: Education; Technology

2142 Texas Cultural and Arts Network

www.arts.state.tx.us

The Texas Cultural and Arts Network provide a "Village," which includes such areas as: Artist Studios, Art and Cultural Organizations, Community Center, Crafts, Folk Arts, Government, Health, Library, Newspaper, Pavilion of Cultures, Public Art, School House K–12 and others

Special Features: Links include Online Web Applications, Grant Programs, Texas Music Project Grant, Texas Arts Exchange, News Flash, Texas Craft Institute

Curriculum: Business; Economics; Government; Language Arts; Health; History

2143 Texas Economics

www.thecitiesof.com/texas/escape/texaseconomics.html

Few states possess as wide a variety of resources as Texas, and few support economic activities of comparable variety. The economy of Texas has closely reflected key technological developments that have occurred during the state's history.

Special Features: Links include more information about the following Texas cities: Austin, Corpus Christi, Dallas, El Paso, Forth Worth, Houston, Laredo, San Antonio

Curriculum: Economics

2144 Texas Environmental Center

www.tec.org

The Texas Environmental Center is a nonprofit organization that produces Web and CD-ROM–based environmental programs. It has been a pioneer in the use of the Internet and developed one of the first online libraries. This Center has received acclaim for producing some of the most creative and appropriate new media based environmental education programs and products in the nation.

Special Features: Examples of Major Programs include: FloodSafety.com. Green by Design CD-ROM, Barton Springs Interactive CD-ROM, Colorado River Trail website, The Texas Environmental Almanac Online, Lower Colorado River Watch Bulletin Board and others

Curriculum: Environmental Studies

2145 Texas Escapes

www.texasescapes.com

The motto of Texas Escapes is, "The reverent, the irreverent and the irrelevant ... dedicated to those who are curious about Texas." This site includes, for example, Texas Scenic Drives, Texas Gulf Coast Destinations, The Painted Churches of Fayette County and much more.

Special Features: Links include Towns and Cities A to Z, Towns by Region, Ghost Towns, Texas Trips, Architecture, Books, Newsletters and others

Curriculum: Business; Economics; Geography; History; Social Studies

2146 Texas Guaranteed Student Loan Corporation

www.tgslc.org

TG Online is a premier source of information, financing and assistance to help all families and students realize their educational and career dreams in Texas. For example, it hosts regional training events and publishes the Integrated Common Manual.

Special Features: One link includes "For Schools," which includes Innovative Solutions and Tools, Information Resources, Individualized Customer Service, Regulatory Information, Default Aversion

Curriculum: Counseling

2147 Texas Hatters

www.texashatters.com

Marvin Emmanuel Gammage, Sr., known to us as "Pappy," began the family tradition of hat making back in mid 1920s as an apprentice hatter at Southern Hat Company in Houston, Texas. His history continues as does the Texas hatting industry.

Special Features: Includes: "Hat Making: A Real Custom Hat," which discusses the methods of hat making used since the early 20th century and more

Curriculum: Business; History

2148 Texas Health Guide

www.texashealthguide.com

Health IT is a physician-driven company dedicated to transforming the delivery of healthcare through Internet technology. It promotes improved communication between providers and patients to empower patients with information to make informed decisions. Health IT created the Texas Health Guide so it could be a significant resource to those in Texas and the rest of the Nation as they search for healthcare-related resources

Special Features: Links include Home, Health Resources, Organizations, Facilities, Vendors, Contact

Curriculum: Health

2149 Texas Heart Institute

www.texasheartinstitute.org

The Texas Heart Institute is a nonprofit organization dedicated to reducing the devastating toll of cardiovascular disease through innovative and progressive programs in research, education and patient care. By browsing its Web pages, one can learn about programs in research and education, highly skilled physicians, medical breakthroughs, ways to reduce risk of cardiovascular diseases and upcoming events.

Special Features: Links include Patient Care Information, International Services, Heart Information Center, Programs, News, History, Milestones, Symbol and others

Curriculum: Health

2150 Texas Historic Trees

www.texasescapes.com/TexasHistory/TexasHistoricTrees.htm

Texas Historic Trees includes images and stories of famous trees such as: Hopewell Magnolia, Wedding Oak, Sam Houston Oak, Goose Island Oak, Evergreen Oak, Auction Oaks, Bandera Tragedy Tree, Hanging Tree and many others.

Special Features: Includes not only Images and Stories of Texas Famous Trees, but also Other Texas Trees and Their Stories, Tree-in-the-Street Sorority, Readers' Comments, Texas Big Tree Registry and others

Curriculum: Science; Social Studies

2151 Texas Home Educators

www.texashomeeducators.com/economics.htm

Examples of Economics lessons include: The Mint, a collaborative effort between the National Council on Economic Education and the Northwestern Mutual Life Foundation that offers lessons, quizzes and activities to teach secondary students basic economics and money management.

Special Features: Links include What's New, Is It Legal, How Do I Start, Online Discussions,

Support Groups, Calendar of Events, Elementary Lesson Plans, High School Lesson Plans and others

Curriculum: Business; Economics

2152 Texas Homeland Security

www.texashomelandsecurity.com

Emergency workers in Texas are well prepared to respond to any type of threat, but every Texan has a role to play in homeland security. Texas Homeland Security provides information about what one can do to protect his or her family and help safeguard the state of Texas.

Special Features: Links include Accessibility, Site Policies, Texas Online, TRAIL Search, Office of the Governor, Be Involved, Be Prepared (for example, assemble emergency supply kit; safeguard your neighborhood)

Curriculum: Economics; Government; Social Studies

2153 Texas Information and Referral Network

www.helpintexas.com

The Texas Information and Referral Network is a system that allows one to search for help with health and human services throughout the state of Texas. Their goal is to provide seamless access to timely, accurate and relevant health and human services information through greater awareness of available information and referral services, along with improved communications among service providers.

Special Features: This website resource system allows one to search for services and programs across Texas; via "guided trails" for novices or "power users" for advanced users of the Internet

Curriculum: Health

2154 Texas Legacies

www.epictexas.com

Texas Legacies is the newest telling of the great stories of Texas. It's not the story you may read about in history books; instead, it is the story of the ordinary folks made great by the greatness of this state.

Special Features: Links include Testimonials, What to Expect, Press, Media, Productions, About Us and others

Curriculum: History; Social Studies

2155 Texas Observer

www.texasobserver.org

The Texas Observer writes about issues ignored or underreported in the mainstream press, in pursuit of a vision of Texas in which education, justice and material progress are available to all. Their goal is to cover stories crucial to the public interest and to provoke dialogue that promotes democratic participation and open government.

Special Features: Links include Current Issues, Archives, Site Map, Search, How You Can Help and others

Curriculum: Business; Economics; Language Arts

2156 Texas Online

www.state.tx.us

Texas Online is the official Web site for the state of Texas. It includes a wide variety of information and links, such as: About Texas, Business and Consumer Services, Education and Training, Environment and Natural Resources, Government, Health and Family Services, Laws and Criminal Justice, Regional and Community Resources and much more.

Special Features: Examples of online service Links include Driver License and ID Card, Driver Record Requests, Vehicle Registration, Renewal and Address change, Pay Taxes, Voter Registration Address Change, Occupational and Professional Licenses

Curriculum: Business; Driver Training; Economics; Environmental Studies; Government; Health; Social Studies

2157 Texas Ornithological Society

www.texasbirds.org

The Texas Ornithological Society was founded in 1953; the purpose of the Society is to promote the discovery and dissemination of knowledge of birds; to encourage the observation, study and conservation of birds in Texas; to encourage the formation of local birding clubs; and to stimulate cooperation among professional ornithologists.

Special Features: Links include Affiliated Clubs, Century Club Award, Meetings, Field Trips, Seasonal Reports, Sanctuaries, Publications, Texas Bird Records and others

Curriculum: Environmental Studies; Science

2158 Texas Programs for the Disabled

www.turningpointtechnolocy.com/Texas%20Programs%20for%20the%20Disabled

Texas Programs for the Disabled include not only these websites, but also: The Medically Dependent Children Program, Community Living Assistance and Support Services Program, Home-Based Community-Based Services, Community-Based Alternatives, Deaf-Blind Multiple Disabilities Program and much more.

Special Features: Examples of Texas Programs for the Disabled websites include: Advocacy, Inc., Caring for Children Program, Education Hot Line, Medicaid Program, The Parent Connection, Texas Parent to Parent Program and others

Curriculum: Special Education

2159 Texas PTA

www.txpta.org

The Texas PTA is a grassroots organization made up of parents, teachers, and others around the state who have a special interest in children, families and schools. PTA membership is as diverse as Texas in cultures, educational levels and parenting skills.

Special Features: Links include PTA's Mission, Purpose of PTA, What is PTS vs. Other Parent Groups, Texas PTA Virtual Exhibit Hall, Texas PTA online Catalog and others

Curriculum: Education

2160 Texas Ranger Hall of Fame

www.texasranger.org/halloffame/HOF.htm

The Texas Ranger Hall of Fame memorializes 30 Texas Rangers who gave their lives in the line of duty or served with great distinction. Examples are John Armstrong, James Brooks, John S. Ford, Jessee Lee Hall, John Coffee Hays, John Jones, Bryan Marsh, Leander McNelley and so forth.

Special Features: Links include Rangers Today, Visitor Information, History, Research Center, Hall of Fame, Student Help, Family History, News and others

Curriculum: History; Social Studies

2161 Texas School for the Blind and Visually Impaired

www.tsbvi.edu/school/index.htm

The Texas School for the Blind and Visually Impaired has been established as part of the public education system to serve as a special school in the continuum of statewide alternative placements for students who have a visual impairment. It is also a statewide resource to professionals and parents who serve these children.

Special Features: Links include Instruction, Technology, Curriculum, Publications, Outreach, Texas Deafblind Project, Space Camp, Statewide Calendar and others

Curriculum: Education

2162 Texas State Aquarium

www.texasstateaquarium.org

The mission of the Texas State Aquarium is to provide educationally enriching, entertaining programming to a diverse audience; to develop entertaining interactive exhibits that engage and inspire; to promote and practice environmental conservation and wildlife rehabilitation; to provide first-class guest services; and to operate as a private, self-supporting organization.

Special Features: Seaside Seashells, the Great Jetty Mystery, Coral Reef Under Construction, Jellyfish, Keepers of the Coast, Sharks and others

Curriculum: Biology; Environmental Studies; Science

2163 Texas State Historical Association — The Handbook of Texas Online

www.tsha.utexas.edu

The Handbook of Texas Online is a multidisciplinary encyclopedia of Texas history, geography and culture sponsored by the Texas State Historical Association. It is a joint project of The General Libraries at the University of Texas at Austin and the Texas State Historical Association.

Special Features: The Education Teaching Tools links presents a collection of instructional resources designed to assist teachers of Texas history. The collection is intended for classroom teachers at the 4th and 7th grade levels. Every teaching tool was prepared by a practicing classroom teacher or by an educator with previous classroom experience

Curriculum: Education; History

2164 Texas Technology Access Project

http://tatp.edb.utexas.edu

Services of the Texas Technology Access Project include: information and advise to individuals and organizations about a wide range of assistive technology issues, training and technical assistance to professionals and others who help people with disabilities access and use technology, and many more

Special Features: This Project recognizes that the explosion of technology is unequaled in its potential to offer people with disabilities opportunities to do more, be more independent or connect with family, friends, and the community

Curriculum: Education; Technology

2165 Texas Travel

www.traveltex.com

Texas Travel is the official site of Texas tourism. Via this website, one can explore 267,000 square miles of the Lone Star State. It includes driving tours, events, Texas regions and much more.

Special Features: Links include Texas Cities, Texas Activities, Texas Events, See Texas, Driving Tours, Links and others

Curriculum: Business; Economics; Geography; History; Social Studies

2166 Texas Women in Law Enforcement

www.twle.com

The vision of Texas Women in Law Enforcement is to strengthen the law enforcement profession through the celebration of diversity, education and awareness. This association fosters a positive relationship between law enforcement and the public they are dedicated to protect and serve.

Special Features: Links include Membership, Board, Vision, Mission, Conference Information, Outstanding Officer Awards Program, Vanessa Rudloff Scholarship Awards

Curriculum: Government; Women's Studies

2167 Welcome to STARS

www.txstars.net/servlet/HSGServlet?page=Home

The State of Texas Assistance and Referral System (STARS) allows one to self-screen for potential eligibility for programs provided by the Texas Department of Human Services and other Texas state agencies.

Special Features: Resource Links include Children's Health Insurance Program, Texas Workforce Network, Office of the Attorney General, Health and Human Services Commission Information and Referral Network

Curriculum: Health

UTAH

2168 America's Serengeti Endangered

www.wasatch.com/~urc/am_serengeti.html

The Great Salt Lake has been called America's Serengeti for birds. As the largest lake west of the Great Lakes, this salt water marvel is the largest wetland area between the Mississippi River and the Pacific Ocean. It is the habitat for over 250 bird species.

Special Features: Links include The Bear River, Water Conservation, Updates, Events, Press

Curriculum: Environmental Studies; Geography; History; Science; Social Studies

2169 American Civil Liberties Union of Utah (ACLU)

www.acluutah.org

The ACLU of Utah was chartered in 1958 to work on constitutional issues that are pertinent to those living in Utah. Their priorities include freedom of speech and expression, the separation of church and state, freedom of religion, the right to privacy, safe prisons and jails and equal protection and due process of Utah's laws.

Special Features: Includes links: Rights Violated, What's New, In the Courts, In the Legislature, In the News, Publications, Take Action

Curriculum: Government

2170 Bluff Utah

www.bluffutah.org

Bluff is a small Utah town located in the San Juan River Valley. It is bordered on the south by the San Juan River and the Navajo Nation. To the north, 300-foot sandstone bluffs, which inspired the name for the town, are a dominant visual element for this community.

Special Features: Links to the Navajo Reservation and Navajo Style — religion, arts, folklore

Curriculum: Geography; History; Social Studies

2171 Children's Museum of Utah

www.childmuseum.org

The Children's Museum of Utah is a hands-on discovery museum for kids of all ages. Visitors will find an interactive playground where a new learning experience awaits them around every corner. Together, children and adults can explore, imagine, create and discover. This Museum features more than 140 permanent exhibits in the arts, sciences and the humanities.

Special Features: Links to: Museum Experience; Online Activities: For Teachers; Helping Hands; Group Events; Future Museum

Curriculum: History; Language Arts; Science; Social Studies; Technology

2172 Economic Development Corporation of Utah

www.edcutah.org

The Economic Development Corporation of Utah is a private, statewide, non-profit organization formed in 1987 to provide a unified and professionally managed economic development program promoting the state of Utah. It specializes in assisting companies who are considering Utah for a business relocation or expansion.

Special Features: Services include: Site Tours, Demographic and labor Market Data, Real Estate Data, Educational Data, Community Briefings, Employment Recruitment Assistance

Curriculum: Business; Economics; Government

2173 Envirocare of Utah

www.envirocareutah.com

The links provided via Envirocare were created to provide individuals with the best information possible about the low-level radioactive waste industry and what is accomplished at Envirocare.

Special Features: Links include Services, Waste Acceptance Criteria, Licenses and Permits, Envirocare Story, In the News, Setting the Record Straight

Curriculum: Environmental Studies

2174 Envision Utah

www.envisionutah.org

By the year 2020, the Greater Wasatch Area of Utah will add a million more residents, two-thirds of whom will be children and grandchildren of current residents. They must breathe the same air, share common resources and use the same roads to travel. Successful growth will require sound planning and strategy.

Special Features: Includes links such as: Promoting Air Quality, Creating Transportation Choices, Preserving Critical Lands, Promoting Housing Options

Curriculum: Business; Economics; Environmental Studies; Government; Social Studies

2175 Hill Aerospace Museum

www.hill.af.mil/museum/history/uahf.htm

This was established to recognize individuals in Utah who have distinguished themselves as aviation pioneers by their accomplishments or by fostering noteworthy advances in Utah's aviation program.

Special Features: Lists all who were recognized with this honor, along with links

Curriculum: Science; Social Studies; Technology

2176 Humane Society of Utah (HSU)

www.utahhumane.org

The Humane Society of Utah is dedicated to the elimination of fear, pain and suffering in all animals. The site quotes George Eliot, "Animals are such agreeable friends, they ask no questions, they pass no criticism."

Special Features: Links include Adoptions, Featured Pets, Animal Listings, Donations, Special Events, Investigation, Newsletter, Press Releases, Dog Training

Curriculum: Social Studies

2177 Labor Commission of Utah

http://laborcommission.utah.gov

The Labor Commission of Utah strives to assure safe, healthful, fair and nondiscriminatory work environments; fair housing practices and the general welfare of employees and employers. It has been in existence for nearly a century.

Special Features: Links include Administrative, Adjudication, Industrial Accidents, Safety Division, Workplace Safety, New Rules

Curriculum: Business; Environmental Studies; Government; Social Studies

2178 Monument Valley — Utah

www.americansouthwest.net/utah/monument_valley

Monument Valley provides perhaps the most enduring and definitive images of the American West. The isolated red mesas and buttes surrounded by empty, sandy desert have been filmed and photographed numerous times. This valley is actually not a valley, but rather a wide flat, interrupted by crumbling formations of sandstone layers.

Special Features: Interesting Links include Arches, Bryce Canyon, Canyon lands, Capitol Reef, Cedar Breaks, Dinosaur, Glen Canyon, Hovenweep, Natural Bridges, Zion

Curriculum: Geography; History; Social Studies

2179 Mountains of Utah (Sponsor: Partners in Flight)

www.blm.gov/wildlife/pl_69sum.htm

North-to-south lying mountains are centered in Utah and extend slightly into Wyoming and Idaho. They consist of the Wasatch and Uinta Ranges and separate the Great Basin from the Colorado Plateau. The four primary vegetation types reflect elevation and are similar to those in the Southern Rockies.

Special Features: Priority Bird Populations and Habitats; material to download; maps to view

Curriculum: Geography

2180 No More Homeless Pets in Utah

www.utahpets.org

No More Homeless Pets in Utah is a coalition of rescue groups, shelters and veterinarians working together to end the euthanasia of healthy, adoptable dogs and cats in Utah. It places an emphasis on increasing the numbers of both adoptions and spay/neuter surgeries in Utah.

Special Features: Links include Adoptions, Spay/Neuter, How to Help, Special Events, FAQs, Our Progress

Curriculum: Social Studies

2181 People for Peace and Justice of Utah

www.utahpeace.org/main.html

People for Peace and Justice of Utah is a grass-roots organization advocating nonviolence and justice — protecting civil liberties.

Special Features: Links include Peace Calendar, Peace Vigil, Peace Pins, U.S. Department of Peace, Texts, Texts of Speeches, Photos, Upcoming Events

Curriculum: Government; Psychology; Social Studies

2182 Pioneer Library: Utah's Online Library

http://pioneer-library.org

Pioneer is Utah's Online Library of electronic resources. It provides statewide access to newspaper articles, magazines, professional journals, encyclopedias, video, photographs, maps, charts and graphics.

Special Features: One could use Pioneer to get help with homework, finish a big paper, prepare to teach a class, keep current, find historical information

Curriculum: Library Media

2183 Pioneer Theatre Company Online (PTC)

www.pioneertheatre.org

The PTC Matinee Program is designed to expose students in grades six through 12 to live professional theatre in such a way that they can develop an understanding of and love for this great art form — drama.

Special Features: A professional theatre at the University of Utah, PTC produces a seven-play season, including classics, musicals, dramas, comedies

Curriculum: Drama; Language Arts

2184 Project ASTRO Utah

www.clarkfoundation.org/astro-utah

Project ASTRO is a national program creating partnerships between teachers and students in grades four through nine with amateur and professional astronomers. The project was created in 1993 by the Astronomical Society of the Pacific and funded by the National Science Foundation.

Special Features: The project's goal is to enhance the core science curriculum for Utah's students. Links include: Goals, Coalition, Schools, Science Snippets

Curriculum: Science

2185 Records Information — Vital, Utah

www.vitalrec.com/ut.html

The Vital Records Information website contains information about where to obtain copies of Utah vital records, such as birth and death certificates, marriage licenses and divorce decrees.

Special Features: Provides information about ancestry, such as: Search Historical Records, Build your Family Tree. Find Locality Resources, Census Records, Databases

Curriculum: Government; Health; History; Social Studies

2186 Southern Utah Wilderness Alliance (SUWA)

www.suwa.org

SUWA's overarching goal is to protect Utah's remaining nine million acres of wild desert lands—lands owned by the American public and administered by the Bureau of Land Management. America's Redrock Wilderness Act will preserve one of the world's most unique landscapes—towering buttes, sweeping plateaus and intimate canyons.

Special Features: Links include Ongoing Works, Alerts and Updates, Campaigns, America's Redrock Wilderness Act, Events, Publications, Press, Goodies

Curriculum: Environmental Studies; Geography; History; Science; Social Studies

2187 Utah AIDS Foundation

www.wtahaids.org

The Utah AIDS foundation strives to help individuals, families, friends and communities with the complex issues surrounding HIV, because they believe that no one should have to suffer alone. They work side-by-side with community members, promoting compassion and extending companionship to every individual impacted by HIV.

Special Features: Links include Services, Information Center, Coming Attractions, Volunteers, Donors

Curriculum: Biology; Health; Sociology

2188 Utah Association for the Deaf

www.uad.org

The Utah Association for the Deaf possesses a long list of accomplishments, such as: development of the Utah Community Center for the Deaf, the Interpreter Service, A bookstore with deaf and hard of hearing products, and a monthly newsletter

Special Features: Links include Announcements, UAD Bulletin, UAD Bookstore, Miss Deaf Utah Pageant, MDUP Sorority

Curriculum: Health; Science

2189 Utah Avalanche

www.avalanche.org/~uac

This website is sponsored by the USDA Forest Service in partnership with: Friends of the Utah Avalanche Center, Utah Department of Public Safety, Salt Lake County and Utah State Parks.

Special Features: Includes such questions as: Is it true Avalanche myths? How fast are avalanches? What kind is the most dangerous? What's it like to be in an avalanche? How long can you live under the snow?

Curriculum: Geography; Science

2190 Utah Beehive State Capital

www.netstate.com/states/intro.ut_intro.htm

When Brigham Young led the persecuted American sect of Mormons into the deserts of Utah in 1847, he found refuge in a land no one else wanted. However, they made the desert bloom through their hard work and skill.

Special Features: Useful Links include Symbols, Almanac, Geography, People, Cool Schools, Marketplace

Curriculum: Economics; Geography; Government; History; Social Studies

2191 Utah Blue Chips

www.ucs.org/ucs_info.php

The Utah Computer Society (Blue Chips is a non-profit organization devoted to helping people with computers and keeping members informed of the latest developments in computing.

Special Features: Links include Monthly Magazine, Special Interest Groups, Corporate Members and Supporters, Virus Information

Curriculum: Technology

2192 Utah Centennial Studies (Sponsor: Utah State Office of Education)

www.uen.org/Centennial/index.html

Utah Centennial Studies were developed to provide teachers with innovative lessons, a wide variety of Utah historical topics and issues that can be adapted for students at any grade level.

Special Features: Extensions are included giving added ideas, as well as additional Utah lesson plan sites
Curriculum: History; Social Studies

2193 Utah Children

www.utahchildren.net/home.html

All children deserve the same shot at health, happiness and success. Utah Children offers everyone the opportunity to make that happen. The great challenge is to place the health and well-being of our children and families at the top of Utah's priorities—ensure children In Utah can succeed.

Special Features: One can select from the following topics: How Are Utah's Children? How Can I Help My Child? Take Action
Curriculum: Government; Psychology, Sociology

2194 Utah Conservation Data Center (UCDC)

http://dwrcdc.nr.utah.gov/ucdc

The Utah Conservation Data Center is the central repository for Utah biodiversity information. Although the UCDC focuses primarily on Utah's rare native species, information on all Utah vertebrate wildlife species, many invertebrate species, and numerous plant species is available.

Special Features: Links include Vertebrate Animals, Invertebrate Animals, Plants, Make a Wildlife Map, GIS Data, Utah Sensitive Species List, The Bats of Utah
Curriculum: Biology; Environmental Studies; Geography; Science; Social Studies

2195 Utah Department of Human Services

www.hsdsa.state.ut.us

One of the Utah Department of Human Service's goals is working to prevent people from abusing alcohol, tobacco and other drugs. Treatment services are offered by local agencies that receive state and federal funding through the United States. They provide research, statistics and general information on many types of drugs.

Special Features: Links include FAQs, Research Reports, Research Statistics, Drug Information, Online Databases, Criminal Justice, Treatment, Prevention
Curriculum: Biology; Health; Science

2196 Utah Education Association Homepage

www.utea.org

The Utah Education Association was organized in 1860 "for the purpose of establishing a society for promoting the educational interests of the community." Today, the Association's mission is to advance the cause of public education by promoting quality teaching and learning and advocating effectively for the rights and interests of its members.

Special Features: Teaching and Learning Links include the UEA Convention, Workshops, Scholarships and Awards, Educator Rights, License Renewal
Curriculum: Education

2197 Utah Festival Opera Company

www.ufoc.org

The Utah Festival Opera is located in Cache Valley, a setting of spectacular mountain scenery. The five-week festival includes four productions of the grand opera, operetta, light opera and musical theatre.

Special Features: Links include Classic Film Series, Inside the Theatre, About the Arena, About Utah Festival Opera, Educational Programs, Auditions
Curriculum: Music

2198 Utah Geological Survey

http://geology.utah.gov

The Utah Geological Survey division is an applied scientific agency that creates, interprets, and provides information about Utah's geologic environment, resources and hazards to promote safe, beneficial and wise use of land.

Special Features: Links include Utah Geology, Maps Online, Publications, Educational Resources, Map and Bookstore, Natural Resources
Curriculum: Environmental Studies; Science

2199 Utah History Encyclopedia

www.media.utah.edu/UHE

The first complete history of Utah in encyclopedia form, consisting of 575 articles and over 200 historical photographs; speaks of individuals, organizations, locations, institutions and topics of importance to Utah history.

Special Features: Utah Collections Multimedia Encyclopedia houses over 9000 digital videos, audio clips, images, maps and so forth.
Curriculum: History

2200 Utah Information Technology Association (UITA)

www.uita.org

UITA has been commissioned to achieve substantial progress in three areas: increasing capital; developing and attracting management talent; and improving the business environment. Through its product offerings and organized advocacy, UITA has had numerous victories.

Special Features: Links include Community Calendar, News, Press Releases, Industry Portal, Corporate Partnerships

Curriculum: Business; Technology

2201 Utah League of Cities and Towns

www.ulct.org

The Utah League of Cities and Towns is a nonpartisan, nonprofit association working through cooperative efforts to strengthen the quality of municipal government and administration. This is accomplished by representing municipal government interests and providing information, technical assistance and training.

Special Features: Includes links about the League, news, events, resources and legislature (including an online library and training programs)

Curriculum: Business; Economics; Government; Social Studies

2202 Utah Lepidopterists' Society

www.utahlepsociety.org

This is a non-profit educational and scientific organization dedicated to the study and enjoyment of all aspects of Lepidoptera, especially in Utah. It affirms that collecting Lepidoptera is one of many legitimate activities enabling professional and avocational lepidopterists to further Lepidoptera.

Special Features: Links include History, Community, Field Trips, Habitat, Kids

Curriculum: Biology; Science

2203 Utah Library Association (ULA)

www.ula.org

The mission of the ULA is to serve the professional development and educational needs of its members and to provide leadership and direction in developing and improving library and information services in the state of Utah.

Special Features: Links include Event Calendar, conference, Newsletter, Jobline, ULA Webteam

Curriculum: Library Media

2204 Utah Museum of Natural History

www.umnh.utah.edu/museum

The Utah Museum of Natural History illuminates the natural world and the place of humans within it. As Utah's state museum of natural history, it fosters an understanding of science as a journey of discovery and wonder, promotes the preservation of biological and cultural diversity.

Special Features: Links include Mission Statement, History, Rent the Museum, Indian Advisory, Museum Links

Curriculum: Environmental Studies; Geography; History; Science; Social Studies

2205 Utah Museums Association (UMA)

www.utahmuseums.org/index.jsp

The Utah Museums Association supports museums as they strive to fulfill their missions. The UMA accomplished its mission by: providing an arena for networking among museums; educating the museum community; and developing awareness of Utah Museums.

Special Features: Offers a Featured Museum, such as Ogden Nature Center, a 127-acre wildlife sanctuary and education center

Curriculum: History; Language Arts; Geography; Science; Social Studies

2206 Utah Native Plant Society

www.unps.org

The Utah Native Plant Society is dedicated to the appreciation, preservation, conservation and responsible use of the native plant and plant communities found in the state of Utah. Their goal is to foster public recognition of the diverse flora in Utah.

Special Features: Links include Calendar, News, Store, Rare Plants, Plant Sources, Newsletters

Curriculum: Biology; Science

2207 Utah Natural Parks and Tourist Guide

www.americansouthwest.net/utah

Utah contains one of the greatest concentrations of spectacular geological features in the world. For hundreds of miles, the landscape is dominated by twisting canyons, delicate arches, sheer mountains and ridges, spires and buttes.

Special Features: Other Place Links include Dead Horse Point, Flaming Gorge, Goblin Valley, Grand Staircase, Kodachrome Basin, Mount Timpanogos, Snow Canyon

Curriculum: Geography; Social Studies

2208 Utah Natural Resources Conservation Service (NRCS)

www.ut.nrcs.usda.gov/about

The Utah NRCS vision is state where every acre is used according to its capability and protected according to its needs. They believe that good management of soil, water and other natural resources will make a more abundant life for the people of Utah.

Special Features: Links include Utah Museum of Natural History, Utah Department of Natural Resources, Utah Locator Map by County Boundaries, Civil Rights

Curriculum: Economics; Environmental Studies; Geography; Science; Social Studies

2209 Utah Parent Center

www.utahparentcenter.org

The Utah parent Center is a statewide non-profit organization founded in 1984 to provide training, information and assistance to parents of children and youth with ALL disabilities, including physical, mental, hearing, vision, learning, behavioral and emotional

Special Features: Links include Mission, News, Upcoming Events, Calendar, Parent Handbook, Shopping

Curriculum: Education; Psychology; Sociology

2210 Utah Rivers Council

www.wastch.com/~urc

The Utah Rivers Council is a community-based, grassroots, non-profit organization dedicated to conservation and stewardship of Utah's rivers and sustainable, clean water sources for Utah citizens and wildlife for years to come.

Special Features: Links include America's Serengeti, the Bear River, Water Conservation, Updates, Events, Press Box

Curriculum: Economics; Environmental Studies; Geography; History; Science; Social Studies

2211 Utah Safety Council

www.utahsafetycouncil.org

The Utah Safety Council is a non-profit organization established to represent and promote safety and health interests on the highway, on the job and in the home. Programs have expanded to now include training, videos, educational materials and other resources to business, industry and the community.

Special Features: Learn about their 18-member Board of Directors who govern the Council and a staff of eight who manage and administer programs

Curriculum: Business; Environmental Studies; Health

2212 Utah Shakespearean Festival

www.bard.org

Presented are Utah Shakespearean Festival's mission, history, latest news, how to obtain information. The Utah Shakespearean Festival education and outreach programs offer chances to enhance one's life, outlook, and understanding of drama; in particular, Shakespeare.

Special Features: Links include Box Office, Group Sales, Gift Shop, The Plays, Membership, Area Events, Press Room

Curriculum: Drama

2213 Utah Symphony

www.utahsymphony.org

Founded in 1940, the Utah Symphony has become a vital presence on the American music scene through its distinctive performances worldwide and its well-known recording legacy.

Special Features: Under the link of Education, Utah Symphony & Opera provides a wide variety of fun and educational programs designed for schools, teachers, families and everyone interested in learning more about opera and orchestral music

Curriculum: Music

2214 Utah Travel Center

http://utahtravelcenter.com/sports

Site includes information about Utah Jazz (National Basketball Team), Utah Starzz (Women's National Basketball Association), Salt Lake Buzz (AAA affiliate of the Minnesota Twins), Utah Grizzles (International Hockey League an others.

Special Features: Professional Utah Sports,

College Sports, Other Sports/Activities, Sporting Events
Curriculum: Sports

2215 Utah's American Indian Tribes

www.utah.com/tribes

Represents the state's original inhabitants—since those ancient days of sacred places, dwelling sites and intriguing rock art messages. Five major tribes include: Ute, Navajo, Paiunte, Goshute and Shoshoni.
Special Features: Includes links, such as: Places to See, Outdoor Recreation, Things to Do, Groups and individual tribes such as the Ute, Navajo
Curriculum: Geography; History; Social Studies

2216 Welcome to Utah! The Official Web Site of the State of Utah

www.utah.gov/main/index

Utah government, living in Utah, visiting Utah, Business in Utah, Working in Utah and Learning in Utah. It also includes online services, such as: Tax Express, Renew Vehicle Registration, Community Services Directory and Find you Legislator.
Special Features: Via this website, one can voice their opinion, view headline news, weather and traffic
Curriculum: Business; Economics; Government; History; Social Studies

2217 Women's Resource Center

www.sa.utah.edu/women/mission.html

The Women's Resource Center, a member of the Division of Student Affairs at the University of Utah, provides educational support services for Women. The Center supports and facilitates women's choices, changes and empowerment through programs, advocacy, workshops, group and individual counseling.
Special Features: Links include Events, Counseling, Groups, Workshops, Scholarships, Resources, FAQs
Curriculum: Women's Studies

VERMONT

2218 American Precision Museum

www.americanprecision.org

The American Precision Museum preserves the heritage of the mechanical arts, celebrates the ingenuity of mechanical forebears, and explores the effects of their work on everyday loves. It now holds the largest collection of historically significant machine tools in the nation.
Special Features: Precision manufacturing touches all of us. Without it, we would not have the mass communication, rapid transportation, modern standards of sanitation and medical care, abundant food and clothing
Curriculum: History; Technology

2219 Billings Farm and Museum of Woodstock

www.billingsfarm.com

The Billings Farm and Museum is a living museum of Vermont's rural past, as well as a working dairy farm. The farm dates back to 1871, when Frederick Billings began importing cows for the Isle of Jersey. His farm has prospered, and today, is still a working dairy, which operates with the renowned farm life museum
Special Features: Links include Visitor Information, Special Events, Billings Farm, 1890 Farm House, Exhibits, School Visits, Group Tours, Museum Shop, News and Publications and others
Curriculum: History

2220 Birds of Vermont Museum

www.birdsofvermont.org

The Birds of Vermont Museum is a place where individuals can learn about birds and their role in the earth's ecosystem. It features over 450 carved birds representing 258 species.
Special Features: Links include Schedule of Events, The collections, Meet the Carver, School Field Trips, Links and others
Curriculum: Environmental Studies; Science

2221 Brattleboro Museum and Art Center

www.brattleboromuseum.org

The Brattleboro Museum and Art Center presents the art of our time in a way that entertains, educates and enlightens audiences of all ages. It is a nonprofit organization that produces frequently changing exhibitions of current art.

Special Features: Links include Information, Links, History, Exhibits, Education, Programs and Events, Membership and Giving

Curriculum: Art

2222 Camp Vermont

www.campvermont.com

The major goal of Camp Vermont is to help campers enjoy their stay in Vermont. Their members include most private campgrounds and all State Parks that offer camping. With more than 100 campgrounds, they offer a wide variety of facilities and experiences throughout the state of Vermont.

Special Features: Links include Campgrounds, Maps, More Information: Weather, Articles, Fishing, Links, Request Guide and others

Curriculum: Geography

2223 Center for Rural Studies

http://crs.uvm.edu

The Center for Rural Studies is a nonprofit, fee-for-service research organization that addresses social, economic, and resource-based problems of rural people and communities in Vermont. It provides consulting, research and program evaluation services; it also serves as the U.S. Census Bureau's Vermont State Data Center.

Special Features: Links include Agriculture, Education, Community Development, Data Bank, Recent Surveys, Search and others

Curriculum: Economics; Environmental Studies; Social Studies; Sociology

2224 Central Vermont Humane Society

www.cvhumane.com

The Central Vermont Humane Society promotes "One at a Time," which offers hope for neglected animals—bringing new families into pet's lives. "Over half of the households in America include an animal companion ... yet each animal shelter takes in 8 to 12 million lost and unwanted pets per year."

Special Features: Links include About Us, Dogs, Cats, Small Animals, Foster Care, Wish List, Upcoming Events, Retail Outlet, Training Classes, Breed Rescue and others

Curriculum: Social Studies

2225 Famous People

www.thingstodo.com/states/VT/famous_people.htm

Examples of Vermont Famous People include: Chester A. Arthur (21st President of the United States), Henry Wells (founder of Wells Fargo and Company), Orson Bean (actor), John Dewey (philosopher), Rudy Vallee (singer), and Elisha Graves Otis (inventor of the elevator).

Special Features: Katherine Paterson (author of *Jacob Have I Loved*, Ben Cohen and Jerry Greenfield (founders of Ben & Jerry's ice cream)

Curriculum: History

2226 Foliage Vermont

www.foliage-vermont.com

Within the Web site of Foliage Vermont, one can find daily foliage updates, including official State of Vermont Foliage information, eye witness reports by leaf peepers visiting Vermont, picture and even beautiful moon-setting foliage movies.

Special Features: Links include The Foliage, Driving Tours, Pictures, Interactive Foliage Map, The Leaves of Foliage, Foliage Forum and others

Curriculum: Environmental Studies; Science; Social Studies

2227 Greater Burlington Industrial Corporation/Cynosure, Inc.

www.vermont.org/gbic

This corporation was incorporated by 50 municipal officials and civic leaders from the Greater Burlington Area in 1954. The incorporators were citizens interested in creating sustainable economic opportunities for future generations.

Special Features: Their vision is a thriving Lake Champlain region with an economic environment providing meaningful employment consistent with a natural environment

Curriculum: Business; Economics

2228 KidsPlayce

www.kidsplayce.org

The mission of KidsPlayce is to foster positive adult-child interactions and to expand children's horizons through interactive exhibits and displays. It was founded in 1981 and serves children up to 12 years of age and their adult care givers in the Southern Vermont region.

Special Features: Links include Playspace, Programs, About Us, Program Calendar, Membership, Community Center and others

Curriculum: Education; Psychology; Sociology

2229 Lake Champlain Region

www.vermont.org

This is the official Web site of the Lake Champlain Regional Chamber of Commerce. The Lake Champlain region is an inspiring backdrop for both work and relaxation. The Chamber of Commerce offers information regarding events, activities, business, travel.

Special Features: Links include Vermont Convention Bureau, Business Directory, Events, Community Services, Frequently Asked Questions, Media Center, Chamber Store and others

Curriculum: Business; Economics; Social Studies

2230 Montshire Museum

www.montshire.net

The Montshire Museum of Science is a hands-on Museum located in Norwich, Vermont, offering dozens of exciting exhibits relating to the natural and physical sciences, ecology, and technology. The building is located on a 110-acre site near the Connecticut River, and the Museums' outdoor environment is a large part of the visitor experience. Science Park is a two-acre exhibit area in a beautiful, park-like setting.

Special Features: Links include Visiting the Museum; Exhibits and Trails; Programs; Montshire Access Project, Volunteering, Mountshire Minute, Press Room and others

Curriculum: Biology; Environmental Studies; Science; Social Studies

2231 Nature Museum at Grafton

www.nature-museum.org

The Nature Museum at Grafton, Vermont, is an institution that is fulfilling its mission for "fostering respect, understanding, and delight in the natural world..."

Special Features: Links include Exploring Nature in the Springtime with Children; Early Education, Calendar of Events, The Nature Almanac, Photo Gallery, Summer Camp and many others

Curriculum: Environmental Studies; Geography; Science; Social Studies

2232 Norman Rockwell Museum

www.normanrockwellvt.com

The Norman Rockwell Museum of Vermont includes a nationally recognized collection of Norman Rockwell's art, established in 1976 and commemorates his Vermont years and the entire span and diversity of his career (1911–1978).

Special Features: Links include Tender Tidbits, Prints, Collector Plates, Figurines, Matted Prints, Framed Prints, Puzzles, Afghans, Four Freedoms and others

Curriculum: Art; History

2233 Northeast Organic Farming Association of Vermont

www.nofavt.org

The Northeast Organic Farming Association of Vermont is a nonprofit association of farmers, gardeners, and consumers working to promote an economically viable and ecologically sound Vermont food system for the benefit of current and future generations.

Special Features: Links include Programs, Organic Certification, Upcoming Events, Organic Farms, Farmer's Markets, Why Organic, Books and Merchandise and others

Curriculum: Environmental Studies; Health; Science

2234 Shelburne Museum

www.shelburnemuseum.org

The Shelburne Museum, founded in 1947, is one of the nation's most eclectic museums of art, Americana, architecture and artifacts. Thirty-nine galleries and exhibition structures display over 150,000 objects spanning four centuries.

Special Features: At this museum, elements of both history and art are fused into a lively combination that has been describes as "a place of the imagination"

Curriculum: Art

2235 Southern Vermont Natural History Museum

www.vermontmuseum.org

The mission of the Southern Vermont Natural History Museum is to foster an interest in nature, the environment, and the natural sciences through exhibitions, research, and educational activities.

Special Features: Exhibits include over 600 native New England birds and mammals in 100 small dioramas, one of the largest collections of its type in the Northeast

Curriculum: Biology; Environmental Studies; History; Science; Social Studies

2236 Special Olympics Vermont

www.vtso.org

The mission of Special Olympics Vermont is to provide year-round sports training and athletic competition in a variety of Olympic-type sports for children and adults with cognitive disabilities.

Special Features: Individuals are allowed to develop physical fitness, demonstrate courage, experience joy, participate in a sharing of gifts

Curriculum: Physical Education; Sociology

2237 This is Vermont

www.thisisvermont.com

This is Vermont has a complete and regularly updated events listings for the Southern Vermont region. It includes information about local events, towns and villages, business, art, culture, theatre and much more.

Special Features: Links include Business Directory; Local Lore, Towns and Villages, Events, Arts and Culture, Publications, Forums and others

Curriculum: Art; Business; Social Studies

2238 Vermont Alliance for the Social Studies

www.vermontsocialstudies.com

The Vermont Alliance for the Social Studies, an affiliate of the National Council for the Social Studies, is a nonprofit educational corporation representing social studies educators including history, geography, political science, economics, sociology, anthropology and psychology.

Special Features: Links include Resources, Stories from the Classroom, Social Studies Inquiry Method, Project-Based Learning and others

Curriculum: Economics; Geography; Government; History; Social Studies; Sociology

2239 Vermont Arts Council

www.vermontartscouncil.org

The Vermont Arts Council provides funding, services and information to artists, arts organizations, schools, communities and the general public. It is the only state arts agency in the U.S. that is also an independent, nonprofit, membership organization.

Special Features: Areas of interest include, for example: Cultural Heritage Tourism Tool Available, Current Issue of Artmail, Citation of Merit Awarded, Danville Project Featured and others

Curriculum: Art

2240 Vermont Assistive Technology

www.dad.state.vt.us/atp

The purpose of the Vermont Assistive Technology Project is to effect systems change to insure the integration of Assistive Technology within all services to Vermonters with disabilities.

Special Features: Links include About Us, What is Assistive Technology, Conferences, Publications, Tryout Centers, Communication, Visual and others

Curriculum: Technology

2241 Vermont Association of Hospitals and Health Systems

www.vahhs.com

The mission of the Vermont Association of Hospitals and Health Systems is to advocate for, lead and serve its members in their efforts to develop and sustain high-quality health services for Vermonters.

Special Features: Links include Calendar, Data, Jobs, HIPAA, Hospitals, Legislative, Links, Newsletter, Vermont Health Policy Perspectives, and others

Curriculum: Health

2242 Vermont Center for Geographic Information

www.vcgi.org

The Vermont Center for Geographic Information is a public nonprofit organization. This organization develops data standards, guidelines and procedures; develops and assist in the development of essential statewide databases; performs outreach and training and much more.

Special Features: Links include Projects, Staff, Board, TAC, Documents, Help, Site Map, Data Warehouse, Technical Resources, Community Resources and many others
Curriculum: Geography

2243 Vermont Chamber of Commerce

www.vtchamber.com

The Vermont Chamber of Commerce was formed in 1950. During the past five decades, the Chamber has grown to become a private, nonprofit organization representing nearly every sector of the state's corporate community. Their mission is to create an economic climate conductive to business growth and the preservation of the Vermont quality of life.

Special Features: Links include Visiting Vermont, Events Calendar, About Vermont, Member Services and Benefits, Business and Commerce, Newsroom and others
Curriculum: Business; Economics

2244 Vermont Covered Bridges

http://vermontbridges.com

The Vermont Covered Bridges Web site offers a wide variety of resources regarding covered bridges in Vermont, such as: Collected Covered Bridge Articles, Bridger Newsletter, Covered Bridge Community Notes and many other interesting resources.

Special Features: Links include The Vermont Covered Bridge Society, Covered Bridge Preservation, Bridge Talk, Covered Bridge Market Place and others
Curriculum: Geography; History; Social Studies

2245 Vermont Department of Economic Development

www.thinkvermont.com

The mission of the Vermont Department of Economic Development is to enhance Vermonters' quality of life through expanded economic opportunities. Inherent in this mission is the implicit relationship between a high performance economy and Vermont's quality of life.

Special Features: Links include Press Room, Publications, Frequently Asked Questions, Sitemap, Information Resources, Business Sectors, Quick Links and others
Curriculum: Business; Economics

2246 Vermont Department of Libraries

http://dol.state.vt.us

The purpose of the Vermont Automated Libraries System is to take advantage of technology to improve library services while increasing resource sharing among libraries, so that citizens of Vermont will have the same type of access to information as their urban counterparts.

Special Features: Links include About, General Assembly Information, Librarians' Resources, Online Library Catalogs in Vermont, Secretary of State's Databases and other
Curriculum: Library Media

2247 Vermont Division for Historic Preservation

www.dhca.state.vt.us/DHP/general/about.html

The Division for Historic Preservation is the public agency designated to be the advocate for historic and prehistoric properties in Vermont. Prehistoric archaeological sites supply information about the lives of the original inhabitants of Vermont.

Special Features: Links include Programs, Partners, Sitemap, Frequently Asked Questions, State Historic Preservation Plan, Vermont Advisory Council and others
Curriculum: History

2248 Vermont Festival of the Arts

www.vermontartfest.com

"Against the backdrop of some of Vermont's highest mountains, the towns and villages of the mad River Valley play host in August to one of the most diverse festivals in New England. With more than 100 arts-related events and activities, the Vermont Festival of the Arts is designed to entertain the soul, enlighten the mind, and energize the spirit."

Special Features: Links include Welcome Center, Visual Arts, Culinary Arts, Drama and Cinema, Music and Dance, Workshops, Literature and Lectures, Tours and Festivities, Kids
Curriculum: Art; Dance; Drama; Music

2249 Vermont Folklife Center

www.vermontfolklifecenter.org

The Vermont Folklife Center is dedicated to preserving and presenting the folk arts and cultural traditions of Vermont and the surrounding region. Through ongoing field research, a multimedia archive and an apprenticeship program, they document and conserve cultural heritage through exhibits, media, publications and educational projects.

Special Features: Links include Events, Exhibits, Books, Music, Stories, Resources, Programs, Education, Services and others
Curriculum: Sociology

2250 Vermont Geological Survey

www.anr.state.vt.us/dec/geo/vgs.htm

The Vermont Geological Survey, also known as the Division of Geology and Mineral Resources in the Department of Environmental Conservation, conducts surveys and research relating to geology, mineral resource and topography of Vermont.

Special Features: Links include Activities of the Survey, Earth Resources, Earth Science Week, Geology of Vermont, Groundwater, Photogallery, Publications and Reports and others
Curriculum: Environmental Studies; Geography; History; Science; Social Studies

2251 Vermont History

www.vermonthistory.info

Vermont History Web site is a quick, readable summary of Vermont's settlement, Vermont's role in the American Revolution and Civil War, and more. "One of the smallest states, Vermont is a mountainous region with large rivers and valleys...."

Special Features: Links include Vermont History Timeline, Vermont History Questions and Answers, Gallery, Books, History Clippings, Movies and Music and others
Curriculum: History

2252 Vermont History and Genealogy

http://home.att.net/~Local_History/VT_History.htm

Vermont History and Genealogy is a Web site created, on a volunteer basis, to explore the world of ancestors who resided in Vermont. It claims that genealogical research is accomplished by learning more about the history of one's ancestors— how they lived as individuals and families.

Special Features: Each county in Vermont is listed, along with the date the county was formed and contact information, for example: Addison, 1785, Sue Waite-Langley
Curriculum: History

2253 Vermont Home Page

http://vermont.gov

The Vermont Home Page is the official site for the state of Vermont. It includes a wide vari-

ety of areas, such as: Access Government, Find the Facts, Living in Vermont, Doing Business in Vermont, Education, Health and Public Safety, Recreation and Travel and much more.

Special Features: Additional useful Links include Kid's Page, Vermont Connections Newsletter, Vermont Life Magazine, Press Releases, Portal Policies, Online Government Services and many others
Curriculum: Business; Education; Government; Health; Social Studies

2254 Vermont Institute of Natural Science

www.vinsweb.org

The mission of the Vermont Institute of Natural Science stresses education as the way to change attitudes and maintain a healthy environment. It now includes over 5,000 members all across Vermont, establishing education programs statewide.

Special Features: Links include About, Education, Nature Center, Wildlife Services and Bird Rehabilitation, Conservation Biology, Programs and Events and others
Curriculum: Environmental Studies; Science; Social Studies

2255 Vermont Journal of Environmental Law

www.vje.org

The mission of the Vermont Journal of Environmental Law is to combine cutting-edge technology with a multidisciplinary approach, including a broad range of environment issues in order to ensure a rapid presentation of the information and to facilitate and enlightened discourse.

Special Features: Links include Articles, events, Roscoe Hogan, Discussion, Submissions, Links and others
Curriculum: Environmental Studies

2256 Vermont Leadership Center

www.vtlc.org

The Vermont Leadership Center's mission is to instill within participants the knowledge, caring and motivation necessary to take responsible action on behalf of themselves, their communities and the natural world.

Special Features: Links include Ecosystem Management Project, School Programs, Community Events, Kingdom Corps, Camps,

Recreation, Onsite Facilities, Partners and others
Curriculum: Economics; Environmental Studies; Science; Social Studies

2257 Vermont National Education Association

www.vtnea.org

The Vermont National Education Association is a voluntary membership organization of Vermont teachers and educational support personnel. This Web site offers fresh, constantly updated information to support the work of educators, encourage the contribution of parents, and nurture the learning of children and young adults.

Special Features: Links include Summer Leadership, Summer Reading for Kids, Educators' Convention, Professionalism in Teaching, Approaches to School Violence and many others

Curriculum: Education

2258 Vermont Opera Theater

www.vermontopera.org

Based in the state capital of Montpelier, the Vermont Opera Theatre features local professional talent in opera, operetta, and original programs ranging from classical recitals to cabaret. It also offers workshops and master classes in classical song.

Special Features: Links include Foliage Art Song, Recent Performances, History, Gallery, For Friends, A Fleeting Animal and others

Curriculum: Music

2259 Vermont Public Libraries

www.publiclibraries.com/vermont.htm

The mission of the Vermont Public Libraries is to serve people with an easy access to the use of public libraries and promote reading. It provides an extremely useful online site for individuals, families, schools and organizations.

Special Features: This site includes links to their thirty-seven public libraries in Vermont

Curriculum: Library Media

2260 Vermont Quilt Festival

www.vqf.org

The Vermont Quilt Festival offers more than 400 antique and contemporary quilts on display in special exhibits. It includes 65 booths full of quilts, fabrics, patterns, books, supplies,

etc. The Festival also offers classes and lectures presented by the best in quilt making.

Special Features: Links include General Information, Merchandise, Contest Quilts, Classes and Registration, Teachers, Activities, Exhibits and others

Curriculum: Business; History; Home Economics

2261 Vermont Renaissance Festival

www.vtrenfest.com

On August 30, 2002, approximately 400 acres of land in Vernon, Vermont was privately purchased for the purpose of creating a permanent Arts site that would be suitable for open-to-the-public events, such as the Vermont Renaissance Festival.

Special Features: Links and Featured Acts include: Message Board, Contests, Press, "Empty hats," "Lord of the Wings," Roderick Russell" and others

Curriculum: Art; Dance; Drama

2262 Vermont Ski Museum

www.vermontskimuseum.org

The Vermont Ski Museum resides in the heart of the Village of Stowe. It is in the Old Town Hall built in 1818 and listed on the National Register of Historic Places. The museum captures moments in skiing history.

Special Features: Links include Vision, History, Exhibits, Hall of Fame, News, Photo Gallery, Calendar of Events and others

Curriculum: History; Physical Education

2263 Vermont Symphony Orchestra

www.vso.org

Right from the beginning, the Vermont Symphony Orchestra was extraordinary in its mission. It dedicated itself to traveling to any gymnasium, armory, racetrack or hillside where an audience could be found.

Special Features: For sixty-eight years, the Orchestra has shuttled from town to town overcoming geography with such energy that it has earned a national reputation

Curriculum: Music

2264 Vermont Technology Council

www.vttechcouncil.org

The mission of the Vermont Technology Council is to foster competitive, profitable enterprise and research and development based on science, technology and engineering, to provide ongoing benefits to the State of Vermont.

Special Features: Links include Science and Technology Infrastructure, Centers of Excellence, Partner Organizations, and others
Curriculum: Technology

2265 Vermont Veterinary Medical Association

www.vtvets.org

Every day our lives are enhanced by animals. To celebrate this unique relationship and to honor and say thank you to these exceptional animals, the Vermont Veterinary Medical Association has established the Vermont Hall of Fame, including amazing and heartwarming stories about animals.

Special Features: Links include Animal Disaster Planning, Animal Hall of Fame, 2003 and 2003, Press Articles, Animal Cruelty, Animal Owners, Veterinary Directory and others
Curriculum: Social Studies

2266 Vermont Wind Energy

www.vermontwind.com

Vermont Wind Energy offers information about both utility scale wind farms and home-sized turbines. Vermont's tremendous wind energy resource, the issues facing wind energy development in Vermont and the latest news reports regarding wind energy are provided.

Special Features: Discussion items include: Wind energy creates jobs, Wind energy revitalizes our local communities, Wind can sup-ply 20% of Vermont's electric energy and many others
Curriculum: Science

2267 Vermont Women in Higher Education

www.vwhe.org

Vermont Women in Higher Education is an organization affiliated with the Office of Women in Higher Education at the American Council on Education. It is dedicated to serving women in higher education at all professional levels. Their mission is to assist women in the pursuit of careers in Higher Education.

Special Features: The central goals of the program are to promote both women's leadership and women leaders by identifying talented women and encouraging and supporting them
Curriculum: Education; Women's Studies

2268 Vermont Women's Fund

www.vermontcf.org/vwf.html

The Vermont Women's Fund is a grant making organization that supports the advancement, self-sufficiency, and economic and social equality of Vermont women and girls. It encourages women to be philanthropists by contributing to the Fund's endowment.

Special Features: Links include About, News and Events, VANPO, Vermont Women's Fund, Upper Valley Community Foundation, Child Care Fund of Vermont, Online Resources and others
Curriculum: Economics; Sociology; Women's Studies

VIRGINIA

2269 American Lung Association of Virginia

www.lungusa2.org/virginia

The American Lung Association of Virginia offers a variety of educational and support programs for children and adults. It focuses on three areas: asthma, tobacco control and environmental health. The Association also offers support programs who suffer with lung diseases.

Special Features: Links include News, Programs, Special Events, Advocacy, Virginia Thoracic Society, Asthma Programs, Tobacco Programs, Environmental Health Programs and others
Curriculum: Health

2270 Black History Museum

www.blackhistorymuseum.org

The Black History Museum and Cultural Center is a permanent repository for visual, oral and written records and artifacts commemorating the lives and accomplishments of Blacks in Virginia. Their goal is to become a statewide resource on the many facets of Black history through exhibitions, discussions and celebrations. The Museum collects documents, limited editions, prints, art and photographs for use in its Black History Archives Program.

Special Features: Links include Director's Page, Calendar, Exhibitions, Historic Jackson Ward and others

Curriculum: History; Social Studies; Sociology

2271 Chesapeake Bay Foundation

www.cbf.org

The Chesapeake Bay Foundation is the largest conservation organization dedicated solely to saving the Chesapeake Bay watershed. Their motto, "Save the Bay," defines the organization's mission and commitment to reducing pollution, improving fisheries and protecting and restoring natural resources such as wetlands, forests and underwater grasses.

Special Features: Links include Environmental Education Program, Environmental Protection and Restoration, Philip Merrill Environmental Center and others

Curriculum: Environmental Studies; Geography, Science; Social Studies

2272 Childhelp USA Virginia

www.childhelpusa.org/virginia

Childhelp USA directly provides help and hope to thousands of children and adults each year whose lives have been traumatized by child abuse. This organization is dedicated to the treatment and prevention of child abuse and neglect.

Special Features: Links include Programs and Services, Prevention, Children's Center of Virginia, Residential Treatment, What is Child Abuse, Community Action, Events Calendar, Newsletter, Pressroom and others

Curriculum: Education; Health; Sociology

2273 Colonial America: Early Virginia History

www.nv.cc.va.us/home/nvsageh/Hist121/Part1/topics/earlyva.htm

Historian Page Smith wrote a full-length history of the United States. His "People's History

of the United States" covers the time from the American Revolution through World War II in eight volumes of 800–1000 pages each. Smith is a thoughtful, careful historian, who sees beyond the mere chronology into the deeper meanings of historic events.

Special Features: Examples of subheadings include: The Period of Colonization, 1607–1700, Themes of the Colonial Period, Population Growth, The London Company, The Jamestown Disaster and others

Curriculum: History

2274 Colonial Williamsburg Foundation

www.history.org/foundation/mission.cfm

Colonial Williamsburg in Williamsburg, Virginia, is the world's largest living history museum. It was restored in the 18th century capital city of Britain's largest, wealthiest, and most populous outpost of empire in the New World. Williamsburg includes a 301-acre historic area with restored, reconstructed, and historically furnished buildings.

Special Features: Links include Explore and Learn, Publications, Museums, History, Reports, Newsroom and much more

Curriculum: History; Social Studies

2275 Commonwealth of Virginia

www.virginia.gov/cmsportal/

This is the official site for the State of Virginia. This source include information about Virginia Communities, Business and Employment, Government, Citizen Services, Business Services, Virginia Tourism, Family and Education and so forth.

Special Features: The Family and Education sections includes links to: Education, Family Services, Just for Fun, Virginia Community Database, Employment, Kids Commonwealth, Media Links

Curriculum: Business; Economics; Government; History; Social Studies

2276 Department of Rehabilitative Services

www.vadrs.org

The Department of Rehabilitative Service's mission is to partner with people with disabilities and their families. The organization also collaborates with the public and private sectors to provide and advocate for the highest quality services that empower individuals with disabilities to maximize their employment, independence and full inclusion into society.

Special Features: Links include Boards and Councils, Public Events Calendar, Publications, Career Center, Virginia Government Sites, Forms Cabinet and others

Curriculum: Business; Economics; Government; Health

2277 Designing the Capitol: The Library of Virginia

www.lva.lib.va.us/whoweare/exhibits/capitor/design

Thomas Jefferson drew his first design for a Virginia Capitol, possibly for Williamsburg, in the early or mid–1770s. He had decided to treat the exterior as a giant Ionic temple and had also thought of using the Capitol to set a model for cubic architecture.

Special Features: Includes selected titles concerning the Virginia State Capitol, such as: "The Making of Virginia Architecture," "Thomas Jefferson: Architect and Builder," "The Evolution of the Virginia State Capitol" and others

Curriculum: Government; History; Social Studies

2278 Geography of Virginia: Virginia Places

www.virginiaplaces.org

Virginia Places offers a wealth of information regarding: The Natural Setting (Rocks and Ridges, Rivers and Watersheds, Climate, Habitats and Species, Wetlands, etc.; The Places of Virginia (Cities and Towns, Exploring Frontiers, Regions of Virginia, etc.; and The People and Development of Virginia (Agriculture, Architecture, Education, Energy, Military, etc.).

Special Features: According to Education, although a state Literary Fund was established in the early 1800s, it was not until the North forced Virginia to adopt a new state constitution that a free public school system was established for all Virginia students.

Curriculum: Business; Economics; Education; Government; History; Social Studies

2279 Hall of Fame Homepage

www.gloucesterva.info/museum/HallOfFame/HallOfFame.htm

The Hall of Fame Homepage includes important personages in the history of Gloucester County, Virginia. For Gloucester County (under the heading of "Courtroom, Country Shrine,"

there are forty-eight portraits and seven tablets describing the twelve Virginia counties where the Western migration began.

Special Features: The forty-eight portraits include, for example, the following: John R. Cary, John S. Cooke, Judge Warner Jones, Col. George Wythe, Dr. Walter Reed, Benjamin Rowe and others

Curriculum: History

2280 Historic Central Virginia

www.cvco.org/tourism/histrich

The Historic Central Virginia website includes information about such historic places and people and places as: George Washington, State Capitol, St. John's Church, Petersburg Battlefield, Maymont House and much more.

Special Features: Includes a Guide to Historic Virginia, Websites of Historical Attraction, including such places as: Barter Theatre, Alexandria Museums, Daniel Boone Trail, Great Falls Park and others

Curriculum: Geography, History, Social Studies

2281 History of Jamestown

www.apva.org/history

"America's only shrines are her altars of patriotism — the first and most potent being Jamestown; the sire of Virginia, and Virginia the mother of this great Republic." (from a 1907 Virginia guidebook The History of Jamestown provides a comprehensive history of the beginning of Virginia — and America's Colonial World.

Special Features: Links include The Virginia Company, Archaeological Research, Sketch of a Fort, Captain John Smith, Pocahontas, John Rolfe, Findings, Exhibits, Visiting, Publications, Resources

Curriculum: History

2282 Library of Virginia

www.lva.lib.va.us

The Library of Virginia provides information for the public, government, libraries, and teachers and students. Links include the following: Services for the Public, Services for the Government, Services for Libraries, Services for teachers and Students, programs and Projects and so forth.

Special Features: Services for Teachers and Students include information such as: Bill of Rights at the Library of Virginia, Lesson Plans

for Cavalcade, Virginia History and Culture Resources on the Internet and more
Curriculum: Library Media

2283 Museum of Culpeper History: Famous People

www.culpepermuseum.com/people.htm

The Museum of Culpeper History includes famous individuals, such as: George Washington, Eppa Rixey, Clara Barton, George Custer, Daniel Boone, J.E.B. Stuart, A.P. Hill, Ulysses S. Grant, Walt Whitman, Robert E. Lee and many others.

Special Features: Links include Culpeper History, Burgandine House, Civil War History, Historical Timeline, Photo Gallery and others
Curriculum: History; Social Studies

2284 Natural Bridge

www.naturalbridgeva.com

Natural Bridge and Niagara Falls were the two wonders of the new world that Europeans visited during the 18th and 19th centuries. Of the two sights, Natural Bridge was the most mysterious—no clear explanation of its formation. Natural Bridge was first surveyed in 1750 by George Washington.

Special Features: Links include The Caverns, The Wax Museum, The Toy Museum, The Monster Museum, Packages and Groups, The Gift Shop, Photo Gallery
Curriculum: Geography; History; Science; Social Studies

2285 Northern Virginia Astronomy Club

www.novac.com

The primary purpose of the Northern Virginia Astronomy Club is to provide enjoyment and education to the public (and ourselves! through amateur astronomy. This organization strives to be a friendly club, with a focus on observing. They are one of the largest clubs in the United States, with almost 1000 members.

Special Features: Links include What's New, Meetings, Public Viewings, Outreach, Resources (Astronomy challenge, The EarthDial Project, Astronomical League, Observing and Drawing Mars and others), Newsletters, Photos
Curriculum: Science

2286 Preservation of Virginia Antiquities

www.apva.org

The Preservation of Virginia Antiquities sites tell the stories of famous Virginians—John Smith, Pocahontas, John Marshall, Patrick Henry, Dolly Madison, Mary Washington and Walter Reed. Its mission is to preserver, interpret and promote personal property relating to the history and people of Virginia.

Special Features: This foundation is the oldest statewide preservation organization in the nation, founded in 1889
Curriculum: Geography; History

2287 Story of Virginia — An American Experience

www.vahistorical.org/storyofvirginia.htm

The Story of Virginia: An American Experience includes: Becoming a Homeplace, Contact and Conflict, Becoming Virginians, Becoming Americans, Becoming Southerners, Becoming Confederates, Becoming New Southerners, Becoming Americans Again, Becoming Equal, and Becoming a New Virginia.

Special Features: In the area, Becoming Equal, for example, it states that: Orra Gray Langhorne of Lynchburg organized a Virginia Suffrage Association in 1893, but the serious push for votes for women came from the Equal Suffrage League of Virginia from 1909 to 1920
Curriculum: History; Social Studies; Sociology; Women's Studies

2288 Virginia Agricultural Experiment Station

www.vaes.vt.edu

The mission of the Virginia Agricultural Experiment Station is to perform basic and applied research on agricultural, environmental and natural and community resource issues related to the future needs of Virginia, the region, the nation, and the world.

Special Features: Links include History, Historical Highlights, Geography, People, Virginia Cooperative Extension, Cooperative State Research, Education, Extension Service
Curriculum: Biology; Environmental Studies; Science; Social Studies

2289 Virginia Art Education Association

www.vaea.org

The Virginia Art Association's mission is to promote, support and advance visual arts education within the State of Virginia through professional development, leadership and service.

Special Features: Links include Divisions,

Regions, Standings and Affiliates, Communication, Student Gallery (Online School Galleries), Calendar, Fine Arts Standard of Learning
Curriculum: Art

2290 Virginia Assistive Technology System

www.vats.org

The Virginia Technology System has received federal funding since 1990 to develop a statewide comprehensive program of assistive technology and to assist Virginians with disabilities in accessing assistive information devices and services.
Special Features: Links include Disability Links, Tech Art Projects, Accessibility Information, Aging, Highlights, Publications, Handbook, Funding Guide, AbleData
Curriculum: Technology

2291 Virginia Association of Museums

www.vamuseums.org

The Virginia Association of Museums, a nonprofit organization established in 1968, has grown to become one of the largest state museum associations in the country. It furthers education and training, fosters development and provides support for museums and their staff.
Special Features: Provides links to all Virginia Museums, such as: Amazement Square, Artisan Center of Virginia, Belle Grove Plantation, Blue Ridge Institute and Museum, Cedar Hill, Cold War Museum, Courthouse Galleries, Edgar Allan Poe Museum and others
Curriculum: History

2292 Virginia Center for Innovative Technology

www.cit.org

The Virginia Center for Innovative Technology recognizes three drives as fundamental issues that require attention: increased competition among universities regarding research funding; advanced purchasing opportunities...; and low survival rates for early-stage technology firms.
Special Features: Links include Programs, Research Investment, Federal Funding, Access to Capital, Small Business Assistance, Events, News, and others
Curriculum: Business; Technology

2293 Virginia Commission for the Arts

www.arts.state.va.us

The Virginia Commission for the Arts is mandated to support and stimulate excellence in all the arts, in their full cultural and ethnic diversity, and to make the arts accessible to all Virginians.
Special Features: Links include Advisory Panels, Announcements and News, Arts Advocacy Information, Commissions Members and Staff, Publications, Reports, Research and Studies, Resources for Artists and others
Curriculum: Art

2294 Virginia Corps

www.virginiacorps.org

Virginia Corps is a new effort to capture the renewed spirit of volunteer service and community preparedness that has emerged since September 11, 2001. It serves as a central clearinghouse for volunteer opportunities across Virginia, linking citizens with a variety of volunteer efforts.
Special Features: Links include Homeland Security, Volunteer Connections, News, Links, Resources, About Virginia Corps, Contact Us
Curriculum: Sociology

2295 Virginia Department of Education

www.pen.k12.va.us

The Virginia Department of Education believes in education for a lifetime. This website includes numerous useful links, such as News, Calendar of Events, Featured Sites, For Students, For Parents, For Teachers, and others.
Special Features: The link, "For Students" includes General Interest Information (such as Blue Web'N, EduHound K12), Elementary and Middle School (such as Bill Nye the Science Guy), Secondary (such as The New York Times Learning Network)
Curriculum: Education

2296 Virginia Department of Forestry

www.vdof.org

The Virginia Department of Forestry is responsible for: protection of 15.8 million acres of forest land from fire, insects and disease; management of 16 State Forests; and assistance to non-industrial private forest landowners.
Special Features: Links include Upcoming Events, Press Room, Forms, FAQs, Links to

Partner Agencies and State Forest Sites, Refor-estation of Timberlands, Forest Inventory Analysis, Fire Situation and others

Curriculum: Economics; Environmental Studies; Geography Science; Social Studies

2297 Virginia Education Association

www.veaweteach.org

The Virginia Education Association is a teacher, a school secretary, bus driver, custodian, cafeteria worker or aide. They are 56,000 people voluntarily associated together to improve the success of every child and to upgrade the profession of teaching.

Special Features: A sample of what they do: Lister for better ideas, provide workshops, produce a monthly professional magazine, work to upgrade salaries and working conditions, provide free parent information

Curriculum: Education

2298 Virginia Educational Media Association

www.vema.edu

The mission of the Virginia Education Media Association is to be the recognized voice for excellence in Virginia's school libraries. Their aim is to promote: literacy, information access and evaluation, love of literature, effective use of technology, collaboration in the teaching and learning process, intellectual freedom, professional growth, instructional leadership and life-long learning.

Special Features: Links include Awards and Contests, Conferences, News and Issues, Organization, Professional, Publications, Colleges, Research, Events and News

Curriculum: Library Media

2299 Virginia Energy Choice

www.yesvachoice.com

Virginia Energy Choice offers information about energy restructuring in Virginia — what is changing, what is staying the same, and how one can make the right choice regarding energy services (electricity and natural gas).

Special Features: Links include What is Energy Choice?, Energy Choice Questions and Answers, How to Choose, Service Providers, Newsroom, Community Educational Toolbox, Business Educational Toolbox

Curriculum: Business; Economics; Science

2300 Virginia Environmental Business Council

www.vebc.org

The Virginia Environmental Business Council is a non-profit organization created to enhance the business and job growth of both established and emerging environmental companies in Virginia.

Special Features: Links include Membership, Events, External Events, Environmental News, Feedback, Search

Curriculum: Business; Economics; Environmental Studies

2301 Virginia Festival of the Book

www.vabook.org

The Virginia Festival of the Book is an annual festival, open to the public that promotes literacy and celebrates the book. Its goals are to organize public programs about books, writing emerging technologies, etc., to encourage programs in schools about books, writing and reading, to foster reading and discussion of books, and so on.

Special Features: Links include Program, Participants, Press Kit, Literary Links and others

Curriculum: Language Arts

2302 Virginia Foundation for Women

www.virginiawomen.org

The Virginia Foundation for Women provides a diversity of opportunities for women across the state to help one another. The Foundation is a community without walls, of and for women, giving and receiving professional and personal support. Its focus is to promote the welfare of women and girls through education, outreach, collaboration and leadership.

Special Features: Links include Programs, Common Threads, Quilt Stories, Current Events, Resources and Links, Corporate Founders, Calendar and more

Curriculum: Women's Studies

2303 Virginia Historical Society

www.vahistorical.org

The mission of the Virginia Historical Society is to collect, preserve and interpret Virginia's past for the education and enjoyment of present and future generations. With education as their primary focus, they offer lectures, seminars, conferences and consulting services.

Special Features: Links include History, Battle

Abbey, Associations, Reports and others. This society maintains a museum, operates a research library and a publications program that has functioned for more than a century

Curriculum: History

2304 Virginia Library Association

www.vla.org

The Virginia Library Association is a statewide organization whose purpose is to develop, promote and improve library and information services and the profession of librarianship in order to advance literacy and learning and to ensure access to information in the State of Virginia.

Special Features: Links include What's New, Calendar, Committees, Forums, Sections, Regions, Awards, Manual, Publications, Listservs, Legislative Action and others

Curriculum: Library Media

2305 Virginia Marine Resources Commission

www.mrc.state.va.us/mrcoverview.htm

The Marine Resources Commission is one of the oldest agencies in Virginia State Government. It was recommended by a legislative study commission in 1867. Until the last decade, shellfish regulation has dominated much of the agency's activities because of the economic and cultural importance of the oyster industry. Private leasing of State bottom for the planting and propagation of oysters began before 1875.

Special Features: Links include Public Notices and Information, Harvest Bulletin, Saltwater Review, Regulations, Newsletters, Marine Resource Links, Historical Highlights, News Releases and others

Curriculum: Environmental Studies; Science; Social Studies

2306 Virginia Museum of Natural History

www.vmnh.net

The Virginia Museum of Natural History is an agency of the Secretary of Natural Resources of Virginia. Educational programs, exhibits and field tours are available to the general public via this museum. It also offers teacher training opportunities, special publications for teachers on natural history and science kits for classroom use.

Special Features: Links include Archaeology,

Books, Children's Books, Curators, Dinosaur Dig, Education, Exhibits, Field Trips, Mammals and much more

Curriculum: Environmental Studies; History; Science; Social Studies

2307 Virginia Music Teachers Association

www.music-usa.org/vmta/main.html

The Virginia Music Teachers Association is an organization of teachers throughout Virginia who are united in promoting music through mutual cooperation. Their main objectives are the advancement of musical knowledge and education and promotion of the general welfare of music teachers in Virginia and neighboring states.

Special Features: Links include Member Areas, Calendar, Certification, News and Workshops, Local Assistants' Reports, Regulations, Photo Links

Curriculum: Education; Music

2308 Virginia Native Plant Society

www.vnps.org

The Virginia Native Plant Society was founded in 1982 as the Virginia Wildflower Preservation Study. It is a statewide organization open to anyone, amateur or professional. Its purpose is to further appreciation and conservation of Virginia's native plants and habitats.

Special Features: Links include Wildflowers across Virginia, Virginia Flora Project, Wildflower of the Year, Invasive Alien Plants, Events, Chapters, Newsletters, Native Plant References

Curriculum: Biology; Science

2309 Virginia Opera

www.vaopera.org

The Virginia Opera Company is one of the finest and largest operas in the nation. The opera performs in Norfolk, Richmond and Fairfax; it has focused national and international attention on Virginia as an important opera center through the quality of its work, its excellent educational programs and history of identifying and presenting fine young American singers.

Special Features: Links include In the Press, History, Terms to Know, Opera 101, The Venues, The Opera and much more

Curriculum: Music

2310 Virginia Parent Teachers Association

www.vapta.org

The Virginia Congress of Parents and Teachers is a volunteer child advocacy association working for all children and you in the State of Virginia. The Virginia PTA is the third largest Congress of the 54 Congresses in the National PTA.

Special Features: Links include Alerts, Latest News, E-Newsletters, Programs, Events and Training, Reflections Gallery, Committees and Services and others
Curriculum: Education

2311 Virginia Politics: Guide to Virginia Government

http://capwiz.com/vapolitics/state/main/?state=VA

Virginia Politics: Guide to Virginia Government includes useful information, such as: Virginia State Officials and Agencies, Local Government, Issues and Legislation, Congressional Delegation, Media Guide and much more.

Special Features: Links include Current Issues, Market Research, Meeting Planner, Virginia Politics, Advertising and others
Curriculum: Business; Government

2312 Virginia Press Association

www.vpa.net

The mission of the Virginia Press Association is to support membership through responsive services and resources. They connect members through valuable business services, effective representation, practical communication and information and relevant education and recognition.

Special Features: Links include Advertising, Association Services, Conferences, Members, Legislative, Newsletter, Professional Development, News Release Services, Newspapers and the Law and others
Curriculum: Language Arts

2313 Virginia Railway Express

www.vre.org

The Virginia Railway Express is a joint project of the Northern Virginia Transportation Commission and the Potomac and Rappahannock Transportation Commission. It provides safe, cost-effective, accessible, customer-responsive and reliable rail passenger service.

Special Features: This Express provides commuter rail service from the Northern Virginia suburbs to Alexandria, Crystal City and downtown Washington, D.C. It is an integral part of a balanced, intermodal regional transportation system
Curriculum: Business; Economics

2314 Virginia Tourism Corporation

www.vatc.org

The goals of the Virginia Tourism Corporation are to serve the broader interests of the economy of Virginia by supporting, maintaining and expanding Virginia's domestic and international travel market — thereby generating increased visitor expenditures, tax revenues and employment.

Special Features: Links include Administration and Finance, Advertising, Customer Service and Industry Relations, Electronic Marketing, Film Office, Marketing and Promotions, Public Relations, Research
Curriculum: Business; Economics

2315 Virginia War Museum

www.warmuseum.org

In 2002, the Virginia War Museum entered into a new partnership with the Company of Military Historians. Their primary interest is in military materials that are culturally related to the Americans. This Company has acquired an impressive collection of uniforms, headgear and accessories as a resource for research and exhibits.

Special Features: Links include Programs, Docents, Pre-visit Materials, Teacher Evaluation Form, Curriculum Guides, Brief History Series, World War One, The Vietnam War, Soldier's Heritage, The Holocaust and many others
Curriculum: History; Social Studies

2316 Virtual Jamestown

www.virtualjamestown.org

The Virtual Jamestown Archive is a digital research, teaching and learning project that explores the legacies of the Jamestown settlement and "the Virginia experiment." As a work in progress, Virtual Jamestown aims to shape the national dialogue on the occasion of the four hundred-year anniversary observance in 2007 of the founding of the Jamestown colony.

Special Features: Links include Jamestown Interactive, Maps and Images, Court Records, Labor Contracts, Public Records, Reference

Center, First-Hand Accounts and Letters, Newspapers

Curriculum: History

2317 VTC Virginia History Facts

www.vatc.org/pr/facthistory.htm

Jamestown is the site of the first permanent English-speaking settlement in North America at Jamestown in 1607. Here, the English met the Powhatans, a chiefdom of Algonquian Indians who lived in central and eastern Virginia. Virginia was the largest, most populous and prosperous of the original 13 colonies.

Special Features: Links include Administration and Finance, Film Office, Marketing and Promotions, Public Relations, Research and others; also includes Virginia's capitals

Curriculum: History

2318 Women Activists of Virginia History Collection

www.library.vcu.edu/jbc/speccoll/women.html

The Women Activists of Virginia History Collection is a manuscript collection that focuses on organizations and individuals significant to the history of women's rights in Virginia. The materials date from the late part of the 19th century to the present and cover topics such as the women's suffrage movement, Equal Rights Amendment, and reproductive rights.

Special Features: Includes resources on women's history, such as Archival Sites for Women's Studies, Library of Congress Manuscripts on Women's History and others

Curriculum: History; Women's Studies

WASHINGTON

2319 Access Washington

http://access.wa.gov

Access Washington is the official Web site for the state of Washington. Quick and useful links on this site include: Cities/Towns, Courts, Emergency Information, Governor Locke, Laws and Rules, Legislature, Licenses, State Agencies, State Facts, State Services, Vital Records, Weather and much more.

Special Features: General links on this Web site include: Public Services, Business, Education, Government, Online Services, Employment and others

Curriculum: Business; Driver Training; Economics; Environmental Studies; Government; Health; Social Studies

2320 Alzheimer's Association of Western and Central Washington State

www.alzwa.org

The Alzheimer's Association of Western and Central Washington State is a nationally affiliated, community-based, volunteer-driven, nonprofit agency. It is dedicated to Alzheimer's research and supporting those affected by Alzheimer's, including their families and friends;

their mission is to eliminate Alzheimer's disease through the advancement of research and to enhance care and support for individuals, families and caregivers.

Special Features: Links include What is Alzheimer's?, How We Can Help, Find a Support Group Near You, View Informative Articles, Free Basic Family Classes, Loss Problems and Care and many others

Curriculum: Biology; Health

2321 American Association of University Women of Washington

www.aauw-wa.org

The American Association of University Women of Washington is the champion of equal rights for women and girls and for quality public education in Washington State. It engages students, schools, and legislatures to ensure accessible and relevant quality education; it also protects the rights of women on campus, at work, at home, and in the community.

Special Features: The mission of this Association is to promote equity for all women and girls, lifelong education, and positive societal change; links include: About, Branches, Scholarships, What's New and others

Curriculum: Women's Studies

2322 Arc of Washington State

www.arcwa.org

In 1936, a group of parents whose children were living in institutions formed the Children's Benevolent League of Washington, now known as the Arc of Washington State. The Arc strives to ensure that all people with developmental disabilities have choices about where they live, work and recreate.

Special Features: Links include Up One Level, Join Us, Local Arts, Board Members, Arc Lawsuit 12.2.02, Meetings, New Items, advocacy, Conferences, and others
Curriculum: Education

2323 Audubon Washington

www.Wa.audubon.org

Audubon Washington conserves and restores natural ecosystems, focusing on birds, other wildlife, and their habitats for the benefit of humanity and earth's biological diversity.

Special Features: Links include Conservation and Action, Birds and Science, Centers and Education, Join and Support, Volunteer Opportunities, News and Publications, Washington State Chapters, Events
Curriculum: Environmental Studies; Science; Social Studies

2324 Bureau of Land Management

www.or.blm.gov

The Bureau of Land Management manages 339,950 acres of public lands in Washington State; it uses a multiple-use approach to managing the public lands of Washington. It also manages wildlife, recreation, timber harvest, livestock, grazing, mineral extraction and other public uses.

Special Features: Links include News, Information, Facts, What We Do, Recreation, Attractions, Directory, Federal Recreation Pass Programs, National Fire Plan, Pacific Northwest File Plan and others
Curriculum: Economics; Environmental Studies; Geography; Science; Social Studies

2325 Core Facts

www.bestapples.com

Did you know that half of all apples grown in the United States for fresh eating come from orchards in Washington State? Core Facts provides information on Apple Varieties, Health and Nutrition, Recipes and More, Core Facts, Meet Your Grower, and Just for Kids.

Special Features: The "Just for Kids" link includes: Kid's Eye View, Apple Trivia, Recipes for Kids, Coloring Book and others
Curriculum: Geography; Health

2326 Department of Agricultural and Resource Economics

www.arec.wsu.edu

Washington State University's Department of Agricultural and Resource Economics includes agribusiness, environmental and resource economics, and management.

Special Features: Links include Overview, Academics, Research, Italy Study Abroad, People, Publications, Announcements, Other Links and so forth
Curriculum: Economics; Education; Environmental Studies; Social Studies

2327 History Guy: Washington State Government

www.historyguy.com/WaStatelink.html

The History Guy: Washington State Government is offered to research the Executive, Legislative and Judicial branches of Washington state government. Links to Washington state political parties and candidates are updated periodically.

Special Features: Links include Civics and Politics, Military History, New and Recent Conflicts Historical Personalities, What's New, Email, About us and others
Curriculum: Economics; History

2328 Just for Kids — Access Washington

http://access.wa.gov/kids

Just for Kids—Access Washington provides useful information for students, including: Homework Help, Government Homework Help, Schools and Websites, Science and Nature, Social Studies and Geography, Just for Fun and much more.

Special Features: Links include Home, Customer Support, Featured Sites, Public Services, Business, Education, Government, Online Services and many others
Curriculum: Education

2329 League of Women Voters of Washington

www.lwvwa.org

The League of Women Voters of Washington includes information about civic participation, current public policy issues, such as election reform, campaign finance reform, health care, education, climate change, growth management and land use, reproductive rights, forestry and children's issues.

Special Features: This organization is a nonpartisan political organization that encourages the informed and active participation of citizens in government, works to increase understanding of major public policy issues and influences public policy through education and advocacy

Curriculum: Economics; Government; Women's Studies

2330 Square Dance in Washington

www.squaredance-wa.org

Square Dance in Washington promotes square and folk dance as a means of recreation and pleasure. Their goal is to foster interest and publicize their activity along with the exchange of ideas.

Special Features: Links include Festivals, Events, Awards, Heritage Center, Councils and Clubs, Classes, Officers and others; it also includes a detailed calendar of events

Curriculum: Dance; Physical Education

2331 State of Washington Sports Hall of Fame

www.washingtonsportshalloffame.com

The State of Washington Sports Hall of Fame members are recognized for their outstanding sports accomplishments and contributions that have brought national acclaim to themselves and to the State of Washington. It currently includes 136 members.

Special Features: Links include Inductees, Fame Staff, Photo Gallery, and sports areas such as: baseball, basketball, boat racing, bowling, boxing, football, golf, hockey, horse racing, skiing, tennis, track and field and others

Curriculum: Sports

2332 Washington Agricultural Statistics Service

www.nass.usda.gov/wa/ssoinfo.htm

The Washington Agricultural Statistics Service's primary responsibility is to prepare official estimates of agriculture for the State of Washington. It collects, verifies and analyzes data that are used to prepare estimates for farmers, ranchers and agribusiness people.

Special Features: This Service publishes several reports, such as: weekly information on crop development, crop acreage, yield and production, inventory of grain stocks, livestock data and others

Curriculum: Business; Economics; Environmental Studies; Geography

2333 Washington Center for Teaching Careers

www.wateach.com

The Washington Center for Teaching Careers was established to recruit qualified individuals to the teaching profession in Washington. This Center is a one-stop information and referral recruitment center for individuals who may be interested in a teaching career.

Special Features: This Center offers a variety of informational and advisor-related services to prospective teachers, such as What It Takes to Teach, Resources and more

Curriculum: Education

2334 Washington Dairy Council

www.eatsmart.org

The Washington Dairy Council contains the Essential Academic Learning Requirements for Health and Fitness for Washington State, approved by the Commission on Student Learning. It has matched material to Benchmarks that address nutrition (one through three).

Special Features: A recent study indicated three action steps for parents: encourage regular intake of calcium-rich foods, increase physical activity and restrict intake of low nutrient beverages

Curriculum: Health

2335 Washington Department of Natural Resources

www.dnr.wa.gov

The Washington Department of Natural Resources is one of the important state agencies that serve the state; their role is to protect and manage valuable assets that belong to the residents of Washington, such as forests, farms, commercial properties and underwater lands.

Special Features: Links include About, Programs and Topics, News and Information, Publications and Data, Business, Recreation, Fire and Natural Hazards, Education and Assistance and others

Curriculum: Business; Environmental Studies; Geography; Science; Social Studies

2336 Washington Geographic Information Council

http://wagic.wa.gov

The Washington Geographic Information Council is recognized as the statewide body responsible for coordinating and facilitating the use and development of Washington State's geospatial information.

Special Features: The Organization link includes: Strategic Focus, Funding Mechanism, Charters and Bylaws, member List, Regional and Site Information, County GIS Contact List and others

Curriculum: Geography

2337 Washington Online Highways

www.ohwy.com/wa/homepage.htm

The state of Washington is divided into three geographic regions: The Cascade Mountains, the Puget Sound Basin and Olympic Peninsula, and the Columbia Plateau. Online Highways provides information regarding travel through the state of Washington.

Special Features: Links include Art, Cities, Education, Events, History, Hospitals, Natural Features, Outdoors, State Parks and many others

Curriculum: Business; Geography, Social Studies

2338 Washington Parent to Parent

www.arcwa.org/parent2parent.htm

The Washington Parent to Parent program provides emotional support and information to families of children with special needs and/or disabilities. Services offered include, for example: Local County Coordinators, Emotional Support for Parents of Children with Disabilities, Current Information on Disabilities, Parent Support Meetings and many more.

Special Features: State Resource Links include Basis Health Information for Washington, Children with Special Health Care Needs, Fathers Network, Help for Working Families, Infant and Early Childhood, Kids Health, and others

Curriculum: Health; Sociology

2339 Washington State Alcohol/Drug Clearinghouse

http://clearinghouse.adhl.org

The Washington State Alcohol/Drug Clearinghouse provides information to the people of Washington State on issues relating to alcohol and other drugs. As the State's designated Regional Alcohol and Drug Awareness Resource Network Center, it links local communities with clearinghouses and information centers worldwide.

Special Features: Examples of what they offer include: A Video Lending Library, Hundreds of Free Publications, Federal and State Report, Prevention E-Briefs and many others

Curriculum: Health; Science

2340 Washington State Association of Counties

www.wacounties.org

The Washington State Association of Counties has worked to advocate for local government needs and support critical county services for nearly a century. The Association provides a variety of services to its member counties, including advocacy and liaison with the Legislature and statewide elected and appointed officials, training and workshops and much more.

Special Features: Links include Policy Positions, Tri-Association Package, Members, Affiliates and Partners, Associate Members, Board of Directors, Staff, Calendar

Curriculum: Business; Government, Social Studies

2341 Washington State Association of Parliamentarians

www.bd123.com

The purpose of the Washington State Association of Parliamentarians is to: promote the study and use of parliamentary procedure and the educational programs of the National Association of Parliamentarians at the state level, promote the growing interest in parliamentary rules and many more.

Special Features: Links include Goals, History, Organization, Bylaws, Parliamentary Law: What is it? Why use it? Who uses it?, Calendar, Publications, Resources and others

Curriculum: Government

2342 Washington State Board of Education

www.sbe.wa.gov

The vision of the Washington State Board of Education is to be a respected leader and trusted partner in developing schools and programs that prepare each student for their future; its mission is to provide leadership, support and advocacy through policy so that each student achieves success in school and life.

Special Features: An example of their beliefs include: student input is essential in order to establish a student vision and for the school to establish a vision for the student

Curriculum: Education

2343 Washington State Coalition Against Domestic Violence

www.wscadv.org

The Washington State Coalition Against Domestic Violence was founded in 1990 by domestic violence survivors and their allies; the Coalition is a non-profit, statewide network of 64 member programs that serve victims of domestic violence in rural, urban and Indian County communities in Washington.

Special Features: Examples of results include: Economic Justice, Support of Domestic Violence Advocacy, Research and Collaboration; links include: projects, trainings, resources and others

Curriculum: Social Studies; Sociology

2344 Washington State Convention and Trade Center

www.wscts.com

The Washington State convention and Trade Center's award winning design integrates the vitality of an international port city with the natural beauty of the Evergreen State.

Special Features: Links include Retain Services, Public Entertainment, Public Art, Public Information, Expansion, Sales and Booking, Public Art Exhibitions, Blue Earth Alliance and others

Curriculum: Business; Economics

2345 Washington State Dental Association

www.wsda.org

The Washington State Dental Association is the primary voice of dentistry in the state and exists to promote oral health of the highest quality. Examples of their activities include: playing a leadership role in the development and implementation of quality assurance programs, providing information about dental issues to dentists and the public, and many more.

Special Features: Links include Consumer Information, Media Relations, Pacific Northwest

Dental Conference, Washington Oral Health Foundation and others

Curriculum: Health

2346 Washington State Department of Agriculture

http://agr.wa.gov

The Washington State Department of Agriculture carries out more than 25 distinct programs that support the agricultural community and promote consumer and environmental protection. It has approximately 500 full-time employees, as well as many others seasonally or intermittently to work in inspection and insect diction programs.

Special Features: This Department's major goals include: To protect and reduce the risk to public health by assuring the safety of the state's food supply; To ensure the safe and legal distribution, use and disposal of pesticides and fertilizers in Washington State and others

Curriculum: Biology; Environmental Studies; Science; Social Studies

2347 Washington State Department of Corrections

www.doc.wa.gov

The Washington State Department of Corrections serves as a partner with victims, communities and the criminal justice system to enhance public safety, administer criminal sanctions of the courts and correctional programs, and provide leadership for the future corrections in Washington State.

Special Features: Links include Index — Facts, Figures and Frequently Asked Questions, Population Statistics, Research Studies, Glossary, and many others

Curriculum: Government; Sociology

2348 Washington State Department of Ecology

www.ecy.wa.gov/ecyhome.html

Ecology is Washington's principle environmental management agency. The mission of the Washington State Department of Ecology is to protect, preserve and enhance Washington's environment, and promote the wise management of their air, land and water for the benefit of current and future generations.

Special Features: Links include About Ecology, Directory, Public Events, Laws and Rules, Publications and Forms, Public Records, Environmental Information, Services, Programs, Contracting, Jobs

Curriculum: Environmental Studies

2349 Washington State Department of Health

www.doh.wa.gov

Public health services are population-based, focusing on improving the health status of the population, rather than simply treating individuals. This responsibility is shared by the Department of Health and 34 local public health jurisdictions serving Washington's 39 counties.

Special Features: Links include Newsroom, Programs and Services, Community and Family Health, Environmental Health, Epidemiology, Health Statistics and Public Health Laboratories and others

Curriculum: Health

2350 Washington State Ferries

www.wsdot.wa.gov/ferries/your_wsf

Washington State Ferries is the largest ferry system in the United States, serving eight countries within Washington and the Province of British Columbia in Canada. Their existing system has 10 routes and 20 terminals that are served by 29 vessels.

Special Features: Links include Traveling to Victoria, Visitors Center, Route Maps, Find Terminals, Ferry Cameras, Our Fleet, History, Photo Gallery, Rider's Gallery and others

Curriculum: Geography

2351 Washington State Fruit Commission/Northwest Cherries

www.nwcherries.com

The Washington State Fruit Commission/ Northwest Cherries represents Northwest Cherry Growers in a wide variety of ways. Examples of links include: Industry Guide — Domestic, International, Contests, Market Information and Consumer Information — Recipes, Health, Weather, Festivals, Children, Varieties, Contests, Fruit Stands and much more.

Special Features: Under the link, "Ask the Cherry Lady," one can compose questions about cherries and receive electronic answers; this site also answers frequently asked questions about cherries, such as "When is cherry season?"

Curriculum: Business; Economics; Geography; Health; Science

2352 Washington State Genealogical Society

www.rootsweb.com/~wasgs

Examples of the purposes of the Washington State Genealogical Society include: provide a combination of individual members and local, county and regional genealogical organizations who share by newsletter and other information about genealogical activities and resources and so forth.

Special Features: Links for Genealogical Research in Washington State include, for instance, Washington State Genealogical Resource Guide, Washington State Archives, Washington State Library and many others

Curriculum: History

2353 Washington State Geospatial Data Archive

http://wagda.lib.washington.edu

The Washington State Geospatial Data Archive is a space to locate geospatial data for the state of Washington; it also contains selected non–Washington geospatial data sets that have been created by students and researchers. This site does not include any digital maps, but offers access to digital geospatial data that can be used to make maps.

Special Features: Links include Home, Download Data, Metadata, About, Resource Links, ArcExplorer, Map Collection Homepage and others

Curriculum: Geography; Science; Social Studies; Technology

2354 Washington State Historical Society

www.washingtonhistory.org

The vision of the Washington State Historical Society is to be a highly esteemed and respected historical organization in the minds of patrons, policymakers, donors, and peer institutions, accomplished by a commitment to excellence, effective communications and strong relationships.

Special Features: Examples of goals include: make historical observances meaningful and memorable, create significant venues for interpretative programming, strengthen institutional capacities and others

Curriculum: History

2355 Washington State History Museum

www.wshs.org

The Washington State History Museum provides people of all ages the opportunity to explore and be entertained in an environment where characters from Washington's past speak about their lives; via exhibits, theatrical storytelling, high-tech displays and dramatics artifacts.

Special Features: Under the Education link, this Museum offers a variety of educational services to schools and educational institutions of Washington State; they support the educator's efforts to teach the techniques of historians and the story of the State of Washington

Curriculum: History

2356 Washington State Holocaust Education Resource Center

www.wsherc.org

The Washington State Holocaust Education Resource Center's mission is to inspire teaching and learning for humanity in the schools and communities of this region through study of the Holocaust.

Special Features: Links include What's New, Online Teaching and Learning Center, Programs and Events, Center and Local Resources, About the Washington State Holocaust Education Resource Center and others

Curriculum: Education; History

2357 Washington State Hospital Association

www.wsha.org

The purpose of the Washington State Hospital Association is to provide advocacy for, and service to, its members. It takes a major leadership role in issues that affect delivery, quality, accessibility, affordability and continuity of health care. This Association also works with others in identifying and responding to critical health care issues.

Special Features: Their goals include: Address the Human Resources Crisis, Assure the vitality of Hospitals and Physician Practices, Assure Access to Health Care Insurance, Promote Regulatory Reform and Administrative Simplification and others

Curriculum: Health

2358 Washington State Institute for Public Policy

www.wsipp.wa.gov

The Washington Legislature created the Washington State Institute for Public Policy in 1983. Its mission is to carry out practical, non-partisan research — at legislative direction — on issues of importance to Washington State.

Special Features: Links include Publications by Policy Area, such as: Child Welfare, Criminal Justice, Education, Employment/Welfare, Government, Health Care, Mental Illness, Prevention, State Economy

Curriculum: Economics; Government; Social Studies

2359 Washington State Labor Council

www.wslc.org

The Washington State Labor Council is a non-profit organization representing more than 550 local unions and trade councils, and offering services via legislative, political and educational programs, as well as in the community, school and media.

Special Features: Examples of services provided by this Council are: Education, Legislative Action, Political Action, Communications, Research and many others

Curriculum: Business; Economics

2360 Washington State Legislature Kid's Page

www.leg.wa.gov/common/kids/default.htm

The Washington State Legislature Kid's Page provides activities and websites for young students to learn about Washington's legislature. Activities include: Learn How a Bill Becomes a Law, Capitol Campus Trivia Game, Washington State Coloring Book, Discover the Symbols of Washington.

Special Features: Examples of websites include: Natural Resources youth Camp, Help for Teen workers, Washington State Fruit Commission, Rural Girls in Science, White House for Kids and others

Curriculum: Government; Social Studies

2361 Washington State Medical Association

www.wsma.org

The Washington State Medical Association works to represent the professional interests of all physicians, on behalf of their patients; in addition, it promotes effective leadership in the evolving health care delivery system.

Special Features: Links include News and Events, Legislative Affairs, For Our Patients, Principles of Medical Ethics, Frequently Ask Questions, Physician Locator and others

Curriculum: Health

2362 Washington State Office of Minority and Women's Business Enterprises

www.omwbe.wa.gov

The vision of the Washington State Office of Minority and Women's Business Enterprises is as follows: "Washington's economic vitality is enhanced by businesses owned and operated by people in all walks of life. Public contracting and procurement in the state mitigates against the effects of race and gender discrimination and promotes the development and growth of businesses owned and operated by all people who may be socially and economically disadvantaged, including women and minorities."

Special Features: Links include Information for State Agencies, Information for Businesses, Directory, News, Frequently Asked Questions, Upcoming Conferences, Seminars and Training, Opportunities and others

Curriculum: Business; Economics; Women's Studies

2363 Washington State Parent Teachers Association

www.wastatepta.org

The Washington State parent Teachers Association is a non-profit, membership association that seeks to bring together the home, school and community on behalf of all children and youth. Examples of their missions include: to support and speak on behalf of children and youth in schools, in the community and before governmental bodies and other organizations that make decisions affecting children.

Special Features: Examples of the objects of the Parent Teachers Association include: to promote the welfare of the children and youth in home, school, community and places of worship, to raise the standards of home life, and others

Curriculum: Education

2364 Washington State Potato Commission

www.potatoes.com

The mission of the Washington State Potato Commission is to serve the potato growers of the state. The main function of the Commission is to work toward the enhancement of marketing opportunities through promotion, advanced production and cultural practices via research, and preserve the rights and enhance the ability of growers to produce potatoes through legislative and regulatory actions.

Special Features: Links include Potatoes!, Recipes, Retain, Foodservice, News, Research, Growers; under recipes, in includes: Consumer, Foodservice, Dehydrated, Frozen, Cooking, Nutrition, Storage and Handling

Curriculum: Home Economics; Science; Social Studies

2365 Washington State Psychological Association

www.wapsych.org

The mission of the Washington State Psychological Association is to support, promote and advance the science, education and practice of psychology in the public interest.

Special Features: Links include Locate a Psychologist, Continuing Education, Calendar of Events, Committees, Links and Resources, Mental Health News, Newsletter, Classifieds and others

Curriculum: Psychology

2366 Washington State Women, Infants, and Children Program

www.doh.wa.gov/cfh/WIC/default.htm

The mission of the Washington Women, Infants and Children Program is to improve the lifelong health and nutrition of women, infants, and young children in Washington State. It is a nutrition program that helps pregnant women, new mothers and young children eat well, learn about nutrition and stay healthy.

Special Features: Links include What's New, Annual Report and County Profiles, Information for the Public, Who's Eligible, Foods, Health Effects and Cost Benefits, Nutrition Education and Physical Activity and many others

Curriculum: Health; Science; Women's Studies

2367 Washington Water Science Center

http://wa.water.usgs.gov

The Washington Water Science Center provides a direct link to all kinds of water resource information. One can locate information regarding Washington's rivers and streams, ground water, water quality and many other topics.

Special Features: Links include Message From Our Water Science Center Director, Newsroom, Outreach and Education, Information,

Employment and Volunteer Opportunities, Directions and Locations Map

Curriculum: Economics; Environmental Studies; Geography; Science; Social Studies

2368 Washington Women in Trades

www.wawomenintrades.com

The Washington Women in Trades was founded in 1978 for women working in trades to gather and share information. The Association sponsors an annual trade fair, where employers can recruit women for trades work. The fair is also an outreach to women who may not be familiar with the high paying jobs available in trade careers.

Special Features: Each Trade Fair offers the following areas: employers, apprenticeship, information, tradeswomen, demonstrations, hands-on activities, guest speakers, educational and vocational training information, employment register, awards, network opportunities, tool and trade exhibits

Curriculum: Business; Economics; Women's Studies

WEST VIRGINIA

2369 American Discovery Trail: West Virginia

www.discoverytrail.org/states/westvir

In West Virginia, the American Discovery Trail ventures through what might be called the "amazement park" of eastern America. Many trails offer scenic vistas, pastoral settings, stirring waterfalls and botanical diversification, which include rafting, kayaking, canoeing, exploration of caves, cliff climbing and much more.

Special Features: Examples of trails and sites include: North Bend Rail Trail, Harrison County Rail Trail, Allegheny Trail, Potomac Highlands, Greenland Gap, Nancy Hanks Memorial, Blackwater River Canyon and Falls and others

Curriculum: Environmental Studies; Geography; History; Science; Social Studies

2370 Kearneysville Tree Fruit Research and Information Center

www.caf.wvu.edu/kearneysville/wvufarm2.html

West Virginia University's Kearneysville Tree Fruit Research and Education Center was established in 1930 and includes 158 acres of mixed tree fruit plantings and corn rotation, a modern laboratory, a historic farm house, a greenhouse and various equipment buildings.

Special Features: The mission of the Fruit Center is to serve the commercial tree fruit industry of West Virginia by conducting research in entomology and plant biology

Curriculum: Biology; Economics; Science; Social Studies

2371 Marshall University Herpetology Lab

www.marshall.edu/herp

Marshall University Herpetology Lab is the headquarters for the study of West Virginia's amphibians and reptiles. Since the 1930s, herpetology in West Virginia has become widely known and studied because of the rich diversity of amphibians and reptiles that occur in this region.

Special Features: One link includes: West Virginia Biological Survey — Amphibians and Reptiles Collection. This museum includes over 13,000 specimens of amphibians and reptiles; the majorities are from West Virginia

Curriculum: Biology; Environmental Studies; Science

2372 Online Guide to West Virginia Politics

www.politics1.com/wv.htm

The Online Guide to West Virginia Politics is a complete directory of West Virginia candidates for Governor, United State Senator and Congress in the current election cycle, state political parties and much more.

Special Features: Links include The Presidency, The States, Political Parties, Calendar,

Campaign Products and Services, Bookstore, Awards and others
Curriculum: Government

2373 Portraits of Women in West Virginia

www.wvculture.org/history/whm1.html

This site is offered via West Virginia Archives and History. Each notable woman offers a photograph, as well as a link to more information about each famous West Virginian woman.
Special Features: Examples include: Ruth Woods Dayton, Fannie Cobb Carter, Dorothy Callison, Mary A. Byrne, Mary Lee Settle, Sharon Rockefeller, Mary Lou Retton and others
Curriculum: Women's Studies

2374 Science Museum of Western Virginia

www.smwv.org

The mission of the Science Museum of Western Virginia is to make science and technology accessible to all people by being an outstanding regional institution that ignites and nurtures lifelong learning.
Special Features: The link for teachers offers to make science and technology an exciting experience for youth — at the museum and in the classroom, including such areas as Live Animals, Planetarium Shows, MegaDome Movies and others
Curriculum: Environmental Studies; Science; Technology

2375 Small Business Administration — West Virginia

www.sba.gov/wv

The Small Business Administration's West Virginia office is located in Clarksburg, an area of industry and growing small businesses. Clarksburg is a unique community rich with economic growth, heritage, and family recreation. Downtown Clarksville is home to the largest legal and financial center in North Central West Virginia.
Special Features: Links include News, Training Calendar, Startup Kit, Financing, Laws and Regulations, Disaster Assistance, Local Resources, Opportunities and others
Curriculum: Business; Economics; Government

2376 State of West Virginia Official Web Portal

www.wv.gov/

Government, business, living/working/learning/wisiting in West Virginia.
Special Features: West Virginia news, weather, tips on finding state information
Curriculum: Business; Geography; Government; Social Studies

2377 Travel West Virginia Trails Online

www.wvtrails.com

Travel West Virginia Trails Online is a comprehensive trails database for the state. From hardwood forests and open farmland to rushing rivers and high mountains, West Virginia provides outdoor enthusiasts with an abundance of trails to explore the beauty of West Virginia.
Special Features: Links include Hatfield McCoy Trail, Trial Search and Maps, Trail News, Trail Facts, Trail Quiz, Mountain Manners, Bookstore, Statewide Trail Plan and others
Curriculum: Environmental Studies; Geography; History; Physical Education; Social Studies

2378 West Virginia Agricultural Statistics

www.nass.usda.gov/wv

The West Virginia Agricultural Statistics Web site includes census, charts, maps, releases and publications, crop weather reports, and much more, all presented for public use.
Special Features: Related Links include NASS Homepage, USDA Homepage, WVDA Homepage, WVU Extension Service, USDA Farm Service Agency, NASS Kids and others
Curriculum: Economics; Environmental Studies; Geography; History; Science; Social Studies

2379 West Virginia Appalachian Music and Literature

www.ferrum.edu/applit/studyg/West/htm/main menu.htm

West Virginia's Appalachian Music and Literature is a self-contained teaching unit by Avis Caynor and Renee Wyatt. There are four major sections of this interesting unit: Welcome to West Virginia, Traditional Appalachian Music and Literature, Come Back Home to West Virginia and Teacher's Guide.

Special Features: This is an online multimedia project that offers a look at selected traditional children's music and stories from West Virginia that reflect Appalachian culture

Curriculum: Language Arts; Music; Social Studies

2380 West Virginia Archives and History

www.wvculture.org/history

The West Virginia Archives and History includes areas such as: Records Management and Preservation Board, Genealogy Corner, State Archives, Daily Trivia, History Center, West Virginia Memory Project, Publications and much more.

Special Features: Under the "History Center," links include (for example: African Americans in West Virginia, Ante-Bellum, Civil War Union Militia, Community Resources, History Heroes, Native Americans, Mine Wars

Curriculum: History; Social Studies

2381 West Virginia Art and Craft Guild

www.wvartcraftguild.com

The West Virginia Art and Craft Guild is a nonprofit membership organization formed in 1963 by people determined to preserve and promote the creative lifestyle in West Virginia.

Special Features: Links include Membership, Newsletter, Spotlight, Exhibition, Calendar, History and others

Curriculum: Arts; Sociology

2382 West Virginia Board of Education

wvde.state.wv.us/boe

The West Virginia Board of Education is established in the West Virginia Constitution. It provides supervision of the state's 834 elementary and secondary schools. The board determines educational policies and establishes rules that carry into effect state law regarding education.

Special Features: Links include Office of Technology. Special Education, Reading for All, Textbook Adoption, Healthy Schools, Adult Education, Learn and Serve and others

Curriculum: Education

2383 West Virginia Bureau for Public Health

www.wvdhhr.org/bph

The West Virginia Bureau for Public Health is aimed at advancing health services in West Virginia. They are based on core values and a shared vision to accomplish excellent health initiatives in the state of West Virginia.

Special Features: Links include information about, for example: AIDS/HIV, Asthma, Cancer, Diabetes Detection Initiative, Food Inspection, Obesity, Smallpox, Tobacco

Curriculum: Health

2384 West Virginia Coal Association

www.wvcoal.com

Located in Charleston, the West Virginia coal Association is a trade association representing more than 90 percent of the state's underground and surface coal mine production. Its purpose is to have a unified voice representing the state's coal industry, as well as increase emphasis on coal as a reliable energy source to help the nation achieve energy independence.

Special Features: Honors people for their important contributions to West Virginia

Curriculum: Business; Economics; Environmental Studies; Geography; History; Science; Social Studies

2385 West Virginia Coalition Against Domestic Violence

www.wvcadv.org

The West Virginia Coalition Against Domestic Violence is committed to the elimination of personal and institutional violence against women, children and men. It provides a safe space and quality service for victims of domestic violence.

Special Features: Links include Faith Communities, People with Disabilities, Batterer Intervention/Prevention Programs, Family Violence Options/Welfare and others

Curriculum: Psychology; Sociology

2386 West Virginia Department of Transportation

www.wvdot.com

The West Virginia Department of Transportation is comprised of more than 6,000 men and women who work in the Division of Highways, Motor Vehicles, Public Transit, Port Authority, Parkways Economic Development and Tourism Authority.

Special Features: This Department provides essential services in transportation, tourism and economic development, including (for example): Safety and Protection, Transportation Services, Revenue Generation, Information and Education, etc.

Curriculum: Business; Driver Training; Economics

2387 West Virginia Dietetic Association

www.wvda.org

The West Virginia Dietetic Association is a professional organization for those who are committed to serving the public through the promotion of optimal nutrition, good health and well-being.

Special Features: Links include Continuing Education, Pyramid, Dietetic Jobs, Board, Licensure, Annual Meetings and others

Curriculum: Health

2388 West Virginia Division of Motor Vehicles

www.wvdot.com/6_motorists/dmv/6G_dmv.htm

The West Virginia Division of Motor Vehicles provides driver information and education through twenty-one regional offices in West Virginia. It includes: Driver's Licenses, Commercial Driver's Licenses, Vehicle Registration, Boating Regulations, Governor's Highway Safety Program and much more.

Special Features: News and Information includes, for example: To Honor All Who Served, Motorcycle Safety Awareness Rally, New Laws for Child Passenger Seat Belt Restraints and others

Curriculum: Driver Training

2389 West Virginia Division of Natural Resources

www.wvdnr.gov

The West Virginia Division of Natural Resources offers a wealth of information, including current and past news, state parks, wildlife diversity, publications and programs, special opportunities, environmental resources and much more.

Special Features: Calendar of Events offers such topics as: Murder Mystery Train at Cass Scenic Railroad State Park, Salute to America at Beech Fork State Park, Fiddles and Vittles Train at Call Scenic Railroad State Park

Curriculum: Economics; Environmental Studies; Geography; History; Science; Social Studies

2390 West Virginia Division of Rehabilitation Services

www.wvdrs.org

The mission of the West Virginia Division of Rehabilitation Services is to enable and empower individuals with disabilities to work and to live independently.

Special Features: Strategies include, for example: Organize and manage an effective and efficient agency, Maintain a skilled workforce committed to the mission of the agency

Curriculum: Education; Psychology; Social Studies; Sociology

2391 West Virginia Education Alliance

www.educationalliance.org

The Education Alliance is West Virginia's statewide public education fund. This nonprofit organization's mission is to create positive, systemic change in public education. Their vision is higher student achievement for every child in West Virginia.

Special Features: Links include Board, Dates, Grants, News, Latest Events, Partnerships, Provider of Giving, Publications, Research, Speakers Bureau and others

Curriculum: Education

2392 West Virginia Education Association

www.wvew.org

The West Virginia Education Association are individuals who teach in kindergarten classrooms and lecture halls, counsel youth, drive buses, coach soccer, direct school plays and so forth. Their purpose is to provide a high quality public education for every child.

Special Features: Links include Newsroom, Professional Issues, Legal Resources, Government Relations, Resources and others

Curriculum: Education

2393 West Virginia Environmental Council

www.wvecouncil.org

The mission of the West Virginia Environmental Council is to facilitate communication and cooperation among citizens in promoting environmental protection in West Virginia, to assist in organizing grass roots groups, to facilitate interaction among established environmental organization and so forth.

Special Features: Links include Newsletter,

Events Calendar, Legislative Updates, Issues, Links and Contacts, Email Alerts Archive and others
Curriculum: Environmental Studies

2394 West Virginia Genealogy and History

www.usgennet.org/usa/wv/state1

The West Virginia History and Genealogy Web site is a central point of entry into independent, genealogical and historical websites. It includes, for example: Hacker's Creek Pioneer Descendants, Vital Records for West Virginia, African-American Research, West Virginia Biographies online and much more.

Special Features: Links include Gramps and the Bushwhackers, Tidbits of West Virginia, Famous People from West Virginia, Early American Pioneers Held Captive or Killed by Indians and others
Curriculum: History

2395 West Virginia Health Care Association

www.wvhca.org

The West Virginia Health Care Association is a trade association for extended care providers of health care in West Virginia. Its member facilities include nursing homes, personal care homes and hospital-based skilled nursing.

Special Features: Links include About, Consumer Information, Member Information, Services, Links, Events Calendar, What's New and others
Curriculum: Health

2396 West Virginia Highlands Conservancy

www.wvhighlands.org

The West Virginia Highlands Conservancy was formed in 1967 to preserve the natural beauty of the West Virginia Highlands; the Conservancy is the state's oldest environmental advocacy organization.

Special Features: The Conservancy has been instrumental in the creation of the Monongahela National Forest Wilderness areas in preventing the destruction of Canaan Valley
Curriculum: Economics; Environmental Studies; Geography; History; Science; Social Studies

2397 West Virginia Hospitality and Travel Association

www.wvhta.com

The West Virginia Hospitality and Travel Association helps individuals and businesses monitor legislation, influence government actions, rules and regulations, convey needs and wishes to various governmental agencies and so forth.

Special Features: Links include About, News and Events, Directors and Representatives, Links, Guest Book Form, Legislative Issues, Educational Foundation and others
Curriculum: Business; Economics; Geography; Social Studies

2398 West Virginia in the Civil War

www.wvcivilwar.com

West Virginia in the Civil War offers a wealth of information regarding West Virginia's role in the Civil War, including Union Regiments, Confederate Regiments, Medal of Honor Recipients, Historic Sites, Recommended Reading, Organizations and Reenactment Groups.

Special Features: Examples of "News" include: Civil War in West Virginia Symposium, Belington Purchases Laurel Hill Battlefield Camp, and others
Curriculum: History

2399 West Virginia Legislature

www.legis.state.wv.us/legishp1.html

The West Virginia Legislature Web site offers a wealth of information such as: Bill Status, Legislative Calendar, Bulletin Board, West Virginia State Code, Personalized Bill Tracking, District Information, Members' Capitol Addresses and much more.

Special Features: Links include Senate, House, Leadership, Joint Committee, Legislative Auditor, Court of Claims, Crime Victims, Acts of the Legislature and others
Curriculum: Government

2400 West Virginia Library Commission

librarycommission.lib.wv.us/#

The West Virginia Library Commission celebrates West Virginia's rich literary heritage. Via this site, one can explore literary services such as: Governor's council on Literacy, Learning Express Library, ALA Office for Literacy and Library Outreach Services, and much more.

Special Features: Links include About, Cataloging, Organizations, Plans and Bylaws, Reference Desk, Services and Staff, State Government, Surveys and Forms, West Virginia libraries
Curriculum: Library Media

2401 West Virginia Museum of American Glass

http://members.aol.com/wvmuseumofglass

The West Virginia Museum of American Glass is a museum with a mission to share the diverse and rich heritage of glass as a product and historical object, as well as telling the lives of glass workers, their families and communities, and of the tools and machines they used in glass houses.

Special Features: Links include How to Find Us, Event Calendar, Museum Store, Catalog Holdings, Gems of the Museum, Library Holdings and others

Curriculum: Art; Business; History

2402 West Virginia Natural Heritage Program

www.natureserve.org/nnp/us/wv

The mission of the West Virginia Natural Heritage Programs is to conserve and enhance West Virginia's natural heritage and ecological diversity by identifying species in need of conservation, maintaining information on these resources and assisting in their conservation.

Special Features: This program was founded in 1975 and conducts an ongoing statewide ecological inventory of rare plant and animal species, wetlands and other biological communities

Curriculum: Environmental Studies; Science; Social Studies

2403 West Virginia Newspapers

http://newslink.org/wvnews.html

West Virginia Newspapers includes, for example, *Beckley Register-Herald, Charleston Gazette, Martinsburg Journal, Parkersburg News and Sentinel, Williamson News, Lewisburg Mountain Messenger, Marlinton Pocahontas Times* and much more.

Special Features: Links include Top Sites, Newspapers, Magazines, Radio/TV, Resources, Search, Update, Feedback and others

Curriculum: Language Arts

2404 West Virginia Office of Environmental Health Services

www.wvdhhr.org/oehs

The mission of the West Virginia Office of Environmental Health Services is to improve environmental health protection for every West Virginia citizen and visitor through quality programs that are designed and administered to serve, education and regulate in the least restrictive and most efficient manner.

Special Features: Examples of how this service will achieve this mission include: taking a leadership role in assessing West Virginia's present and emerging environmental health needs, and many others

Curriculum: Environmental Studies; Health

2405 West Virginia Office of Technology

http://access.k12.wv.us

The West Virginia's Department of Education, Office of Technology includes such areas as: Basic Skills/Computer Education, SUCCESS, Grants, Reinventing Education, West Virginia Virtual School, MarcoPolo in West Virginia, Internet and K–12 Intranet, Information Technology, Technology Planning and much more.

Special Features: Forms include: Basic Skills/Computer Education, Email West Virginia K–12 — Educators and Students, Electronics Rack Installation Summary, Reinventing Education and others

Curriculum: Education; Technology

2406 West Virginia Plant Fossils

www.geocraft.com/WVFossils/

The West Virginia Plant Fossils Web site includes articles, links to other sites, what's new, search, translate and Plant Fossils of the Pennsylvanian Period" Articulates, Lycopods, Cordaites, and Ferns and Seed Ferns.

Special Features: "Ferns and Seed Ferns" include: Alethopteris, Eremopteris, Mariopteris, Neuropteris, Pecopteris, Sphenopteris, Rhodea

Curriculum: Biology; Science; Social Studies

2407 West Virginia Press Association

www.wvpress.org

The West Virginia Press Association includes: General Advertising in West Virginia, Statewide Classified Network, Display Network, Political Advertising, Press Release for All Media in West Virginia, Resources Links and much more.

Special Features: Links include Ads Online, Association, Foundation, Newspapers in Education, Newspapers Online, Newsletter, Legal Ads and others

Curriculum: Language Arts

2408 West Virginia Rails to Trails Council

www.wvrtc.org

The West Virginia Rails to Trails Council is a collection of individuals, civic groups and organizations who have joined together to promote the development and enjoyment of Rail-Trails in West Virginia.

Special Features: Rail-Trails have gentle grades and wide rights of way suitable for multiple uses such as walking, bicycling, horseback riding and others

Curriculum: Geography; History; Physical Education; Social Studies

2409 West Virginia Regional History Collection

www.libraries.wvc.edu/wvcollection

The West Virginia Regional History Collection possesses field recording of folk music that are extensive in volume and diverse in subject matter, recorded in West Virginia from the 1930s to the 1980s.

Special Features: In their collections, one can find accompanied and unaccompanied vocal and instrumental music for various combinations of fiddle, guitar, banjo, dulcimer and other instruments

Curriculum: History; Music

2410 West Virginia Rivers Coalition

www.wvrivers.org

The mission of the West Virginia Rivers Coalition is to seek the conservation and restoration of West Virginia's exceptional rivers and streams.

Special Features: Links include Merchandise, Anglers, paddlers, Watershed Groups, Mountaintop Removal, Potomac Headquarters and others

Curriculum: Economics; Environmental Studies; Geography; Physical Education; Social Studies

2411 West Virginia Rural Health Education Partnerships

www.wvrhep.org

This mission of the West Virginia Rural Health Education Partnerships is to achieve greater retention of West Virginia trained health science graduates in underserved rural West Virginia communities.

Special Features: Links include Consortia, Calendar, Committees, Directory, Policies, Reports, Informatics, Scholarships and others

Curriculum: Health

2412 West Virginia State Farm Museum

www.pointpleasantwv.org/FarmMuseum.html

The West Virginia State Farm Museum is a non-profit organization that strives for the preservation of West Virginia early pioneer and farm life heritage. Its purpose is to collect artifacts of their rural past and use them to education youth about how their ancestors lived.

Special Features: This Museum is a great asset to the State and surrounding community; providing a wealth of knowledge and education via visual and demonstrative history.

Curriculum: History; Social Studies

2413 West Virginia State Museum

www.wvculture.org/museum

The West Virginia State Museum of the Division of Culture and History is located in Charleston. The purposes of this museum is to collect, document, present, preserve and promote the State of West Virginia in every aspect of its archaeology, art, culture, geology, history, paleontology and socio-economic backgrounds.

Special Features: Links include Exhibits in the Museum, Exhibits Online, Education, Collections, Tips for Conserving Quilts, Curiosities, Museum Links and others

Curriculum: Geography; History; Sociology

2414 West Virginia State Parks and Forests

www.wvstateparks.com

West Virginia State Parks includes numerous parks and forests such as: Audra, Babcock, Beach Fork, Bluestone State park, Camp Creek, Cathedral, Holly River, Kanawha, Lost River, Panther, Seneca, Watoga and many others.

Special Features: Links include Lodging, Recreation, Calendar of Events, Conferences, News and Events, Park Programs, Resource Center and others

Curriculum: Environmental Studies; Geography; History; Science; Social Studies

2415 West Virginia State Police

www.wvstatepolice.com

The West Virginia State Police includes areas such as: Colonel's Welcome, Missing Children,

Sex Offenders, Crime Lab, Legal Division, Road Conditions, News Releases, Traffic Safety and much more.

Special Features: Includes a section "Need Help (Provide Anonymous Information " and a list of areas and locations, such as: missing person, stolen checks, attempted abduction, hit and run victim and others

Curriculum: Government; Social Studies

2416 West Virginia Travel and Outdoor Recreation

http://gorp.away.com/gorp/location/wv/wv.htm

West Virginia Travel and Outdoor Recreation offers exciting places to visit for educational, recreational and entertainment purposes Examples of the "Best of West Virginia" include: Monongahela National Forest, Civil War Battle Sites, New River Gorge, Gauley River and many more.

Special Features: Links include Summer Guide to Outdoor Fun, Unbeatable Urban Hikes, The Norwest Quest, California Beach Camping, Tour de France Preview and others

Curriculum: Economics; Environmental Studies; Geography; History; Physical Education; Social Studies

2417 West Virginia Web

http://wvweb.com/wvso

Special Olympics West Virginia is a non-profit organization that is part of a year-round international movement of sports training and athletic competition for people with mental retardation.

Special Features: Their goal is to bring all persons who are mentally challenged into the larger society under conditions whereby they are accepted, respected and given a chance to become useful and productive citizens

Curriculum: Education; Health; Physical Education; Sociology

2418 West Virginia Women's Commission

www.wvdhhr.org/women

The West Virginia Women's Commission promotes the status and empowerment of all West Virginia women through advocacy, research, education, and consensus building. The Commission exists to foster women's economic, political, educational and social development; to ensure their full participation in society and to recognize their achievements.

Special Features: Links include Upcoming Training Events, Staff and Commissioners, Mission, West Virginia Women's Resource Directory, Policy Statements, History, Publications and others

Curriculum: Women's Studies

2419 Wonderful West Virginia Magazine

www.wonderfulwv.com

The Wonderful West Virginia Magazine is the premier magazine about the Mountain State, published monthly by the West Virginia Division of Natural Resources. It includes photographs and interesting articles about West Virginia.

Special Features: Links include Bookshelf, Photo Gallery, Coming Attractions, Send Comments, Online Shopping, Submission Guidelines and others

Curriculum: Language Arts; Social Studies

WISCONSIN

2420 The American Cranberry (Sponsor: University of Wisconsin–Madison)

www.library.wisc.edu/guides/agnic/cranberry/

The American Cranberry (Vaccinium macrocarpon). Wisconsin produces about half of America's annual crop of cranberries. Basic information on cranberries can be found on this page including: marketing, cultivation, nutrition and recipes, harvest, production, environmental issues and directory of handlers.

Special Features: AskCranberry and email option to question experts on cranberries, extensive links to other cranberry sites

Curriculum: Business; Environmental Studies; Home Economics; Science

2421 Blind Readers' Page

http://blindreaders.info/

Over two thousand three hundred annotated links about alternative information formats (Braille, recordings, large print, web audio, etc.) with a special collection of Wisconsin resources. Designed for people with print disabilities, dyslexia, visual or physical handicaps. Sites organized by subject.

Special Features: Searchable site
Curriculum: Language Arts; Sociology

2422 Board of Regents of the University of Wisconsin

www.uwex.edu/wgnhs/

Wisconsin Geological and Natural History Survey dates back to 1897. The survey provides basic data for resource, land use and environmental management through such medium as maps, records and reports. Online publications include educational series, Geoscience Wisconsin and maps.

Special Features: Listing of current research programs, news, data, other earth science links
Curriculum: Environmental Studies; Geography; Science

2423 Capital Newspapers

www.madison.com/

Madison.com is the capital city news page. Find out what is happening in the city and surrounding communities. National and local news, sports, business and entertainment. Extensive related links dealing in local businesses, jobs, and classifieds.

Special Features: Local weather, searchable, real estate
Curriculum: Business; Geography; Social Studies

2424 Children's Hospital and Health System

www.chw.org/display/jhome.asp

Wisconsin's leader in pediatric care is Children's Hospital and Health System. Find pediatric physicians, clinics, and outreach programs. Use the "Learn About Health" link for health and safety information such as injury prevention, immunizations, nutrition, growth and development, parenting issues, and car seat safety. Site also provides a glossary of medical terms.

Special Features: Medical glossary, health information sheets
Curriculum: Health; Psychology; Science

2425 Circus World Museum

www.circusworldmuseum.com/

The Circus World Museum is located in Baraboo, Wisconsin, the "home" of the Ringling Brothers wintering quarters; a national historic landmark. It is dedicated to preserving the history of the American circus. It also includes a library and research center and is owned by the Wisconsin Historical Society. Website offers a brief history of the museum and descriptions of outdoor displays. Circus memorabilia and artifacts.

Special Features: Interactive map, seasonal programming
Curriculum: History

2426 Council for Wisconsin Writers, Inc.

www.wisconsinwriters.org/

Council for Wisconsin Writers is a nonprofit organization dedicated to enhancing awareness of the state's literary heritage and to encourage today's writers. The CWW was founded in 1964 and is operated by volunteers. CWW hosts an annual writing contest; past contest winners are listed online.

Special Features: Membership application, newsletter, links of interest
Curriculum: Language Arts

2427 Council of University of Wisconsin Libraries, Wisconsin Historical Society

http://libtext.library.wisc.edu/wipionexp/

"Wisconsin Pioneer Experience: A digital collection of original sources documenting nineteenth century Wisconsin history." A collection of diaries, letters, reminiscences, speeches and personal narratives of people who settled Wisconsin. All artifacts are digitized and available for browsing or searching. Includes Native American narratives.

Special Features: Searchable collection, digitized images, text request form
Curriculum: History; Language Arts; Social Studies

2428 Door County Chamber of Commerce Visitor and Convention Bureau

www.doorcounty.com/

Door County is located east of Green Bay on a thumb like peninsula sticking out into Lake Michigan. The peninsula has more than two hundred fifty miles of shoreline, ten lighthouses, five state parks and is known for having "culture in the country." A true state treasure, Door County is a special vacation destination.

Special Features: Vacation planner, maps, community and business directory and photo gallery

Curriculum: Art; Business; Geography

2429 Folk Dance Association, Wisconsin Folk Dance

www.folkdancing.org/wisconsin.html

Ethnic dance is a great hobby, a source of exercise and good way to socialize with others. The Wisconsin Folk Dance site lists organized groups who hold dances featuring numerous kinds of ethnic dance. Read over listings of classes and sessions in different regions of the state.

Special Features: Wisconsin links, national folk dance directory, contact information

Curriculum: Dance; Sociology

2430 Green Bay Packers, Inc.

www.packers.com

The official web page of the National Football League team, the Green Bay Packers. Find out the inside news on the team. Hall of fame, game day events, news, team roster, history, fans, tickets, and more. Sign up for Packer e-news to have the latest breaking team news delivered to your mailbox.

Special Features: Statistics, stockholder information, fan surveys, searchable

Curriculum: Sports

2431 Milwaukee Public Museum, Northern Prairie Wildlife Research Center

www.mpm.edu/collect/vertzo/herp/atlas/welcome.html

The Wisconsin Herpetology Homepage is an informational resource on the reptiles and amphibians of the state. Provides a herpetological atlas of the species accounts and sightings in the state by common name, scientific name and status. Each reptile or amphibian may include photo.

Special Features: Site offers information of Great Lakes amphibians, timber rattlesnakes, bibliography, audio/video and laws and regulations

Curriculum: Biology; Environmental Studies; Science

2432 Mushrooms (Sponsor: University of Wisconsin–La Crosse)

http://botit.botany.wisc.edu/toms_fungi/

Tom Volk's Fungi. Extensive and educational information on mushrooms/fungi. Learn about medicinal and scientific uses for fungi. Each fungus of the month explains the fungus and its importance to society, nature or science. Lesson plans for educators, images, research and basic information available.

Special Features: Searchable, images, fungus history

Curriculum: Biology; Science

2433 National Fresh Water Fishing Hall of Fame

www.freshwater-fishing.org/

Located in Hayward, the National Fresh Water Fishing Hall of Fame and Museum strives to collect, preserve and display the artifacts and history of freshwater angling. The building of the museum is in the form of a giant muskie. Inside the giant leaping fish resides the hall of fame. The mouth of the fish is an observation platform. Kids' link includes how to tie fishing knots and river conservation.

Special Features: Contact information, related fishing links, museum and grounds details

Curriculum: Biology; Science

2434 Office of the Governor

www.wisgov.state.wi.us/

Find out about the state governor. A biography of the current governor and their spouse is available. Read through recent press releases, speeches, and web broadcasts. Take a virtual tour of governor's residence Maple Bluff dating back to 1927. The mansion has thirty-four rooms and employs nine people for household duties and maintenance.

Special Features: Audio clips, trade information, task forces, budgeting

Curriculum: Government

2435 Outagamie County Historical Society

www.foxvalleyhistory.org/index.htm

Harry Houdini claimed Appleton, Wisconsin his hometown. It is also the home of the Outagamie Museum and neighbor to the Kaukauna located Charles A. Grignon Mansion. The mansion was built in 1837 out of the fur trade era and as a wedding gift. Harry Houdini was actually born in Hungary, but moved to Appleton as a toddler and referred to it as his hometown.
Special Features: Historical articles and photos
Curriculum: History

2436 RENEW Wisconsin

www.renewwisconsin.org/index.html

RENEW Wisconsin promotes clean energy strategies for the state in a responsible manner. RENEW is made up of business educators, farmers, agency officials and concerned citizens. Website offers information on renewable energy policy development, information exchange and project facilitation. Read through such environmental topics as wind farms, green power, and the oil crisis.
Special Features: Latest news, publications, reports, legislative actions, related links
Curriculum: Business; Economics; Environmental Studies; Science; Technology

2437 Robert M. La Follette School of Public Affairs, University of Wisconsin

www.lafollette.wisc.edu/publications/otherpub
lications/LaFollette/LaFLegacy.html

Alice Honeywell is author of the article, "La Follette and his Legacy." Progressivism was an authentic reform movement that suggested government should improve society. Robert M. La Follette was a Progressive politician known for reducing the power of railroad barons after the turn of the century. This article is a short history of his life and times.
Special Features: Historical photos, bibliography
Curriculum: Government; History; Sociology

2438 State of Wisconsin

www.wisconsin.gov/state/home/app?COMM
AND=gov.wi.state.cpp.command.LoadPortal
Home

The official website of the state of Wisconsin. Find basic Wisconsin facts such as the state symbols; take a virtual tour of the capitol, maps, statistics, demographics, and FAQ's. Information about government, public services, business, education, health and safety, and tourism is available. An agency index and subject directory is also included.
Special Features: Text only version, searchable, site map
Curriculum: Business; Economics; Geography; Government; Social Studies

2439 University of Wisconsin, Center for Perinatal Care at Meriter Hospital Madison, Wisconsin

www.pediatrics.wisc.edu/childrenshosp/paren
ts_of_preemies/

A webpage dedicated to parents of premature babies. Although all personal medical issues should be addressed to local physicians and nurses, the Parents for Preemies page answers many frequently asked questions. Some issues addressed include: common problems and diseases, special problems, common drugs, understanding preemie development, emotional support and questions after discharge form the hospital.
Special Features: Child safety, family issues, related links, support sites
Curriculum: Health; Psychology

2440 University of Wisconsin-Madison Department of Astronomy

www.astro.wisc.edu/~dolan/*constellations*

"The Constellations and Their Stars." By Chris Dolan. A collection of pages about constellations, stars and our galaxy. Information includes the solar system, myths of Greeks and Romans, moon phases, and pronunciation guide. Wonderful information for the beginner astronomer. Includes references, resources and links.
Special Features: Milky Way photos, alphabetical listing of constellations, the twenty-six nearest and brightest stars
Curriculum: Science

2441 University of Wisconsin-Madison Department of Botany

www.botany.wisc.edu/herbarium/

Wisconsin State Herbarium. Founded in 1849 the herbarium contains over one million dried and labeled plants of local, national, and international importance. Over one third of the collection is Wisconsin native plants. The herbarium is used for education in ecology, biodiversity, environmentalism, and botany. Read over current projects and data sets.

Special Features: Searchable by name, habitat, common names, genera, and family

Curriculum: Biology; Environmental Studies; Science

2442 University of Wisconsin-Madison Libraries

www.library.wisc.edu/libraries/WomensStudies/

Today, most librarians, almost eighty three percent, are women. The University of Wisconsin System Women's Studies Librarian's Office is long to pronounce but easy to understand. It is simply, a librarian who assess library materials dealing specifically in women's studies. The office opened in 1977. Articles are available on the office and what it provides.

Special Features: Extensive bibliographies, history of the position, presentations, links to other women's studies resources

Curriculum: Library Media; Women's Studies

2443 USS Wisconsin Association

www.usswisconsin.org/

The USS *Wisconsin* is a BB-64 battleship launched in 1943. The battleship served in World War II, Korea and the first Gulf War. It is now at anchor at the National Maritime Center. Website offers history of the ship, crewmember photos, general information and veteran reunion information.

Special Features: Historical photos, ship's history, deck logs, gun information

Curriculum: History

2444 Wilson Alwyn Bentley Photograph Collection (Sponsor: University of Wisconsin–Madison)

http://mail.ssec.wisc.edu/snow/index.html

Wilson Alwyn Bentley photographed snow crystals, dew, frost and ice crystals. The Bentley Collection is the digitized collection of his photographed works. Articles on snow crystals and their history and classification. Biography of Bentley and his work is included.

Special Features: Digitized photomicrographs, browse or searchable site

Curriculum: Art; Science; Technology

2445 Wisconsin Academy of Sciences, Arts and Letters

www.wisconsinacademy.org/

The academy was founded in 1870, separate from government and university affiliations they strive to celebrate thought and culture and explore solutions to common problems. Some of the issues the Academy addresses include: Wisconsin water, Center for the Book, publications, and writing contests.

Special Features: Writing contests, news, reports

Curriculum: Environmental Studies; Language Arts; Sociology

2446 Wisconsin Arts Board

http://arts.state.wi.us/static/

Since 1973 the Arts board has supports and promoted arts in Wisconsin. Website offers grants, news, publications and organization listings. Look for arts and craft fairs, art museum listings and traveling exhibits.

Special Features: Calendar of events, featured artists

Curriculum: Art

2447 Wisconsin Beef Council

www.beeftips.com/

Beeftips.com is dedicated to the cooking, serving, and teaching all about beef. The site is separated between beef and veal. Look through recipes and cooking tips. Food safety and nutrition is also covered. Find something new in the new products link.

Special Features: Email an expert, news, find a restaurant, and buy veal online

Curriculum: Business; Home Economics

2448 Wisconsin Council on Children and Families

www.wccf.org/

As an advocate for promoting the well being of children and families in Wisconsin the WCCF offers educational conferences and projects. Projects and topics include: welfare and economic support, child brain research, juvenile justice and family law.

Special Features: Breaking news, publications, bill news

Curriculum: Government; Health; Sociology; Women's Studies

2449 Wisconsin Dells Visitor and Convention Bureau

www.wisdells.com/

The Wisconsin Dells is an eighteen square mile family vacation area located in south central Wisconsin. Named in 1931 the Dells has grown into a nationally known vacation spot. Some attractions include water parks, golf courses, live performances, resort hotels and spas. Natural attractions to the area include unusual rock formations and sandstone cliffs.

Special Features: History of the area, news releases, community and school facts and lodging

Curriculum: Business; Geography

2450 Wisconsin Department of Agriculture, Trade and Consumer Protection

http://datcp.state.wi.us/index.jsp

Serving the state, the Wisconsin Department of Agriculture, Trade and Consumer Protection (WDATCP is responsible for food safety and quality, fair business, agricultural conservation, plant and animal welfare, and commerce. Wisconsin strives to be a leader in agricultural productivity, profitability, and growth.

Special Features: Site map focuses on issues such as animals, crops, land and water, chemicals, farm center, business, food, marketing, unfair competition, consumer protection, animals, environment, insects, plants, inspections, and trade

Curriculum: Biology; Business; Economics; Health; Science; Social Studies

2451 Wisconsin Department of Health and Family Services

www.dhfs.state.wi.us/

The WDHFS is divided into five areas: children and family services, disability and elder services, public health, health care financing and management and technology. The EDHFS serves the public through educational programming, collecting and reporting data and disseminating information. Site offers search engine for health issues.

Special Features: hot topics, telephone hotline numbers, directory of services and larger font option

Curriculum: Government; Health; Sociology

2452 Wisconsin Department of Natural Resources

http://dnr.wi.gov/

The Wisconsin Department of Natural Resources or WDNR is responsible for implementing laws to protect and enhance natural resources. Some of the WDNR's areas of responsibility include: outdoor recreation, natural resources, environmental protection, licenses, permits and registration, environmental education and training.

Special Features: Weekly top headlines, just for kids web pages, magazine articles, searchable, Wisconsin wildlife

Curriculum: Biology; Environmental Studies; Science

2453 Wisconsin Department of Public Instruction

www.dpi.state.wi.us/

The WDPI ensures every child in the state of Wisconsin has an opportunity for a quality education through small class sizes, quality teachers and staff including parental involvement. The DPI is made up of five divisions: academic excellence, finance and management, equity and advocacy, libraries, technology, and community learning, reading and student achievement.

Special Features: Meet the state superintendent, directory of schools and libraries,

Curriculum: Education; Government

2454 Wisconsin Department of Tourism

www.travelwisconsin.com/

The Department of Tourism provides leadership to Wisconsin's tourism industry to ensure contributions to the state's economy and the quality of life. The official tourism site offers indoor and outdoor activities, maps, free guides of the state, multicultural news, and schedule of events. Sign up for e-news to get the latest events within the state.

Special Features: Travel packages, special events, fun stuff for kids, golf course links

Curriculum: Business; Economics; Geography; Social Studies

2455 Wisconsin Fast Plants Program (Sponsor: University of Wisconsin–Madison)

www.fastplants.org/home_flash.html

The Fast Plants Program was founded in 1986 by the University of Wisconsin to promote science education kindergarten through college and facilitate networking between teachers, scientists, and educators around the world. Fast plants are a rapid cycling plant that illustrates the life cycle in about 35–45 days. Teacher and student resources available online

Special Features: Online lesson plans, growing instructions, history of the plant

Curriculum: Biology; Science

2456 Wisconsin Historical Society

www.wisconsinhistory.org/

As one of the oldest publicly funded historical societies in the nation the Wisconsin Historical Society strives to engage the public in the relevance of history in our everyday lives. Research the past is made easy through library archives, genealogy links, historic buildings, museum collections, and online collections. Visit historic attractions such as Old World Wisconsin, Wade house, Villa Louis and Pendarvis.

Special Features: News, events, attractions, services, publications, kids' page

Curriculum: History; Social Studies

2457 Wisconsin Humane Society

www.wihumane.com/

Striving to create a community that values animals and treats them with respect, the Wisconsin Humane Society has existed since 1879. The virtual tour inside the society includes wild animals and domestic. See how wildlife rehabilitation works. Many programs are offered. These include: adoption and sterilization, telephone tip lines, summer camps and therapy dogs.

Special Features: Adopt a pet, wild animal information, kids pages, ask an expert, newsletters

Curriculum: Psychology; Sociology

2458 Wisconsin Humanities Council

www.wisconsinhumanities.org/

The Wisconsin Humanities Council or WHC was established in 1972 to bring the public programs that explore human culture, ideas and values. The WHC supports libraries, museums, universities, historical societies, schools and other nonprofit organizations through grants. Some well known programs funded by WHC include the Wisconsin Book Festival and the Speakers Bureau.

Special Features: Book discussions, listing of current programs offered by the WHC

Curriculum: Art; Education; Language Arts; Library Media; Sociology

2459 Wisconsin Interscholastic Athletic Association

www.wiaawi.org/

The Wisconsin Interscholastic Athletic Association or WIAA is the oldest high school athletic association in the country dating back to 1895. Today the WIAA promotes and regulates boys and girls high school events across the state. The site provides regulations, publications, official's licensure and rule changes, sportsmanship reference guide, and scholar athletes.

Special Features: Downloadable forms, events calendar, health issues, middle level handbooks and information

Curriculum: Health; Physical Education

2460 Wisconsin Library Association

www.wla.lib.wi.us/

Networking people and libraries, the Wisconsin Library Association is dedicated to legislation and funding, public information, leadership and professional growth, staff diversification and qualification. Read through news releases, and conference reports. Check the WLA units for individual interests such as media technology, reading, adult services, technical, and youth services.

Special Features: Searchable site, library hot topics

Curriculum: Library Media; Technology

2461 Wisconsin Maritime Museum

www.wimaritimemuseum.org/

The Wisconsin Maritime Museum is located in Manitowoc on the shore of Lake Michigan. The USS *Cobia* is a WWII U.S. Navy submarine now part of the museum available for touring. Some of the exhibits include: 1840's shipbuilding replica, scale model ship gallery, sixty-five ton steam engine, children's waterway room, and art gallery.

Special Features: Library and archives, newsletter, contact information

Curriculum: Art; History; Technology

2462 Wisconsin Milk Marketing Board, Wisconsin Dairy Producers

http://producer.wisdairy.com/

Wisconsin is known for its high quality dairy products. Look up any information about cheese and diary products, recipes, or nutritional information. Take a virtual tour of cheese making, use the cheese data for presentation, or look up cheese terms in the glossary. Tips for serving milk products to the lactose intolerant.

Special Features: News on osteoporosis, calcium, flavored milk, cow and farm data, breaking news, FAQ

Curriculum: Business; Health; Home Economics

2463 Wisconsin Newspaper Association

www.wnanews.com/

Established in 1853 the Wisconsin Newspaper Association or the WNA offers an inside look to how and what it takes to run a newspaper. Legislative updates, paper recycling, schedule of events for new coverage, advertising standards, and more. Includes careers in newspapers, collegiate presses, and conventions and workshops.

Special Features: Related newspaper links, contact information

Curriculum: Business; Language Arts; Sociology

2464 Wisconsin Public Radio

www.wpr.org/

Since 1917 Wisconsin Public Radio (WPR) has offered stimulating and entertaining programming to the radio listener. Experience such ideas as car humor, comedy quizzes, global affairs, medical advice, health information, pet care and local news. Searchable site offers keyword searching.

Special Features: Listener feedback, newsletters and reports, program index, volunteer opportunities

Curriculum: Health; Language Arts; Music

2465 Wisconsin State Cartographer's Office (Sponsor: Board of Regents of the University of Wisconsin)

www.geography.wisc.edu/sco/

The Wisconsin State Cartographer's Office or SCO gathers, maintains, and disseminates mapping and geo-spatial information about the state. The first state cartographer was appointed in 1974. Information offered on site include: maps, surveying basics, satellite imagery,

aerial photos, and digital orthophotography. Links and references available.

Special Features: News, events, publications, searchable maps

Curriculum: Environmental Studies; Geography; Technology

2466 Wisconsin State Legislature

www.legis.state.wi.us/

Take a virtual tour of the capitol, look at maps or find a legislator. Legislative activity is chronological or by subject. Full text Wisconsin constitution and the U.S. Declaration of Independence are offered. Election statistics, glossary of terms, census, links to other sites available

Special Features: Text only option, site map, citizen's guide, searchable

Curriculum: Government; History; Social Studies

2467 Wisconsin Wildlife Federation

www.wiwf.org/

Started in 1949 the Wisconsin Wildlife Federation or WiWF strives to educate the public about conservation to sustain the environment for future generations. Educational materials are available for teachers and organizations. Traveling education trunks include pelts, videos, skulls and more to teach such subjects as biology, habitats, predator prey relationships and endangered species.

Special Features: Backyard habitat program, meeting minutes, legislative issues

Curriculum: Biology; Environmental Studies; Science

2468 Wisconsin Women's Network

www.wiwomensnetwork.org/

The Wisconsin Women's Network is a statewide organization that strives to improve the status of women through communication, networking, promoting equity and justices for women. The WWN supports the following task forces: child care, economic security and aging. Read online newsletter for latest topics and issues.

Special Features: Calendar of events, contact information, related links

Curriculum: Business; Women's Studies

2469 Wistravel.com

www.wistravel.com/

Prepare for travel on Wistravel.com. Find out the latest activities going on in the state or find the nearest craft show. Print off free coupon for various vacation spots or find a map to the nearest of five hundred golf courses. Site includes such interests as: maps, accommodations, activities, team sports, antiques, crafts, casinos, dog tracks, state parks, campgrounds or education.

Special Features: Maps, weather, road conditions, extensive travel links

Curriculum: Business; Economics; Geography; Social Studies

WYOMING

2470 Buffalo Wyoming Community Directory

www.buffalowyoming.com

This site provides an electronic tour of Buffalo, Wyoming. Buffalo is located in an historic and recreationally rich area between the Black Hills of South Dakota and Yellowstone National Park. Buffalo is located on the historic Bozeman Trail and near numerous Indian Battlefields and western sites.

Special Features: Links include Frontier History, Outdoor Recreation, Lodging and Services, Religious, Shopping, Internet Marketing

Curriculum: Economics; Geography; History; Social Studies

2471 Bureau of Land Management: Wyoming

www.wy.blm.gov

The Bureau of Land Management in Wyoming manages over 18 million surface acres of public land and an additional 23 million subsurface acres of mineral estate. These lands are held in trust for the employment of, and use by, the American people. Its mission is to sustain health, diversity and productivity of the public lands for the use and enjoyment of present and future generations.

Special Features: Links include BLM Facts, Recreation, Minerals, Photo Library, FAQs, What's New

Curriculum: Economics; Environmental Studies; Geography; Social Studies

2472 Cody, Wyoming — Buffalo Bill's Town

www.comp-unltd.com/~rodeo/cody.html

Cody, Wyoming, was founded in 1896 by William F. "Buffalo Bill" Cody. The "Cody Nite Rodeo" has been hosted by Cody since 1938; the rodeo can be seen every night. It is the Rodeo Capital of the World! Cody is a short drive from Yellowstone National Park — the Wapiti Valley, Trail Town, Buffalo Bill Reservoir, and the Buffalo Bill Historical Center.

Special Features: Access to additional information regarding Red Canyon River Trips, Yellowstone National Park, Buffalo Bill Historical Center

Curriculum: Geography; History; Social Studies

2473 Education in Wyoming

www.k12.wy.us

One of the main goals at the Wyoming Department of Education is to serve the public through enhanced customer service. This site includes links to: Professional Teaching Standards Board; Wyoming Public Schools; Wyoming Education Association; Private Schools and Licensing; University of Wyoming; U.S. Department of Education; and the Wyoming Education Gateway.

Special Features: Includes links such as, Legislature, Superintendent's Office, Goals, Education Rules and Regulations, and State Board of Education

Curriculum: Education

2474 Genesee and Wyoming, Inc. (GWI)

www.gwrr.com

GWI is a world-class provider of rail-freight transportation and its supporting services. It functions as a holding company with subsidiaries that own and operate regional freight railroads.

They own or have interests in more than 20 railroads in five countries, over 8000 miles of owned or leased track, with access to an additional 3000 miles through track-access arrangements

Special Features: Links to GWI Worldwide Map, Governance, Press Releases, GWI History, For Railroad Buffs (including a Merchandise Depot)

Curriculum: Business; Economics; History; Science; Social Studies

2475 Historic Preservation in Wyoming

http://wyoshpo.state.wy.us

The Wyoming State Historic Preservation Office's mandate is to promote the preservation of cultural resources and to explore all alternatives for their preservation. The Wyoming SHPO carries out activities to accomplish this mandate — preserving and promoting Wyoming's heritage.

Special Features: Links include Online Data, State Parks, Cultural Resources, Public Education, General Information, Emigrant Trails, Digital Collections

Curriculum: Environmental Studies; Geography; History; Social Studies

2476 Jackson Hole Wildlife Film Festival

www.jhfestival.org

The Jackson Hole Wildlife Film Festival's mission is to encourage production or natural history programming around the world by providing nonfiction filmmakers and broadcasters with an international forum to conduct business, test new equipment, refine program production techniques and continue to seen new and effective ways to promote awareness and sensitivity to the conservation of wildlife.

Special Features: Links such as: News Center, Mailing List, Delegates, Technical Symposium Event, Film Festival Event

Curriculum: Social Studies

2477 KidCare CHIP

http://kidcare.state.sy.us

KidCare CHIP is a State of Wyoming program designed to ensure that children and teens of both working and non-working families can have the health insurance they need. CHIP offers health insurance coverage for Wyoming's children and teens through age 18 who are uninsured and meet income and eligibility guidelines.

Special Features: Links include Department of Health, EqualityCare, Wyoming Covering Kids, Immunization Schedule

Curriculum: Health

2478 Office of the Wyoming Attorney General

http://attorneygeneral.state.wy.us

The purpose of this website is to provide information about the work of the Attorney General's Office and to provide resources to the people of Wyoming. The Attorney General's office, by law, provides legal opinions only to elected and appointed state officials.

Special Features: Links include Administration Division, Human Services Division, Civil Division, Consumer Protection Unit, Criminal Division, Medicaid Fraud, Water and Natural Resources Division

Curriculum: Business; Economics; Government; History; Social Studies

2479 Petroleum Association of Wyoming (PAW)

www.pawyo.org

PAW is Wyoming's largest and oldest petroleum industry trade association, dedicated to the betterment of the state's oil and gas industry and public welfare. Through the PAW network, it monitors and responds to day-to-day activities vital in oil and gas areas.

Special Features: Useful Links include Headlines, Association Information, Committee Activities, Oil and Gas Facts, Industry Links

Curriculum: Business; Environmental Studies; Science; Social Studies

2480 Red Desert (Sponsor: National Wildlife Federation)

www.nwf.org/reddesert

Tucked away in southwestern Wyoming, the Red Desert remains one of the last high-desert ecosystems in North America. Long before the West was settled, this region played a significant role in the lives of native peoples, such as the Shoshone and Ute tribes.

Special Features: Explores the Red Desert via a virtual tour, unearths the deserts of the world, offers Meet the Animals that call the Red Desert home

Curriculum: Environmental Studies; Geography; History; Social Studies

2481 University of Wyoming: Art Museum

http://uwadmnweb.uwyo.edu/ArtMuseum

The University of Wyoming Art Museum was established in 1972 to preserve, exhibit and interpret the breadth of the visual arts and cultural artifacts throughout time. Supported by public and private funds, the University of Wyoming Art Museum was created to serve the people of Wyoming and those who visit there.

Special Features: Links to the Museum include: Academics, A–Z Directory, Calendar, Research, Feature Exhibitions

Curriculum: Art

2482 University of Wyoming, Department of Atmospheric Science

www-das.uwyo.edu

The University of Wyoming Department Of Atmospheric Science contains items which people should find useful. It also offers information about the research activities and facilities that are at the heart of this department. Anyone with an interest in the atmosphere and weather will find something new to view at this website.

Special Features: Useful Links include Research, Weather, Flight Center, What's New

Curriculum: Geography; Science; Social Studies

2483 USGS Water Resources of Wyoming

http://wy.water.usgs.gov

The USGS provides maps, reports and information to help others met their needs to manage, develop and protect America's water, energy, mineral and land resources. It assists in finding natural resources needed for tomorrow, and supplies scientific understanding required to minimize and mitigate the effects of natural hazards.

Special Features: Links include Real-time Data, Stream flow Data, Water-quality Data, Ground-water Data, Water Data Reports, Maps and Publications, Projects and Studies

Curriculum: Business; Economics; Environmental Studies; Geography; History; Science; Social Studies

2484 Welcome to the State of Wyoming

http://wyoming.gov

This is the official site for the state of Wyoming. It includes government, business, education, tourism, news and a virtual tour. This site also provides Wyoming information (State capital, motto, etc.), facts about Wyoming, a narrative about Wyoming, historical dates, heritage resources, the State Constitution, and the Wyoming Geographic information Advisory Council.

Special Features: KidsPage includes Wyoming School Kids, Stories about Wyoming, Wyoming Wildlife, Puzzles and Fun Stuff, Dinosaur Quiz Page

Curriculum: Business; Economics; Education; Geography; Government; History; Social Studies

2485 Wyoming Agriculture in the Classroom

www.wyoagcenter.com/waic/classroom.html

The mission of Wyoming Agriculture in the Classroom is to raise the awareness and understand of its natural resources among educators and students to enhance the value of agriculture to society. Their vision is a future in which the interdependence of people, agriculture and natural resources is recognized and valued.

Special Features: Great links for the classroom: Discovery Tool chest, Teacher Workshops, Student Contests, Agriculture Literacy in Wyoming, Ag Literacy Quizzes

Curriculum: Economics; Environmental Studies; Geography; History; Science; Social Studies

2486 Wyoming Arts Council (WAC)

www.wyoarts.com/

The Wyoming Arts Council includes events in the following areas: archaeology, children's, conferences, workshops, classes, dance, fairs and festivals, literary, music, humanities, paleontology, state parks, historic sites, theatre and visual arts.

Special Features: Under the area of children's, one can view events for the month, such as Children's Super Saturday at the Museum — Railroads and Wyoming State Museum — Wee-Ones

Curriculum: Art; Dance; Drama; History; Language Arts; Music; Social Studies

2487 Wyoming Art Galleries and Gallery Guide

http://art-collecting.com/galleries_wy.htm

This website offers the Wyoming art gallery guide and listing of fine art galleried located in Wyoming. These galleries feature contemporary art, traditional fine art, fine art photography, glass art, prints, sculpture and numerous other visual arts.

Special Features: Provides online access to several art galleries in Wyoming, including the Jackson Art Galleries

Curriculum: Art

2488 Wyoming Association of Municipalities (WAM)

www.wyomuni.org

The purpose of WAM is to build strong communities. Each person in Wyoming lives, works, studies, recreates, shops, conducts business, or just spends time in their 98 incorporated cities and towns. WAM strives to make their communities the best possible for the citizens who live there.

Special Features: Links such as, Advocacy, Allied Members, Events, FYI, National League of Cities, Publications, Trail Mix

Curriculum: Business; Economics; Geography; Government; History; Social Studies

2489 Wyoming Attractions: Roadside America

www.roadsideamerica.com/map.wy.html

Roadside America visits and reviews weird sites along the highways of Wyoming. Examples include the World's Largest Elk, Tree in the Rock, Daily Street Gunfights, Ride a Jackalope, Old West Wax Museum, House-made Dinosaur Bones, the World's Largest Turbine and Sundance Kid Exchange.

Special Features: The Dinosaur Bone House: Medicine Bow. Made of 26,000 fossils—the oldest cabin in the world stands next to the dinosaur graveyard

Curriculum: Geography; History; Science; Social Studies

2490 Wyoming Business Council

www.wyomingbusiness.org/home/index.cfm

Facilitating Wyoming's economic growth, this council includes business information and resources. Working with the Business Council will assist one to become business ready. It offers links to travel and tourism in Wyoming, an Interactive Business Center and Commercial Properties Database.

Special Features: Regional Offices: Agribusiness, Business and Industry, Investment Ready Communities, Technology, Mineral, Energy and Transportation, Film and Arts

Curriculum: Business

2491 Wyoming Children's Action Alliance

www.wykids.com/

A non-profit organization which administers several programs encouraging the well-being of Wyoming children. Desired outcome is that Wyoming will have a strong, well-trained early care and education workforce to meet the physical, social, emotional, language and cognitive developmental needs of young children.

Special Features: A Statewide Training and Resource System (WYStars) and an Apprenticeship program, a mentoring program that encourages child care providers who have been in the business for several years to be available to new child care providers just entering the field

Curriculum: Education

2492 Wyoming Coalition against Domestic Violence and Sexual Assault

www.users.qwest.net/~wyomingcoalition

The Wyoming Coalition against Domestic Violence and Sexual Assault supports its members so that they can accomplish more together than alone to provide advocacy and safety for victims of domestic violence and sexual assault in their communities. Their goal is to provide a state level voice for local programs and participate in policy and planning activities with other state level governmental private agencies.

Special Features: This coalition strengthens and energizes member programs by providing resources, training and technical assistance to ensure quality public education to every community

Curriculum: Sociology; Women's Studies

2493 Wyoming Coalition for the Homeless

www.vcn.com/~wch

The Coalition was founded in 1990. In 1995, Publication of StreetViews began, followed In 1996 with writing workshops and poetry readings. In 1997, this coalition began making sleeping bags for adults, later for children on

Indian Reservations and refugee programs. A clothing closed opened in 1999; an Annual Walk in My Shoes to make money for the homeless.

Special Features: Links include Services Available, Funds Needed, Homeless Memorial Day, Street News Service, Street Papers, Wyoming Shelters and Services

Curriculum: Economics; Social Studies; Sociology

2494 Wyoming Companion

www.wyomingcompanion.com

The Wyoming companion is an online magazine and visitor's guide. Useful links include: Today in Wyoming, Free Weekly Newsletter, From the Banks of the Firehole, Wyoming Communities, Wyoming Web Cameras, Yellowstone Picture of the Day, and Best of the West.

Special Features: The Wyoming Companion offers: Wyoming Twilight Photo, Wyoming Guides, Wyoming Arts Guide, The Year in Photos, Outdoor Recreation, Yellowstone National Park Picture of the Day

Curriculum: Geography; Social Studies

2495 Wyoming Dinosaur Center and Dig Site

http://server.1.wyodino.org/index2.htm

This site includes a World-Class Museum, with interpretive displays, dioramas and life-size mounts, as well as exhibits covering all facets of early life and preparation laboratory observation. In addition, it offers Active Digsites, with over 60 identified dinosaur digsites in a 500-acre area.

Special Features: Programs and Activities: Digsite Tours, Dig-for-a-Day Programs, Kids' Digs

Curriculum: Biology; Geography; History; Science; Social Studies

2496 Wyoming Energy Council, Inc.

www.nonprofitpages.com/wec

The Wyoming Energy Council, Inc., is a nonprofit corporation chartered in 1981 as the Albany County Energy Council. The name changed in 1996 to reflect an expanded scope of operations throughout the State of Wyoming. Currently, it is active in eight counties. Its mission is to encourage energy conservation and energy alternatives in the State of Wyoming.

Special Features: Links: Wyoming Weatherization Assistance Association, Weatherization Managers Association, Energy Efficient Builders Association, EPA Energy Star Ally Program

Curriculum: Business; Economics; Environmental Studies; Social Studies

2497 Wyoming Head Start Collaboration Project

http://wind.uwyo.edu/headstart/

Wyoming Head Start State Collaboration Project (WHS-SCP) is located in the Wyoming, Wyoming and focuses on childcare, education, health, welfare reform, family literacy, and disabilities. Mission is to strengthen partnerships in Wyoming, which foster a comprehensive and quality early childhood system firmly grounded in the Head Start principle of serving children and families.

Special Features: A quarterly newsletter (*Collaboration Comminique*), a list of head start programs in the state, related Internet sites and the Wyoming Institute for Disabilities (WIND)

Curriculum: Education; Special Education

2498 Wyoming Libraries

http://gowyld.net/wyoming/education.html

Comprehensive website provides information about the Wyoming Department of Education, Wyoming Higher Education, Wyoming K–12 Schools, Wyoming Comprehensive Assessment System (WyCAS), Wyoming Teacher Education and Certification, Wyoming Education Organizations, Literacy in Wyoming, Preschool and Homeschooling, Education Statistics.

Special Features: Information about WyCAS, WyCAS results, sample questions and frequently asked questions; the Wyoming Education Statistical Report; and Northwest Literacy Information and Communication System (LINCS)

Curriculum: Education

2499 Wyoming Library Association (WLA)

www.wyla.org

The vision of the Wyoming Library Association is that the educational, cultural and economic conditions of Wyoming will be advanced through greater use of libraries and an enhanced awareness of the vital role libraries fulfill in society.

Special Features: Links include WLA Committees, WLA Sections, Boards and Trustees,

ALA Councilor, WLA Newsletter, WLA Membership
Curriculum: Library Media

2500 Wyoming Livestock Roundup Online

www.wyoagcenter.com

This site is a weekly news source for Wyoming's farmers, ranchers and agribusiness communities. It includes current information, including From the Publisher, From the Editor, Classifieds and Wyoming Properties.

Special Features: Useful Links include Market Reports, Sales and Auctions, Cowboy Bookmark, Inside this Week
Curriculum: Business; Economics; Social Studies

2501 Wyoming Medical Society

www.wyomed.org

The Wyoming Medical Society was founded in 1903 to provide representation, advocacy and service to Wyoming physicians. It serves Wyoming physicians and their patients in two ways: advocates for physicians and quality health care for patients and improved public health for all Wyoming residents.

Special Features: Links provided include Physician Finder, Current Issues, Legislative/Regulatory, Links of Interest
Curriculum: Health

2502 Wyoming Mining Association

www.wma-minelife.com

The Wyoming Mining Association represents 24 mining companies who operate 50 mines, producing a variety of minerals essential to the nation's economy. It serves as a unified voice, providing value at a reasonable cost to its membership, by communicating, influencing and promoting issues on behalf of the mining industry.

Special Features: Links to Bentonite, Coal, Trona, Uranium, Reclamation
Curriculum: Environmental Studies; Geography; Science; Social Studies

2503 Wyoming Music Educators Association (WMEA)

http://uwacadweb.uwyo.edu/BRINKMAN/wmea.htm

The Wyoming Music Educators Association (WMEA) is the Wyoming affiliate of MENC —

Music Educators National Conference. Members include Kindergarten through 12th grade, college/university and private music instructors throughout Wyoming.

Special Features: Links, such as MENC (National Organization), Standards, Music Ed Links, K–12 Schools; as well as the state magazine, *Windsong* and possible scholarships
Curriculum: Music

2504 Wyoming Nature Conservancy

www.tncwyoming.org

Wyoming is a land of rich natural diversity, wide-open spaces, abundant wildlife and few people. This poses a rare conservation opportunity to choose a future path that will sustain this extraordinary land. Because Wyoming still retains much of its original character, it is a great opportunity to maintain the tapestry of this natural world.

Special Features: This site includes: The Way We Work, People conserving Wyoming, Where We Work, News and much information about hunting, fishing and wildlife of Wyoming
Curriculum: Biology; Environmental Studies; Geography; Social Studies

2505 Wyoming Outdoor Council (WOC)

www.wyomingoutdoorcouncil.org

WOC is Wyoming's largest statewide conservation organization and the state's leading natural resources conservation and environmental protection. WOC works to safeguard the national parks and protected areas, vast national forest, blue-ribbon fisheries and air quality. WOC's work encompasses a broad range of conservation issues that affect Wyoming.

Special Features: Links include Programs, News, Library, Conservation
Curriculum: Economics; Environmental Studies; Geography; Social Studies

2506 Wyoming Pets Directory

http://wyoming.uscity.net/Pets/

The Wyoming Pets Directory includes links such as: Puppymill Rescue, Paw Print Pet Stockings, Allpets, American Veterinary Medical Association, Humane Society of the United States, Pet Blessings, Pets Warehouse and the American Society for the Prevention of Cruelty to Animals.

Special Features: Under Pets Services Directory, one can view: American Humane Associ-

ation, Just4Pooches, National Association of Professional Pet Sitters, People for Ethical Treatment of Animals, the Pet Wellness System
Curriculum: Social Studies

2507 Wyoming Project Nova

www.wytec.org

Project Nova's mission includes a strategy for integrating technology, collaboration, research and real world activities into education. It is also intended to improve the scientific and technological literacy in the United States and around the world.
Special Features: This site includes the following links: Virtual Field Trips, Mobile Classroom, A Universe of Resources, Workshops, Videoconferencing, Training School
Curriculum: Science; Technology

2508 Wyoming Public Libraries

www.publiclibraries.com

The Wyoming Public Libraries' mission is to serve people with easy access to the use of public libraries and promote reading. This goal is made possible via participation of local libraries. This site is resourceful for individuals, families, schools and organizations.
Special Features: Includes a directory of all Wyoming Public Libraries, as well as State, University, Presidential, National Libraries
Curriculum: Library Media

2509 Wyoming Rural Development Council (WRDC)

www.wyomingrural.org

The WRDC, a collaborative partnership, serves as a forum to address a full range of issues, opportunities and potential solutions in the rural communities of Wyoming. One current project seeks participants to help low-income families create sustainable income through entrepreneurship.
Special Features: Another special grant program supports arts-based rural community development projects, helping demonstrate the importance and value of the arts in rural areas
Curriculum: Art; Business; Geography; Government; Social Studies; Sociology

2510 Wyoming School Boards Association (WSBA)

www.wsba-wy.org

WSBA is the official voice of its member local school boards. It is dedicated to improving educational opportunities for all of Wyoming's public school students through the improvement of local school board governance.
Special Features: Links include Wyoming Association of School Business Officials, Wyoming Parent Education Network. Wyoming State Department of Education
Curriculum: Education

2511 Wyoming Small Business Development Center

http://uwadmnweb.uwyo.edu/SBDC

The Wyoming Small Business Development Center's mission is to strengthen Wyoming business and create economic growth by providing excellent management assistance, educational programs and helpful resources for the state's small businesses and entrepreneurs.
Special Features: Links include Consulting (personalized consulting service), Training Programs (workshops, conferences and courses), Resources Library (books, videos, periodicals), Referral Programs
Curriculum: Business

2512 Wyoming State Geological Survey

www.wsgs.uwyo.edu

The Wyoming State Geological Survey's mission is to promote the beneficial and environmentally sound use of Wyoming's vast geologic, mineral and energy resources, while helping protect the public from geologic hazards. It contributes to economic growth and improvement in the quality of life for Wyoming's citizens.
Special Features: Featured Links: Digital Map Series, 2003 Results, information on Yellowstone Lake Bubble, Wyoming Educational Coal mine, Realtime Earthquake Information
Curriculum: Economics; Geography; Science; Social Studies

2513 Wyoming State Museum

http://wyomuseum.state.wy.us

Founded in 1895, the mission of the Wyoming State Museum is to serve as an educational, historical and cultural institution, whose goal is to collect, preserve and interpret artifacts that reflect the human and natural history of Wyoming.
Special Features: Links to Programs and

Events, Exhibits and Galleries, Educational Programs, Trivia Questions

Curriculum: Art; Science; Social Studies; Sociology

2514 Wyoming Tales and Trails

www.wyomingtalesandtrails.com

Tales include, for example, Stories of the Central Overland and California Pony Express, Haunted Places in Wyoming, Tale of Old Fort Laramie and the Hole-in-the-Wall Fight. Examples of trails are the Oregon Trail, Overland Trail, Mormon Trail, Cherokee Trail and Bozeman Trail.

Special Features: Over 700 historical photos illustrating the history of Wyoming

Curriculum: Geography; Language Arts; Geography; History; Social Studies

2515 Wyoming Territorial Park (WTP)

www.wyoprisonpark.org/prisonmuseum.htm

WTP is a unique living history/cultural heritage facility in Laramie, Wyoming. The centerpiece of the Park is the Wyoming Territorial Prison Museum, which was built in 1872 and restored in 1989. This was the only prison to house Butch Cassidy, among other ruffians that intimidated the people of the Wyoming Territory.

Special Features: Includes Frontier Town (western-style entertainment), Ranchland Exhibit (view of life in the prairie in the 1800s, Horse Barn Dinner Theater

Curriculum: Drama; Language Arts; Geography; History; Social Studies

2516 Wyoming Travel

www.travel-to-wyoming.com

Wyoming is a state where names memorialize struggles to settle the West, Spring Creek Raid at Tensleep, the Bloody Bozeman Trail, Crazy Woman Creek and more. These frontier museums display unparalleled pioneer treasures and historical reenactments. Wyoming is a state of legend and intrigue.

Special Features: Useful Links include History, Events, Recreation, Museums, Activities, Maps

Curriculum: Geography; Social Studies

2517 Wyoming Women's Foundation

www.wycf.org/wyowomens.html

The Wyoming Women's Foundation is an endowed fund of the WYCF that supports economic self-sufficiency and access to opportunities for women and girls in Wyoming by raising funds, making grants and providing leadership. "Reality for Wyoming's women and girls can be as harsh as the climate."

Special Features: Foundation notes that women: are more likely to be homeless, live in poverty, more likely to be unemployed, face violence and fear, suffer inadequate housing and health care

Curriculum: Economics; Sociology; Women's Studies

2518 Wyoming Writers, Inc. (WWI)

www.wyowriters.org

WWI is a not-for-profit corporation focused on helping Wyoming authors achieve their full potential. Organized in 1974, the organization has helped a full generation of writers develop expertise, receive recognition and find their true voice in the American West.

Special Features: Links include Events and Programs, News Board, Constitution and By-laws, Member Sites, Sites for Writers

Curriculum: Language Arts

Appendix A:
Sites for All States

2519 American Cancer Society

www.cancer.org/asp/search/mla/mla_global.as
p?sort=name

Click on a state and find American Cancer offices in that state. Information about Prevention and Early Detection, State Facts and Figures, Research.

Special Features: Message Boards, News, PDFs
Curriculum: Health

2520 American Educational Guidance Center

www.college-scholarships.com/index.html#
State_Pages

Over a thousand college sand universities by state, college scholarship and financial aid searches, SAT and ACT test preparation tips.

Special Features: Information on graduate schools, GRE and GMAT examinations, community colleges, and other help
Curriculum: Counseling

2521 American Folklife Center

www.loc.gov/folklife/roots/

A Local Legacies Project in which the Library of Congress collected information from over a thousand community and cultural events which help capture the "Uniqueness of our nation and the pride of its citizens in their heritage." The states are represented as well as the District of Columbia, American Samoa, Guam, Puerto Rico, and the Virgin Islands. Local festivals, parades, barbeques, and other grassroots activities are among those represented.

Special Features: Picture of featured events
Curriculum: Art; Music; Social Studies

2522 The American History and Genealogy Project (AHGP)

www.ahgp.org/states.html

An unincorporated not-for-profit network of independent sites devoted to history and genealogy hosted by individuals within each state which covers various aspects such as newspapers, famous people, cemetery records, cities, major events, counties.

Special Features: Each state presents itself differently since it has different creators and webmasters
Curriculum: History

2523 State Trees (Sponsor: Athenic Systems)

www.treeguide.com/State_trees.asp

The official symbolic tree of each state in the United States. For most of the states you can obtain a list of all tree species known to be native or naturalized in that state. From that list, you can get natural history descriptions, range maps, photographs and other information about the trees.

Special Features: Includes scientific names
Curriculum: Science

2524 Children's Bureau

http://nccanch.acf.hhs.gov/general/statespecifi
c/index.cfm

National Clearinghouse on Child Abuse and Neglect Information resources includes state by state access to laws governing child abuse and neglect, and conferences and training such as: State Statutes, Disclosure of Confidential Records for this state, Definitions of Child Abuse and Neglect for this State, Reporting Laws for this State, Mandatory Reporters for this State, Reporting Penalties for this State, Central Registry/Reporting Records Expungement for this State, Grounds for Termination of Parental Rights for this State.

Special Features: A–Z Index, e-mail contact, Professional Section, Spanish option

Curriculum: Counseling; Education; Psychology; Social Studies

2525 Cooperative State, Research, Education, and Extension Service

www.csrees.usda.gov/qlinks/partners/state_partners.html

Provides educators with innovative ways to enhance educational programs in the classroom, after-school programs, child care programs, and communities. Students gain firsthand knowledge through experiential learning activities in areas such as healthy diet and weight, financial planning and management, the community, the environment, and safety.

Special Features: Information is geared to state needs

Curriculum: Business; Health; Home Economics; Social Studies

2526 Documents Center, University of Michigan Library

www.lib.umich.edu/govdocs/stats.html

Wide selection of statistical resources in broad categories as Agriculture, Education, Health, Transportation that include states and cities such as: *Statistical Abstract of the United States*. Information can be accessed: Frames Version, or No Frames Version. PDF files.

Special Features: Information featuring the current month topics in the news such as state-by-state marriage laws, state primary elections by state

Curriculum: Math; Social Studies

2527 Educational Resources Information Center (ERIC)

www.eduref.org/Eric/

ERIC is the world's largest source of education information, funded by the U.S. Department of Education. The database is updated monthly and provides access to ERIC documents from 1966. Use the searching tips, place the state you are looking for and information will be retrieved.

Special Features: Topics A–Z, Site Map

Curriculum: Education

2528 Extension Disaster Education Network

www.agctr.lsu.edu/eden/default.aspx

EDEN links educators from across the United States enabling them to use and share resources to reduce the impact of disasters. Covers such aspects as food safety, physical and psychological impacts.

Special Features: Current Topics such as West Nile Virus, Homeland Security. Each state's website reflects government resources, contacts of officials, educator resources

Curriculum: Social Studies

2529 Federal Citizen Information Center

www.kids.gov/

The U.S. government interagency Kids' Portal developed and maintained by the Federal Citizen Information Center. It provides links to Federal kids' sites along with some of the best kids' sites from other organizations grouped by subject. By clicking State Sites, the sites relating to states appears.

Special Features: Each state provides a variety of information, including downloading opportunities, homework guides.

Curriculum: Social Studies

2530 Federal Resources for Educational Excellence (FREE)

www.ed.gov/free

About fifty federal agencies such as the Advisory Council on Historic Preservation and the Department of Army, The White House, formed a working group, FREE, to make hundreds of federally supported teaching and learning resources easier to find. Each month new teaching and learning resources are added. Access what relates to each state by using search option.

Special Features: Teaching materials from a federally supported consortium is also available

Curriculum: Education; Library Media

2531 FedStats

www.fedstats.gov/qf/

Profiles by state, county, federal judicial district, congressional district by over 100 federal agencies. Access to such statistics as: population, births, deaths, language spoken, education level, persons below poverty as compared with national standard.

Special Features: Kids' pages on agency websites

Curriculum: Social Studies

2532 Fiftystates.com

www.50states.com/news/

For the state you select, it brings you to the newspapers for that state: name of the newspaper, city of publication. Online editions with graphics.

Special Features: Study Tools, College Links

Curriculum: Language Arts

2533 Global Information Locator Service (GILS)

www.gils.net/

The goal of the Global Information Locator Service is to make it easier for people to find information based on title, author, publisher, date, and place. Among its most common forms are those dealing with public access to government information.

Special Features: The Clearinghouse for Geospatial Data helps searcher for maps and answer questions

Curriculum: Geography; Social Studies

2534 The Henry J. Kaiser Family Foundation

www.statehealthfacts.kff.org/cgi-bin/healthfacts.cgi?action=profile&area=Arkansas&category=Demographics+and+the+Economy&subcategory=Geography

State Health Facts Online includes state comparisons, state profiles for such areas as: Demographics and the economy which includes topics like adult poverty; Women's Health; Minority Health, Health Costs and Budgets.

Special Features: Fact sheets, glossary

Curriculum: Health; Sociology

2535 Humane Society of the United States

www.hsus.org/ace/352

Searchable state by state. For example, when Michigan was entered, 57 articles covering recent legislations, news about a wide range of animals was available for that state.

Special Features: Link to the Humane Society of the United States Regional Office serving your state. Educational materials designed for the classroom and library

Curriculum: Government; Social Studies

2536 National Agricultural Statistics Service

www.usda.gov/nass/sso-rpts.htm

American agriculture is continually counted, measured, priced, analyzed, and reported to provide the facts needed by people working throughout this vast industry. Each year, hundreds of surveys and prepare reports cover U.S. production and supplies of food and fiber, prices paid and received by farmers, farm labor and wages, farm aspects of the industry. State-by-state access.

Special Features: Today's Reports bring the latest news

Curriculum: Business; Social Studies

2537 The National Assembly of State Arts Agencies

www.nasaa-arts.org/aoa/saadir.shtml

A state arts agency directory: click on any state to access information about the arts; includes the title of the agency, U.S. Postal Service address, telephone, fax, agency's website, officers. Also includes regional arts organizations such as: Arts Midwest, Mid Atlantic Arts Foundation. Includes U.S. Jurisdictions such as Guam, Virgin Islands. Offers publications for leaders.

Special Features: Includes such links as: State Spotlight, Arts Over America, Artworks

Curriculum: Art

2538 National Center for Education Statistics

http://nces.ed.gov/globallocator/

Search for schools, colleges, and libraries by state. Selection can be made by public schools, private schools, colleges, public libraries, or all of the institutions. Browse for city option. Names can be sorted by name, city, or state. Option of distance in miles from a zip code.

Special Features: Provides name, address, phone, name of county, grades, enrollment by race/ethnicity, student/teacher ratio and related facts

Curriculum: Social Studies

2539 National Historic Landmarks Program

www.cr.nps.gov/

States may be searched for National Historic Landmarks in the National Park Service. Each landmark's location is given and if it is district, structure, or building landmark. Includes date it was designated, pictures, and why it is significant, and related information.

Special Features: Teaching With Historic Places Lesson Plans

Curriculum: History

2540 National History Day Organization

www.nationalhistoryday.org/

National History Day program promotes systemic educational reform related to the teaching and learning of history in America's schools, combining creativity and scholarship for grades 6–12. Select a state to get in contact with your state's volunteer coordinators. The National History Day program is a year-long education program that culminates in an annual national contest in June.

Special Features: PDFs to download

Curriculum: History

2541 National Park Service

www.nps.gov

Federal source for parks under the National Park Service. Locate parks by using the: Visit Your Parks alphabetical listing by name, or use the search option by entering a particular state.

Special Features: Learn NPR for Teachers and Learners; Nature Net

Curriculum: Social Studies

2542 National Women's History Project

www.nwhp.org/tlp/performers/performers.html

The National Women's History Project is an educational nonprofit organization to recognize and celebrate the diverse and historic accomplishments of women by providing information and educational materials and programs. Resources includes: Teachers Lounge; Student Center; History Quiz, and other resources. States may be accessed for performers that includes a description of the performer, what states they cover, their website, and other ways of contacting them.

Special Features: Tips for program planning

Curriculum: History; Women's Studies

2543 NSTATE

www.netstate.com/states/index.html

State symbols, almanac-type survey information, geography, map, people, forum, news, schools, state ranking, lists such as the state's birds and trees.

Special Features: Quizzes for each state

Curriculum: Geography; Social Studies

2544 Office of Juvenile Justice and Delinquency Prevention

http://ojjdp.ncjrs.org/ojstatbb/html/POPULATION.html

State by state information on such topics as: high school completion rates, juveniles living in poverty, birth rates for mothers 15–17, juvenile population by race.

Special Features: Publications available by HTML, PDF, print

Curriculum: Social Studies

2545 Office on Violence Against Women

www.ojp.usdoj.gov/vawo/stategrants.htm

State-by-State Offices on Violence Against Women Grant Activities administered by the United States Department of Justice's formula and discretionary grant programs authorized by the Violence Against Women Act of 1994. Archives by fiscal year, publications, press releases, information about sexual assault.

Special Features: Help numbers for domestic violence

Curriculum: Women's Studies

2546 School Information Partnership

www.SchoolResults.org/

A partnership is a public-private collaborative of the U.S. Department of Education, Standard & Poor's School Evaluation Services, National Center for Educational Accountability's Just for the Kids, The Broad Foundation to provide timely and comparable education data on schools, school districts, and states nationwide. Data tables such as reading and math assessments by grade, yearly progress, teacher qualifications, enrollment.

Special Features: Interactive analytic tools allows users to create side-by-side comparisons and search schools or districts within the state based on selected criteria

Curriculum: Education

2547 State and Local Government (Sponsor: Piper Resources)

www.statelocalgov.net/

State and Local Government on the Net is a frequently updated directory of links to government sponsored and controlled resources on the Internet created by Piper Resources providing access to the websites of thousands of state agencies and city and county governments. Each state begins with a state home page, directory, statewide offices, branches of state government, boards and commissions, regional groups, a listing of counties, cities, charter townships, villages, state groups.

Special Features: Includes libraries
Curriculum: Government; Library Media

2548 State by State (Sponsor: Software Solutions)

www.thingstodo.com/facts.html

State by state: Attractions, National and State Parks, State Histories, Interesting Facts, State Symbols, News Resources, State Event Calendars. For example, under State History, about two printed pages worth of information that includes a timeline.

Special Features: Famous People includes capsules with access to more complete biography and added photos
Curriculum: Social Studies

2549 State Information (Sponsor: Pearson Education)

www.infoplease.com/states.html

Select a state and obtain such information as: capital, median age, elected officials, history, state motto, name origins, counties, and related information from Infoplease. Printable maps, flags. Summary biographies of famous people include links to where they appear in The Columbia Electronic Encyclopedia.

Special Features: Homework Center; Infoplease for Teachers
Curriculum: Social Studies

2550 State Summaries (Sponsor: The Library of Congress)

www.americasstory.com/cgi-bin/page.cgi/es

For the state you click, a summary that includes how it got its name, some of the state symbols such as the state bird and flower, is provided as well as articles about that state's famous people and history to choose.

Special Features: Site Map; Jump Back in Time; See, Hear and Sing links
Curriculum: History; Music; Social Studies

2551 State Port Laureates (Sponsor: The Library of Congress Main Reading Room)

www.loc.gov/rr/main/poets/poetlist.html

States may be accessed to see the poets laureates for the state. The name, date the poet was named, official action regarding the naming. Those having none are noted.

Special Features: Bibliographies and Guides, Search Option, Ask a Librarian
Curriculum: Language Arts

2552 United States Census Bureau

www.factfinder.census.gov

Census statistics are fascinating as presented under the Kids' Corner section. Each state may be accessed for fun facts covering the last two census figures in such areas as: Median Age, Average Family Size, Total Housing Units, Farm Population.

Special Features: Includes each state's capital, date of statehood, flower, tree, bird. Main screen includes: Bureau's Latest News, Population Estimates Program
Curriculum: Math; Social Science

2553 United States Department of Agriculture

www.agclassroom.org/teacher/stats.htm

Agriculture in the classroom: teacher resources. You will need Adobe Acrobat Reader 4.0 or above to read the PDF files, which you can download. Agricultural State Profiles. Agriculture in the Classroom Consortium, Conferences.

Special Features: Kids Zone, Teen Scene. Teacher Resources includes lesson plans, science projects, awards, grants, resource directory
Curriculum: Science; Social Studies

2554 United States Department of Commerce

www.commerce.gov

The federal department includes various offices and bureaus. Click on a state featured on the map of the United States (including Guam and

Puerto Rico) and reports are available from such sources as: The Census Bureau, International Trade Administration. Includes latest economic indicators.

Special Features: Today's weather within each state from the National Oceanic & Atmospheric Administration; Official Time in Your Area from the National Institute of Standards and Technology

Curriculum: Science; Social Studies

2555 United States Department of Education

www.thegateway.org

The Gateway to Educational Materials (GEM) provides educators with access to resources found on various federal, state, university, nonprofit, and commercial Internet sites. Search by state using the keyword search and obtain several sites about the state; when I looked for Alaska, I got eighty-three.

Special Features: Grade levels from Pre-K through Higher Education may be selected

Curriculum: Library Media

2556 United States Department of Health & Human Services

www.dhhs.gov

This federal agency's information may be accessed by one of its ten regions or by state. Some of the agencies that are within this department include: Administration for Children and families, Administration on Aging, Agency for Toxic Substances and Disease Registry, and Health Resources and Services Administration.

Special Features: HHS Pages for Kids; Are You a Working Teen?; The Surgeon General's Report for Kids about Smoking

Curriculum: Health

2557 United States Department of Labor

www.bls.gov/oco/oco20024.htm

Links to state labor employment security agencies that provide information such as: location of local offices, unemployment benefits, job training, jobs needing licenses, wages and salaries, employment outlooks and projections, jobs for veterans and those with disabilities.

Special Features: *Occupational Outlook Handbook* provides labor information for the nation as a whole

Curriculum: Business; Counseling

2558 United States Fish and Wildlife Service

www.fws.gov

Federal source for information about the agency responsible the nation's fish and wildlife. Search by state provides a state map locating ecological service offices, national wildlife refuges, wetland management districts, national fish hatcheries, fishery resource offices, law enforcement offices. Links to each, phone numbers, and updates about current programs.

Special Features: Kids/Education; Endangered Species

Curriculum: Science

2559 United States Forest Service

www.fs.fed.us/

Accesses national forests within each state that has them; the national forest's location is shown on a state map. Publications, upcoming events, photo, visitor information, mailing address, projects relating to that national forest are included.

Special Features: Just for Kids includes fun activities

Curriculum: Science

2560 United States General Services Administration

www.pueblo.gsa.gov/crh/banking.htm

State by state banking authorities who answer general questions about banking and consumer credit. The officials regulate and supervise state-chartered banks. U.S. Postal Address, telephone number, fax number, e-mail address, web site are provided.

Special Features: Middle School Lesson Plans

Curriculum: Math; Social Studies

2561 United States Geological Survey

www.usgs.gov

Federal source for the science about the earth, living resources, natural hazards such as floods, earthquakes. Each state may be accessed under: USGS Information by State.

Special Features: Students and Teachers; Maps

Curriculum: Geography

2562 United States Government Printing Office

http://bensguide.gpo.gov/

Ben's Guide to U.S. Government, an award winning service of the Superintendent of Documents, is designed for kids, parents, and teachers. The material for children is divided into: K–2; 3–5; 6–8; 9–12. State information includes state's motto, bird, when it became a state, largest cities, state song and related information.

Special Features: Includes a picture of each state's congressperson, e-mail links
Curriculum: Social Studies

2563 United States House of Representatives

www.house.gov/

Access each state representatives. For example, the seven representatives for Alabama may be accessed, which is followed by the one representing Alaska. States are listed alphabetically and representatives for each state are included alphabetically with their district.

Special Features: What is on the current House Floor
Curriculum: Government

2564 United States Senate

www.senate.gov/

Senators for any state may be located by selecting a state. Once selected, their party is given, address, phone number, and web address. Each is given a classification which indicates the year their terms expire.

Special Features: Biographical Directory about any senator. Organizational Chart showing the relationships among the leaders and officers managing the flow of legislative and administration Senate affairs
Curriculum: Government

2565 State Facts (Sponsor: University of Michigan)

www.ipl.org/div/kidspace/stateknow/

Basic facts about any state of the Union and the District of Columbia. Includes such facts as: capital, population, governor, when it entered the Union, motto, major industries, points of interest, bordering states, a picture of the state flag, and others. Charts to compare size and population.

Special Features: Ask a Question; Fun Stuff; Teachers & Parents
Curriculum: Social Studies

2566 The USGenWeb Project

www.usgenweb.net/statelinks.html

A volunteer effort to provide non-commercial Internet websites for genealogical research in every county and every state in the Untied States. Includes state histories, maps; click the state you are interested for resources.

Special Features: Suggestions for using the Internet as a research tool
Curriculum: History

2567 Welcome to America (Sponsor: Roger Johnson)

www.welcometoamerica.us/index.html

State flags, songs, highest points, picture of state capitols, pictures of state features, state fairs, state welcome signs, executive mansions are some of the points covered for each state. District of Columbia features Washington, D.C.

Special Features: Photo of the Month
Curriculum: Social Studies

2568 The World Almanac

www.worldalmanacforkids.com/explore/states.html

Click on any state for quick tips designed for kids such as: Land and resources; Population; Education and Cultural Activity; Government and Politics; Economy; History. Each of these categories are divided: for example Education and Cultural Activity is grouped by Education, Cultural Institutions, Historical Sites, Sports and Recreation, Communications.

Special Features: Kids Speak Out Contest; Printable Fun Quizzes; Ask the Editors
Curriculum: Library Media

Appendix B:
Sites for Washington, D.C.

2569 The Brookings Institution

www.brookings.edu/index/about.htm

"The Brookings Institution, one of Washington's oldest think tanks, is an independent, nonpartisan organization devoted to research, analysis, and public education with an emphasis on economics, foreign policy, governance, and metropolitan policy." This site posts news events and transcripts, lists Brookings' research topics, and outlines their approach to research. Appropriate for advanced students.

Special Features: Brookings' Publications and Programs

Curriculum: Economics; Government; Language Arts

2570 Discovery Creek Children's Museum of Washington

www.discoverycreek.org

"Discovery Creek Children's Museum of Washington is committed to helping all children experience, appreciate and become stewards of the natural environment." Camps, weekend and school programs, and ongoing special events are listed. The Children's corner includes games, fun facts, and every day tips.

Special Features: Curriculum Resources and Professional Development for Teachers; Outreach Programs

Curriculum: Biology; Environmental Studies

2571 The Folklore Society of Greater Washington

www.fsgw.org

The Folklore Society of Greater Washington presents over 200 folk events in the Washington, D.C., area every year. Music festivals, dancing weekends, storytelling workshops all aim to "further the understanding, investigation, appreciation, and performance of the traditional folk music and folklore of the American people."

Special Features: Calendar of Events; Links to Participating Organizations

Curriculum: Dance; Language Arts; Music; Sociology

2572 Foreign Embassies

www.embassy.org

This Electronic Embassy guide features each of the embassies in Washington, D.C., with links to Web-based resources. Resources include a virtual library, a virtual gallery, and a quick index to the embassies.

Special Features: Diplomatic Quotations; Embassy Row Tour; Stories of Washington's Historic Diplomatic Buildings

Curriculum: Government

2573 Guide to Historic Neighborhoods and Monuments

www.cr.nps.gov/nr/travel/wash

This National Park Register Guide to Historic Neighborhoods and Monuments of Washington, D.C., profiles the twenty-seven designated historic districts throughout the city. "Visitors will learn not only about the famous national landmarks and monuments of Washington, such as the White House, the Capitol Building, and the Mall, but will also learn about the historic neighborhoods and local landmarks that make the city so unique."

Special Features: City Maps; Mayor's Welcome

Curriculum: Geography; History

2574 Joint Center for Political and Economic Studies

www.jointcenter.org

The Joint Center for Political and Economic Studies strives to "improve the socioeconomic status of black Americans and other minorities, expand their effective participation in the political and public policy arenas, and promote communications and relationships across racial and ethnic lines to strengthen the nation's pluralistic society." Site includes a comprehensive warehouse of data on racial populations, information on the Joint Center's international activities, and access to recent publications.

Special Features: Youth Network

Curriculum: Economics; Government; Social Studies

2575 Library of Congress

www.loc.gov

The Library of Congress acts as the Nation's library, the U.S. Copyright Office, research center for the nations lawmakers, and a center for international studies. This rich Internet resource boasts, "Thousands of special features, millions of educational items, billions of hits annually".

Special Features: Ask a Librarian; News & Events; Teacher Resources; Today in History

Curriculum: Library Media

2576 National Gallery of Art: Educational Resources

www.nga.gov/education/index.shtm

The National Gallery of Art's education page strives to bring art into the classroom. NGA Classroom offers a place where "teacher and students can connect art and curriculum." NGA Loan Materials offers free learning materials from the National Gallery of Art's Division of Education.

Special Features: Online Tours; Teacher, School, and Family Programs

Curriculum: Art

2577 National Zoo

http://nationalzoo.si.edu/default.cfm

The National Zoo is part of the Smithsonian Institute and provides a home to more than 2,700 individual animals and 435 different species. This site provides numerous educational resources ranging from articles on endangered species to interactive programs on the conservation of animal habitats.

Special Features: Conservation Corner; Zoos: A Historical Perspective

Curriculum: Biology

2578 Official Tourism Site of Washington, D.C.

www.washington.org

A guide to enjoying Washington, D.C., "From its celebrated symbols of patriotism to its undiscovered neighborhoods, the sights and sounds of the nation's capital inspire millions of visitors every year. Packed with famous sights, free attractions, and an endless calendar of special events, Washington, D.C., offers year-round inspiring experiences."

Special Features: Area maps; Community Links; Visitor Information

Curriculum: Government; History

2579 The Shakespeare Theater in the Nation's Capital

www.shakespearedc.org

Provides information on current productions and the season's events (including free shows), opportunities within the theater, and links to theater-related resources. Audience enrichment programs strive to expand the enjoyment of classical theater through discussion and seminars.

Special Features: Photo Gallery; School and Community Programs; Virtual Tour

Curriculum: Drama

2580 Smithsonian Center for Education

www.smithsonianeducation.org/educators

The Smithsonian Center for Education and Museum Studies produces a variety of programs, services, and resources for the education and museum communities. Educational resources include a grade-specific resource library, access to Smithsonian published curriculum guides, and recommended sites for students.

Special Features: Lesson Plans; E-newsletter; Professional Development

Curriculum: Art; History; Language Arts; Science; Technology

2581 The Textile Museum

www.textilemuseum.org

The Textile Museum's mission is to further the understanding of mankind's creative achievements in the textile arts. Site includes Calendar of Events, programs for children and families, and links to related sites.

Special Features: Educational Programs; Textile of the Month

Curriculum: Home Economics

2582 Washington National Opera

www.dc-opera.org

Renowned for its staging of high quality productions and championing lesser-known works, The Washington National Opera also offers school-based-programs and other resources to promote opera to children and young adults.

Special Features: Current Productions; Education and Community Programs; Opera Insights

Curriculum: Music

2583 Weather Underground: Washington Forecast

www.wunderground.com/US/DC/Washington. html

Provides comprehensive coverage of Washington, D.C., weather. Includes information on extended forecasts, air quality, and seasonal weather averages. Also provides access to personal weather stations.

Special Features: Forecast; History and Almanac; Moon Phases; Meteorology

Curriculum: Geography

Index

Curriculum subjects such as Art and Biology are in **bold** as are official state sites. Numbers refer to entries, not page numbers.

7/05